Modern Methods in SECONDARY EDUCATION

JEAN D. GRAMBS

and

WILLIAM J. IVERSON

Stanford University

Illustrations by

ROBERT M. THOMAS

Brockport (N.Y.) State College

THE DRYDEN PRESS · NEW YORK

Typography and format by
LEONARD W. BLIZARD

Manufactured in the United States of America

First Printing, May 1952
Second Printing, December 1952

Preface

In our own generation the high school in America has become the school for all the children of all the people. It is now the "common school," just as the elementary school was the common school in earlier days. The change has been sudden and without parallel in the rest of the world. No other nation comes even close to sending seventy percent of its youth to secondary schools, so the American high school has had little precedent to guide its phenomenal growth. And, regardless of precedent, it has had little time to pause and reflect on its role in American life. Yet the high school is slowly and steadily adjusting its structure and its practice to the magnitude of its task.

Today, less than one-fifth of our high-school graduates will ever finish college. Important as this one-fifth is to the Nation, it is not so important that the other four-fifths must be sacrificed. For the four-fifths, high school offers the last opportunity for a general education to fit them to be good workers, good parents, good citizens.

Of all societies democracy alone insists that each of its citizens has enduring worth just because he is a human being. Democracy places a high premium on significant individuality and rightly so, for democracy needs differentiated capacities, developed to the full, in order to maintain its strength. High schools therefore can no longer concentrate on those who are preparing for college and neglect those whose talents are other than academic. No one who works with high schools pretends that this problem has been mastered, but at least the job is more clearly defined than ever before.

As part of this job, the high-school curriculum is currently being subjected to careful analysis. Hand in hand with curriculum reorganization must go changes in classroom teaching practices. Experimentation during the last decade has provided a wealth of new methodology which can be applied in many different kinds of learning and applied to achieve a unity of purpose which has heretofore been lacking. The methodology comes from many fields: from anthropology, psychology, sociology, and political science. We need now to put it to work.

It is not enough for a beginning teacher to be told what he ought to do. He wants to know how to do it. This book is the result of our efforts in "how to do it." It is the product of long-time experimentation with our students—experimentation that resulted in sound improvement in our students' teaching.

In the book we have tried first to set forth the overall job of the high school clearly. Then we have attempted to show exactly what this means in everyday teaching, and we spell it out in detail. Further, to make the book effective, we have endeavored to face honestly the hard realities in present-day high schools, high schools that are attempting to adjust to the enormity of their problems. Our students have forced us to remember that today's high school has many limitations. They have told us in no uncertain terms that if we ignore these limitations, we cannot help the high school realize its potentialities. So we have worked to give beginning teachers sympathetic understanding of the problems of modern high schools along with many practical suggestions about what to do about them.

Specifically, then, we have gone beyond the usual methods text in attempting to bridge the gap between theory and practice. Democratic classrooms? Yes, but what are the specifics of teacher behavior that produce such classrooms? The details are here. Similarly, we have given a large amount of space to discipline, knowing from our own work with beginning and inexperienced teachers that this is an area of great concern and insecurity. One further illustration. Some readers may be slightly mystified by the sequence of the chapters on evaluation. Here too, we have drawn upon our experience with students: their first question is not, "What are modern theories of evaluation?" but "How can I make up a good test?" When satisfied that they can build good tests, students want to know how test results fit into grading practices. Only after they have solved these testing and grading problems are students ready to examine theories of evaluation. Thus, throughout the book we have attempted to follow the practical needs of the student-teacher.

In the book we have drawn liberally on the researches of others, and we wish to acknowledge our great indebtedness to them and to their publishers for generous permission to quote from their findings. Thanks for encouragement throughout the painful, albeit stimulating, experience of writing a book are due our students and our colleagues in the Stanford School of Education. We owe a special debt to Dr. Lucien B. Kinney for many helpful suggestions. For patient understanding and assistance we wish to thank Sheila Buckholtz, Adelaide Iverson, and Harold Grambs.

J. D. G.
W. J. I.

Stanford University
April, 1952

CONTENTS

SECTION II: MATERIALS AND ACTIVITIES FOR LEARNING

SECTION IV: EVALUATING LEARNING

Introduction

SOME of the best and some of the worst people you have known have been teachers. And now you want to become a teacher. You have begun to ask yourself: Will I become a good teacher? In some respects, becoming a good teacher is the easiest thing in the world, and in some ways it is the most difficult. Teaching seems to be done by feel and also by intensive and serious study and inquiry. What is a good teacher like? How did some people become good in this job? Can *I* become a good teacher?

These are questions that every aspirant toward the teaching profession will ask himself over and over again. And each one will have a different answer, an answer that fits his own unique personal history. For there are many kinds of good teachers. In the succeeding pages is a brief description of some of the kinds of good teachers that we find and some of the kinds of things that they do. The balance of the book is devoted to the practical details of modern teaching. Not all of what is described can be done by any one teacher; but each good teacher will find some practices that, in terms of his own personality pattern, will equip him best to provide democratic learning situations for the youth of today.

The Teacher as Guide for Learning

The classroom. We enter Room 15 in Middlefield High School. We see walls brightened with photographs, bookcases loaded with books, tables lined with well-thumbed magazines, bulletin-boards splashed with colorful displays. There is a sense of orderliness, a feeling of efficiency in the room. This is a kind of laboratory for learning, waiting for the work of young minds.

The teacher. I've taught United States history six years now. I like to see young people face the serious issues of our times. I want to develop the ability of my students to think clearly because one day soon they will be our adult citizens.

I plan out in careful detail my work for the year. Each year I try to weave in new approaches to our old problems. I leave nothing to chance. I am not opportunistic in my teaching; I know where I'm going. Sometimes I worry about those of my students who are less mentally alert. They flounder a little but I'm convinced they need to meet these challenges as best they can. I know John Young, whose room is down the hall, has his troubles with students of that type. But somehow I never do. Discipline? I bring my students to the long search for knowledge; that takes care of discipline.

The students. I remember the first time I saw Mr. Franklin. I remember I'd never cared much about history and as I looked at him, I wondered why the students said he was such a good teacher. But they were right. He *is* good. He makes history interesting and exciting. He makes you work hard. I don't think even in college I'll work any harder. I had to learn to think.

The parent. I appreciate the thoughtful planning Mr. Franklin does for his work. He's a real scholar. Sometimes he treads on controversial ground, but I must say he is very careful to have the facts. He isn't much of a mixer in town affairs, since he spends so much time on photography. He gives my boy a lot of homework, but I think it may be good for John to get down and dig.

The principal. Henry Franklin isn't much of a leader, but I must say I respect his competence in the classroom. I suppose no one in the school knows the history of this country better than Henry Franklin. Of course, sometimes I think he carries this preoccupation with his subject matter too far. Last time I tried to get the president of the student body out of his class for a meeting, he raised cain for a week. But he is a crackerjack teacher. His file of resource materials is nothing short of amazing. It represents years of work in gathering all kinds of teaching aids. Oh, we've learned to go a little easy on assigning noncollege students to his classes, but for the better people he just can't be beat.

The Teacher as Counselor

The classroom. Across the hall is George Verplanck, who teaches general science. He runs a laboratory for learning, too, but the orderliness apparent in Henry Franklin's room is missing. The students don't seem to mind, though. Any time you look in George

Verplanck's room there are busy students around—busy around George Verplanck, that is.

The teacher. I can't keep up with my work. Henry Franklin always has things so well in hand. Every time I sit down to get organized, three students come in. Of course, I like to see them and I think the little personal problems they want help with are really more important than the stuff I give them in general science. You need a sympathetic ear at their age. I don't mind listening, but even my evenings are getting invaded. And Mary, my wife, sometimes gets a little irritated when parents want me to come to see them, but really this is the heart of my work. I want to use my teaching to help people understand themselves. I suppose that's as good science teaching as any.

The students. Verplanck's a teacher you can turn to when you have troubles. He'll listen to you like your parents never will. And he has good advice too,—none of this goody-goody stuff some of these teachers try to hand you. I guess he isn't the best science teacher in the world. We never do get to where we're supposed to in the book. But I think it's more important that he always supports the students. He comes to our games; he brings his wife to our dances. He's more a friend than a teacher.

The parents. We appreciate George Verplanck. George ought to be dean of boys if the school were large enough. He is, unofficially. Sometimes we get a little concerned about how much science Joe's learning with George, but Joe will go to him when he won't come to us. And we feel easier for having him around.

The principal. I'd like it better if I could get Verplanck to a few committee meetings, but I suppose it's my own fault. I always send him the problem children, and I must say he sets straight more of them than anybody else I've seen. And while he doesn't make all the meetings, he still is good to have around on a faculty. He makes for good morale.

The Teacher as Mediator of the Culture

The classroom. At the end of the hall is the art room. This is Katherine Heron's domain. Maps, scale drawings, model houses are everywhere. Apparently Miss Heron is engaged with her students in some community beautification program. We see scale replicas of "before" and "after" stages in the planning.

The teacher. Art for me is the expression of people: in line, shape, color, sound and texture—expression of their feelings about their way of life. I like to tell my students that perhaps the least important part of what most people call "art" is sketching or painting or sculpturing. Much more significant in our culture is the shape of an automobile, the color of a living room, the texture of a cloth coat. Why, my students redecorated the Community Center buildings, designed the furniture, planned the new landscaping. When I take them on sketching tours we concentrate on ways of bringing new line and color to our town. One night a week I sponsor craft classes for parents and their children. We work on simple ways to bring new beauty into their homes. I know I sound like a one-man art department. I'm not. John Mareat and Helen Hagan, the other art teachers, do much more than I. Anyway, together I think we're giving art more of the touch of everyday living, or maybe I should say giving everyday living more of the touch of art.

The students. Yeah, I know what you're thinking, what's a football player doing in an art course. That's what people new to our school always wonder. Well, that's because they don't know Happy Heron. Why, she knows more about streamlining a plane fuselage than the Air Force. You take a hot rod—Happy's the one to go to when you want to strip a car and she'll give it a clean, fast look. Yeah—she can talk about more than muscles in marble. She knows a little football, too. And you ought to hear my old man rave about the radio cabinet she helped me and him design and build. Happy's all right.

The parents. I suppose we were a little suspicious of Miss Heron when she first came and started talking about beautifying our community. It looked pretty good to us as it was. But when we saw what her students did with murals for the school cafeteria, we didn't shy away quite so nervously when she talked about working over the Community Center. Now we think it's amazing what she and those high-school youngsters were able to do. The old Center is brighter and more attractive than many newer buildings we've seen. And she doesn't stop with public buildings. Her students do layouts for new homes, prepare redecorating schemes, and work to help carry them out. In a way Miss Heron and her students have become art consultants to our community.

The principal. Katherine Heron is the best public relations medium I have. She knows just about everybody and she makes few enemies. I believe she belongs to more things than I do. If I'm ever a little unsure about the public pulse rate, I check with Katherine. Sometimes others in the faculty gripe because I don't put her on many school committees. She does her committee work for the school down town.

The Teacher as a Member of the School Community

The classroom. There isn't anything very remarkable about Mrs. Averill's classroom. On the bulletin board she has posted all the school notices and bulletins. During the height of the football season, there was a graph with the scores of the opposing teams. But her room is not one to catch the eye of the casual visitor. It's neat and orderly—but ordinary.

The teacher. "I know I have a great deal to learn about teaching," Mrs. Averill wrote a friend, "but in a school like ours everyone is helpful. I have found my main concern now is to learn the routines of attendance records, passes, study hall, and all the other paper work of the school. I have made a point of visiting other classes during my free period so I can understand the contributions of subject fields other than my own. I've also talked with the counselors, the librarian, school nurse—it sounds as though I've made myself a regular pest around here!"

The students. Mrs. Averill is good, as new teachers go. The thing we like about her is her interest in our activities. She is at all our games, comes to our plays, attends the school dances. We know that she wants to be part of what we are doing. They always make the new teachers sponsor one of the classes. She's done a swell job as sponsor for the junior class. Many people think our school elections are just kid stuff, but Mrs. Averill really appreciates how important they are. We feel she is really a part of our school.

The parents. Mrs. Averill? Oh yes, she is the new teacher. We don't know much about her yet. She seems to know a lot about the school, though. Bill says she was a great help in outlining his program. She knew more about the rules and regulations and policies than even some of the old-timers. At Open House last month when we were inquiring about the recent fuss over the bond election campaign, she really knew what had happened and told us, without trying to pass the buck. We like a teacher who takes a real interest in the school.

The principal. Now there is one new teacher who appreciates the importance of getting reports in on time. I think this is because she is really interested in her profession. Teaching isn't just a job to her; it is a career. She always does her share, cooperates very well with others. She even gets along with Miss Miller who seems to enjoy picking fights with the new teachers. I have also appreciated her attendance at PTA meetings and her willingness to help out with their programs. So many teachers seem to think that PTA is for parents only.

Do these teachers sound familiar? Several of them may be teachers you yourself have known in high school. Some may sound like teachers you have read about in books. But what is important about these teachers is (1) that each one is an example of a real teacher; (2) that each is a good teacher in his or her own right; and (3) that each has a place in the high school.

Sometimes there is a feeling among beginning teachers that there is only one kind of good teacher. But the fact is that so far we are not able to say, "This, and this only, is the master teacher." Perhaps we may never be able to say it. Just as children come in an infinite variety of shapes, sizes, and temperaments, likes and dislikes, talents, and interests, so do teachers. Until children all come in the same pattern, we will always want to have many kinds of good teachers. In this book we will seek to describe in detail the different kinds of emphases good teachers bring to their classrooms. It is important, however, to remember that some of these methods and techniques will be more useful and more meaningful to a Mr. Franklin than to a Miss Heron.

Each of these teachers we described was especially able in one of the roles of the teacher. The teacher must guide the learning activities of young people; the teacher must be one who can give good counsel; the teacher must be a vital member of the community; the teacher must be alert to his professional responsibility. These are all part of the job of teaching and each is important. Yet no one teacher can expect to be a master in every one. The beginning teacher must be aware of all the roles of the teacher. He may do a *superior* job in those areas where his particular talent lies, but he should strive to do at least a *good* job in the others.

1. Recognizing Student Differences

ARE high-school students more alike than they are different? High-school students have many important characteristics in common, yet at the same time each student is very different from every other student. In planning instruction for any course, the teacher is balancing and weighing the common qualities against the differences. Some teaching seems to lend itself to general attack by the whole class, while at other times it seems more appropriate to differentiate so that each student or group of students is doing something particularly suited to some special need, ability, or interest.

It is no accident that this book begins with a consideration of the ways in which high-school students may differ. We cannot have good education unless we take care to recognize these differences. Why are differences important? In our American culture, we prize the individual. It is basic to democratic processes that we foster those differences which make for good government. After all, if every person felt and thought alike, there would be no need for discussion or election. We are also concerned in education with the development of those significant differences among individuals which make unique and creative additions to group living. But, says the teacher, how can I help each one of forty youngsters be a different sort of person? It is hard enough to keep them all quiet for ten minutes, let alone try to indulge in the luxury of special projects for each special need. It is true that teaching to meet individual differences effectively is most difficult, but it is also most essential.

This kind of teaching demands (1) knowledge of how individuals can differ, and (2) ability to use a variety of teaching approaches to meet these differences. The ways in which students can differ may be described in the following four areas:

1. Differences in growth and maturational patterns;
2. Differences in backgrounds of experience;
3. Differences in needs, interests and abilities;
4. Differences in school level: freshman to senior.

In this chapter, we shall attempt to outline briefly those ways in which youth at large in the culture are apt to differ in general and to show the ways in which youth at hand in the classroom will differ in detail. On the basis of the research findings we will then suggest methods that the teacher may use in obtaining information about the students in the classroom. In later chapters we will describe how to capitalize on the findings to promote learning.

Differences in Growth and Maturational Patterns

To teach any student anything, the teacher must consider those many diverse factors that converged to produce a student at this point in time, sitting on the first seat in the third row. The teacher must know the general patterns of maturation for the level he is teaching as well as for those that precede and follow. The more the teacher knows about the general factors that have been operating up to this particular moment in the personal history of Joe Robinson, the better able will he be to speak to Joe in language that makes sense to the young man and that will influence him toward increasingly more mature patterns of behavior and growth.

Let us consider how Joe grew. In childhood, the young boy grew rapidly in body height, weight, surface area. This growth came quite fast until about eight or nine years of age, then seemed to stop or at least to slow down to a very slight amount. Then, during adolescence, the rate of growth again increased at sometimes astonishing rates, followed by another decline in growth rate. If one were to chart this growth, it would look like an elongated S curve with two rapid growth points, and two plateaus.

When Joe sits in your class, anywhere from the age of twelve to eighteen, he may be undergoing the latter of the growth spurts. Or the growth may have occurred prior to high school or may be delayed until nearly the end of high school. In any event, this factor of growth is a vital one to the adolescent boy; and, in another kind of context, it is also vital to the adolescent girl. A boy seeks to be tall as a special cultural need; he has to be taller than the girl he takes to dances; he ought to be taller than the girl he marries. If he wishes to be a good basketball player, height is important. If growth occurs sooner than it does with the rest of his playmates, Joe will feel gawky, all arms and legs, and wonder whether something has gone wrong with his glands. Or, if he does not grow when others seem to be getting taller and taller, he will become worried over his small size, feel left out of the bigger boys' games, and become a special problem to himself and often to others because the culture says he is too small.

> Paul, the biggest boy physically, seemed insecure. He didn't seem to belong. He was noisy and constantly disturbing others by borrowing paper and books. To call more attention to himself, he experimented with the typewriter by pushing all the keys down at once, typing without paper in the machine, slamming the carriage return. He was doing all he could to overcome his troubles by trying to be the center of attention, even if it meant a reprimand from his fellows and the teacher.*

With girls, the problem of maturity of appearance corresponds to the boys' height problem. If a girl develops the outward appearance of a young lady before others in her group do so, she is likely to develop mixed feelings of self-consciousness and pride. She will be treated according to the way she looks; if she looks old enough to be dated by older boys, she may find herself in personal situations for which her experiences have as yet not fitted her. On the other hand, if her body is slow to develop into that of a woman, she may become overly concerned about her abnormal appearance and again develop feelings of embarrassment and social isolation.

Why are these ideas regarding growth so important to the teacher? During adolescence, as the youth sees himself more and more clearly as an adult, he strives to fit himself into the adult stereotype. The hard fact is that no one even approximates what he thinks he ought to be at all moments in his life. With the adolescent, caught between the need to conform and the need to feel independent, we often find extreme and unpredictable behaviors. Here is where the teacher is well advised to understand and appreciate the growth patterns of the boys and girls in his classroom. When John

* All classroom anecdotal material is taken from observation records, unless otherwise noted.

suddenly becomes shy and reticent where before he was always seeking the limelight, when Susan suddenly (it seems) develops a case of the giggles no matter what is said, when George combs his hair at least five times during ten minutes, then adolescence has come to the classroom.

> Jack sits to the right of Pat in the typing class. He is a senior who is removing a condition from his grade and attempting to make a good rate of speed. He is about 5 feet 10 inches tall, thin, and awkward. He works erratically—typing a few words, jumping up to sharpen a pencil, typing some more, experimenting with his machine, jumping up again to ask the teacher questions, wandering around the classroom, and talking to others. He is restless and painfully aware of his ungainliness.

But even more important than the numerous minor overt behavior manifestations that we are all familiar with as the "teen-age" type, are the genuine concerns and confusions of the young person. These years of important body changes, of awakening of new and important personal and social drives, and of growing sensitivity to a wider world produce within the student less of a desire to study the routine subjects of the school and an increasing need to seek reassurance and to obtain guidance in these deeply personal areas. The frequently observed apathy, lack of responsibility, seeming boredom and distaste for the important learnings that the school has to offer will plague every high-school teacher. "They just don't seem to want to try, or to learn, or to pay attention," is the recurrent cry. At the same time, teachers will report extraordinary spurts of energy, enthusiasm, and persistence when dances and football games are suggested. We must not forget that these high-school years are years of intense self-concern. Adolescents seem to be the most self-centered beings in the world, while still at unexpected moments the most idealistic of any other group. The major point for the teacher to remember is that the activities of the school can gain great impetus by starting with those matters which are primary in the personal world of the student. Then, and only then, can the teacher skillfully draw the attention of the student to less immediate problems and finally work with the student on the kind of problem that will be of persistent interest long after the turmoils of youth are forgotten.

Noting health needs. The matter of good health is closely allied to the mental and emotional problems of adolescence. It is obvious that the high-school student cannot profit much from instruction if he is ill. Teachers are not physicians, but often they can see the need for a physician's help before family and others do. Here are some important points for observation:

General

General impression of physique
Vigor or listlessness

Face and lips, arms and hands

Pallor
Flush of fever
Signs of skin disease

Eyes and vision

Squint
Complaints of headache, blurred vision, dizziness
Holding book too near or too far
Congestion or sties

Ears and hearing

Slow response
Presence of discharge

Nose, throat and chest

Chronic discharge from nose
Frequent sore throat
Chronic cough
Rapid breathing after slight exertion[1]

Assembling the data. Now where will information on the short and the tall, the plump and the thin, the sick and the well, be found? Many school systems will have cumulative record cards on which the growth of students will be charted. More often no such record has been kept for all students, although school physicians and nurses may have some information about those who have the more unusual physical developments and abnormalities. However, when teachers find no such record or, as is often the case, incomplete records, information can often be obtained through observation in the classroom, through questionnaires, or through informal interviews with students, parents, and family physicians. Other teachers who have taught the students will often be able to supply useful, informal information about earlier stages of growth.

Outside the school and the home, various social agencies may be

[1] Adapted from Rogers, J. F., *What Every Teacher Should Know about the Physical Condition of Her Pupils* (Washington, D.C.: U.S. Office of Education, 1945).

able to supply missing data. The YMCA's and YWCA's, the church youth groups, the Boy Scouts and Girl Scouts, the community recreation agencies are usually happy to give whatever assistance they can.

Obviously the busy teacher cannot make exhaustive searches for data about all his students. But he will want to get into the habit of collecting data rather than nourishing prejudice. Just as important as the recording of the facts of growth is the recording of anecdotal incidents which reveal the effects of growth. It is important then to preserve in a central classroom file easy-to-record, easy-to-use cards with whatever information the teacher is able to assemble.[2] Otherwise the information gets lost on miscellaneous pieces of paper in various drawers and cabinets.

Some teachers will want to experiment with the use of the Wetzel Grid.[3] This provides a standardized graph on which to record physical growth and development.[4] The grid makes possible quick identification of those who are deviating from their normal growth curves. In larger schools, such a record may be maintained by the school health service or by the physical-education department. More important than maintaining the record is using the data to make significant differences in the way the student is taught.

Differences in Backgrounds of Experience

Students in high school will bring to the class very different ways of living. They will belong to different socioeconomic groupings. They will have developed under very different psychological climates. Both the sociological and the psychological environments will affect directly the goals they have in high school.

The speech sounds of a student, for example, are given characteristic qualities in part by maturation of the speech organs but also by efforts to achieve the kinds of sounds heard in family and neighborhood. Sometimes vocal quality achieved by this interplay is not that which teachers consider most desirable. Even more crucial for the student is the language he has learned to make with these speech sounds. The "right" language caste is a very real asset to students in their homes and in their neighborhoods. But the student who comes from the "wrong" sociological grouping may find the comfortable diction of his home and neighborbood strongly deprecated in the school. He may be called publicly to task for "poor" English by his

[2] This card may also be used for guidance notes as suggested in Chap. 18.

[3] Wetzel, N. C., "The Simultaneous Screening and Assessment of School Children," *Health and Physical Education,* 13:576-577 (December, 1942).

[4] Copies of the grid may be ordered from Newspaper Enterprise Association Service, 1200 West Third St., Cleveland, Ohio.

teacher, and yet be taunted by his gang if he tries on them the "good" English prescribed by the teacher.

And we know that the gang is an especially strong influence during the adolescent years. Besides speech and language habits the gang affects importantly almost every small and large detail of daily living: dress, posture, food habits, habits of personal cleanliness, recreation habits (sports, reading, motion pictures, radio and television programs, hobbies), attitudes toward family, church, and school, and attitudes toward one's own and the opposite sex.

It is of some importance to the teacher, then, to know what kind of gang Joe or Mary belongs to, or whether Joe belongs to any gang at all, or whether Mary belongs to a clique of three and has no other social contact. It is also important to the teacher to know what the gangs and the cliques prize highly, what they are indifferent to, and what they scorn. For the teacher who does not know how the gangs and the cliques feel courts trouble.[5] This does not mean that he has to follow the attitudes and values of the gangs and cliques; it does mean, however, that he has to be keenly aware of what they are.

There is no intention to minimize the influence of family. But then it is the rare teacher who does. Indeed, there is a rather good chance that the teacher will ascribe more areas of exclusive dominion to the family than it has retained in our culture. Still, even though authority is now so largely shared, the teacher is justified in looking to the family for the primary psychological and sociological climate out of which boys and girls come to the classroom.

If it is a warm psychological climate, if there is a good feeling between mother and father, between parents and children, between brothers and sisters, the sense of well-being will furnish a ready fund upon which to draw in facing the frustrations of school life. But if children live in turbulent atmosphere, even small crises in the classroom may be enough to upset them completely. For example:

> There was Don who sat and just watched the rest of the class. If he were asked a question he would bitterly answer, "Naw, I don't know." And if pressed, he might either go into a rage or refuse to say anything.
>
> I later asked Mr. Dickson about Don. He said that Don had had a poor home life, where he was made to feel inferior. His older sister Mary had always done well in school. She was constantly held up to him as a model. Don's mother had a strong competitive spirit and wanted everything about her family to be "most and best."

[5] Hollingshead, A. B., *Elmtown's Youth* (New York: John Wiley & Sons, 1949), Chap. 9, "Cliques and Dates."

The sociological atmosphere in the family is just as pervasive as the psychological. Here a boy learns the difficult lesson of how a boy must behave to be accepted as a real boy. It is just as important that he learn to become a man as to become a nondrunkard. For a girl the learning task is also difficult. The family teaches the boy and the girl their cultural roles. But the larger culture is much less decided about how the boy and the girl should behave. Often they are torn between what they see everyone else doing, and what their family says they must not do, as in the following:

> My mother and dad got too many old-fashioned ideas. She's from another country. I'm from America, and I'm not like her. With Mexican girls they want you to sit in the house like *moscas muertas*, dead flies, like that. If you tell them what the teachers say, they say the teachers don't know, and what they tell us will only get us in trouble. They think they know what is good, not the American teachers. And even if we do take our parents to school to explain them—our parents don't hear. They only know from Mexico.
>
> I remember when me and my sister told my mother we wanted to dress neat and American they beat us and said no, to dress like they wanted us to, in old Mexico. So after a while it's no use.[6]

Both boys and girls learn their ideas of what is worth while and what is not from their families. If one student seems intent on getting very good grades, despite average ability, even when it means giving up many social activities, we may be sure that somewhere at home there has been developed a major emphasis on high scholastic standings. Another student, with superior ability, may loaf on the job—often, to the teacher's hurt surprise, being openly happy at getting a poor mark because in the cultural milieu where he was raised it was a mark of dishonor to do what the teacher expected. Some students are highly ambitious, others content with a future that might seem very drab and dull. These different personal and life goals are not to be easily dismissed by the teacher and should not be, since they are important in developing the significant differences that we prize. Suppose that a teacher asks Joe if he doesn't want good grades so that he can go to college, and Joe's immediate reply is, "Ah, that's a lot of hooey; I'd rather work any day in the Smith garage." Then the teacher must seek motivations that are more inclusive, incentives that appeal to many kinds of student from many kinds of background. The schools have traditionally motivated effectively those students who clearly are headed for the upper social and economic strata of our culture, but they have only

[6] Griffith, Beatrice, *American Me* (Boston: Houghton Mifflin Company, 1948), p. 151.

recently begun to understand the motivating goals of others with modest ideas of their future social roles.[7]

What have we been saying? We might summarize in two sentences. The way boys and girls feel about themselves, about their families, about their gangs, and about the level of society at which they live has a direct effect on how and what they will learn in school. The characteristic sociological quality of boys' and girls' families, gangs, and living levels (independent of the way boys and girls feel about them) has a direct effect on how and what they will learn in school. This is the incontrovertible implication of research.

Conscientious teachers have always been aware that they ought to know more about these primary feelings and relationships which make the boys and girls what they are. But teachers have generally thought themselves unequipped to gather the information they needed or to interpret it if they had it. Moreover, they commonly said that they had more to do now than they had time for.

Assembling the Data. In the last decade, we have learned a great deal about collecting and interpreting the kind of data we have been discussing. Now we are more prepared to help with assurance both beginning and experienced teachers in these techniques. In addition, we can now honestly tell teachers that *taking* time for appraisal will *save* time for learning. Granted, as we said about collecting data on physical growth, *no* teacher in any one year can make intensive studies of *all* of his students. Still, if every year each teacher made detailed studies of *some* of his students, most students in any school system would be covered over the period of twelve years of schooling. The dividends in reduced frustration and induced understanding for both teachers and students would make these years incomparably more effective and satisfying.

There are many devices that may be used to assemble data about the differences in psychological and sociological backgrounds. They include non-directive interviews, projective tests, case studies, and sociometric techniques, which are discussed in detail in Chapters 17 and 18.

Differences in Needs

Out of the mental-hygiene movement and cultural-anthropology studies has come emphasis on basic needs and their influence on human behavior. Stolz[8] has classified them as follows:

[7] Davis, Allison, *Social Class Influences on Learning* (Cambridge: Harvard University Press, 1948).

[8] Stolz, Lois M., Department of Psychology, Stanford University, Stanford, California.

1. *The need for functioning as an individual*—the need for air, sunshine, food, rhythm of activity and rest.
2. *The need for psychobiological completeness*—the need for complementary relationships between boys and girls, the need for good family relationships.
3. *The need for other personal-social relations*—the need for supporting relationships with people of the same age and with adults.
4. *The need to understand the world*—the need to develop concepts of self and the place of that self in the universe.

Obviously these needs are closely interrelated while retaining distinctive identities.

There is good evidence that those whose needs have been met well during the growing years have a backlog of security that helps them through troubled times. It should be noted at once that there are many ways to meet these needs, just as there are great differences in the way these needs express themselves in individuals. We know now that the needs of students do not give automatic blessing to any subject matter or way of teaching. They are blessed only if, as, and when they help students meet their needs.

Assembling the data. A number of simple methods for collecting evidence on the needs of students have been developed. We have already suggested a brief growth and development record where information on the functioning of the individual may be recorded. The autobiography, when it is written under relaxed classroom conditions, can furnish useful clues. The teacher can thus often learn about the adolescent's problems as boy-girl relationships become more important. The case study (see Chapter 18) is a good guide to family relationships. Some teachers have had good results reading aloud brief selections of poetry and prose about man's eternal quest for the meaning of things. Lively discussions and free writing periods may bring revelation of student hopes, fears, aspirations, and system of values.

Beginning teachers will also want to be aware of the Prescott Child Study Movement described in detail in *Helping Teachers Understand Children.*[9] Some high schools have organized child-study groups following the patterns suggested by Prescott. The needs of youth in their classes are studied by teachers through anecdotal records, home visitation, sociometrics. (For discussion of these techniques, see Chapters 18, 19, and 20.) Group discussion on data is led by experienced guidance personnel. Ten steps are recommended to interpret data on the needs of the student:

[9] Commission on Teacher Education, *Helping Teachers Understand Children* (Washington, D.C.: American Council on Education, 1945).

aptitude in handwriting, arts and crafts, or drawing is not clea singled out.

Intelligence quotients are also closely related to ability to ma ter vocational tasks of increasing complexity. Not only does th relationship exist between different vocational groups, but withi vocational groups as well. That is, the intelligence quotient will usu ally indicate whether the student can learn the job of a shippin clerk or the job of an accountant—jobs in different vocationa groups. Furthermore, the tests will usually distinguish betwee ability to do bookkeeping and accounting—jobs within the same vocational group.

On the other hand, the correspondence is only fair between intelligence and social skills: understanding, getting along with, directing other people. Indeed, those who score the very highest on intelligence tests often are not "big wheels" socially. Characteristically, these students are somewhat at a loss to understand why they are different from the ordinary students, and, in turn, the ordinary students find them a little odd.

Similarly, social adjustment, in the sense of lack of involvement in delinquency and crime, is not too well indicated by intelligence tests. Although delinquents as a group are somewhat below average, delinquency occurs along the whole range of intelligence.

Probably out of all this research about the predictive qualities of intelligence tests, one conclusion needs special emphasis. The intelligence quotient does not comprehend the whole complex of abilities that men and women need to live satisfying, effective lives. There is no body of significant data which licenses teachers to relegate those who score below average on this single instrument to a kind of second-rate status in the classroom. Teachers need to remember that we do not have a differential tally at the ballot box. The so-called "dull normal" also elects congressmen. He has a right to a fair share of time, skill, and consideration from his teachers and a right to the opportunity to develop *his* capacities, some of which may register very imperfectly on intelligence tests. All too often an intelligence quotient that is below average brands the student in the eyes of the teachers. Over a period of years he may be invested with a reputation that makes it psychologically impossible for him to gain equitable opportunity to learn. And his teachers, if asked to explain his fringe existence in the classroom, simply point to the IQ penciled in red in the classbook. "What do you expect?" they say. "Look at his IQ."

1. Arranging the facts in accordance with an organizing framework for information.
2. Checking the facts.
3. Looking for clues and uncovering blind spots.
4. Identifying and testing recurring situations and patterns of behavior.
5. Spotting significant, unique events.
6. Forming a series of hypotheses to account for particular patterns of behavior.
7. Relating hypotheses about different patterns of behavior to each other in order to understand the youth as an organized whole and as a developing personality.
8. Checking hypotheses against an organizing framework of explanatory principles in order to discover contradictory, oversimplified, or biased interpretations.
9. Planning practical ways to help the individual.
10. Evaluating hypotheses and plans on the basis of the effects of practical attempts to help the individual.[10]

Differences in Interests

Stemming from these needs are patterns of interest which research has identified. Since motivation is a prime problem in learning, knowledge of these characteristic interests is most useful. Teachers who do not point these latent sources of energy toward important learning needlessly handicap themselves.

For convenience, we may distinguish three main interest structures: interest in intellectual and aesthetic achievement; interest in the current social scene; interest in the cultural heritage. Perhaps we may best gain a sense of continuity if we follow each of these structures as it changes during the high-school years.

Intellectual and aesthetic achievement. On entering adolescence, responsiveness to sensory impressions is intensified. Neither interest nor ability in fashioning understandings is strong unless closely allied to direct experience through the senses. It is a rare young adolescent whose interest is captured for long by purely intellectual or aesthetic appeals. By mid-adolescence an upsurge in interests often occurs in intellectual and aesthetic matters. This interest is commonly expended in many directions with no single direction very well defined.

Depth and continuity of interest in dealing with abstract considerations come usually with the later adolescent years. Mature reasoning ability can consequently be expected more confidently. This new proficiency is often directed toward crystallizing and specializing vocational aims.

[10] *Ibid.*, p. 426.

Current social scene. As adolescence approaches, interest in group cooperation is more readily engaged. Then experience in group action toward goals quite removed from the immediate peer culture but of importance to the larger community may profitably be begun. Given this earlier guidance, by mid-adolescence group activity should be increasingly self-directed, and by late adolescence groups should be able to focus on social issues with a minimum of teacher direction.

Concurrently with this enlarging interest in group solution of social problems runs the much publicized interest in boy-girl relationships. Neither teachers nor parents need research to remind them how engrossing this interest can be. And yet it is strange how little constructive guidance either teachers or parents give to this interest. Both groups recite countless moral strictures about what cannot be done, but neither is willing to take time to show what can be done to develop understandings in these crucial human relationships.

The cultural heritage. Even in early childhood there is often considerable interest about the facts regarding past societies, but it is usually about the time of adolescence before a consistent understanding that this age stands on the shoulders of other ages is developed. There is commonly a wide interest in the fact that men make the culture in which they live. This budding interest can be nurtured if the drama and adventure of the long struggle is brought to them. It often withers in the arid climate of purely political chronicles.

This description of interest structures is couched in broad generalizations. It can only be a very general guide to the kind of interest patterns which are often found around the adolescent years. Now there is nothing inviolate or sacred about interests. The good teacher does not haphazardly follow the interests of students. Instead, he plans with them to use what he can of those interests which seem to be most common and most abiding and most important. There are thousands of fleeting interests passing through the adolescents he teaches which will not be helpful for learning. Nor does the teacher discharge his responsibilities unless he helps arouse some common abiding and important interests. Someone has said: "What interests the students bring are our opportunity; what interests the students carry away are our responsibility." Ingenious teachers almost literally strew the course of instruction with interesting items to stumble over. Gathering information about interests will be undertaken willingly by students if they are convinced this is a

necessary prelude to planning with the teacher how bes
can be conducted. It is vital that from the beginning s
cept the idea that they have heavy responsibility for t
of their education.

The use of student interest may seem a remote poss
some classes—mathematics for example—but even in this
teacher can relate mathematics to future vocational go
Chapter 20), can determine if any students are puzzle fier
even perhaps develop a mathematics hobby club.

Assembling the data. Ways of ascertaining just what i
are already present in a specific class are numerous. One of tl
is to encourage the students themselves to take a census of int
Hobby exhibits are also useful in discovering interests. Particip
in extracurricular activities (perhaps better called co-curric
sports, and out-of-school clubs should also be noted. Sometin
time log that lists for each student his activities for the week
how he budgets his time is revealing.

Differences in Abilities

Needs develop interests. Interests channel abilities, and th
abilities, in turn, develop further interests. Some abilities have be
recognized early in the student's school career, especially tho
which were engaged to advantage in school activities. But othe
abilities may be dormant, at least as far as the school is concerned.

Here it may be useful to classify abilities on two levels:
(1) aptitudes—potentialities that *will* profit by training; and (2)
achievements—measurements attesting that students *have* profited by training. Common instruments for indicating aptitudes include intelligence tests, musical aptitude tests, and mechanical aptitude tests. There are achievement tests available in all the usual subject-matter areas; for example, English, social studies, mathematics, science.

Research has indicated that intelligence tests are very good indices to potentialities that will profit from academic training, especially where that training requires linguistic ability and the ability to manage abstract ideas. This theory is applicable from the elementary school through college. Thus, at any level of education, students of high intelligence quotients generally do superior work in written composition, reading, spelling, English, social studies, science, and mathematics. But where mechanical aptitude is a more important component of the training, the prediction of talent by means of these instruments is not nearly so marked. For example,

THE POOR SCHOLAR'S SOLILOQUY[11]

No, I'm not very good in school. This is my second year in the seventh grade, and I'm bigger and taller than the other kids. They like me all right, though, even if I don't say much in the classroom, because outside I can tell them how to do a lot of things. They tag me around and that sort of makes up for what goes on in school.

I don't know why the teachers don't like me. They never have very much. Seems like they don't think you know anything unless they can name the book it comes out of. I've got a lot of books in my room at home—books like Popular Science Mechanical Encyclopedia, and the Sears' and Wards' catalogues—but I don't very often just sit down and read them through like they make us do in school. I use my books when I want to find something out, like whenever Mom buys anything second-hand I look it up in Sears' or Ward's first and tell her if she's getting stung or not. I can use the index in a hurry.

In school, though, we've got to learn whatever is in the book and I just can't memorize the stuff. Last year I stayed after school every night for two weeks trying to learn the names of the Presidents. Of course I knew some of them like Washington and Jefferson and Lincoln, but there must have been thirty altogether, and I never did get them straight.

I'm not too sorry though, because the kids who learned the Presidents had to turn right around and learn all the Vice Presidents. I am taking the seventh grade over, but our teacher this year isn't so interested in the names of the Presidents. She has us trying to learn the names of all the great American inventors.

I guess I just can't remember names in history. Anyway, this year I've been trying to learn about trucks because my uncle owns three and he says I can drive one when I'm sixteen. I already know the horsepower and number of forward and backward speeds of twenty-six American trucks, some of them Diesels, and I can spot each make a long way off. It's funny how that Diesel works. I started to tell my teacher about it last Wednesday in science class when the pump we were using to make a vacuum in a bell jar got hot, but she said she didn't see what a Diesel engine had to do with our experiment on air pressure so I just kept still. The kids seemed interested though. I took four of them around to my uncle's garage after school and we saw the mechanic, Gus, tear a big truck Diesel down. Boy, does he know his stuff!!

I'm not very good in geography either. They call it economic geography this year. We've been studying the imports and exports of Chile all week, but I couldn't tell you what they are. Maybe the reason is I had to miss school yesterday because my uncle took me and his big trailer truck down state about 200 miles, and we brought almost 10 tons of stock to the Chicago market.

He had told me where we were going, and I had to figure out the

[11] This soliloquy first appeared in *Childhood Education*, XX, 219-229 (January, 1944).

highways to take and also the mileage. He didn't do anything but drive and turn where I told him to. Was that fun! I sat with a map in my lap and told him to turn south, or southeast, or some other direction. We made seven stops, and drove over 500 miles round trip. I'm figuring now what his oil cost, and also the wear and tear on the truck—he calls it depreciation—so we'll know how much we made.

I even write out all the bills and send letters to the farmers about what their pigs and beef cattle brought at the stockyards. I only made three mistakes in 17 letters last time, my aunt said, all commas. She's been through high school and reads them over. I wish I could write school themes that way. The last one I had to write was on, "What a Daffodil Thinks of Spring," and I just couldn't get going.

I don't do very well in school in arithmetic either. Seems I just can't keep my mind on the problems. We had one the other day like this:

> If a 57-foot telephone pole falls across a cement highway so that 17 3/6 feet extend from one side and 14 9/17 feet from the other, how wide is the highway?

That seemed to me like an awfuly silly way to get the width of a highway. I didn't even try to answer it because it didn't say whether the pole had fallen straight across or not.

Even in shop I don't get very good grades. All of us kids made a broom holder and a bookend this term and mine were sloppy. I just couldn't get interested. Mom doesn't use a broom anymore with her new vacuum cleaner, and all our books are in a bookcase with glass doors in the parlor. Anyway, I wanted to make an end gate for my uncle's trailer, but the shop teacher said that meant using metal and wood both, and I'd have to learn how to work with wood first. I didn't see why, but I kept still and made a tie rack at school and the tail gate after school at my uncle's garage. He said I saved him ten dollars.

Civics is hard for me, too. I've been staying after school trying to learn the "Articles of Confederation" for almost a week, because the teacher said we couldn't be good citizens unless we did. I really tried, because I want to be a good citizen. I did hate to stay after school, though, because a bunch of us boys from the south end of town have been cleaning up the old lot across from Taylor's Machine Shop to make a playground out of it for the little kids from the Methodist home. I made the jungle gym from old pipe, and the guys made me Grand Mogul to keep the playground going. We raised enough money collecting scrap this month to build a wire fence clear around the lot.

Dad says I can quit school when I am fifteen, and I am sort of anxious to because there are a lot of things I want to learn . . . and as my uncle says, I'm not getting any younger.

The fact that intelligence tests do not neatly sum up all of a student's potentialities has led to extensive research in developing instruments to measure other aptitudes. We now have aptitude tests in mechanical arts, fine arts, music, clerical work, physical dexterity.

But this is an infant science, and the yields in most of these fields are only rough approximations of aptitudes.

In music, Carl Seashore of Iowa devoted years of research to devise talent tests. These tests sample such components of musical ability as sense and control of pitch, time, rhythm, timbre, musical memory and imagination, musical intellect and feeling. Probable ability to manipulate tools, machines, and materials is measured in the Stenquist Mechanical Aptitude Tests, the O'Rourke Mechanical Aptitude Test, and the Minnesota Mechanical Ability Tests. As yet these tests can be used only in combination with other data as useful predictors. The two best known tests for ability to discriminate among artistic values are the McAdory Art Test and the Meier-Seashort Art Judgment Test. These tests are of some assistance in sorting out those who can *judge* work of artistic merit but of less aid in indicating those who can *produce* work of artistic merit. The Rogers Physical Capacity Tests and the Brace Motor Ability Tests are often used with fair success to gauge probable ability in athletics.[12] Again, the most important outcome of research in aptitude testing is that these tests can be used by teachers only with caution and in the light of other qualifying data.

Earlier in this discussion, achievement tests were defined as instruments for measuring whether students *had* profited by training. They may measure such different aspects of achievement as power or speed or accuracy and, regularly administered, can tell the teacher just what the strengths and weaknesses of his class are in necessary skills and understanding. In Chapter 15 we shall discuss their advantages and limitations in more detail.

Differences in School Level

Freshman into senior. Think back to your own high-school days. Didn't you once look with awe upon the seniors, who knew so much; and didn't the sophomores seem irritatingly smug just because they *thought* they knew so much? So, too, each generation of high-school students imbibes a certain atmosphere that goes with the status of freshman or junior. Let us briefly characterize the different years in the high school, bearing in mind as we do, however, that schools will vary widely and that within each grade level many students will not fit the pattern.

Freshmen. Some teachers say, "I prefer the freshmen. They are

[12] All these tests are described and reviewed in Buros, O. K., *Mental Measurements Yearbook* (New Brunswick: Rutgers University Press, 1949).

so scared you can do anything with them!" True, the high school to many freshmen is a very awe-inspiring place. As the freshmen come from small elementary schools, some with only one or two teachers at most, into the larger high school, with many teachers and several hundred—or even several thousand—other students, they feel bewildered and overwhelmed. The transition from elementary school to high school is abrupt. The patterns of high-school teaching are vastly different from those of most elementary schools. Some elementary schools may have partial departmentalization in the upper grades, and the students may have been used to changing rooms or teachers once or twice a day. But that is nothing like the changes of five or six periods in the high school with an equal number of changes of teacher. Thus the freshmen face two major adjustment problems: to become a part of a much larger group of students and to adjust to five or six different teachers.

There are additional problems; the rules that keep the machinery of the school going in the high school are both more restrictive in some ways and more easygoing in others. But in any event, there are many *new* rules to learn. There may be special traffic problems in crowded halls; the use of lockers may be a new experience, as are eating in a cafeteria and traveling a long distance in a bus. Each new situation has its related set of regulations, and "It just isn't done that way" is heard over and over. The freshman sees around him hundreds of other students apparently very competent in dealing with this complicated world, and he feels very strange, lost, and, often, unhappy.

Entering high school may mean that the student has to learn to adjust to groups that have never before been part of his life: groups with different ethnic backgrounds, other religious groups, lower or upper class groups. The smaller elementary school often tends to be more homogeneous because the neighborhood is smaller. Towns, cities, and rural areas are settled in patterns, and individuals with similar incomes and ways of earning a living and similar social and cultural backgrounds will tend to find homes near by. Housing restrictions often freeze one group in one neighborhood only; particularly is this true of nonwhite groups and foreign-language speaking groups. In the high school, however, which includes students from several elementary schools, the student may face for the first time close association with students whose backgrounds are far different from his own. He does not know quite how to react. Should he be afraid of them, will they hurt him, will they be friendly, will they excel him in schoolwork? All these questions perplex the freshman as he looks over the numerous strangers that he suddenly finds in every class—and a new set of strangers to be dealt with every hour. How can I ever learn all their names? he asks himself. No one will know me, either, he whispers deep inside. I shall be lonely, I won't have any friends.

The freshman is faced with some basic new choices. Shall he take the vocational curriculum, the college preparatory, the general? These are very vague and difficult concepts, and yet somehow very important. He knows he must choose his courses, but often he is completely at sea as to the basis for such a choice. He rushes around to find out what courses his friends from the elementary school are taking, and he will then take it too. But he is pursued by anxiety as to whether this was or was not a wise choice.

In some schools the freshman runs the special hazard of teasing or hazing by the sophomores. While this particular form of torture is not seen too often on the high-school level, the new student does run a chance of being subject to special kinds of attention merely because he is new. In some junior high schools the incoming seventh-grade boys have to have special protection from the attacks of the eighth- and ninth-grade boys during the first few days of school. It is also possible that in schools where a new minority group enters the high school from the more homogeneous elementary schools, there may be occasional intergroup fights among the freshmen and with the other, older school members. The problem is less severe with the girls. The initiation of freshmen seems to be the special interest of the male.

What about secret societies? In many school districts across the country the secret society—the high-school version of the college sorority and fraternity—is banned, but in some places they are accepted as part of the school situation. In the latter case, the entering freshmen, both boys and girls, are likely to get rushed by some of these secret clubs. Sometimes this rushing has gone on before the student even came to high school, but more often new members will be chosen among the freshman class during the first few months of school. Thus, there is another element of anxiety among the freshmen; will they or will they not make the ranks of "The Sword and Flame", of Sigma Sigma, or of "The White Roses"? Usually only the socially ambitious and the socially established elite will be concerned with this problem, but the effects on the total freshman group may be seen in a heightened sense of personal insecurity and a corresponding lack of interest in classroom routines.

A number of school systems, in recognition of this transition problem, attempt to introduce the eighth- or ninth-grade student to the high school while he is still in elementary school or junior high school. There may be intervisitation programs; a special teacher or counselor may help each child arrange his program; a handbook on the high school and its program may even be given to each child and his parents. Some high schools have a special course entitled "Orientation" that is designed specifically for the freshman group to aid them in dealing with these problems. Nevertheless, each classroom teacher who has a freshman class will want to bear in mind the fact that the freshmen have a special kind of problem in their adjustment to the high school. Specifically, the teacher might try to keep these in mind:

1. *It will take several weeks for the students to learn and remember the rules.* The teacher will want to discuss with the students any special rules that are particularly difficult for the newcomers to follow, such as hall traffic regulations and behavior on the buses. Repetition will often be very necessary. Spending several minutes of each day with a freshman class to answer their questions about the school, the classwork, clubs, will make them feel more at ease and able to concentrate on classwork.

2. *Help the students get acquainted.* Early utilization of group techniques will quickly aid the freshmen to find friends to give the personal support that each needs. Various socializing devices would be helpful. Early in the fall a class Halloween party will not be amiss and will give the students a chance to relax together.

3. *Visit the elementary schools from which the students come.* By observing the classroom methods in these schools and the kinds of students in them, the teacher may quickly see areas where trouble may originate. If the elementary school has been very relaxed and has not used departmental instruction, the teacher may find it expedient to take over a few of the elementary practices into the freshman classes in order to help the students feel at home and at ease, so that the transition is not too abrupt. Although the students expect high school to be different and indeed would be disappointed if it were not, the teacher cannot automatically assume that the students fresh from the elementary school can adapt to high-school ways of thinking without some help and assistance.

4. *It is a good idea to be familiar with the clubs and organizations* other than the secret social groups that are available to the new student. By making every effort to guide the freshmen into extracurricular activities of their interest it will be possible to mitigate in some measure the exclusiveness and snobbery that accompanies overemphasis upon the secret social groups to the neglect of other far more personally rewarding activities.

Sophomores. Being sophomoric is such a widely observed phenomenon that we hardly need to explain its application in high-school teaching. This particular cultural expression does not occur only at the college level, but is often seen at the high-school level too. It is the "know-it-all" year. The students are no longer frightened, as when they were freshmen, and it gives them a great feeling of spurious superiority to observe the green look on the faces of the newcomers. The exuberance of the sophomore may well be a reaction of relief—they actually lived through that first dreadful year of being lost, of not knowing the directions, and it was not so bad after all. Now they scurry around the halls being very sure of themselves, which of course infuriates the incoming freshmen. The conflict between sophomores and freshmen may well lie in this need on the part of the sophomores to assert their security and the anger of the freshmen who know very well how much is to be learned about the school culture. While "hazing" seems to be passing out of the picture in many colleges (the returned veterans after World War II scorned this childishness and waste of time), there are some instances where it is cropping up in the junior high or senior high level. The sophomores therefore may need special guidance in the proper attitude to take to the incoming class.

Sophomores seem to be happy. The prospect of graduation and the burdens of adulthood are quite remote, and they have survived the freshman year. They are still young and with many immature ways about them. Only a few are concerned with the serious problems of adolescence; they play at being "in love" and going steady. They may even try being "fresh" to the teacher and seeing if they can get away with it. They throw themselves with zest into school functions and make good joiners.

There may be some special problems similar to those encountered with freshmen where there is a junior high school in the district. Then the sophomores have the same apprehensive approach to the high school, but it does not last quite so long as with the freshmen. The junior high has prepared them for high-school procedures and often there is little difference between the ninth grade and the sophomore year in so far as programming is concerned. The major problem with the transfer from junior high school is the higher level of sophistication. Many activities that used to be the exclusive possession of the high school are gradually filtering into the junior high, so that much of the high-school program is "old hat." The junior-high transfer is apt to be more sophisticated than the typical sophomore in an 8-4 system, less exuberant, more intent on his social activities.

The teacher with sophomores will want to—

1. *Enjoy their good spirits.* The sophomore is in a secure state in the total school hierarchy, and the teacher would do well to help the students enjoy and make the most of this period. Good friendships can be fostered,

and teachers can come closer to the students because of this relative security.

2. *Look for potential school leaders.* During the settling down period of the sophomores it is possible to note which individuals may emerge as school leaders in the junior and senior years. The social cliques will form during this year, and the school can benefit or suffer if these are not guided wisely.

Juniors. Having weathered one or two years of high school, the junior class has acquired a certain mature stability that is a welcome relief after the exuberance of the sophomores and the insecurity of the freshmen. This class will often be the backbone of the school. Having become well versed in the school routines, knowing the program and having made the vital academic choices already, the majority of the junior class works fairly steadily, supports school activities, and responds to more adult treatment by teachers.

From this class will come the leadership of the senior year, and already one can spot the more ambitious who are looking ahead for greater glory as senior class president, student body president, chairman of the social committee, or what not. There is likewise greater interest in schoolwork itself. The response to new ideas seems keener and more mature, and there is evident a development of interests that will endure for some time as against the somewhat flighty and haphazard interest of the younger students. Most of the enterprises of the juniors seem to be more seriously undertaken, with a better chance of completion and follow-through. The leadership can be trusted to perform according to its promises; there also seems more realistic planning of projects within the limits of the situation.

The giddiness of the sophomore seems to disappear during the intervening summer vacation. While there is continuous interest in the opposite sex, it is less likely to degenerate into a massive case of the giggles. Dating is somewhat more serious; students more and more pair off into "steady" couples; the social life includes more of the students, not just the socially precocious as was true of the earlier years. And from time to time a boy or girl may drop out of school—married. Such early marriages are usually frowned upon, but they are not so rare as we sometimes imagine. Some of the older boys will drop out also for jobs or to enter the armed services, not waiting for graduation.

The status achieved by the juniors is reflected in their behavior. It is often useful to call upon juniors to help orient the incoming freshmen class. They respond well to the protective role and are not completely preoccupied by their own affairs, as are the seniors.

Teaching a class of juniors is quite rewarding. Nevertheless, the teacher may find these suggestions useful:

1. *Treat them with more awareness of their adult status.* This group can and will respond well to reasoned explanations; they can participate actively and intelligently in planning many kinds of activities. Assignments can be more challenging and new ideas can be debated with greater show of general interest.

2. *Work toward discrimination in choosing of leadership.* A teacher who discusses from time to time the qualities of good leadership with a junior class is laying the foundation for a stable senior program and a well-organized student body, since from the junior group will come the future most important student leadership. Providing in class many opportunities to try out leadership is thus very vital for the junior group.

3. *Encourage serious class discussion about such things as choosing a vocation,* selecting a college, dating, problems of foreign and domestic policy. The juniors are more ready to consider these larger decisions and, with encouragement, can develop objective opinions and attitudes toward them. The groundwork for some important decisions to be made in the senior year can be laid now with some expectation of carry-over.

Seniors. The high and mighty seniors! In some ways the seniors are the most interesting and the most exasperating of all the classes. They appear to others as terribly sophisticated adults one moment, and as frightened children the next. Behind them are three successful years of high school and all of the other students look up to them, but ahead of them lie the vast unknown stretches of adulthood unprotected by the womb of the school.

Seniors can be very annoying because of their know-it-all attitude. The feeling of looking down on the childish interests of the high school is typical of one segment of every senior class. This small group is seriously engaged in becoming adult. It is probably the group that will go directly into jobs and very shortly thereafter into marriage. In many ways they are already grown up, having often worked in afterschool hours, and actually quite eager to be gone from the classroom. This desire to be out in the world is exactly what the school has been trying to foster, but sometimes when the students express it blatantly in class, by acting either smart-alecky or bored, the teacher finds it difficult to avoid being irritated. Where the senior has really set some goals after graduation, goals that do not relate very closely to success in school, he probably will be very difficult to motivate in class. After all, what does it really matter if he gets an *A* or a *D* in senior English when he has a full-time job already lined up at Joe's drugstore as a soda-clerk, a job that does not depend on any particular grade in English. And Susy, who also looks and acts equally bored is really daydreaming about her fiancé, Frank, and speculating on just how long it will be before he will earn enough for them to get married. Frank has been out of school several years and is doing fairly well as an assistant cashier in the credit department of one of the downtown stores. For her, also, obtaining a good grade hardly seems worth the effort compared with the important personal problems that she has to face.

This group may produce some fresh youngsters, who, seeing the end so close, and suddenly realizing the limited power of teachers and of all other adults as well, try to explore a new freedom. They may answer back, ask shocking questions, and in general refuse to cooperate with rules and routines. The sanctions of the school are relatively meaningless to this group; if they have so far not learned to *want to learn,* there are few threats that the teacher can produce that will have any effect. Cajolery, appeals to reason or affection or personal loyalty, and praise—these are probably the only effective tools left to the teacher. The two kinds of students noted above, the bored and the aggressive, are usually the hard core that makes life difficult with a senior group.

But the other seniors make up tenfold for all the trouble caused by these few. For between the junior and senior year a new purpose has blossomed. Most of the seniors have suddenly seen themselves on the brink of growing up, and life assumes a different complexion. A number of them look forward to junior college or college or university work. The senior year becomes a last period to concentrate on schoolwork to raise a drooping average; grades become almost too important. At the same time, many of the college-bound group are likely to withdraw somewhat from school affairs because they are already looking ahead to new fields to be conquered in the college of their choice. The glories of high-school recognition already seem a bit unimportant, and to get crazily excited about a school election or a big game is not nearly so appealing as it was a year or so before. Others, however, in this college-bound group respond quite differently. College seems like a new and terrifying challenge; the chances for failure are again very, very real in prospect. The senior who intends to go to college knows that he can succeed in high school; he has done so already. But what about college? Thus, he tends to become very devoted to high school; it is such a comforting place to be, where all the challenges are within one's range of talents. The eagerness to excel is redoubled; never have they debated so brilliantly or given the team so much energy and power.

The end of the year for the seniors is probably the most exciting, most excruciating, most wonderful time in the whole high-school life of the student—and for the teacher as well. Everything now centers around graduation. Students are called out of class for rehearsals of this and that, and there seem to be literally hundreds of things that seniors have to rehearse for. Valedictorian must be chosen; the senior play rehearsed; the senior ball staged, with all the fanfare and heartbreak and joy that goes into it. Each week brings something that will be done "for the last time." The last class party, the last examination, the last noon rally. Even the most bored, cynical, and eager-to-be-out-of-school seniors are caught up in this whirl and the sentiment that engulfs them. The nostalgia of four years spent together in the old school even includes the teachers and the administrators; students are more kindly, more responsive, more helpful during these last few weeks; and discipline actually becomes less strenuous.

The important problems of who will go with whom to the senior ball, of what is to be worn at this dance, of what is to be worn at graduation, what parties are being planned and who is being asked to come to celebrate the end of high school—these problems crowd out the most interesting schoolwork completely for some students and provide very tough competition even for the most serious. A wise teacher will plan, with seniors, to finish the big part of the term work well before the senior whirl starts, and then devote the last few days to developing short, interesting, significant topics that do not demand extended study or concentration. It will not be possible to get it without terrific pressure, painful and intolerable to both student and teacher.

In working with seniors, then, the teacher will need to remember:

1. *The senior group will sharply divide itself into college-bound and noncollege-bound students.* Don't try to give them all the same treatment. Among the former, study will be more diligent than ever, more serious, more determined, though not necessarily better. Among the latter, one will expect to find a mixed reaction; some students will express boredom or aggression; others will be fearful and reluctant to leave high school. The motivation that works with one group will not work with another. Do not rely on previous devices that worked, but experiment with new ones.

2. *Share their excitement with them.* The teacher of a senior class who refuses to enter into their feelings during the last weeks of school, and even earlier, will only earn the concentrated dislike of the students and the title "old fogey." This does not mean releasing them completely from school restraints, but it does mean a sharing of interest with them and a sympathetic cooperation when senior activities disrupt the usual routines.

3. *Recognize their imminent new worlds.* Some students are going di-

rectly into the adult work world and need guidance and assistance in this venture. Others face college, where they must start all over to win status and recognition. Either prospect is terrifying to almost anyone at some time or another, no matter how much desired, and the good teacher will share his own past experiences, will have "bull sessions" with his students about their present feelings and problems. The students are perhaps never so receptive as now to advice from an adult who genuinely seeks to understand their situation. But advice given in a patronizing, superior, sarcastic manner will not be accepted. These students consider themselves quite grown up, and, in many ways, they are. Acting on that assumption will get a teacher further with them than any other approach.

4. *Expect to be shocked.* The senior is often experimenting with socially disapproved ways of behaving. Although some students will be old hands at smoking and drinking, these departures from the code of behavior will become more and more widespread. Dating involves more sexual exploration, with dire consequences from time to time. The wild party is something to boast about, and students may seek distant and remote towns in which to misbehave so as to be able to tell about it all next day in school. The best students from the best families will be drawn into some of these activities. Don't be surprised! Dating college boys is an ambition of most of the girls, or dating boys that have been out of school for a while and have jobs and money to spend. And the money will be spent, often unwisely, often dangerously. These are the undercurrents that stir the senior class and compete with the academic routine.

General Implications of These Differences for the Teacher

Now obviously no teacher can alone remake the social and psychological worlds in which a student lives. But he *can* do his part in his classroom and in informal contacts with students. He can plan with the staff a consistent program and arrange for regular interchange of information. He can often get understanding classmates to help. He can himself, or through the administration of the school, obtain the assistance of other community agencies when appropriate, especially where problems center in the family.[11]

Here are some suggestions about specific assistance that the individual teacher can give:

1. *Make his own living healthful, balanced, satisfying.* Teachers who feel good because of good food, good rest, good fun, and good companions are more likely to make students feel good. This helps all students but especially students with problems.

2. *Make his attitude toward students relaxed, friendly, understanding.* Teachers who *expect* to find friends in the classroom are more likely to have cooperation and good will. This means reducing to a minimum a rigid, moralizing manner which concentrates on what students must *not* do and then waits grimly for them to do it. Of course, expecting behavior that contributes to good order and effectiveness does not mean disruptive be-

[11] For more detailed consideration see Chapters 17, 18, 19.

havior never occurs. The very best teachers have their troubles. It does mean, when trouble comes, trying hard to remain calm, trying to place the trouble in proper perspective (minor disorders are often best ignored), trying to remember that the trouble is caused. Especially when disruption comes from students who are known to have basic problems, good teachers try not to add to burdens which may already be almost too heavy to bear.

3. *Make the learning jobs attempted meet the differences represented in the classroom.* Teachers who know how students have lived are more likely to help students choose learning jobs for which they have the needed experience. The boy whose family has few good books or magazines, who was never sold on using the library in either home or school, who now reads comic books and not much more, probably does not have the experience with good literature to get much satisfaction from the standard works prescribed in the English class. It will not help to thrust him into the kind of reading he ought to do, if he is not ready for it. On the other hand, although building reading from where the boy is to where he ought to be is slow business, it is one good way to help the boy gain in self-insight.

4. *Make a special effort to build rapport with students who have problems.* Teachers in whom students have trust and confidence are more likely to hear about impending troubles. The kind of aloof dignity and cold authority in which many teachers clothe themselves discourages students from discussing their problems. Habitual use of force and fear, whether primarily physical or psychological, drives away those most in need of help.

Good teachers are good listeners. They have time to let students talk out their problems. They are happy to hear about successes, however small, and are sympathetic about failures, however large.

5. *Try to develop the rapport between students with problems and other students.* Teachers who know who likes whom in their classrooms are more likely to be able to help students make needed friendships. Students with problems are often social isolates. Good teachers involve them in class projects with others socially well accepted. Often parents are unaware that their children are not sought by other children and are very willing to try to make their homes places where the gangs will want to gather.

Summary

High-school teaching must take into account both the common qualities and the differences in students. We have always been much more aware of the sameness in students than of their individuality. This individuality is important to good government and good group living. We need to direct our education more toward developing significant individuality. To do this, we must be aware of these basic differences:

1. In growth and maturational patterns.
2. In backgrounds of experience.
3. In needs, interests, and abilities.
4. In school level.

For each of these differences, techniques have been developed in collecting information. The skillful high-school teacher gathers data through observation, case study, autobiography, interest inventory, aptitude and achievement testing. He recognizes the fact that unaided he cannot know all about all his students. He meets too many every schoolday. But he does what he can, realizing that, if each teacher adds to the personnel file of some students, all students eventually will be known better. Knowing students better is essential to teaching students better.

Selected References

Blos, Peter. *The Adolescent Personality*. New York: Appleton-Century-Crofts, Inc., 1941. A careful study of the psychology of the adolescent.

Caswell, Hollis L. (ed.). *The American High School.* Eighth Yearbook, John Dewey Society. New York: Harper & Brothers, 1946. Chap. II, "Youth Problems in Peace and War," pp. 18-30; Chap. V, "The Developmental Tasks of Youth," pp. 70-99. Discussion of today's problems as faced by the growing adolescent.

Frank, Lawrence K. "This Is the Adolescent," *Understanding the Child,* 18:65-69 (June, 1949). A direct and concise statement of the major confusions and anxieties of adolescents, with excellent recommendations to adults as to how to meet these problems.

Ginsburg, S. W. "Adolescence Is Hard on Everyone," *Child Study,* 28:12-33 (Winter, 1950-1951). Maturational problems faced by adolescents as they affect others.

Havighurst, Robert J. *Developmental Tasks and Education.* New York: Longmans, Green & Co., 1950. 86 pp. Shows both the personal and cultural demands made on young people with suggested implications for educational practices.

Havighurst, Robert J., and Hilda Taba. *Adolescent Character and Personality.* New York: John Wiley & Sons, Inc., 1949. Reports the findings of an extensive study into adolescent value systems, their source, and effects; includes a description of techniques used.

Hollingshead, August B. *Elmtown's Youth.* New York: John Wiley & Sons, Inc., 1949. A fascinating report by a social anthropologist of the role of the adolescent in a typical American community.

Landis, Paul H. *Adolescence and Youth.* New York: McGraw-Hill Book Company, Inc., 1950. A well-written and comprehensive text on adolescent development.

National Society for the Study of Education. *Adolescence.* Part I, Forty-third Yearbook. Chicago: University of Chicago Press, 1944. A wide range of chapters covers the physical, mental, emotional, and social-growth needs and expectations of the adolescent period.

Quillen, I. James, and Lavone A. Hanna. *Education for Social Competence.* Chicago: Scott, Foresman & Company, 1948. Chap. 2, "The Nature and Needs of the Individual," pp. 25-45. The relationship between individual and social needs in terms of the educational task of the high school.

Riesman, David. "How Different May One Be," *Child Study,* 28:6-8 (Spring, 1951). Focuses on a problem for adolescents particularly.

Segel, David. *Intellectual Abilities in the Adolescent Period: Their Growth and Development,* Bulletin No. 6. Washington, D.C.: U.S. Office of Education, 1948. Very important material on growth characteristics of high-school students, showing what the teacher can expect as to variations among his classes.

Strang, Ruth. "Manifestations of Maturity in Adolescents," *Mental Hygiene,* 33:563-569 (October, 1949). Specific case reports of the needs and problem areas of adolescents as they grope toward maturity.

Thayer, V. T., C. B. Zachry, and R. Kotinsky. *Reorganizing Secondary Education.* New York: Appleton-Century-Crofts, Inc., 1939. Part II, "Meeting the Needs of Adolescents in a Democracy," pp. 91-358. Excellent presentation of personal-social needs of adolescents and the challenge they present to the school.

"The Environment and School Health," *Health Bulletin for Teachers,* Vol. 21, No. 2 (January, 1950). Metropolitan Life Insurance Company, New York. The health of the student as a major factor in his school adjustment; a guide to teachers of what items are significant.

Watson, Goodwin B. *Youth after Conflict.* New York: Association Press, 1947. A comprehensive study of the effects of war and its aftermath on youth.

Zachry, Caroline. *Emotion and Conduct in Adolescence.* New York: Appleton-Century-Crofts, Inc., 1940. A basic reference for all teachers of adolescents—very penetrating and stimulating.

2. The Curriculum of the High School

WE BEGAN with the high-school student and his differences. We learned how to assemble data on these differences and then discussed how to use these data to promote learning. But is it enough to meet the individual's problems in development? Learning does not occur in a vacuum. The individual grows and develops in a society, and the culture, as well as the individual, has needs that must be satisfied. Therefore there must be an organized scheme of learnings. With a plan, we can see to it that neither is slighted—neither the individual's needs nor society's needs.

Once this organized framework—the curriculum—is agreed upon, we must see how the guidance of the learning tasks can be divided among the high-school staff. Such guidance will require detailed planning for the day, the month, the year. It will also require active consideration of the kind of classroom into which this planning must fit. But these related matters will be discussed in later chapters. Here we will concentrate on the over-all structure in the curriculum of the high school.

The Curriculum of the High School

The curriculum should be a meeting ground for the needs of society and the needs of the student. It is extremely important that the high-school student understand these double demands. Early in high school he should realize what society will require of him and what he will need from society. On his way through high school, he must always see clearly that what he is doing will make him better able to live effectively as a person in a society.

The dual responsibilities of the high school have not always been clearly seen. Consequently, the curriculum has not always been concerned with what the *student* needed as a person. Curricular patterns have not always taken into consideration the differences that we discussed in the first chapter. The high-school curriculum has been much more concerned with what *society* needed of the student. As we shall see in a moment, the high school has not always moved fast enough to satisfy the real societal expectations, but at least high-school curriculum makers did direct their best efforts to this end. As a rule they were *not* primarily concerned with students' needs.

Historical Backgrounds of the Curriculum

Let us see how the new emphasis in the high-school curriculum came to be. The high school has inherited a heterogeneous array of traditions and patterns, some imported, some typically American. The whole story of the American school system is that of an institution slowly adapting itself to changing social need. Several particularly significant historical factors must be kept in mind when considering the curriculum of the modern high school:

1. In eighteenth-century America, education above the "reading, writing, arithmetic" level was primarily thought to be for the gentlefolk, and for the special occupations pursued by gentlemen: the ministry, law, letters, medicine, teaching.
2. Nineteenth-century America felt that the opportunity to be among the gentlemen should be open to all. Public education became mass education. Still, even in 1890, the high schools enrolled only about 200,000.
3. Twentieth-century America became increasingly aware that democracy implies a concept of intelligent choice among genuine alternatives. Only literate individuals can understand the issues involved. Therefore, everyone needs to be educated. This concept also became a cornerstone of the proposition of universal compulsory education.
4. As the prosperity of twentieth-century America increased, the need for the labor of children and youth decreased. Idleness is not acceptable, particularly among the young, who are developing the habits of a lifetime. The harder it is for young people to get jobs, and the less desirable society deems it for young people to work, the more likely we are to find them in school. By 1950, the high-school population numbered over 6,600,000.

How do these historical social forces, briefly summarized above, find expression in the curriculum? Two of them are especially important: first, the tradition that the real task of the high school is to prepare students for college; second, the countering force of vast new numbers of students who do not intend to attend college.

The earliest high schools were attended for the most part by students whose parents could afford advanced schooling. The subjects taught were, by and large, useful for those who were going to practice the professions of the day. As high-school education became accepted as part of the system of free public education—indeed, as part of the compulsory school pattern in many parts of the nation—more and more parents sent their children on to high school. The previous pattern of highly selected student bodies no longer existed. With more of the bright children, also came more of the average and dull. More children came from homes where learning had little, if any, place, and where parents themselves could scarcely read or write, where books and even newspapers were unknown.

The High School and Social Trends

What did the schools do in response to this new population? The central fabric remained virtually untouched, but assorted pieces were now attached. The college-preparatory emphasis scarcely diminished through the decades, but at the same time various sequences were grudgingly added. These sequences were not specially intended to meet the needs of students but to satisfy the needs of society. Commercial majors, general majors, and majors in industrial arts, home economics, agriculture, and other fields became organized sequences so that the student not preparing for college might also obtain a diploma. Unfortunately special courses in these sequences, such as business English and general mathematics, and sometimes the entire sequences, were often used as repositories for the academically inept. Only rarely did these other means to high-school graduation gain the status of the college-preparatory curriculum.

It is interesting to note that where a high school is small—and the average high school in the United States has only 289 students and 13 teachers[1] —the basic curriculum, the one that remains when all other courses are shorn away because of the lack of money, is the college preparatory.

> One remote mountain high school enrolled, at the beginning of the year, about 150 students. At the end of the year this had usually dropped to about 120 or 110 as the spring round-up or marriage attracted various members of the student body. Of this school, about five students went on to college, two of them to the university, the rest to nearby junior colleges or state trade schools. The curriculum was fairly standard. Students had to take four years of English. Latin was of-

[1] *Statistics of Public High Schools, 1945–1946* (Washington, D.C.: Federal Security Agency, U.S. Office of Education, 1946), p. 5.

> fered, and one year of Spanish. Four years of social studies were required. As electives, the school provided two business courses, algebra and geometry, plus two art classes, two home economics, two industrial arts, and physical education. The sciences consisted of biology and chemistry in alternate years. The force of circumstances had made it necessary to have a course called general mathematics, since few of the students could succeed in the college-preparatory mathematics. And yet the graduates of this high school became ranchers, housewives, small businessmen, miners, fathers.

This curriculum represents common practice. Where schools have adequate finances, they add courses to the basic college-preparatory core: where they lack funds, only the college-preparatory courses are offered. Yet what percentage of high-school students actually go on to college? The over-all figure for the United States is less than 20 per cent, less than one fifth of the student population. The rate differs by districts, of course; some suburban high schools send as many as 75 per cent of their students to universities, colleges, and junior colleges, while many rural high schools send but 1 or 2 per cent.

The other important effect of large numbers of students upon the curriculum has been the crystallizing into almost institutional form of the unit system of separate subjects and the setting up of 45- to 50-minute periods for each subject, five days a week. This method has meant that each teacher could be a specialist, teaching one subject six hours a day, five days a week, to 150 or more students. The period is an accepted pattern for the American high school, where students may spend the first period in English, the second in music, the third in physics; lunch in the fourth period; United States history in the fifth, physical education in the sixth; and then home.

Yet we know that learning takes in the whole personality of the learner. It includes what he had for breakfast, the feelings he demonstrated when he got top score in an exam the period before, the fact that the chair he sits in is too small, the idea he has that the teacher likes Bill better than himself, the statement of his father that "I never understood that stuff myself." In other words, he learns in one piece. Even if he would, he cannot present only that part of him best suited to the learning job. Yet in the high school we have tried to cut the student into pieces much as we cut up the school day. Around each piece we have erected a fence that is called variously "a logical sequence of subject matter" or "a prerequisite to . . .," but whatever rationale is used, we seem to assume that the problems of the adult citizen are faced in tightly bounded areas of English or mathematics or social studies. We forget that it is the same student who goes from class to class, being presented with bits of this and bits of that, largely unrelated concepts, skills, and attitudes. Somewhere the relationships he has to see as an adult need to be developed. Thus, the accretion of the years in the high-school curriculum has been a collection of temporary structures jointed to the existing structure, rather than a real building to meet students' needs either as individuals or as members of a society.

It must always be kept in mind that in the United States we have attempted to bring secondary education to all the people, whereas no such pattern existed any place in the world. Furthermore, we undertook to complete this expansion of the high school within a comparatively short time. Although the population has only tripled since 1870, the number of high-school students has multiplied ninety times.[2] When an institution grows so fast, many solutions to important problems are bound to be based on expediency. So it is with the curriculum of the high school. More people than ever before are "exposed" to the important ideas of our culture and to the important tools needed by an industrial civilization, yet we are not teaching at maximum efficiency. Much time is wasted on studies that have long since lost their significance in meeting either individual or societal needs.

Examining the Purposes of Secondary Education

Any curriculum needs to be examined carefully in terms of fundamental objectives for education in a democracy. We should ask constantly about the total school pattern and its curricular components:

1. Do they contribute to producing better citizens, better workers, better parents, better human beings?
2. Do they improve daily living now, as well as adult living later? Do they help students meet some social or personal problem?
3. Do they serve those who will be the leaders today and tomorrow as well as those who will be the followers?
4. Do they make students desire to learn more or do they kill all desire to continue education once school years are over? Do they make students increasingly better able to direct their own learning?
5. Do they broaden the individual's view of himself in the world or do they strengthen his provincialisms and prejudices?

These fundamental purposes have been stated in detail by the Educational Policies Commission:

[2] *General Education in a Free Society* (Cambridge: Harvard University Press, 1945), p. 7.

The Objectives of Self-Realization:

The Inquiring Mind. The educated person has an appetite for learning.

Speech. The educated person can speak the mother tongue clearly.

Reading. The educated person reads the mother tongue efficiently.

Writing. The educated person writes the mother tongue effectively.

Number. The educated person solves his problems of counting and calculating.

Sight and Hearing. The educated person is skilled in listening and observing.

Health Knowledge. The educated person understands the basic facts concerning health and disease.

Health Habits. The educated person protects his own health and that of his dependents.

Public Health. The educated person works to improve the health of the community.

Recreation. The educated person is participant and spectator in many sports and other pastimes.

Intellectual Interests. The educated person has mental resources for the use of leisure.

Esthetic Interests. The educated person appreciates beauty.

Character. The educated person gives responsible direction to his own life.

The Objectives of Human Relationship:

Respect for Humanity. The educated person puts human relationships first.

Friendships. The educated person enjoys a rich, sincere, and varied social life.

Cooperation. The educated person can work and play with others.

Courtesy. The educated person observes the amenities of social behavior.

Appreciation of the Home. The educated person appreciates the family as a social institution.

Conservation of the Home. The educated person conserves family ideals.

Homemaking. The educated person is skilled in homemaking.

Democracy in the Home. The educated person maintains democratic family relationships.

The Objectives of Economic Efficiency:

Work. The educated producer knows the satisfaction of good workmanship.

Occupational Information. The educated producer understands the requirements and opportunities for various jobs.

Occupational Choice. The educated producer succeeds in his chosen vocation.

Occupational Efficiency. The educated producer maintains and improves his efficiency.

Occupational Appreciation. The educated producer appreciates the social value of his work.

Personal Economics. The educated consumer plans the economics of his own life.

Consumer Judgment. The educated consumer develops standards to guide his expenditures.

Efficiency in Buying. The educated consumer is an informed and skillful buyer.

Consumer Protection. The educated consumer takes appropriate measures to safeguard his interests.

The Objectives of Civic Responsibility:

Social Justice. The educated citizen is sensitive to the disparities of human circumstance.

Social Activity. The educated citizen acts to correct unsatisfactory conditions.

Social Understanding. The educated citizen seeks to understand social structures and social processes.

Critical Judgment. The educated citizen has defenses against propaganda.

Tolerance. The educated citizen respects honest differences of opinion.

Conservation. The educated citizen has a regard for the nation's resources.

Social Applications of Science. The educated citizen measures scientific advance by its contribution to the general welfare.

World Citizenship. The educated citizen is a cooperating member of the world community.

Law Observance. The educated citizen respects the law.

Economic Literacy. The educated citizen is economically literate.

Political Citizenship. The educated citizen accepts his civic duties.

Devotion to Democracy. The educated citizen acts upon an unswerving loyalty to democratic ideals.[3]

It is evident here that individual and societal needs have been placed in balance. As objectives, then, these are sound. But how shall we translate these objectives into curricular structures for the high school?

Curriculum Reorganization: But How?

In the period after World War II there appeared two basic reports on high-school education which tried to do exactly that. One was a report by the Harvard University faculty, *General Education in a Free Society.*[4] The other was published by the same Educational Policies Commission which sponsored the statement of objectives cited above. This report was called *Education for All American Youth.*[5] The Harvard group saw no great advantage to rebuilding the high-school curriculum. Instead, the committee believed, larger

[3] Educational Policies Commission, *The Purpose of Education in American Democracy* (Washington, D. C.: National Education Association, 1938), pp. 50, 72, 90, 108.

[4] Op. cit.

[5] Educational Policies Commission, *Education for All American Youth* (Washington, D.C.: National Education Association, 1944).

unity of purpose among the curricular course offerings and better methods of instruction would achieve the objectives sought.

The NEA report, on the other hand, proposed a number of basic modifications. The school day was to be made more flexible, allowing larger blocks of time where needed. Into some of these longer periods was to go a core course. The course was called "core" because it focused on the core social processes: family living, governing, distributing goods and services, consuming, communicating, appreciating beauty. Toward these central concerns of individuals and societies were to be directed the concepts, skills, and attitudes from many fields of study. The course was to be called "Common Learnings" because it cut across many of the old separate subjects of the high school to provide a commonly needed general education.

We can see the contrast in curricular emphasis by a glance at the accompanying charts.

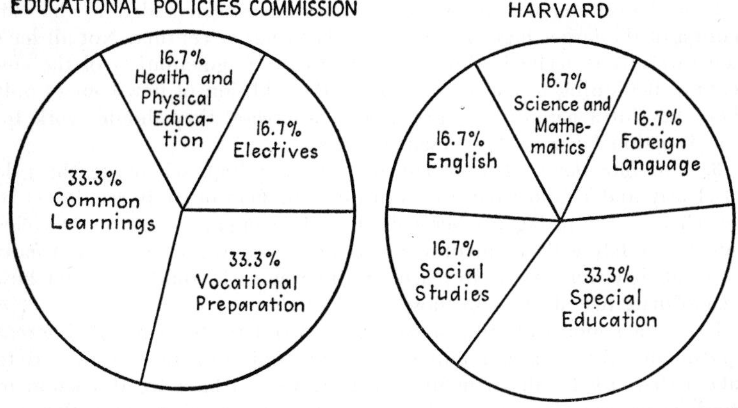

Both plans consider that they are providing for two thirds of general education and one third of special education. In the Educational Policies Commission report, however, the special education is more strictly vocational in intent. Within the provisions for general education are differences we already have noted. English, social studies, science, mathematics, and foreign languages disappear as required separate general-education courses in the EPC plan. All may appear, of course, either as elective courses in general education or in vocational preparation.

The Teacher Implements School Purposes

How can beginning teachers work within the framework each report endorses? Let us begin with the Harvard plan. Basically, most high schools retain the kind of curriculum endorsed by the Harvard plan. Remember the Harvard committee was convinced that the objectives of the high school could be achieved by developing larger unity of purpose and better methods of instruction. Other sections in this book discuss at length how better methods of instruction can help make these objectives realizable. Here we can concentrate on ways for the beginning teacher to help build coordinated effort in the curriculum:

1. *Change the content of courses.* It is the rare school system which prescribes exactly what must be taught. Suggested outlines of instruction abound. Nevertheless within these outlines there is more freedom than most teachers accept. Teachers are usually relatively free to shift emphasis, to rearrange organization of topics, to expand or contract the time suggested for topics. It is more often than not rationalization when teachers say, "They won't let me." The "they" is nebulous but convenient. Good teachers use the freedom they have to point the content of their courses directly toward the real objectives of the high school.

2. *Add new courses.* Many new courses have been added to the curriculum of the larger high schools in the last quarter century. Not all have been carefully conceived. Many just add to the fragmentation of the curriculum. Beginning teachers can support the addition of new courses only when they fill a gap in the curriculum; otherwise, they should work for more functional use of the present courses.

3. *Correlate the content of courses.* In many high schools teachers do not clearly understand what others in the same field of study are doing. In one school a beginning teacher volunteered to organize a series of coffee hours where fellow department members were encouraged to tell informally just what they were trying to teach. In this way each could see better how to coordinate his efforts with those of the others.

It is much more difficult, of course, to correlate the work of different departments. But it is not impossible. One beginning teacher offered to make a chart for his department head to serve as a basis for discussion in interdepartmental meetings. The chart looked something like the one below.

Courses

Objectives	English 1	English 2	English 3	U.S. History	World History	Social Problems
Self-realization Speaking clearly Reading efficiently and so on						

The beginning teacher's department met with only one other department that year and listed on the chart just which content applied to each objective. Only the barest beginning in cross-fertilization of content had been made at the end of the year. However, it was a rewarding effort because in a number of small ways the two departments helped each other with their problems.

In another school a young teacher discussed with his students the objectives of the high school. He asked them not only to help him keep the work in his course directed toward these objectives but also to call to his attention at any time the work of other classes in this direction on which his class could lend assistance.

4. *Fuse the content of courses.* To achieve the broad purposes of the high school, some courses belong together. We have seen a gradual trend toward these "broad fields" courses: general science, social living, general mathematics. Beginning teachers are often called upon to teach these new courses because others are reluctant to undertake the burden of planning a new field of study. If beginning teachers accept these assignments willingly and carry them out successfully, they will make a genuine contribution to a better high-school curriculum.

Now let us turn to the NEA report to see how beginning teachers can help implement it. Here the task is obviously more difficult. To break down the tight compartments of the present high-school curriculum calls for courage and tenacity.

The Teacher and Curriculum Change

Teachers themselves have long been trained in colleges and universities whose departments strictly maintain the same course boundaries. English teachers, for example, do not leap at the opportunity to teach "common learnings" courses where they must cope with social studies, science, and mathematics. Furthermore, there are no textbooks, or, indeed, other instructional materials, designed especially for core courses. Still, exasperatingly slow as progress must be toward curricular revision as fundamental as this, the beginning teacher should not be persuaded to abandon the attempt before he has even begun to try.

"To begin to try" means usually that the beginning teacher must first establish himself as a good teacher under the present curriculum. Then his colleagues, both teachers and administrators, will be more willing to listen to his suggestion for curricular revision. This is also important for the public relations of the school. Experienced teachers and administrators know that the quickest way to arouse community criticism is to revise the curriculum. But if the beginning teacher knows his community and the community knows him as a good teacher, the danger is at least minimized.

Too often the beginning teacher has forgotten how very traditional high schools are. He may not have been reminded of this fact at all by the department of education in which he prepared for teaching. Consequently, when the beginning teacher tries to apply the good ideas he gathers in departments of education before he has been accepted as a good teacher, he is rudely shocked by the cold resistance he encounters. In all too many cases then, he joins the older teachers in dismissing the good ideas as "educational theory" and reverts to the kind of education he has had most of his life. It is better to face the facts of high-school life from the beginning and calculate the mortality risks in proposing curricular experiments.

What are the steps in preparing a community and its high school for curriculum revision? What part can the beginning teacher play?

1. *Study successful attempts to revise the curriculum.* The beginning teacher can become well acquainted with projects like the Eight-Year Study and the community school. Then when the opportunity arises, he is prepared with the facts. He should know facts like these about (A) the Eight-Year Study* and (B) the community school:

A. The purpose of the Eight-Year Study was to see whether high schools, freed from dependence on college-entrance requirements, might not develop some newer curricular patterns that would prepare students equally well for college, but, more essentially, provide them with richer educational experiences. The study did demonstrate clearly that students could do just as well in college if the kinds of experiences in high school were quite different from the typical required courses. The cooperating schools produced some unique and challenging programs. Two careful appraisals of experimental programs in secondary education pointed out some decided advantages in these new approaches.[6]

B. The community-school movement fosters the idea that the high school is a community institution and that communities differ in their needs and problems in the same way that individual children differ. The high school, therefore, needs to be aware of the community, to serve it and educate the total community as widely as possible in the understanding of modern problems of living. Furthermore, to the degree that subject matter can be seen in the daily community setting, to that degree will students learn the lessons of the classroom. No subject matter can be truly meaningful that does not touch upon some aspect of the pupil's everyday world. A growing body of literature attests to the interest among school people in developing units, topics, courses, and even whole school programs that relate to the community. (For details, see Chapter 21.)

2. *Review the present curriculum.* Faculties may be ready to appraise the limitations of the present curriculum if they are reminded often enough of the successful experiments in curriculum. Parents' committees

* See *Thirty Schools Tell Their Story* in bibliography.

[6] Wrightstone, J. Wayne, *Appraisal of Experimental High School Practices,* Bureau of Publications, Teachers College, Columbia University, 1936.

Leonard, J. P., and A. C. Eurich (eds.), *An Evaluation of Modern Education* (New York: Appleton-Century-Crofts, 1942).

should assist in this review as in all subsequent steps toward curriculum revision.

3. *Summarize the key societal needs.* The understandings, skills, and attitudes developed in high school should build ability to meet the needs of the culture. The connection cannot be assumed and should be made explicit.

A continuous awareness of the problems of society is needed in curriculum construction for a realistic perspective of its objectives. A clear understanding of the foremost social problems may also serve to suggest focal points around which to organize classroom instruction. For example, a clear understanding of the family structure and problems in family living builds better understanding of the learners and their life problems. It also suggests what in this area needs to be considered in school and which facts and understandings are likely to be both useful and educative, which attitudes most desirable.

These pressures, problems, and values manifest themselves generally in the world society as well as in unique ways in local communities. Therefore, it is not enough for a curriculum-maker to acquaint himself with the general results of research or with analyses made by frontier thinkers. He needs also to study his own local community to uncover the unique manifestations of these problems, and, therefore, of the unique responsibilities of education in a given community. For example, while conservation of human and natural resources is the common problem for the "great" society, soil erosion may represent a specific illustration of that fundamental problem in one community, while preservation of mineral resources is most acute in the next one. Both can be used as gateways to the understanding of conservation.[7]

4. *Determine the basic developmental needs of the individual.* It is just as important that the understandings, skills, and attitudes developed in high school meet the needs of the individual as that they meet societal needs. Again, this necessary relationship cannot be taken for granted.

Whatever the high school does, the basic developmental tasks must be met, if not with the help of the high school, then in spite of it. If the tasks are attempted without the help and guidance that a good school can give, some of the tasks may be completed in ways not desirable for the adolescent or for society. Some of these important tasks of adolescence are:

(1) Coming to terms with his body and its changes.
(2) Working out a picture of himself consonant with these changes and being able to communicate this to others.
(3) Achieving a satisfactory role in the new adolescent society including the new kind of relationships with members of the other sex.
(4) Trying to gain a sense of independence from parents yet needing some security from them.
(5) Searching for a possible vocation.
(6) Striving to weave all these adjustments together into a pattern of values.[8]

[7] Taba, Hilda, "General Techniques of Curriculum Planning" in *American Education in the Postwar Period,* Forty-fourth Yearbook, National Society for the Study of Education (Chicago: University of Chicago Press, 1945), pp. 86-87.

[8] Adapted from Tryon, Caroline, and William E. Henry, "How Children Learn Personal and Social Adjustment," in *Learning and Instruction,* Forty-ninth Yearbook, National Society for the Study of Education (Chicago: University of Chicago Press, 1950), pp. 171-178.

Some promising, concrete planning to meet these developmental tasks has been undertaken by the Commission on Life Adjustment Education for Youth. The U.S. Office of Education and the National Association of Secondary School Principals, together with several other interested organizations, initiated the Commission in 1947. Since then state departments of education and cooperating high schools have tried to reorganize the curriculum so that it was something more than college preparatory. Special efforts have been extended to attempt to retain in school the large numbers of youth who drop out of high school before they are really ready for full-time occupations.[9]

5. *Identify the key objectives of the school.* Out of examination of individual and societal needs may come a desire to express for this school the really pertinent understandings, skills and attitudes to be developed.

Many high-school curriculum committees have found it helpful in this connection to look again at the statement of *The Purposes of Education in American Democracy* which was cited earlier in the chapter as an example of a formulation of goals where individual and societal needs were placed in balance. First the committees have sat down to ask themselves honestly, "Just *why* do we teach this?" And often the committees have had to confess they had never really faced that searching question before. In the first embarrassment, they have often turned to the pat statements of the professional literature in their subject fields. They have said, "Of course, this is why we teach this." But as they have tried to connect what they did in their classrooms with what the professional literature said were the ends sought, more often than not, as honest people, the curriculum committees have ruefully admitted some serious doubts. And so they have begun to look for ways to redirect their energies in the classroom in order to be more confident they were really moving toward these *Purposes of Education in American Democracy.*

Sometimes the curriculum committees found it useful to turn to a supplemental statement of the Educational Policies Commission in *Education for All American Youth.* The statement in *Purposes of Education in American Democracy* was intended for all levels of education, but the later statement was drawn particularly for the high school. And as such, the later statement gave more specific guidance to committee efforts:

(1) All youth need to develop salable skills and those understandings and attitudes that make the worker an intelligent and productive participant in economic life. To this end, most youth need work experience as well as education in the skills and knowledge of their occupations.

(2) All youth need to develop and maintain good health and physical fitness.

(3) All youth need to understand the rights and duties of the citizen of a democratic society and to be diligent and competent in the performance of their obligations as members of the community and citizens of the state and nation.

[9] Willis, B. C., "Life Adjustment Education for Youth," *Bulletin of the National Association of Secondary School Principals,* April, 1949, pp. 95-106.

Douglass, Harl, *Education for Life Adjustment* (New York: The Ronald Press Company, 1950).

(4) All youth need to understand the significance of the family for the individual and society and the conditions conducive to successful family life.

(5) All youth need to know how to purchase and use goods and services intelligently, understanding both the values received by the consumer and the economic consequences of their acts.

(6) All youth need to understand the methods of science, the influence of science on human life, and the more scientific facts concerning the nature of the world and man.

(7) All youth need opportunities to develop their capacities to appreciate beauty in literature, art, music, and nature.

(8) All youth need to be able to use their leisure time well and to budget it wisely, balancing activities that yield satisfactions to the individual with those that are socially useful.

(9) All youth need to develop respect for other persons, to grow in their insight into ethical values and principles, and to be able to live and work co-operatively with others.

(10) All youth need to grow in ability to think rationally, to express their thoughts clearly, and to read and listen with understanding.[10]

6. *Agree on an over-all design for the curriculum.* In any revision, a careful review must be made to see that the development of skills, attitudes and understandings is achieved in a graded sequence and without important gaps. The revision of the curriculum must not permit less thorough learning of the necessary understandings, skills, and attitudes.

Here the beginning teacher should familiarize himself with several authoritative discussions on high-school curriculum reconstruction. For example, he will find in Harold Alberty's *Reorganizing the High School Curriculum* (Macmillan, 1947), J. Paul Leonard's *Developing the Secondary School Curriculum* (Rinehart, 1946), and the Stratemeyer, Forkner, McKim book *Developing a Curriculum for Modern Living* (Teachers College, Columbia University, 1947) many concrete suggestions on curriculum design. He can assist curriculum committees in his school out of many impasses by tactfully suggesting some of the alternatives proposed in these careful analyses by experienced curriculum consultants.

7. *Prepare curricular resource materials.* The revision cannot succeed unless materials with which teachers and students can work have been carefully prepared. The resources will, of course, not be complete, but they ought to be extensive enough to give each class a good start.

The National Council for the Social Studies has issued a series of resource pamphlets which will provide good models for curriculum committees.[11] Perhaps the best discussion of the resource unit is in Quillen and Hanna's *Education for Social Competence.*[12] Over a period of years many of the nation's schools systems have developed excellent resource materials which can usually be obtained for the guidance of new curriculum committees.

[10] Educational Policies Commission, *Education for All American Youth* (Washington: National Education Association, 1944), pp. 225-226.

[11] National Council for the Social Studies, *Problems in American Life Series* (Washington, D.C.: National Education Association, 1942).

[12] Quillen, I. J., and Lavone Hanna, *Education for Social Competence* (Chicago: Scott, Foresman & Company, 1948).

This step-by-step approach to curriculum revision presumes years of patient effort. Too much cannot be expected too fast. The beginning teacher can best play his part if he helps the cycle of revision to begin. He cannot be expected to be the main source of momentum once it has begun. Momentum will come only if the public, the students, the other teachers, the administrators all work together. Even then change will be slow.

Factors Opposing Curriculum Change

Why do the schools change so slowly? Why are the findings of research often accepted only years after they have been published and accepted? Within the classroom, the high school today is in many ways as outdated as the buildings that are still in use in some parts of the country. Why is that?

First, we must remember that people are essentially conservative in those areas of life that affect them most deeply, such as religion, government, and education.

Second, many people remember their own schooling; it is familiar to them, and it is difficult to foresee how newer methods could work or be effective. There is rarely *overwhelming* experimental evidence to substantiate proposed changes, and where there is, the cases are often not typical—or so we tend to think.

Third, those very factors that assist in giving the curriculum its framework, such as the textbook, the courses of study, and the hour periods, affect many other aspects of the school and the school system. To change a given teacher's course may have far-reaching effects on many other persons and programs. The more people who are affected by such change, the more difficult it is to make the change.

Fourth, teachers themselves find it difficult to strike out in new paths. The reasons are not easily dismissed:

1. Teachers have trouble keeping in close enough touch with students to know whether newer practices really are acceptable to students or really make their teaching more effective.

2. Where direction has always come from some "authority," the teacher feels diffident about striking out alone in untried paths.

3. Newer approaches are usually more difficult: outcomes are less certain; criticism is not so easily answered; materials are not always available; more unexpected things are likely to occur.

4. The teacher is not always sure that the students are really "learning," since often the content and emphasis are very different from the traditional subject field.

5. The students as well as the teacher often do not "know what is being

expected" and this sense of lack of direction, lack of following established routines, is very unnerving for all involved.[13]

Since it is the individual classroom teacher who may, within limits, effect the important curricular changes, it is especially important for beginning teachers to develop an attitude of mind that welcomes new ideas and is willing to work for them.

Facing a New Challenge

Today many powerful forces have banded together to fight against proposed changes in the curriculum. The schools are under more savage attack than ever before. The reasons for this attack are many, but we can list only a few here:

1. Unprecedented increase in school enrollments.
2. Inflationary aspects of economy including increased taxation and cost of living.
3. Increased world tension, with concomitant increase in personal anxiety and insecurity.

The confluence of these forces has put the schools in the unfortunate position of being the scapegoat. It is highly important that those entering the teaching profession today be alert to the temper of public opinion in order to be able to detect that criticism which is intended to strengthen school programs, and that criticism which is aimed to destroy. Educators must not allow American public schools to be undermined by capricious and destructive critics who speak for only a vociferous minority. The profession must constantly seek for more and more avenues of communication among all levels of the community in order that, together, school and community may best find democratic solutions to the recurrent problems of education.

Summary

In order to further the needs of both the individual and society, the learnings of the high school are organized into a curriculum. The high-school curriculum has always been more concerned with the demands of society than with the needs of the individual. But even in attempting to meet society's demands, the curriculum of the high school has failed to keep pace. The old societal demand used to be for college preparation in the high school, but now less than one fifth of the high-school students go on to college. Still, the college-preparatory curriculum predominates. Furthermore, the

[13] Thelen, H. A., "Resistance to Change of Teaching Methods," *Progressive Education,* XXVI: 208-214 (May, 1949).

courses within the curriculum are rigidly compartmentalized. The curriculum needs more unity of purpose and effort.

Two proposals came out of the years after World War II to meet these deficiencies. One was prepared by the faculty of Harvard University, the other by the Educational Policies Commission. Each recognized that the high school has larger purposes than merely to prepare students for college. These purposes, the reports agree, can be separated into those belonging to general education and those belonging to special education. The purpose of general education is to prepare all citizens to think critically, discriminate among values, communicate effectively; that of special education is to prepare students for vocations or for advanced study. The Harvard Committee believed both general and special education could be provided without changing the present curricular framework, even though it has been largely pointed toward preparation for college. All that was needed, according to the Harvard report, was to point the courses toward broader purposes and work to achieve unity of effort among the courses. On the other hand, the Educational Policies Commission saw the need for basic revision of the curricular framework. The school day was to be made more flexible. Into some of the larger blocks of time now provided were to go courses cutting across the old course boundaries. These common-learnings courses were to focus on the core social processes (family living, governing, distributing goods and services, and so on), drawing in, as needed, the concepts, skills, and attitudes from many fields of study.

Whichever point of view is held, teachers have responsibilities to work toward the accepted goals of the high school. Within the old curricular framework, for example, teachers can work to change the content of courses, to correlate courses, and to fuse courses. In more thoroughgoing reorganization, curriculum committees will need to study such promising experimentation as that of the Eight-Year Study and the community-school movement. As new objectives and new curricular designs are built, teachers must invite community assistance and take the long-term view. Change will come slowly. It is especially important that beginning teachers recognize this hard fact without defaulting on their responsibility to work for a better curriculum for the high school.

Selected References

Alexander, William M., and J. Galen Saylor. *Secondary Education*. New York: Rinehart & Company, Inc., 1950. Chap. XV, "Core Curriculum

Plans" pp. 371-396. Detailed suggestions about how to carry the kind of common learnings course envisioned in *Education for All American Youth.*

Cary, Miles E. "Learning Comes through Living," *Educational Leadership,* 4:491-495 (May, 1947). A brief presentation of a curriculum centered in basic social functions.

Caswell, Hollis L. (ed.). *The American High School.* Eighth Yearbook, John Dewey Society. New York: Harper & Brothers, 1946. Chap. VI, "Assets and Liabilities of the High School," pp. 100-114; Chap. VII, "The Changing Curriculum," pp. 115-134; Chap. VIII, "Curriculum Proposals for the Future," pp. 135-157. Leading curriculum planners speak of needs, hopes, and plans for the high school.

Core Program in World Culture—A Progress Report of the Haverford Township High School. In University of Pennsylvania, *Schoolmen's Week Proceedings,* 1947. Philadelphia: The University, 1947. pp. 177-188. "How and Why the Program Was Started," by Oscar Granger; "The Growth, Methods, and Outcomes," by W. Breuninger; "The Approach of the History Teacher," by Lilly Reichmann; "The Approach of the English Teacher," by Theodore Huber. A correlated history-English core.

Faunce, Roland C., and Nelson L. Bossing. *Developing the Core Curriculum.* New York: Prentice-Hall, Inc., 1951. The most recent and complete coverage of this whole area in practical terms.

Harris, L. E. "Developing a Community School in Floodwood." *North Central Association Quarterly,* 23:334-338 (April, 1949). A three-hour general-education program, grades 7 through 12, is reported by this small northern Minnesota high school. Emphasizes school-community relationships and contribution of the general education program to community-mindedness.

Leonard, J. Paul. *Developing the Secondary School Curriculum.* New York: Rinehart & Company, Inc., 1946. In Chap. 11 are a number of illustrations of communities who worked out curriculum designs with careful regard for sequential development of understandings, skills, and attitudes.

MacConnell, Charles M., Ernest O. Melby, and Christian O. Arndt. *New Schools for a New Culture.* New York: Harper & Brothers, 1943. Chapters 3, 4, 5, and 6 relate to the core program—getting it started, carrying it on, and setting standards—with New School of Evanston Township High School (Illinois) used as illustrative material. Chapter 6 answers questions and objections most commonly raised by those seeking information concerning New School's experiment.

Manley, C. Benton. "Life Adjustment Education in Springfield Senior High School," *Education Outlook,* 22:173-182 (May, 1948). A description of how one high school tried out life-adjustment education.

Quillen, I. James, and Lavone A. Hanna. *Education for Social Competence.* Chicago: Scott, Foresman & Company, 1948, Chap. 4, "Content of Instruction for Social Competence," pp. 69-106. A stimulating volume containing much helpful advice about resource materials for the high-school curriculum.

Rolnick, Gladys. "The Experience Curriculum at Midwood as the Teacher

Sees It," *High Points,* 30:27-34 (January, 1948). Discusses pupil-teacher planning and work in a democratic classroom and describes briefly a typical day in a core class.

Smith, B. O., W. O. Stanley, and J. H. Shores. *Fundamentals of Curriculum Development.* Yonkers: World Book Company, 1950. Part Four, Chaps. 16-24, "Patterns of Curriculum Organization," pp. 376-614. One of the most discerning of the new books on curriculum.

Stratemeyer, F. B., *et al. Developing a Curriculum for Modern Living.* New York: Bureau of Publications, Teachers College, Columbia University, 1947. Recommended to beginning teachers when they are asked to serve on curriculum committees.

Thirty Schools Tell Their Story. New York: Harper & Brothers, 1943. Adventure in American Education, Vol. 5. Report of their experimental curriculum practices by schools in the Eight-Year Study.

Wright, Grace S. *Core Curriculum in Public High Schools: An Inquiry into Practices, 1949.* Bulletin No. 5, 1950. Washington, D.C.: U.S. Office of Education, 1950. Gives a statistical report on the number and kind of core programs with descriptions of some outstanding examples.

General Education in the American High School. Report of Sub-Committee of the General Education Committee Commission on Curricula of Secondary Schools and Institutions of Higher Education of the North Central Association of Colleges and Secondary Schools. Chicago: Scott Foresman & Company, 1942. An excellent series of essays by Havighurst, Hand, Prescott, Redl, Tyler, and others on various aspects of the curriculum of the modern high school and related problems.

Understanding School Criticisms

Association for Supervision and Curriculum Development. *Building Public Confidence in the Schools* (1949), and *Laymen Help Plan the Curriculum* (1946). Washington: The Association. Two excellent pamphlets showing how schools can make positive use of public interest in education.

Beale, Howard K. *Are American Teachers Free?* New York: Charles Scribners Sons, 1936. A well-documented study of pressures on teachers from many sources.

Bossing, Nelson L. *Principles of Secondary Education.* New York: Prentice-Hall, Inc., 1949. Chap. I, "What Criticisms Are Frequently Made of the Secondary Schools?" pp. 3-15. A good statement that places the general over-all criticisms of the high school in perspective.

Governor's Fact-Finding Commission on Education. "Do Citizens and Education Mix?" The Connecticut Report. Hartford, Conn.: Office of the Governor, 1950. An impressive report of how 85 Connecticut community-school committees worked together to improve education in each locality.

Hulburd, David. *This Happened in Pasadena.* New York: The Macmillan Company, 1951. A highly readable and accurate account of the upheaval in Pasadena that ended with the resignation of the superintendent and started a nation-wide inquiry into the methods and motives of the critics of the schools.

Melby, Ernest O. *American Education under Fire.* Freedom Pamphlet. New York: Anti-Defamation League of B'nai B'rith, 1951. Who the critics are and how they may be handled.

National Citizens Commission for the Public Schools. Miscellaneous publications. 2 West 45th St., New York, 19, N. Y. This Commission is an excellent source for recent material on methods of promoting positive school-community cooperation.

3. Developing Democratic Behavior in the Classroom

A CURRICULUM is only a piece of paper until it reaches the classroom. There it comes alive. But the gift of life is not always the same. In one classroom, it may be quickened to the needs of individuals working out their common problems. In another, it may be charged with the needs of a regimen working its will on individuals. The teacher may honestly believe he is carrying out the same curriculum in both of these classrooms. And it may be a curriculum carefully dedicated to those accepted purposes of the high school in a democracy—purposes on which a committee like that of Harvard or that of the Educational Policies Commission could agree. Each teacher may be able to say with complete sincerity that he is laboring to develop the kind of democratic behavior envisioned in those purposes. Each may be honestly convinced that he himself is a democratic teacher.

Of course, in our culture it would be difficult for any teacher to defend a way of teaching that could not be called "democratic." But here is the difficulty. What do we mean by "democratic?" It is most difficult to frame a definition on which we agree in the only way that really counts—in the way we act. Nations use the word in very different ways.[1] Similarly educators have difficulty in identifying the democratic classroom or the democratic teacher. Part of the trouble may be that so few of us have ever experienced a democratic classroom.

Defining the Democratic Classroom

Typically, our schools, although taught by people of good will, are not necessarily democratic. As a matter of fact, one of the first things to remember is that good will in itself is not synonymous with democracy. Let us first look at two classrooms:

> Mr. Giffin thought of his students in Spanish 2. He wanted to be certain they understood this language was a key to the culture. Suppose he broached the subject of bull fights? He might fill in some of the outlines of this traditional spectacle. Then, if he had caught them up in the excitement of this other world, he might open up a number of alternatives to them for further pursuit. Some might want to see a motion picture playing the neighborhoods, *The Brave Bulls.* Others might want to check out those newspaper accounts from *La Prensa* which he had in the file. Then the library had a number of short stories in Spanish. The old Spanish-American residents in South Town would welcome a group of students in an interview about their memories of the toreadors of their youth. There would be other possibilities the students themselves would suggest. They could work up the final plans for the unit together.
>
> Mr. Conley was also planning his next week's work. Now, said he to himself, we have just finished the first real introduction to irregular verbs. Let me see—quickly he picked up the textbook and checked the next chapter. Ah, a discussion of the passive tense. Well, I guess next week we will spend time first on a review of the irregular verbs. It's so hard for those slow students who sit near the windows to remember anything. Then, after a quiz—I'll spring that on them so I can see who has really been studying—I'll go over the material in the next chapter. I guess they can do the exercises by Tuesday, the paragraph translation by Wednesday, and Thursday we will have oral drill. Then Friday—Friday is the day of the game. I know they'll be all excited so I guess to keep them in their seats I'd better have a test ready to come about the last half of the period.

Now both of these teachers are doing a job of planning. Both act with good will. But let us look at the difference: one plans with his subject matter in one hand and his students in the other and tries to see the best meeting ground between them. The other has his subject matter before him and tries to fit the students to it, never

[1] See "On the Meanings of 'Democracy': The UNESCO Inquiry," *Journal of General Education,* 4:54-67 (October, 1949).

concerned with students' needs. Which one is it easier to be? It is, unfortunately, easier to be Mr. Conley than Mr. Giffin. Mr. Giffin has to be flexible, to be aware of students, to have a great variety of teaching resources at hand. Mr. Conley can build the mold for weeks with a minimum consideration of students as persons and with the barest essentials in teaching materials.

But does that make Mr. Giffin democratic? Mr. Giffin had the class under control; he would suggest the choices and they might not *vote* at all! This is a legitimate point and one that needs careful consideration. After all, the classroom is not at all the area of politics where citizens of equal voting stature discuss, debate, and then cast a ballot. The teacher has knowledge, the teacher is an adult, the teacher is vested by law with authority, and the teacher is surrounded in part with the aura of the parent. These "authorities" of the teacher, both open and hidden, make an important difference. The students had no say in choosing Mr. Giffin to be their teacher. Neither of course did Mr. Giffin choose belligerent Tim Atkins or arrogant Jane Boothe for his class. Reluctant subjects and arbitrary leadership do not, in our usual sense of the word, make for a very democratic situation. Thus we need to redefine our terms somewhat if democracy can legitimately be joined to education.

The anthropologists and social psychologists have some light to shed on this subject. As Ruth Benedict has pointed out, there are many kinds of folk systems that one can call "democratic" because each member of the group is able to live a good, protected, productive, individual existence. Yet they may look very different from our own political democratic system.[2]

Democratic education, then, must not be considered as a *political* system, but as a *social* system, a concept that embraces human interrelations, not merely methods of control and organization. If the needs of students are being met, if they are progressively more able to cope with their world, if they are developing increasing self-direction in the conduct of their own affairs, if they are able to seek more learning as a result of these present learning experiences, then probably it is a democratic classroom. And the teacher who arranges for such things to occur is then a democratic teacher. Yet there may not be a single vote taken the whole time. Confusing? Not democratic?

[2] Benedict, Ruth, "Recognition of Cultural Diversities in the Post-War World," *Annals of the American Academy of Political and Social Science,* 228: 101-107 (July, 1943).

Misconceptions About Democratic Classrooms

As a study in contrast, it might be useful to look for a moment at what a democratic classroom is *not.*There are two common misconceptions of the democratic classroom. One is that in a democratic classroom the students decide everything. No activity, no subject, no assignment is made without student consent. In fact, unless the students want to do something, they do not have to do it. This is obviously not democracy, but the most ordinary kind of anarchy. The second misconception is that in a democratic classroom students must be protected from their immaturity. Therefore, a benevolent and wise leader must decide in order that the students may be adequately prepared for adult living. After all, the adults know what is best; therefore, let those who know best make the decisions. This is not democracy, either. It is benevolent autocracy.

Democratic Classrooms

We have said that neither of these classrooms is democratic. Although we cannot have any kind of social group without rules, we also cannot have any kind of self-direction on the part of the group unless members of the group have some vital part in making these rules. This kind of balance between freedom and security within the classroom is one measure of the democracy of that classroom.

Freedom within rules. A democratic classroom has an orderly procedure established; there are rules that apply to various activities. If someone is giving a report, others listen; if a group member has an assignment, he must see that the assignment is completed because the group will need it. These and similar rules govern social living in any group, and certainly are acceptable in a classroom.

But what happens if the teacher establishes a rule that the students do not like?

> In a science class, the teacher had stated that all of the class would have to finish every experiment in the unit being studied before anyone could proceed to the next unit. Three students finished very much before the others and spent a week in the library while the rest of the class caught up. But even at the end of the week, two students were still several experiments short. This meant postponing the next unit of work for another two or three days. The students felt that the teacher's rule had been arbitrary and should not be applied to succeeding units of work.

Obviously, the teacher had a good reason for this rule. Some general class instruction would be necessary before the whole class could proceed to the experiments in the next major unit of work. It would be very inefficient to give the same class instruction to two or three students at a time, not to mention the difficulty of having supplies out for a number of different experiments at the same time. However, the students also had a good point; the present rule rewarded only the slowest students and penalized the fast ones for being ahead in their work. "Why get your work done ahead of time, or even on time," said the students, "you still have to wait for the others." Here is where the democratic teacher discusses with the class the reasoning behind the making of the rule, the possible problems that might arise, and requests from the class a more acceptable solution. The class and the teacher may very well agree that all work should be done by a certain time, and that when most of the class has done the required work, those who are still incomplete may come in at stated hours before and after school, during study hour or lunch period, to get their assignments out of the way. Those who were ahead could have an option of helping others or doing special related reading for the next unit and making a class presentation.

What if the rule is a school rule and such deviations and compromises are not allowed? The students are then in no position to change it. In that case the whole problem of rules and what to do about them should be aired. Why do we have rules anyway? In a game there are very definite rules, and these are what make the game. We do not change the rules just because they put a temporary handicap on our side. Rules are used in a democracy to ensure good order and fair play. Students need to make an objective examination of this function of rules in a democracy. In this study they will discover that when a rule is contrary to common sense and actually impedes the purpose it was to achieve, an orderly way of changing the rule is sought. This way we may have freedom within security.

Rules are only one part of the kind of classroom security that produces a democratic atmosphere. Another kind of security is that both students and teacher have a clear-cut definition of the other's role and areas of responsibility. The teacher who seeks to have a democratic classroom must not fool his students into letting them believe they have more freedom and power than he is really willing to grant.

> Miss Willow was dissatisfied with the routine of the classroom that she had inherited in mid-term from another teacher. In this class the schedule was: Read assigned chapter Monday and Tuesday, answering questions at end of chapter. Wednesday, discuss questions. Thursday,

> have more question recitation, then a short quiz. Friday was current events. Miss Willow suggested a more active kind of learning situation, with projects, debates, different kinds of readings, etc. After some talk in class, the class voted; and they voted to keep their usual routine. At this Miss Willow became angry at the class, and told them they would have to try things her way anyway. The students became rather bitter over her previous fine comments on democracy and freedom.

This teacher was not genuinely willing to let the class choose, and yet she had provided the freedom for the class to choose. The class learned to mistrust her. The class had no security regarding the teacher's role in the class. The teacher, in a democratic situation, must be willing to take the consequences of freedom granted. If the students cannot reasonably be expected to make a wise choice, through lack of necessary experience or knowledge, then obviously the teacher should not offer the choice.

Genuine choices. The first criterion of a democratic classroom, then, is *freedom within rules;* the second criterion is that choices are available. After all, freedom does mean freedom to choose. But among what kinds of things can students choose? First, the choices must be real. When people vote in totalitarian countries, they only vote "yes." We do not want Miss Willow's democracy in our classrooms.

The concept of choice is essential to democratic teaching in the same way that it is essential to a democratic society. What kinds of choice does the democratic teacher provide? How can he tell whether the choices he provides are those that could be called genuine? We know that young people do not know all of the consequences of their acts. If students had their own way about it, how many would stay in school everyday for the required length of time? The student does not choose whether or not to come to school—he has to come. It is all the more important, then, that classrooms give him many opportunities to develop ability to make wise choices in those realms of social and personal affairs where he does know the consequences. Otherwise, one essential democratic skill will not be developed.

Of course, the teacher by virtue of age, training, experience, legal authority, and tradition must establish some limits in choices of subject matter and method. For many choices it is the teacher who knows best. Obviously, we would not want young people to choose whether to study for six weeks spelling and nothing else or lyric poetry and nothing else. Of course, these are not realistic alternatives. The teacher, however, may discuss with the class the importance of having reasonable amounts of both activities. Then the class may choose, perhaps, the days for spelling, or methods of getting spelling lists that include the most troublesome words, or ways of presenting the poetry for maximum enjoyment.

Suppose that a teacher decides to discuss with a class alternatives to a final examination. What criteria have we to guide us in this kind of choice situation? First, the teacher may well explain to the class why a final examination is to be given. He will say, for example, that he needs this information about the progress that individuals have made in the class. However, the students may point out that there are other means of obtaining evidence about their progress. The teacher who seeks to be democratic has an obligation to think through with his students the common goal that they have, and then examine carefully the means that are available to achieve that goal. The discussion might sound like this:

TEACHER: A final exam helps you organize your thinking.

STUDENTS: But we could do the same thing in a paper, and that would give us more time to show really what we could do.

TEACHER: In college you will need to take many final exams; it helps to learn how to work quickly and accurately.

STUDENTS: But many of us are not going on to college; perhaps only the college-bound students ought to take the final.

TEACHER: I need some comparable evidence, however; it wouldn't be fair to judge a few on a final exam and the rest on a written report—the results might be so different.

STUDENTS: Then could we all do both activities, and you take the highest grade that an individual makes, whether on the exam or the report, since some of us do better on reports and some on exams.

This interplay provides a framework within which democratic education may operate. If student needs are ignored or suppressed and only the opinions and demands of the teacher and the institution are followed, there can be no democracy. Thus the answer to the question above—Do students have a right to vote against a final examination?—is a question that can only be answered when both teacher and students are informed of the needs, interests, motives, limitations, goals of the other. After students are helped to recognize the consequences of their choices, only then are they fully able to make choices. The democratic teacher's function is to guide students so that they become increasingly more able to choose among increasingly more significant alternatives. After all, the major decisions in life are somewhat above the level of spelling vs. the lyric poets. In life the boys and girls themselves are choosing whether to disobey their parents and stay out with the gang, whether to spend their money on a new dress for an important date or save it for some possible college expense three years from now. Such choices do have broad implications for the young people involved; the democratic classroom provides essential experience to develop the ability to consider choices intelligently.

Let us not confuse the concept stated above with the requirement that *every* time a decision is to be made, the whole class must participate. This kind of "democracy" is just as futile and frustrating as no democracy at all. One can take a lesson from society itself; many decisions are so obvious, so insignificant, that often we do not know we are making them. We do not consciously decide whether to put on our left shoe rather than our right shoe first. This is habit. Nor in a classroom must all learning stop while the class ponders the problem of whether books should be passed up the aisle from the left or from the right. The concept of orderly living can and must pervade the classroom much as it pervades a home. In a classroom, however, there are thirty youngsters and one adult to be managed, and the average home only deals with two children and two adults—a vastly different problem in management of human patterns. Because of this complexity, the democratic classroom does demand many group decisions. These are accomplished quickly and satisfactorily to the degree that the group has had experience in such group thinking; the group follows the steps in logical thinking as described in the section on discussion (Chapter 7): What is our problem? What possible alternatives are there? What are the consequences of any given alternative? What additional facts do we need in order to evaluate the alternatives? In the light of the facts we have, which alternative do we choose? How shall we put this choice into operation? These steps guide the class in making democratic choices.

Besides developing an essential democratic skill, the opportunity to choose means better motivation of the learner. He is involved from the beginning because he has a voice in the direction the learning will take.

> The literature book used in a tenth-grade English class started with *Beowulf* and progressed chronologically to modern essays and stories. The teacher had found that to start at the beginning of the book was a great handicap, since *Beowulf* was one of the most difficult selections in the whole book to read. Therefore, at the beginning of the semester, he would pass out the textbook and ask the students to look the book through carefully. Then he would discuss the various sections of the book, pointing out some of the more interesting and important selections to be found. He answered questions about the book that the students raised. Almost a whole class period was spent in this exploratory

> experience. Toward the end of the period, he asked the class to gather in small groups of four. Each group was to reach a consensus about where in the text they would like to start. These reports were then given to the teacher who proceeded to start his work in literature on the basis of the student choices. The interesting thing was that while no two classes ever wanted to start in the same place, he found that he covered the same ground. But by starting with an area in which most of the students had some interest, the class was more amenable to following his lead into areas of lesser interest.

Choice here became a facilitating factor in learning. Choice meant active *participation.* In an election people often say that their candidate is just the lesser of two evils, but nonetheless, the fact that they express preference for one candidate over the other endows the whole process with considerably more interest. So it is in learning. Even though students may have had at the outset little interest in literature, the very process of choosing makes them evaluate, makes them look at the possibilities and seek something "good" about one or the other. Then, having chosen, the students develop a stake in the subject area; the students feel it is *theirs,* because they had an active role in selecting it. The teacher may of course find that in spite of this student interest lags. The wise teacher would not then say, "What is wrong with you? After all, *you* decided to study this material." It will not help to flail the class for being unable to sustain its own choice. Having once created a situation in which students make a positive choice toward some learning experience, the teacher must help in sustaining this expressed interest. Merely allowing a class to choose and then expecting the expressed interest to solve all further problems of motivation would not only be very foolish—it would not work. Nevertheless, by providing the springboard of choice, the teacher has at least obtained an initial impetus moving students toward worth-while learning.

But, says the skeptic, what if the students choose to do nothing? Is that not one of the alternatives we must allow them in a democratic framework? Of course not. A person has no choice in a democracy about whether or not he will obey the law. Law is the framework that makes it possible for everyone to have maximum freedom. Without laws we would be at the mercy of the whims and passions of anyone, and the most powerful and most selfish would destroy the others. Thus in the classroom: students cannot have the alternative *not to learn* as a conscious choice, though often it is an unconscious decision of which the teacher must be aware. Part of the personal obligation of living in a society is that one is educated in the ways of that society. The obligation of the teacher is to stretch every possible resource to bring this learning to every student. The teacher cannot let the student choose *nothing!* Probably many teachers who would accept the necessity of choice in democratic procedures outside the classroom balk at allowing much choice in school, fearing that students would choose not to learn. But to the extent that we can justify what we teach both psychologically and sociologically, we can say that a democratic classroom does not permit the decision not to learn; it does permit and encourage the exercise and the development of the ability to choose various paths to learning, various objects of study, various methods of evaluating learning, various goals toward which one may strive through learning.

So far we have discussed two major criteria of democratic education, with some of the implications for classroom practice. These two are—

1. Creation of freedom with rules.
2. Providing significant areas of choice.

There are four more that must be considered—

3. A democratic classroom also provides for participation by all members;
4. Creates a feeling of responsibility on the part of all members;
5. Creates a feeling of being valued;
6. Uses the experimental approach to subject matter.

Participation by all. It is obvious that the discussion of choice as a factor in the democratic classroom implies active participation on the part of the class members in the direction of the learning. It is not possible to have genuine choices presented without an active response on the part of the students. There are, however, even broader implications. Students not only enter into active choice regarding the class, its procedures, and its content, but are given the opportunity to increase their participation as they grow in skill, insight, and understanding.

A democratic teacher starts slowly, allowing students to expand their area of activity as they demonstrate ability to do so. Democratic ordering of society is one of the most demanding kinds of social control that man has ever devised. In a democratic classroom, students *grow into* wider and wider spheres of participation. Also as individuals, there are different amounts and types of participation. Some students are more able to lead, and these students are encouraged to assume more and more leadership; other students have the best solutions to problems, and these students are expected more and more to share this ability with the class. Not only is participation encouraged, but it is something won within the group; that is, a student is able to provide as much leadership as the class is willing to relinquish to him. We may have, as we often do, the case of the bright student who knows all the answers, or the bully, or the exhibitionist. None of these are true leaders but have a long hard path to travel in order to achieve the true stature of democratic leadership. And in a democratic classroom such students learn that leadership does not come because one talks loudest or longest or most insistently, but because the group accepts one as a leader. How does the teacher provide for this to occur? It happens when teachers allow students to get to know each other in many intimate work situations, with both small groups and large, short-run and long-range, and where many kinds of leadership opportunities are provided—collecting papers, reading notices, taking roll, leading a discussion, reporting on special research, making plans for a trip, serving on an evaluation committee—right up the ladder toward full and significant participation in what is going on.

But in the emphasis on participation the democratic classroom is not concerned only with leadership, but with *relationship*. In such a classroom, few students can hold back, can be passive observers, having nothing to do with learning or with the teacher or with fellow students. The teacher does not win such active participation by all students merely by requesting it. Nor can the teacher punish with a "zero" those who do not speak up in a discussion. Rather, the teacher provides again many ways in which many different talents may manifest themselves—cutting out pictures for a bulletin board, rearranging the seats at the end of the hour, becoming an expert on some special topic of personal interest that in some way is related to the major content of the course. These and countless other small devices eventually provide an avenue for every student to become a participant. A democratic social order needs the intelligence of everyone to function; even though this intelligence may not be verbal, it at least is educated in self-knowledge.

There is an idea current that participation, or activity, is an end in itself. Mere activity is not and never could be called democratic. In the larger society governing bodies do not indulge in activities merely to look as though they were doing something; there are too many vital projects demanding the best talent and intelligence of the leaders for them to be wasting time in mere running around to look busy. Similarly, in the democratic classroom there are so many vital and significant areas for student participation that there is no need to manufacture them.

Only through actual participation may the teacher learn about the total student personality. If the teacher knows the student only from the problems finished, from the test results, from a few recitations in class, obviously the teacher is not fully informed about his students. But students who are asked to become judges of what subject matter to start with, whether a panel discussion of a topic is preferable to individual reports, what standard shall be accepted on student papers as to neatness, legibility, and content—such students tell the teacher, through their actions and their ideas, a great deal about themselves. This gives the teacher considerable knowledge to use in guiding individual students. The physical education program, for instance, offers many opportunities for participation. Students who are less athletically inclined may serve as student managers, taking care of equipment, keeping score, setting up tournament schedules. The members of the team themselves work *with* the teacher or coach in discussing the best plays to use under various conditions, may talk and decide together the problems of training, team relations, sportsmanship.

In mathematics, often considered a very routine and logical subject, the same participation may be utilized. Students can be encouraged to see real-life applications of problems in mathematics; groups can explore the community to find ways in which mathematics is used by workers and in what areas; the organization of the classroom as far as distributing paper, collecting assignments, checking roll, keeping the room orderly, provide opportunity for extensive student participation. Examples of these kinds of student activity are discussed throughout this book; and wherever students are actively brought into their own learning experience, there we find a democratic classroom in operation.

Development of responsibility. What does participation do to students? The more they can affect the world around them, the more they feel responsible for what they do. The great complaint of adults about youth today is that "they have no feeling of responsibility." And how, one asks, could they acquire a feeling of responsibility in a world that allows youth to make so few important decisions, that gives youth so few important jobs to do? There is a direct relationship between participation and responsibility; it is certain that responsibility cannot be learned without participation. This sense of responsibility is increased when participation is related significantly to the adult world. Too often the students feel that there are two distinct worlds—the in-school world and the out-of-school world, and the one that is most important is out-of-school. The teacher therefore needs to seek constantly those bridges between school and community that relate the learning of the classroom to daily living.

All feel valued. In our democratic society the phrase, "all men are created equal" points to a fundamental assumption regarding human nature: that all individuals are equal in being deserving of respect and being given the protection of the social group. People are far from equal in talents, in contributions to society, in an infinite number of other characteristics. But in a democratic social order each human being has a value merely because he is a human being. Similarly, in the democratic classroom, every student feels that he, as a person, is given as much consideration as any other. Each student recognizes that his needs, interests, motivations, goals, wholly personal and subjective and unique, are carefully considered in the whole learning process. How does this differ from our usual classroom?

> A high school separates the college-preparatory group from the non-college-preparatory group. Both groups take the same required English and United States history courses. The major difference is that few if any of the non-college-preparatory students get good grades; college-recommending grades are reserved only for those intending to use them.

As the example above shows, respect for the individual here means respect only for the goals and motivations of those going to college, in terms of the rewards given by this school. What kind of a picture of themselves are the noncollege-preparatory students going to get? They will feel inferior; they will feel that society has put a low ceiling on their efforts. As one teacher in the above school said, "I don't see why the noncollege prep students work at all—they can't expect good grades anyway." A democratic classroom does not distribute its rewards on such a narrow basis. Grades are incidental rather than primary. On the other hand, accomplishing significant classroom learning is most important. In this process each person is given maximum opportunity to achieve learning *in his own way.* True, these individual differences make democratic teaching difficult, since reading, for example, may vary in one classroom from fourth-grade level to twelfth-grade level. The teacher who genuinely values each student as a person has an obligation to find reading materials suited to each extreme and to help those at each extreme to better performance. What we feel about ourselves is one key to our happiness; if we feel that we are good, that others like us and our particular characteristics, then we are more able to deal successfully with the problems of home and job. The school has an obligation to give each person a clear view of himself, but in that process to help him feel that he is a good person. Delinquents among young people are often those students who feel that no one likes them and who in turn do not like themselves. Consequently, they hit out at society through antisocial acts of one sort or another. The democratic classroom therefore creates situations in which each student feels valued, feels that he *does* have a genuine contribution to make to something that others, his peers, deem important.

The experimental approach to learning. A final criterion which may be used in the evaluation of the democratic classroom is actually implicit in what has already been discussed. The democratic procedure depends to a greater and greater extent on the experimental approach. In this approach, nothing is known until it is tried out. We, of course, accept this thesis in the realm of athletics. We would not expect a student to learn tennis by reading a book about it. We know that he cannot know the game until he has had much contact with tennis racquets, balls, courts, rules. Democratic education utilizes this inquiring approach in dealing with subject matter. In United States history the teacher will develop an understanding of government through intensive interviews in the field with governmental functionnaires of all kinds rather than depending merely on the textbook for the discussion of government. In English the radio, newspaper, magazines, current novels, and literary criticism become the basis for developing judgments about good writing, rather than just selections in the English text anthologies.[4]

Democratic education, it is clear, is not merely a matter of method and relationship, nor merely a matter of content: democratic education utilizes both content and method to achieve democratic ends. Some observers have attempted to see a difference here, and to put either method or content in a prior position. But a careful analysis of what actually happens to the student in the classroom shows clearly that the best method will fall far short of its fullest promise if the content is sterile, and the best content will be rendered ineffective if the method of instruction is inappropriate.

[4] Childs, John L., *Education and Morals* (New York: Appleton-Century-Crofts, Inc., 1950), pp. 158 ff.

Guideposts of the Democratic Classroom

Beginning teachers are interested in having available some immediate guideposts to give them an indication of the "degree of democracy" that is being exercised in any classroom. We will try to suggest below some of the things to look for in observing classes. One warning, however, must be carefully heeded. Democracy in education is a *developmental concept.* Students are not naturally democratic. It is, of course, a learned behavior. And learning democracy is one of the hardest of all learnings, since it demands so much of every individual in the way of actual selflessness, responsibility, and objectivity. Many teachers must start with groups of students who are very unskilled in democratic procedures and relationships. Also, it must be remembered that democracy in the classroom will *look different* depending on the age of the students and the subject. After all, seniors in high school can usually be given much more freedom of choice than freshmen. With these warnings in mind, observers may ask of a classroom the following questions:

	The democratic answer
1. Are students able to make choices?	Yes
1.1 Are significant areas of choice provided in terms of developing more adult discrimination among alternatives?	Yes
1.2 Do students always select the alternative the teacher had in mind?	No
1.3 Does the teacher seem genuinely open-minded regarding which choice the students may make?	Yes
1.4 Does the teacher follow through on the choices that the students make?	Yes
1.5 Do students, in talking about their classwork, often use the phrase, "We decided to do this," or "When we chose that. . . ." ?	Yes
2. Do students have freedom?	Yes
2.1 Do students have freedom of movement? Are they able to move in and around the room on purposeful activities?	Yes
2.2 Is there a relaxed interaction among students not only about the material being studied but about other personal and school affairs?	Yes
2.3 Is the freedom used by students to express resentment (i.e., walking to pencil sharpener when someone is talking to the whole class)?	No
2.4 Do students seem tense and nervous? Is the class *too* quiet?	No
3. Are students participating in all classroom activities?	Yes

	The democratic answer
3.1 Is participation limited to a few of special talent?	No
3.2 Does participation include planning important phases of the program?	Yes
3.3 Does participation include evaluation of class and individual learning?	Yes
3.4 Is there daily evidence of student leadership in a variety of activities?	Yes
3.4.1 Is this leadership shared by most of the students during a semester?	Yes
3.4.2 Are the criteria for selection of leadership increasingly dependent on individual contribution rather than social popularity?	Yes
3.4.3 Is the leadership more skillful at the end of the semester than at the beginning?	Yes
3.4.4 Do the results of leadership appear as group effort, in which accomplishment is experienced by all members of the group?	Yes
3.4.5 Do those not in leadership roles at any given moment actively work with and gladly support their own student leaders?	Yes
3.5 Is there an atmosphere of belonging to a group in which each student has an important place?	Yes
3.5.1 Do the students talk about the classroom as "*our* classroom"?	Yes
3.5.2 Do the students refer to the class as "*our* class in. . . ." ?	Yes
3.5.3 Do all the students early in the semester get to know the other class members through actively working together?	Yes
3.5.4 Is there a feeling that all class members "belong"?	Yes
3.5.5. Does there exist an "in-group" and one or more "out-groups" either in terms of social patterns or class leadership roles?	No
4. Are students developing responsibility in relation to their age?	Yes
4.1 Can the teacher leave the room for any period of time and expect class routines to continue relatively undisturbed?	Yes
4.2 When students agree on a project, do they follow through on that decision and complete the work with a good standard of workmanship without prodding through grades or other threats?	Yes
4.3 Do students increasingly take responsibility for each other by volunteering to help those needing special assistance?	Yes
4.4 Do the students and teachers share responsibility if something goes wrong with their class plans?	Yes

	The democratic answer
4.5 Are the students increasingly able to plan reasonable rules for class conduct and help each other live up to them?	Yes
4.6 Do the students express more reasonable judgments as to life goals and personal decisions? Are they more objective in discussions of other people and controversial issues? Do they seek facts and then form opinions?	Yes
4.7 Is the out-of-class conduct of the students becoming more like in-class conduct?	Yes
5. Do the students feel valued as individuals?	Yes
5.1 Do the students like to come to this class?	Yes
5.2 Do students express anxiety about their ability to succeed in this class?	No
5.3 Are lowest ability students taking an active part in class activities?	Yes
5.4 Are superior students making unusual contributions to the class?	Yes
5.5 Are opportunities available for special interests and talents to develop?	Yes
5.6 Do students feel that their personal emotional problems will be adequately taken into consideration even if classwork has to be sacrificed at times?	Yes
5.7 Are student interests, such as big games, rallies, student affairs, given recognition in this class; and, when warranted, is class time provided for discussion of crucial problems among the student groups?	Yes
5.8 Are student relations with the teacher sound? (Is there an absence of "apple polishing" reactions when students approach the teacher?)	Yes
5.9 Do students feel a lack of favoritism in the classroom? Are all students helped by the teacher when and if they need such help?	Yes
6. Does the subject matter relate to significant democratic goals?	Yes
6.1 Is subject matter at every possible point related to real-life situations faced by youth or adults in our culture?	Yes
6.2 Are the ethical bases for democratic processes made explicit continually during the course?	Yes
6.3 Does subject matter utilize wherever possible the experimental approach?	Yes
6.4 Is the textbook, where one is used, supplemented by a variety of instructional materials?	Yes
6.5 Is subject matter continually reviewed in light of changing social needs and changing classroom composition?	Yes
6.6 Does most of the subject matter have intrinsic interest in terms of adolescent experiences and needs?	Yes

The preceding list is rather formidable. The beginner may feel completely discouraged by the assumption that each one of these conditions must be met in order to be "democratic." In one sense this is true; in another sense, the democratic teacher is striving toward these goals, though some may be achieved sooner than others. A quick glance at the pictures of teachers presented in the Introduction clearly shows that, in terms of the democracy practiced, these "good" teachers would be stronger in some areas than others. Where one teacher will be better able to relate content to daily living, another teacher may be better able to give students a real sense of being valued. Each teacher has strengths worth conserving; the democratic teacher recognizes these strengths and seeks to minimize those areas of lesser competence.

Democratic versus Autocratic, or Laissez-faire, Leadership

At this point, it may be useful to see what happens to students under democratic leadership in contrast to autocratic or laissez-faire leadership. This will make apparent why all teachers must work toward democratic leadership, even though no one teacher can hope to realize that kind of leadership perfectly.

> Under the authoritarian leader, members seek approval from the leader rather than from one another; there is marked rivalry for the leader's attention. When all rewards and punishments come from one omnipotent source, only the relationships with that person become important. Other members in the group are looked upon as being in the way, or as competitors, or as persons to whom one hopes punishment will be diverted. Under such leadership, member-member relationships are not likely to be constructive. . . .
>
> An autocratic leader makes many, though not all, members fearful or angry. Since he may seem too powerful to rebel against, members of the group get relief for their pent-up feelings by attacking another member of the group. The autocratic leader fosters attacks on scapegoats and thus keeps tensions in the group directed away from himself.
>
> Under a "democratic" leader, activity and responsibility are shared among the members. The leader behaves not like the Omnipotent One, but like one of the members of the group, though one who has special skills and knowledge. Failure as well as success is shared, and another's rewards are one's own. The leader's accepting attitude toward members fosters their respect for one another. They show a healthy balance between mutual dependence and independence.
>
> A leader may . . . be too permissive. In such a group the child feels that anything goes; nothing is definite. The leader seems indifferent to the members and what they do. Members feel a strong need for leadership, and they may seek an autocrat. There may be rivalry among them to organize the situation in some fashion or other. In many ways, members show their dissatisfaction with the anarchic situation.[5]

[5] Maas, Henry S., *Fostering Mental Health in Our Schools,* 1950 Yearbook, Association for Supervision and Curriculum Development, National Education Association, "Understanding Group Processes," Chapter 17, p. 289-290.

Classroom Leadership versus Leadership in Voluntary Groups

This summarizes well the differences between the democratic group leader, the authoritarian, and the laissez-faire leader. But is the democratic teacher exactly the same as any other group leader? In the voluntary youth groups, such as YMCA, Boy Scouts, 4-H, Campfire Girls, we see exercised a kind of democratic group leadership.[6]

What are some of the unique features of this relationship?

1. The group members are self-directing. They have their own officers, committees, procedures.
2. The program is group selected.
3. Discipline is group determined.
4. The adult is very much on the side lines, giving advice and suggestions, throwing in new ideas, working with the leadership to make them more able in their roles, working with individuals in the group in a guidance capacity.

Can the teacher be a similar kind of leader? This question is a very important one, since the youth groups by and large have evolved a pattern of leadership that could be very useful to the schools. But the teacher's role does differ in some important respects from that of any other group leader:

1. The teacher has legal authority; the students are compelled to attend.
2. The teacher is in the classroom because of special knowledge and skill; the students *expect* to *learn.*
3. The teacher must grade the students.

In addition, the teacher shares some of the special features of any adult with a group of young people:

4. The teacher is older.
5. The teacher is a quasi parent.

All these characteristics of the teacher inhibit to a great extent the kind of group leadership that emerges in voluntary groups. The school as an institution has a cultural role of authoritativeness; the students develop a deep expectation of "being run." This expectation of authoritarian procedures is a major problem for the democratically oriented teacher. In a youth group, of course, the expectation is different—the students, for the most part, expect to run themselves. In the classroom, we have created an institutional tradition about who is boss.

[6] Wittenberg, Rudolph M., *So You Want to Help People* (New York: Association Press, 1947).

These special conditions make it difficult for classroom leadership to emulate voluntary group leadership. In some way, probably classroom leadership must always be different. Once this difference is admitted, we can look for basic similarities that do exist and seek out the school adaptations and applications.

Guideposts of the Democratic Teacher

The teacher who seeks to be a teacher-leader will have some basic differences in method, content, and attitude. As the list of democratic classroom situations shows, a democratic classroom includes many important relationships not often found elsewhere. The list as presented on pages 70 to 72 emphasized the democratic classroom as seen from the student's point of view and illustrated how an observer might see such a classroom. Little mention was made of what the teacher was like or what the teacher did. It may be helpful now to try to give some of the characteristics of a democratic teacher-leader. The teacher who is democratic—

1. Gets a genuine satisfaction out of seeing the group do for itself something that the teacher may previously have done (e.g., lead a class discussion; set up rules for a field trip).
2. Considers all learning as a means of meeting individual and societal needs.
3. Is willing to take a back seat as often as possible in order that students may learn how to exercise self-direction.
4. Is patient with the seeming slowness of the discussion and joint-planning approach.
5. Is sensitive to student need for security and guidance and therefore is not afraid of providing a firm touch as often as required.
6. Recognizes the variety of human personalities to be found in any classroom; does not penalize students for being from different class levels or different racial or ethnic groups, or of different abilities.
7. Encourages creative thinking on the part of students; recognizes that any given unit of learning may be approached from an infinite number of ways.
8. Is able to respond objectively to student aggression; recognizes that the leader does not need to overreact to personal attacks by young people.

This list corresponds in many ways to a list of characteristics of the good teacher. But these characteristics are particularly crucial in defining the *democratic teacher.*

Hazards in Democratic Teaching

It seems obvious to many students that there should be no question about the need for democratic teaching. But then, the question arises, why is democratic teaching so difficult to achieve in the average high school? There are a number of significant reasons for this that might be pondered by the new teacher, since they constitute genuine barriers to implementing our basic idea:

1. ***Institutional traditions.*** As has already been mentioned, the school as an institution derives from eras when authoritarian relations were the rule in families, in governmental systems, in religious institutions. Teachers who seek more democratic ways of teaching sometimes find a number of their colleagues very opposed to their new approach. Classrooms have always been teacher-dominated; it is the pattern most familiar to us. The students know exactly how to respond in such situations; so teachers resist breaking the familiar routines.

2. ***Difficulties in finding legitimate areas of choice.*** Democratic education depends to a great extent on affording young people important areas for the making of decisions after group discussion, fact finding, and evaluation. However, the traditional curriculum presents a course of study, from which is derived a logical sequence of the subject matter. Thus, the teacher feels frustrated in seeking some important choice situations. Students may make some decisions and choices regarding rules of conduct, but the democratic learning is limited if this is all the choosing that they are allowed to do. Selection in terms of content and methodology is highly important; therefore, teachers may in some instances need considerable retraining in the resources they bring to teaching in order to be able to present legitimate choices to students.

3. ***Inability of students to accept freedom.*** Very often where students have been fully conditioned to a repressive school environment, the least deviation produces chaos. And democracy cannot flourish in chaos. Many times teachers, with the best will in the world, begin a class with democratic procedures without finding out first how capable the group is in self-direction and self-discipline. Where order has always been imposed, students will not be able to discipline themselves without a very gradual induction.

> In a class where very strict routines had always been followed—the read-recite-quiz sequence—a student-teacher decided to introduce a small element of self-direction. He suggested that a bulletin board committee might take over the bulletin board, with contributions from class members, particularly those who had done poorly in the usual work. The idea, relatively simple though it was, took about half an hour of class time to convey. When the committee was appointed, by the teacher, with two top students in it, he was amazed to be bombarded constantly with numerous petty questions: What color shall

we use? Can we use pins or thumb tacks? Who will put the material up? These students were so unskilled in self-direction that any teacher would have to move very slowly with them.

Too often when a teacher does have such an experience, the conclusion reached is that the class just cannot have democracy in education. This is an unfortunate and unjustified conclusion.

4. ***Inability of teachers to share with class the significant areas of self-direction.*** Undoubtedly there are individuals attracted to teaching because they see opportunity for authoritarian roles. Because of this, everyone who enters teaching and seeks to be a democratic teacher will need to do some self-examination. Those who feel a need to be tyrants have no place in education. Of course, there are other facets to this problem. Teachers are often fearful about allowing students too much freedom of choice because "one never knows what the little demons will do next." This uncertainty is a genuine hazard; the adolescent is unpredictable—moody and stubborn one day, sunny and cooperative the next. The teacher who is sensitive to these forces, as well as the teacher who suspects that the ill-repressed primitive urges in adolescents may at any moment get the upper hand, often feels compelled to exercise a rigid and unrelaxed control over the classroom. Teachers who do feel this way, however, are not giving due credit to the positive, civilized, socialized habits that young people have already acquired. By emphasizing the latter, the former are more easily dealt with. It is necessary to bring to teaching, however, a real tolerance for the unexpected. Fear of emergencies and unusual events must not so paralyze us that we cannot be democratic in our teaching.

In an English class during a period devoted to drama, two students were in front of the class reading a dramatic selection. It was a warm day—all the windows were wide open. As the selection reached its climax, one character was supposed to depart precipitately. He did. He dived out the nearest open window. The teacher, who had only been on the job two months, suddenly remembered that she had never noticed how far the window was from the ground (though it was on the first floor). However, she kept her presence of mind, and went on to lead a class discussion on the selection. A few moments later the student walked in the door and took his seat. After class she suggested that there were better ways of making a sudden exit than diving out the window! Interestingly enough, no other student has ever tried to repeat that performance; the teacher's complete calm and unmoved reaction took some of the exhibitionistic appeal out of the episode, so that other students were not tempted to try the same thing.

5. ***Student frustration and aggression.*** Teachers who use democratic approaches to teaching are often surprised at the violence of reaction of some one or two students who for no obvious reason become genuinely upset. It must be remembered that democratic procedures put a great burden on the individual to be self-disciplined, to adhere to group-made standards, to share his own talents with the group. Many individuals in our culture find these disciplines very severe. Sometimes the reactions have come directly from homes where a harsh and rigid parent or, surprisingly enough, an overindulgent one, prevented the development of independent self-control on the part of the individual. We call these people authoritarian personalities.[7]

In a democratic situation latent hostilities to authority may come bursting forth; again, the teacher is likely to think that the fault lies in democratic teaching procedures rather than in the individual's own social adjustment. Democratic teaching may permit more direct aggression upon the teacher than repressive teaching. Agression is also produced under repressed teaching, but is usually displaced upon scapegoats, such as minority group members, other classmates, brothers and sisters. In a democratic situation the more permissive atmosphere allows the aggression to be directly focused on the teacher who appears to be the source of frustration. A teacher who wants to be democratic must be very alert to these signs of frustration. If too many securities are taken away from the students, without first providing substitutes, aggression may become widespread. For instance, where students have been used to working for grades, the teacher may suggest that grades are not so important and spend much time discussing grades in class. Eventually he may bring the group around to setting somewhat more realistic evaluation devices; yet, in a short time the teacher may find the class agitated and rebellious. They complain they don't know how they are doing in the classwork. The new methods sounded good intellectually, but they were not emotionally meaningful. Consequently, a careful and slow approach is often wiser where a group is not used to self-direction.

6. ***Undemocratic school administration.*** Teachers who are themselves subject to authoritarian methods may come to believe that students should be treated in the same manner.

> Observers had noted a very tense atmosphere in all the classrooms of a suburban high school. Students were reprimanded for merely

[7] Adorno, T. W., *et al, The Authoritarian Personality* (New York: Harper & Brothers, 1950).

> slouching in their chairs. Whispering to anyone was a cardinal offense. Later, a faculty meeting was visited. There the principal treated the faculty as the students were being treated. He shouted at them, shook his finger at them, and in general conveyed the impression that the faculty were to be ordered around. Interestingly enough most of the faculty seemed to feel that their school was much superior to all neighboring schools; that rigid discipline, limited textbook study, few extracurricular activities and a "tough" marking system meant better education.

In other cases, teachers themselves may reject a principal who tries to be democratic. Why doesn't he tell us what he wants, they say. Wherever the attitudes originate, it is difficult to maintain democratic relations at either level, teaching or administrative, without the support of the other.[8]

7. *Competition or cooperation?* The spice of competition is present in most of the social and work situations where people find themselves; but we sometimes forget cooperation must also be present wherever people work and live together. In the usual classroom, competition has tended to overshadow cooperation; in the democratic classroom this is reversed. Also, the competition that is encouraged is between groups rather than between individuals. Moreover, the goals are of a different kind—competition is not for prizes or money or grades or special dispensations, but for higher achievement, more adequate solving of a group problem, finding a more acceptable alternative for group choice.

Students and teachers sometimes feel that the props have been pulled out from under them if competitive situations are made less important. Teachers often feel that students do the classroom work only out of a desire to get ahead of someone else, rather than from any real interest in the learning. The democratic classroom is viewed with alarm simply because cooperative enterprise is substituted for individual competitive work. Teachers do not see how it can accomplish the same units of learning. It is possible that democratic education will not produce the same learning, but it may produce just as much learning of a rather different sort. A democratic teacher may use competition when different groups have bulletin board displays, and the class is asked to judge which group made the best display. Will the group that made the best one get an *A?* Where a pervasive grading system is in operation, this may be necessary; a democratic teacher would strive to produce a learning situation where the recognition of one's peers was all the reward desired, since adult life

[8] Grambs, Jean D., "Do Teachers Want Democratic Administrators?" *Nations Schools,* 46:40-41 (November, 1950).

awards no grades as such, merely recognition. It is also true that the democratic classroom emphasizes cooperative skills to a very high degree. Working with others is essential in family life, in citizenship roles, in work relations. Too few students are skilled in this kind of participation in high school. True, this can be overdone; cooperation should not be maintained to the exclusion of genuine individual accomplishment. Still the unique feature of democratic education is the emphasis on the group working together.

Summary

A democratic society rests upon democratic education, which in turn depends on the processes and attitudes prevailing in each classroom. Yet this *practice* of democracy is one of the hardest things for us to accomplish in education.

What are the earmarks of democratic education? For the student they include a chance to learn responsibility through participation in directing significant areas of his own learning. This means valid choices are provided for him among the possible pathways toward goals of importance to him and to the social order. The student, furthermore, feels a sense of freedom in his school experiences because there are reasonable rules and limits which he shares in setting. Finally, he feels that he as an individual is valued because this participation, these choices, this freedom can only function when the basic worth and significance of personality and individuality is recognized.

Because of long-standing expectations of how teachers should behave, these democratic human relations in the classroom have been made difficult to attain. It is far easier to use to the full the authority and power traditionally delegated to teachers. But, however difficult, it is clear in this troubled time that the effort to practice democracy must be made. It must be the continuing task of the teacher to appraise the growth of students in ability to direct intelligently their own learning. The teacher is only democratic when he sees himself becoming increasingly dispensable, less needed by his students.

Selected References

Baxter, Bernice, and Rosalind Cassidy. *Group Experience—The Democratic Way*. New York: Harper & Brothers, 1943. A graphic description of democratic patterns of working together against autocratic ones.

Benne, Kenneth. *A Conception of Authority*. Contributions to Education No. 895. New York: Bureau of Publications Teachers College, Columbia University, 1943. A tightly argued discussion of the vital role of authority in democracy; essential to a real insight into a fundamental educational problem.

Bode, Boyd. *Democracy as a Way of Life.* New York: The Macmillan Company, 1943. Excellent, lucid and brief statement identifying some of the crucial democratic concepts of significance to us as citizens and educators.

Booker, J. A. "Democracy in the Teens," *National Parent-Teacher,* 43:4-6 (February, 1949). A straightforward presentation of what democracy means in terms of the human relationships involved between adult and adolescent.

Childs, John. *Education and Morals.* New York: Appleton-Century-Crofts, Inc., 1950. A basic inquiry into the moral implications for education of a democratic philosophy of teaching.

DeHuszar, George B. *Practical Applications of Democracy.* New York: Harper & Brothers, 1945.

Dewey, John. *Democracy and Education.* New York: The Macmillan Company, 1924.

———. *Experience and Education.* New York: The Macmillan Company, 1938.

———. *Individualism, Old and New.* New York: Minton Balch & Company, 1930.

Modern teaching stems in the main from Dewey's formulations; these references are all useful to the teacher. The second one is particularly important.

Douglass, Harl R. (ed.). *Education for Life Adjustment.* New York: The Ronald Press Company, 1950. Relating education to life problems as illustrated in the major subject fields.

Educational Policies Commission. *Learning the Ways of Democracy.* Washington, D.C.: National Education Association, 1940. How schools actually can and do present democratic concepts and practice democratic processes in every area of instruction.

Ferguson, Charles W. *A Little Democracy Is a Dangerous Thing.* New York: Association Press, 1948. A small volume that cogently presents some of the reasons democracy is so hard to live and to learn.

Hartman, G. W. "Democratic Behavior and the Educative Process," *Review of Educational Research,* 19:21-31 (February, 1949). A review of the literature and research in this area; extensive bibliography.

Justman, Joseph. "Democracy in Education: A Study in Meaning," *Bulletin of the National Association of Secondary School Principals,* 26:71-84 (February, 1942). An analysis of four points of view on "democratic education"; points out the implications for practice of each version.

Lewin, Kurt, Ronald Lippitt, and Ralph K. White. "Patterns of Aggressive Behavior in Experimentally Created Social Climates," *Journal of Social Psychology,* 10:271-279 (May, 1939). The differences in behavior that arise from democratic, autocratic, and laissez-faire leadership situations.

Newlon, Jesse H. *Education for Democracy in Our Time.* New York: McGraw Hill Book Company, Inc., 1939. An experienced educator presents a program for the schools implicit in the democratic theory.

Rugg, Harold. *The Teacher in School and Society.* Yonkers: World Book

Company, 1950. Chap. 4, "The Child in American Culture," pp. 78-115. A good overview of the growth of American democracy.

Stiles, Lindley J., and Mattie E. Dorsey. *Democratic Teaching in Secondary Schools.* Philadelphia: J. B. Lippincott Company, 1950. A textbook on high-school teaching based on a democratic viewpoint throughout; especially Chap. 5 for criteria of democratic classroom methods.

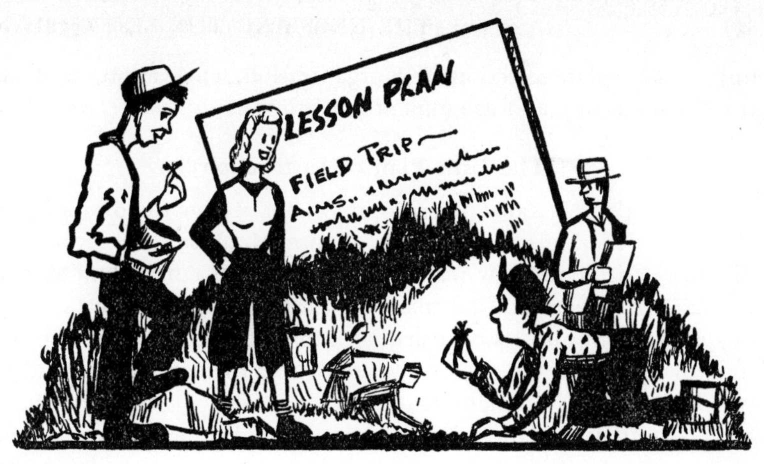

4. The Unit and the Lesson Plan

Some Special Instructional Procedures

LIKE the success of a building plan, the success of a school curriculum depends upon the materials selected and the skill with which they are utilized. The way in which the individual teacher selects learning experiences and fits them together determines the success of the curriculum. What happens to the curriculum in the classroom may well determine whether high school students develop into citizens able to carry out the responsibilities of a democracy. Implementing the curriculum to this end is the great task of the classroom teacher.

The basic building element of the curriculum is the unit. The teacher's job is both to weld units together in accordance with the over-all purposes of the curriculum plan, and to act within units according to specific planning for the month, the week, and the day.

Once the materials are selected and the sequence sketched in by the teacher, three significant activities are required: (1) developing interest on the part of the students in the unit and the daily lesson—the problem of motivation; (2) planning with students how the unit and the lesson should be carried out; (3) assigning work to carry out the plans agreed upon.

In this chapter, then, we will consider the related problems of unit, lesson plan selection and organization, motivation, student-teacher planning, and assignment procedures.

The Unit Plan of Instruction

Just as there is a division of opinion about how the over-all curriculum of the high school should be organized, so there is marked disagreement about how instruction within this curriculum should be planned. There are not many advocates left for the old day-by-day assignment and lesson learning. Most educators now affirm the unit plan of teaching. But, as we shall see, the kind of unit advocated may be quite different.

The unit is a plan of instruction centered on a significant area of learning. Instead of disconnected lessons, then, each day is devoted to exploration of this area of learning. If it is a good unit, the plan will have taken cognizance of the differences among members of the class. In fact, it will have involved these different students in the planning from the beginning. To meet the differences, a variety of activities and materials (See Chapter 5) will have been provided in the planning.

But a unit can be all these things and still begin with a quite different premise. On the one hand, the assumption may be that the goals of the high school can be reached through the presentation of logically arranged knowledge. In that case, the unit will center in a subject-matter topic: the halogens; the short story; the Civil War. This is sometimes called a subject matter unit. On the other hand, the assumption may be that the goals of the high school can be reached through experiences enabling students to meet their needs—individual and societal. In that case, the unit will center in problem solving: How can we prepare for good family living? How can we make democracy work better? This is sometimes called the experience unit.[1]

Obviously, the second kind of unit, is by far the more difficult to conduct. It takes more skill in planning. It demands a wider range of activities and materials and requires greater elasticity in time allotment. Furthermore, the school administration may be primarily concerned with subject-matter outcomes. These expectations may be reinforced both by school-wide testing programs and by the desires of fellow teachers. It may be difficult to force the same outcomes from experience units as from subject-matter units. The beginning teacher

[1] For further details on subject matter units and experience units, see Thut, I. N., and J. R. Gerberich. *Foundations of Method for Secondary Schools.* New York. McGraw-Hill Company, Inc., 1949.

may also find it difficult to get an experience unit rolling in the short high-school period and even more difficult to maintain continuity. He may find fellow teachers complaining because his students get involved in the unit at the expense of other assignments. In short, the beginning teacher who believes in the experience-unit approach may have to make some compromises, at least until he gains experience. He may have to content himself with only a few experience units a semester.

On the other hand, the difference in classroom implementation between the two units need not be so sharply drawn. Subject-matter units can take account of student and societal needs, can orient subject matter goals to these needs, can choose materials and activities to meet both the short-term subject-matter expectations and the long-term goals of the high school, and can include a broad evaluation program. And wherever he can, the conscientious beginning teacher, who finds he must teach subject-matter units a large part of the time, will direct his teaching toward this kind of learning.

As each division of the unit and the lesson plan is described, it will become apparent that many practical details have been omitted. In this chapter, the objective is merely to give an over-all view of the structure of the unit and the lesson plan, but the methods of carrying out each section in the classroom are the substance of much of the remainder of the book. So in each of the following brief descriptions of parts of the unit and the lesson plan, many references will be made to those later chapters which give the necessary "know-how."

Preparing the Unit

When the beginning teacher undertakes a unit of instruction for the first time, he should rough out a complete, if tentative, plan. We have said a good unit is planned cooperatively by teachers and students. So it is. But the beginner has to guard his uncertain skill against chaos. He may be able to maintain orderly direction in his instruction only if he sees some distinct goals, some definite activities, some specific sources of materials, some well-defined evaluation measures which may be used. True, he should base his tentative choices on the data he has collected on student differences and on his best estimate of what experiences will meet the students' needs. Moreover, he should expect to modify his rough plans in accordance with his students' suggestions. But it is unwise, at least in the early efforts, to venture far without plans.

The unit may be said to progress through four stages of development:

1. Initiating.
2. Planning.
3. Conducting Research.
4. Culminating.

We will discuss each briefly.

Initiating Stage

The initiative stage is crucial to the success of the unit, for, unless student interest and purpose are genuinely involved, the unit becomes a hollow shell. (See a later section on motivation in this chapter.) Good units do not just happen. If the teacher has done his work well, he will have an accurate profile of his class. He will know intimately the heterogeneity there, and this knowledge will exercise a limiting effect on proposing areas from which the problem is to be selected. In addition, he will have considered what learning activities and materials are feasible and available (Chapter 5). Nothing is quite so devastating to class morale as a stimulating introduction that is followed two days later by a terse announcement that the unit has to be abandoned because of lack of resources. But, suppose the teacher has calculated his risks carefully, what then? To capture student interest and purpose, some teachers use the current-materials approach.[2] They adapt problems being aired in the newspapers and periodicals, or use a field trip, a community survey, or resource visitors (see Chapter 6); others use a rousing discussion or a challenging sociodrama (see Chapter 7), or audio-visual materials (see Chapter 5). Whatever the resource, good teachers take steps to ensure genuine group acceptance of the problem (chapter 7).

> Mr. Manley fumbled through the personnel data cards that he had made for his class. These were ninth-graders. It was spring—beautiful weather—ideal for baseball. The class met right after lunch. They came perspiring and exhausted from the noon-hour activities. They'd go to sleep unless he managed to involve them in something they thought important. Or else some of those girls would just get the giggles.
>
> He stopped the aimless toying with the cards. Most of these kids lived in South Town—been having some trouble out there at the drive-ins—never had been enough recreational facilities out there—might start a discussion around that last drive-in fracas. Ask them to

[2] For details, see Chapter 5, and Kinney, Lucien, and Katharine Dresden, *Better Learning through Current Materials* (Stanford: Stanford University Press, 1949).

list some of the grievances—pretty sure the recreation problem would come out—need something, though, to suggest a way to tackle this thing—might be a good article they could read together. Better check the library.

Mr. Manley strode out of the room and into the corridor. There's Mr. Hill, the principal. "Hello! Say, been thinking about turning my ninth-grade gang loose on recreation facilities in South Town. Think it's all right? Don't want your office stormed by unhappy taxpayers."

The principal thought a minute. As a matter of fact he believed the Lions were going to look into the problem anyhow. "Maybe your crew could work with them. I'll call Hal Wolfe." They went into the office together. Mr. Hill called Hal Wolfe on the phone, and he was all for the plan.

"Going to show a movie—*Leaders for Leisure*—at the next luncheon. Bring Manley along."

The movie was good. Mr. Manley brought it back to class. He brought them smack into the recreation problem in South Town. He started a brisk discussion, then showed the movie. Out of it came plans for a community survey in collaboration with the Lions. They were off!

Planning Stage

Once the problem center has been chosen, the blueprint to indicate scope and sequence of study must be drawn. The scope is usually indicated by dividing the problem into principal subquestions. Beginning teachers often have trouble at this stage bebecause the limits of the problem are not clearly defined. Usually both teacher and students are anxious to get into the problem if the initiating stage has been well devised. They see no point in mulling over how key questions should be stated. It seems like a waste of time. On the contrary, unless the energies of the group are well directed, they will be expended in a hundred directions and never bring the unit to a satisfactory culmination. The sequence of study is equally important. It must be perfectly clear how the data necessary to answer the key questions will be collected and who will collect it. Much of this work will be done in groups. Guidance of group activities requires great skill. In Chapter 8 we will discuss in detail the requisite abilities for both teachers and students, and in a later section of this chapter we will expand the specific problem of student-teacher planning.

Researching Stage

Once the battle is joined and the combat teams have their missions assigned, it is up to the teacher to tend to the logistics. He must see to it that the matériel is kept flowing to his teams. The unskilled group chairmen may need suggestions now and then about what activities and materials will gain the group's ends. Will it be discussion (Chapter 7)? Or a field trip (Chapter 6)? Will it call for individual assignments (see section at end of this chapter)? Does his group need to see a motion picture or listen to recordings of interviews or cull the newspapers and periodicals (Chapter 5)? As these questions arise, the chairmen should have access to the teacher's resource file. The teacher will want to check regularly with the group chairmen as individuals and as a kind of executive committee (Chapter 8). Sometimes the teacher will want to call for a general class discussion to review common problems and ensure that the goal is still clear (Chapter 7).

Culminating Stage

Certainly the emphasis in the unit should be on the quality of the process rather than on the end product. We do not want to evaluate a unit solely on a beautifully illustrated or dramatic report. The processes of learning leadership and followership, developing good group attitudes and skills, fostering problem-solving abilities, and encouraging student self-direction deserve primary consideration. (See Chapters 6, 7, 8, and 14.) If some of the gathered facts slip away in the ensuing years while these essential processes remain, the efforts will have been justified. A good culmination includes much evaluation by both teacher and students. In Chapters 15, 16, and 17 we shall have more to say about the possible range of evaluation. It is sufficient, for the present, to say that the success or failure of a unit cannot rest entirely on a paper-and-pencil test.

The Plan for the Day's Work

In the experience unit, the old lesson plan mapped out solely by the teacher is inappropriate. The subject-matter unit assumes that the teacher chops up the topics into fifty-minute pieces and plans his tactics accordingly. The experience unit requires of the teacher long range planning for resources and materials, but the significant day-to-day planning is shared with the student groups.

However, in introducing the experience unit we said that only the rare beginning teacher would be able to conduct more than a few experience units a semester. Until he has had some experience, he may have to teach several of the more conventional subject-matter units. Here his responsibility for day-by-day planning is much more direct, and he will need lesson plans. This is not to say that in his lesson plans he cannot still engage in cooperative planning or group work or joint evaluation. But it does mean that the range of choices is less extensive, because the preliminary screening has been done by the teacher. This kind of lesson plan will be discussed on four levels: (1) Lesson purposes; (2) Activities and materials; (3) Assignment; (4) Evaluation.

Lesson purposes. The plan should take cognizance of the long-term goals of the high school in order to place the immediate objectives in perspective. The daily objectives must be realistically modest. Both teachers and students tend to overestimate what can be accomplished in fifty minutes. Certainly the teacher should help the students choose objectives in terms of their differences. The students themselves are usually not aware of how different they are. It is a good technique to help students phrase their purposes in the form of questions because responsibility for action may be implied in a question. The questions should stress concrete problems rather than abstractions. Problems can be made concrete if conceived in terms of every-day applications (Chapter 7).

Activities and materials. Of course there can be no hard and fast rules about how many activities and what materials are required for a high-school period. But it is certain that there should be some variety of both within the hour. The class should rarely discuss all period or listen to the teacher all period or even meet in groups all period. However, orderly transition from one activity to another requires explicit forethought on the part of both students and teachers. Much time, energy, and motivation can be lost if transitions are allowed merely to happen. (Chapters 7, 8, and 9.)

Because not everyone in the class comes equipped to learn the same thing in the same way, a variety of instructional materials must also be planned. But again, it is imperative to know when and how each material is to be distributed and used. It is obvious that the teacher should have some familiarity with the materials before they are used. Beginners sometimes go through embarrassing moments over motion pictures, maps, or chapters of text that they have not seen (Chapter 5).

Some kind of time budget will be necessary. Nothing is so awkward as a slice of idle time—idle because nothing has been planned. The beginning teacher should always have a number of alternatives in his plan. He will regularly have need of these extras. He invites disaster if he trusts to his ability to extemporize.

Assignment. As the work progresses, there will need to be regular restatements of the key purposes to discover whether the class still knows its direction. If assignments are used to carry the day's work forward, they need to make clear what to do, how to do it, why do it. They must be specific: who is to do it, what difficulties are involved, when it is to be done. They must be made at the right time: on the basis of inadequacies in discussion, group work, problem solving; when they will lead to further learning. Assignments are never successful when they are mechanically conceived and applied. Because the assignment is a crucial spot in carrying out the plan for learning, and also one of the chief areas of conflict between student and teacher, it will be discussed in greater detail in the final section of this chapter.

Evaluation. Evaluation of the day's work does not imply merely a five-minute quiz or grading the assignment or conducting an oral question and answer period. Each of these may have its place. But the good teacher will take equal note of how well the student worked in his group, what pictures he collected for the bulletin board display, the quality of the questions he asked. As we shall see in Chapter 17, these ways of observing behavior belong in a sound scheme of evaluation.

How Much Planning?

Variations in the amount of planning by competent teachers are as great as in any other component of teaching. Some teachers do a great deal of planning, others little or none. A wise beginner, however, takes care to do a thorough job of planning for the first year or two, until he discovers his own strengths in teaching. Good organization for learning does not just happen; it must be part of a well-thought-out long range plan for activities and materials. It is unfortunately true that planning takes time; many textbook-centered teachers, whose classes are monotonous and dull, are merely lazy. Getting away from the read-recite-test cycle requires time and thought on the part of the teacher. But once a teacher has done a really thorough job of planning a unit, he has at hand a wealth of ideas for succeeding classes and can dip into this reserve for new ways of meeting the needs of new and different students.

The new teacher should also seek out those resource units that are already available to him through the school system where he teaches. An excellent series entitled "Problems in American Life" (see bibliography) covers twenty-two different subject areas of vital interest. Another series on consumer problems[3] is an excellent source. Many of the major school systems publish resource units,

[3] *Eleven Teaching-Learning Units for Secondary School Students, 1947–1950,* Consumer Education Study, Washington, D.C.: National Association of Secondary School Principals, NEA, 1950.

and these are available at curriculum centers in all parts of the United States. The nearest university or college engaged in teacher education will have many that can be borrowed for teacher use.

Planning for Motivation in the Unit and Lesson Plan

The unit, of course, is useless unless it provides for efficient learning. One factor in getting student and content into close and happy proximity is typically called "motivation." It is the extra *push* that impels young people toward the hard work of education. Primarily this push comes from inside the student. Real motivation is said to arise when a thirsty man sees a tall glass of cool water. The teacher must try, therefore, to establish the process of learning as the goal that will satisfy the real and abiding hungers, or needs, of students.

Some teachers refer to motivation as a special activity; actually it embraces all that makes for good teaching. Beginning teachers are often appalled and frightened at the apparent apathy and disinterest of adolescents. But this need not be. A number of means to motivation that will start active learning have been implied in the earlier discussion of individual differences. It may be helpful to illustrate some of them again.

The *first means of motivation* is *recognizing* student needs. Here the teacher draws upon all he knows of adolescents in general and those in his class in particular. He identifies those needs relevant to *his* course content and experience. For example, the biology teacher knows that adolescents need to understand and accept bodily growth changes. Therefore, where biology content gives students a chance to understand their own physical equipment better, they will be motivated to learn (see Chapter 1).

But often the things we need, we do not *know* we need! Thus it is with adolescents. They have no *need* to learn about lenses and refraction of light in a physics class, but a skilled teacher, by showing them all kinds of lenses—in eyeglasses, microscopes, car headlights, binoculars, can excite their curiosity and create a "need to find out" why and how light can be bent. A *second means of motivation* then, is, making students aware of their needs. Creating such an awareness in a psychologically sound manner means that the teacher has a medium for widening the experience field of the student. If a teacher wishes to interest students in bettering their oral skills, he may provide motivation by recording several job interviews and then asking the class to judge who would get the job—and *why*. Thus, he provides a springboard into concentrated practice in self-improvement.

The liberal use of problem solving as a method of teaching also helps to make students more aware of their needs. The problem-centered unit is, in a sense, its own motivation. Such a unit takes its focus from a significant question; it is the teacher's task to see to it that the problem is of deep concern. Adolescents readily respond to the real article and just as readily reject a substitute that is only a pretense at a "problem."[4] One reliable test of what is a good problem in this sense is the alacrity with which the students comprehend it. If the teacher has to do all the work of building enthusiasm over the exciting material, then it can be assumed that the problem is *not* really centrally important to the adolescent. It is obvious that the teacher will need to sketch in for the students some of the reasons why a study of conservation has important implications for them, but unless these reasons take root in student acceptance, no problem unit can eventuate. We can, therefore, state the *third means to motivation* is conveying enthusiasm for learning. Enthusiasm is contagious. Some teachers kill off their own subject because they forget to share with students their own interests in it.

A *fourth means to motivation* is setting goals important to students. Too often the real thing a student works for is a grade. Actually, of course, this is motivation too—students can and will work very, very hard to get a good grade. But the result is low-level learning. The student actually is not concerned with *what* he is learning or even *how,* but only with a status label. Good motivation establishes goals that in themselves are important: to be able to read better, or fix simple electrical circuits, or appreciate the culture of a foreign people, or have greater skill in taking dictation. A further discussion of grades as motivation devices will be found in Chapter 16, but suffice it to say here that enduring learning must be based on more than the grade to make learning worth the effort to many of our young people.

A *fifth means to motivation* is relating the goal to the student's range of abilities. Setting a goal too difficult or too easy to achieve will destroy a good job of arousing interest. Aspiration levels commensurate with student abilities can be identified through variations in assignments, as described later in this chapter. Students enjoy working hard at tasks in which they can gain personal satisfaction from a sense of being actually *able* to do it. The problem of adapting goals to slow and fast learners is discussed in Chapter 11

[4] In Chapter 8 this distinction is discussed under the general problem of questions that provoke real discussions and those that do not.

and is basic to motivating such divergent groups to maximum learning effort.

The *final means* of motivation that we shall discuss in this section is ensuring a reasonable amount of success to students. This means is closely allied to the preceding one. There we said that students should be challenged toward goals that lie within the range of their ability. Here we are pointing out that a task remains challenging so long as the student is fairly certain he can do it and do it with some pride in accomplishment. Success must taste good, must not be too cheaply won, and must leave important resources for further learning.

What Motivation Is Not

Good motivation is positive and based on learning situations that are sociologically and psychologically justifiable. Motivation is *not* negative. Too often the motivation used by a teacher may take one of the following forms:

If you don't do this well you will have ten additional problems.

We'll have a test tomorrow if you waste this study period.

We can't stay on this topic all semester; you'd better start studying harder or you'll flunk the exam.

Since you did so badly on that last test we'll have to spend more time on this material.

Such phrases and their underlying negative approach to learning do *not* provide good motivation. Whenever the teacher expresses such attitudes he builds student antipathy to learning. And from then on it is a dull and dreary struggle for both teacher and student to plow through the drab desert of history, or chemistry, or French, or bookkeeping, or what you will.

In the pages of this volume we have attempted to present a variety of ways to make teaching and learning an exciting and worth-while experience for all concerned: *this* is *motivation.*

Student-Teacher Planning in the Unit and Lesson Plan

Much of the planning for unit and lesson plan discussed in this chapter has emphasized what the teacher must do *before* entering the classroom. But to achieve optimum learning, students must be encouraged to take an active role in reshaping and reconstructing these plans. In other words, the teacher's plan should be only tentative: the final plan for action should be conceived jointly by students and teacher.

The planning will revolve around such questions as, "What are the divisions of this problem?" "How shall we go about finding out how people feel on this subject?" "What rules do we need in order to go on that trip we proposed?" These are questions of classroom procedures, of student conduct, and of choice of subject matter. Such planning is fundamental to democratic teaching. Democracy involves planning; not planning by one person, but planning by everyone concerned. The debates in Congress, the discussions of the city council or the recreation commission—these are all part of planning in a democracy. Here citizens come together to decide what they think ought to be done based on a reasoned consideration of alternatives.

In the classroom, the teacher who undertakes this kind of project needs a strong conviction that such planning, if successfully carried out, achieves a better quality of classroom control and motivation for learning. This teacher assumes that each class differs, and therefore each class needs to advance on any body of knowledge from a different vantage point. The teacher's role, then, is to help the class see what the choices are and to analyze them; to see the consequences of the choices; and then to outline a plan.

> A history teacher decided to start the semester's work at the level of interest held by his students. But he was not sure just what did interest them. He arranged with the two local papers to have sufficient copies of both papers in class when school opened so each student could have one to read. The first two days' assignments were to read the paper carefully and then come to class with a suggestion about some topic of such importance that class time should be spent on learning more about it. Quite a variety of ideas were named. These were written on slips of paper, and while a committee started tabulating them, another committee helped pass out the textbooks for the course. There were three different texts to choose from, so again the students needed to leaf through them and decide which one they found most appealing. (The three books were on different reading levels and the teacher sought to help those who needed fast or slow books to choose properly.) Finally, the committee on current events reported that most of the class felt that recent happenings on the state level prior to a coming special election were of most concern. A discussion was then conducted by the teacher about this special election. From here, plans were made to get additional information. It was found that many students did not know about the machinery of state elections. Plans were made to read in the text about how state government operates. . . .

In this sample of *planning* the teacher deliberately set up a procedure where choice was needed. He did not himself care how the students attacked the actual history lesson. He knew that every contemporary event has its historical roots, so he saw no reason why the students could not choose the beginning topic. Similarly, they could easily see what more needed to be learned—with his guidance. Planning of what content to study—within the limits set by the course and by the instructor—involved the students in an important activity. The subject matter became alive. After all, if you choose to study Arabs rather than Egyptians, Phoenicians, or Babylonians, you probably are going to be somewhat more interested in this than in a formal assignment. This emphasis on desirability provides positive motivation.

Often teachers have found that students also get a greater sense of genuine participation in the conduct and direction of their own learning if they are allowed to help judge their own achievements. This acts as a very important incentive to follow through on what the group has agreed upon. The influence of group decision on individual action is potent for the very reason that the decisions and choices are now theirs. It is interesting to note also that students will give themselves more severe punishment and often more difficult assignments if they are helped to set good standards for themselves. Moreover, it is encouraging to see how concerned they are to make decisions fair to all. This incident is typical:

> A class once decided that since they had all done such good work they all deserved *A*'s. In a somewhat joking fashion they told this to their instructor. She received it in the proper spirit and said that, since they had done the work, they knew better than anyone else what sort of a grade they had earned. Accordingly, she suggested a real class discussion of the problem. Some of the consequences of everyone's receiving *A* were described. Under student leadership the class ranged over the whole subject and finally agreed that all had not deserved a uniform grade, but that they would like their own evaluation of their work, plus that of the instructor, to be part of the grade they would receive. This was adopted and at the final marking there were fewer dissatisfied students while some poor students were stimulated to try harder.

One word of caution must be given in the use of student-teacher planning: avoid overdoing it. The constant insistence on student choice can be just as frustrating as the denial of student choice. There should be time set aside for student-teacher planning shortly after the initiation of the new unit. There should be short planning sessions for the day as the work progresses. The evaluative sessions are important in keeping standards of work and conduct at an acceptable level. But the balance of the class time should be devoted to problem discussion, study and research, and individual and small group work. The planning sessions themselves need to be stimulating and well paced; that is, the students should feel that this opportunity to choose and evaluate is real and should be considered seriously and carefully. The teacher himself must bring a genuine enthusiasm to the planning sessions, showing his own eagerness to learn and evaluate progress along with his students. He must see exciting opportunities for learning in even the most mundane and naïve suggestions of his students.

Can planning be applied in such logically organized classes as algebra, geometry, chemistry, or physics? The answer is *yes*. Although some teachers do not develop units in these subjects revolving around large problem areas, there is still ample room for student-teacher planning. Such questions as, "How much time do we need for study in class?" "Should we do lab work in pairs, groups, or individually?" "How much credit should be discounted on homework if papers are messy and untidy?" are best answered by teacher and students working together and are pertinent in any and all classrooms. While valuable class time must, of course, be spent on such planning, the teacher will find that much less time will be needed later in pushing reluctant students and checking up on undone assignments.

The Assignment in the Unit and Lesson Plan

> It was near the end of the period in a junior class in high school. Bored students were slowly closing their books, mentally calculating just exactly how many more minutes were left to the hour. The minute hand jerked on with slow, dull clicks. Miss Jones always waited until the last possible moment to make the assignment for the next day. Often the crucial words were spoken as the bell shrilled out, effectively drowning her voice. Then students anxiously and irritably demanded, "What pages were we supposed to read?" Today she seemed particularly labored in giving the assignment: "Now I want you all to read Chapter III in your text. That is about 40 pages. You should be able to do that at home in about an hour. Be ready to answer questions on the chapter and perhaps we'll have a short quiz if you aren't prepared well enough. I'm going to check in my record book and call on those of you who haven't been doing much in class lately." This time Miss Jones beat the bell. She finished her unpleasant remarks just as the period ended. The students straggled out, complaining about what they had just heard. Clearly there were few students in this class who looked forward to returning to Miss Jones's class the next day.

Does this description seem overdrawn? Or is it a typical episode in hundreds of high-school classrooms? Let us look for a moment at a teacher who is performing the assignment function at a somewhat higher level:

> It was near the end of the period in a junior class in high school. A student was in front of the room answering questions about a report he had made on a visit to the telephone company. He had brought back some advice from the personnel manager on what high-school students should do to prepare for work in his company. Questions were being fired at him from right and left. He was having difficulty remembering all of them. Just then Miss Murphy interrupted: "Bill, I think our time is about up. That was a splendid report and there are many more questions to be asked. Since we haven't time now to answer the questions, how about each student jotting down tonight three or four really important questions he would like answered about the visit Bill made. We'll ask Bill to answer them the day after tomorrow." She turned to the board, and wrote: Assignment for Period II, Wednesday: Three or four questions on the telephone company visit. "Also," she continued, "there are some books here and in the library on how to prepare for a job. After we hear from Fred and Mary tomorrow on their visit to the cannery, it would be helpful to have some summaries of these books for those who could not make trips. Suppose each of you takes one article or book and prepares it for Thursday. Anyone else interested can see me." This was written on the board, with the names and the topic. There still remained a few moments of class. Students gathered their books: John, Bob, and Harry came up to the shelf and discussed the books they would choose. The teacher briefly chatted with them, and made an appointment to talk with them during the first few moments of class the next day.

The second example shows a different approach to the assignment. This teacher has capitalized on what was occurring in the class at the moment. Specific students were given special work to do. No threats were made; instead, the assignment was so stated that it followed naturally out of the discussion.

Current practices in assigning this out-of-school work leave much to be desired:

> The meager, vague, unanalyzed, wholly inadequate type of assignment predominates in the secondary school, practically to the exclusion of all other forms. One investigator reports that more than four-fifths of the procedures—in the social studies of all places—involved nothing more than page assignments to a single textbook! . . . Despite fifty years of attack by competent critics armed with unlimited, valid evidence, there persists the wholly unexplained assignment aimed only at "covering the text." *It would be difficult to devise an educational practice so grossly ineffective, so certainly calculated to interfere with learning, as a page assignment to a single text followed by a formal*

verbal quiz. Yet, this is the practice used by the great majority of secondary school teachers.[5]

Participation by students in developing assignments is provided by only a minority of teachers. Assignments developed in terms of the varying interests, abilities, and needs of the students are also still too rare.

What is a Good Assignment?

Perhaps before we complain further about the poor assignment, we ought to define the good assignment:

1. *The assignment should motivate substantial units of work.* One teacher divided the number of textual pages in the book by the number of teaching days, and found that if the students read five pages every night they would finish the book by the end of the year. This daily assignment took absolutely no cognizance of any relationships in the unit.

Spending half a period on a significant assignment is far better practice than five minutes every day for piece-meal, fragmentary assignments.

2. *The assignment should be developed through discussion between teacher and students.* Extensive discussion with the class about the assignment will help them understand its meaning. The teacher should also provide room for student modification and addition to the assignment. Perhaps the teacher has given too short or too long a time for completion. Perhaps an additional topic to be covered has been omitted. An assignment that represents a joint enterprise is a sounder investment of time and energy.

3. *The assignment should arise from an important problem where additional data is needed to go forward with the work.* To expect students to learn very much from trivial tasks is to expect the impossible. The student needs to see a genuine relationship between the assignment he is expected to complete and some significant purpose.

POOR: List the five main reasons why brushing teeth is important. See pages 25-35 in your text.

BETTER: Arrange an interview with a dentist or dental hygienist. Ask for the following information:

Does diet affect tooth decay?

Does brushing teeth help prevent decay?

What does the fluorine treatment do? Are there any similar discoveries that we ought to know about?

Read one of the following articles and tell whether you agree or disagree, or explain what difference the conclusions make in what you do every day regarding diet and care of teeth.

4. *The assignment should include alternatives to meet the varying needs and interests and abilities of the class.* The usual assignment assumes a dead level of need and ability in the class. Everyone has to learn the same thing and in the same amount. Yet we know this will not work. The

[5] Burton, William H., "Implications for Organization of Instruction and Instructional Adjuncts," in *Learning and Instruction,* Forty-ninth Yearbook, Part I, Chap. IX, National Society for the Study of Education (Chicago: University of Chicago Press, 1950), p. 227.

assignment should provide a number of pathways to learning, not just one. The various pathways can *complement* or *supplement* or *parallel* each other.

A Complementary Assignment: Choose one of the following three areas and prepare a summary to present to the class:

1. The weather problems in our locality.
2. How the weather bureau operates in this area.
3. How weather changed the course of history.

(Selected references and activities suggested)
(Due date: one week in advance)

A Supplementary Assignment: Students may review the material pertaining to the contributions of immigrant groups in general to American culture (selected references listed) or may choose to trace the story of one immigrant group in our locality or one they are particularly interested in.

Maps may be drawn showing: (1) historical pattern of migrations or (2) major settlements of various ethnic groups today for the nation or for our state.

A Parallel Assignment: Following is a list of the books and the chapters that cover the material on electricity. This we need to study in order to continue with the experiment on a-c and d-c current. You may read any one chapter: the books are listed in order of difficulty; the simplest at the top of the list and the most advanced and detailed at the bottom. Sign up for the book you want.

5. *The assignment should be clear and concise.* A vague problem is worse than no problem at all. A brief statement of what is to be done, who is to do it, when it is to be completed, should be placed on the board at the end of every assignment period. Often a teacher will find it useful to allocate either bulletin board or blackboard space to each class where all assignments can be posted and can remain during the time when the assignment is being completed. Students can check themselves off as each assignment is finished through a simple method of posting a list of all class members, their assignments, due dates, and providing a place for checking when the teacher has received the completed work. As each assignment is finished, the sheets can then be removed and placed in the teacher's file, where he can record the evaluation of each student's work. Duplicating such class lists at the beginning of the semester will facilitate this kind of routine.

6. *Flexibility should exist for special assignments according to varying class experiences.* The example of Miss Murphy on page 97 showed a teacher capitalizing on class interest for an immediate assignment. However, we cannot always count on some event in class that can be conveniently turned into an assignment. Therefore the teacher will have to plan a number of possible assignments several days in advance, always being alert, however, for a superior alternative arising out of the daily activity. Using class events rather than teacher preplanned assignments usually means tapping a greater student motivation. It is often useful to have several possible assignments in mind and then use the one that seems to reflect student interest of the moment.

7. *The assignment should have variety.* The old textbook assignment

routine was deadly in its monotony. It assumed that there was only one way to learn the material. In a mathematics class, for example, the assignment in the text could be varied by problems in real life, problems from other books, readings in the lives of mathematicians.

8. *The assignment should include planning with the class about what constitutes good performance* (see Chapter 17 on evaluation).

9. *The assignment should not overload students.* Some teachers derive great satisfaction from boasting about the 50-page research papers their sophomores turn in. The value of engaging in enterprises to impress fellow teachers may be questioned.

10. *The assignment should be made when it does not interfere with major out-of-school activities.* Teachers only invite hostility by scheduling assignments which interfere with student participation in the big game, the big dance, the big play. It is just good sense to make allowances at times like these.

11. *The assignment should help students learn adequate study habits.* By scheduling study periods in class so students can get started on the assignment, the teacher can observe whether the students have the skill to attack the problem, and can provide aid to those who need it. Supervised study is a vital adjunct to adequate assignment procedures. It is especially important to those students whose home conditions make study difficult, if not impossible.

Using the Textbook

What do we do with the textbook if these assignment principles are followed? Clearly, the textbook is here regarded as providing (1) a quick overview of the problem, or (2) a handy reference guide, or (3) a useful minimum assignment for students who cannot be stimulated to explore other ways of learning. The place of the textbook in relation to other learning resources is further discussed in Chapter 5.

Assignment Patterns

We might, for convenience, view the assignment procedure as a changing pattern from common assignments, to individual assignments based on interests or abilities, to small group assignments, and then back again to common assignments. A diagram of this pattern which will make it more graphic follows on the next page.

Using Questions in Assignments

Another common device in assignments is the use of a list of questions to be answered upon the completion of the research section of a lesson or unit. These questions, by pointing out things to look for, may be used to guide reading. Common practice is to assign a number of questions at the end of a textbook chapter. Such textbook questions often seek information that is trivial. The student

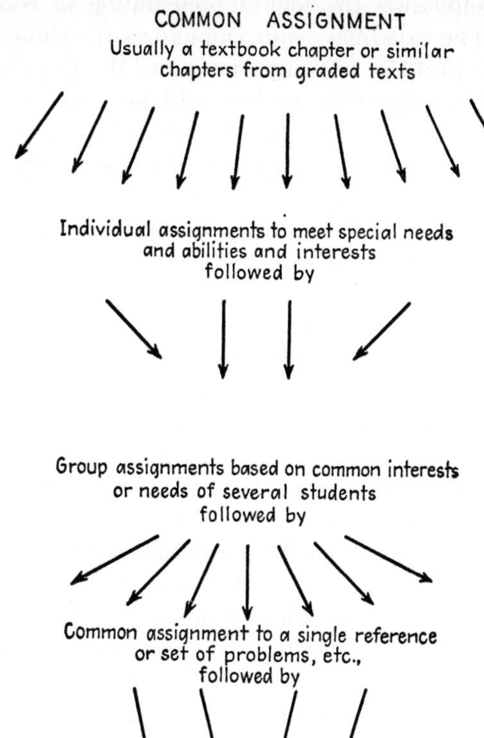

will be asked to discuss problems that are not problems to him, not now or ever, to concentrate on details that even the teacher barely remembers from semester to semester. Whenever the question device is employed as an assignment technique, the teacher should always ask himself, "Is the answer to this question worth remembering?"

The time for formal education is short, and the complexity of ideas and concepts and knowledge that we hope to introduce to young people is overwhelming. Assignments should seek out those most basic, significant, enduring major concerns, instead of wasting precious time and destroying interest by digging for detail that is of concern only to the academician.

Summary

The basic element in the building of the curriculum is the unit. Though there are many variations, in general, units can be divided into two categories: subject matter and experience. The subject matter unit emphasizes the logical presentation of content as an end in itself. The experience unit emphasizes the choice of experiences within a problem area as a means to the goals of the high school. Very few beginning teachers will be able to teach many experience units in their first years. But the subject matter unit can be modified so that in many ways it comes close to the experience unit.

Whatever kind of unit is taught, its structure includes at least four sections: initiating, planning, conducting research, culminating. In this chapter, only an overview of these sections is presented. The practical details necessary to carry out the sections comprise most of the remainder of the book.

The day-by-day work of the unit must also have its plan. In the experience unit the formal teacher-derived lesson plan is inappropriate. Planning is over longer periods of time and considered to be the joint responsibility of teacher and students. But, as we have said, most beginning teachers will be teaching many subject-matter units. And even when these units are guided toward the experience type of unit, some daily lesson planning will be needed. These lesson plans, however, do not prohibit student-teacher planning, even though the teacher may take more responsibility than in the experience unit.

Lesson plans include as prime elements: purposes, activities and materials, assignments, and evaluations. As in the unit, we have treated here only the outlines of the lesson plan, referring to later sections and chapters for the classroom techniques.

In both unit and lesson plans, the first problem is centered in motivation. Though many more could be given, this chapter has presented six ways illustrative of the best paths to motivation. These include recognizing student needs, making students aware of these needs, conveying enthusiasm for learning, setting goals important to students, relating these goals to the abilities of students, and ensuring a reasonable amount of success in achieving these goals. Good motivation, then, is positive and constructive. Learning is not best served by threats and punishment.

Once the purposes of students are engaged, plans must be made to carry out the purposes. The best planning, and also the most difficult, is planning shared by teacher and students. In this chapter we contented ourselves with indicating why student-teacher planning is most effective. Later chapters tell how to do it.

Planning involves delegation of responsibility. Willingness to accept responsibility is of prime importance in a democracy. But developing the willingness is not easy. Students do not characteristically carry out assignments without much help in learning how. In the process, friction will arise unless the assignment is jointly planned, represents an important problem, and meets the differences in student ability.

With the section on assignments, the chapter on the unit and the lesson plan is concluded. We go forward now to learn how to carry out these plans so that good learning will be effected.

Selected References

Building and Using Units

Alberty, Harold. *Reorganizing the High School Curriculum.* New York: The Macmillan Company, 1947. Chap. VIII, "Unit Teaching: Its Evolution and Present Trends," pp. 221-248; Chap. IX, "The Resource Unit in Curriculum Reorganization," pp. 249-270; Chap. X, "Developing Resource Units," pp. 271-288; Chap. XI, "Problems of Living in the Air Age: An Illustrative Resource Unit," pp. 289-334. Excellent and comprehensive coverage of unit preparation, with an example given in detail.

Billett, Roy O. *Fundamentals of Secondary School Teaching.* Boston: Houghton Mifflin Company, 1940. Part Three, pp. 459-579. Major emphasis on teaching procedures that implement unit organization of content with many specific examples.

Douglass, Harl R., and Hubert H. Mills. *Teaching in High School.* New York: The Ronald Press Company, 1948. Chap. 7, "Planning for Teaching," pp. 120-138.

Krug, Edward A. *Curriculum Planning.* New York: Harper & Brothers, 1950. Chap. V, "The Development of Specific Teaching-Learning Aids," pp. 158-191. Describes in detail the organization and planning of a teaching unit and a resource unit.

Michener, James A., and Harold M. Long. *The Unit in the Social Studies.* Harvard Workshop Series No. 1. Cambridge: Harvard Graduate School of Education, 1940.

Problems in American Life Series. 22 Resource Units for Teachers in Secondary Schools. Washington, D.C.: National Association of Secondary School Principals and National Council for the Social Studies, 1942.

Quillen, I. J. *Using a Resource Unit: Manual for Teachers.* Washington, D.C.: National Association of Secondary School Principals and the National Council for the Social Studies, 1942. An excellent practical guide for the teacher, covering the steps in building and using a unit in the classroom.

Quillen, I. J., and L. Hanna. *Education for Social Competence.* Chicago: Scott, Foresman & Company, 1948. Chap. 7, "Techniques of Teaching: Preplanning." Resource Units, pp. 184-234. Detailed coverage of content selection and teaching methods useful for resource units in *all* subject fields: pp. 509-539, Sample Resource Unit; pp. 540-551, Sample teaching unit showing assignment sequence.

Sands, Lester B. *An Introduction to Teaching in Secondary Schools.* New York: Harper & Brothers, 1949. Chap. X, pp. 219-24, "Planning Your Lessons," covers the major points to be considered by the teacher in planning the daily lesson.

Smith, B. O., W. O. Stanley, and J. H. Shores. *Fundamentals of Curriculum Development.* Yonkers: World Book Company, 1950. Chap. 23, "The Unit Organization of Instruction," pp. 554-581. Consideration of the theory of unit organization and the basic assumptions underlying various types of units.

Thut, I. N., and J. R. Gerberich. *Foundations of Method for Secondary Schools.* New York: McGraw-Hill Book Company, Inc., 1949. The subject-matter unit, pp. 193-235; The experience unit, pp. 269-317. Discusses organization, content, and methods appropriate to different kinds of units of learning.

Assignment Procedures

Burton, William H. *The Guidance of Learning Activities.* New York: Appleton-Century-Crofts, Inc., 1944. Chap. 11, The Improvement of Assignments, pp. 312-324. Concise coverage of instructional problems in making good assignments.

Butler, Frank A. *The Improvement of Teaching in Secondary Schools.* Rev. ed. Chicago: University of Chicago Press, 1946. Chap. IX, "The Assignment as the Beginning Point in Teaching," pp. 170-181. A brief discussion of some of the factors basic to good assignment procedures.

Cochrane, John J. "A Three-Level Assignment for General Science," *School Science and Mathematics,* XLV: 523 (June, 1945). Example of an assignment to meet varying needs.

Hilgard, E. R., and D. Russell. "Motivation in School Learning," in *Learning and Instruction.* Forty-ninth Yearbook, Part I, National Society for the Study of Education. Chicago: University of Chicago Press, 1950. Chap. II, pp. 36-68. See especially the discussion of rewards and punishments, pp. 46-52, and the general discussion of goals and goal-setting as vital to motivation in the whole assignment-making process.

Rivlin, Harry N. *Teaching Adolescents in Secondary Schools.* New York: Appleton-Century-Crofts, Inc., 1948. The Assignment, pp. 175-189. A brief coverage of general principles regarding assignment procedure.

Tompkins, E. E. "Richard's Reluctance," *Bulletin of National Association of Secondary School Principals,* 32:139-142 (April, 1948). Recommendations of a faculty group on how to make assignments more meaningful.

Student-Teacher Planning

Alberty, Harold. *Reorganizing the High School Curriculum.* New York: The Macmillan Company, 1949. Chap. XII, "Curriculum Reorganization Through Teacher-Student Planning," pp. 337-375. Detailed presentation of different approaches to classroom planning.

Educational Policies Commission. *Learning the Ways of Democracy.* Washington, D.C.: National Education Association, 1940. For excellent descriptions of examples of student-teacher planning, see the following pages: 114-18, 149-161, 181-184, 235-238, 239-240, 275-280.

Giles, H. H. *Teacher-Pupil Planning.* New York: Harper & Brothers, 1941. Basic discussion of total process; a well-argued statement on the importance of this kind of activity.

Group Planning in Education. Washington, D.C.: Department of Supervision and Curriculum Development, National Education Association, 1945. Describes many levels of planning and how they can most effectively be developed with students.

Horace Mann-Lincoln Institute of School Experimentation. *The Teacher's Role in Pupil-Teacher Planning.* New York: Bureau of Publications, Teachers College, Columbia University, 1947. 27 pp. A practical and concise guide to planning with some verbatim reports for analysis.

Mendenhall, C. B., and K. J. Arisman. *Secondary Education.* New York: William Sloane Associates Inc., 1951. Chap. X, "Planning for Learning," pp. 303-349. Provides a lengthy detailed description of the planning process that will be of help to a beginner.

Stiles, Lindley J., Mattie F. Dorsey. *Democratic Teaching in Secondary Schools.* Philadelphia: J. B. Lippincott Company, 1950. Chap. 13, "Teacher-Student Sharing," Chap. 14, "Examples of Teacher-Student Sharing." Theory and practice of the planning process. See Chap. 14 for detailed report on many different situations where teachers and students planned together.

Trecker, Harleigh B. *Group Process in Administration.* Revised and enlarged. New York: Woman's Press, 1950. Chap. 12, "The Planning Process," pp. 232-245. A concise description of the what and how of group planning, with significant carry-over for the teacher.

5. Providing Materials for Learning

GOOD teaching can never be routine. It can never be organized like an assembly line in a factory. Neither the students nor the teacher can afford to do the same things day after day. In the first place, interest would be stifled, and motivation is essential to efficient learning. But much more important, a standard pattern of instruction could not possibly meet the individual differences among the students. Nor could the same way of teaching day in and day out develop all the learnings that youth needs to deal with this complex world.

Reasons for Providing Variety

There are many sound psychological reasons for having a variety of learning experiences in a classroom. Many of us have experienced the sort of routine that goes as follows: Monday, read textbook chapter and answer stated questions; Tuesday, recite, with teacher asking questions, students answering, no discussion; Wednesday, quiz on previous day's material; Thursday, the cycle may start all over again with the assignment of a new section of the text. The most fascinating material can be killed for students by such treatment. Nor are teachers who fall into this kind of rut happy in their classrooms. An enjoyable, exciting, satisfying learning situation is as good for the personal morale of the teacher as for that of the students.

Planning for Variety

How can the teacher plan to include variety as well as everything else he is supposed to do! Actually, variety in learning experiences follows very naturally when planning starts with student interest and experiences. The reason for this is that student interest and experiences are themselves different at different times. For instance, a teacher of social problems might plan a discussion on developing worth-while leisure-time interests (in order to lead into a study of the problem of leisure and recreation in an industrial civilization). He might talk over with students the degree of their satisfaction with a recent vacation. Several important points would probably arise: first, recreation costs money; second, there are not enough recreation facilities in our town; third, our parents won't let us do the things we want to do in our leisure time. On the basis of these points a teacher could foresee such *variety* of activities as:

1. *Community study* to see how much recreation costs.
2. *Use of encyclopedia* on recreation and related topics.
3. *Library research* to see if anything has been written about this subject.
4. *Interviews* with local recreation commission to see what is available in the community.
5. *Panel discussion* on the findings from above activities.
6. *Quiz* on how much do you know about recreation in your town.
7. *Individual oral reports* on findings.
8. *Essay examination* on problem topics in area of recreation.
9. *Poster and bulletin board displays* on desirable recreation activities.
10. *Written report* on specific phase of subject or survey.
11. *Individual scrapbook* of advertisements, newspaper clippings, and so on, on recreation and health.
12. *Diary* by student on own recreation habits.

This list indicates some of the many experiences that can come out of a single unit of work when instruction starts with immediate student interests and activities. In the sequence of class days the unit might follow through some such outline as this:

MONDAY: Class discussion in which problem is presented through stimulating questions by teacher. Analysis of problem shows a number of areas of interests. Class is divided into study groups. Groups elect chairmen and discuss and delegate reponsibilities.

TUESDAY: Small group study on various areas of interest. Some use materials in the room; some go to library. Whole class reconvenes. Class hears preliminary reports from groups as basis for planning.

WEDNESDAY: Supervised study: groups plan work, individuals study in library to get information and prepare for community survey. Homework is either continued study in text or library sources, or interviews.

THURSDAY: Preliminary panel report on group findings after brief group meetings at beginning of period. One group has arranged an exhibit and bulletin board display.

FRIDAY: Quiz section: class discussion of results. Follow-up discussion by class on activity to date and plans for a field trip Saturday morning.

Thus, a week's work in this unit presents to the students a variety of learning situations each day and over the whole week. Students are more likely to learn lasting lessons in this class. Each day presents some lively participation activity without neglecting time for quiet study and thought.

Variety in Different Fields of Study

Variety is all very well and good, some teachers may say, but how can we have this "variety" when the subject matter is strictly limited, such as is the case with algebra, or typing, or foreign languages? Variety is not only possible in these fields but highly necessary. Here are some illustrations:

An algebra class

MONDAY: The class was excitedly discussing the last football game as the teacher entered the room. He had planned to start the unit on Ratio, and found this a good place to begin: "How would you like to make a model football field for this room and we could discuss some of the good and bad plays?" The boys agreed enthusiastically. From this came a discussion of how to make a scale drawing which led into the problem of ratio.

TUESDAY: Since not all the class was eager to do the football-field problem, and since it would not need more than five or six at the most, the teacher enlarged the discussion the next day to other areas where ratio was important. Out of this discussion came several more interest groups: one group decided to show the proportionate size of the world according to the time taken by different transportation and communication media to circle the globe, from historical periods to modern times. Two groups of girls decided to see if they could set up a series of recipes for large numbers, and then submit them to the cafeteria management in order to improve the bill-of-fare.

WEDNESDAY: The mathematics of ratio was explained and discussed. Examples from the text were worked out. Homework on ratio was assigned and started in class.

THURSDAY: Groups met on their projects. The football-field group went down to get the school blueprints to find out what the dimensions were. The girls worked on recipe books brought from home. The world-size group was in the library doing research.

FRIDAY: An architect was invited by the teacher to show how ratio enters into his work; he brought along a number of house drawings and industrial plans. The groups agreed to complete their work by the following Wednesday. A quiz on ratio was planned for Tuesday, and Monday was to be a class review of ratio problems in the homework.

A typing class

MONDAY: A businessman was brought in to explain the importance of good appearance, accurate spelling and punctuation, and careful phrasing in a business letter.

TUESDAY: Several business letters were diagrammed on the blackboard and spacing problems discussed.

WEDNESDAY: The class did a sample letter together while the teacher gave individual assistance.

THURSDAY: The students undertook business-letter assignments individually from the typing manual.

FRIDAY: The class picked out some business firm to whom they might write for free literature, catalogues, a mail-order purchase. They typed the letters, exchanged, criticized, and mailed them.

A foreign-language class

MONDAY: The students used practice records in which a native speaker spoke the phrases and they chorused a repetition.

TUESDAY: Simple songs were sung (where the teacher is self-conscious about his singing, he uses a student leader or a phonograph record to lead the singing).

WEDNESDAY: Displays were fashioned from travel agency materials (or from organizations like the French Information Services with offices in principal cities) and from materials collected from community families.

THURSDAY: Slides on the country where the language is spoken were viewed.

FRIDAY: A restaurant scene was improvised. Small groups took turns going through: greeting the head waiter, being seated at the table, ordering from the menu, discussing the table arrangement and the food, paying the bill.

Variety from Year to Year

One more point before we proceed. Variety is important not only for any single class, but year after year different approaches to the same subject matter are needed. Each class is different. No two junior groups in United States history can be quite the same. Each has a different assortment of boys and girls with different home and school problems and interests. Therefore if in one year the class studied the Civil War in the light of present-day consequences in the thinking and socioeconomic structure of the South, in the next year the class might compare the Civil War and its results with modern wars and their probable consequences in other lands. The second reason for such a change in approach is the effect on the personality of the teacher. To do the same things five periods a day for ten months, year after year, would be bound to have a deadening effect on the spark and interest of the teacher. In terms of sheer self-preservation as a person, the teacher should seek different approaches to the subject matter so that his own interest is kept alive following a new pattern of learning.

Although in this section emphasis has been put upon variety of experiences, upon the idea of the "change of pace," the importance of routine is not meant to be overlooked. There are some very essential routines that need to be kept constant, and these will be elaborated in Chapter 10 on classroom management. Routines give students a feeling of security; of knowing what to expect; of being at ease because of familiar orderliness. The teacher should be sensitive to the need for security and familiar patterns. Sudden crucial situations, such as examinations or oral presentations before visitors, should not be sprung on a class. Shifts in tactics are naturally part of providing variety in experiences, but anxiety-producing changes should be avoided. Of course, too rigid a schedule is as undesirable as one that changes with every whim of teacher or pupil. The best plans are those that are clear without being arbitrary and flexible without being formless.

So, variety in experience is necessary if learning is to be efficient. There are a number of good reasons why classrooms must have this variety:

1. Higher interest is maintained.
2. Mental and physical hygiene is improved.
3. More differences in maturation, experience, needs, and abilities are met.
4. The classes and the world in which they live are different from year to year.
5. Teacher morale is better.

Variety in Learning Materials

For the purposes of discussion, learning may be said to depend on experiences with materials and activities. Materials include: books, newspapers and periodicals, animate and inanimate objects and specimens, models, motion pictures, slides, filmstrips, still pictures, recordings, maps and charts. Activities include: discussion, sociodrama, group work, study and review, field trips, and community surveys. In later chapters the techniques for using a variety of learning activities will be detailed, but here the emphasis will center on materials for learning.

Each material has unique advantages in promoting learning. For example, with a motion picture you can watch and listen to events unfold and processes evolve. By using records you can hear in the classroom famous actors play the great roles of dramatic literature. Newspapers stay for a moment the rushing tide of history. Books organize whole fields of knowledge for study and reflection. But unless the full range of instructional materials is used, neither the full range of human differences can be met nor the full range of learnings mastered.

For the sake of convenient later reference, instructional materials will be discussed in three principal groups:

1. Audio-visual materials.
2. Newspapers, periodicals, and free materials.
3. Textbooks.

Each of these groups will be discussed under advantages for instruction, criteria for selection, and techniques for use in the classroom.

Why Use Audio-visual Materials?

Some promising approaches to harnessing differences in students for better learning have been developed in the audio-visual movement. This movement has re-emphasized the importance of using the full range of instructional materials now available: motion pictures, radio, television, recordings, filmstrips, slides, models, charts, and pictures.

> Fundamentally, learning experiences should be varied rather than repetitive, as for arbitrary associations. Meaning is not extended or deepened by engaging over and over again in the same experiences, as by reciting the exact words of a definition ten times. The nonsense word "gostifluven" is as truly nonsense after fifty repetitions as after two. Instead, the child needs—and the teacher should provide—an abundance of experiences differing somewhat but all related to the pattern of meaning under development.[1]

The effectiveness of these materials of instruction was established beyond question in the vast laboratory of World War II. There, where efficiency was at a premium, clear and consistent learning economies were effected in almost every kind of teaching from developing social attitudes to building physical skills. These gains held for almost every kind of learner from the very slow to

[1] Brownell, W. A., and Gordon Hendrickson, "How Children Learn Information, Concepts and Generalizations," in *Learning and Instruction*. Forty-ninth Yearbook, Part I, National Society for the Study of Education. (Chicago: University of Chicago Press, 1950), p. 114.

the very fast. In high-school classrooms these same advantages pertain. A few illustrations will serve to demonstrate how audio-visual materials help to meet basic differences in learners and to provide important means of motivation.

Differences in needs and interests. We said earlier that one of four basic needs is to have good personal-social relations with others. Basic to satisfaction of this need is, of course, direct experience with other persons. But experience must lead to an understanding of how good relations are furthered. For some students, keys to understanding can be wrought out of study of printed materials which interpret their direct experience; for others sight, sounds, and feeling tones must be reproduced in a motion picture before the necessary concepts are fixed; and for still others the human-relationship problems can be comprehended only by dramatic participation.

> Mr. Bertoth's class was finishing a unit on "Getting Along with Others." Each member of the class had brought in one of his problems in establishing good relationships with people. These were grouped under five subtopics:
>
> 1. How to get along with parents.
> 2. How to get along with brothers and sisters.
> 3. How to get along with other adults.
> 4. How to get along with members of the opposite sex.
> 5. How to get along on a job.
>
> Five groups of students had agreed to work on the subtopics. Joe Agransky's group took a tape recorder and collected interviews with parents. The day the group presented the recording, three parents came along to be available for the discussion. Mary Roder's group delved into the psychology books and periodicals. Out of these they singled out the most common types of problems of brothers and sisters. Then they wrote a playlet around these persistent troubles based on their own experiences. The motion picture "Dating Do's and Don't's" was used by Hank Schmitt's committee to start a rousing discussion. Jennie Marsh persuaded one of the local radio stations to loan her group a transcription of a program they had produced called "Meet the Boss." Harry Penn's group had not reported yet.

For an illustration of how these materials help to meet differences in interests, let us take one kind of interest: interest in the current social scene. We all know democracy places large faith in the ability of common people to get the facts about their problems and to make sound judgments on the basis of these facts. Today young and old alike are bombarded with a thousand sources of information. Of course, no one is born with the ability to distinguish a source that is clear and objective and one that is foggy and prejudiced. So all have to learn. There are two basic problems in this learning: (1) to know the range of sources and (2) to use this range to touch on all the important concerns of the social scene. The first problem includes showing high-school youth how to realize that they are relying on too few sources for all their opinions on current events. Some may depend on a single radio news commentator. Others may trust one newspaper, and still others may speak out of one periodical. The second problem is concerned with those students who are interested only in sports or music or the social whirl or, indeed, politics, if such there be. The other important matters covered in our superb mediums of communication just get no attention from these students. The virtues of audio-visual materials in making certain that our youth know they need many sources of information on today's world are obvious. Good teachers show the boy who relies on the newspaper what he can learn from the motion picture and the girl who depends on the radio what she can gain from the periodical. Equally valuable are audio-visual instructional tools in enriching the interest range. The student who feels drama only in football may sense climax and dénouement in history when he sees expert re-enactment in a motion picture.

> Joe Martin was tired. Yesterday's practice had been tough. He ached intolerably. If you had to take physics, he wished they would give you comfortable seats. He listened dully to Chesty Thornborough talk about the work for the day. Atoms—nuclear fission—bombs. Bombs! Joe shifted his hulking frame. Chesty sure was serious today. Ah! Curtains being drawn. Movies. Nice comfortable darkness. Now he could doze. "One World or None." Spooky music. The guy on the film wasn't helping him rest, either. Too grim. All those crosses in the cemetery. Might as well sit up.

Differences in abilities. In our first discussion of abilities we noted two levels: aptitudes (potential abilities) and achievements (developed abilities). Aptitudes, we noted, vary widely in individuals. Some of our students have special talent for handling the abstract, for dealing with verbal and quantitative symbols. Our high-school instruction has always depended heavily on this kind of ability. But some of our students do not have a marked verbal or quantitative potential. In such cases we have been prone to say that they were without any aptitude. Actually, they may have other important gifts—aptitude for the mechanical or for the artistic or aptitude in dealing with people. Unless the full range of instructional materials is used the full range of aptitudes cannot be developed. Those whose ability lags in *writing* a good paragraph about technological development in the early twentieth century may still be far ahead in *building* replicas of 1910 automobiles. Those whose skill is retarded in figuring the costs of producing *Our Town* may still be advanced in ability to play George or Emily with insight and feeling. Of course, everyone needs at least a minimum of ability to express himself in writing and to solve arithmetical problems. However, it is certainly overlooking a prime asset to learning if these existing aptitudes are not used to further other needed abilities.

> Mr. Maybee's ninth-grade mathematics class was studying the topic of measurement. First they tried out some problems in measurement of their classroom, then the school. Mr. Maybee showed them a simple way to find the distance from one corner to another of the building without cutting through the walls. Then they studied how homes were planned to conserve space. George Holt's father was a builder. So he brought blueprints in of some new houses being built. With Ozzie and Ben, George built a scale model from one of the plans. George's father said he'd like to use it in his sales office at the tract. It was really a fine model, even though none of the three had ever been too good in mathematics.

Audio-visual materials are equally useful in developing those aptitudes which are not so marked. While the potential for some students in reading, writing, and arithmetic may be low, we have, of course, no license to neglect these necessary abilities in high school. But frequently we do. For often we say that the skills should have been developed in the elementary schools, or that if the students cannot do high-school work, they ought not to be in high school. But if we are honest, we know neither statement will bear close examination. We may be sure that the elementary schools have done their best to develop these abilities as fully as they could. We know that our society needs these abilities developed at least to the point where its citizens can meet their everyday problems of making a living, raising a family, taking part in their government. There is no present likelihood that these abilities will be developed for all the children of all the people without high-school training. Sometimes the boy who reads badly is suffering from malnutrition of experience. He cannot bring experience to many symbols he sees because even in high school he simply has not had it. He needs to have this deficiency remedied before he can develop skill. If he cannot visit the scene of the symbols, at least he can see and hear and feel something of their reality in a good motion picture. Sometimes the girl who flounders in arithmetic never connected the multiplication tables with cooking or clothes or cars. She needs to work out this relationship in matters important to her. She may be helped by a problem of dress design progressing from the first sketches to the exact measurements of the pattern. As she pursues her goal of converting an idea for an attractive dress into a pattern from which material can be cut, accurate arithmetical skill will become quite important to her.

> Bert Hogan never had liked history. History teachers always wanted you to read a lot. Bert just couldn't keep up. Now here they were studying the Westward Movement. Old Pisenki seemed to get pretty steamed up about it. Always talking about "pioneer spirit" and "winning order out of the West." Bert just couldn't see it. The words stayed flat and empty on the page of his book. And this movie they were going to see today sounded about as dull as the book. "Due Process of Law Denied." What a title. Bert slouched a little lower. But wait a minute! That's Henry Fonda. And there's Dana Andrews. This is a pretty fair horse opera at that.
>
> By the time the last lines about "the conscience of mankind" lingered in the taut silence of the room, Bert Hogan had felt life in history for the first time. Did this kind of thing happen very often? Could a guy get hung then even if they didn't really prove he'd done anything? Hey, could they see that thing again?

Differences in maturation and experience. In adolescence the sharpest differences in maturation are usually noticed in sexual development. We have discussed the fact that in many ninth grades there are boys and girls and men and women sitting side by side. Often these obvious differences give them private concern. Too often the community has not allowed the high school to discuss these changes at all. Some important changes in this attitude have been effected by carefully designed motion pictures. For example, Dr. Lester Beck, when he was at the University of Oregon, went out into the communities to find out just what communities would permit. He found he was able to produce motion pictures to which there has been remarkably little objection, for example, "Human Beginnings" and "Human Growth". The motion pictures are set in the classroom and take a straightforward, natural approach which seems to satisfy most parents. Many communities foster family viewings of the pictures, so that father, mother, son, and daughter see them together. Certainly this is only a beginning toward meeting a most difficult problem, but we have every reason to expect more materials now that these pioneer films have succeeded so well.

We have alluded to the great differences in experience youth brings to the high school. There are, for example, students who have traveled throughout the United States and students who have never been ten miles from home. The history of our country may be dead on the pages of a book unless some of the color and grandeur of its "purple mountain's majesty" are more than words in a patriotic song. Slides, filmstrips, and pictures can bring this beauty closer.

Audio-visual materials are useful not only because they help meet differences in learners, but also because they furnish good means of motivation. Two means of motivation will be used to illustrate. Others, of course, could be cited. One means of motivation is to obtain active participation of the learner; another is to show the learner how much he has progressed in his struggle to learn. Here in brief is how audio-visual materials assist both means of motivation.

Active participation in learning. One reason passive learning lingers in the high school is because it has the sanction of tradition. But there is another good, practical, and perhaps more immediate reason. Most high-school teachers face five classes a day. To so change the learning environment five days a week that 125 or more students are moved to join actively in building new skills, understandings, and attitudes is a task to try the mettle of the most ingenious. Sunny charm and a golden voice are not enough. But suppose the mathematics class is studying the cost of extending social security. What better stimulation than a tape recording of a rousing debate on the radio program, "Town Meeting." Or suppose the school orchestra is preparing for the spring concert. What keener challenge than a recording of some of last year's successes.

Knowledge of progress. Later we shall see that one of the reasons grades gives students, parents, and teachers so much trouble is that they are very complicated symbols. In other words, grades stand for so many things that it is difficult for anyone to single out any specific meaning. One way to give more meaning is for students and teachers to plan together what exactly anyone should be able to do to show he has "learned" a unit of work. Then in order to be fair to the different talents of the class, several ways of displaying these agreed-upon basic behaviors are listed (and it is understood other ways conceived during the unit by class members will be allowed). It is not enough to assemble a single test for everybody, though that may be part of the scheme. In addition, some may devise a bulletin board display, or take a series of photographs, or build a model, or make a recording. So audio-visual materials become not only a means to learn but a means to demonstrate that learning has occurred. A description of what the student did thus gives meaning to the grade or may take its place entirely.

There is good evidence, then, that audio-visual instructional materials can furnish important assistance in creating the desire to learn. This help is, fortunately, available in most areas of the curriculum.

Some qualifications are, however, necessary. The materials accomplish no miracles. Some claims have been made for them that are not borne out by evidence in research. For example, broad statements are sometimes made that a definite percentage of saving in time is assured or that a definite percentage of greater permanency in learning is guaranteed. Of course, such gains do not hold for all learners encountering any kind of learning. The materials are good and useful enough without pretending that they end teaching problems everywhere. To get sound learning, teachers and students still have to plan and work hard, even with audio-visual materials. The necessity for good mental and physical hygiene in the classroom, for opportunity to review and apply learning, for efficient classroom management, to name just three of the multitude of factors affecting learning, is just as crucial as ever. Nor is an audio-visual material good just because it is audio-visual. For example, motion pictures are sometimes shown whether or not they have a place in the unit of work. They are shown because they are in the building that day.

> It was Friday morning. Miss Adams was tired. The week had been long and harried. She dragged open the school office door and shuffled in. What would she do in her classes today, she wondered? Especially that last hour. By then, she knew she would really be beat. She walked by the bulletin board. Her eyes skidded over frowsy sheets of ancient directives and stopped. Movies! That paper stuck up in a corner said there were movies here today. If you wanted your class to see them, call Harris. Let's see—*Ancient Peru, Science All around Us, Nation's Capitol, Henry Wadsworth Longfellow, Greece.* The last hour was just about up to the 1890's in U. S. history. Better give them *Nation's Capitol.* She'd find some way to tie it in. The kids wouldn't care anyway. Better call Harris.

Of course, any instructional material—book, periodical, chart, recording, or motion picture—is only really useful if it "belongs" in the curriculum.

To help teachers know the sources of audio-visual materials, colleges maintain basic references. It will be helpful to gain familiarity with the principal catalogues and their different systems of indexing. For example, every teacher ought to know the *Educational Film Guide* and its regular supplements. He ought to know the catalogue is indexed by film title and by subject-matter area. Most larger school systems will have their own catalogues of audio-visual materials. Small school systems may draw upon county libraries or libraries maintained by state colleges and universities, and some borrowing may be made from federal, state, and municipal agencies. The Red Cross, the American Cancer Society, and many other public organizations and foundations have materials for lending. Commercial firms have become increasingly intelligent in the kind of materials they offer to our schools. The earlier overloading with advertising has diminished to an encouraging extent. All in all, for the teacher with initiative, there is a wealth of these materials to be had. But, first, teachers have to learn where and how the materials are listed as well as the requisitioning procedure that each source employs. Some exploratory work with the standard catalogs will be time well spent.

Why Use Newspapers, Periodical Materials, and Free Materials?

In the United States we have the largest variety of newspapers and periodicals in the world. Unquestionably they exercise great influence on the attitudes and actions of our people. There is a significant percentage of the population who read little beyond the daily newspaper and popular magazines. Such important sources of information and opinion belong in the classroom. There the advantages and limitations of the mediums can be explored. Students can be taught how best to use these resources now and as adults.

No teacher can afford to neglect the wealth of instructional materials available with little or no cost from the federal, state, and local governments, from public service organizations, from foundations, from business and labor organizations. The advantages that accrue to the teacher who uses newspapers and periodicals may be supplemented with these resources. There are exhibits to be had, posters, pictures, pamphlets, maps, and books. The great majority have been issued without objectionable, partisan propaganda. A list of major current sources of free and inexpensive materials will be found in the appendix.

Moreover, it should be apparent at once that these are valuable materials to meet individual differences and provide motivation. In less detail this time, we can check through again to see just how newspapers and periodicals may contribute.

Differences in interests. Part of the need to function as an individual is satisfied by a feeling of status and recognition. Often this can be gained by capitalizing on long established interests. Interests in such subjects as horses, stars, boats, and Indians may have been pursued to the point where students are experts in the field. There is mathematics in these interests (how do you determine good "lines" for a boat); there is English (what was the quality of Navajo literature); there is science (how far into the firmament have we been able to see); there is history (when were Arabian horses introduced into this country).

Horses, stars, boats, and Indians figure in the newspapers, periodicals, and free materials regularly. It is relatively easy to get students to explain these articles to the class or to begin a scrapbook collection or to organize an exhibit.

Differences in abilities. The range in reading abilities commonly appalls beginning high-school teachers. The textbooks do not begin to meet the variant skills, but there is newspaper, periodical and free material on about every level. Several of the popular magazines (for example, *Reader's Digest*) issue special editions for less able readers. These have the great advantage of meeting the maturity of their interests and the immaturity of their reading skill.

Differences in maturation and experience. Newspapers, periodicals, and free materials are designed to appeal to every degree of naivete and sophistication. They have a flexibility of format, content, and style not to be equaled by the usual instructional materials. Some teachers have organized clipping committees who cull the magazines contributed by the class for articles of current or potential interest to the group. These are pasted on cards and filed by topic.

Active participation in learning. Before we can get active participation in learning, we must first have reception and reflection. Too often the learning cycle does not even begin because students have not "tuned in" on the problem. They sit listening to the teacher, but they do not hear; they look steadfastly at the book, but they do not see (much less read). But if we can just ride a frequency that reaches where they live (for example, an editorial decrying the "hoodlumism" of youth), the change is instantaneous. All the marvelous intensity of adolescence flashes over the room. And learning begins.

Knowledge of progress. The infinite variety of newspapers, periodicals, and free materials furnishes a kind of many-runged ladder of achievement. For some the steps will be slow; others will scorn to take each small gradation but clamber over several at a time. The point here is that where these materials are used, we do not have lock-step education. We can make more allowances as each seeks his own pace, but with a lesser range of materials, such allowance is not possible. As the student climbs his way, we do not have to tell him that he made four rungs this month. He can see his progress himself.

Why Use the Textbook?

European visitors have long been impressed with the extent that the textbook is used in American education. Probably more varieties are available for each area of the curriculum than anywhere else in the world. Nor does any other country demand such attention to classroom pretesting, to attractive format, to visualization of content, to frequent revision.

Although we have reserved this discussion of the textbook until last, we cannot say that the textbook is last to meet the maturational problems induced by individual differences. It is only last when the instruction of a whole group of different people is tied to one textbook. But then the same could be said of any instruction using only one teaching material. Instruction is better when more than one textbook is used and best when the textbook is used in combination with many other kinds of instructional materials.

Choosing Materials for Learning

The basic determinant of the adequacy of a material for learning is the curriculum. In the curriculum each high school codifies its beliefs about men and society. In terms of these beliefs, the specific task of the high school is defined. The task will include a comprehensive range of concepts, skills, attitudes, and appreciations. To develop these concepts, skills, attitudes, and appreciations, a pattern of learning experiences is developed. These learning experiences involve both materials and activities.

Here the discussion has been confined to learning materials. And we can say of a learning material, it is effective or ineffective, appropriate or inappropriate to the degree that it promotes or does not promote the concepts, skills, attitudes, and appreciations stated as goals in the high-school curriculum. In other words, a material for learning derives its primary validity from the curriculum. Of course, this assumes that the curricular design has taken realistic cognizance of the dual demands of society and the individual. This is another way of saying that the objectives of the curriculum must be sociologically and psychologically sound. Furthermore, the task undertaken by the high school must be feasible. The high school cannot undertake all responsibility for the development of youth. Other agencies have their responsibilities, too. (For details on this point, see Chapter 17 on evaluation.)

If the goals are assumed to be psychologically and sociologically sound as well as feasible, then learning materials may be judged by their ability to provide the means of implementing the curriculum. On this basis a series of criteria can be established to determine proportionate amounts and kinds of materials for the curriculum:

1. *Materials appropriate to the general objectives of the curriculum.* Each material should have its definite part to play in the curriculum. No one kind of material (books alone, or newspapers alone, or motion pictures alone) can be expected to provide the means to accomplish all the objectives. With each objective it is important to ascertain just what concepts, skills, attitudes, and appreciations each material can best help further.

2. *Materials appropriate to the specific objectives of the course of study and to a specific group of learners.* The general objectives of the high school are a shared responsibility. In each class the teacher has his specific objectives. As each class is made up of different individuals, the way to reach these specific objectives will be different. The materials for learning must be appropriate to this way.

3. *Materials that bridge in and out of school experience.* As each class makes its own way toward its specific objectives, the learning materials must help relate the objectives to the daily lives of students.

4. *Materials that emphasize student activity.* Learning materials should be a spur to student initiative. They should encourage creative discovery rather than memorizing readymade solutions.

5. *Materials that belong in a graded sequence.* Learning materials should be chosen to fill a place in a planned sequence of extending and strengthening the concepts, skills, attitudes, and appreciations as they are required in the curriculum pattern.

6. *Materials that provide stress on learning, not on entertainment.* The present emphasis on providing a variety of instructional materials should not be construed as an invitation to convert the classroom into a vaudeville show. The material should promote learning. This goal should not be obscured by overindulgence in tricks or devices which do not engage relevant purposes.

These are general criteria to guide teachers in the selection of any kind of material for learning. Here are some additional suggestions to illustrate how further screening can be employed for each of the major groups of materials.

Audio-visual materials: the motion picture and the television program. The motion picture and the television program are similar in the kind of learning materials they can provide. Both have the unique ability to show the world in action through sight and sound and color. It is possible to watch the drama of human relationships, real and imagined. It is possible to transport the viewer to places and events, distant in time or in space. Microscopic life can be made to fill the screen. An explosion of a bomb, which in reality took a fraction of a second to occur, can be studied for minutes through slow-motion photography. Conversely the unfolding of a flower which in reality took hours can be seen in a few moments through time-lapse photography. The complicated workings of a giant machine can be simplified as the camera focuses on one relevant operation at a time. The operation can even be viewed from within through animation photography, as in the case of the cylinders of an internal-combustion engine.

The first criterion of selection for the motion picture and the television program therefore is that it should exploit these unique advantages. An instructional motion picture or television program ought not to be merely a photographed lecture or, in effect, a series of still pictures. It ought not to be consumed with commentary about action that is never seen on the screen.

As the motion picture and the television program have unique advantages, so they have special disadvantages. Both present the material for learning at a fixed pace. The student must perforce move along at the speed determined by the producer of the material. Some of this can be overcome in the motion picture, since the film and scene within the film can be reshown. But to achieve most efficient learning, both motion pictures and television programs should always take account of the psychological principle of pacing. In simplest terms, this means that material of intellectual complexity or emotional intensity must be presented with deliberately planned intervals which permit the viewer to mull over what he has seen, heard, and felt. If enough time is allowed, the learner is ready then to accept another difficult or tense sequence. But if he is hit hard again and again without time to recover between hits, his preoccupation with the first hit may shut off further receptivity. In other words, the viewer stops learning.

This problem is particularly striking in the motion picture and the television program because these are expensive media. There is a great temptation to load the typical ten-minute motion picture or the fifteen-minute television program with learning material just because it costs so much to provide these few minutes. The idea seems to be to appeal to the greatest number of teachers. If enough concepts or skills or attitudes or appreciations are packed in, the argument runs, almost everybody will see something in it that he teaches. Of course, this is the very falsest kind of economy for learning, because when films and programs are so concentrated, they pass by most learners.

One other special problem with the motion picture and the television program needs brief mention. We have long been a moviegoing people. Most of our children begin to see motion pictures in the neighborhood theater in their very first school year, if not before. By the time they reach high-school, they have seen many motion pictures. During the last few years the increase in television sets in American homes has been astonishing. Because of the technical difficulties many rural areas will not be able to join the television audience for some time, but in many metropolitan areas, the sale of television sets is phenomenal. In the case of both the motion picture and the television program, then, we can expect high-school students, by and large, to be quite sophisticated, if not blasé. They are conditioned to commercial motion pictures and television programs produced with far larger budgets than the education counterpart ever enjoys. Educational motion pictures and television programs employ less expensive actors, sets, costumes, properties. They use minimal musical mood setting, or none at all. And students are very critical of the result. They compare what they see in the classroom with last week's feature movie or leading commercial television program. Unless they are given very careful preparation for the film or program, they may attend to it only half-heartedly. However, it is only fair to say that the quality of educational motion pictures and television programs has improved markedly in the last few years. Unquestionably, some of the materials now made available facilitate learning in ways that are impossible to duplicate with any other instructional medium.

One last suggestion about choosing motion pictures and television programs—select one with a good teaching pattern. For example, sound means of motivating the student should be employed. This may mean setting unfamiliar material in familiar surroundings to facilitate engaging the students in the problem. Sometimes just a regular classroom setting serves the purpose. Or it may mean using as actors people the same age as the students. To sustain interest, the film or program should challenge the students to work along, at least mentally, as the action unfolds. Corollary problems not covered in the film or program may be suggested directly by the actors or commentator. In the closing sequences, the film or program may well have the actors or commentator speak directly to the students about their responsibility for further exploration of the problem.

Radio broadcasts and recordings. Unquestionably radio broadcasts and recordings do not have the impact of motion pictures or television programs. The appeal of these media to learners is primarily aural, and thus the hold on attention is not nearly so tenacious. Still, radio broadcasts and recordings are quite useful in the classroom. As yet only a comparatively few schools are equipped with television receivers, and thus the radio is the only medium able to present the events of the day as they happen. Classes can still gain much by listening to the President addressing Congress, to informed men debating the issues of the day, to the leaders of sister nations speaking to the American people.

Now by means of tape recordings any school can preserve a radio broadcast for release in the classroom at the appropriate time. Moreover, the same tape can be used over and over again. This means that fine dramatizations of historical events and literary masterpieces can be recorded and held at very small cost until they are most timely or useful. A wealth of music from the radio can also now be made availabe for convenient listening times.

A great deal of valuable material, some originally produced for radio and some not, is also available on disc recordings. In addition, the commercial companies have produced over the years a wide range of recordings, especially, of course, in the field of music. These recordings, unfortunately, have never been fully exploited in the classroom.

Teachers will find that recordings of student-prepared radio programs, either simulated or real, make excellent motivating devices. The tape recorder permits the teacher to record a complete program and use the program once or a hundred times without impairing the tape or the quality of the recording. The tape can then be erased and used over again many times for entirely new programs. Erasing and splicing also make judicious editing possible so that mistakes and extraneous sounds can be eliminated. History teachers can re-create great events and personalities with student scripts and student actors. English teachers can present plays, short stories, excerpts from novels. Science teachers can develop panel discussions, popular science programs, or science-in-everyday-life series.[2] Many community radio stations will be happy to release these tape recordings over the air. Then parents and other inter-

[2] For another stimulating use of tape recordings, see Spitler, R. Conway, "Being Two People at Once," *California Journal of Secondary Education,* 26:224-225 (April, 1951).

ested members of the community can listen and learn more about the activities of their schools.

The first criterion for selecting radio broadcasts and recordings derives from the ability of radio and recordings to bring to the classroom the manifold sounds of living: trains, planes, people, music, and the ability to take out of the classroom the creative expressions of the students in drama, discussion, song, and story. True, this medium does not see the fullness of life; it only listens to it. But at least it can be listening to living and not just to the teacher. The tremendous audience of radio before the competition of television indicates the power that is there. Until motion pictures and television programs become much less expensive, radio and recordings will be the more practical media for many instructional purposes.

Of course the limitations of listening must be recognized. In general, the attention span is shorter than when the eye also is engaged. The emotional hold is also less powerful. Students can be distracted easily when listening to radio and recordings. The teacher will need to make realistic estimates about whether the program or recording can hope to engage the attention at all and, if it can, for how long.

Attention is engaged longer and the effect strengthened if the program or recording has an easily recognizable structure. The outlines of what the student is to understand or appreciate should be joined in a coherent organization. He should be told early and explicitly just what the point of the program is and should be reminded as the program develops. He should be assisted by summation as the program ends. In dramatization, for example, the number of scenes and characters in each program should be sharply limited, unless the group has had much training in listening (see Chapter 12). Each scene and each character needs careful introduction because if the student fails to make the essential identifications, his interest plummets. Sudden shifts in time and place are to be held to a minimum for similar reasons. And at the end, brief comments or suggestive questions by the announcer about what happened in the drama make learning more efficient.

Within these coherent program patterns, the radio broadcast or recording should limit the number of concepts introduced in any one presentation. The limitation should be even more severe than those imposed in motion pictures and television programs. For example, the twenty-minute motion picture, "Due Process of Law Denied," excerpted from the full-length feature picture "The

Oxbow Incident," easily includes materials for three or four 15-minute radio dramatizations.

When the class is expected to retain much detail, that program or recording should be chosen which provides repetition of detail in a variety of ways. For example, if the radio program hopes to establish several qualities in the character of President Wilson, each of these qualities may have to be seen in two or three revealing episodes.

The last criterion will be obvious as soon as it is mentioned; yet it is crucial to the success of this medium. The voices of narrators, speakers, or participants in drama must employ good diction and clear enunciation. The presentation is to the ear alone, but if the ear cannot clearly distinguish the words, no learning can take place.

Filmstrips and slides. Slides and filmstrips are similar to radio programs and recordings in that they appeal to one sense only, but they are different in that they permit study and discussion at any point and for as long as the class wishes. Filmstrips and slides, therefore, ought to be chosen for their adequacy in stimulating study and discussion. For example, they can arrest the processes involved in making speech sounds, or they can magnify views of flowers and insects or catch the climactic moment of a news event.

To accomplish this kind of stimulation, the amount of detail or the number of captions and labels in any one slide or picture in a filmstrip should be limited. Otherwise the impact will be diffused. For example, so many parts of the flower may be labeled that the student either becomes confused or his attention is never gained at all. In a series of slides or of pictures in a filmstrip, the appeal can be strengthened by variety of treatment. Close-up, medium, and long photographic shots can be employed. The possibilities of diagrams, cut-aways, exploded views, graphs, and cartoons should not be overlooked.

Newspapers and periodicals. There are two kinds of newspapers and periodicals used in the classroom: those especially prepared for the classroom and those published to sell in the general adult market. Obviously the problem of selection with the first kind is much simpler. They are produced by experienced educators who are fully aware of teachers' problems. Of course, not all succeed uniformly well, so, there is still some room for choice.

Probably the most important consideration with the newspaper or periodical designed for the classroom concerns the quality of its interpretation and selection in its news stories, articles, and library materials. These newspapers and periodicals do not pretend to be abreast of each day's events. When they reach the classroom, the news is somewhat dated. Students will be familiar with a good many of the facts from reading adult newspapers, listening to the radio, viewing television, and hearing the conversation of their parents and others. A simple record of the news, then, is not enough. Succinct restatements of facts will still be needed to refresh memories and to ensure a common background of information. But much more important is the placing of these facts in perspective. Students need interpretive comment to start them thinking about the significance of the facts, and the quality of this comment should be the first criterion of selection.

Naturally, it is equally important that the interpretive comment be nonpartisan. Opposing points of view should be fairly stated. It is not the purpose or concern of this kind of publication to propagandize for one side or the other.

Next in importance to the teacher is the vocabulary of the material. The reading experts have made available a number of readability formulas, and a good classroom newspaper will have been checked for readability in order to avoid an unrealistic vocabulary burden.

Some attention ought also to be paid to the make-up of a classroom newspaper or periodical. It ought to invite attention through good design, avoiding arrangement of articles like tombstones in solemn rows. Pictures, cartoons, maps, and graphs ought to be used liberally.

Finally, classroom newspapers and periodicals can be chosen for the quality of the teaching guide offered. This supplemental sheet published for the teacher should emphasize how the teacher can guide his students in developing increased discrimination in reading newspapers and periodicals.

When the teacher comes to select adult newspapers and periodicals for the classroom, the problem is much more difficult. In the first place, the number of publications available is overwhelming, and in the second they manage to violate most of the precepts just listed as guides to the selection of newspapers and periodicals published especially for classroom use. They are rarely nonpartisan, the vocabulary is not gauged for the classroom, the make-up ranges from the sensational to the ultraconservative.

Still these are the materials on which these students will depend to an important extent when they are adults. It does not seem wise to exclude them from the classroom, for where but in the classroom will youth learn to penetrate prejudiced information or to graduate from the cheap and superficial? The important consideration is that a comprehensive sampling from these materials be offered. In many communities only one newspaper is published. Students should become acquainted with other newspapers of varying quality and temperament in order to be able to view their own community newspaper in proper perspective. In many homes, the only periodicals read are chosen from the five or six national leaders in circulation, and in still other homes, no periodical material of any kind is read. Students therefore need to examine and compare in the objective atmosphere of the classroom not only the popular favorites but some of the lesser known magazines.

Free materials. Many millions of dollars are spent by commercial firms and public and private agencies on materials to influence public opinion. A large portion of the materials is aimed at the classroom. But whether or not specially tailored for the schools, the materials comprise a valuable resource. Certainly they cannot be used without careful education of students to discern bias and slanting of information. As was noted earlier, the sponsors of these materials are becoming increasingly intelligent in learning to refrain from extravagant singing of their own praises. But the materials would not be sponsored so widely unless they still offered some opportunity to plug for special interests.[3] However, as in the case of adult newspapers and periodicals, the students will be assailed by special-interest materials all their lives. They must learn discrimination somewhere.

Textbooks. Beginning teachers will not often have a hand in choosing the textbooks for their class. Nevertheless, they need to know how to judge the strengths and weaknesses of the books selected for them. Perhaps, first of all, teachers should look to see how well the authors of the textbook seem to know the adolescent. Does the book relate the interests, needs, abilities, backgrounds of experience of adolescents to the content presented? Is the style brisk and alive rather than dignified and dead? Is the format attractive? Are the illustrations abundant? Unless the book is thus aware of the adolescent, the textbook deters, rather than encourages, learning.

Some evidence should be offered by the publishers that the material has been tested in the classroom so that development of concepts, attitudes, and skills is carefully calculated. This evidence should include analysis of the vocabulary burden; systematic pro-

[3] Patterson, Franklin K., "Free Teaching Aids in California Schools," *California Journal of Educational Research,* 1:165–168, 210–214 (September, November, 1950).

vision for repetition, summary, and review; and suggestions for a wide range of supplemental materials and activities.

Using Materials for Learning

Learning is never induced automatically. Whether the instructional material is a motion picture, a newspaper, or a textbook, teachers and students have to plan for and work with it. There are current too many unfounded claims of miraculous gains with instructional materials. There is often the implication that this particular motion picture or classroom newspaper or textbook will guarantee better learning, whatever the class or its teacher is like or whichever way they are going. Of course, this is nonsense. Teachers and students need to work as hard as they ever did. With a better range of instructional materials, a better range of learnings is possible. But it is not guaranteed.

Audio-visual materials. A basic pattern of instruction needs to be followed with audio-visual materials. This is especially important in those materials which follow a constant pace in presentation once they are begun: motion pictures, television programs, radio broadcasts, recordings. Motion pictures and recordings can be interrupted, but not without dangers of inducing discontinuity and confusion—at least during the first run with the class. Television programs and radio broadcasts (unless recorded) cannot be interrupted. By and large, then, with these four materials, the student must keep pace. This places greater premium on readiness for learning, acceptance of responsibility for active participation, and follow-up activities for evaluating learning. But even with slides, filmstrips, and other audio-visual materials these three elements in a basic pattern of instruction are important.

1. *Develop readiness.* No learning material should be used until a purpose for it has been clearly established. A motion picture must fit into the course of instruction just as a textbook or a periodical must. The learning material should be related to previous activities and materials. A motion picture on slum clearance, for example, might be related to a chapter in the textbook or to a filmstrip.

2. *Develop responsibility for active participation.* Some anticipation of the learning job in the new material should be provided. For this purpose teachers and students must preview the materials, then vocabulary difficulties can be met in advance. Guide questions suggesting the key concepts in the material can be suggested. Auxiliary problems and materials for the follow-up activities can be planned. In the United Nations recording, "Document A777," for example, many of the historical characters will be new to students. Brief discussion can lead to posing for the students

questions like this: Listen carefully to see why this person is introduced.

3. *Conduct follow-up activities.* The amount of learning achieved should not be taken for granted. There should always be evaluation to see just what was learned. The pace of presentation of the material for learning may have been too swift. Some students may have been left behind; others may have not completely understood the material; still others may have gained quite false impressions.

Any of these may require re-presentation of the material or turning to another material or activity. Even when the learning seems to have been developed efficiently, the opportunity to move into new materials and activities should not be neglected. No material should be regarded as an end in itself. The filmstrip "The Atom," for example, pictures a number of laboratory demonstrations. Most of them need further explanation. Students could turn to reference works and periodicals and prepare reports. Charts illustrating the points in further detail could be made. Some simple experiments could be carried out.

Newspapers, periodicals, and free materials. To utilize newspapers, periodicals, and free materials each teacher needs to organize a resource file. Here can be placed pictures, clippings from newspapers, articles from magazines, pamphlets, the smaller charts, and maps. (The available motion pictures, filmstrips, slides, recordings, television and radio broadcasts can also be listed.) Names of useful newspapers and periodicals as well as sources of appropriate free and inexpensive materials can be noted. References to chapters in textbooks, supplementary and reference books bearing on the teaching topic should be there.

One way to organize the file is by common large topics or problems into which a field of knowledge may be organized. Within these larger divisions, subtopics can be selected. Some teachers obtain a number of courses of study of the kind they expect to teach. From these they select the recurring themes or centers of instruction, which become the main divisions of the file. Other teachers leaf through some of the widely used textbooks to locate a pattern for organizing the file.[4]

This logical system of filing instructional materials should not be confused with the pattern for teaching. It is simply a way to locate readily those materials for which teacher and student together find need in their plans for learning. The materials will be used in different order and with varying emphasis for each class. The goal is to stimulate and forward the learning jobs attempted but not to limit what they will be.

[4] For additional suggestions, see Chapter 10 and *Materials of Instruction*, Eighth Yearbook, Department of Supervisors, National Education Association. New York: Columbia University Press, 1935, pp. 140-148.

Certainly the students should be encouraged to add to the resource file. They will find pictures, pamphlets, charts, and articles to an extent much beyond the teacher's necessarily limited search. Often they will be more meticulous than the teacher in the maintenance of the file. Sometimes the students can even build simple files out of orange crates or boxes for the teacher whose room does not have sufficient filing equipment.

However they are built up, resource files represent long-term, continuous projects. It is not possible overnight to know the sources of materials, to appraise their worth, to index their possible uses in instruction. This is the work of a lifetime. No one can begin too soon.

Once a system for managing the materials is organized, the beginning teacher can begin to make his plans with his students for their use in instruction. It is unwise to plunge into extensive use of these materials, unless plans and facilities for filing and storing are made. Many teachers will want first to try their skill with the materials as supplemental resources. Later, whole units of instruction can be centered in the materials.

As a supplemental resource, newspapers, periodicals, and free materials are useful in a number of classes. In social studies classes, for example, the regular ten-minute news period may be used to encourage more discerning reading. Student chairmen may be used to conduct these periods and evaluation committees organized to plan ways to check the understandings that are developed. Sometimes the students may organize programs simulating one of the many radio and television quizzes. In English classes, the materials can be used both to develop reading skills and to extend general collateral reading. Some of the periodicals issue tests for reading skills. But teachers and students can easily develop their own simple exercises: in vocabulary, in locating key ideas, in skimming, in summarizing.

For collateral reading teachers can organize clipping committees to cull good articles and stories from a variety of sources. These may be mounted on large cards with several articles or stories around the same topic or theme on the same card. Science teachers find newspapers, periodicals, and free materials an especially rich resource for bulletin board displays. In this connection there has been developed the concept of the display area. This recognizes the limitations of the bulletin board and uses whole classroom walls for display. The techniques of the commercial display artisans in retail merchandising can be used to great advantage in this kind of display. Occasionally local firms will loan these skilled people to demonstrate their techniques.[5] Mathematics classes may look for the application of mathematics in articles and advertisements. The materials are particularly useful in providing examples of graphic representation of quantitative data.

The management of a whole unit of instruction dependent upon newspapers, periodicals, and free materials takes mature teaching skill. But the quality of learning achieved can be of high caliber. An English class can undertake to study modern media of communication: the motion picture, the radio broadcast, the television program. These media cannot be studied adequately without recourse to newspapers, periodicals, and free materials. And certainly careful appraisal of the influence of these media in the attitudes and understandings of the public needs undertaking in our public schools. In the sciences, vital units of instruction like conservation, atomic energy, and electronics must depend on materials more current than any textbook can be. Of course, in the social studies the possible units of instruction are almost without end.

In order to protect themselves while developing the skill required to use newspapers, periodicals, and free materials, beginning teachers should check their preparation well. Here are illustrations of the kinds of preparation that need to be made:

1. Survey the possibilities of assuring an adequate supply of materials, especially to see there is a balance in the supply where controversial issues are attempted.
2. Be sure the administrators in the system have been informed of what is being attempted.
3. Look again to see that the system and facilities for filing and storing are adequate.
4. Tell other teachers, especially those in the same department, of the plans. Solicit their advice. Then, if students in other classes ask to try the same materials, the teachers will at least not be caught by surprise.
5. Prepare an exceptionally careful scheme of evaluation (see Chapter 17). Evidence should be ready that students learn something with these materials.

The textbook. In a sense, the best way to use the textbook has already been discussed, that is, to use the textbook in alliance with other instructional materials (and, as will be apparent in the chapters that follow, in support of many instructional activities). The guides for teachers that are issued with many textbooks include

[5] For details on this and other techniques with these materials, see Kinney, L. B., and Katharine Dresden, *Better Learning through Current Materials* (Stanford: Stanford University Press, 1949).

good suggestions for this kind of balanced instruction. Too often these guides are overlooked or forgotten by beginning teachers.

The beginning teacher can help his students to realize the most from the textbook by discussing at the beginning of the year how the book is organized and showing them the section and chapter organization. He ought to remind them of the many aids planned for their assistance: illustrations, maps, graphs, paragraph subheads, supplementary references, discussion questions, and index. A little time spent in this way may help the students to realize how much can be learned from a good textbook.

Without question, for most beginning teachers, the textbook will be a basic material for instruction. As he grows in teaching skill, he ought, of course, to become less dependent on it. Although in the beginning, the teacher starts much instruction with the textbook, he does not, however, have to start *and* end there. Each time that he turns to the textbook he should ask himself: What other materials and activities are feasible for this class? At first, because he is overwhelmed by his five or six classes a day, he may have energy to try only a few. A history teacher may see a reference to Lafayette in the text and be reminded of a new biography on that interesting Frenchman. Can he interest a student to report some anecdotes from the book? The English teacher may recall a new filmstrip on "Emerson's New England" as his English class approaches that writer. Can he obtain it from an audio-visual center? Gradually the beginning teacher should be able to see that the textbook does not always have to be the center of instruction. And one day he ought to have the courage to try some other materials for learning.

Summary

The many different kinds of students have come to the high school with different expectations of what high school can mean to them. They have many common tasks, but they cannot all meet these tasks in the same way. To "motivate" these students means to meet their differences in ways that will enable them to master these tasks in some measure. Motivation of this quality and extent can be obtained through selecting a variety of learning materials and activities. Variety of learning activities may range from community study to sociodrama. Learning materials may vary from motion pictures to textbooks. With this range, learning is more efficient because of higher interest; meeting more differences in maturation, experience, needs, and abilities; better mental and physical hygiene within any one class; meeting differences from year to year in all classes and the world in which they live; improved teacher morale. In addition, there are unique advantages in promoting learning which each kind of activity and material enjoys.

In this chapter, three groups of learning materials—audio-visual materials; newspapers, periodicals, and free materials; and textbooks—have been discussed in detail. For each group, the advantages for instruction, criteria for selection, and techniques for use in the classroom were presented. In the next chapters, ways to use a variety of learning activities will be described.

Selected References

General

Dale, Edgar. *Audio-Visual Methods in Teaching.* New York: The Dryden Press, 1946. Particularly useful for its discussion of the importance of a variety of instructional materials.

Kinder, James. *Audio-Visual Materials and Techniques.* New York: American Book Company, 1950. Helpful, practical details about using visual and auditory materials in the classroom.

McKown, Harry, and Alvin Roberts. *Audio Visual Aids to Instruction.* New York: McGraw-Hill Book Company, Inc., 1950. Suggestions about planning for instructional materials in a number of subject-matter fields are included.

National Society for the Study of Education. *Audio-Visual Materials of Instruction.* Forty-eighth Yearbook, Part I. Chicago: University of Chicago Press, 1949. An authoritative discussion of materials of instruction with comprehensive bibliographies.

Filmstrips, slides and flat pictures

Dale, Edgar, *et al. How to Teach with Pictures.* Informative Classroom Picture Publishers, Grand Rapids (Mich.), 1947. A small pamphlet packed with teaching ideas about the use of pictures.

Falconer, Vera. *Filmstrips.* New York: McGraw-Hill Book Company, Inc., 1948. A comprehensive guide to selection and utilization with organized sections devoted to the common fields of instruction in high school.

Hamilton, G. E. *The Stereograph and the Lantern Slide in Education.* Meadville (Pa.): Keystone, 1946. Another pamphlet with many good suggestions about hand-made slides.

Motion pictures and television

Elliott, Godfrey. *Film and Education.* New York: Philosophical Library, 1948. A symposium by the experts clarifying the special advantages for instruction of the motion picture.

Gable, Martha. "Teacher! Here Comes Television," *Educational Screen,* 28: pp. 68-70 (February, 1949). A report of how one large school system has produced and used television programs to improve instruction.

Radio and recordings

Levenson, William, and Edward Stasheff. *Teaching through Radio and Television.* 2d ed. New York: Rinehart Company, Inc., 1952. One of the best discussions of the potentialities for motivation of the simulated and actual broadcast.

Woelfel, Norman, and I. Keith Tyler. *Radio and the School.* Yonkers: World Book Company, 1945. Two pioneers in the field of auditory materials of instruction provide some concrete advice about recordings in the classroom.

Newspapers, periodicals and free materials

Clark, Delbert. *Current Affairs and Modern Education.* New York: The New York Times, Inc., 1950. Use of newspapers by teachers is described in detail.

Junior Town Meeting League. *Using Current Materials.* Columbus: The League, 1950. A free pamphlet with good suggestions about classroom techniques.

Kinney, L. B., and Katharine Dresden. *Better Learning through Current Materials.* Stanford: Stanford University Press, 1949. This volume recounts exactly how teachers have used newspapers and periodicals in many subject fields.

Patterson, Franklin K. "Free Teaching Aids in California Schools," *Calif. Journal of Educational Research,* 1:165-168, 210-214 (September, November, 1950). Current practice in schools regarding selection of free materials pointing out some of the dangers as well as possibilities of these materials.

Sinclair, Thomas. *A Report about Business-Sponsored Teaching Aids.* Dansville (N.Y.): F. A. Owen Publishing Co., 1949. This is a research report investigating purposes, content, and methods of evaluation of free materials.

Weeks, Ruth M. *Using Periodicals.* Chicago: National Council of Teachers of English, 1951. Many stimulating ideas about using periodicals which have application in a wide range of subject fields.

Textbooks

Clement, J. A. *Educational Significance of Analysis, Appraisal and Use of Textbooks in Junior and Senior High Schools.* Champaign (Ill.): Daniels Photopress, 1939. A careful study of the textbook in American education.

Cartwright, William H. *How to Use a Textbook.* No. 2, "How to Do It Series." Washington, D. C.: National Council for the Social Studies, 1947. A brief but valuable pamphlet showing how the teacher may best use the textbook in a good teaching program.

Lampkin, Richard H. *Variability in Recognizing Scientific Inquiry: An Analysis of High School Science Textbooks.* Teachers College Contributions to Education No. 955. New York: Teachers College, Columbia University, 1949. A careful study of one of the major emphases sought in science classes to determine to what extent textbooks actually aid the development of scientific inquiry.

Pierce, Bessie L. *Civic Attitudes in American School Textbooks.* New York: Charles Scribner's Sons, 1930. A classic study of the selectivity of material to be found in textbooks. Comparing findings of those books to today's is very interesting.

Stewart, Maxwell S. "Prejudice in Textbooks," *Public Affairs Pamphlet* No. 160. New York: Public Affairs Committee, 1950. An excellent brief summary of the larger study made by a committee of the American Council on Education of the extent to which certain groups in America are given a differential treatment in school text material.

Thompson, Craig. "How Are Your Child's Textbooks Selected?" *Collier's,* Nov. 18, 1950. An interesting report of the textbook industry and its relations to the public schools.

6. Learning Activities: Community Resources

THE basic medium for learning is direct experience. From the day of birth, our fundamental concepts issue out of the stuff of day-to-day living, while in the classroom teachers have long been accustomed to stay away from direct experience. Of course, it is not feasible to conduct all learning out of direct experience, even though the primary meanings come from there. But, on the other hand, it is not efficient to operate most of the time on a plane of abstractions far removed from everyday living.

The best teaching ranges up and down through many levels of experience from direct to abstract and back again. It is possible not only with learning *materials,* as was discussed in the last chapter, but with learning *activities.* In the following chapters, the teacher will see how the full range of learning activities from sociodrama to group work may be employed. It is only natural that the first chapter on learning *activities* should begin with the very best source of direct real-life experience: the community. Here is where the young people have been raised, learned their modes of behavior, and where many of them will find their future. It is important that the lessons of the school contribute to ongoing community life.

We have noted earlier that the high school loses many students who might benefit from continued schooling. Why do they leave? Because school offers them fewer worth-while experiences than does the world of work. Were the school to derive its major curricular problems from the immediate community, more of our students would find the school meaningful and important for a longer period of time.[1]

Community Resources and Course Objectives

The first step in utilizing community resources is for the teacher to look over the basic course objectives. With these in mind, he can plan with his students the major problems to be explored. After teacher and students have clearly in mind the major topics, their question is: What community resource can we find that will make this content relevant to our daily life?

For instance, if the course of study includes a consideration of governmental structure, local, state, or national, the teacher has at hand in any community representation of government in action on all of these levels. With his students, he may make an inventory of all the units of government represented in this town or city neighborhood. The class might plan visits by teams from the class to the courts, the fire and police stations, the offices of welfare bureaus, the various federal agencies with branches in that area. Such a study might lead also into an examination of the extra-governmental agencies that perform services for the community, such as the private charities, the boys and girls group-work agencies, the service clubs for adults, and so on. These excursions into the structure of the community would be both enlightening and informative, far more useful in the long run than learning the diagrams from a reference book.

An art course might include various handicrafts for student exploration. It would be of great value, in terms of developing worth-while out-of-school avocational interests, for the young people to find out such things as (a) the sources of handicraft supplies in this area; (b) what artisans are working in this or surrounding communities in these crafts; (c) what organizations are there for weavers, silversmiths, ceramicists, artists in general, and what does one obtain through membership in such an organization; and (d) where are exhibits of similar handicraft products held and are they near enough for a visit. These questions may have as much

[1] Gaumnitz, Walter H., and Grace S. Wright, "Broadening the Services of Small High Schools," *Bulletin 1948,* No. 9, Federal Security Agency (Washington, D.C.: Office of Education, 1948).

long-term value for the individual as the development of the art skill itself. And, furthermore, while obtaining answers to such questions, the students are learning about their own community and the means of obtaining information in any community.

These examples could be multiplied a hundredfold. Each subject area is rich in possibilities for utilizing the community. The references at the end of the chapter describe only a few such experiences; each teacher, by keeping informed on the literature in his own field, will find many descriptions each year of teachers who have successfully drawn upon the community for stimulating learning resources.

Building a Community Resource File

The beginning teacher may well have to depend on his own initiative and that of his students to build a file of sources in the community, since it is highly probable that few other members of a typical high school faculty will be making full use of the community. The first prerequisite is an open mind and an alert eye. The swamp that lies along the highway may be a fine place for finding polluted water, or for various decorative grasses, or for interviewing families who live in the no-man's-land of barges and river boats. The second step is to organize a file of these resources. The file should be accessible, easy to use, abundantly cross-filed. A source useful for one kind of activity may be also very useful in another context for another class. The teacher will wish to organize his own file cards. Some suggested headings follow:

1. Unit of study
2. Name of resource   Address
3. Place: travel directions as needed
4. Person to contact   Telephone
5. Suggested use in class
6. Limits on use
7. Evaluation: when and how used: results: recommendations for use next time[2]

The file entry should include both good and poor resources for a particular topic or theme. This saves considerable wear and tear on the memory. It is often difficult to remember just what did happen when so-and-so came to class, or whether the students gained much from a visit to the X plant. A good resource file refreshes the memory at a glance.

[2] A good file card form is reproduced in *Fifty Teachers to a Classroom,* Committee on Human Resources, Metropolitan School Study Council, (New York: The Macmillan Company, 1950), p. 43.

Excursions and Field Trips

Much has been written about the value of the field trip. Yet many students go through high school with no field trip experience. Why is this? The most significant factor is the way in which the high-school day is organized. When the student has only one 50-minute period with a teacher, obviously it is going to cause a major disruption if a teacher wishes to undertake a field trip lasting for more than a single class period. However it is also clear that few worthwhile field trips can be conducted within such a short space of time. Moreover, the teacher himself must face another class each hour and in good conscience cannot often shove his responsibility off on any other faculty member or even assign them to the library. The actual physical barriers to the use of the field trip in the high school are the major obstacles to its use. Can these barriers be overcome? The co-operation of other faculty members is essential. If a field trip means encroaching on the class time of another teacher, then clearly no teacher is justified in asking for such a dispensation very often. If, however, a good reciprocal relationship can be established ("If you let my students out for a biology field trip, then I will gladly excuse your students to practice the senior play"), the field trip can be more generally used.

Planning the Field Trip

The actual planning of a field trip is time-consuming, and for this reason too a teacher can rarely take many a semester. For example, if the teacher has five classes, he is confronted with all the mass of detail for five different field trips. The very thought of this kind of planning is enough to discourage most teachers. The planning problems may, however, be solved in a number of different ways. First, the preplanning may be done almost wholly by students. With functioning student committees, the teacher may find that most of the work can be done for him. A simple outline, planned by teacher and students, will suffice for a framework:

1. What is the purpose of the field trip?
2. Where can we go?
3. What places will allow our class to visit?
4. How do we get there?
5. What transportation is needed? Where can we get it? How much will it cost?
6. How long will it take?
7. Whose permission must we have? Has this been obtained? How? (principal, parents, other)

8. Can students be excused from other classes?
9. What are we to look for?
10. How will the trip be reported?
11. What study should we do before we make the trip to make it more meaningful?

This list will set a framework around which to assign specific individual or committee responsibility. With a few days of exploration, the committees may report back to the class. After some consultation with the teacher, the trip is practically arranged. If the teacher has previously collected a few suggested community resources for possible field trips, the students are able to plan with a minimum of fumbling around. Much of the student planning can be done after school, or a few students can be dismissed for one hour. In arranging the field trip for the whole group the students save time for the teacher and are given practice in assuming genuine responsibility.

> They used to let us out of class to do our community study (one student who participated in the Eight-Year Study reported), and I thought this would be a good chance to get away with something. But you know, it was surprising how interested we got in our projects. The teacher must have seen to it that the groups investigating different aspects of the New Deal became somewhat competitive, because we all worked like dogs, even if we weren't in class, trying to collect our data from the community sources we had ourselves unearthed.

To obtain time beyond the class hour, field study may be made a substitute for textbook homework. Groups of students living in the same general vicinity may be asked to interview some local residents; teams may be assigned the job of visiting downtown stores to check price differences; or others may go to city offices to talk with officials or to watch courts in action. The community-centered assignment takes the place of more passive kinds of learning. And what about those who do work after school? Their assignments may be geared to the weekend, rather than to the work week, or they may be excused from this kind of study. The idea that all students have to do the same thing all the time is a strait jacket that modern education refuses to wear. Cooperative planning with students will make clear what responsibilities each may best undertake. (See the section on the assignment in Chapter 4.)

Cost is an important problem to consider in planning field trips. The average student in high school has very little extra money. It is wise for the teacher to think ahead about such problems so as not to exclude from a valuable trip a student who may be unable to pay his way. Some teachers place a collection box in the front of the room so that anyone can make his contribution without others knowing if it is less than what was asked for. The teacher should be prepared to make up a deficit which probably will be slight in any event. Even this can be eliminated by telling the class as a whole that a dollar or so more is needed and then the field trip money will be all in. In this way students lacking the financial wherewithal can still participate, and those who need such learning most are thus enabled to benefit by it.

Each school will have its own regulations regarding field trips; whether or not school buses may be used, how long students may be away from school, what costs may be covered by student contributions. The new teacher should be certain to study basic school policies before planning field trips. Sometimes the regulations on transportation and costs discourage teachers. But there is a further resource: the parents. Parents are usually more than happy to help out. Parents can often provide needed transportation. The more parents are called on to help schools with their problems, the more understanding they are. This tactic can be an important source of community good will. Here again the arrangements for parent assistance should be planned with students after consultation with the school principal.

The wise teacher tries out any contemplated field trip before any suggestion is made to the students. He will then have seen at first hand the administrative and other problems that are likely to arise. If students overlook some vital point in their planning through sheer lack of experience, he will be able to suggest further checking. He will also have thought of what alternatives he must have, if, for any reason, the field trip can not be taken.

The field trip is a significant means for improving public relations. The teacher will therefore want to be sure that the students observe the amenities when requesting permission to make a visit. A proper phone call, polite note, or personal visit should be carefully planned in advance. A preview of the proper address in telephoning might very well be a class exercise. It is amazing how few adolescents know the adult forms of requesting a favor. A letter asking for permission to visit might be submitted to the whole class for approval and will provide a real-life demonstration of correct letter-writing form that will not soon be forgotten. If the field study involves interviewing, a practice interview might be tried and procedures criticized by the group. The thank-you message is equally important. Both students and teachers are prone to overlook this. Yet on just such small courtesies—or lack of them—the community may judge the school. Some teachers find it helpful to have a check list on permanent display in front of the room when field studies are in progress. As each essential activity is accomplished, it is checked off. Thus no important items are overlooked. Such a check list might include:

Item	*Person responsible*	*Date to be accomplished*
1. Transportation arranged		
2. Request letter written		
3. Preliminary visit		
4. Principal's permission obtained		
. . . . .		
8. Thank you letter written		
9. Resource file card filled in		

Field trips are enjoyed by most students. They lend color and life to the content of instruction. They show that what is learned in the classroom is closely related to everyday activities. With some thought and with faith in the ability of students to take mature responsibility for their own affairs, every teacher can use field trips in his field of instruction.

Resource Visitors

The use of resource visitors in the high-school classroom is probably more common than almost any other method of using the community. Some community workers make numerous trips to schools as a regular part of their work. Police chiefs, probation officers, traffic court judges, fire chiefs, health officers, directors of recreation, all recognize the importance of informing future citizens about the kind of community service they perform. There is a certain glamour about seeing and hearing the police chief in person; he is both more formidable, and also more human, than the students anticipate. The law becomes more than just "Thou shalt not . . ." In the same way many of the lessons of science, mathematics, foreign language, history, and English are enlivened through the resource visitors. Often they can say to the class things the teacher cannot say, are believed when the teacher may be doubted, are able to inspire young people when the familiar school-ma'am goes unheeded. In addition, the resource visitor often has special knowledge, as of a foreign country, or a special expertness, as in building roads or directing criminal investigations or administering relief programs, that the average teacher cannot hope to have. And thus the vision and knowledge of the students are enlarged. Knowledge that such people live in his area also inspires the young person to take more interest and pride in his own community, gives him goals to strive for as a maturing adult, shows him in flesh and blood the complexity and fascination of this modern world.

However, for all that the resource visitor brings, he is often an utter failure. Remembering these harrowing hours, teachers sometimes become cynical about using resource visitors at all. Yet the fault as often as not lies with the teacher and his students. Few visitors are in touch with adolescents; they do not know much about them, their interests, ideas, or levels of understanding. We invite into our classrooms those people who are successful in their own life sphere, but this very success may take them out of touch with high-school students. Many experts cannot share their expertness without using language which may be so much mumbo-jumbo. Sometimes the teacher may have to interview such persons himself and transmit the special knowledge to the students. Prior to inviting an expert, teachers and students should make his acquaintance; if this is not feasible, at least his "student appeal" should be checked with other members of the faculty and with students.

In evaluating a future visitor teachers and students might consider some of these suggested queries:

1. *Is he interested in adolescents or does he have a negative attitude about young people?* If he feels that high school students are not very admirable people, his attitude will show when talking with them. Whatever message he may have will not get across, but his attitude will.

2. *Does he ordinarily speak in an overly academic fashion?* A person who speaks formally in a complicated and abstruse way will never be able to drop this manner before a classroom and should not be invited.

3. *Does he ramble and constantly get off the subject?* A raconteur may be all right for a social event, but if certain content is to be covered, this kind of individual is hopeless. He cannot be counted on to stick to his subject and the hour may be lost in a maze of irrelevant comments.

4. *Is he a jokester?* While this may keep the class amused for an hour, it will not enlarge the students' knowledge. We do not have to be deadly serious at all times, but if the content is serious, we don't want someone who is merely amusing.

5. *Does he express strong prejudices?* It is fine for a person to be sold on his hobby or his job. But sometimes visitors use an audience situation to express pet hates. If these are directed against any group represented in the class, it can be very unfortunate. Moreover, we do not want the class used for propaganda purposes unless both sides can be heard.

6. *Will student questions rattle him or offend him?* It takes a great deal

of poise sometimes to answer the innocent questions of youth. We do not want to expose a community member indiscriminately to such questions unless we know he can stand up to them with poise and humor. If he gets incensed because young people ask "such dumb questions," then he probably will not make a good visitor.

With these and other questions in mind, teachers and students can interview a prospective resource visitor and be fairly sure of the degree of success he would have with the class.

Many of the speaking faults that would lose a teacher a job are permissible in a visitor. After all, the students only have to listen to him for a few minutes and if his voice is nasal, if he has odd mannerisms, if he breaks the rules of good public speaking, we can easily overlook such things if, in the main, what he has to give the class is important.

Insuring Success with Resource Visitors

But whatever his speaking abilities, the resource visitor will need guidance if he is to meet the expectations of the group. There are several devices which may be used:

1. *Brief the visitor ahead of time.* A list of student questions can be made up by a student committee and presented to the visitor. Probably the questions should be presented personally, since the visitor at that time can go over the questions with the students and make sure he understands what it is the students are interested in.
2. *Prepare the introduction.* When the student or teacher introduces the visitor to the class, he should make it clear that the visitor will speak for 10 minutes, or whatever the time allotment agreed upon (the shorter the better), and then will answer questions. Stating the time period to the visitor with the class as audience is a kind of gentle blackmail. It takes a rugged individualist to overlook this kind of time limit. Often a visitor is more aware of a student chairman than of another adult and more likely to comply with his requests.
3. *Request permission to interrupt.* Either the teacher or the student chairman can ask the visitor, with the class as audience, if it is all right if he or a member of the class interrupts if something doesn't seem clear. The visitor can do nothing but answer yes. This provides a needed tool if the speaker gets off the track, gets boring, or gets too academic.
4. *List questions on the board.* The questions that have previously been given the speaker may be written on the board and the speaker placed so that he and the class can see the list. This keeps the speaker from spending all his time on one question, since it is clear to everyone that there are five more to go.
5. *Use a group interview.* A group of students may be specially prepared in the field that the visitor is to discuss. The students have read about it and are ready with intelligent and significant questions. Then the visitor

and the interviewing group are placed in the front of the room and encouraged to proceed as though no audience were present. This prevents the visitor from making speeches and ensures that student questions will be answered.

6. *Prepare the class.* In discussing the area on which the visitor is to speak to the class, the teacher or student committee may make a point of raising important issues. The class may then be divided into groups. Each group will write out questions and assign responsibility to students for asking the questions. This ensures that student questions will get asked and that the visitor will not forget his real mission.

Several of these devices may be used together in order to present the visitor to the best advantage. There are very few adults who can keep an audience of adolescents enthralled for a full hour by just lecturing. More often the students become bored and restless. The reason is not impoliteness but that the visitor is too remote from the life of the adolescent. An attentive and educated audience is something the community likes to know about, and the reputation of a class can be enhanced by doing some planning such as that outlined above. Then both class and visitor have an enjoyable and educational interchange.

Expression of appreciation to the visitor is very important. A student-written letter of thanks can be easily arranged by a committee. The teacher would also be wise to send a personal letter of his own. When the visitor finishes his class appearance, the teacher should assign a student to escort him out of the building. It is surprising how many adults feel lost in the modern high school, having rarely entered one after their own graduation. As a good host always accompanies his guest to the door, so a teacher, who cannot leave his classroom, can make the same gesture by having a student host or hostess guide the visitor out.

Should the visitor be evaluated by the class? If he is good, this is a fine idea, but what if he was not good? He may be related to any number of students in the class, who will promptly run home and tell their parents, "You know, Uncle Joe came to class and we all voted he was just awful." It is probably better to review with the class the important things learned from the visitor, even though he may have fallen short of expectations. We cannot expect young people to respect adults unless we express that respect ourselves. On the other hand, we must not lose sight of the adolescent's quick penetration of the shoddy or the pretentious. To protect future groups, the teacher will want to enter in his resource file a note about the effectiveness of any visitor. If the file is open to students for use, however, this note should be diplomatic. Uncomplimentary remarks must not find their way into community gossip channels to the detriment of good school-community relations.

Parents and Recent Graduates As Resource Visitors

The preceding discussion of resource visitors assumed a rather limited type of contribution to the class—someone who can present purely verbal information. It may be useful therefore to take a broader definition of resource personnel. For example, a class might want to try some gardening experiments in order to test soil fertility. A parent who knew gardening might work well with such a group of students on this technical problem. The more parents who can be brought into the classroom, the more support they will provide for the school program.

> A ninth-grade orientation class was finishing a unit on personal problems, one of which had been "getting along with parents." As a final activity, three parents were invited to the class, two of them housewives and one a minister. Each met with a subgroup of the class to talk together about the problems of youth in the home, which the class had previously discussed. The young people were happy to have "real parents" to talk over the problems with and get the point of view, while the parents were delighted with the intelligent give-and-take that occurred.

If experts are needed, it is more valuable to use an expert who is the parent of a student in the class or in the school than a community stranger. For one thing the bond between adolescent and parent will be strengthened as the adolescent sees his parent in a new light. When the adolescent sees other adolescents according respect to his parent, he is more apt to do likewise. The idea of the parent "room committee" is often used in the elementary grades; it would be a very useful adjunct to the high-school classroom also. Such a committee of parents could help get needed supplies, canvass for magazines, participate in a paint-up day or clean-up day, sponsor end of semester parties, help in transportation when a field trip is planned.

> The home economics program at the Community High School, Frost, Texas, utilized over 40 local people during 1945-1946. A few of the activities demonstrated by the local women are upholstering chairs, refinishing old furniture, framing pictures and cutting glass, hairdressing and other beauty parlor operations, and caring for physical fitness needs of girls and women.[3]

[3] Gaumnitz and Wright, *op. cit.*, p. 5.

When the teacher makes up his file of community resources he may also include a file card that covers the parents of his students. Such a card might include:[4]

NAME	
PARENTS' OCCUPATIONS: *Mother*	*Father*
SPECIAL INTERESTS OR HOBBIES:	
Mother	*Father*
TRAVEL EXPERIENCES:	
Mother	*Father*

Another kind of resource visitor is the recent graduate. The experiences and reactions of those who are near the students' own age are often more meaningful and significant than any read in a book. When a class is studying vocations, assessing the value of a high-school education or trying to determine what is the best course of study to take, a panel of recent graduates can be very helpful. Similarly, such graduates can tell students about some of their job-hunting experiences, what they have learned by actual experience in the big world, the problems of home financing and budgeting, the adjustment to college life.

The resource visitor is a relatively easy method of enriching the content of instruction. The time element is not as much of a barrier as it is for the field trip. With some thought, the teacher can ensure a successful experience.

Community Study and Survey Techniques

Both field trips and resource personnel may serve as the means to introduce extensive studies of the community. Here are a few ex-

[4] See also Sutherland, Miriam, "A School Survey of Personal Resources," *Educational Method,* 28:275-278 (March, 1939).

Another helpful reference on using parents' participation in classroom activities is: *Fifty Teachers to a Classroom.* Committee on Human Resources, Metropolitan Study Council (New York: The Macmillan Company, 1950). It includes excellent parent-resource questionnaires and file-card forms as well as specific ways to utilize parents' interests, skills, professions.

amples of community projects that will show the variety and success that are possible.

1. Floodwood Community School, Floodwood, Minnesota. During the school year 1939-1940, the general science classes made a survey of wells in the community. More than half of the wells of the community were found to be contaminated. The completed report was turned over to the village authorities and helped in the campaign to obtain community water and sewage system.[5]

2. Part of the orientation course for the ninth-grade students included learning about the community. The students asked such questions as: What are our major industries? What churches are there? What form of local government do we have? What are the services provided by our community? What are our recreational resources?

3. Seniors studying vocations conducted a survey of the community to find out what employers wanted in the young people they hired.

4. A high-school sociology class decided to study the standard of living of their own community. A questionnaire was developed by the class around the major areas of living and distributed to the students in the high school. The results were analyzed and studied by the class as a whole with genuine interest developed on the part of the students.[6]

5. A public opinion poll was conducted by two ninth-grade classes in order to see how the local community felt about national issues of importance.[7]

The community survey, like the resource visitor, is a means to a variety of exciting experiences. The face-to-face encounter with public opinion gives the young student more real feeling about current issues and what they mean in everyday living than any class discussion can possibly arouse. As an illustration, checking neighborhoods for unsanitary backyards will leave a lasting impression upon future homemakers regarding the importance of home cleanliness. Talking with employers about local employment needs impresses the future worker with his own imminent maturity and the appropriate behaviors he must acquire.

The conducting of a survey requires the total energies of a class for an extended period of time. It is possible that several students may make a small survey of one aspect of community life, but such activity might be more in the nature of field work, or field assignment, and not necessarily a survey in the sense the term is generally understood and used here. However, the problems and techniques

[5] Gaumnitz and Wright, *op. cit.*, p. 12.

[6] Olsen, Edward G., *School and Community Programs* (New York: Prentice-Hall Inc., 1949), p. 250-253.

[7] *Ibid.*, pp. 260-261.

are just as useful for a few students as they would be for the whole class. The advantage of the community survey conducted by the whole class is the opportunity to make use of a variety of talents. Some students can do library research on the background of the problem; others can type up and mimeograph the questionnaires; others may do the interviewing. The mathematicians in the class can tabulate the data and analyze it statistically; the artists can present graphic charts to show the data; the photographers can take pictures of typical findings. Such a variety of activities means considerable class planning with the teacher so that time is used efficiently and productively. A time plan for a full-scale community study worked out by the teacher and the class might look like this:

1st Week:

1. Initiation of survey: student presents visitor, motion picture, or other current provocative material. There is preliminary discussion of the problem and its subproblems.

2. Class study in selected references or text material.

3. Reconsideration of problem areas. First designation of committees:
   a. Background information: three or four subproblem groups.
   b. Questionnaire: one group.
   c. Sources of information in community: one group.

4. Study by groups as designated above.

5. Reports from groups and plans for further study.

2nd Week:

6. Questionnaire group pretests questionnaire. Rest of class continues study.

7. Out-of-class teams assigned. Survey deadline set: all interviews to be completed by following Friday. Interview practice for those who are to use the questionnaire.

8. Continue interview practice.

9. Reports from first interviews. Class evaluates progress.

10. Study continues in broader aspects of problem in text or related references.

3rd Week:

11. Class discussion to formulate major ideas of problem area.

12. Quiz: review of material known by class in area.

13. Reports on progress: questionnaire tabulation begun; groups given assignment for tabulation.

14. Maps constructed; preliminary charts and graphs begun; background material written up by groups responsible.

15. Class evaluates work to date; reports of groups as above. Group assigned to invite community leaders in for final report.

4th Week:

16. Final tabulations: charts and graphs completed.

17. Introduction and background sections written. Class reviews.

18. Class considers data assembled. What are the conclusions?

19. Conclusions agreed upon. What action is recommended?

20. Community leaders invited in to hear summary and report.

5TH WEEK:

21. Evaluation of total experience. What would we do differently next time?

22. New unit begun.

A time plan like this will, of course, have to be flexible. Often more time is needed for study. In a science class, laboratory periods may continue in class while out-of-class work is mainly concerned with the community survey. An English class may set aside certain class days for routine drill periods on skills needed in the conduct of the survey. In a foreign-language class the survey may become a long-range out-of-class project with sufficient time devoted in class to keep the group informed and interested. The time plan suggested above involves complete concentration of class time on the survey until completed. Probably it would be wisest for a beginning teacher to use this plan, since it is usually too difficult at first to keep track of several different activities at once.

If one group in the class completes its portion of the project ahead of the others, several alternative procedures are suggested. First, let the students work with the other groups who are not yet through. Second, assign them responsibility for one of the final phases of the project, such as inviting in community leaders to hear the report. Third, allow the students to use class time freely on whatever they wish. Or, fourth, let them do preliminary study on the next unit of work. The teacher needs to have a plan for such students, as there will always be a few who will finish anything ahead of time!

Selecting Problems for Community Study

How can the teacher select a problem for community study? There are excellent suggestions to be found in Edward Olsen, *School and Community,*[8] and in Harl Douglass, *Education for Life Adjustment.*[9] The problem area selected should conform to the demands of student interest, practicability, and community mores. It would be unwise to consider a survey problem to which the students were indifferent, one that required reference material that could not be readily obtained, or one that offended major portions of the community. In addition, the view of the administrator of the school should be sought. The teacher may find that the administrator himself does not understand the values of community study and would

[8] New York: Prentice-Hall Inc., 1946, Chap. 9.

[9] New York: Ronald Press Company, 1950, Chap. 20.

need to be informed and convinced. And in districts where the school and community have had disagreements, it would be wise not to attempt community study until more cordial relations have been established.

The beginning teacher is well advised to try community study with only one class at a time, particularly in the first few years of teaching in a new community. The teacher should select the class with whom he has the best rapport, the class that seems most responsible and responsive. This does not mean that he should use his "best" class or his "slowest" class. Sometimes we hear arguments that only the most intelligent profit from community study, or, just the opposite, that only the slow student need have concrete experiences of this kind. Both arguments are fallacious. Community study is valuable in meeting all kinds of individual differences. For this reason the teacher will want to choose a class, not on the basis of fastest or slowest learning, but on the basis of work habits, and teacher-student relationship. While teachers find community study very rewarding, it would be an impossible task to have five classes all studying the community at once.

In preparing for the survey, the teacher will find two techniques are central to the success of community study. These are—

1. Interviewing.
2. Making and using questionnaires.

The Interview in Community Study

Much of the success of a community study will depend on the way in which students are able to conduct themselves in interviews. While some community surveys involve merely observation of community facilities and no contact with adults, most surveys do involve talking with community members. The average adolescent is not very skillful in this particular area, nor is the typical adult! The teacher can use interview training to develop many more insights than the mere gathering of information. As soon as the students have agreed that it will be necessary to do some interviewing, the teacher can set up some short and illuminating role-playing episodes. (See Chapter 7 for directions on role-playing.) One student, for instance, who may have lived in a remote part of the country, can be the person being interviewed. The object of the interview is to obtain his views of this locality. Three class members can be the interviewers, being called on one at a time to obtain the needed information. The teacher can designate someone to act as the "secretary" for the interviewee in order to have a means for cutting short interviews that might go on too long. It is almost certain that the three different interviewers will obtain three different sets of information, three different versions, particularly if the student being interviewed is instructed not to give any information unless asked. Out of such a role-playing situation the teacher can then move into a class discussion around the following points:

1. *What information is desired from the interview?* It is valuable to have a list of two or three lead questions so that each interviewer obtains similar material. This will focus the task of the students. A group may be given the job of listing the kinds of questions to be asked in the interviews.

2. *What should be worn to the interview?* The careless dress of the adolescent is often the despair of the teacher. Actually, the high-school boy (less usually the girl) sees no particular reason for dressing in a very neat fashion. Yet in many of the areas where young people seek work, appearance will be vital. Thus, in discussing what should be worn in interviewing for a community survey, other attitudes can be built.

3. *How will rapport be established in the interview?* The key steps will need to be stressed: state who you are, what you are there for, what information you would like, what you intend to do with the information.

4. *Should notes be taken during the interview?* An analysis of the person being interviewed and the purpose of the interview are relevant in order to answer this question. The need for accuracy in quoting community members is vital. Most high-school students will need careful coaching in the need for accuracy and objectivity in reporting the results of interviews.

5. *How should the interviewer behave during the interview?* The interviewer should never argue with the person being interviewed. An attitude of interest should be demonstrated by leaning forward in the chair, listening, not interrupting, nodding to encourage the speaker to continue.

6. *When should the interview be terminated?* The interviewer should be aware of the cues of the interviewee indicating that he would like to close the interview. Observe a moderate time period for the interview—a ten-minute interview should not last longer than that. Be sure to be appreciative of assistance of the person interviewed, even when the information is not all that was desired. A graceful exit and a warm "thank you" are very important aspects of a good interview.

7. *What should be done about disagreeable situations?* Students need to be given protection against possible unpleasant occurrences in interview studies: people who slam the door in the face of the student, individuals who use the occasion to attack the schools, persons who get angry or annoyed at the questions. By role playing a few such disagreeable incidents the students will learn objectivity and some methods of dealing with this kind of individual.

8. *How can interview experiences be exchanged?* After a few class members have made some interviews, reports to the class on how they went are very valuable. Other students gain security and learn techniques.

9. *Should the interview be conducted by one or by two students?* It is usually desirable to have students interview in teams of two. The students support each other, particularly if they are nervous or uneasy. One student

can remember something the other may forget; thus, each can check the other's impressions.

Some teachers use actual interviews before the class to demonstrate techniques.

> In helping a group of new students in a ninth-grade orientation class the teacher planned with the students to interview several teachers and student leaders. A list was made of those to be interviewed, and two students assigned to contact the individual and arrange for class time. Then, when the individual came to the class the two team members conducted an "interview" with the class as observers. After the planned interview was over, the rest of the class joined in, asking questions not covered by the team. After each such experience a brief evaluation of the technique of each team was conducted. By the end of a few weeks the students were becoming very skillful in interviewing.

A significant value of the interview experience is the carry-over into the vocational interview. Where students have had extensive community-study experience, they have learned how to conduct themselves with poise and assurance in the crucial job-application interview that face them later. Here experience in interviewing may compensate for some lack of job experience.[10]

Using Questionnaires in Community Study

A good questionnaire requires considerable thought and planning. For the kind of community study that a high-school class ordinarily conducts, the questionnaire will hardly be the elaborate, scientifically tested instrument of the trained social scientist. Nevertheless, the teacher will want to make sure that the students obtain fairly valid and fairly reliable data, otherwise, the whole experience may produce either unwarranted faith or complete cynicism about questionnaire studies. We live in a world of statistics, yet the average citizen knows little about how they are derived or how applicable they may be. The high school as its contribution to intelligent living in a modern world needs to equip young people with understanding of data-gathering techniques. The making of a questionnaire should be a group undertaking, based on as careful study as possible.

In developing a questionnaire the teacher and the class will want to have clearly in mind the purpose of the questionnaire. Then every question can be clearly related to a purpose of the survey:

[10] See also National Council for the Social Studies Ninth Yearbook, *Utilization of Community Resources in the Social Studies* (Cambridge, Mass.: The Council, 1938), pp. 8, 77-78, 82.

Purpose	*Questions*
1. To determine reading interests of adults in our town. What do people read and where do they get their reading material?	
a. Newspapers b. Books c. Magazines	a. What newspaper do you read? What part of the paper do you read? What part do you like best. And so on.

It may be found that the purposes that seemed desirable cannot be achieved through a questionnaire. Either the questionnaire will get too bulky and unmanageable or the questionnaire will not reveal the kind of data sought. Having a permanent statement of the purposes of the total survey against which to check each technique used is very valuable in keeping the group focused on the problem at hand. Then the teacher can say, "Do we need to ask that question? What purpose does it relate to?"

Questionnaires should be organized in terms of the usability of the data. Very often questions are asked in a survey that are highly interesting and important, but when the time comes to tabulate the replies, it is almost impossible to find what the concensus was. On the other hand, questions that are too simple and obvious will provide meaningless results.

Since the survey of the community will often revolve around a questionnaire, whether it is used for interview purposes or mailed out to be filled in by individuals in groups, it is important that the teacher help the students understand how a good questionnaire is developed. The pretest is a vital part of this development. It is considered best practice to pretest the questionnaire on a few individuals who resemble the ones that are eventually to constitute the sample group. Thus, if one is interested in the high-school students' attitude toward community recreation facilities, then the pretest might include administering the questionnaire to twenty or thirty high-school students, tabulating the results, and finding out if the answers to the questions are adequate to the purposes of the study.

In the pretest situation, the instructions that will be used should be tried out also: "Please answer the following questions as briefly and quickly as possible . . . etc." Often the instructions themselves are unclear. The pretest group can give its reactions to the instructions. The time needed for the fastest and slowest to fill out the questionnaire should be checked. When using a questionnaire it is important to be able to tell the individuals responding with confidence: "This will take only ten minutes to fill out." After the questionnaire has been completed by the pretest group, the respondents should be asked to give any comments or suggestions about the questionnaire: Were there any ambiguous questions? Were some questions too long? Were some important questions omitted? Was it easy to answer? And so on.

In devising a questionnaire, the following are typical errors to be avoided:

1. *Loaded questions.*

Do you think the community should enforce quarantines of people with communicable diseases?

Obviously everyone will answer "yes"—no one would dream of taking the negative on such a question.

2. *Questions with double negatives.*

Is it not true that most adolescents today are no worse than a generation ago?

A "yes" or "no" answer to this could easily mean the same thing.

3. *Invading taboo areas.*

Questions regarding religion, income, attitudes toward sex instruction, and so on, are very often taboo. Individuals will not give opinions or answers and will be offended at being asked.

4. *Asking for respondents' names.*

It is usually best to keep questionnaire responses anonymous in this kind of community study. Sometimes signed questionnaires are used in social research, but with a high-school group it is probably best to use questionnaire techniques that do not require identifying responses by individuals.

By tabulating the pretest, it often becomes apparent that the tentative form of the questionnaire does not lend itself to ease of tabulation. For instance:

Poor

1. What do you do after school?
2. Do you go to playgrounds?
   Yes —— No ——
3. What playground do you go to?
4. What do you like to do best at the playground?

Good

1. What do you do after school?
   Check the following:
   1. Go home ——
   2. Go to job ——
   3. Play on playground ——
   And so on.
2. What playground do you go to?
   1. Central ——
   2. Emerson ——
   3. High ——
   And so on.
3. What are your favorite activities at the playground?
   1. Baseball ——
   2. Tennis ——
   3. Swimming ——
   And so on.

When questions are aligned on the page so that tabulation may be made from one side only, the possibilities for error are decreased. Tabulation forms that make cross-checks possible are also helpful in eliminating errors.[11]

The use of the questionnaire in the survey provides an extensive opportunity to cooperate with other members of the school faculty. The mathematics instructor can be called on to help in the statistical analysis. As a matter of fact, many mathematics courses might be greatly enhanced if community surveys were part of the instruction. The art instructor can be called upon to help set up colorful charts and graphs, to give instruction in lettering techniques, to act as consultant for bulletin board displays, to illustrate the findings of the survey. The science instructor or photography specialist on the staff can help the students in taking pictures, enlarging, mounting. The shop instructor can help in making models of various aspects of the community observed: making relief maps, building exhibits. Of course, beginning teachers must work slowly and carefully to get this kind of cooperation. Fellow teachers can not be drafted; they must volunteer.

Some Warnings about Surveys

The survey is an excellent educational resource, but the teacher should be aware of some of the pitfalls. For one thing, the students may report data inaccurately. If such data are circulated in the community, someone will protest. Students may not know what is important and what is not and very often will include much that an adult would discard. Students may also fail to distinguish between fact and fancy. Often the chief value of a survey is to show the students how careful one must be in judging from inadequate or superficial evidence. The teacher will need to watch carefully what aspects of a survey are reported back to the community. Sometimes it will be wise not to publicize the findings of a study since the community leaders will misjudge the student effort. On the other hand, in the effort to be wholly accurate, the teacher may put too many rigid limits on the survey and its genuine educational value will be lost. The students will then be engaged only in a mechanical kind of activity that they will not understand. The margin for error is large where students have a great role to play in the planning. But it is just this margin for error that makes for

[11] Further practical suggestions about constructing and using questionnaires are to be found in L. V. Koos, *The Questionnaire in Education* (New York: The Macmillan Company, 1928). See additional references in Bibliography at end of chapter.

the richest kind of learning. The teacher could probably set up a very adequate survey, but, if he does it for the students, they will be cheated out of a very important learning.

Publicity for survey findings should be carefully considered. The students will often get very enthusiastic about their study, particularly if it is controversial or startling. This attitude is the beginning of citizen responsibility and is something to be fostered and prized. But a whole school program can be endangered by one bad mistake in facts, or one distorted quotation. When the report is finished, trusted "friends of the school" could well be brought in to discuss the findings with the class and then, in consultation with the teacher, help to determine whether the report merits further community publicity. If so, the local newspaper is almost invariably cooperative in publishing student findings.

During the course of the interviewing it is also important that the teacher discuss with the class the ethical approach to information received. It is doubtful that students will be given much confidential information, but any kind of survey may uncover some material that, if broadcast, could injure some person or program. Thus, the teacher will find it advantageous to have general class agreement about the ethics of revealing social survey findings without proper clearance.

Service Projects

One element of the community school often discussed in theory but rarely carried out in practice is the obligation to provide service to the community. In preceding sections of this chapter it can be clearly seen that the school is utilizing community resources to further the learning of young people, but it is either incidental or accidental if the community itself benefits from what is done. Developing responsibility in young people means acquiring a sense of obligation to society. The idea of "me first" is unfortunately ingrained through much class instruction. Each student works and is evaluated only as an individual; hence, he is concerned only with what *he* gets out of it. Such an attitude restricts the development of broader community concern and may in part account for the apathy with which so many youth view the events of the world around them. By involving young people in community-service projects during their school careers a community conscience may be created in students. Moreover, through such projects, students learn more about ways in which communities do need the energy and talent of their citizens.

Typical service projects are of two kinds: those that develop out of the curriculum and those that are extracurricular. These may be further subdivided into those that service the school community, and those that service the larger adult community.

The junior and senior girls in a home economics class perform both kinds of community service; they volunteer their services to elementary teachers for a specified period, and they also help out where families in the community need home care. For instance, a teacher may ask them to help decorate a room, designing and making curtains. Or they may help supervise the mid-morning milk period, prepare a tea for new mothers, conduct health surveys among the children. In the community the girls are available to help in the home if the mother has been taken ill, to make dolls for sick children, to provide entertainment for mothers of different classes.[12]

The senior commercial students studying office practice render a useful service to the teachers: whenever a teacher needs a stencil cut and run, typing done, and other clerical services, the students, under their own student Chief Clerk, perform the task. In this way the students not only learn the problems of managing flow of work in an office, but are performing a worth-while task for the school that might otherwise not get done.[13]

An art class was concerned with improving home decoration. In cooperation with the agriculture teacher, they learned some of the basic principles of landscape gardening. The public was invited to a series of home-garden beautification talks presented by the agriculture and art students, after the speech teacher had helped them develop good oral skills. Then the students acted as consultants to families who wanted to follow up the suggestions made in the public discussions. As a result many home gardens were both more productive and more beautiful. Several students developed a new vocational interest. The community was really appreciative of the school service provided.

An English class became interested in the lost art of story telling. One girl reported how cleverly her mother made up stories to tell the younger children at home, so much so that neighbor children dropped in to hear them. The girls in the class became interested in learning how to tell stories and then going to the various playgrounds for a story hour. After considerable community exploration, which was taken by the boys as their responsibility, the cooperation of the recreation department was secured. Some visits from the library story teller were arranged. The class work then became a project in finding good stories to retell and also writing new ones. Even the boys were interested. They had quickly decided that most of the stories were "too sissy." At this the girls challenged them to get better ones. The class divided into story-writing groups. Out of it came a series of very imaginative and

[12] Educational Policies Commission, *Learning the Ways of Democracy* (Washington, D.C.: National Educational Association, 1940), p. 131.

[13] *Ibid.*, p. 130.

original stories for young people. The girls of the class have found the playground work most satisfying and enjoyable.

The teacher of public speaking and the advanced public-speaking students set up a speakers bureau. The community organizations were canvassed to find out what topics of interest student speakers might present. Some organizations did not have very set ideas about speakers. If the students had some good topics, they would be quite happy to consider using the students as speakers from time to time. Other organizations had definite suggestions: some wanted technical speeches; others wanted inspirational or humorous; others liked the idea of debates or panels. The speech classes had enough material to work on for several semesters. Every kind of talent and interest could be tapped.

The mathematics class knew that the community as a whole felt that mathematics was abstract and remote from real life. The teacher had done an excellent job of bringing in many illustrations from actual jobs to show mathematics in use. Students had been encouraged to do independent study on such topics. As a result, many examples were available. Why not put on an exhibit at the library to show how we use mathematics in everyday life? The students responded very happily to this suggestion and a series of very attractive panels were made, with the help of the art and industrial arts teachers.

The Spanish Club suspected that the Mexican-American mothers in the community felt left out of many community affairs because of their inability to speak English adequately. The club decided to hold a series of mothers' teas for this group in their own neighborhood and frankly made the purpose of the teas to help these mothers feel more at ease in English-speaking situations.

Once a school builds a reputation for providing community service, it is relatively easy to find abundant outlets for the energy and talent of the students. Churches, civic organizations, and city officials often have many problems of community welfare that, with the help of volunteers, could be met more effectively. Some surveys of community opinion, for example, could help a city decide whether or not it was feasible to call for an election on a new bond issue for expanded recreation facilities, or whether such an election needed more community discussion. If the school district needs to conduct a school census in order to determine needs for new facilities, properly trained students can do the job adequately. There are innumerable problems that arise, once the teacher is alert to see them. However, are all such service projects worth student time? Care is needed to avoid work on trivial and merely glamorous projects; to steer clear of projects that are identified with special-interest groups; to stay away from projects that are purely exploitive of student time and contribute very little to their experience.

Furthermore, the teacher will want to work closely with his school administrator and, even more important, with community leaders to create an atmosphere of genuine community teamwork. Using community citizens as planning-committee members for all service projects helps to ensure the community acceptance of young people, their efforts, successes, and failures, and also protects the school from adverse criticism of favoritism or undue interference in community affairs.

It is difficult to see that a school may be guilty of an excess of zeal in performing community service at this time, since the error has been so gross in the opposite direction. Community service is so rare and so slight when performed that teachers need constant encouragement and assurance in going boldly into the area of community service. The rewards in terms of enhanced social learning and increased student maturity are considerable.[14]

Summary

The teacher who has discovered the rich resources of a community will find himself and the students continually challenged and stimulated by new experiences. It is as important to the mental health of the teacher as it is for that of the students that learning be satisfying and various. Community utilization can certainly be a source of an unlimited variety of problems, procedures, outcomes, and new ideas. But working with a community requires imagination and sensitivity on the part of the teacher. He needs to guide students wisely as they first begin with community interviews; he must prepare them carefully to receive a resource visitor; he must be ready for any emergency when he embarks on a field trip or excursion. Finding significant community-service projects can become one of the central contributions that a teacher can make to the citizenship education of young people; but again, care in selecting such projects and close cooperation with school officials and community leaders is essential to the continuing success of this kind of program.

The more we can use the community as the real stuff of education the more enduring will be the lessons of education. But mere use of the community is no cure-all for every educational need; it is merely one more significant and valuable resource the modern teacher uses judiciously.

[14] Olsen, *op. cit.*, Chap. 12, "Service Projects," has excellent teaching-methods approach, specific and pointed; also many excellent examples from Olsen's *School and Community Programs,* Section 9, Service Projects.

Selected References

General

Alexander, William M., and I. Galen Saylor. *Secondary Education.* New York: Rinehart & Company, Inc., 1950. Chap. XIX, "School-Community Activities," pp. 478-499. Contains many specific suggestions of areas of community study that contribute to high school education; provides a brief guide for utilizing the community.

Clark, Delbert (ed.). *Current Affairs and Modern Education.* New York: The New York Times, Inc., 1950. Chap. 3, "Community Resources," pp. 42-61. Shows how a variety of materials and activities in a community are utilized by alert teachers; particular emphasis on the role of the local newspaper.

Commission on Secondary School Curriculum. *Science in General Education.* New York: Appleton-Century-Crofts, Inc., 1938. Chap. V, "Meeting the Needs of Adolescents in Social-Civic Relationships," pp. 183-234. Basic generalizations to guide the science teacher in school-community relations.

Department of Supervision and Curriculum Development. *Toward a New Curriculum,* 1944 Yearbook. Washington, D.C.: National Education Association, 1944. Chap. 4, "Educating through Community Service," pp. 41-55; Chap. 10, "Community Organization and Cooperation," pp. 141-168. Many detailed examples of significant school-service projects; also a provocative list of questions as guides to evaluate such participation.

Dewey, John. *The School and Society.* Chicago: University of Chicago Press, 1900. One of the earliest formulations of the theory behind the need to bring the community, as subject matter, into the schools.

Douglass, H. R. (ed.). *The High School Curriculum.* New York: Ronald Press Company, Inc., 1947. Chap. 8, "Community Life as Curriculum," pp. 165-188. A number of typical and recurrent community problems are discussed, showing how these may become the focus of learning activities; presents a general introduction to community understanding.

Douglass, Harl R., and Hubert H. Mills. *Teaching in High School.* New York: The Ronald Press Company, Inc., 1948. Chap. 18, "Utilizing Community Resources in Teaching," pp. 353-379. Gives suggestions for the teacher in planning surveys, excursions, and work experience. Lists some community activities by content fields for high-school subjects.

Educational Policies Commission (NEA). *Learning the Ways of Democracy.* Washington, D.C.: National Education Association, 1940. Chap. V, "School Activities in the Community," pp. 263-330. Short descriptions of many school programs that bridge the gap between school and community, including service projects, parent conferences, camping, and many others.

Enriched Community Living: An Approach through Art and Music in Adult Education. Wilmington: Division of Adult Education, Delaware State Dept. of Education, 1936. A stimulating report of the role art and music can play in the total community.

Committee on Human Resources, Metropolitan School Study Council. *Fifty Teachers to a Classroom.* New York: The Macmillan Company, 1950. 44 pp. An attractive and stimulating pamphlet showing how to find resource persons in a community to enrich classroom teaching.

Kaulfers, Walter, Grayson Kefauver, and Holland Roberts. (eds.). *Foreign Languages and Cultures in American Democracy.* New York: McGraw-Hill Book Company, Inc., 1942. Teachers describe ways to utilize foreign-culture elements in the American scene to promote greater and deeper understanding of language and culture.

Mort, Paul R., and William S. Vincent. *Modern Educational Practice.* New York: McGraw-Hill Book Company, Inc., 1950. Practice 13, "Community Resources," pp. 273-289; Practice 19, "Coordination with the Home," pp. 357-374; Practice 20, "Coordination with the Community," pp. 375-388. Brief paragraphs describing many different ways to use and work with the community for both the regular curriculum and the extracurriculum.

National Council for the Social Studies. *Utilization of Community Resources in the Social Studies.* Ninth Yearbook. Cambridge: The Council, 1938. A basic reference for teachers of the social studies.

Olsen, Edward G. *School and Community Programs.* New York: Prentice-Hall, Inc., 1949. A case-book paralleling the major sections in the author's *School and Community* showing in actual practice how the techniques were implemented.

Olsen, Edward G., *et al. School and Community.* New York: Prentice-Hall, Inc., 1946. A basic guide for the teacher in specific techniques for using the community.

Quillen, I. James, and Lavone A. Hanna. *Education for Social Competence.* Chicago: Scott, Foresman & Company, 1948. Chap. 11, "Using Community Resources in Social Studies Instruction," pp. 284-319. Detailed guide of value to all teachers on conducting excursions and making surveys in the community.

Smith, B. O., W. O. Stanley, and J. H. Shores. *Fundamentals of Curriculum Development.* Yonkers: World Book Company, 1950. Chap. 22, "The Community School and Curriculum Patterns," pp. 533-553. Excellent discussion of the theory underlying curricular emphasis on community-school interaction. Discusses the different ways of viewing the role of the school in the community.

Young, Theodore. "An English Class Explores the Community," *Education,* 63:639-644 (June, 1943). In conversational manner, describes a high-school English class that uses the community as a basis for English classwork.

Community survey guides

American Women's Voluntary Services. *Know Your Community.* New York: AWVS, n.d. A brief list of key questions to assess community resources and problems.

"Community Self-Surveys: An Approach to Social Change," *Journal of Social Issues,* Vol. 5, No. 2 (Spring, 1949), pp. 1-65. Describes the technique of surveys designed to aid a community in resolving its own problems; can be adapted for high-school use.

Goodykoontz, Bess. "Know Your Community," Fed. Sec. Agency, Leaflet No. 57. Washington, D.C.: Office of Education, 1941. 35 pp. Outline of pertinent questions to guide a teacher in community understanding.

Hand, Harold. *What People Think about Their Schools.* Yonkers: World Book Company, 1948. A well-tested community study form to discover public reactions to the schools; includes summary of findings from surveys using this questionnaire form.

Porter, Edna H. *Community Wise.* New York: The Woman's Press, 1947. 64 pp. A workbook for a community survey, as used by the YWCA.

7. Discussion, Sociodrama, and Related Techniques

THE term "activity school" was coined to describe the new kind of school that John Dewey's early followers produced because in these schools the predominant idea was freedom to learn. Some schools, indeed, made activity an end in itself, and modern educators have been living down the sad results of this kind of misinterpretation of Dewey ever since. But the fundamental idea that learning is an *active* process has been substantiated by observation and research in countless classrooms. If the learner sits and lets knowledge flow over him, like water over a rock, nothing is going to happen to him. It is only when a genuine interaction between the learner and the "stuff" of education takes place does any observable change occur. We do not mean, by interaction, merely running around. We mean the activity that occurs when thinking occurs; when facts are sought, weighed, sorted, ranked; when generalizations, conclusions, and solutions are proposed. How then can we ensure such interchange?

In the following chapters we shall present several important classroom techniques designed to bring the learner into a more active role in his own learning. These techniques are problem-solving class discussion, sociodrama, and allied techniques; small group work; classroom games and other review and drill procedures.

This chapter will describe the pattern of class discussion and the utilization of sociodrama. The succeeding two chapters will cover the other topics noted.

Classroom Discussion

There are many times when the teacher wishes to treat the class as a whole group, to develop in each student a desire to discuss common problems. For even the experienced teacher this procedure demands special skill. How can the teacher help all the students feel part of a group inquiry?

First, he must select a problem that is really "common" to students, not just "common" to teachers. Second, he must be convinced that the problem selected can best be attacked by thinking aloud. Thinking aloud together is a kind of learning experience that is uniquely valuable. Ideas often become more meaningful to students when they must chew them over, defend them, modify them, explain them to others. As they struggle to frame concepts in their own words, the implications of the problems presented become personalized; for they have committed themselves publicly before their peers. In such joint thinking individual errors in judgment have to be revised. Each is encouraged to contribute his little bit of knowledge or experience to make up a more accurate picture. Alternatives not known to any one person come to light as others speak out. Students learn to express ideas so that they are understandable and persuasive while still "conversational" in tone and language (a most important skill to the adult in his social world). A tolerance for a wider point of view than that held by students' own provincial groups is acquired.

In terms of learning, the verbal expression made aloud, however haltingly, is usually more lasting than the unvoiced concept. This kind of verbalizing is not memorizing, but actual reworking of ideas and concepts to the point where the student can express the essential in his own fashion. In this manner, a whole group works together so that while each shares in the common solution of the problem, still the concept achieved also belongs to each individual in his own fashion.

What is Discussion?

The teacher's role in the development of good discussion is tremendously important, for it is all too easy to prevent any real thinking. We might start with a consideration of what discussion is *not*. Suppose we listen to this history class:

TEACHER: We have a real problem to discuss today. I wonder how many of you have thought about why we have an electoral college.

GEORGE: Because people in those days hadn't done much voting.

TEACHER: Well, that is not *exactly* right.

JOHN: Because someone suggested the idea and no one could think of a better reason.

TEACHER: No. Can anyone give us the real reason?

SUSAN: Did it have anything to do with transportation?

TEACHER: Now let's not guess. This is a real problem. Can't we discuss it?

MARY: I think it was because the leaders didn't want the people to vote for president.

TEACHER: Now you are getting on the right track; any other good reasons?

The above exchange is really little more than a guessing game. The teacher suggested a problem which in reality is no problem. Real problems for discussion need to have several equally plausible solutions, each of which needs careful examination to find the one most fitting. On the other hand, the history problem to which we listened had one "right" answer. The students were trying to figure out what, in the teacher's mind, this "right" answer was. There was no group thinking; in fact, it was not *group* activity at all.

Before we proceed, we might list some other things discussion is *not:*

1. It is not just talking by people who know little and care less about the subject being discussed.
2. It is not a debate in which different factions try to "win" by fair means or foul, completely disregarding right and wrong.
3. It is not an opportunity for one or two to show off how much they know while everyone else listens in bored silence.

What is a genuine discussion? Let's listen to the same problem in another classroom:

TEACHER: We have a real problem to talk about today. There has been much discussion recently about abolishing the electoral college. What do you think about it?

GEORGE: Well, I think it has outlived it usefulness.

TEACHER: That is a good point, but John, would you agree with George?

JOHN: No—not entirely—uh—after all, the electoral college is part of our traditions, and in these times I think we should keep to our traditions, instead of doing away with them.

SUSAN: Well, but John, if something isn't useful anymore, why should we keep on doing it? After all, you wouldn't keep on riding a horse and buggy if you had a car just because your grandfather did it!

MARY: But the people must have had some good reasons for putting in the electoral college.

GEORGE: Except the only trouble is those reasons never worked. Don't you remember when we were reading about the—what was it?—Convention —Constitutional Convention I think—

TEACHER: Let's see, John, there seem to be two sides here. Will you have a try at saying what they are?

Here the teacher has skillfully encouraged some discussion by deliberately asking for student opinion. The students have done the talking—not the teacher. At this first stage in any discussion, the thinking is muddled, but the teacher is careful to keep in the background so that difference of point of view can be freely expressed. Students can feel that they have a real part to play in seeking good answers, not merely guessing what the teacher thinks to be the "right" answer.

Here is another example of "recitation" as opposed to "discussion."

It was the first period after lunch, and the crisp autumn air and warm sunshine came through the open windows of Miss Abbott's classroom. Feet shuffled and pencils dropped as 33 seventh-grade geography books were opened to page 198. During the next fifteen minutes, some students kept their eyes glued to their books; others tapped on their desks with their pencils and stared moodily around the room or out the window; others whispered to their neighbors.

Miss Abbott looked up from her desk and said, "Close your books. This afternoon we are to discuss foods produced by the Middle Atlantic states, which you read about in today's assignment. What foods are produced in the northern part of this section?" Four hands went up. "Mary Jane?"

"New York state produces an abundance of dairy products, and New York and Pennsylvania raise barley, corn, and buckwheat," recited Mary Jane.

"What else is raised in those states, Ben?" Ben shifted in his chair, frowned, but did not answer. "Barbara?"

"Fruits of all kinds, pears, peaches, apples. Also cabbage, potatoes, maple syrup, and poultry," answered Barbara.

"What foods do we find grown in the states along the coast, Edgar?"

"Ah, ah, well, ah—" began Edgar, but Miss Abbott broke in. "Why, Edgar, don't you even know what is grown in your own state?" Miss Abbott turned to Mary Jane and said sweetly, "Will you tell the class, please, Mary Jane?"

As this pattern of question-answer pseudo-discussion continued, more and more of the questions were directed or referred to Mary Jane, Barbara, and three or four others who responded with memorized answers. The rest of the class shuffled their feet, nudged or whispered to one another, or stared into space.

Twenty minutes later the bell rang. Class members made a grab for books and papers and jostled each other as they pushed out of the room to their next class. Miss Abbott's face relaxed as if she were expressing relief that the period was over.

Another Way

Another seventh-grade social-science class some miles distant was having a very different experience even though the printed course of study furnished to this teacher was the same as the one used by Miss Abbott. Miss Jameson for many years had felt that she could do a better job of teaching if she knew more about the out-of-school activities and experiences of her students.

She listened as the students talked in groups about their experiences over the weekend. Occasionally, she dropped in at some of their homes to chat for a few minutes. More often she walked down the streets or drove past the farms where her students lived, all the time observing and later jotting down descriptions of the woods, the creek, the back alleys, the houses, factories, hatcheries, railroads, wharves, and even the ages and descriptions of the people in each neighborhood. Thus, she gained a clearer understanding of each child's total environment and potential experience—his life space.

Her observations indicated that poultry raising was important in the lives of these children. In their study of the food raised in the Middle Atlantic states, this seventh-grade social-science class decided to study the poultry industry.

The class talked freely for several minutes in relating what they already knew about chickens. Finally, Miss Jameson said, "Let's get some real facts down. I'll write them on the board. Now, where should we begin?"

ANNE: My father works at Mangum's Hatchery. It is the largest hatchery in the world. The eggs are shipped there by trucks. When the eggs reach the hatchery, they are *trayed.*

MISS J: I wonder if everyone knows what *trayed* means. I do not.

VERA: After a certain number of days, the eggs have to be turned.

MISS J: Why is this so?

CAROL: This is so the heat will be distributed evenly to every side.

ANNE: The temperature must remain at 97 degrees in the incubator.

NEIL: Miss Jameson, is that the temperature of a hen?

MISS J: I really don't know, Neil. I wonder how we might find out the answer to Neil's question?

NEIL: I'll ask the ag teacher.

MISS J: Good, Neil, you can report on it tomorrow.

ESTHER: How long do the eggs remain in the incubator?

BOBBY: Three days.

MISS J: I believe it is much longer. Does anyone know?

DAVID: My science book says 21 days. Here are some pictures of the process of development of the chicken.

BOBBY: Well, my mother went to get chickens on Thursday, and the man at the hatchery told her she could get them on Monday.

ANNE: The hatchery has eggs to hatch every Monday and Thursday. That is because they set eggs at all times during the month.

Just then the bell rang. Class members slowly arose from their seats, picked up their books, and continued the discussion in groups of two or three as they left the room.[1]

Arguments Against Discussion as a Way of Learning

The value of this kind of classroom activity seems beyond question to most educators; yet many classrooms have relatively few discussions. Why is this? Here are some of the arguments advanced against using the discussion. First, the discussion takes much more time than the usual recitation. It is true that a teacher can efficiently summarize the arguments for and against a given point of view and then quickly resolve the difficulty. Whether it is best to save time or to take time must be decided with a given problem. Where the exercise of real critical thinking is desired, only taking time for discussion will do. After having really argued through an important problem the students have moved one more step toward ability to do mature thinking. Moreover, as teachers soon observe, the amount of time taken depends upon the experience of the class. Students who are used to discussion can quickly think through new problem situations as they arise. An inexperienced class will falter and flounder all around the problem in the attempt to think clearly as a group.

The second argument against discussions is that the same students always do all the talking. This objection is real with groups not used to discussion, since here the leadership is usually unaware of how to distribute participation. Of course, there are always students with greater oral ability than others. While these students need a chance to continue to develop this ability, it must not be at the expense of others.

Sometimes it is argued that in discussion the teacher cannot tell exactly how much or what the students have learned. It is true that some of the outcomes of discussion appear very intangible. How, for instance, can growth in critical thinking or ability to express ideas convincingly be measured? The discussion often moves so fast, so the argument goes, that the teacher has all he can do to follow the trend of thought, much less remember whether Johnny was better today than he was in the discussion the week before. But actually, these intangibles can be measured. As the teacher becomes skillful in discussion leadership, he needs to give less of his attention to the mere mechanics of leadership and can better distinguish

[1] Perkins, Hugh V., Jr., "Your Pupils' Life Space," *NEA Journal,* 39:447-448 (September, 1950).

among the *kinds* of contribution made by individuals. As he leads the same class in discussion several times a week, he soon recognizes the roles taken by different students. He notes that a dogmatic, irritating, overconfident student is beginning to depend less upon the loudness with which he expresses a point of view and more upon facts and clear thinking to support his statements.

After helping a class learn how to discuss together, the teacher is able to relinquish the leadership to various students and to take a place at the back of the room to observe individuals as they participate. Then actual notes about the contributions made by individuals can be taken, notes that can later guide the teacher in individual or group instruction. Sometimes he uses paper-and-pencil tests of subject matter to find out whether the content of a talk by a resource visitor, a text assignment, or a discussion was remembered best. In this way he can make direct comparisons of the effectiveness of his teaching procedures. Many teachers skilled in developing class discussion have found that content which is the subject of genuine discussion is remembered longer and more accurately than the content developed through other learning experiences.

Teachers sometimes complain that during discussions the class fails to keep to the point. This is the fault as much of the leader as of the group. Inexperienced leaders may assume that one topic is of chief importance when actually the group has defined another problem, or another aspect of the problem, as of major concern. Thus, "getting off the track" may allow the class to talk about those concepts of real concern to its members. In that way a teacher may learn a great deal about the basic interests of his class. As for "not covering the material," there is *never* enough time to teach all we would like to teach! Teachers must pick and choose content, whatever method they use. Furthermore, not all subject matter can be discussed, not all of it should be discussed. But some subject matter *ought* to be discussed!

Selecting Discussion Questions

In planning for a discussion in the classroom, the teacher clearly needs something that is controversial, that is not an open-and-shut case. Here is a series of opening questions proposed by a group of teachers as provocative:

1. Do you suppose Beethoven worried about this aspect of harmony?
2. If Congress refuses to pass legislation asked for by the President, what could be done to persuade Congress?

3. Should insurance be carried by everyone?
4. One third of us will die of heart disease. Can we do anything about it?
5. Why did some fish feel compelled to come out of the water and become amphibian? How did it happen? What caused it?
6. Should there be censorship on the quality of movies produced by Hollywood?
7. Who was the world's first chemist? What do you think he did?
8. What makes up good choral singing?
9. Why do not rats have a gall bladder?
10. What important factors should be considered in choosing a vocation?
11. Why should anyone take algebra?
12. Are women healthier than men?
13. How many of you agree with the statement that a juvenile delinquent is born, not made?
14. Do you think the T formation is better than the single wing?

A quick glance at this list poses some interesting problems. Which of the above questions do *you* think would interest *you,* assuming you knew something about the subject matter? Sometimes we are startled to realize how essentially dull the "problems" are that we present to young people; and if these problems are dull for adults, they must be even more so to youngsters.

Each of the above questions suggests some sort of an inquiry. But notice the way in which each is framed. Let us take one example:

> How many of you agree with the statement that a juvenile delinquent is born, not made?

What sort of a response will the teacher get? The request is for "how many?" Probably the students will just raise their hands if they agree with the statement. Obviously this reaction will not provoke discussion. The teacher must search for a stimulating question. Suppose he tries again: "How many of you disagree?" Again, a sprinkling of hands. No, another tack must be tried; "Why do you disagree?" Now we have the germ of discussion. From here the students can proceed to analyze one facet of the nature-nurture controversy, a problem that could easily arise in social studies, biology, or English classes.

Perhaps this approach seems roundabout. Does it seem that there ought to be a more direct way of initiating the discussion? A moment's reflection, however, will show that to ask for a clear-cut decision on a controversial issue, even before the issue has been discussed, will alarm some students and cause them to doubt their own ability to think. Many students will not have made up their minds about the question as asked. Yet the teacher may assume by his question that each student has already reached a decision. Furthermore, taking sides at the outset should be discouraged, rather than encouraged. Some students will "vote" one way or the other because a friend took that position, or because one of the bright students indicated his opinion. The teacher is thus encouraging superficial habits of thinking.

A more direct approach might have been:

Some people think that juvenile delinquents are born, not made. If some friend of yours got into trouble for stealing, would you say it is his fault, or the fault of society?

Or:

If you had to list the things that contribute to crime among teen-agers, what things would you feel come at the head of the list and which come at the bottom?

Or:

Are young people your age really responsible for their own behavior; if they commit crimes such as stealing, should they be punished like adults?

Any of the above variations will strike at essentially the same idea. The important point to observe is that the questions are phrased to provoke interest and to provoke thought. The issue is not black or white. Variations in judgment are expected, and, what is more important, the problem has significance for young people.

Let us examine a few more of these questions. The questions that ask for facts, pure and simple, are hardly likely to stir much interest. The students who have the facts will smugly wave their hands, while those who did not read the assignment will sit silent, barely aware of the topic suggested. These questions are:

5. Why did some fish feel compelled to come out of the water and become amphibian? How did it happen? What caused it?
7. Who was the world's first chemist? What do you think he did?
9. Why do not rats have a gall bladder?

Other questions in the list require a reporting back of a series of concepts that are not very debatable. These questions are:

1. Do you suppose Beethoven worried about this aspect of harmony?
2. If Congress refuses to pass legislation asked for by the President, what could be done to persuade Congress?
4. One third of us will die of heart disease. Can we do anything about it?

If discussion arises from such questions, it will be only as a result of teacher prodding. Furthermore, the morbid tone of question 4 is probably not the best approach for adolescents.

Some of the questions will provoke undesirable student responses unless very carefully handled. For example:

11. Why should anyone take algebra?
12. Are women healthier than men?

This sort of question is almost too good to be passed up by the classroom clown. Unless the teacher desires a light touch or is prepared for a raucous session, such questions should be avoided.

Questions such as the following are more apt to move a class toward a real discussion:

3. Should insurance be carried by everyone?
6. Should we have censorship on the quality of movies produced by Hollywood?
14. Do you think the T formation is better than the single wing?

These questions indicate that there are several good answers possible. Besides, the problems are currently significant to young people, and have been discussed widely in many other places besides the school. The students may already have encountered various points of view on the controversy in newspapers and current magazines, so that some groundwork is already laid for exchanging ideas.

Criteria for Good Discussion Questions

Out of the preceding analysis some criteria for good discussion questions may be assembled:

1. The question implies a genuine interest in divergent points of view. It suggests the existence of differences of opinion and indicates that such differences are respectable.
2. The question probes an area of experience that is of immediate, as well as more remote, concern to young people. A question including some present-day reference but also by implication embracing more general aspects of the problem will encourage discussion.
3. Discussion questions imply values and the process of evaluations of known facts, rather than a memory search for right facts opposed to wrong facts.
4. Questions that ask for: most, least, best, worst; which would you rather do; is it better to; and the like, encourage a sorting and evaluation process that promotes exchange of knowledge as well as ideas.

The beginning teacher would be well advised to practice the procedure of asking provocative questions.

The tone of voice used by the teacher is important to good discussion. Not only framing good questions but asking them in a *tone of inquiry* is essential. A dull, bored, sarcastic, or dogmatic tone of voice can kill student expression of opinion, no matter how good the question.

Other Ways of Starting Classroom Discussions

Of course we should not assume that discussions come only out of a teacher-posed question. Discussions emerge from any stimulating activity, initiated by either teacher or student. Any of these materials and resources may be utilized to develop class discussion:

1. Motion picture or filmstrip (see Chapter 5).
2. Bulletin board displays (see Chapter 5).
3. Odd or unusual objects brought to class.
4. Resource visitors (see Chapter 6).
5. Newspaper items (see Chapter 5).
6. Pictures (see Chapter 5).
7. Local events: school, community, national.
8. Commemorative days, for example, United Nations Day.
9. Radio recordings (see Chapter 5).

In using any of the above devices there are a few warnings to be noted:

1. The teacher should be alert to the controversial aspects of the resource used. If an unusual object is brought to class, it should be displayed because it will excite curiosity and open up an important area of inquiry. It is essential, then, that the teacher preview the material and assess the discussion possibilities of any such resource.

2. The medium used to promote discussion may itself take up all the available time. This is particularly true of motion pictures, visitors, and recordings. If any of these take the whole class period, there will not be time to exploit the interest aroused. The next day may be too late.

3. The medium used may raise more questions than the teacher is interested in opening for discussion at this time. The teacher may be startled and upset to find the students interested in some other area than he anticipated.

The Leader Is Important

Once the discussion has been started, it is the job of the teacher as leader to keep it moving forward toward consensus. A discussion may, it is true, have so much vitality that it will go on regardless of anything the leader may or may not do. When students have become accustomed to talking together about live issues in the classroom, there may seem to be no leader at all. In fact, after the class is over, the discussion will rage on, in hall, lunchroom, or library or on the stairs. Certainly it is good education when students are so consumed with a desire to talk together about important things that discussion continues whether a teacher is present or not. To get this process started and keep it moving ahead takes sensitive direction. Let us look at some of the factors to consider in leading a discussion.

The Three Roles of the Leader

The role of the discussion leader may be described this way. First, the leader acts as a *"back-stop,"* tossing questions back to the group much as a back-stop bounces the ball back to the person practicing his tennis stroke. Second, the leader acts as a *traffic policeman,* directing the flow of questions and making certain that individuals take their turn in crossing the issue. And third, he acts like a *guide with a road map,* stopping from time to time to show the group the road they have taken, the branches that have been sketched in but abandoned, the wrong turnings, the fork in the road that now approaches, and pointing toward the goal of the travel.

The leader as back-stop. The first activity of the leader needs constant emphasis. A good leader rarely if ever answers a question, unless it is a petty question retarding good discussion. He sees to it that the group answers the important questions. After all, the discussion is being held in order that the members of the group may together answer the questions that arise in the process of problem solving. Many would-be discussion leaders cannot resist the temptation to answer, to explain, to clarify. That is what the group must do for itself. When a student says, "Now isn't it better to spend our tax money on hospitals than on schools," the teacher should answer, "That is a good question. What do you think about it, Henry?" "Sue, what is your opinion?" "We haven't heard Jim on this problem yet." "Donald's father is manager for a local hospital; what do you think, Donald?" Of course, simple matters of fact that are not worth wasting group time may be answered by the teacher. A question of semantics or a quibble over whether a report is in error or not should not be allowed to impede the process of group thinking.

A cardinal principle of good discussion leadership, and the one that is probably most often broken, is that the leader be very sure that all important and vital questions are tossed back to the group. Otherwise, the discussion becomes a series of little conversations between the teacher and members of the class. The discussion pattern which is merely dialogue would look like this:

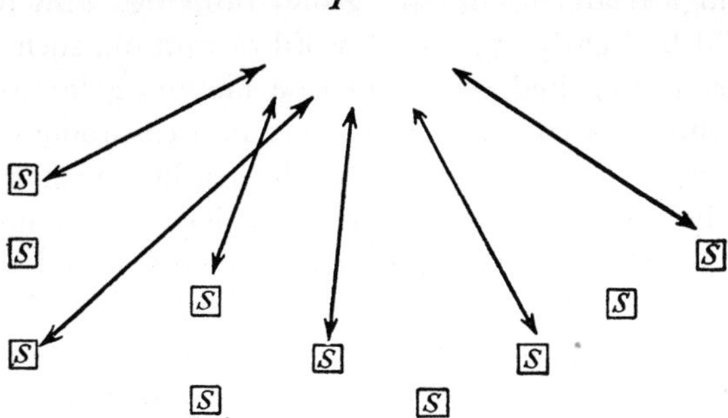

A picture of participation in a discussion where real group thinking was going on would look more like this:

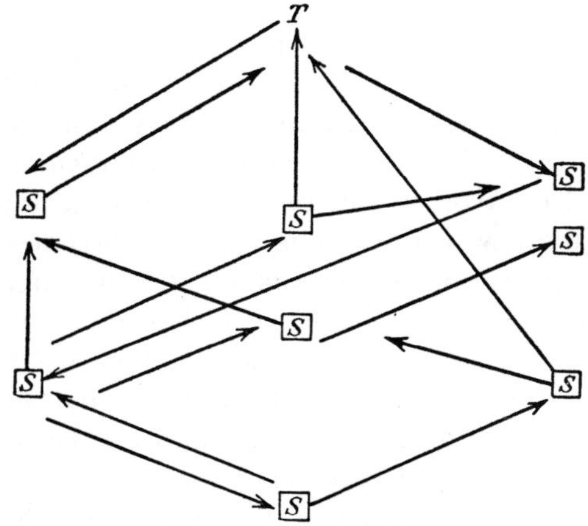

The leader as traffic policeman. The second role for the leader to take, that of "traffic policeman," implies the guidance function that must occur. This is when the teacher uses his leadership prerogative to direct questions to specific members of the class, to see to it that the more verbose do not dominate the discussion, to keep voices down to a reasonable level of volume, and finally, to see to it that only one person is speaking at a time. These latter disciplinary functions are highly important, but need to be exercised with care. A teacher who pounces on a class the first moment a slight rise in temperature is noted, the first moment a voice becomes a bit shrill in argument or when small bits of conversation spring up in answer to someone's statement, will soon thwart the genuine student interest in discussion. A really good discussion is bound to generate some heat. The teacher must see to it that this rise in interest does not interfere with logical and productive group thinking. This restraining hand should be lightly applied. A word of caution, such as, "Now, let's not get *too* excited, yet!" can ease mounting tension and remind the students that after all they are in a classroom engaged in an intellectual discussion. Similarly, the teacher must be alert to guide the discussion toward students who have as yet not contributed, to interrupt—judiciously—those students who tend toward speechmaking, using every bit of knowledge he may have about a student as a method of helping that person make his best contribution. Knowledge of a given student's interests, out-of-class activities, father's or mother's occupations, and travel experiences is very useful when the teacher seeks a strand, no matter how tenuous, to weave the interest of a student into the conversation going on about him.

This policeman function, therefore, is not only keeping the traffic of ideas flowing, but seeing that each contributor gets his full share of attention and opportunity to express himself. Student observers, keeping checks on how many times individuals make contributions and the type of contribution each makes, are invaluable assistants to the new teacher. The class also becomes much interested in charts of its own discussion. Such reports, treated with objectivity, are among the most effective devices to keep the loquacious students in check. They can for the first time see themselves in perspective and realize without too much ego damage how much more time they have taken of the total allowed the class than they deserve. A participation record, used to encourage those who do not participate and keep in check those who tend to talk too much is one of those indirect, group-centered disciplinary devices that will help the new teacher in class control. Such devices will do far more than any teacher's admonition, or even the less pleasant prod of a grade.[2]

The leader as discussion guide. The third major function for the leader to perform is to act as over-all guide for the direction of group discussion. Thinking of a discussion as an unfolding map may clarify the nature of the process. With our first experience of trying to keep thirty or forty lively minds focused on a single problem, we have seen how rough the going may be. So many ideas are suggested! And for every idea there are at least three objections, complaints, asides, personal comments, or amendments. Where does the question asked by Jimmy fit into the remark made by Joan three minutes earlier? Such problems arise every other moment during

[2] See Chapter 8 for use of forms for measuring participation.

the course of a lively discussion. Thus, the teacher as guide is involved in helping the class perform the various steps in problem solving. Briefly, these steps are as follows:

1. *What is the problem?* At this stage, the teacher may have recourse to the blackboard. It is useful to get agreement from the whole class at the very outset about the limits of the topic that has sparked the discussion. Then, if an irrelevant comment is offered, the teacher—or other students as they gain in facility—may point to the statement on the board and say, "Is that part of our problem?"

2. *What are the major issues?* Here, again, teacher and students should use the blackboard to list the things upon which significant disagreement occurs. Matters of fact need to be listed in a separate column as topics for further research. It may be—and often this occurs—that a discussion must be temporarily suspended at this level. It is found that what has appeared to be a disagreement is merely difference of opinion about the facts on a given problem. Then the teacher may utilize student interest in solving the problem, to motivate them to study and research to find the answers *in fact* to the various areas where apparent disagreement occurs.

3. *What are the possible solutions?* As the issues are clarified and as the most important are separated from the less important, the focus of the discussion is on solutions for each major issue. Suggested solutions are then posted on the blackboard. Again, additional research may be called for on the solution level to determine whether a given solution is feasible.

4. *What are the consequences of possible solutions?* The test of feasibility must be applied. Can the proposed solutions work? Are they in accord with what we know about human beings and society and the physical world? At this stage proposed lines of action or syntheses of arguments are discarded and those that the class as a whole finds agreeable are chosen.

5. *What consensus is reached?* In a real discussion it is usually both unnecessary and undesirable to have a vote. With sufficient freedom of interplay the leader can usually tell when general agreement has been reached. Constant voting on each point would be both a waste of time and a useless interruption. In this last stage of discussion, where the sense of the group is finally attained, there is a feeling of satisfaction and relief. The leader may step in to summarize and point out where the group has traveled in its thinking.

6. *What action is planned?* This stage is not always reached. Where a discussion involves merely an intellectual exchange of somewhat abstract ideas or general principles, no action is likely to occur. However, where a discussion starts on such topics as, "What play should the seniors pick for the last school assembly?" then some plans for action should result. Sometimes committees are selected to carry out the plan. Other outcomes may be writing a letter to the local Congressman, preparing a skit for a PTA meeting, or setting out a plan for study for the succeeding six weeks.

These steps in the process of group thinking form the fundamental structure for problem solving. As the teacher gets accustomed to thinking in this sequence himself, it is relatively easy to help others to follow through these steps. The teacher can make explicit which step the class is approaching as an aid to logical thinking. He can say, for example, "We must define our problem before we go on to discuss where and how we disagree," as the class approaches the first step; or, as the group edges around step two, "Now let's be sure we know what the issues are in this problem before we try to find out what a good solution would be."

As a road guide, the teacher can also assist in the appraisal of contributions. When a student makes a suggestion that is supposed to be pertinent, the leader will want to ask, "Now is that your opinion, or is that a fact?" so that the difference between what is true and what is believed or felt becomes clear in the minds of the students. Moreover, the source of information is significant: a student contribution may be more or less reliable, depending upon his source of information. Developing a critical use of standard sources of information is a major result of learning. Did the newspaper report the event accurately? Why does this paper's report differ from the one in this magazine? How did the radio or television report the same event? Such questions will develop out of discussion when the leader directs attention to the quality of individual contributions. As students gain facility in discussions, they will learn to discriminate among authorities, to think objectively rather than emotionally about facts and to modify opinions in the face of sound logic.

Finally, the teacher or student leader of discussion in his role as guide, is interested in keeping the group moving toward its goal. "Needling" the group to sharpen its thinking, getting it back on the right track, challenging it to new ideas when the discussion seems to be bogging down are all parts of the art of leadership. To serve these purposes, a series of questions or queries may sometimes be formulated prior to the discussion by the leader. Obviously these stimulants need to be administered judiciously lest the leader get too far ahead of group thinking. It is important to check frequently with the group with such remarks as: "Do we all know what the point is under discussion?" or, "Was that last issue clear to everyone?" before moving on to newer fields. The teacher may find that while the interest and vitality of a few keep a discussion moving swiftly forward, a good portion of the class may have lost the thread of the argument several twists back. A group with widely differing intellectual abilities is apt to make the faster students impatient, or move too quickly for the slower ones. A teacher may want to use some of the smaller-group techniques outlined in Chapter 8 in order to bring up the skill level of the whole group, impressing particularly upon those who think most quickly that the need to wait till the slower ones catch up is an essential quality of democratic group thinking.

Personal Qualities for Discussion Leaders

To carry out the roles of the leader as a "back-stop," a "traffic policeman," and a "road guide," some special personal qualities are needed:

1. *A personal and lively interest in the subject under discussion.* Good leaders do not try to promote a discussion about topics that they find boring or dull. Excitement generated by the teacher is most contagious and will help enliven a classroom group. Choosing for leaders those students with a more-than-usual interest in the subject will also help to promote student discussion.

2. *An open mind about the outcomes or the pattern to be taken by the discussion.* Group thinking changes as groups change. While one class arrived at one decision, another class may arrive at an opposite one. When choices are to be made, it is not wise to have a personal stake in any one choice; this is apt to spoil the genuineness of leadership. Students soon descend to the guessing-game level of participation under this kind of leadership.

3. *A sense of the humorous as well as a sense of the serious.* Being able to shift from low gear to high, from the light to the heavy and back again, is part of the leadership art. Ability to laugh at the unexpected remark or retort will keep young people with the leader in the more serious parts.

4. *A real interest in the opinions of young people.* Some adults enjoy discussions with other adults, but become bored when youngsters express naïve, bigoted, or ignorant ideas. Discussion does not flower in this sort of an atmosphere.

5. *An ability to repress the expression of his own opinion most of the time.* Students are quick to detect what the teacher thinks is the correct point of view unless the leader is skillful in summarizing impartially both sides of an issue. As rapport is established, the teacher may, however, use the assertion of an opinion in order to encourage disagreement. However, this technique should be used carefully.

Jacques Barzun has described very vividly the role of discussion on the college level; much of what he says is just as appropriate for the high-school teacher:

> Handling a discussion group requires a special talent. . . . The hour's discussion must not go off in all directions like a leaky hose. It must have a pattern, beginning at a given point and logically reaching another, from which to start again the next day. Now it is relatively easy to impose a pattern on a lecture; the scheme of it can be written out beforehand and even memorized, because no one will interfere with it. But in a discussion, every one of twenty-five or thirty men has a right to shove the tiller in any direction he pleases. Since there must be an atmosphere of freedom, the instructor must not act like a priggish moderator with a gavel. He must be willing to go up sidetracks and come back. His imagination must swarm

with connecting links, factual illustrations, answers to unexpected questions. He must, moreover, know how to correct without wounding, contradict without discouraging, coax along without coddling. Every once in a while, a group of men will contain a crank or a fanatic: he must be turned to good teaching use without being made to feel a goat. Every once in a while, the class will want to take the bit in its teeth and hold a political or ethical debate, none too close to the issue. This must be tolerated. Every once in a while, the instructor will feel so strongly on a given matter that he will want to lecture. This must be nipped in the bud.

An advanced discussion group . . . is a test of any discussion leader. His role is that of an orchestra conductor, except that neither he nor his men have a score before them. Yet the result of the evening's noise must be as intelligible as a symphony. This takes mutual accustoming on the part of leader and led. Calling on the right man for the right thing, balancing opinions, drawing out the shy and backward, keeping silent so that the group itself will unwind its own errors . . . is an art that only comes with long practice. It calls for the best teachers in their prime and I am convinced furthermore that it accomplishes more than any other form of teaching.[3]

The teacher will seek to develop his own skill in leading discussions, but all that has been said here should be passed on to students in order that they too may become more skilled in thinking through problems cooperatively and giving leadership to such endeavors. The more the teacher is able to let student leaders preside during appropriate discussion periods the greater will be the opportunity for students to gain in poise, responsibility, and maturity of reflective thinking.

Controversial Issues: What Can One Discuss?

Some issues are controversial only in the sense that they are considered inappropriate for immature minds. Other problems are considered controversial because there is such grave divergence of opinion about the right and the wrong that deep emotions become involved. It is often felt that areas of such public and personal reaction are not suitable for our schools, since the process of education ought to be based on fact and objective truth.

Then, we know that what is controversial in one part of the country may be taken as a matter of course in another part. It is possible in some sections, for instance, to discuss interrace relations and do much toward developing greater understanding. But in many sections such a discussion would disturb community groups and lead to serious criticism of the teacher. Similarly, research on and discussion of such topics as unions, local political problems,

[3] Barzun, Jacques, *Teacher in America* (Boston: Little, Brown & Company, 1945), pp. 40-41.

communism, historical bases of religion, evolution, and divorce will be apt to upset some communities. Should the teacher avoid such issues? Most of the questions we have mentioned are in the realm of the social sciences, but obviously there are controversial issues in every field of study. Any teacher who encourages discussion may find himself teetering on the edge of a controversy.

Controversial issues may arise whenever subject matter is concerned with contemporary events. Even a mathematics class in discussion of statistics and percentage problems may bump into a topic like "What is a fair rate of return on a capital investment?" Obviously this is a controversial subject in the minds of many people. Yet current problems like this one are important in any curriculum where young people are being encouraged to think critically about the modern world.

Many teachers are understandably wary of allowing classroom instruction to veer off into these "controversial issues." They fear that community opinion will not approve; they will be accused of being "radical" or "immoral" or of putting the wrong ideas in the minds of youth, and that fear brings visions of loss of job. Or teachers may fear that students will start expressing ideas that are inappropriate, getting into topics where the teacher himself feels uneasy because the problems are unresolved. As a result many teachers keep their courses on the dull and even keel of dry facts, uninspiring recitation, or memorizing. Actually the alternatives need not be so sharply drawn. It is possible for most teachers to engage in classroom discussion of some controversial issues. Of course, teachers who are biased, who are untactful and undiplomatic, will run into difficulties in this field just as they would in any situation that demanded mature appraisal.

Some criteria may be suggested here to guide the teacher in the choice of those controversial issues which ought to be discussed in classrooms:[4]

1. Is this issue of significance to my students now? What is of concern to adults may not be important to young people, and perhaps ought not to be important to them until they grow into maturity. Let us not foist all of our perplexities upon youth!

2. Is this issue one that students may be able to understand? The special ideas and even the vocabulary of some problem areas may be too far outside the realm of experience of your students.

3. If the issue interests the students, is it possible for them to seek additional information to answer the kinds of questions they may raise?

[4] Adapted from Junior Town Meeting League, 400 South Front St., Columbus 15, Ohio, *Teaching Controversial Issues,* 1948.

It is unwise to open up debate upon a question of importance in order to encourage young people to get the facts, and then not have sources of information from which facts may be obtained. Those issues that have no factual solution whatsoever are often merely frustrating for the whole class.

4. Will this problem, if discussed in class, help or hinder the long-run aims of the school in this community? The teacher may feel very strongly about a problem which, however, a given community is not yet ready to face. If such a problem is discussed in the class and the community objects, the teacher may have done basic damage to any further education along such lines in this community.

Finding Areas of Interest

One of the broad purposes of education is to provoke thinking. Unfortunately, this purpose cannot be accomplished without some people becoming irritated. But being capable of irritation is, after all, a sign of life! We would encourage all teachers to examine carefully the material they intend to teach and seek those controversial issues that meet the criteria we have suggested. This is not an easy task. Many subjects, such as music, art, science, mathematics, languages, do not seem on the surface to include any controversial issues. However, it is possible to make a beginning of a list here and let each student, in his own subject field, continue it for himself:

1. Art:

Who should say what is good art? The people, who are untrained, or the artists, or the critics?

Advertising is really not art.

Only good art should be studied in schools, since we see so much bad art outside of school.

A great artist must also be a great person.

2. Music:

Jazz is very superficial music and therefore should not be studied in school.

Modern music, like modern art, does not seem to make sense.

People should sing for their own enjoyment, not to uplift others.

3. Mathematics:

Mathematics should be required of all students, no matter what they intend doing in adult life.

Science could not advance without mathematics, but mathematics can advance without science.

We should adopt the metric system rather than retaining our present English system of measurement.

4. Science:

Atomic energy research should be controlled by private industry rather than by government.

There should be international regulation of all work in atomic energy.

There is no such thing as "pure" science.

The scientist need not be concerned with politics.

5. Social studies:

There should be an amendment to the Constitution giving equal rights to women.

Divorce laws should be made more stringent.

If Americans had been more patient, the American Revolution need never have been fought. We would have been farther along the road to world peace had this been true.

The voting age should be lowered to eighteen in all elections.

Avoiding Common Errors in Discussing Controversial Issues

Although the teacher should be alert to the usefulness of arousing discussion in areas of controversy, he will, of course, run into trouble if he is unfair to any particular point of view. The teacher must himself have an open and unprejudiced mind, since the students in his class may represent all shades of opinion and attitude. The teacher will be criticized if he fails to give a fair hearing to all points of view. Then, if criticism arises, the teacher can point out that the democratic process insists on an "open market-place for ideas." Obviously the teacher should beware of needlessly stepping on toes. Otherwise, the idealistic teacher becomes a Don Quixote, tilting with ideological or personal windmills, and his long-run effectiveness is lost in a maze of recrimination and suspicion.

The discussion of controversial issues, or of any important subject, for that matter, has one special hazard for the beginning teacher—this is the embarrassing question.

> Mr. Doyle was finishing a unit on race tolerance. There had been much lively discussion, and students had been very interested. He felt that it had been a highly constructive experience all around. The film "Americans All" from the *March of Time* series had been chosen as a kind of summary of the democratic point of view. There were a few moments of class time left after the motion picture, and discussion was somewhat desultory. The group was pretty well talked out on the subject. Then Phillip, who could usually be counted on to do something to provide a jolt to the group, raised his hand: "Mr. Doyle, would you marry someone who wasn't of your race?"

What happens next! This is the kind of question that teachers fear, some of them so much that they will not risk raising the issues at all. Yet, there are always ways to handle these questions. Here are some of the ways in which Mr. Doyle might have replied:

> "Well, Phillip, I think that is a very important question. Frankly, I don't have an answer to it. I would like to give you a good answer, and not just the first thing that pops into my head. Let me think about

the problem, will you, and then perhaps we can come to an understanding of it."

"That is a serious question you raise, Phillip. It is asked by many people whenever we discuss this subject. I think I know what I would do, but before I give you my opinion, I would be interested in hearing what other members of our class think."

Oh, says the reader, the teacher is just stalling for time. Yes, the teacher is asking for more time; he is trying to arrange his ideas so that he can give a reasoned answer, a response that cannot be misinterpreted. The motives of students who ask these questions may be suspect, but the issue still needs to be faced. The teacher cannot allow himself to become confused or upset. Here is the moment when clear thinking is most needed. Yet the atmosphere is so charged with emotion that it is often most difficult to think clearly. So the teacher should be ready to turn the discussion back to the class, while both he and they work out their thinking. There is great wisdom in not answering immediately. Admitting that a pat answer is not at hand may be the most convincing evidence of honesty.

We admit, then, that there will be many uncomfortable moments for the teacher whose class discusses controversial issues. But we need still to remember:

> A majority of people end their formal school period on or before graduation from high school. Therefore, if the majority of our pupils are ever to consider and discuss controversial issues under conditions which normally exist in the school room, this must be done during the high school period.
>
> An individual may best be inducted into a consideration of controversial issues under conditions prevailing in a public school classroom. Here partisanship and propaganda are much less in evidence than outside the classroom, and scientific techniques of attack on social, political, and economic problems are not only used but their uses are likewise taught.[5]

Indeed, in democracy there must be a marked emphasis on freedom for the discussion of controversial subjects. As the Educational Policies Commission stated:

> Freedom of discussion of controversial subjects is more than a right. It is a requisite of democratic institutions and democratic ways of living. In a democracy, public policy is ultimately determined by the will of the people. To deny the right of consideration of controversial questions to any portion of the people, or to place any question outside the pale of free discussion, is to strike at the heart of democratic institutions.[6]

[5] Educational Policies Commission, *Learning the Ways of Democracy* (Washington, D.C.: The Commission, 1940), p. 367.

[6] *Ibid.*, p. 171.

Sociodrama, Role Playing, and Related Techniques

When we were all very young we used to play "Let's Pretend" and forthwith produced fascinating versions of school, family, cowboys, historical stories. This play acting can be seen among all young children; an observer may often gain new insights into the child's view of the world by hearing a group of four-year-olds "play house." The "mother" will discipline the "children" much as these children are actually disciplined; the father role emerges according to the view that the child has of his father—sometimes rather different from that of the adult in question! Not only do the observers learn about the child's world, but the child is going through an interesting learning experience; he is trying out the various real-life or fantasy-life characters that he sees or dreams about. By pretending to be a fireman, the child learns a great deal about what it is actually like to be a fireman. Dramatic play of this sort, both creative and realistic, is utilized in elementary schools to provide teachers with insight and to develop on the part of the young people a new dimension for learning.

The technique applied to the high-school class is also a useful device serving similar purposes. We call the technique "sociodrama" when we are concerned mainly with the development of deeper understanding of social relations. The technique is called "psychodrama" when it refers to the deeper personal-emotional problems encountered by the individual in his own life. The latter technique is used mainly by therapists and psychologists and should be used only by those trained in dealing with deep emotional problems. For the high-school teacher, sociodrama is the more appropriate tool.

Sociodrama is unprepared, unrehearsed dramatization. A class discussion may be focused on the issue, "If the United States has a surplus of food, to which country should it go and under what terms?" The teacher may assign some members of the class the problem of portraying the role of spokesmen for various countries in need of food, while other students represent the United States. Then these "pretend diplomats" meet to present their points of view as might occur among real statesmen. By the time the sociodrama is finished, the teacher has gained insight into 1) how meaningful the subject matter was to the young people; 2) what concepts they had developed about foreign viewpoints; and 3) how well the individual student could relate subject matter to the real people involved.

Sociodrama may center in the student's version of the dramatic moments from a book that is being read in class. The book may concern historical figures, may be biography or autobiography, may be in a foreign language. Some teachers have had students give their own version of Shakespeare's plays spontaneously, thus gaining an idea of what elements of the story remain in the students' minds. Sometimes current events may be portrayed in "live" action—some local controversy over taxation, some debate in Congress over foreign policy, some conflict in the United Nations over China. One very effective use of sociodrama has been in the development of democratic attitudes toward people of minority groups. Here students take the roles of these people in their daily lives in order to gain greater understanding and appreciation of their problems.

Sociodrama differs from the usual type of dramatic work in that no script is needed, no memorizing of parts, no rehearsal. In fact, the value of sociodrama as a teaching device lies in the spontaneity of presentation. The action comes directly from the individual's creative use of his own experience.

There are only three prerequisites needed for good classroom sociodrama: (1) the class should have a cooperative group feeling and a common interest in the issue at hand; (2) the participants should have the issue clearly in mind; and (3) the experience should be regarded as a means of learning, not entertaining. The following specific examples will show how the technique can be used:

> In a United States history class, the material being studied had to do with George Washington's selection as the first President. After reading the text and having a brief discussion about it, the teacher asked one student to be George Washington and two students to be the committee who called upon him to ask his acceptance of the nomination. At first the students were unable to portray the roles, but after further class discussion as to how George Washington actually would have felt and would have answered, after consideration of the appropriate arguments that might have worked, the little drama was reenacted to the satisfaction of the class. Here could be seen one of the prime usefulnesses of the technique; making remote and fairly abstract situations come alive in the present-day moment for the young people.
>
> A journalism class was discussing interview techniques. In order to make the lesson clear, the class described various kinds of persons one might interview: the high-handed celebrity, the sobbing mother, the tough politician, the frightened child, the garrulous gossip. Then members of the class practiced different interview approaches to each such situation. The discussions after each presentation often resulted in a replaying of the interview with different performers as criticisms

or suggestions came from the class about different and better ways of showing the method to be used. The teacher discovered that some students had more insight than others into the ways in which real people act, and that those with less insight learned a great deal by having to think through the problems presented.

A group of music teachers felt the need for variety of activities in their classes as a means of solving problems of discipline. Among the new techniques that were suggested and used with success was sociodrama. One teacher reported that prior to the visit of a noted pianist, some episodes from his life were read to the class from an article in a current music periodical. The teacher then asked: "What episode was most interesting and dramatic? Could we re-enact it as it must have occurred? Who would like to be the pianist? What about the other characters?" The class response was very rewarding; music and musicians took on new life.

The specific steps to be taken in putting on a sociodrama are described below.[7] These steps are merely suggested. After one or two tries, the teacher probably will want to alter or adapt them to suit his own situation.

1. ***Selecting the situation.*** The situation should, first, be a fairly simple one, revolving about one main idea or issue. Secondly, the situation should be one involving personalities. The issues should be those that arise because people have different desires, beliefs, hopes, and aspirations, or they should be problems that arise from the inability of people to understand the point of view of others. When introducing this technique for the first time, the teacher should have an idea for a sociodrama situation clearly in mind. Later, the class members will be eager to describe situations of their own choosing and select the roles that should be taken. Situations that require from two to four characters are easiest to begin with. Larger numbers are confusing until students know more about what they are supposed to do.

The teacher, with the help of the class, should describe each of the roles to be taken. As an illustration, suppose the sociodrama concerns the problem of incorporation of an agricultural community. Opinion is divided; to some residents the increased services do not seem sufficient to counterbalance the increased tax load; to other residents, incorporation offers distinct advantage. A petition is being circulated. The sociodrama then revolves around the various characters that might be concerned with such a problem. Farmer Jones is then selected as one role to be portrayed. The es-

[7] See Grambs, Jean D., and Lucien B. Kinney, "Sociodrama in High School Classes," *Social Education,* 12:341-343 (December, 1948).

sential details of his role are sketched in: he is married, has lived in the area about fifteen years, and has never made very much money—just enough to live nicely. Other details may be added as appropriate: he is stubborn; or he is a sharp bargainer, or he is very slow and ignorant. After one portrayal the teacher and the class will learn how much description of each role is necessary. Then the teacher and the class should set the situation: Mr. Jones is visiting Mr. Smith in order to get his signature on the petition, or Mr. Jones has come to ask Mr. Smith's advice about the local controversy.

2. ***Choosing participants.*** When first trying out sociodrama, the teacher should select students who are fairly well informed on the issue to be presented, and who are imaginative, articulate, and self-assured. The "show-off" often freezes up or clowns absurdly; the shy student feels insecure and inadequate. Both types can be assisted in their own personality adjustment by first being given minor prop roles, such as that of secretary or doorman, and later being allowed to take larger roles. It will also be found that those with dramatic training are not necessarily the best participants in spontaneous dramatics, since sociodrama draws upon the individual's own resources of feeling and imagination.

It would probably be advisable not to ask for volunteers for sociodrama until such time as the students initiate the program themselves. In selecting participants, the teacher should also make use of his knowledge of each student's background and needs, placing the student in roles and situations that will be of benefit to him.

3. ***Setting the stage.*** When the participants have been selected, they should be sent out of the room or to some quiet corner for about two minutes. They should be instructed to "think themselves into" the role they are to take. The participants may want to decide together how the scene will look, where the furniture will be, who will enter first, and other details of staging. Later, the class as a whole may describe the complete setting before the participants are selected.

4. ***Preparing the audience.*** While the participants are out of the room for their two minutes of thinking, the teacher should direct the class to observe the action as though each one were acting in it. The students should ask themselves: Is this the way these people act and feel in real life? The students should be concerned with how a housewife would act and what she would say when defending her interest in soap operas, rather than how Harriet Smith acted as the housewife.

Emphasis upon the exploratory nature of the sociodrama should be clear to both the participants and the audience. It should be understood that no finished product is expected, but that, in fact, everyone will learn more if the participants are considerably less than perfect.

5. ***Acting out the situation.*** When directing sociodrama the teacher becomes a cross between director and audience. When a student seems to be slipping out of his role, the teacher should remind him of what he is trying to do. When the students seem to reach a dead end, the teacher should cut the situation short. However, the teacher should otherwise allow the action to follow its own pattern as completely as possible, since this very naturalness, the feeling of freedom to become wholly involved in the situation, contributes immeasurably to the reality and the success of the sociodrama. Few sociodramas will last more than five minutes, unless the situation is very complicated or the students have a great deal of information.

6. ***Follow-up.*** When the situation is finished, the class will be eager with comments. This stimulation of discussion, centering on how people feel and why they act as they do, is one of the basic contributions of sociodrama. The students may have so many ideas for a re-enactment of the situation that it may be appropriate to go through it again with new actors. On the other hand, the students may feel that more knowledge is necessary before trying again and may want to do more reading and study about the personalities involved. This outcome, of course, is most desirable, and the alert teacher will make the most of his opportunity.

The participants should also report upon how they felt as they acted through the sociodrama. This feeling will provide a clue to the teacher of the depth of insight of the students into the wellsprings of human emotion.

In the follow-up, as in the preparatory period, the teacher should always stress that no one is expected to do a perfect job in sociodrama. The teacher should make a point of expressing pleasant surprise at how well the students have succeeded in the task. Sociodrama can, in this manner, be an effective learning medium, providing both students and teachers an opportunity for joint creative experience.

Now we are ready for an illustration of a complete sociodrama.

> There had been much concern in this school about intergroup relations. There seemed to be some covert conflict between the Spanish-American group and the other students. The English teacher,

Mrs. Morgan, felt that some dramatic enactment of a related situation might help clarify the immediate school problem. At the start of one class she announced that they were going to try a new kind of dramatics; they would make up a play as they went along and see how it worked. She then presented to the class the "plot."

> The son of one of the leading ranchers in the area, Sidney Stuart, had been killed during World War II while serving as a Marine in the South Pacific. In memory of his son, Mr. Stuart said he would like to award annually a $50 prize to the student in the school who was considered the best citizen by a student committee. The first year the award was made, the committee, composed of George Green, Doris Bacigalupi, and Tony Nevin, chose Bill Thompson. Bill did very good schoolwork, was one of the track stars of the school, and just the previous semester had, at great personal risk, saved a whole family from disaster. Bill was a Negro. When Mr. Stuart heard who had been given the first award he was furious. He told the principal that under no circumstance could he agree to the award being given to a Negro student. "Isn't there a white student who is a good citizen?" he asked. He said he would even give another $50 award and let Bill keep the one he was to get. The principal, Mr. Jenkins, agreed to call the student committee back together again and explain Mr. Stuart's position.

The sociodrama took up at this point. Students were selected for the various roles, and the "committee" met with the "principal." The members of the first committee were assigned specific roles by Mrs. Morgan. The student to play George Green was told to take the position that Mr. Stuart was right, that another award should be selected and then they could have two awards. The student who played Doris felt that this was absolutely wrong and was opposed to a second award. The student who played Tony carried the burden of the committee decision. The class listened to the description of the situation, and then, after the role assignments had been given, there was marked rise in interest and alertness. This problem assumed great reality, and everyone leaned forward to see what the "committee" would work out with the "principal."

This committee carried on a rather extensive argument with the principal. The students playing the roles found it difficult to reach agreement. The principal seemed to favor Mr. Stuart's proposal. The meeting finally was called to a close by the "principal" who suggested that they think it over until the next day, since they obviously were having difficulty deciding.

At this point, when Mrs. Morgan, the teacher, turned to the rest of the class for their reaction there was an immediate hubbub of comment. Mrs. Morgan merely waited, without saying a word. One by one students started to voice their opinion of what they had seen. One student finally stated that he knew what he would have done if he had been the principal. This sounded like a good idea to Mrs. Morgan, so she called him up to be the principal, quickly picked a new committee from the class members, and they went through a new sequence.

As the new principal worked toward his solution, which was not a very ethical one, the teacher turned herself into a secretary, announced that Mr. Stuart was waiting to see him. Without warning she called one of the class members up to be Mr. Stuart. Then a new situation evolved, with Mr. Stuart reacting to the proposal of the principal. This discussion grew quite heated as the student playing Mr. Stuart flung himself into the role of a highly prejudiced person. The teacher felt enough had been said and, again being the secretary, told the "principal" that he was wanted on the telephone. Then the sociodrama ended for the time being.

A lively discussion ensued. The students by this time were very deeply involved in the problem. Two major ethical points had emerged, one regarding attitudes of tolerance, and one regarding the justification of a lie. The lie had been the last principal's solution, which then became the focus of class discussion. By the end of the period, the teacher felt that the groundwork had been laid for a follow-up discussion the next day regarding tolerance and understanding of others. Eventually she hoped to open up the immediate school problem of understanding and working with the Spanish-American students in the school.[8]

Where a teacher is alert to sense student reactions, there can be a very rich sociodrama experience. In the example, the teacher captured a student idea regarding a solution and "tried it out". By seeing their suggestions in practice, the students gained a deeper insight into reality.

Other situations are given below to illustrate the kind that are possible in high school classrooms:

1. Jean Talbott is an eighteen-year-old girl who was very close to her parents until she overheard them discussing her boy-friend, Ted Green, and discovered that they didn't care for him at all. Jean is very fond of Ted, who has asked her to marry him when she finishes school next summer, and she finds she must either reconcile her parents to Ted or make the decision to marry him against their wishes.

2. The young people in a small community have started a youth group. They meet for a few weeks at a local church. Even the minister agrees with them that social dancing is an appropriate activity for them, but because of local tradition, he does not feel free to have them dance at the church. Failing any other meeting place, the young people decide to approach the high school principal for the use of the local school building after hours. The principal is responsible to a tough school board, which includes church members.

3. Ted works for his father on the farm. He knows that the war years have been the first financially easy ones his parents have ever had, and that every penny of the family is accounted for in advance. He gets a moderate

[8] Problem situation adapted from Shaftel, George, and Fannie Shaftel, *Toward the Democratic Personality* (tentative title), Stanford University Press, to be published.

allowance from the profits, but, since he last year chose the farm as his life's work, he feels that some more businesslike arrangements should have been made with his father. For example, he may want sometime to marry or to have a car of his own when he can afford it. Right now both seem impossible. He does need more allowance, however, because he has a girl he's known for a long time and whom he's just asked to go steady.

4. Larry has been working hard to become financially independent of his parents by raising and selling some livestock of his own. While he is having a late breakfast with his father and mother on Sunday morning, a hot-tempered neighbor storms in to accuse Larry of letting a bull get out and destroy his vegetable garden. Neither Larry nor his parents have even met the neighbor, who keeps vicious dogs around his place and discourages visitors of any kind.

5. Since finishing high school John Rowan has worked with his father at farming. The family is well enough off, and John has been thinking for a year or so about going to college. He could take agriculture, but lately he's thought he might like to be a veterinarian, or perhaps, a rural sociologist. He is an only child, and his parents have always thought of him as wanting to stay at home. John's father, too, hasn't much patience with college education for farmers and is supremely happy that John seems never to have mentioned wanting to go away from home. With John's help, now, Mr. Rowan is sure that he can take it easier around the farm. Finally, John can just take over, but that will not be for some time.

6. Bruce Schaeffer and his wife Mary are both interested in leadership jobs in their rural community. They want to begin by organizing not only the young people but the parents into some community recreation. A major problem is how to approach all the different religious and cultural groups (each with different attitudes) in the town. Many difficulties are encountered in getting all these groups working together. Parents are harder to bring together than the young people.[9]

There are a number of variations on the technique which the teacher will soon discover for himself. Teachers who are interested in trying this method might do well to form a small group and run through some sociodramas of their own in order to know how it feels. Teacher-principal, teacher-parent, teacher-student problems are fitting subjects for such practice. An experience in a sociodrama is the best way of discovering what this method accomplishes for the participants.

Evaluating Sociodramas

Teachers who have made much use of this technique find that it works better if frequent evaluation periods are held. One history teacher assigns portions of the textbook chapter to groups of two or

[9] Harshfield, H. W., and J. P. Schmidt, *Playing Out Our Problems in Sociodrama* (Pamphlet) (Columbus: Ohio State University Agricultural Extension Service, 1948).

three to enact. After each series of enactments, an evaluation committee reports on how well the sociodramas were presented, and suggests improvements for next time. From the committee came suggestions like these: "Don't turn your back on the audience"; "Make clear to the group just what each person is supposed to represent"; "Don't giggle or act silly"; "It helps when something exciting is selected." These provide impetus toward doing a better job next time. Through constant encouragement to improve, the students learn discrimination as well as gain in poise and freedom in front of a group.

Sometimes the sociodrama group is requested to summarize in writing the main principle that it hopes to project. Then the group has a definite focus. The principle is not announced in advance, of course, but the audience is alerted to its responsibility to capture the major idea. A brief check-up quiz after a series of sociodramas used for review can be used to show how well each group made its point. The success of the groups in projecting concepts may furnish guides for continuing training in selecting problems for sociodrama.

Role Playing

Role playing is another term that has been used recently to denote a technique very similar to sociodrama. As the name indicates, the emphasis is on the role, whereas in sociodrama the emphasis is on the problem. The use of role playing has been found particularly effective when the role has immediate carryover into real-life situations. For instance, when developing the idea of working in a group, the teacher can use role playing to show the class how different people assist or impede the process of group thinking.

> A teacher had been concerned about some of the group projects in her class. Several of the groups were working very well together, but in two groups there was dissension due to dominating leadership as well as to disagreement over what the group was trying to do. Therefore, at the beginning of one class hour, the teacher said that she was going to ask several members of the class to be a "pretend" group. She called up five students and gave each a separate slip of paper, cautioning them not to tell anyone what was on the paper. The slips were as follows:
>
> 1. You are very eager to be chairman of the group.
> 2. You don't like anything that is suggested.
> 3. You are very enthusiastic about almost any project suggested.
> 4. You refuse to take sides in a discussion.
> 5. You are eager to see the group working together on almost anything.
>
> She then asked the students to pretend that they were a group

similar to one in class and gave them a project to plan that paralleled those being worked on. The students threw themselves into the roles with great vigor, to the amusement and chagrin of various of the class members who saw their own group roles being portrayed. After about ten minutes, when it was obvious the group wasn't getting very far, the teacher called the group to a halt and then threw the problem open to the class to discuss. She started by asking them to identify the *roles* each person had taken.

Where individuals have developed inadequate or difficult personal roles for themselves, role playing may help them to find a more adequate behavior pattern.

Role playing is especially useful in any situation where various kinds of leadership problems are being discussed. A teacher who is the adviser to the student council may need to aid the president of the student body in appropriate role behavior. The president may need help in developing ability to be fairly assertive, poised, able to interrupt long-winded speeches, to turn aside provocative comments, to encourage and praise. By acting out some of the typical experiences in presiding, the president may become better equipped to carry out his responsibilities. Similarly, a team captain may be able to work out appropriate ways of encouraging the members of the team. In sessions of role playing a sympathetic audience can say, "Bill, you shouldn't be so sharp when you tell Joe about his mistakes." Or, "I think, Bill, you might try another kind of comment when George hogs the ball." Then Bill can try out a few different phrases or comments and see if the group feels these are better ways of working with the team members.

Role playing can often be used in guidance. A group of boys may be unable to participate in social affairs because they completely fear the tête-à-tête situation with a girl. Sometimes a visitor can act the girl's role, since it might be difficult to get a student to act this role without feeling embarrassed. The boys then try out how they would ask "her" for a date, what they might say at a dance, how they would make a graceful exit at the end of the party, and other crucial social relations. This kind of role playing may be preceded by make-believe telephone conversations to a girl. The telephone conversation situation is most appropriate for role playing because it is such a common problem situation for adolescents.

Writing Skits, Radio Scripts, and Plays

In the two techniques presented above—sociodrama and role playing—the classroom teacher has two very simple but effective tools with which to build some original and dramatic presentations. Such presentations require carefully thought out and detailed scripts, but the informal sociodrama and role playing help get the scripts going.

> An assignment had been given to try to write a simple one-act play. One student chose the scene where Ann Boleyn said farewell to her daughter just before she (Ann) was to be beheaded. The student asked various class members to take the few roles needed and to ad lib the parts. The students, after a quick briefing, threw themselves with a will into the scene. The conversation that ensued had the real breath of life in it. As a result, the student playwright had the basic structure of her play set up, and also obtained some important clues about how people might interact in a crisis like this.

This technique is applicable in almost any situation where a script or playlet is to be written. Radio scripts provide good motivation for writing in classes where writing is not the primary aim. They can be easily tape-recorded and played back to the class, and local radio stations can sometimes be persuaded to use the better efforts.

> A journalism teacher had taken her class on a field trip to a newspaper plant. When they returned, the teacher suggested a follow-up activity involving the preparation and recording of a script describing the field trip and what was learned. The class divided into groups: one group were the *experts,* to check the script written by the *writers* for accuracy of facts and scientific soundness; another group, the *sound engineers,* arranged for the recording equipment and studio; another provided background music and sound effects; and still another became the *critics* to see that the whole thing was an effective presentation and could be used for PTA, assembly, and other journalism classrooms.

The idea of the "living newspaper," in which a group of individuals trained in sociodramatic techniques, act out current happenings for an audience may also be very readily adapted to the school-assembly program. For this, too, preparation of the script requires a minimum of technical skill.

Conversation Periods

Adults spend more time conversing with others than in any other kind of oral communication. The ability to carry on an interesting, logical, informative, and enjoyable conversation is therefore a valuable asset in social situations. To develop this skill some teachers have several students who are prepared on a given topic put on a "conversation" for the class. Some principles of good conversation can thus be illustrated. The class sees that a conversation is an informal talking together about something of interest to the participants. It becomes clear that good conversation depends on rapid give and take of ideas rather than on prolonged speech making, and that it utilizes humor as well as serious argument. Students also observe how sensitive conversation is to personality interaction.

Conversation as a teaching device in developing oral skills tends to reduce fear of an audience, since it stimulates a situation familiar to most students and emphasizes natural behavior and relaxation. Students who can learn to converse in front of a group will soon be able to stand up alone and give an informative and enjoyable talk. Learning conversation skills prior to beginning with panel discussions may also help make the panels more genuine discussions.[10]

Use of These Techniques by Beginning Teachers

When should the teacher use these more dramatic teaching techniques? This question will be raised often by the beginning teacher. There seem to be so many different ways of presenting material, how can the teacher know which to use when? The techniques described in this section—sociodrama, role playing, script writing, and conversation periods—may best be used when the teacher is fully assured of class control. Sometimes the freedom implicit in these devices is too much for students to handle who are used to more rigid methods. The teacher will want to develop the idea of using this approach with the class and assess their readiness to try something new. The teacher himself will want to have some experience in the techniques. Beginning teachers would do well to try them out with fellow beginners where no students are present. Some of the problems and possibilities can be realized only through active participation and cannot be adequately experienced by just reading about them.

Summary

Efficient learning requires genuine interaction between the learner and the content of education. No high-school student retains long the learning handed him by others. To harried beginning teachers it may seem to save time to organize learning for the student and deliver it to him in a concise lecture. But research is ada-

[10] National Council of Teachers of English, *Conducting Experiences in English,* Monograph No. 8 (New York: Appleton-Century-Crofts, Inc., 1939), pp. 121, 132. Also, Kinney, Lucien, and Katharine Dresden, *Better Learning through Current Materials* (Stanford: Stanford University Press, 1949), p. 35.

mant on this point. Learning that is not reworked, reshaped, rediscovered by the learner never becomes a part of the learner and soon washes away.

In this chapter, discussion, sociodrama, and allied techniques have been presented as effective ways to engage active participation by students. Discussion is sometimes not used as a means of learning because it appears to take so much time; because the same students always seem to do the talking; and because it is difficult to measure the amount of learning. Actually discussion may, in the end, save time, and, with the right kind of leadership, participation can be distributed and the amount of learning measured.

The use of discussion inevitably involves the teacher in controversial issues. Most controversial issues can and should be discussed in the classroom, although each community will undoubtedly have its own taboos. The decision to discuss or not to discuss should be resolved on the basis of what promotes best the long-term aims of the school in the community. Thus, the kind of issue that can or cannot be discussed will vary considerably from community to community. In any community it does not take extraordinary perception to discover the tender spots, but no community prohibits discussion of all controversial issues by its teachers. As the Educational Policies Commission says: "Freedom of discussion of controversial subjects is more than a right. It is a requisite of democratic institutions and democratic ways of living."

Like discussion, sociodrama ensures active student participation. Sociodrama invites students to act out the roles of people in the social world. After a social relations problem has been posed, students take their parts without rehearsal or script. Each tries to feel, act, and talk as he imagines the real-life participants would. In this way, the teacher can determine how meaningful the content was and how well it is related to the problems of real people and what values the student holds about human relations.

The teacher also has available the allied techniques role playing, writing plays and radio scripts, and conducting conversation periods.

Selected References

Discussion

Association for Supervision and Curriculum Development. *Group Planning in Education.* Washington, D.C.: National Education Association, 1945. Many examples of teachers and students planning joint enterprises for more effective learning.

Benne, Kenneth D., Leland P. Bradford, and Ronald Lippit. *Group Dynamics and Social Action.* Freedom Pamphlet Series. New York: Anti-Defamation League of B'Nai B'rith, 1950. The principles of group discussion as basic to group action and interaction presented via a case study of a group.

Deering, Ivah. *Let's Try Thinking.* Antioch: Antioch Press, 1949. A challenging presentation of the need for skill in group solving of current problems, and how to do it.

Lasker, Bruno. *Democracy through Discussion.* New York: H. W. Wilson Company, 1949. Sets forth with graphic illustrative detail the lessons of thirty years of experience with group discussion, pointing out how difficult discussional situations were met—or might have been.

Learning through Group Discussion. Junior Town Meeting League, 400 South Front St., Columbus, Ohio, no date. A valuable, free handbook on using group discussion in classrooms.

Litchen, Ruth E. *How to Use Group Discussion.* "How to Do It Series," No. 6. Washington, D.C.: National Council for the Social Studies, 1949. A short and useful guide for the teacher.

McBurney, James H., and Kenneth C. Hance. *Discussion in Human Affairs.* New York: Harper and Brothers, 1950. Excellent basic presentation of discussion techniques.

Problem Solving. Detroit: The Citizenship Education Study, 1949. A brief and graphic presentation of the major elements in the problem-solving process basic to free discussion.

Salt, George. *Thinking Together: Promoting Democracy through Class Discussion.* Pamphlet Publications, No. 6, National Council of Teachers of English. Chicago: The Council, 1942. 26 pp. Discussion topics and techniques for use by English teachers and others with actual discussions presented as examples.

Social Leadership. Vocational Division Bulletin No. 231, Defense Training Series No. 4. Washington: U.S. Office of Education, 1945. Suggests some excellent demonstrations of discussion leadership methods; also discusses ways of developing discussion leadership skill in class members.

Controversial Issues

Clark, Delbert (ed.). *Current Affairs and Modern Education.* New York: The New York Times, Inc., 1950. Chap. 2, "Community Pressures and Controversial Issues" pp. 15-41. Problems and issues faced by teachers who bring real-life situations into classrooms.

"Controversial Issues," *Educational Leadership,* Vol. 6: entire issue (November, 1948). Theoretical and practical considerations for the handling of live social problems in teaching.

"On Teaching Controversial Issues," *NEA Journal,* 39:29 (April, 1950). Things to do and things to watch out for.

Rothstein, Edward. "The Techniques of Teaching Controversial Issues," *Social Education,* 13:82 (February, 1949). Helpful and practical suggestions for the classroom teacher.

Sociodrama

Association for Supervision and Curriculum Development. *Fostering Mental Health in our Classrooms.* 1950 Yearbook. Washington, D.C.: National Education Association, 1950. Chap. 16, "Sociodrama as an Educative Process," pp. 260-285. A good statement on the value of sociodrama.

Chapman, E. N. "Role Playing in Cooperative Retail Training," *California Distributive Educator,* 2:22-25, (Fall, 1950). Shows role of this technique in specific business-education situations.

Clark, Margaret W. "Role-Playing in a Group Guidance Class," *California Journal of Secondary Education,* 26:34-36 (January, 1951). Tenth-grade guidance class uses role playing to gain insight into some elementary psychology concepts.

Ferreira, Margaret B., Frances P. Arnold, and Doris V. Wilson. *How Girls Grow Interpreted through Creative Dramatics.* The Girls' Friendly Society, 386 Fourth Ave., New York 16, N. Y. Though this is for girls' groups, the situations and discussion of the technique can readily be adapted to mixed classes. An excellent handbook on sociodrama.

Gilchrist, Robert S., Lothar Kahn, and Robert Haas. *Building Friendly Relations.* Adventures in Education, University School Series No. 4. Columbus: Ohio State University, 1947. A good teachers' guide illustrating many new techniques, including sociodrama, for helping students develop insight into each other.

Greenleaf, Walter J. "Sociodrama as a Guidance Technique," *California Journal of Secondary Education,* 26:71-75 (February, 1951). Specific guide for classroom use of sociodrama. Gives step-by-step directions for the teacher-director.

Haas, Robert B. (ed.). *Psychodrama and Sociodrama in American Education.* Beacon, N.Y.: Beacon House, 1949. Many examples of classroom practices using these techniques.

Hendry, Charles E., Ronald Lippitt, and Alvin Zander. *Reality Practice as Educational Method.* Psychodrama Monograph No. 9. Beacon N.Y.: Beacon House, 1947.

Kay, Lillian W. "Role Playing as a Teaching Aid," *Sociometry,* 9:263-274 (May-August, 1946).

Lippitt, Ronald. "The Psychodrama in Leadership Training," *Sociometry,* 6:286-292 (August, 1943). Can be adapted to classroom leadership training.

Schuman, Claire S., and Oscar Tarcov. *. . . to Clarify Our Problems: A Guide to Role Playing.* Chicago: Anti-Defamation League of B'Nai B'rith, 1950. One of the best brief guides to role playing, providing specific step-by-step directions.

Shellhammer, Lois B. "Solving Personal Problems through Sociodrama," *English Journal,* 38:503-505 (November, 1949). Use of sociodrama in seventh-grade English to gain insight into students' problems.

"Sociodrama Workshops in Puerto Rico," *Understanding the Child,* 19:85-89 (June, 1950). The use of sociodrama for increasing teachers' understanding of children's needs.

Strauss, Bert and Frances Strauss. *New Ways to Better Meetings,* N. Y. The

Viking Press, 1950, "Role Playing." Illustrates the use and value of role playing to improve group situations.

Taba, Hilda. *Curriculum in Intergroup Relations for Secondary Schools* Washington, D.C.: American Council on Education, 1949. pp. 109-125 The use of sociodrama with interesting illustrations.

Zander, Alvin, and Ronald Lippitt. "Reality Practice as Educational Method," *Sociometry,* 7:129-151 (May, 1944). Shows the significant learning to be derived from such techniques as sociodrama and role playing.

8. Group Techniques in the Classroom

VARIETY adds zest to good teaching. There is virtually no limit to the number of teaching techniques available to the imaginative teacher. This chapter describes in detail an approach to teaching which offers a rich resource for the teacher. Group work not only provides for many kinds of new learning experiences, but also is unusually effective in deepening student understanding. The use of this technique facilitates social interchange among young people and at the same time utilizes cooperative problem-solving skills.

Two kinds of group methods will be discussed: short-run groups and long-run groups. The techniques of selecting appropriate problems for group attack, of choosing group membership, establishing a time schedule for group work, and evaluating the outcomes of group learning will be analysed. The specific problems surrounding the reporting of group accomplishment will be described. Special consideration will be given to the panel discussion as a means of reporting group thinking.

What Are Group Techniques?

By group techniques we mean any kind of classroom activities that involve interaction among students in cooperative enterprises. The activity might well be the project in which two or three students are interested; it might involve the whole class as a group under student guidance; it might mean the committee on a community study or a class party. In these group techniques students work for a common goal that they have selected and planned. Once the plans are carried out, they evaluate themselves, using the teacher as an expert or consultant.

In the previous chapter we presented the techniques essential in treating the class as a total group, namely, in using group discussion and the related technique of sociodrama. In this chapter the emphasis will be upon the smaller group composed of three to seven individuals in which the teacher's primary role is in setting the stage. The group leadership devolves upon the student participants.

Before describing some of the specific elements of this technique, let us watch some "group" work in a classroom.

> It was third period. While Mr. Betts was introducing the topic for the day, he noticed a livening of interest. At one point, several hands were raised at once, and several voices called out ideas without waiting for the teacher to give them the floor. There seemed to be the spark here for starting a good discussion. Mr. Betts raised his hand for quiet and suggested that since this seemed like a very vital topic to many in the class, and since everyone obviously couldn't talk at once, he would let them discuss their ideas together in groups of five for the next ten minutes. At the end of that time, he would ask for one report from each group (there would be about six such groups in the class) giving their consensus regarding the topic.
>
> He set up his groups of five according to the natural seating of the class. Their desks were movable, and they were able to make small circular groupings all over the room. Some groups were quite close together, but so intent were the students on giving their ideas they hardly noticed each other. Mr. Betts reminded them that they were to talk as quietly as possible but so that all could hear, and he would help them keep quiet if need be.
>
> He walked round the room, giving a fact here, helping provide a word there, watching the level of participation in each group. He noticed that Mary said nothing at all in her group; in fact, she looked ill and tired. Joe was talking volumes in his meeting, but Sidney managed to tell him to keep still since everyone wanted a chance, too. In Bill's group, the students generously suggested that he report their views since he was a shy, quiet, but pleasant boy. Thus, Mr. Betts learned some things about his students that no written examination would reveal.

At the end of the ten minutes the talk was still going strong. Only one group had organized their ideas; so Mr. Betts gave them all five more minutes. When time was called, each group's representative presented the views of his group. A list was made on the board, and soon it was evident where the real issues lay, what the class as a whole thought. Mr. Betts had material for leading further total class discussion on the problem, skillfully pointing out how more study and research would help everyone in determining what was the best solution of the issues.

What kind of a class was that? Was it biology, history, or art? Actually, it could have been any of these, and many more. In biology the class might have become interested in the problem of heredity vs. environment; in history, whether political or economic problems were basic causes of the Civil War; in art, the question of popular taste as against critics' judgment about what constitutes a work of art. This technique is sometimes called the "buzz group" technique. The name, of course, comes from the hum of conversation that arises in a room where many people are talking together. It has been used successfully in schools and in groups of adults as well. Is such a use of classroom time appropriate? Does it increase students' learning? How can a teacher utilize this technique?

Why Group Work?

A number of studies have explored the efficiency of group learning. In one, an attempt was made to see if individuals or groups were able to solve arithmetical problems more accurately and more efficiently.[1] In this experiment, a number of graduate students in social psychology were first assigned the task of solving some problems individually, then, as members of five groups of four members each, were asked to solve similar problems as a group. The outcomes are interesting: groups seemed assured of a much larger percentage of correct answers than individuals because the group was able to reject incorrect answers and check errors. It was found that other members of the group would tend to detect the incorrect suggestion made by another member. Groups did not err so soon as does the average individual. From this, it would seem that where there are more heads, there are likely to be more chances for arriving at a good answer. Students thus could learn correct, rather than incorrect methods and solutions.

[1] Shaw, Marjorie E., "A Comparison of Individuals and Small Groups in the Rational Solution of Complex Problems," in *Readings in Social Psychology*, edited by T. M. Newcomb and E. L. Hartley (New York: Henry Holt & Company, 1947), pp. 314-315.

In the famous studies of boys' groups under different types of leadership,[2] one group of boys was helped to plan and work cooperatively, setting their own goals as a group, choosing from several alternatives the best method to proceed, selecting their own work partners. The quality of the work was superior to other types of work situations, even though the quantity was not so great. It was also found that in this group atmosphere the boys liked each other better, liked the work they were doing better, and liked the leader better.

Since learning ultimately can only be seen to the degree that behavior is modified, it is interesting to note that group decisions have a more significant effect upon behavior than do other learning situations.[3] A study of food habits during the war illustrates the point. Housewives were instructed, via lecture and via group discussion and decision, regarding the importance of eating some of the less desirable portions of meat. Housewives who participated in group decisions followed the decisions of the group. Housewives who were given the lecture material were much less apt to do as directed.[4]

Some of the most striking effects of group membership on learning are reported in the literature on group therapy. Alcoholics Anonymous is one familiar utilization of the principle that group membership can help individuals, where isolation and punitive or even medical treatments will not. The same idea is suggested for school practice in the prevention of delinquency. It has been found that the delinquent is often the student who is failing in school. This failure may have its roots in social rather than academic participation. The youth who is outside the group, outside society, tries to hit back. The teacher needs to assist these "peripheral" youth to find something to which they belong, a place where they are needed and where their contributions are valued and respected.

We have implied a number of reasons for employing group techniques. Now let us state these directly and suggest some others:

[2] Lippitt, Ronald, and R. K. White, "An Experimental Study of Leadership and Group Life," in *Readings in Social Psychology,* edited by T. M. Newcomb and E. L. Hartley (New York: Henry Holt and Company, 1947), pp. 315-329.

[3] Many of the concepts from which the specific suggestions for practice have been derived have been formulated by the group of social psychologists working with the National Training Laboratory for Group Development, now associated with the National Education Association Department of Adult Education. For an excellent collection of basic writings see *Human Relations in Curriculum Change,* Bulletin No. 7, Illinois Secondary Curriculum Program, 1950. (to be published by Dryden Press in book form, 1951)

[4] *The Problem of Changing Food Habits,* Bulletin No. 108, 1943, National Research Council, Washington, D. C.

1. Group learning may be more efficient than individual learning.
2. The quality of work is often improved by cooperative effort.
3. In a group, one is more apt to accept what the group accepts, rather than accept something one is told by one in a position of authority.
4. Leadership is learned through helping one's associates obtain the goals important to them.
5. Each person needs to belong to a group. The delinquent is often one who has been unable to adjust to a normal social group of his peers.
6. An individual will be more willing to do significant work if the work is part of a meaningful plan which he has had a share in building.
7. Because of the small families of today and the increased mobility of families, it is difficult for individuals to develop social skills and to make significant contacts with others unless helped through the school or other social agency.
8. The recognition for achievement accorded by one's peers is more meaningful in the long run than the praise of a superior.
9. Individual variations in abilities, needs, interests, and goals are so different that no one general requirement in method or content of learning can suffice.
10. Group work assists young people in establishing sound heterosexual relations.

This last reason for group work needs some discussion. Typically, boy meets girl for serious discussion in our modern culture only under the most exceptional circumstances. The contact is usually restricted to a few undercover words in class, a brief conversation in the hall, and then the bantering chit-chat at the soda fountain. Instead of criticizing the lack of significant ties binding husband and wife or the readiness with which young people contemplate divorce today, it might be better to examine some of our teaching practices to see whether the fault might not lie there. Until recently we have made it very difficult indeed for boys and girls to talk normally together about important things.

We need to provide in all our classroom situations more and more opportunity for young people to learn about each other as they try together to understand the problems of modern civilization. Group work can assist adolescents in their consideration of important human relations. In pioneer life the mutual sharing by man and wife of the burden of solving important problems contributed to the solidarity of the family. Practice in this skill should be provided by the modern high school.

But what is life like in many classrooms? Each student is a separate island. Little real interchange is permitted, though much goes on that is under cover. The students learn together the same common material, some lagging far behind, others impatiently surging ahead of the rest. This dead level of learning has earned many high schools the condemnation of teaching for mediocrity. Such criticism need no longer be merited. One of the contributions of approaching teaching as a problem in "group" learning is to meet the varieties of personality present in every classroom in terms of intellectual, social, and emotional differences.

Setting the Stage for Group Work

In beginning group work we note the importance of knowing what the experience of the class has been in previous classrooms. Have the students done committee work before? Do they know what the responsibilities and functions of a chairman are? Have they ever helped each other to find answers to the same problem with the encouragement of the teacher? The usual high-school class has had some experience with committees, where students led special school activities, particularly assembly programs. Few, however, have experienced the kind of group work that is being discussed here. Let us set up, then, some of the basic principles that underlie the use of group work as it is conceived here before we proceed to a description of how it may be used in a real classroom:

1. The goals for the group activity are set jointly by teachers and students.
2. The group is mainly concerned with doing together something that as individuals they could not accomplish as well.
3. The group is able to choose its own leadership after a short period of introduction to group methods.
4. The group is responsible for its own members, helping them where necessary or disciplining them with the help of the teacher.
5. The group is able to look at its activity objectively and evaluate how well it has worked toward achieving its goals.
6. The group provides an opportunity for each member to make a contribution in terms of his ability in accomplishing the group goal.

Where the teacher can see that there has been little previous opportunity to learn to work together, it is wise to start very slowly. The teacher begins, in a new class, with assigning some minor jobs to a few reliable students. As these become routine, he may suggest from time to time that a student lead the class discussion in a topic where he has special knowledge. A Spanish teacher, for instance, may allow a student to lead class discussion about some of the cultural aspects of Mexico where the student has perhaps lived or traveled. As the occasion arises, the teacher may select three students to carry out some special project, such as presenting a topic to the class as a whole. This first group project may be so designed that the students cooperating in it can meet with the teacher after class so he can give them special aid as they try out a new venture.

Some teachers find it helpful to demonstrate group procedures before the class. The first time the teacher himself may act as chairman. In a later demonstration a student may replace the teacher as chairman. The teacher may then become a group member to help demonstrate how a good group member acts. Still later the teacher may drop out of the demonstration group entirely and assist the rest of the class in noting the group processes.

Other teachers may use tape recordings of radio discussion groups to demonstrate procedures, or they may record on tape their own group discussions for later analysis. Assistance can also be obtained by teachers from the Junior Town Meeting League of Columbus, Ohio.[5] The organization provides without cost pamphlets and other materials on group discussion.

Once the stage has been set, and the teacher feels relatively assured that a cooperative group enterprise is possible for the whole class, he will be able to develop group projects both over a short-run period of time and over a longer period of time. These two kinds of group activities will be described separately below.

It is important that the *first group experiences be successful and enjoyable.* Personalities are tender; adolescents in particular are tremendously awkward as they try to make friendships. The teacher must go slowly and carefully at first, helping these awkward yet tremendously intent youngsters learn a new technique of human relation. Sometimes using the concept of the "team" helps to set the psychological pattern of cooperation in an intellectual atmosphere. This is a familiar term. The students can readily see how on a team each must help the others or none can succeed. The idea of "teamwork" has been bred into them from earliest days of group play. It is appropriate in the classroom also, where joint efforts are important. Again, teamwork develops an appreciation of the value of differences among students as they contribute to group goals and provides for acceptance of the variation in each person's role in the group.

After several projects by selected groups have been seen by the class, the teacher might discuss with the class the value of providing everyone with a chance to work on a group project. By this time the teacher has tried to create in the class the general idea that it is more important that we help each other than that anyone hoards his knowledge for himself.

[5] 400 South Front St., Columbus 15, Ohio.

How does the teacher develop this idea? His own words and actions are the clue. The teacher may say, "This is your class as much as mine; what do *you* want to do in studying the next unit?" Or, "Marjorie, you have done a great deal outside of class on your hobby of stamp collecting. I think the class would enjoy your telling them some of the historical background of our present-day stamps." Or, "Many of the class missed the point on that last exam. Let's ask George and Mary, who saw the point of the last question, to explain it to the class." Or, "Now this homework assignment is pretty tough so I am going to suggest that you discuss it now in small groups and see whether by exchanging all our ideas everyone in the class can do a fine job on it."

These comments point to a kind of activity that encourages sharing and working together, that says that knowledge is the important thing, not any one person's secret information. As the teacher manages to impress this sharing on students, through his own actions and attitudes, it becomes relatively easy to move into the more complicated group activity described at the beginning of this section.

Short-Run Groups

If the teacher wishes to use the "buzz group" idea, it is important that at first he plan it very carefully. The selection of a live issue is crucial. Find some topic that will excite most of the students to express an opinion. The most likely topics are those nearest home: "Can you learn more in school than on a job?" "Should women work outside the home after they have children?" "Should girls be allowed the same freedom as boys?" "If boys are drafted for a war, should girls be also?" And similar topics. It is wise to avoid any topic that will produce a silly, superficial response. It is also wise to be aware that some classes will be very serious about a problem that to another class may provoke raucous laughter.

After the issue has been clearly stated, the class can be divided; a group of four or five is about the maximum for this type of short discussion. It is a good idea to put on the board the question around which their discussion should center.

The *time* element should be clear, for it keeps the group members vigorously at work. The time for a buzz group should be as short as possible, commensurate with allowing the members to explore the topic. It is better, however, to allow too little time than too much, because, after a topic is exhausted, students easily turn to horseplay and noise. The teacher may have to "call time" before he planned if his prediction of the time necessary to discuss the topic is erroneous. He will then, of course, say to the class that he overestimated how long it would take them to get their ideas in order and that actually they did not need as long as he had expected. It is also possible that the time will have to be revised in the opposite direction. If the teacher has given the groups five minutes to arrive at a statement of their position on a given issue, but discovers that there is too much to be said before group consensus can be reached, then he can announce, "This topic gets bigger all the time; let's take another ten minutes for the group discussion."

Each group should have a reporter who is appointed by the teacher or by the group. The use of a reporter from each group channels the group's thinking. It also adds the requirement that what the spokesman says is agreeable to all members, thus furthering the need for group consensus. In order to facilitate the choice of reporter when groups are still new to this technique, the teacher can follow this procedure. When the buzz groups are announced, the teacher can walk down the aisles, count off the class by fives, and hand to one student a small card, or a sheet of paper on which the buzz-group topic has already been indicated. That individual then acts as the group reporter. Choosing at random helps to draw in some of the more silent and peripheral students. Sometimes it will be necessary to select as reporter some student who will help move the group along, but not dominate it by talking too much himself. In the first trials, the student reporter may need to be someone relatively secure in addressing the class.

To facilitate reporting, the teacher should designate the groups by number immediately after they are organized. "This five will be group 1, and this group of five here will be group 2," and so on. Then when the time comes to call for reports, the possibility of confusion is lessened. Sometimes it helps to place a seating chart on the blackboard and indicate what sections of the room will be used for each group.

We have mentioned group "consensus" in talking about the product that the buzz group is seeking in these short-run discussions. By "consensus" we mean that the group has a general acceptance of the point of view expressed. The teacher will want to talk over the concept of consensus *after* one or two such short group experiences have been provided. After all, it seems somewhat foolish to have a group of five students vote on each minor point. In such a process a "majority" of three is meaningless. Discussion should be encouraged until a genuine middle ground is achieved. However, the teacher and the class should consider the problem of the minority position. If in a small group like this one or two students feel very strongly about some point, so strongly that consensus is impossible, they should have the right and the opportunity to register their different point of view. The reporter for the group will then include a minority report.

When the time set for the groups is up, the teacher and probably later a student chairman will call for a report from each group. A student can be posted at the blackboard to tally the results or to list the various ideas expressed. The individual calling for the reports will want to ask for a full report from one of the groups. After this report, the chairman will ask, "Does group two have anything to *add?*" if this is a problem in which the listing of ideas is important. If it is a two-sided debate, then each group would of course merely report, "Our group felt we should support the X Bill in Congress," and another group would say, "Our group felt we should not support the X Bill." For those problems where one can list ideas, as in the support of a particular bill, the groups might give reasons for or against such support. Then, as each group reports, the chairman asks for "additional contributions." This method speeds the reporting and reduces repetition.

After the reports are made, the teacher will want to summarize what has been stated, and perhaps indicate additional areas for general discussion, group discussion, or individual study in reference material. When group activity has been successfully used, it is also wise to ask the class how they liked the experience. The teacher will want to ask for suggestions of ways to improve such group discussions in the future. If the class responds well to the technique, the teacher may ask a committee to draw up some rules for future buzz-group discussions. These could be posted, so that the class is led on the way to self-discipline.

> A substitute teacher was faced with a class of seniors who had been studying some of the problems of vocational selection. Although the substitute was entirely new to the class, and the class to him, he felt that anything would be better than the usual teacher-student battle that goes on when a substitute comes in. So he took the class by surprise. He asked them to shift their chairs into groups of five, and to list as a group some of the problems they felt they would face when they entered the world of work after June. The class took up the discussion with vigor, and, when the time was up, a very provocative list of problems had been put on the board. The class was led into a discussion of "Which problem is most important now?" and then, "Which problems can we do something about ourselves, and which can we get help on from the school?" Next day, when the substitute returned, the class demanded another buzz session.

The short-run group in the form of the buzz-group technique as we have outlined may be used in other ways as well. Early in the term buzz groups may discuss questions that they would like to have answered in the course. Sometimes when students have few questions regarding the course, the teacher may outline the variety of possible topics to be covered. This list should be longer than can be taught. The problem for the groups then is to select those that they would like to study. This device gives the students a chance to think critically about the course work ahead, gives them a feeling of proprietorship in the course work to be covered, and also provides a chance early in the semester for them to meet others in the class.[6]

Another use for the short-run group is in working out routine problems or exercises together. For instance, students may spend a part of a period selecting from a list the sentences that they consider most "vivid." Or they might grade the quality of a set of anonymous compositions, giving them significant practice in critical judgment. The same sort of group situation is useful in judging various musical compositions, artistic productions, lettering charts, floor plans, breakfast menus, recreation habits, propaganda slogans, and the like. One teacher has utilized this device by allowing students in groups to correct their examinations together. Where morale is high and competition for grades has been de-emphasized, this procedure minimizes the chance and the need to cheat or fabricate. It also provides the students with a chance to learn the right answer, not just to find out theirs was wrong.

Short term group activity may be devoted to the group game. This is particularly useful in those classes where a certain amount of drill is needed. The imaginative teacher can devise simple games (see pages 236 to 242) that small groups may play while the rest of the class is doing other activities. Or the whole class may play them together in small groups. This latter method ensures maximum practice for all, not merely for the most apt or the most backward. It also makes routine drills somewhat more palatable.

The small group activity, then, lasting for not more than one school period and usually for less may be used (1) to discuss some provocative issue; (2) to select course material or help plan future course work; (3) to do exercises together; and (4) to take part in drill games.

In setting up the short-run groups, the natural seating of the students should be the first basis used. Students ought to be allowed to

[6] Van Hoesen, Ralph, "Pupil-Teacher Planning in the Social Studies and Its Psychological Aspects," *School Review*, 58:29-37 (January, 1950).

sit near their friends. Communication is easier with those we know. After the students are used to the group idea, the teacher may suggest that students join other groups. He may actually reshuffle the class from time to time so that groups are better balanced. In this way, too, students are weaned away from their own small clique or friendship group. The use of a sociometric questionnaire (see Chapter 19) is of great help in setting new group patterns, though not quite so vital for the short-term group as for the more extensive group projects to be described below.

Can this sort of group activity, as well as more elaborate ones, be used in rooms where the seats are fastened to the floor? In rooms where every desk is filled and there are no empty corners? These conditions make group work harder, but not impossible. Of course it is better if there are small tables and chairs around which students can sit. But even with fixed chairs, groups of four can be set up relatively easily by asking students to twist around in their chairs. This they do with facility most of the time, anyway! The teacher may let a group gather around his desk, thus freeing some seats so that a few feet of space separate the groups.

A final word from a teacher who used buzz techniques:

> It is important to realize that introduction of group work techniques must be gradual. The first time we had a buzz session, the class acted as though I were eccentric. The second time, however, they were enthusiastic. In evaluating their group work afterward they felt they had achieved much more than they would have in discussion with the entire class. Their main conclusion was that discussion in small groups helped to clarify their thinking.[7]

Arranging for Long-Term Group Activities

In the long-term activity, groups attack extended problems and work together until the completion of the project. When students are in such groups for several days, weeks, or even months, new problems of social relationships appear. What kinds of projects can be undertaken? How should the groups be organized? How can the teacher and the groups differentiate within the group between those who did the most work and the best work and those who did a minimum of work or fell down on their responsibility entirely? These are vital questions in using long-term group work in the classroom.

What kinds of projects are suitable to long-term group activity? To answer this question we need to see how the class can be

[7] Virginia Hearn, teacher, San Jose, Cal.

grouped. There are many ways of dividing a class, but these categories include most of the bases for setting up groups:

1. Interest.
2. Ability.
3. Special skill.
4. Personal differences (national origin of parents, place of residence in the school district, travel experiences, amount of classwork accomplished, and the like).
5. Sociometric information (natural social groupings).
6. Arbitrary decision (all those sitting in a given row, everyone in the first five seats, equal parts of the class alphabetically, or some other plan).
7. Student choice (student chairmen who choose own groups).

Some projects would fall naturally into one of these headings. For instance, some projects depend on differences in *interests* on the part of students. Some projects need special *abilities.* Writing a radio script might be a group project in which some students would do the writing because of superior ability; others would do the sound effects; others would check the factual information needed; others would take care of the electrical equipment for recording. Groups may be arranged *in different ability levels.* In mathematics the group may be divided according to different levels of skill or achievement. Students may be separated according to reading ability in a social-studies class and given different textbooks accordingly. Under the fourth category would come groups where some *common factor,* such as vocational choice, would reveal important differences. Each subgroup may be challenged to relate current learning to their future goals. *All boy* and *all girl* groups, where different points of view might be expected, are very interesting to young adolescents.

Sociometric tests provide a fifth way of dividing a class. This technique is discussed in Chapter 19. It gives the teacher important clues about which students already belong to a natural group, which ones are outside the central groups, and which are rejected by the class in general. Using this knowledge, the teacher can arrange groupings for special guidance purposes, particularly in helping those outside the group to learn group skills and become known to those on the inside.

Arbitrary groupings make it possible for the teacher to rearrange the usual working groups in the classroom. Thus, if the same students seem always to be together, are not developing a wider range of acquaintance, some mechanical device for grouping may help to lead them out of their own tight circle. Such devices as alphabetical procedures, arrangement by rows, lining the class up by height and counting off may help to widen student's range of friends without seeming to be directed at any one person or group.

This analysis of the many ways to divide a class demonstrates one important function of group activity. Used imaginatively, for different kinds of projects, these groupings make it possible for a student to achieve recognition for some particular skill or attribute or idea, allow individual differences to be met, and, finally, make it possible for all members of the class to learn to work together with every other member of the class on some common basis.

The kind of project that the group works on will, to a large extent, determine the composition of the group. Not all subject matter can be dealt with through the group process. Not all students are capable of their best work in a group, just as some students are unable to work alone. Let us look at some typical classrooms to see how teachers have used group techniques in the different subject fields.

1. Science:

A biology class was studying communicable diseases. A question arose about which parts of town were the most sanitary. The students at this union high school came from over half the county; so the question was broadened to include the whole county. By a show of hands, it was found that most of the students fell into natural groupings according to their home addresses. A map of the school district was obtained from the principal, and rough districts were drawn. All those living in a given district agreed to explore their section as to sanitary conditions. By planning with the students, the teacher was able to set up five groups of from four to six members for each section of the map. The groups were then given the remainder of the hour to list the things they thought they should look for. The next day, each group submitted its list. A master list was then compiled. The teacher suggested further reading in the text and some additional references so that the students would know how to recognize danger areas. Thus a group project was launched.

2. History:

A world history class was studying Egypt. They became interested in the kind of schools that children went to in ancient times. Students expressed interest in various phases of the problem. The teacher listed on the board some of the things they suggested as material that might be worth bringing to class. These included: what the students wore to school; what subjects they studied; what a typical school looked like; what kinds of children went to school. Some were interested in: whether there were special kinds of schools for the kings and the nobility; whether there were separate schools for boys and girls; whether their schools were better or worse than ours today. The students were asked to indicate which topic interested them most. The teacher pointed out that some topics might be illustrated by models or drawings; some might be dramatically portrayed to the class. One or two topics demanded research in the main town library, since they were very obscure.

As he looked over the names of the students who had signed up for the various topics, the teacher could easily see how the natural interests and abilities of the students had determined the group they chose. Johnny, who liked to carve wood and was interested in very little else, had chosen to work on what a typical school looked like. Polly, who designed her own dresses, chose the group on clothing worn by the students in those days. Tom, with the high IQ, chose the topic on the subjects studied, which might require work at the main library where he practically lived anyway. And so on around the class.

He noticed that several close friends chose the same topic, although only one of them could conceivably be interested in it. He also noticed that some of the youngsters from the bottom of the hill were in the same group with Mary Jane, who was a rather aloof and somewhat snobbish child from the top of the hill where the "old families" lived. The two Negro students in the class who seemed always outside of things had chosen different topics. He foresaw a chance for them to move out of the unconscious barriers that always seemed to place them together in a far corner of the room. It was planned by the class that ten minutes of each period would be allowed for the groups to show what progress had been made on their projects; to arrange after-school meetings if needed; to ask the teacher for help; and to meet other important problems. The class felt that they would need about three weeks to do the needed work. Meanwhile, the class continued its study of the Mediterranean world.

3. English:

The senior English class was very much concerned about passing the English entrance examinations for the state university. Much emphasis was therefore being placed on gaining competence in grammatical usage, reading comprehension, and facility in composition. The teacher gave the class several achievement tests in English and clearly saw the major weaknesses of each student in these three areas. He suggested to the class that he might arrange groups for them in which they could work together on these weaknesses. This seemed to the class to be a good idea. It was agreed that Tuesday and Thursday would be the days when the "problem" groups, as they were to be called, would meet together. Workbooks and special exercises would be provided by the teacher. The other days of the class would be devoted to regular class instruction in the main skills in the areas being studied.

After this plan had been operating for several weeks, the students suggested a revision. It was clear that some students were very good in one area where others were weak. It was also clear that the teacher could not get around to all the groups each period to work with them on their problems. They asked if every other time one of the better students would be assigned to the groups as a sort of teacher's aide. This meant that a number of the students did not meet with their own groups, but worked as experts with slower or less adept students. Then the situation would be reversed; a student who was skillful in grammar, might be poor in reading for understanding in poetry; then he would be given assistance by another student who had mastered this art.

As the semester progressed, many shifts in groupings occurred. The teacher kept a record of the problem groups and their memberships; he also noted those students who acted as teacher's aides. He found that almost every student had worked on at least one aspect of each skill area, and, in addition, all but five students had been able to develop sufficient proficiency in some special topic to be asked to work with a given group for one or more periods. The students felt that this had been a very interesting experience.

4. Business Law:

This illustration shows how problem solving can be accomplished through group methods. It is a report by a student teacher who tried for the first time to use these methods in his teaching. After a preliminary pep talk on "team play," the class was divided into five groups. The few boys in the class were put into the girl groups on the basis of relative aggressiveness. The quiet girls were put in with talkative ones, and high-scoring students with low-scoring ones. The first time the groups worked together, they were given one problem to solve, which took only 1½ minutes, to the surprise of the student teacher. From then on, after a few minutes of discussion of each day's work, the groups proceeded to solve the problems. It was found that the brightest students needed the most help in learning how to cooperate.

Some of the other things that this student teacher learned were: (1) interest in solving problems had increased markedly; (2) individualists were learning how to compromise with the demands of others; (3) more actual work was being done than by any other methods—more reading of the text and more problems solved; (4) short lecture periods were appreciated and the teacher obtained full attention all the time; (5) the time of the teacher could be devoted to individual problems; (6) only 5 papers needed to be graded each day instead of 25; and finally, (7) new social behaviors were emerging, cliques were dissolving, and noncooperative students were learning how to get along in the classroom with others. This approach could also work in mathematics classes.

5. Oral English (Speech):

An eleventh-grade English-history core class was working on strengthening its ability to communicate orally to a group. The teacher assigned an article to a group of five to read together, and then prepare a summary that would hit the high spots for the class. (These articles could all relate to the same topic, or short stories could be used. It would be necessary to have material that was either quite short, so that it could be read aloud to the subgroup, or to have enough copies prepared for each member to read silently to himself prior to preparing the group summary.) Then the teacher had the option of calling on anyone in the group to give the oral report. This served as a great aid to those who did not speak well before the class because they had the help of four others in the group to write the speech and their moral support in presenting it.[8]

6. Beginning and Advanced Bookkeeping:

After testing a class in advanced bookkeeping on the material they retained from their beginning class, the teacher prepared a set of problems that would involve applying old principles and learning new ones. On

[8] Robert Eaton, Social Studies Teacher, Stockton High School, Stockton, Calif.

the basis of the screening test, the class was divided into two groups, "Bookkeepers," and "Assistant Bookkeepers." As the "assistants" developed skill and understanding, they could be "promoted" to the status of bookkeepers. With this promotion went a lowering of the amount of homework expected, as a kind of "increase in pay." The same method was used later in the semester with the beginning class in bookkeeping. The slower students felt more secure as they could receive help from their classmates, and the faster students progressed as rapidly as they could. There were few absentees and no problem of cutting class. This teacher is really enthusiastic about her success.[9]

These examples show the successful use of group techniques. It must be remembered that for every report of success, there will be many trials and mistakes and failures. Some of the typical mistakes that are made are:

1. Rushing into group or committee work without careful preparation on the part of students or teacher.
2. Failure to provide needed materials. If groups are to do research, the materials of research must be available.
3. Inability of the teacher to guide the groups because of individualization of previous training. To develop group spirit, it is necessary to treat the group as a whole, but often we see only individuals, rather than group relations.
4. Projects too complicated, or too simple. If timing is wrong on the group project, the group is liable to disintegrate rather quickly.
5. Putting the wrong people together. Often a teacher needs to experiment with various ways of grouping the class before he will find out which grouping will click in his class.

Thus far some of the important general principles and techniques of using group processes in classrooms have been discussed. These general concepts apply to almost any purpose for which groups may be used.

Evaluating Group Techniques

Since this approach to learning is relatively new, it is important for the teacher to know whether it is working satisfactorily. One of the more obvious ways of evaluating the success of group methods is by a subject-matter test. Do the students know as much as one expects them to know from use of other classroom methods? If the subject matter seems to be acquired to the same extent, then one is assured of one measure of success of the group approach. What other ways of evaluation are there? Recent studies of group

[9] Wholey, Ellen J., "Room 308a—Our Classrooms Can Be Like It," *The Balance Sheet,* Vol. 3 May, 1950, pp. 395-397.

processes indicate that one important measure of success may be the extent to which the group itself can appraise its progress. That is, if the youngsters in the class stop and look at themselves as a group and report objectively about their progress, then one important new outcome has been achieved. A new growth toward adult behavior has occurred. From an objective view then comes the prescription for what might be done to make the group function better.

Through observing the behavior of his students, the teacher can sometimes tell rather accurately to what extent the group work is affecting students. If those students who previously had no friends now appear to have someone to talk with when class is over, then the groups may have had an important socializing effect. The use of sociometric questionnaires (see Chapter 19) is also extremely useful, not only in helping set up new groups, but in knowing to what extent group experiences have actually affected the social relationships of youngsters.

Preliminary to all evaluation, however, there must be some basic understanding between teacher and student about what constitutes good work. When using group techniques, the teacher might well pause, after the first classroom experience with this method. He can discuss with the class whether they enjoyed the experience, what things made it good, what things made it less than good. The basic question: What makes a good group? then becomes important to everyone. Periodic re-evaluations help the class to grow in skill and insight. *How are we doing now?* and, *What can we do to improve?* are important follow-up questions that the class could help the teacher answer.

Planning with the Class about What Constitutes a Good Group

How does one grade a group product? Here again some pupil-teacher agreement is very useful; in fact, it is mandatory. Since not everyone contributes alike to any group project, there must be room for both individual and group recognition. This can be accomplished by having a group grade on one end-product, say a report or an oral presentation, while also having an individual grade on some common assignment, such as a quiz of subject matter that the group is covering, a written report of individual reading or interviewing, and so forth. Students will be very intent on knowing how the grades will be weighted. It is therefore important to give the group product sufficient weight in the total grading to encourage the best effort of everyone. But in order to account for individual differences and other imponderables, some provision is needed for an individual assessment of growth.[10]

One interesting method of evaluating the "attractiveness" of a given group is to ask the members of the class, individually, to report how much weight they feel should be given to their group as against their individual projects. Where the groups are successful in doing a good job, the students will tend to assign more weight in the final grading; where the groups are not functioning so well, the students will wish their own individual work to get the greatest share in the total grading.

In evaluating the success of the group approach, the teacher may profitably utilize some of the following specific aids:

1. ***Meeting-evaluation form.*** At the end of a period when the groups have been meeting for some time, the teacher might use a very simple form in order to get a quick check on the level of satisfaction with their meeting:

How Good Was Our Meeting?

Name ______(or group no. or group topic)______

1. Check on the line below at the point which best indicates your feeling about your group meeting:

____

Very Good   Good   All Right   Not Very Good   No Good

2. What was the best thing about the meeting?
3. What was the main weakness of the meeting?
4. Comments and suggestions:

These forms may need to be anonymous, using only group number or project in order to protect individual respondents. After the teacher has studied them, it may be useful to give the reports to each group to review. Or a summary of the reactions of all members of the group can be reported to the individual groups or to the whole class in order to increase group morale and intergroup competition to be "the best group."

2. ***Group-participation records.*** These records of group participation may be filled in either by the teacher as he or she observes the groups, or they may be filled in by a member of the group with that special assignment. An example of a form that can be used is given below. This will help the teacher as well as the group see to

[10] For some evaluation techniques of group work, see Pearl Spinks, "Life Brought to Literature through Group Work," *English Journal*, 39:201-205 (April, 1950).

what extent certain individuals are doing either too much or too little in the group's life. Various kinds of observational forms may be devised by the class itself for special purposes.

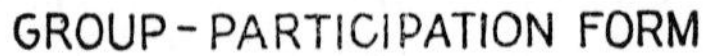

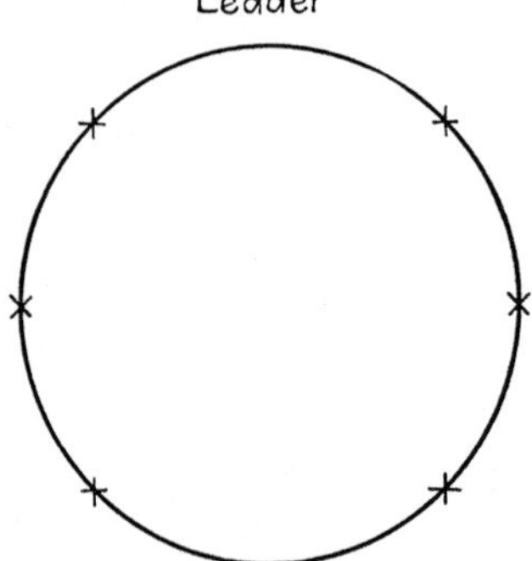

Put the names of group members around the circle. Whenever a person makes a contribution his name is checked. The group-participation pattern may be recorded in any one of three different ways:

1. Quantity-participation record: A tally mark is recorded after each person's name every time he makes a contribution. This gives a sum of contributions.

2. Quality-participation record: As each person makes his contribution, an evaluative mark is put after his name. These marks are:

plus = a contribution that aids the group thinking
minus = a contribution that delayed or interfered with group progress in thinking
zero = a remark that neither aided nor hindered—a "blah" remark
? = individual asks a question

In using this scoring method, it is often difficult for observers to put down many minus remarks, since it is likely to hurt the feelings of those so evaluated. However, if the discussion about the scoring is objective and everyone sees that a minus score might mean just lack of skill in group participation, then the negative factors may be recorded without damage to morale.

3. Group-interaction record: An arrow is used to join the names of individuals whenever they talk to anyone else. When an individual addresses a remark to the group as a whole, the arrow should point out toward the edge of the paper. The pattern recorded here is one of the most interesting, since it is possible to note whether the leader or chairman is dominating the discussion, or whether two people are carrying on a personal argument to the exclusion of everyone else. (See section on discussion for more on this aspect of discussion patterning.)

3. *Use of group observers.* It may be helpful to use group observers, assigning one student to each group as an observer. These observers then can report to the whole class on how well the group

was able to work together. The role of the observer provides excellent training. As soon as an individual is outside the group, watching only for group interaction and evidences of progress toward the goal, he learns a great deal about how to be a good group member. The task of observer is often useful with students who have particular difficulty in working with a group.

4. ***Use of group recorders.*** The function of the group recorder can be to report both to the group and to the teacher or class about the group's progress. This recorder is more than just a secretary and should be an assignment for boys as well as girls. The recorder also helps the group to think toward its goal. The leader of the group, either elected or chosen spontaneously, can help balance the discussion and include those who are least verbal. But besides the leader, one person is often needed to help keep the group thinking focused. The recorder asks such questions as: "Now what is the issue we are discussing?" "Is this an accurate statement of what we decided to do?" "I am not sure that we covered the point raised by John a while back regarding. . . ." Thus, he or she helps keep the group moving forward. From the record made in this fashion, the teacher as well as the group has a sense of where it is going, and how.

5. ***Methods of appraising individual participation.*** Often the class as well as the teacher may be dissatisfied with giving a whole group the same grade for the group report or group product, whatever that may be. It is obvious that some students will do better work and more work than others. As a method of helping to assess the work that is done in the groups, as well as appraising individual efforts, teachers may ask the members of the group to evaluate each other. Each may also evaluate his own progress. A form similar to that given here may be used.

The teacher will find it most useful to develop such a rating form with the assistance of the total class. When the students aid in building such evaluative tools, they are learning some very important lessons in social skills. In addition, they are learning to discriminate among ideas to establish sound values, and to view behavior—their own and others—objectively. It is easier for students in the class to fill in such a rating form intelligently if the items and the form itself have been phrased and designed by them. The words are their words—the ideas are phrased in terms understandable to the class members, and it is clear to them just what it is they will do with the rating form. Students often fail in following directions, filling in workbooks, completing exercises because they have no sense of re-

Members of the Group	Effort	Leadership	Quality of Work	Coopera-tion
1.				
2.				
3.				
4.				
5.				

DIRECTIONS: In the spaces after each name, put a letter grade to indicate how well, in your opinion, each member of your group demonstrated the particular item listed. Include a grade for yourself in each category.

sponsibility for the materials. Opportunities such as those provided in building evaluative rating scales help to develop this important feeling of responsibility for learning.

Reporting on the Group Project

While some of the long-term groups described in this section will not have anything to report to the rest of the class (for instance, the problem-solving groups in the business-law class), others need to share with their classmates the results of their research. Experience with group reports has been gratifying wherever the groups have been encouraged to try new ways of educating their classmates. The following steps should be taken with the class prior to group reporting:

1. Set a deadline for groups to report. Some groups may report earlier than others, or all groups may be asked to be ready for reporting by a certain date. This date may be shifted forward or back depending on the progress of the groups in obtaining the needed information or performing the assigned tasks.
2. Agree on the function of the group report. If the report is to inform, then the group must emphasize facts, must seek ways of discriminating between important and unimportant facts, should find media for presenting factual material so all can see it at once, such as graphs, charts, slides. If the report is to stimulate discussion, then a panel, a debate, a dramatic introduction of some sort is called for.
3. Discuss what it means to educate others. The class will need very

often to analyze the difference between that which is educational and that which is merely novel, entertaining, or startling. Turn the thinking of the class upon what their classmates *need* and *want* to know.

4. Encourage originality. Point out the mis-educative effects of a dull, boring, and confused presentation. Suggest some things that groups can do to enliven their report and attract the interest of the class.

Some tenth grade students who were reporting on their vocational choice, elementary school teaching, recognized that they were shy and fearful about facing their classmates. Therefore they borrowed the school recording machine, and, in the privacy of a quiet room, they merely conversed about their findings. The next day in class the recorded report had a freshness and vitality that pleased everyone.

5. Review the material on good oral reporting. Since the success of many group reports will depend on the skill of the members in oral presentation, some class discussion of oral report forms is very useful.

6. Arrange for responsibility for evaluation of information contained in the report. It should be clear just what the class audience will be asked to recall as a result of the presentation. The teacher may announce that the group will make up exam questions on the basis of its reports, that he will himself take this responsibility, or that designated members of the class will be asked to make up questions for a later quiz. Or, the class may be directed to take notes on the presentation, or to summarize the main points presented by the group. This is a vital aspect of ensuring class attention to the report, but the teacher will want to be careful not to make the audience so anxious about every minor fact that they spoil the major points the group is seeking to get across.

7. Designate clearly the teacher's role during the group report. Sometimes the teacher may request a few moments at the end of the report to add or summarize or emphasize some point the group may have overlooked. Or the teacher may want to do a brief evaluation of the report. Once in a while a discussion gets so lively or a report is so amusing that the class gets somewhat out of hand; then the teacher should step in. If a group member ties up completely with stage fright the teacher may want to come to his rescue rather than leave it up to a chairman.

Remember that it is not always necessary for a group to report directly to the class. Sometimes too much time is taken in listening to other students report. The use of the group report should be a significant activity, and each report must be carefully worked out. Sometimes using bulletin board displays or circulating a written report is a satisfactory substitute for the oral report. Too frequent group reports can become monotonous and may be as inefficient as too few.

Since the panel discussion is used so frequently as a method of group reporting, this technique will be discussed in some detail in the next section.

Panel Discussions as a Special Method for Reporting Group Accomplishment

Panel discussion is one of the methods of imparting new knowledge through group presentation. A panel usually is composed of three or four persons who have made a special effort to be informed on various phases of a problem; they are the experts. It is their function to share their expert knowledge with the audience, who may have opinions on the subject, but lack specific information and facts. A panel may do one of two things: it may increase the interest of the audience in the topic and stimulate a desire to enter the discussion; or it may be a series of short speeches as a result of which the audience is less interested in the topic than before. Certainly our hope would be to avoid the latter. Probably most of us have sat through panel discussions that were very far from being discussions at all. Either the panel members were too ill-informed to have anything to say or were determined to give a speech rather than contribute to a discussion.

How can we set up a panel discussion that really stimulates wider learning on the part of the audience? The teacher who would use the panel-discussion technique probably can help his students most by first discussing what the panel ought to do, then having a panel presentation, and finally appraising the result to see how it might be done differently the next time. This "trial by fire" approach serves two purposes: (1) it helps the teacher see the level of competence of his students in order to *train them further* in the necessary skills; and (2) it brings the students into an active role in developing their own skills and setting their own standards for adequate performance.

The preliminary training for a panel discussion involves some understanding between teacher and students about the purpose of the discussion. If a group has developed some special knowledge in an area of importance to the whole class, it may be feasible to have a panel presentation. Thus the purpose is to "share expert knowledge." How can this best be done? Primarily, the teacher will want to guide the students toward establishing a problem basis for the presentation of their special information. Perhaps they have been studying health problems in the United States. It would be possible, of course, to have four separate topics presented: trends in major diseases, prevention of disease, the government's role in this field, health education. Each topic in itself is of some interest, but given as four speeches, the topics could be intolerably dull and incoherent. It would be better to pose a problem such as, "How healthy are we Americans?" and then have the experts discuss this problem before the class. The problem-solving sequence is then the framework for the panel presentation, and a genuine discussion occurs that will stimulate audience interest. The purpose of the panel may be to present different sides of a problem; but here again, set speeches will inhibit the development of lively interest. The pattern that has been found stimulating on such radio programs as the Chicago Round Table might well be brought into class to help in training panel members.

In preparing for a panel presentation, the members should have clearly in mind the specific contributions that they wish to make. It is the responsibility of the panel chairman or moderator to know what each panel member wishes to contribute. It is then the function of the chairman to see to it that the different members are allowed to make their contributions at the appropriate times during the discussion. Finally, the panel chairman senses the right time to throw the discussion open to the floor and invite audience comment and questions. When panels are used in classrooms, the teacher usually tries to get student leadership for the panel chairman or moderator. However, it might be advisable if the teacher acted in this capacity until the pattern of panel discussion was understood by the class; then leadership can be passed on to the students.

The panel serves an excellent function in helping develop oral skills in many different kinds of classrooms. The teacher will need to work with each group of students and the class as a whole in building up a series of criteria for effective presentations of oral material. It is often useful to have two or three students especially assigned to the task of observing the panel discussion for presentation effectiveness and to make a report at the end of the hour to the whole class as to how well this panel functioned. With such student evaluations, the stress should be placed on "These things were particularly good," and "These things might be improved next time." Such problems as talking to the windows, slavish reading of notes, dull and uninterested reporting, mispronunciation of words, talking too much and too long, boring the class, should concern the student evaluators.

The panel provides an opportunity for students to make and use their own audio or visual materials. An effective panel often uses graphic presentation of complicated data, then each student speaker can point to the implications of these facts which remain vividly before the audience the whole time. Thus, a panel can utilize student talent beyond effective oral speaking; students who can paint, or letter, or even just paste pictures neatly on a background. Models, charts, graphs, special displays, exhibits, all may be utilized as part of a panel presentation.

The panel is a very important method of focusing the kind of long-range group projects discussed in the preceding section. Students who have worked for some time as a group collecting a body of information or knowledge, will want to share it with others, if only to show what a lot of work they have done! However, days of group reports can be very dull indeed. It is important that the teacher plan to have a group report, followed by some other class activity, then another report, rather than subjecting the class to one report after another. It is also useful to encourage groups to use original and different methods of presenting their material, so that the panel presentation is only one of several possibilities, rather than just the only one.

Summary

Learning with others is an important pathway to better understanding of how to live with others. In group learning adolescents may learn not only the subject matter of the curriculum, but the skills of working in a social group.

Although the significance of individual achievement in learning must never be forgotten, our high schools have for too long promoted this learning in isolation from fellow learners. The very fact that young people so successfully evade our dicta "Do your homework by yourself"; "Do not help your neighbor on his experiment"; and so forth, demonstrates that in some ways they are wiser than we in recognizing the gains from mutual help and discussion. But using group techniques in a classroom requires more than merely setting up committees; it involves deliberate manipulation of social relations to maximize individual adjustment and group achievement. Careful planning by the teacher with the class and with each small group is necessary for successful utilization of the principles of group dynamics.

Selected References

Association for Supervision and Curriculum Development. *Toward Better Teaching.* 1949 Yearbook. Washington, D.C.: The Association, 1949. Chap. 3, "Promoting Cooperative Learning." Ways in which group experiences can be utilized in many kinds of classroom situations.

Bergh, Donald. "Planning in the Core Class," *Educational Leadership,* 8:208-214 (January, 1951). Describes the use of a planning group of students to help direct classroom experiences; focus is on helping the group itself function best.

Bernstein, Saul. *Charting Group Progress.* New York: Association Press, 1949. 24 pp. A brief and useful guide to methods of helping groups see where they are going and how well they are doing.

Bradford, Leland D., *et al.* "Group Dynamics in Education," a series in *NEA Journal,* 1948-1949. Reprinted under the above title, by Division of Adult Education, NEA, Washington, D.C. The theory and practice of group situations from several different vantage points: classroom, individual student, faculty committee.

Buxbaum, Edith. "Transference and Group Formation in Children and Adolescents," *Psychoanalytic Study of the Child.* New York: International Universities Press, 1945. I, 351-365. A different and stimulating view of the meaning of "belonging" in the growth of the individual.

Cunningham, Ruth, and Associates. *Understanding Group Behavior of Boys and Girls.* New York: Bureau of Publications, Teachers College, Columbia University, 1951. A major contribution to understanding group life in the classroom and how teachers utilize these understandings in directing learning.

Langer, Ruth. *We Work in Group.* A Curriculum Resource Guide for Teachers, 10th Grade Common Learnings, Mimeographed. St. Paul (Minn.) Public Schools, Curriculum Bulletin No. 36, September, 1950. An excellent resource unit showing how a consideration of group life in American democracy can be organized and developed.

Lewin, Kurt. *Resolving Social Conflicts.* New York: Harper & Brothers, 1948. Excellent theory on various aspects of group and intergroup relations by a very stimulating mind in modern psychology.

Maas, Henry S. "Understanding Group Processes," Chap. 17, in *Fostering Mental Health in Our Schools,* 1950 Yearbook. Washington, D.C.: Association for Supervision and Curriculum Development, NEA, pp. 286-299. A stimulating general statement regarding the role of group relations as basic to sound educational programs.

Naas, Norman. "Group Work: Popular Feature of Social Living Course," *Clearing House* 25:147-148 (November, 1950). A brief report on how and when group work can be used in an average classroom situation.

Slavson, S. *An Introduction to Group Therapy.* New York: The Commonwealth Fund, 1943. Describes the dramatic effect of special group situations on individual adjustment.

Strang, Ruth. "Prevention of Delinquency through Guided Group Experience," Chap. IV in *Juvenile Delinquency and the Schools,* Forty-seventh Yearbook, Part I, National Society for the Study of Education. Chicago: University of Chicago Press, 1948. pp. 66-97. Excellent discussion of need for group experience in classrooms as an important contribution to normal social adjustment.

"Symposium on Group Dynamics," *National Association Deans of Women Journal* 12:99-113 (March, 1949). Good specific accounts of classroom use of group methods.

Thelen, Herbert A., and Watson Dickerman. "Stereotypes and the Growth of Groups," *Educational Leadership,* VI, 309-317 (February, 1949). Some interesting comments on how groups grow and change.

Thelen, Herbert A., and Ralph W. Tyler. "Implications for Improving Instruction in the High School," Chap. XII, in *Learning and Instruction.* Forty-ninth Yearbook, Part I, National Society for the Study of Education. Chicago: University of Chicago Press, 1950. pp. 304-333. A clear statement of the central need for well-developed group procedures for high-school classrooms.

"The Dynamics of the Discussion Group," *Journal of Social Issues,* Vol. 4, No. 2 (Spring, 1948). Entire issue devoted to basic research on interpersonal relations in a small group.

Wittenberg, R. *So You Want to Help People.* New York: Association Press, 1947. A basic text for developing sound leadership attitudes and practices.

9. Toward More Permanent Learning

MERE survival in this complex world of ours requires having ready for use a vast amount of attitudes, concepts, and skills. And one of the basic functions of the secondary schools is to develop much of this needed facility in young people. Only half the job is accomplished, however, if this facility is forgotten as soon as it is presented. How can we ensure greater retention? This is a recurrent question that pursues every teacher. In this chapter the problems of helping students develop retention through various drill, study, and review procedures will be discussed, and some useful games for drill purposes described.

Distinguishing Between Drill and Review

Review and drill may be considered supplementary concepts. *Review* may be defined as *reconsideration of learning* to deepen understanding of relationships. The separate elements of these relationships may require drill. *Drill* provides *intensive repetition* of *elements* to ensure swift, accurate response. Drill is intended to establish associations that are available without a "thinking-through" to derive them each time the associations are needed. Thus, we need to know arithmetical combinations without each time reasoning out the answer. Obviously not everything we study is a fit subject for drill. But once drill is proved to be appropriate, the learning established is retained best when it becomes part of a larger pattern of understanding. This larger pattern is furnished by review.

Perhaps this differentiation seems purely academic. It is not. Many long hours are still wasted in high-school classrooms drilling materials that are never needed as automatic responses. And still more hours are consumed drilling materials that really do need drill but failing to place the drill in a setting that will give it meaning to the student.

An example may help to make concrete the difference between review and drill. It is necessary to drill some words in spelling. But these ought to be the words needed by the student to express himself in writing. He does not need drill on words that he never uses in his writing. Even those words on which drill seems justified will only be retained correctly if they are re-used in further writing. This writing is the best kind of spelling review.

It is clear, then, that students need both drill and review. For each there are distinctive procedures. These procedures have been generalized in the following discussion so as to be applicable in most high-school classrooms.

Drill Procedures

Before considering any procedures, it is well to remember the limitations of drill:

1. All students may not need repetition of the same material.
2. The inevitable monotony of repetition may involve both teacher and student in a situation that breeds misbehavior on the part of the student and punitive or threatened counter-reactions on the part of the teacher.
3. Drill should be reserved for those few essentials in any field where automatic response is desirable.
4. If too many materials are selected for drill, not only will the content that can be treated be severely limited, but retention of materials will be poor.

If these limitations are considered, drill has an important place in learning. Here are suggested procedures for making drill efficient:

1. Select only an absolute minimum of concepts for drill, material so vital that not to learn it will seriously handicap the student. In most subjects this will be very nominal.
2. Provide drill periods in line with demonstrated individual needs. It is not necessary to have all students drill over the same material when it is

clear that some have already grasped it fully. Drill must be individualized in terms of individual needs and ways of learning.

3. Provide a setting for drill that reduces the monotony of the situation. Using games as suggested in a later section of this chapter will effectively overcome the boredom that usually accompanies drill work.

4. Space drill periods in line with research findings on spaced practice. These findings indicate that shorter periods of drill, spaced over a period of time, are more effective than longer drill periods, with longer intervals of time between them.

5. Be sure that all students realize the function of the drill procedure. The material covered should be clearly related to other aspects of the course in well-integrated fashion.

If these principles are used by the teacher in setting up drill procedures and selecting the content for drill, then many of the limitations will be overcome.

Review Procedures

Review gives meaning to drill. School content is shifting to focus on the development of attitudes and understandings. Skill development is seen as a means to this end. Students will learn to write and to read, we now believe, because writing and reading are essential tools for solving the problems of learning that are important to them; the skills themselves are only incidentally the focus of student and teacher. When the lack of skill interferes with effective solving of a problem, then we concentrate on developing that skill to the point where it can aid us in reaching our primary goal. The object of review, then, as distinguished from that of drill, is to go back over the ground covered by the class and ask such questions as these:

1. What were the major things we learned in this unit?
2. Which of these are of enduring significance to us in our lives now and later?
3. What outstanding new concepts, understandings, or processes did we encounter?
4. How did we gain insight into these new concepts? What process of problem solving did we use? How well did we use it?
5. What conclusions can we draw about our world on the basis of this material?
6. How does this material relate to what we have learned previously—this semester, last year, when we were younger?
7. What is the next step?

In essence, then, review is concerned with *What do we know?* and *What does it mean?*

How can teachers best use review? There are two major uses of review that are of basic value: One is the review that occurs daily, and the other is the review that is scheduled at the end of a psychological or logical unit of time or content.

The daily review is an important aid to students, particularly to those who learn more slowly. This review encompasses, first, a brief statement by a student or group of students to the class or to some group within it of the material covered the day before, or the assignment that had been made, or the plan that had been laid out for the succeeding day's work. This serves to recall to the whole class the setting for the day's work. When the students have five or six subjects a day, none of which have any organic relationship to any other, it is no wonder that they find it difficult to keep any one subject in order. This apparent lack of order also accounts in part for the fact that slower students may like mathematics best, even if they do poorly, because each day's work progresses inevitably from the previous day's work. In the social sciences and language arts classes, on the other hand, the sequences often involve a grasp of a larger structure in which each day's work fits. But in any field, the daily preview that involves recall of the previous day's work is a great help to the student.

Review may also occur at the end of the period. To many teachers the few minutes before the bell rings is a period of confusion and impatient waiting. Instead of losing these minutes, the teacher can prepare the class for the bell a few minutes early, ask students to review what was done in class, and agree with the group about the plan for the next day's work. Sometimes this is the strategic moment to agree on assignments for out-of-class work. The review of the day's work should include such specific items as:

1. What were the major facts or processes that we learned today?

2. Why are they important to us?

3. Are there some aspects of the material that we still do not understand?

Review at the end of a unit will cover in detail the seven questions listed on page 233. The purpose of the review should be clearly stated: Is the review in preparation for an examination or quiz? If so, what is the nature of this test? The review procedure should be related to the evaluation procedure. It is frustrating to have a review over broad concepts when the students know that they will be quizzed on specific details. Or the review may serve the function of demonstrating the over-all organization and logic of the subject matter and provide the basis for student-teacher planning of next steps.

The object of the review is, obviously, to involve all of the students in considering the subject matter covered. The maximizing of student participation in review is the crucial problem for the teacher. So often only those already well versed in the subject are able to recall what has been learned; the slower ones are left on the outside or, if asked to participate, merely reveal their ignorance. How can the participation of all be made possible? Several review procedures may be briefly described that will encourage all students to think about the larger areas of subject matter:

1. Set up a review assignment. This should be more than merely a blanket request, "Go over the last three chapters." Instead, a review assignment might be: "Make up ten quiz questions on the last three chapters." Or, "Select the five most important new ideas you obtained from this unit."
2. Set up a classroom group situation and have each group summarize together the main items in the material, or write five examination questions on the chapters read. (See chapter 8).
3. Use a classroom game for review in which students write the questions to be asked and evaluate the answers. (See the following section of this chapter.)

Probably the least effective review procedure is the recitation, the teacher–student-response situation or the oral quiz. In such a situation only the one student being quizzed by the teacher is actively involved; the others are nervously wondering what question will hit them! If the teacher, instead, uses the review period to summarize with the whole class the material covered, making liberal use of the blackboard to write down the major points agreed upon by the class, then greater involvement is possible. In this procedure the teacher may lead a class discussion whose content is the material already covered. Then the process of discussion is used and would be as follows:

1. What points did we cover in this unit of work?
2. Which ones are most important to remember?
3. What specific new information did we learn?
4. What is most important for us to remember?

In this fashion the teacher can challenge the whole class to recall what was learned and to evaluate it in terms of long-range value, and, by listing these items on the blackboard, he can provide a simple summary for all students.

Review and drill procedures are important aspects of aiding students in retaining the material learned. But these teaching devices should be used with care and discrimination, or the purposes sought will not be achieved. In the next section we will consider an approach to drill procedures through the use of games.

Games

The class had just finished a unit in Biology. It was time for review and evaluation. In preparation for this review, the teacher had placed in the front of the room a box labeled "Quiz Questions." This box had been there for a week, and the students were to write out quiz questions and put them in the box. These questions would then become part of their review work, and the best ones would be included in their unit test. It was apparent to the students that the more questions each put in, the more likely he would be to get in the test a question that he knew. With this incentive, the box became filled quickly. The period for review came; each student had a chance to draw a question from the box and give the answer orally. For this review, the class had been divided into teams, and a score was kept of right answers; by the end of the period considerable review work had been done and the class had enjoyed the whole process. The added spice of competition between the two sides of the room had increased the students' concentration on the answers.

From this description of a game in a classroom, it is easy to see why games have an important part to play in assisting the learning process. We can list some of the reasons:

1. Games break classroom routines in a pleasant way.
2. They provide an opportunity to see familiar material in a new relationship.
3. They are excellent motivation for the kind of learning where drill is needed.
4. They assist the uninterested to become part of the class in learning.
5. They are useful in review for fixing details in the students' minds: they contribute to more permanent learning.
6. They are fun.

In all classes, there is a certain amount of material that is, in itself, not very interesting—connecting a name with a date or an incident in history; spelling new words or names of objects; remembering sequences of events or processes; learning definitions. These and similar kinds of material are easily adapted to game situations. The students learn the material more readily, since the atmosphere of the classroom is encouraging rather than discouraging.

Teachers in the elementary grades have found games to be an essential part not only of learning skills and content, but in helping children work together as part of a group. In the high school, the technique is not used as much. There is an unfortunate impression that using games is "kid stuff" or "sugar coating." The attitude that learning, to be genuine, must have more unpleasant than pleasant aspects is all too prevalent in our culture. However, such an attitude is a denial of what we know about how people learn; namely, that they learn when they wish to learn; that more is learned from success than failure; that more is learned from pleasant than unpleasant experiences. It must also be remembered that high-school students are not very far removed from childhood. They enjoy many activities common to both stages of development.

Most high-school teachers who have used games in their classes have had good student response. In one remedial English class where students with repeated histories of failures in reading, writing, and spelling had been segregated, the youngsters begged the teacher to let them "fish." And what was this exciting game? A stack of cards with words written on them was placed face down on a desk. One student was the "game warden." The others, usually five or six in number, sat around the table and each drew a card in turn. The student who drew had to make up a complete sentence, and a correct one, using that word. The warden judged the sentences. And these sixteen- and seventeen-year-old boys played the game together very intently, learning a great deal about meaning in context and good usage. How much more pleasant this simple device made the exercise! Students who had balked at writing or reciting orally, who refused to do their homework in English, were very happy to "learn" their English skills through a simple little game.

The imaginative teacher can make up his own games, but here are some examples of games that can be adapted to many classes:

1. ***Who Am I?*** A ninth-grade world history class after a study of Greek and Roman history was divided into two teams, one taking the Greek historical figures and one of the Roman. Each team decided on the figures to present, one for each student. That student then gave to the other team one or two clues as to his identity; the other team was allowed a certain number of questions to help guess. If they failed to guess in the stated time after using up all their questions, they did not make a point. The teams alternated in asking each other to guess the identity of a character.

Adaptations:

Science—to guess the properties of the different chemicals; the characteristics of different kinds of insects, diseases, germs, plants.

English—to identify characters in a book; parts of speech; authors; books or poems.

Music—to identify musicians, instruments, selections from recordings.

Art—to identify artists, paintings.

Twenty Questions is a variation of the "Who Am I?" type of game. One teacher has used this method successfully: A master of ceremonies and four experts seat themselves at the front of the room. The M.C. starts the game by announcing the subject he has chosen for himself—animal, vegetable, or mineral, person, place, or idea, according to the particular class and subject. On the board, hidden from the experts, the exact item is written. The object of the game is to see whether the experts can then guess the identity of the M.C., using only twenty questions among the four of them and framing questions that can be answered directly by "yes" or "no." The class is in on the secret, since they can see what the M.C. has taken to represent. Using only four students as the questioners and a different M.C. each time lessens the possibility of confusion in the class. Fewer students are actually participating; the rest are audience. By having the M.C. and the experts represent one of two different teams previously set up in the class, the level of audience interest is raised. Scores can be kept on how often each group of four from each team is able to guess correctly within the required number of questions. The number of questions, of course, may be reduced or increased according to ability and knowledge of the class.

2. ***Football and Baseball.*** These games are very similar, merely changing the sport according to the season. Basketball and track rules can also be used.

The class is divided into two teams and a captain is chosen either by the team or by the teacher. The teacher or the students or both have previously composed a series of questions on the material the class has studied. The questions are sorted into three groups by the teacher or by a committee of students: easy, hard, very hard. In baseball, a correct answer to an easy question gives the team a one-base hit; a hard question, two bases; very hard, three bases; and some extra difficult questions can be added for home runs. Each side gets its innings; three wrong answers are equal to three outs. Then the other side is "up at bat." The role of the captain is to decide the "batting order" and what kind of a hit the student is going to try for —a one-base hit (easy question), two-base, or home run, as the case may be. The members of the team may of course want to agree with the captain about each person's probability of being successful at the level of question he is to ask for. A diamond placed on the board and a scorekeeper will assist in keeping track of the game. The teacher should be the umpire; otherwise, student squabbling over a right or wrong answer can spoil the game. It is important to establish the rules clearly before the game starts. The students invariably know the rules of these games very well, so it is not difficult to clear up the possible points of controversy. In baseball, it is important to decide whether, if a man is on first base and the next student hits a two-base question, that puts the first man on third base or gets him home for a run for his team. The class can decide this issue quickly before the game starts.

In football the questions are ranked by number of yards according to how hard the question is. Each team gets four questions (four "downs") before the ball is handed over to the other team. A wrong answer is a "down." The farther down the field one team gets toward the goal line, of course, determines how much added distance the other team has to carry the ball back down the field in the opposite direction. Again, if the team makes a touchdown in two or three downs, rather than four, they may agree to give that team four more downs.

Adaptations:

The two teams may previously have had a chance to think out the questions to be asked; thus, the drill is made doubly effective, since the students must know the material in order to ask the questions to begin with, then must know it in order to answer. The teacher or the students may decide the degree of difficulty of the questions; the teams may get only the questions asked by the other team, or the questions may be mixed and thus each team has a fifty-fifty chance of getting their own questions.

Evaluation may be carried on by the teams or by selected members if the questions are submitted prior to playing the game and are reviewed for pertinence, clarity, and significance. The teacher may choose to review the questions and the team that submitted the better set questions may receive an extra reward of some sort.

Answers to the questions may also be provided by each team, before the game is played, for the teacher to check; this provides even more opportunity for review.

Instead of having the teacher give the questions, each team may do so; one person being pitcher and tossing the ball (question) to the batter on the other team; then the next person in line takes the floor as pitcher, next batter; and so on.

Penalties: Each team may be penalized for infractions of the rules such as getting too noisy, illegal coaching, asking questions that had previously been ruled out, and similar faults. The teacher may also choose to penalize a team for poorly thought-out questions, superficial questions, and so forth. This use of penalties may be invoked after the class has become used to playing the game.

We remember observing two eleventh-grade United States history classes, one slow and one average in ability, playing the baseball game as part of review before a quiz. Both classes enjoyed the game very much; the slower class was easier to control and did not get so excited or full of "team spirit" as the other class. When the game was halted for another activity (hearing a recording), the two classes were reluctant to stop, even though the material had been relatively uninteresting and remote in time. The students paid close attention to both the questions and the answers in order to be sure their team was getting the plays called right.

3. ***Quiz Kids.*** A quiz master introduces the Quiz Kids. These students may be representatives of teams or groups in the class, may volunteer for the game, or may be chosen by lot by the teacher so that anyone and everyone has a chance and an obligation to participate. The Quiz Kids are replaced at regular intervals during the game. The Quiz Kids are seated at the front of the room. From a box the quiz master draws a question that has been prepared previously by a committee or by the class groups or teams. Any one of the Kids may answer the question, the one usually answering is the one who first raises his hand. If a student once raises his hand, he cannot withdraw it. For each correct answer, the Quiz Kid gets a tally which may be his personal score or part of his team score. If none of the Quiz Kids can answer, audience volunteers may try, thus getting a chance to add to their team score. However, if the questions have been prepared by the teams, they should be so marked in order that a team member does not try to answer a question he has himself prepared.

4. ***Card Games.*** We are all familiar with the game of Authors. In this game, a set of cards is made up with the names of famous books and plays and the authors of these productions. The cards are shuffled and passed out equally to all players (4 to 6) so that each has a certain number of cards (6 or 8). The rest of the cards are put face down on the table. Each person tries to match author and book. Each such pair is placed in front of the player and gives him 1 score point. Each person must draw one card from the pile and discard one card. He has an option of drawing from the discard pile (those left face up) or from the pile that is face down. However, if he draws from the discard pile, he must take either the top card, or, if he wants one of the other cards, he must take all preceding it. The student who rightly matches all the cards in his hand first wins.

Variations of this game applicable to other fields are obvious: Names, dates, events can be matched in history and social-studies classes. In science, matching names and properties of materials can be arranged. In English and foreign-language classes, such a game can assist in vocabulary drill, in learning the parts of speech and producing good usage.

The teacher probably should prepare the first few cards, but it would also be a worth-while student project. Thus both the students who make and use the cards are gaining practice in review with a special kind of recognition for talent in making neat cards for the game. In fact, some students may select the items for the test; others may check the items for accuracy, relevance, and coverage; and, finally, a group may elect to cut and letter the cards. In this way, many talents are used at many levels of intellectual competence and cooperative effort.

Another application of card games is to use this idea in pinning down various sequential processes or logical steps in problem solving. Thus, one part of the cards may be a number series and the other part a set of historical events; the object of the student then is to put the cards in the right sequential order. This variation might best be done by a student alone, then checked by another for accuracy as a quick method for individual practice and review. The same idea can be applied to geometry problems and matching right theorems and axioms.

Limitations in Using Games in the Classroom

In team games, choosing sides presents its problems. The process of having the captain choose his team, for example, involves some mental hazards. Those who are chosen last go through moments of anguish; they are left seated while one by one their companions are asked for. Conspicuous to themselves and to everyone else is the fact that they are "not wanted." Certain students may almost always be the last chosen. Obviously this increases the individual student's feeling of being rejected, left out, or actively disliked.

At least one aspect of the old-fashioned spelling bee, and similar games, does not make for very efficient learning. Those who are least successful, those who are least adept at the type of problem presented, are those who go down first. Those who know the most are the best spellers or reciters and get all the practice! Those who are dull or slow or poor in the subject are quickly singled out *through failure.* Such youngsters are those who have already known failure most often. Those who have succeeded continue to succeed; they continue to get the practice of answering correctly and obtain the rewards of recognition and approval from both the teacher and the team.

These descriptions of games that are useful for learning cannot be concluded without a word of warning. These games all assume a body of detailed subject matter that is to be learned. While it is important to provide students with the tools of the various subjects, the important ideas and facts, it is also evident that persistent overemphasis on the details of learning will interfere with more basic kinds of learning—development of attitudes, general understandings, logical thinking, critical and discriminatory tastes, sound value judgments. The teacher should carefully examine the content of such games as are used and constantly ask himself, "Is this content really worth learning?" And, "Am I really confident that, if the students learn this material, they will be more competent adults?" And, "Could the time being spent in learning this material be better spent in considering some broad problems related to the student's life here and now?" Games are a very effective method of making drill interesting and enjoyable, but it is still important to know that the drill is directed toward genuine learning.

Summary

Too often drill or review wastes the time of the students because either the material is so monotonous that students do not pay attention, or so irrelevant to the function it is to perform that it is learned in a meaningless vacuum. To overcome some of these problems, it is suggested that teachers create some group competitive situations in which all students participate in the review, maximizing the possibilities for learning because of the increased student interest.

Review and drill are important aspects of the total teaching plan, but they alone will not suffice to ensure student learning. Helping young people study is a prerequisite for later recall. In the next section we will discuss the ways in which the teacher can provide help to the students in learning appropriate study skills.

Supervising and Guiding Classroom Study

Teachers can develop interesting and significant classroom work and provide well thought-out assignments to meet many individual differences, but if students do not know some of the basic methods of study, such planning is to no avail. In preparation for drill or review periods, students will need techniques of concentrating on the material already covered in order to make use of the review period.

In most classrooms, the materials to be studied are reading materials. Thus an understanding of reading problems precedes any consideration of developing study skills. (See Chapter 12) A student who cannot read obviously cannot study assigned chapters. Once a minimum of reading ability has been demonstrated, and the teacher has considered the specific reading problems of the assigned material, he can proceed to a consideration with students of how most efficiently to study and to learn.

Many high-school teachers in the academic subject fields today plan each period to allow time for in-class study. The out-of-school competition for the student's time means that often home study is either not accomplished at all, or is done rapidly and carelessly. In addition, if students do not know how to study, the teacher cannot provide the needed guidance, unless he can observe the study habits of the students.

But whether study is to be in or out of class, the importance of teacher supervision must be emphasized. Supervision begins with preparing the class to use study time to advantage. Such preparation includes:

1. Agreeing with the class as to the purposes of the study period. Often motivation for use of study time is on the rather low level of "If you don't do this in class, you will just have to do it at home." This implies that learning is a distasteful enterprise best terminated at the earliest possible moment. A better approach is to point out the importance of the material being studied. Then the study time in class becomes an opportunity rather than a chore.
2. Providing specific things to be gained from the study: that is, questions to be answered, concepts to be understood, problems to be solved, information to be collected.
3. Identifying clearly the specifics that are to be sought. List directive questions either on the blackboard or on a study-guide syllabus. For a teacher to say, "Read the next chapter and be ready to answer questions in it" is, for the average student, a very vague and nearly useless kind of instruction.
4. Helping the students set goals as to the time needed to accomplish the study task: that is, "Let's try to get the first five questions answered in class, and then you can continue and finish the rest at home." Remember, however, that variation in student ability will mean that much more will be accomplished by some and much less by others. But emphasis should be on efficient use of the study time provided.

Additional preparation will be needed to guide out-of-class study time. Many students have not learned to plan their time well by the high-school years. The teacher should discuss with the class the conditions that make for efficient home study. These should include:

1. Reviewing work in class to see what, if any, difficulties may be encountered at home and checking with the teacher for help in these areas.
2. Arranging a specific time and place at home for uninterrupted study. This is often not easy for young people who live in crowded or disorganized homes. Such students may need special time in class or even a home visit to help parents help the student in his study needs.
3. Reviewing in class, after the home study has been accomplished, any special problems of study that may have arisen.
4. Considering the importance of learning habits, of individual concentration and responsibility for one's own learning tasks and relating this to later vocational needs.
5. Providing a period in class for students to exchange experiences about the methods of study that they find most helpful, so that students can help one another. Advice from a peer is often more acceptable than advice from an adult or teacher.

When study time is offered in class, individual supervision should be provided. While the students are studying in class the teacher should:

1. Walk around the room to observe student study habits.
2. Use this opportunity to discuss with individual students any problems of study that arise.
3. Watch how student work is going. The teacher may find it advisable to call the attention of the whole class to some particularly difficult passage or interesting point that should not be missed.
4. Ask students about their progress. Do not wait for unfinished or continuously poor work to indicate a trouble spot.
5. Note different ability levels. Check with superior students regarding extra projects or reports that may be done in lieu of homework.
6. Be attentive to the class during study time. Thus the teacher aids in creating a workmanlike atmosphere of quiet and concentration.

When the teacher has established a study routine in class and has been able to work individually with most of the students on their own particular study problems or needs, then the teacher may utilize this study time for individual guidance conferences as suggested in Chapter 18. But even if such conferences can occur without disturbing the class during a study period, it is very important that the teacher use several of the weekly study times for supervision.

How much in-class time should be allowed for study? As has been pointed out, variety in a class is as important as regular routine. And neither should be sacrificed for the other. Time for study should be carefully planned for in the over-all plan, but at the same time it is important to vary the daily schedule enough so that students remain alert and interested. Establishing the practice of a weekly planning session with the class aids in allocating needed class time for study, adapting to different rates of progress of different classes over similar material and adjusting to varying student interests. It is as unwise to have an inflexible rule of "20 minutes every period for in-class study" as it is to have no plan for helping in developing student study skills.

Summary

We spend so much time teaching young people that we like to think that, in years to come, they will remember some of the important details of the subject. Yet so much is forgotten! Students need help to remember for immediate use the lessons of the classroom. Even they need to have readily available some minimum concepts and facts for utilization in adult living. The teacher has at hand several important techniques which, if well used, produce high returns in amount of recall of material. These tools—drill and review—must be used with discrimination and with care.

Drill should be confined to separate elements which need to be available as a kind of automatic response. Review should reinforce the relationships of separate elements of learning. Some of these elements will have been drilled and some will not.

One way of involving all students in drill procedures is to use learning games, in which students review the pertinent material, prepare the content of the quiz game, and then are alerted to see that correct answers are provided by each of the groups or teams involved. A greater use of such games is recommended, since they do increase the range of participation of students in drill, involve extensive and penetrating inquiry into subject matter, and are fun.

Learning how to study is another key to effective drill and review. The teacher must be constantly alert to opportunities to aid students in learning how to study and working closely with those who have special personal problems, particularly in out-of-school study assignments.

Selected References

Drill and Review

Butler, Frank A. *The Improvement of Teaching in Secondary Schools.* Rev. ed. Chicago: University of Chicago Press, 1946. Chap. XVI, "Drill, Review, and Pupil Participation," pp. 331-344. When and how to use drill and review for maximum results. Brief but practical.

Mort, Paul R., and William S. Vincent. *Modern Educational Practice.* New York: McGraw-Hill Book Company, Inc., 1950. Sect. 15, "Varied Drill Devices," pp. 309-324. Many examples of ways of making drill more effective.

Rivlin, Harry N. *Teaching Adolescents in Secondary Schools.* New York: Appleton-Century-Crofts, Inc., 1948. Chap. X, "Improving the Permanence of Learning," pp. 295-319. The many ways a teacher can utilize opportunities to review material for more permanent retention.

Schorling, Raleigh. *Student Teaching.* New York: McGraw-Hill Book Company, Inc., 1949. Chap. 9, "Drill," pp. 232-241. Practical do's and don't's for effective drill experiences.

Classroom Games for Drill

Burkhart, Russell S. "On Warm Spring Days," *The Balance Sheet,* 31:252-254 (February, 1950). Some games that can be used in a typing class.

Buscher, M., and I. R. Wilkerson. "Games in the Classroom," *Educational Method,* 22:324-325 (April, 1943). Some simple games for social studies and language development.

Hollenbeck, E. Irene, and E. N. Stevenson. *Selected Procedures in Teaching Biology.* Corvallis, Ore.: Oregon State College, 1950. Studies in Education and Guidance, No. 3, 1950. "Games," pp. 20-31. Extensive coverage of games that can be used in biology, most of which can be easily adapted to other fields. A particularly useful guide for teachers using learning games.

Kieffer, Elizabeth M. "Christmas Typewriting Games," *Journal of Business Education,* 26:120-121 (November, 1950). Games that help to keep student interest and develop skills at crucial times.

Nunn, C. "Games Lighten Learning," *Sierra Educational News,* 40:24 (October, 1944). Describes card series games for elementary school use that can be adapted for high-school situations in which any process or sequence or matching of concepts is necessary.

Perrine, K. "They Play Football in Class," *Social Education,* 8:355-356 (December, 1944). A description of the basic pattern of this game procedure in classroom and the values of its use.

Van Detta, James F. "Organizing a Competitive Learning Situation for a Basic Business Course," *The Balance Sheet,* 31:262 (February, 1950). Describes how team question-and-answer situations speed up the learning phase of business education and make the actual performance level higher.

Supervised Study

Burton, William H. *The Guidance of Learning Activities.* New York: Appleton-Century-Crofts, Inc., 1944. Chap. 12, "The Development of Independence in Study," pp. 325-350. Improving student study habits requires specific teaching techniques, as outlined in detail here.

Butler, Frank A. *The Improvement of Teaching in Secondary Schools.* Rev. ed. Chicago: University of Chicago Press, 1946. Chap. XII, "Assisting Pupils to Grow through Independent Study," pp. 222-246. Thorough presentation of how the teacher helps students learn appropriate study procedures.

Dodes, I. A. "Teaching Them How to Study," *High Points,* 29:77-80 (May, 1947). A lesson on how to study as used to introduce mathematics courses.

Douglass, Harl, and H. H. Mills. *Teaching in High School.* New York: The Ronald Press Company, 1948. Chap. 8, "Directing the Study of High School Pupils," pp. 139-157; Chap. 9, "Teaching Pupils How to Study," pp. 158-179. Also covers assignment procedures and related problems.

Gruhn, William T., and H. R. Douglass. *The Modern Junior High School.* New York: The Ronald Press Company, 1947. "Improvement of Pupil Study Methods," pp. 214-219. Some of the pressing needs for instruction in study skills for the younger school group.

Mort, Paul R., and William S. Vincent. *Modern Educational Practice.* New York: McGraw-Hill Book Company, Inc., 1950. Sect. 18, "Study Techniques," pp. 347-356. Examples of classroom practices in improving study skills.

Rivlin, Harry N. *Teaching Adolescents in Secondary Schools.* New York: Appleton-Century-Crofts, Inc., 1948. Chap. IX, "Developing the Ability to Work and to Study Effectively," pp. 267-294. Makes a strong case for increased attention to teaching good study habits and suggests how this may best be done.

10. Managing the Classroom for Effective Learning

CLASSROOMS are laboratories for learning—places where we experiment, try out, and test. We have made our great advances as a people because we were willing to take the methods of science to our problems, new and old. The basic procedure of science is to take a problem and state its limitations, collect data within these limits, formulate an hypothesis out of the data, try out the hypothesis, modify the hypothesis on the basis of the tryout, and keep modifying and trying out until the hypothesis states accurately how the problem is resolved. This is a creative way to learn because it involves constant attempts to create explanations that work. It is also a lasting way to learn because it calls upon the learner to propose his own answers, to try them out, to keep trying until the answers test out. If any of his proposals are made without care and thought, he knows he will probe just that much longer working out the right answer. The great virtue of the scientific method of learning is that it places responsibility for sound learning squarely upon the learner. This way he gets no ready-made answers. Too long our classrooms were hearing halls. We repeated words that summarized what others found out for themselves. This was not genuine learning; the words lay only on the surface of memory and were brushed away by the efforts of the learner to find out something he really wanted to know.

As long as our classrooms were listening rooms, we needed little equipment: desks and chairs and a blackboard. We needed few materials: the textbook, paper and pencils, pen and ink, chalk. Our problems in management were small. The desks and chairs were bolted in neat rows. Each student had his book and his writing supplies. For the most part students sat, occasionally advancing to the front of the room to speak. Students spoke from their seats only when given specific permission by the teacher. The classroom was orderly and quiet—and dead.

Laboratory Facilities for Learning

When we began to allow the noise and movement of living in the classrooms, of course, we multiplied our problems. Equipment had to be added (even a Victorian sitting room had more equipment than the old classroom) and materials. Ways for active students to use the equipment and materials efficiently had to be found.

We have already seen the variety of materials now used in modern classrooms: models, specimens and samples, motion pictures, still pictures, filmstrips, slides, recordings, radio, television, charts, maps, graphs, newspapers, periodicals, free and inexpensive materials and books. The variety of methods designed to employ these materials for deeper learning: demonstration, discussion, sociodrama, group work, and games have been reviewed. We have noted what the teacher must know about his students before he can guide choices in materials and methods: differences in maturation and experience; differences in needs, interests, and abilities; differences in goals and aspirations. We have not yet examined what differences in the physical equipment and facilities of the classroom are entailed in the fuller use of methods, materials, and personnel information.

Let us take the additions in materials first. A good laboratory has to have facilities for storing materials where they will be readily accessible. If the materials are to be used effectively, they can be neither neatly stored in a remote part of the building nor piled in confusion right in the classroom. Facilities in the good laboratory for learning include:

Cupboards for	models specimens samples paper crayons water colors mucilage rulers scissors pencils pens ink	Cupboards for	free and inexpensive materials individual student and group collections and projects
Racks and tables for	maps periodicals pamphlets books	Filing cases for	pictures clippings personnel records student papers teacher resource unit outlines
Easels for	newspapers charts graphs student work display	Cabinets for	filmstrips slides recordings

Because of their cost, filmstrips, slides, and recordings are usually stored only temporarily in classrooms. Motion pictures ordinarily are there for one period only and so require no storage. The special equipment needed for their use is also commonly shared within the school.

Now consider how the new scope in method has changed the classroom. A good laboratory has to allow flexibility in the ways in which materials and equipment are used to attack problems. For example, we cannot use the same arrangement for group work as for discussion. So the laboratory for learning has movable furniture. It has more space to allow for group work, sociodrama, games, individual study. It has exhibit cases, extended blackboards (or chalkboards, as they may more properly be called now that they are no longer black), and enlarged bulletin boards (or tackboards, as they may more properly be called now that they display more than bulletins).

The modern classroom has working counters with cupboard space below. An augmented system of natural and artificial lighting assures light intensity evenly distributed throughout the room and adequate for all the learning tasks. The contrasts in brightness are held to a minimum so that glare does not produce eyestrain. The whole room is done in cheerful color, in warm reds and oranges for the sunless rooms and in cool blues and greens for the sunny rooms. Even the furniture departs from the old drab browns and comes now in blonde shades of wood or in light enamels for steel. An automatic heating-ventilating system has been installed to maintain constant temperature. The room has been treated acoustically to dampen sound.

Remember that this range of material and method is for the benefit of the learners. A good laboratory is arranged to permit full application of the talents of its research staff on the problems at hand. We have discussed at some length just how we find what the capacities of the students are. The details of their differing abilities need to be registered in the room where they work. Often the abilities of students have been charted, but the records are secreted in some administrative office. There they rest and gather dust instead of being used to guide the development of the students in the classroom. On the other hand, very little good comes of bringing the records to the classroom if they have to be stuffed in the teacher's desk drawer or piled on the floor of the closet. The laboratory for learning has filing cases where anecdotal records, aptitude and achievement test results, summaries of interviews and home visitations provide a profile of abilities at a moment's notice. Even when teachers move from room to room, as they often do in larger schools, there ought to be one room a teacher can call "home" where these records can be filed.

Let no one say, "But we don't have a classroom like this." Very few have. Sometimes the only models we have are those we make ourselves. The only specimens and samples are those our students collect. The only motion pictures are those we borrow without cost. The only pictures are those we mount from magazines. The only filmstrips are those some company sent our school. In short, without grubbing and scratching we would have very little. No argument. Far more important, however, is our realization that we should seek to increase the kinds of materials we use in teaching. Perhaps the school systems *should* supply us with more than they do. But it will not be too damaging to us as teachers if we have to stretch a little for what we need.

But what about these cupboards and racks and easels and filing cases and cabinets? We may have to improvise here too. Sometimes the school shops will be able to help us a little. Often parents' groups will lend us a hand. And our own students may prove to be surprisingly good craftsmen.

Our classrooms will not frequently be lighted, painted, ventilated, and acoustically treated as a good laboratory should be. In many cases they will be smaller than they ought to be. The chalkboards may be of poor quality and the tackboards dingy and small. With much of this, we will simply have to take the long-term view. Meanwhile, it is very important that the community knows what facilities a modern classroom needs. Beginning with the late 1950's, the high-school population will grow tremendously as the large elementary-school enrollment of the post-World War II years moves in. New classrooms will have to be built in great numbers. Unless the lay public is made aware of how the classroom-laboratory concept has changed school buildings, we may get bright new 1900-style mausoleums. Teachers must know what they need and let the community hear.

Management Routines Within the Laboratory

Sometimes in this profession there is confusion about the way modern learning operates. A few have gained the impression that instruction now is completely *laissez faire.* The teacher merely stands aside in order not to restrict the liberty and fine spirit of individuality. Of course, this is complete nonsense. If classrooms are laboratories, if good learning follows the methodology of science, then instruction must be orderly—but it need not be silent and dead.

Preparing the Room

Just the way a classroom looks does much to build or weaken good management. Even if the classroom is not the most modern, if it is clean and neat, it will help set the tone for businesslike performance. Here good relationships with the custodial staff are imperative. Many a young teacher has needlessly added to his troubles by treating the custodian in a high-handed, discourteous manner. He finds himself the victim of little reprisals: the wastebasket not emptied, the chalkboard not washed, furniture neatly arranged in exactly the wrong way. But treated as a friend, the custodian can make the teaching life more pleasant in innumerable ways.

Where teachers have the same room for the day, much can be done to make it ready before the school begins. Materials and supplies can be checked and set out for the day. The chalkboards and tackboards can be prepared. Some schools have arranged with their art and home-economics departments to help make rooms more attractive with flower arrangements, pictures, and student-made drapes.

Establishing Instructional Routines

Even for experienced teachers, the first days with a new class can be hectic. The students and teachers both have a host of adjustments to make. In a sense, a new social organization is being born and it is inevitably attended with some pain. For these days well-planned routine is imperative, since impressions are being formed and exchanged by the students which may help or hinder long afterward. Sometimes it helps to be at or near the door of the classroom before class begins to make a deliberate effort to speak to some of the students by name. This shows from the beginning a recognition of individuality. A quick briefing on activities in and out of school in which class members are engaged helps to provide impromptu remarks to class members. Of course, these casual conversations need not be limited to before and after class; whenever and wherever class members are seen, they should be recognized and something said to give them assurance that the teacher knows them personally. Just a few bonds established in the first days provide a skeletal framework around which the social organization can take form. It is while the social organization of the class remains formless that there is danger of chaos.

Seating the students. It is a temptation to seat students alphabetically to assist in roll taking and name memorizing. Some teachers think they help the cause of good order by seating by size—short in the front, tall in the rear. Others try segregating boys and girls. Probably none of these devices helps very much, and they may easily give the class a rigidity that will make any kind of spontaneity difficult to generate. Let them sit where they like. Sometimes explosive combinations may have to be separated, but then only as a last resort. Separating good friends when there is no good reason only tempts them to elaborate subterfuges in maintaining communication. It is not an unreasonable request to ask students to retain the seats they chose at the beginning of the course, at least for the first days, in order to facilitate roll taking and the learning of names by both student and teacher.

Beginning the class. From the beginning, students should be led to expect a prompt starting of class activity. It helps beginning teachers sometimes to have at once an activity in which all take part. This settles the class down to business. Meanwhile, attendance can be taken. It is important to understand thoroughly the school's system of reporting attendance before the new term begins. In many states, funds are distributed to school districts on the basis of average daily attendance. But whether this pertains or not, school administrations always lay great stress on knowing exactly where each student is during each hour of the school day. Beginning teachers can avoid much official displeasure by being meticulous about attendance records. Reliable student assistants can later relieve the teacher of this chore.

Establishing routines. A useful activity for one of the first days is to distribute duplicated statements describing basic routines of the class (distributing and collecting materials, forms for reports, checking out reference books, and so on). The statements should be regarded as a basis for discussion. It should be understood that the routines may be modified as the class devises more efficient procedures. Sometimes a group can be appointed immediately to codify management patterns to be presented later to the class. *The more the class can devise its own routines, the better the routines will be observed.*

Varying seating arrangements. For the different activities during the class hour, some changes in seating arrangements will be necessary. Even if the seats cannot be moved, the students need not be immovable for the hour. They can and should move, to facilitate discussion, for group work, for project and study activities. Of course, it is even more important that the teacher not be fastened to the front of the room, for this encourages the old recite-for-the-teacher pattern. Where there is room, the teacher's desk is best moved to the rear of the room; supervision is more efficient from this vantage point, private conversations with students are facilitated, and the teacher domination of the classroom is less to be expected. Where the furniture is movable and where the class is working as one group, seats may be arranged in quarter circles facing away from the windows from left front to right rear so that no one has a direct light glare. In small-group activity, work around tables or at desks arranged in squares or circles is, of course, most efficient because face-to-face working facilitates group unity. The diagrams on page 255 illustrate some possible room arrangements.

Handling materials. Next to seating arrangements, the handling of materials and supplies is most likely to undo the unwary. Before the school year begins, it is very useful to know how materials and supplies for the classroom are requisitioned. If it is done annually in spring and largely on the basis of requests of the department

SUGGESTED ROOM ARRANGEMENTS

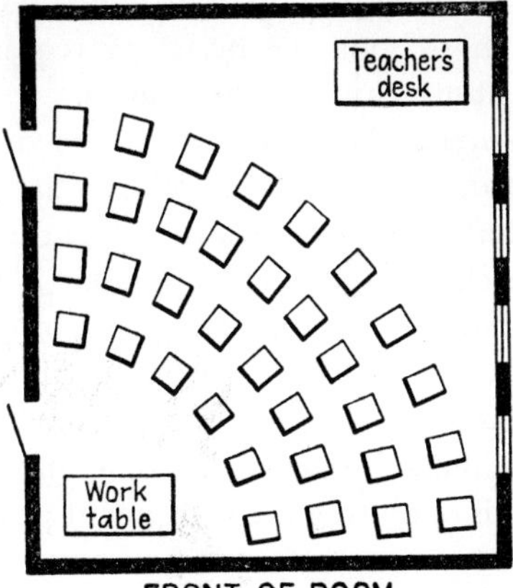

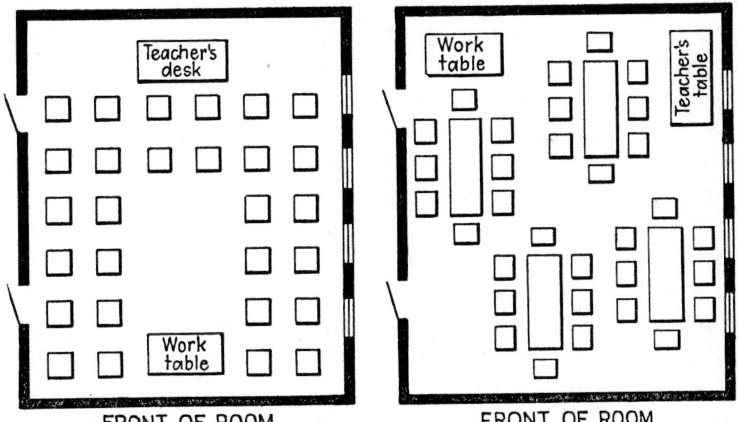

chairman, new teachers do not add to their status by complaining loudly in the autumn about the oversights. If regular reordering is done during the year, it helps to know about it. Then new teachers can get in their bids for additional materials.

Among the audio-visual materials, motion pictures most often present requisitioning problems. Usually the films must be ordered long in advance of the date on which they will be used. Teachers who plan instruction with their students will have difficulty predicting just when a motion picture may be needed. Compromises will be inevitable. But better compromises can be effected if it is known at the beginning of the school year just how and when films may be requested. Larger high schools may have an audio-visual coordinator to assist with the scheduling. Even then, the coordinator will appreciate the teacher's familiarity with the catalogues of the principal supply sources for the school, the necessary requisition forms, and the other required administrative procedures.

Securing equipment. Many of the audio-visual materials require equipment: projectors, recorders, playbacks. Most, if not all, of the equipment will also require advance scheduling. Another quick way for the new teacher to become unpopular is to remember just before class time that he must have a piece of equipment. Many schools will have student service clubs who distribute and operate the equipment. But it is still advantageous for the teacher himself to know how the equipment is operated. Then, at least, he will know whether the student is operating the equipment properly. The equipment is not difficult to master (contrary to a common teacher complaint). Certainly it is far less complex than driving an automobile (and less dangerous to life and limb). In a few hours' time, any teacher should be able to operate any of the school's audio-visual equipment.

Managing newspapers and periodicals. Newspaper and periodicals present special problems in financing. Obviously the best practice is to have the materials purchased through school-district funds. The cost is relatively small; it is simply a matter of educating lay citizens, boards of education, and administrators to see the wisdom of the expenditure. However, in many schools students may be able to afford subscriptions without hardship, or parent organizations and service groups may agree to finance the purchase. Many newspapers and magazines may be secured from the homes of students as soon as the family has read them.

In the classroom, students will need some cautioning about handling such current materials. They are easily torn; pages become detached and lost from an issue. Teachers whose classrooms have tables for students rather than small individual desks have a real advantage. The materials can be spread out and given better protection from excessive wear and tear.

When it comes time to clip and file, storage will be a perplexing problem. In order to make room, student committees should cull out-dated material at the time the new material is filed. Relatively satisfactory supplementary filing cases can be fashioned from cardboard cartons or orange crates. In some schools, the file of clippings and pictures may be maintained by the library.

Inventorying materials and supplies. Before beginning the school year, an inventory should be taken of all the materials and supplies in the classroom. With books, in particular, it is wise to note the amount of wear and tear. There should be a definite place for all materials and supplies. By such a simple device as affixing a label on each drawer and shelf, the teacher can avoid misplacing valuable materials. This also assists student helpers in replacing items used. It should be a matter of routine, which can be easily handled by a student, to check materials before the end of each hour and return them to their proper places. Both distributing and collecting can be systematized under student assistants. It should be clear to both teacher and assistants at the beginning of each hour exactly what materials will be needed, where the materials are, and when during the hour they will be used.

The teacher might well place a list of what materials will be needed on the blackboard before class convenes. A list might look something like this:

Period I: Maps, references on shelf A, scratch paper.
Period II: Examination paper.
Period III: Workbooks, scratch paper.
Period IV: Maps, references on shelf A, scratch paper, and so on.

Budgeting time. This also implies that the variety of activities within the hour needs careful management. Time budgets need to be made for each activity, even though much flexibility will have to be allowed. Transitions from one activity to another must be prepared for if they are to be executed with minimum confusion. The less mature the class, the more explicit the preparation for change in activity must be.

Special care should be exercised to see that activities do not waste the students' time. In practice and review exercises, for example, students should not spend long periods receiving dictation or copying material from book or blackboard. Duplicated materials should obviate this time-consuming practice.

The teacher's time also can be uneconomically expended. Beginning teachers especially tend to assign so many papers and reports that they cannot even pretend to read them. Or they administer many unnecessary tests. Teachers cannot be well-rounded, happy, alive people if they spend all their out-of-class time correcting papers. Many reports and tests can be corrected by the students in class, and others can be appraised by student assistants. Some papers and tests, of course, must be examined by the teacher himself, but these ought not to be so numerous that they dominate all out-of-school time.

Using student assistants. From time to time, during this discussion of instructional routines, we have mentioned student assistants. Wisely used, student assistants can relieve teachers from the supervision of much necessary routine. This help need not be exploitation. It is a part of sharing in responsibility for learning which students should have. Many will gain status and develop maturity from the experience. Because it is an educative experience, student assistance should be rotated. It should not be the exclusive property of the academically gifted. Nor should it gain the reputation of being awarded to the teacher's favorites. The responsibility enjoyed by any one student should be limited both in scope and in time, and division of responsibility among the assistants should be clear. Students themselves should have a voice in who does the jobs, what the responsibilities are, and how long they should be enjoyed.

Ending the class. Before the class hour ends, a few minutes spent in general housekeeping is well justified. It helps the next class to come into a neat and orderly room. This is especially important when the room is shared by several teachers. The incoming teacher's morale will be helped by clean blackboards, bookshelves in good order, chairs or desks in place, floor clear of papers. At the end of the day, the custodian will be appreciative. Furthermore, the beginning teacher will earn a reputation for being a good manager.

Maintaining Records

In the first chapter, we noted how good teaching depended upon knowledge of the differences of individuals in any class, and earlier in this chapter we spoke of the equipment needed to maintain personnel records with this information. There are, in addition, in even small high schools, many reports to be made to the administration. Questionable as the practice is, many administrators judge teachers to a large extent on the promptness and accuracy with which these reports are rendered. Obviously the reports do represent part of a teacher's competence, but they are not the major part. Still teachers have to recognize the facts of administrative practice. For most teachers, it is good policy to keep a calendar marked with warning dates and due dates for the reports. Some system of collecting data for the reports as the teacher goes along is essential if the due date is not to cause frenzied scrabbling for the information. Student assistants can often be used both for the collecting of data and the assembling of the report. There is a commendable trend in larger schools to provide clerical staffs in the administrative office to assist teachers with these reports. This trend stems from a belated recognition that it is, after all, inefficient to use highly trained teachers to do routine clerical work. Teachers do not have limitless resources in personal energy. If they expend large amounts on reports, they will have less to use in classroom instruction.

General Principles

We can arrive at several useful generalizations out of our discussion of good management in the laboratory classroom. These are general criteria which may help to guide in developing any program of routinizing the details of instruction.

1. The development of habits of good management and of sharing responsibility is an important part of good education. Teachers and students together should agree on those details of instruction which should be made matters of routine.

2. Routines are useful when they help teachers and students do common tasks with economy of effort and a minimum of confusion, when teachers and students understand why the routines are advantageous, and when they free teacher and students for the major activities.

3. The greater the maturity of the group, the greater should be its responsibility for establishing and maintaining routines.

4. The larger the class the more necessary are good management procedures.

5. The classroom laboratory that looks neat and is well arranged helps induce habits of good management.

6. Basic routines must be begun from the first day the class meets, in order that at once the expectation of good order in the laboratory will be developed.

7. Teachers and students should hold to basic routines in the beginning, adding procedures as they are needed. Too many rules may induce rather than reduce disorder.

8. All the work of the class must not become mechanical routine. Teachers and students should not hold to such rigid patterns that they know exactly what will happen at a given time every day. Individual initiative and creative learning will be destroyed by too much routine.

Selected References

Billett, Roy O. *Fundamentals of Secondary School Teaching.* Boston: Houghton Mifflin Company, 1940. Chap. XIX, "The Classroom Laboratory and the Teaching-Learning Cycle," pp. 580-609. A detailed discussion of how a teacher can transform a traditional classroom into a materials laboratory; points out why this is so important.

Boicourt, G. "A Classroom Designed for English," *English Journal,* 40:94-98 (February, 1951). A plan for an ideal English classroom.

Burton, William H. *The Guidance of Learning Activities.* New York: Appleton-Century-Crofts, Inc., 1944. Chap. 22, "Classroom Management and Control," pp. 549-586. Good organization is essential to good learning, and this includes the classroom environment and materials as well as content.

Heiss, E. D., E. S. Obourn, and C. W. Hoffman. *Modern Science Teaching.* New York: The Macmillan Company, 1950. Chap. 11, "The Science Classroom and Laboratory," pp. 247-269; Chap. 12, "Equipment and Supplies for Teaching Science," pp. 270-278. Suggested arrangements for science classrooms; problems of administration of laboratory and laboratory equipment are discussed.

Keliher, Alice V. "Mental Hygiene in the Day's Work: A Day in the Life of the Teacher," *Mental Hygiene,* 34:455-464 (July, 1950). A careful review of the many demands made on a teacher that are above and beyond the task of actually teaching.

Kinney, L. B., and Katharine Dresden. *Better Learning through Current Materials.* Stanford: Stanford University Press, 1949. Chap. VIII, "Administering Current Materials," pp. 131-139. A practical discussion of room-management problems when a teacher uses numerous sources for teaching.

Rivlin, Harry N. *Teaching Adolescents in Secondary Schools.* New York: Appleton-Century-Crofts, Inc., 1948. Chap. XI, "Managing a Classroom," pp. 320-343. Routine housekeeping and clerical tasks of the teacher described, with suggestions for how to deal with these recurrent demands most easily.

Roberts, H., and Laura K. Martin. "Classroom Libraries in the School Library Program," *Education,* LXI:42-46 (September, 1940). The importance of making books available in each classroom, not only in the general school library.

Schorling, Raleigh. *Student Teaching.* New York: McGraw-Hill Book Company, Inc., 1949. Chap. IV, "Principles of Routine and Classroom Management," pp. 115-133. A very practical guide to aid the beginning teacher in dealing with classroom detail efficiently.

Stearns, Gertrude B. *English in the Small High School.* Lincoln: University of Nebraska, 1950. "The Library in the Small School," pp. 266-293. Basic mechanics for a simple library system that will be very useful to any teacher who desires to maintain a room library.

Webber, Frank D., and Byron H. Atkinson. "Dynamic Classroom Control," *California Journal of Secondary Education,* 24:350-352 (October, 1949). Well-established routines, cooperatively planned, are vital to a good learning situation.

11. Special Problems in Learning

Slow and Fast Learners

ONCE we get to know the members of any group as individuals, we find it extremely difficult to consider any of them average or typical. This observation is particularly apt for the teacher in the classroom. As soon as names and faces become sorted, he remembers that Johnny's father is dead, or that Mary's mother works evenings as a movie usherette, or that Susan has had rheumatic fever, or that Bill has a very high IQ but is still the youngest in class. Each person stands out as unique, special, different. We have seen that the best teachers are as much aware of individual differences as they are of the common qualities of all children. There are, however, some differences among students that present very special problems to the teacher, problems that can be dealt with only by means of highly developed skills and understandings. For the purposes of discussion, these problems may be arranged in three categories: aptitude for learning, achievement in basic skills, adjustment to school life.

In this chapter and in the following three, these special learning problems will be separately considered. First, we must consider the unique and difficult problems of the very slow and very fast learners. Such students need individual attention both in personality adjustment and in specially tailored content and learning procedures. Next, in Chapter 12, attention will be focused on students who are particularly handicapped by inadequate skill development in the areas of general communication—reading, writing, speaking, listening. Since our instruction depends in such large measure upon at least average ability to understand and impart verbal understandings, any skill deficiency in these areas can seriously interfere with what the individual student can learn.

Finally, in Chapters 13 and 14 we will consider the problems of behavior adjustment to school situations specifically and to growing up in general. In the classroom, we usually call these "discipline problems." Some individuals find it easy to take in their stride the various pressures and demands of being an adolescent and of going to school; others find it extremely difficult. Most young people fluctuate between periods of adequate adjustment and periods of rebellion and dissatisfaction. These adjustment struggles cause the teacher many moments of anxiety and concern. Fundamentally, they are problems of personal adjustment to the world of the school and the larger society, and in this sense present problems similar to those presented by the slow learner or the slow reader. Logically, then, these four chapters form a unit around the general concept of dealing with special learning problems.

The Size of the Problem

In today's high school are found about half of all the youth between fifteen and nineteen. In some states school attendance is compulsory until high-school graduation or until age eighteen. Thus, many students who in former times would have left school early now go on to high school. Holding them back or failing them would result in retarding a large percentage of the school population. For this reason, elementary schools tend more and more to promote all students. (See Chapter 16.) The high school inherits many students who do not meet the old academic standards either in native ability or in amount of previous learning. At the same time the policy of allowing bright children to skip grades has decreased. Schools learned that such promotion tended to retard their social development. Now fast and slow learners progress side by side through the grade levels, bringing to the high school their varying degrees of competence in reading, writing, and arithmetic. In this chapter we are concerned with the few very bright and the few very slow, and how the teacher can best meet their special learning problems.

General Problems with Fast and Slow Learners

Very often the group made up of the extremes in learning ability creates the most difficult discipline problems. No child likes to be bored, and a child who cannot do what the others are doing will be bored. If the material is too hard for the slow student to grasp, he will, unfortunately, often molest other students, annoy the teacher, or keep himself busy in some other undesirable fashion. Similarly, the very bright student who has been able to do all the classwork in half the time it takes the other students will look for new interests. Some very good students have been actually kept from promotion because of their "bad behavior"; yet these students were behavior problems only because their very high intelligence was not properly guided.

The teacher may very well be able to handle the discipline problem of the dull child by means of either intimidation or busy-work. But this tactic does not provide these children with the special preparation that each needs for his future role in society. The slow student who sees no chance to be a useful citizen may become delinquent. Although all delinquents are not retarded or dull children, a majority has failed in school, and many are below average in mental ability. Good teachers need to look regularly to see whether or not experiences in their classrooms may help to produce delinquents.

To the very bright student, the teacher has an even more urgent social responsibility. Many of the leaders in business, the professions, government, will be drawn from the ranks of superior students. The world can never have enough people with trained intelligence. Those with the ability to lead in intellectual or active pursuits need to be helped to develop the qualities of responsible leadership. It is not enough to keep the bright child busy; he needs to understand his social obligation and the right uses of his intellect for the good of all.

The teacher's concern, then, is that the slow students will not impede and that the bright students will help to maximize class progress. These goals are not abstract. They can be translated into the practical everyday classroom teaching by using principles like the following:

1. All students who deviate markedly from the norm feel conspicuous. If the student is too bright, too slow, or is markedly behind in his school performance he feels that everyone else is aware of his difference. For this reason these students are often either very aggressive, as though to say, "I'll

tell you all about myself before you can find out," or very shy and retiring, as though to shrink into a psychological corner where nobody can really see them. In either case, the shyness or aggression should receive minimal reaction from the teacher. The teacher should do his best to handle the fast or slow learner as if that learner were acting just like everybody else.

2. All individuals who are different from the majority are more sensitive than the average. Even the very dull student is apt to respond in an unexpected way to what he considers undue attention. This heightened sensitivity is also to be found among students from minority groups, and in many ways those with special problems react very much like individuals in a minority group. The teacher, aware of this feeling on the part of the student, often overreacts. In this same way the teacher is apt to be too nice to a Negro student in an attempt to show that he does not really bear the student any prejudice. Yet this overniceness is not accepted by the person toward whom it is directed. Another parallel illustration may be seen in a study of injured veterans.[1] The research showed in part that the injured individual wanted most of all to have others face his injuries normally. If he were blind or crippled, he did not want others to ignore this condition, but neither did he want pity or worry because he was handicapped.

3. Any kind of exceptional endowment has significant repercussions in the whole life of the student.[2] Both very bright and very dull students pose special problems to their own families. Often these students have been overprotected by their parents who have sought to smooth the path for them. This sort of treatment may be all very well in the confines of the home, but the total effect on the individual is to keep him a child far longer than his classmates.

At the other extreme are young people with a special problem whose parents have found this problem more of an irritant than anything else. The difficult quandary of parents with a slow-learning child is to accept his mental deficiency and still give him as full love as any other child in the family. Unquestionably these students are more trouble at home. Some parents respond by rejecting and neglecting them. This in turn may result in serious personality repercussions in the slow learner. The teacher, therefore, will want to gain insight into the home situation of all such children in order to see clearly how they have been treated at home.

4. The goals for the normal child may not seem appropriate to the too fast or too slow students. The teacher who suggests life choices that presume a normal endowment will sometimes be perplexed because some students react so negatively to what appear to be very reasonable aspirations. The reason is that such aspirations are felt to be either completely beyond their

[1] Army Medical Research and Development Board, "Social Psychological Rehabilitation of the Physically Handicapped: Adjustment to Misfortune," Final report, April 1, 1948 (Washington, D.C.: Office of the Surgeon General, War Department, 1948).

[2] "Parents' Problems with Exceptional Children" in *The Education of Exceptional Children,* Forty-ninth Yearbook, Part II, National Society for the Study of Education (Chicago: University of Chicago Press, 1950).

range or beneath their abilities. The very superior student, for example, may scorn what appear to be very low-level ambitions. Motivation of these students is directly affected by goal-setting. Thus, the teacher who has such students should study them intensively as individuals to help them set goals which they can accept as reasonable.

Homogeneous Groupings for Fast and Slow Learners

With the development of tests to show the variations in students' abilities, it became more and more common for schools to start separating students into slow and fast groups. Sometimes three different levels for the same grade were distinguished on the basis of intelligence and reading tests. Other schools set up vocational, general, and college-preparatory courses that served the same purpose. The practice is less common in schools with enrollments of 250 or less, but about three fourths of the schools in the country with enrollments over 500 have ability groupings.[3] The elementary schools have been abandoning the practice in recent years, but in the larger high schools it is still common.

Is the practice of ability grouping educationally wise? Does ability grouping promote academic learning and social development? While the evidence is not clear-cut, there is more and more weight on the side of abandoning ability groupings. The use of intelligence test scores for such groupings assumes that intelligence is a single variable. However, a glance at any intelligence test is enough to demonstrate that intelligence as measured by the tests is made up of such different factors as verbal, spatial, problem solving, manipulative, and imaginative aptitudes. Thus, students who excel in one aspect of intelligence may not do so well in another. This variation may not be revealed by the gross score. There is also some evidence that the intelligence tests as developed to date emphasize certain cultural learnings that derive from socioeconomic advantages and do not therefore really measure innate ability to learn and to solve problems.[4]

Since intelligence tests are heavily verbal, and particularly group intelligence tests, children with generally superior abilities but lacking in verbal facility are penalized in homogeneous grouping. They

[3] Sorenson, Herbert, *Psychology in Education* (New York: McGraw-Hill Book Company, Inc., 1948), p. 237. Also, Smith, B. O., and A. J. Dolis, "Recent Developments in Grouping: A Minimum Bibliography," *Educational Leadership*, 4:403-411 (March, 1947).

[4] Davis, Allison, *Social Class Influences Upon Learning* (Cambridge, Mass.: Harvard University Press, 1948). See also Davis, Allison, *Intelligence and Cultural Differences* (Chicago: University of Chicago Press, 1951.)

will be placed with similarly less verbally skillful students and may never learn to develop verbal facility. In a heterogeneous group, their special aptitude can be rewarded at the same time that they are learning from others whose skills are different.

Some evidence has been found that homogeneous grouping will inhibit rather than promote academic learning. In subjects like social studies, where variety of experience, background, and point of view provide the meat of lively learning, ability groupings limit the interchange of experience and thus reduce the possibilities for learning.[5] So complex is the human organism, so various the needs of any given adolescent, that the skillful teacher, rather than seeking homogeneous classrooms based on IQ will do better to set up subgroups in his classrooms based on many kinds of needs, functions, and activities (see Chapter 8). Thus the slow child will find himself working in several different groups through a semester, will avoid the stigma of being in a slow class, and yet at the same time will be given a chance to work at his own speed.[6]

Although we have indicated that there are important personal and social reasons why it seems unwise to encourage homogeneous grouping, it is not realistic to ignore the fact that homogeneous grouping is found in most of the larger high schools. In a later section of this chapter we will discuss how the teacher who finds himself with a class made up mostly of fast or slow learners may best proceed (see pages 272 and 277).

Teaching the Slow Learners

The slow-learning student is one whose intellectual ability as measured by the standard intelligence tests falls in the range between 70 and 91.[7] Children falling below an IQ of 70 are usually cared for either in state institutions or in special classrooms in large school systems.

It must be remembered that some students may be slow learners because of factors other than limited intellectual capacity. For example, this happened in a Michigan classroom.

> Janice was accepted by her teachers, her classmates, and her family as being not very bright. She seemed to have trouble with her school-

[5] Corey, Stephen M., R. J. Havighurst, and D. A. Prescott, "Grouping Children: A Discussion," *Educational Leadership,* 4:365-373 (March, 1947), p. 371.

[6] See entire issue of *Educational Leadership,* Vol. 4, March, 1947. Also, National Society for the Study of Education. *The Grouping of Pupils,* 35th Yearbook, Part I (Bloomington, Illinois: Public School Publishing Company, 1936).

[7] Featherstone, W. B., *Teaching the Slow Learner* (New York: Bureau of Publications, Teachers College, Columbia University, 1941), p. 2.

> work, could not read very well, and, in general, seemed destined for routine jobs. About the middle of her high-school career one teacher, after observing her rather closely, suggested that her eyes be tested. It was found that she was very nearsighted. Glasses were given her and Janice found that she could read the blackboard for the first time. She could read her schoolbooks without tiring quickly. Her problems did not disappear overnight, but by graduation she was a better than average student.

Many schools provide physical examinations that usually detect such gross physical handicaps as that just described. But it is important to remember that some slow-learning students may have physical difficulties of a less obvious nature. When students appear to be working at a lower than normal rate, it may be advisable for the teacher to suggest more extensive physical examinations.

Sometimes emotional troubles impede learning. Conflict in the home or poor adjustment to age-mates makes the world so unpleasant or so disturbing that the student cannot, no matter how hard he tries, take in very much of the material of the classroom. Sometimes students have had some bitter experience with failure, and, rather than feel that terror again, they will not take any kind of role in the classroom. Thus, they are actually *afraid* to learn, rather than incapable.

Although both physical and emotional factors may make a normally endowed child appear to be a slow learner, here we are especially concerned with those students who really do have limited learning capacities. How can these students be detected and what can be done to improve their opportunities to learn?

Identifying the Slow Learner

What does a slow-learning child act and look like? Sometimes there is a stereotype of the vacuous, glazed look of the very dull. These are the students whose faces look empty—there is no spark or life in their expression. They rarely respond to the moods of a class. When the other youngsters are laughing at a joke, the dull student has not understood what it was all about. They are the last ones to open their books, have usually forgotten pencils and paper, usually do not know what the assignment is, and cannot follow the teacher's directions.

However, this dull look is not so typical as we think. The slow learner is often a very happy, gay, extroverted sort of person. His sense of the world is that it is a relatively simple, pleasant place, and he is apt to be less worried by the future, since he understands fewer of the consequences of his own actions. What appears to be irresponsibility is actually a somewhat more restricted view of the world so that fewer things worry him. Teachers often find that slow learners can be the happiest, pleasantest, most well-adjusted students when classroom tasks are appropriate to their abilities. Since most teachers tend to be concerned about the larger world, aware of the many problems that life presents, such students may seem very out of place and most unnatural. Some teachers may go so far as to try to make these happy youngsters worried and anxious, since they feel that it is not "normal" for students not to care about the future. These teachers would do better to try to understand the differences between slow learners and themselves, rather than try to make the students over.

What other behaviors identify the slow-learning child? For one thing, they are often very responsive to personal attention. If treated with kindness, they freely respond with greater effort in school tasks.

> Joe was very far behind the rest of the class in all his work. He was never busy when the others were. He interrupted with foolish questions. Miss English berated him constantly. One day she noticed that he, as usual, was not working. She caught his eye. She smiled. He looked very startled, grinned weakly, even made a gesture toward working. She decided to keep trying good will and good humor. He was not quick to respond, but she persisted. And he did change. He tried to get his schoolwork done, though his success was still not notable.

But the greatest difference in behavior between slow-learning students and other students, of course, is in the way they think. Most teachers have had little, if any, close contact with people of average or below-normal mental processes. By the very selection of the teaching profession, by his broad education, the teacher has put himself in a superior group of individuals. Probably it is only with other people of similar advantages that he has associated closely for many years. It is therefore often extremely difficult for the teacher to grasp the way in which the average or below-average mind learns. The problems facing a business education teacher are illustrative:

> Most teachers are of above average intelligence. They can therefore understand the intellectual and motivation problems of those who should be learning shorthand. However, teachers find it very difficult to understand the type of mentality of those who will be undertaking the routine clerical work, and therefore they fail to see the kind of training the students need.[8]

[8] Tonne, Herbert A., "Clerical Training for Low Ability Students," *Balance Sheet,* 31:249-251 (February, 1950).

The slow learner actually puts facts together differently, generalizes differently, thinks differently. He can retain few details, few facts. He remembers attitudes, feelings, emotions, more than data. He can report on his reactions but has little insight into why he responded as he did. Abstractions are difficult for him; he works from one concrete situation to another concrete situation, but cannot very often make the generalized connection between them. For example, if asked to find out why the United Nations is more apt to succeed than the League of Nations, he will probably fail miserably.

Precautions in Handling Slow Learners

Intelligence has many facets. A student who is very creative in writing may be very slow in arithmetical reasoning. Another student who responds very well to the orderly sequence of material in a science class may become very confused when asked to see the order in social data. The teacher must exercise great care about assuming that the slow-learning student in his class is a slow student in all classes. Although this assumption is true of many of the slow students, it must not be applied indiscriminately to all. In any classroom, there should be opportunities for all *types* of abilities to be rewarded, as well as for all *levels* of abilities to succeed.

Frequently the teacher who identifies one of the slow-learning students will suggest that he be given the chance to do shopwork, or be placed in clerical and business training classes, or put in music and art courses. The teachers of these fields are likely to begin to feel that their classes are dumping grounds for the misfits of the school. This method of dealing with the slow student is a mistake for two reasons.

First, this policy assumes that these manual arts or even the fine arts require less native ability than do the other academic courses. Actually, it takes a high degree of a rather special kind of intelligence to make a good secretary, a good mechanic, a good artist or musician. The lack of verbal skill does not mean that these slower children will necessarily be more interested in less verbal areas. It is untenable to assume that merely because a student does poorly in reading, he therefore will be interested in and do well in mechanical skills.

Second, if the slow learners are moved completely into the so-called vocational courses, they are prevented from having as broad cultural backgrounds as those with greater verbal ability. Furthermore, the slower student is more apt to run into conflict with society simply because it is so difficult for him to understand its complexities. It is therefore more important, rather than less, that he be given a full share of education in the basic courses that lead into social understanding. The real job of the teachers of literature, social science, history, science, and mathematics is so to arrange their learning experiences that the slow as well as the average or bright student can become a well-educated citizen, a competent worker, and a good parent.

The Background of the Slow Learner

When dealing with the slow-learning student in the high school, the teacher should bear in mind constantly the kind of school history that student has probably had. It is tragic but true that for many of these slower students, school has become a place of terror, or boredom, or cruelty, or painful embarrassment, or all of these. These students have known failure before; usually they started falling behind early in their elementary-school career. Sometimes their first failures came as the result of being out of school because of prolonged illness, after which they were never able to catch up. Perhaps a particular subject was failed, and the failure has permeated their whole educational attitude. There may have been a traumatic experience with a given teacher, so that the student felt that learning was too painful for him. Sometimes the parental attitude toward the slow learner has had a bearing upon his ability to progress in school. It has been observed that where parents press the child beyond his ability to produce, the slow student often retreats and will not even work up to whatever capacity he does possess.

How can the teacher gain insight into the background of the slow student? Several sources are available. Consultation with his previous teachers often turns up valuable information, while school records may show where the first evidence appeared of inability to progress at the expected rate. Interviews with the student, of course, should prove important sources of information. (The procedure of student interviews is described in Chapter 18.)

When the slow learner is being interviewed, several admonitions need to be kept in mind. First, the interview should be as routine as possible. The slow learner needs reassurance. He will be suspicious if he is treated differently until he learns that this treatment will aid him. It is best to interview all the students in the classroom, even though the real purpose is to interview only a few;

then no student will feel singled out for special and perhaps at first unwanted attention.

Second, in the interview itself, the teacher should indicate genuine interest in the student's problems. At no time should the teacher show disapproval, disappointment, or censure of the information given by the student in the interview. Understanding and acceptance of the student's report of his reasons for his failure is a prerequisite to gaining insight into the true cause. Probably the student will have his own protective explanations for his failure, built on a variety of obviously spurious circumstances. Thus, he protects himself from facing any damaging truth about himself. The teacher should not take this self-protection away from the student by questioning whether he has the right view of his own problem. Rather, the teacher should accept the student's explanation and from there work on the recognition of a learning problem that the teacher and the student together can solve.

Before turning to the fast learners, let us review the problem of the teacher who must deal with a few slow learners in a class of average and above-average ability (heterogeneous grouping) and consider the problem of the teacher who must deal with a class made up principally of slow learners (homogeneous grouping).

The Slow Learner in the Heterogeneous Class

The preceding portions of this chapter indicate in general what the teacher can do when a few slow learners turn up in the average classroom. To these general principles can be added some specific practices that have proved helpful:

1. Try to have the slow learner become as much a part of the on-going class activities as possible. That is, wherever the slow learner can make a contribution to any aspect of the classroom, he should be given the opportunity to do so. He can run many errands, perform many clerical and other routine tasks around the room, be scorekeeper for review games, act as monitor, timekeeper, shelf straightener.
2. Make available special materials for the slow learner. Simplified texts, special readings, shorter problems, should be prepared ahead of time by the teacher for the slower student. It is not enough to keep him out of mischief; he also should be helped to learn.
3. Provide a variety of classroom activities for learning. Making of models, charts, and bulletin boards, giving oral reports, taking care of room arrangements, room libraries, files of current materials, and similar duties all give the slow learner an opportunity to use his somewhat limited talents in some constructive fashion.
4. Use group techniques to provide the slow learner with an opportunity to learn by a kind of osmosis. If he finds it hard to answer problems

or do assignments, much of the assigned work can be done in small study groups made up of both bright and slow students. The slower ones then can benefit by observation, association, and actual assistance of others.

5. Provide an atmosphere of sympathetic understanding. Too often the busy teacher becomes impatient and overcritical of the slow learner, who never seems to get the point, who always has to ask the question that was just answered. The teacher must constantly remember the handicap that restricts such children and treat them with *consistent* patience and good humor.

6. Use some of the very bright students as coaches or tutors to work with the slower students. Used judiciously, this procedure makes the most of the talents of both very fast and very slow students and takes some of the burden of individual instruction off the teacher's shoulders. At the same time it provides a chance for the slow learner to keep up with the class.

7. Discuss the student's progress with him as often as possible, pointing out his strengths and being realistic about his weaknesses. Where grading is on an absolute level of achievement, it is important to cushion for the slow student the inevitable low grade. This can be best accomplished by individual conferences.

8. Plan to give from time to time a test or examination that is designed to provide the slow learner with a chance to get a good grade. By putting in very easy questions, very obvious problems, the slow learner may have a few success experiences and obtain a somewhat better personal feeling toward trying to learn. The test has shown him that he, too, is capable of learning something.

The Slow Learner in the Homogeneous Class

Some teachers find a whole class of slow learners a challenge; others dread it. Admittedly the problems are many. The class is often characterized by a general apathy, the students being usually less than interested in classroom work, particularly in the academic subjects. The slow progress of the class makes severe demands on the teacher's patience. Sometimes such classes also include brighter students who have behavior or remedial difficulties but who have failed to keep up with the work of their classmates. They are thus placed with the slow group, and they are the worst problem the teacher can have when dealing with slow learners. Appropriate guidance for such students is the only recourse the teacher can have, or they will effectively disrupt all learning.

For a class made up predominantly of very slow students, these suggestions should be helpful:

1. Select text and other learning material very carefully. Such students should not be expected to read the text material used in average or rapid classes. If no additional texts are available, extensive use should be made

of current materials, and other instructional materials that are both more popularly written and of generally greater intrinsic appeal.

2. Consider the course content very carefully, and decide on a minimum of content and concepts to be covered during the semester. Keep reading assignments to a minimum, and do not expect a high level of proficiency in spelling.

3. Plan class time for ample supervised study. Use this time to help each student as much as possible. Many slow students simply will not study at home or come from homes where study is impossible. In-class study is therefore extremely important.

4. Provide many situations in which success in subject matter may be experienced.

5. Make abundant use of field trips, visitors, audio-visual materials and other outside activities to provide a number of different avenues for learning.

6. Never make remarks about the intellectual capacities of the class. Interclass comparisons should not be made. The students are already only too keenly aware of the segregation that has put them in a special class.

7. Focus content on life applications at all times. Weave into the activities and materials references to their part-time jobs, their hot rods and motorcycles, their heroes in sports, motion pictures and television.

8. Be prepared to go over the same material many times. This demands considerable patience on the part of the teacher and is often irritating to the bright mind of the average teacher. To avoid this personal frustration and also to help the slow learners, the teacher should plan out at least three different ways of presenting the same concept. In this way a needed variety is achieved and the mental hygiene of both teacher and student is sustained.

9. Bear in mind the fact that the slow learners have as rich an experiential life as any adolescent. Exploit it fully in every phase of subject matter. Ask students, "Have you ever known people like this?" Or, "Did any of you ever hear someone say that?" Or, "Did anyone in your family ever travel to such a place?"

10. Spend time early in the semester to get to know the background and individual problems of each student. This is essential with slow learners as pointed out previously. It will repay the teacher in later rapport with the students and in conferences with parents and school counselors.

11. Use bulletin boards liberally for displays of student material. Be sure that it is not always the same students who get their work put up. It is often useful to put up *everything* that was done by everyone in the class—or a random sample of this work—so that even the least able can gain some satisfaction out of seeing his work on display.

12. Plan for short learning units. The slow learner absorbs more if it comes in small doses. Do not expect much carry-over from day to day. Call on students to summarize each day's work and to recall for the class what was covered the day before.

13. Do not overlook the fact that the slow learner can and should work just as hard as any other student, even if the total amount learned is less, and the learning pace is slower. A challenging, working atmosphere is as essential here as with faster students.

The Slow Learner in Non-academic Courses

Teachers of "non-academic" courses have some special problems not covered by the suggestions listed above. First of all, such teachers have a personal problem in their relation with other members of the faculty. They must guard against building up defensive attitudes. And they should not, as a counter-reaction, make their courses more academic than the traditional academic courses. Some art teachers, for instance, who resent the patronizing attitude often taken toward art courses—the attitude that these courses are primarily for those who cannot learn the solid courses such as English and mathematics—may be tempted to make their art courses as difficult as those in advanced art schools. In this case, of course, slow learners are quickly exposed as inadequate and fail the course.

The teacher of non-academic classes must also avoid neglecting the slower students, particularly when there appear a few of the bright or talented. It is a temptation to get personal satisfaction out of close work with these rarer students and doom the majority of the class to dull and fruitless activity. It is also all too easy to threaten students with "because this is a noncollege prep course you should not think that you don't have to work." The slow, of course, cannot cope with heavy assignments.

It is obvious that there must be some place for the slow learners, for they are as much a part of our society as the fast learners. The teacher who finds them flocking to his courses should realize that, even though these students seem less rewarding, at the same time the teacher can give them some greatly needed support. In art, for instance, the slower students can enjoy freedom to use color, to try unusual materials, to work on such practical problems as redecorating their own rooms at home, of collecting pictures that they like from current magazines, of making Christmas cards, valentines, or simple designs for block-printing materials. These may require a minimum of talent, but they can add substantially to the life of the slow learner.

Summary

The slow learners need our attention perhaps more than most students because of their own sense of failure and social inadequacy. In keeping them from becoming dissatisfied members of society and from making drastic mistakes in their own life decisions, the teacher can play a highly significant role.

These principles illustrate how the teacher should work with slow-learning students:

1. Check to see that slowness in learning is really due to low intellectual capacity and not to physical or psychological deterrents.

2. Remember that the seeming irresponsibility of the slow learner is directly attributable to his limited ability to foresee the consequences of his actions.

3. Try kindness and appreciation. Slow learners often have had long years of unpleasant treatment from teachers and others.

4. Keep learning materials on a concrete level.

5. Slowness in one area of learning does not necessarily mean slowness in all areas. See how the student is getting along with the rest of his studies; then capitalize on his strengths.

6. Give the slow learner more rather than fewer opportunities to develop an understanding of our world.

7. Keep in mind that the more insight you have into the slow learner's background and the more contact with his out-of-school life, the better able you will be to help him.

Teaching the Fast Learners

Consider the following students:

> Johnny has all the answers. Before Miss Brown is finished explaining the contribution of Einstein to the development of the atomic bomb, his hand is waving wildly in the air, ready to launch into a vivid, accurate, rapid, half-hour lecture of his own on $E = mc^2$.
>
> Annabelle never has to study. Her papers come in with the regularity of a ticking clock; neat, polished, perfect. She has an aloof and bored expression during the hour's discussion of King Lear. Yet, when asked to write a theme on the major issues raised, she does so effortlessly and with remarkable insight.
>
> Gordon is a pest. He gets every assignment done in one tenth of the time it takes the rest of the class. His work can be quite good, but it is usually sloppy, careless, tossed off in a hurry. Then he spends the rest of the time making life miserable for Mr. Jones, Mrs. Gray, Mr. Snyder—in fact, for every teacher he has. He can think of more ways to annoy teachers than a whole school of adolescents.

What do the above students have in common? It is this: they are all very bright. They have intelligence quotients ranging from 140 on up. Their problems, at times, seem very similar to those of the slow learner and sometimes very different. While work for the slow learner needs to be simplified and slowed down, work for the fast student needs to be accelerated, made more complex.

There are some popular notions about geniuses that should be dispelled. According to observers[9] the very bright student is usually physically as healthy as any other child, if not more so, is apt to be as stable emotionally, as other students if not more so—in general, he is a picture of superiority in many areas, not merely in in-

[9] National Society for the Study of Education, *The Education of Exceptional Children,* Forty-ninth Yearbook, Part II, Chap. III, pp. 62-46.

telligence. It is popularly expected that the very bright will somehow be peculiar; yet, research studies contradict this notion. It is true that the very bright child is often to be found associating with older persons. His interests have grown faster than those of his contemporaries, and his mind can grasp more mature matters. At the same time, his social maturity may not have kept pace.[10] In the schools examples of this will often be seen. In addition, the brightest in a class will very often be the youngest, and this difference in age may make him feel awkward, out of place, odd. Of course, the very bright cannot be singled out merely by looking about the room for the most serious, the squirmiest, the thinnest. By appearance alone the bright student will not be detected.

Some of these fast learners have particular difficulties because of the cultural patterns for the sexes. We hold up different standards, different roles for boys and girls. The adolescent is more insecure and more sensitive to these different roles than adults who have become used to their social position. It is not unusual to find very bright girls refusing to demonstrate their intelligence. They may refuse to do more than the minimum of schoolwork; they prefer to get by on very average performance, and even deliberately do poorly in subjects they know well. Why is this? It comes most directly from an attitude common among adolescents that women are not supposed to know so much as men; that boys prefer the "dumb blonde." In one school where the grade averages of all the students are published annually, the girls openly admit that it would be very dangerous for them as "date material" to get grade averages that were too high. The boys become afraid of them and won't ask a "brain" out for a coke or a dance. Against such social pressure, the teacher may easily feel helpless. The question may be raised as to whether the teacher is doing that girl a disservice by demanding that she use her superior brain; by that token, she may alienate herself from her social group; she may be educated out of adjustment to her own concept of her proper role. On the other hand, the teacher may feel that the set of values that says that women must hide intelligence is a poor one, since our society needs all the educated talent it has to deal with the great problems of today's civilization.

The problem of the girl who will not work to capacity is very similar to that of the boy who may use his intelligence only selectively. He may be the star in the football field because of his photographic memory for plays and his keen, quick mind in figuring

[10] Educational Policies Commission, *Education of the Gifted* (Washington: National Education Association, 1950), p. 50.

strategy. But when it comes to analyzing geometric proofs, he just won't be bothered. Or, like the girl described above, he will refuse to discuss or consider poetry or music or art because he thinks of it as "sissy stuff." The problems that such youngsters raise are not easily solved. All teachers are reluctant to see a bright student sit through classes without applying his intelligence to the material at hand. But teachers need to recognize the fact that to keep his self-respect a boy must try to grow up into his vision of what a real man is—a vision that reflects some of the problems and distortions of the adult world.

The Fast Learner Under Homogeneous Grouping

School practices with fast learners vary about as much as those with slow learners. The advantages and disadvantages of ability grouping for fast learners have been debated at length. In commenting on the psychological impact of this grouping, Caroline Zachry says:

> Little is to be gained by homogeneous grouping. Not only does this often leave out of account the differing rates of learning among the gifted which stem from physical and emotional factors. More important, much may be lost by such grouping in opportunity for social development and for learning to give and take in other life situations. The segregation of gifted students places an improper emphasis upon the value of a single aspect of personality often without giving these young people opportunity to appreciate other potentialities in themselves or differing qualities in their peers. It is likely to offer but little incentive for putting to practice that added responsibility to others that is an obligation of superiority in any form of endeavor.[11]

To minimize these limitations, the teacher with a class of the upper range of intelligence quotients can plan programs around the following major principles:

1. Recognize individual differences in interests and needs. While ability of the group may be generally superior, there will continue to be great differences in interests and needs.
2. Establish a high level of performance that challenges the abilities of the group. There should be a constant attempt to help them establish a standard of workmanship that makes them uncomfortable with an inferior piece of work. This is best accomplished by group discussion, by inquiry on the part of the teacher as to what more could be done, by de-emphasis on grades and heavy emphasis on performance, by having available a rich range of resources and possibilities.

[11] Zachry, Caroline, *Emotion and Conduct in Adolescence* (New York: Appleton-Century-Crofts, Inc., 1940), p. 247.

3. Devote special attention to the development of adequate social skills. The brighter the student the more apt he is to be out of step with his fellows. The teacher may use material that emphasizes social understanding, and classroom techniques that promote cooperation and interchange.

4. Encourage individual initiative and a variety of student leadership. The bright student will acquire leadership roles often just because he is bright, not because he is a sound leader. Responsibilities of leaders for being sensitive to the needs and feelings of the followers is an important aspect of the education of the very bright. Such understanding comes through being given opportunities to take responsibility.

5. Do not let the class get a false idea of superiority. The practice of segregation may produce in the bright students a spurious sense of their own position at the top of the group. Showing the students how much more they have to learn and demonstrating the lessons to be learned from others, regardless of IQ, will help reduce this possibility.

6. Set a high level of expectation regarding self-discipline, self-control, and self-direction. The class of bright students can go a long way in educating themselves and in running their own affairs with a high level of maturity if an opportunity is provided for making mistakes under guidance. The bright student needs the mature adult as much as a slow student, but the former can more quickly learn from his experiences.

The Fast Learner in the Heterogeneous Class

In classes where the bright students are found with all the other varieties of intelligence and personality, the teacher should be on the alert to give them special aid and help. Critics of public education sometimes say that too much of our time in school is devoted to protecting the dull and teaching the mediocre. It may be that we should give more attention to the needs of the gifted. The total society benefits when its gifted members are well trained to use their talents for the good of the larger group.

The bright student profits from an enriched program. While the bright student follows the curriculum pattern of his classmates, he should be expected also to explore many side avenues of interest. Some classroom techniques for meeting the needs of fast learners in mixed classes are summarized below:

1. Materials on an adult level covering the material of the course should be available in the classroom. These should be particularly recommended to the bright student as a substitute for textbook material wherever possible.

2. Do not allow bright students to monopolize the teacher's time. Sometimes the response of the bright student is so rewarding that the teacher gears a whole class to these few. This does the rest of the class a disservice and, moreover, is apt to interfere with the optimum adjustment of the bright students.

3. Allow bright students to develop all their talents. Too often the bookish interests of the bright student are exploited as though that were

the only demonstration of intelligence that really counted. The superior student is often superior in other ways. This should be recognized by the teacher in making assignments. The overbookishness of the superior student can be a major handicap in later social and personal adjustment.

Identifying the very bright students is a major responsibility of the teacher. By using school records carefully, such students can be spotted early. Sometimes the maladjusted student who is very bright is not recognized because of his gross classroom behavior. However, if his superior intelligence is given some recognition, the behavior problem can be met. The teacher will do the most to aid the superior student by enriching his intellectual fare while facilitating his acceptance as a desirable member of the class.

Summary

Slow and fast learners present special problems for the teacher. An early recognition of these significant differences will make classroom instruction more rewarding for all concerned. When the teacher plans his work, gathers materials, selects content, he should bear in mind always the differing needs of the very fast and very slow and make adequate provision for them. Each subject field provides different problems to be solved for both slow and fast students, and also provides different opportunities for significant learning experiences. The bibliography at the end of this chapter includes some references to adaptations in different fields that have been successfully used for both slow and fast learners. There are many more such accounts to be found in the professional literature. They will be an invaluable source of help for the teacher in providing maximum learning for these students.

Selected References

General

Garrison, Karl C. *The Psychology of Exceptional Children.* New York: The Ronald Press Company, 1950. A good basic reference that includes other special problems of learning met when teaching students with physical as well as mental handicaps.

Greenberg, H. A. "Problems of Parents of Handicapped Children," *Journal of Exceptional Children,* 17:1-70, (October, 1950). Patterns of parent reaction to children who present special problems in growth or adjustment.

Heck, Arch O. *The Education of Exceptional Children.* New York: McGraw-Hill Book Company, Inc., 1940. A broad coverage of the field of adapting instruction to special needs.

National Society for the Study of Education. *The Grouping of Pupils,* Thirty-fifth Yearbook, Part I. Bloomington: Public School Publishing

Co., 1936. The pros and cons of ability grouping ably presented by a number of experts.

National Society for the Study of Education. *The Education of Exceptional Children.* Forty-ninth Yearbook, Part II. Chicago: University of Chicago Press, 1950. Another good general reference.

For Slow Learners

Blaha, M. Jay, *et al.* "The Slow Learner in the Secondary School," Secondary Curriculum Monograph: M-70, Los Angeles County Schools, Division of Secondary Education, Los Angeles, Calif. Mimeographed. 69 pp. Specific recommendations for adjusting classroom practices for the slow learner. Extensive bibliography.

Boland, Ruth F. "High School Pupils with I.Q.'s below 75," *Understanding the Child,* 16:11-14 (January, 1947). Special problems of the extremely retarded student who occasionally is found in regular high-school classes; stresses parent needs also.

Burt, Cyril. *The Backward Child.* New York: Appleton-Century-Crofts, Inc., 1937. A standard work covering the major problems of the slow child.

Davis, Delpha. "Heart, Mind and Indignation," *Clearing House,* 23:333-335 (February, 1949). A teacher describes how she adjusted ninth-grade English to the special needs of 31 students with IQ's from 62-90, ages fourteen to eighteen.

Featherstone, W. B. *Teaching the Slow Learner.* New York: Bureau of Publications, Teachers College, Columbia University, 1941. A careful, nontechnical discussion of the over-all problem of the slow learner in the school, with special emphasis on the younger age group.

Lass, A. H., and F. A. Smerling. "The English Teacher and the Slow Learner," *High Points,* 29:5-12 (February, 1947). Characteristics of slow learners and specific teaching techniques to deal with these.

National Education Association. "High School Methods with Slow Learners," *NEA Research Bulletin,* 21:59-87 (October, 1943). A survey of opinion and practice in meeting needs of slow learners; special methods in different subject areas are also described.

Rickert, Mary O. "Motivation for Slow Learners," *English Journal,* 38:43-44 (January, 1949). Using field trips as a basis of English skill work proved very effective with a class of students of below average ability.

"Symposium—Special Services for Slow Learners," *California Journal of Secondary Education,* 26:5-28 (January, 1951). Five articles dealing with varied methods of meeting the needs of slow learners in secondary schools.

Tonne, Herbert A. "Clerical Training for Low Ability Students," *The Balance Sheet,* 31:249-251 (February, 1950). Some of the special learning needs in this area for the teacher to note.

For Fast Learners

Bobbitt, Blanche. "What Science Teachers Can Do for Gifted Pupils," *Clearing House,* 22:267-269 (January, 1948). A supervisor of science tells what opportunities there are for the high-school teacher to enrich the curriculum for exceptionally bright children, including science-club activities, extra time in the laboratory, acting as laboratory assistants, special experiments, social and professional contacts with scientists, and others.

Educational Policies Commission. *Education of the Gifted.* Washington, D.C.: National Education Association, 1950. A direct challenge to the schools to find and educate those of superior intelligence for responsible democratic leadership.

"Gifted Child, The," *Understanding the Child,* 17:33-64 (April, 1948). Entire issue devoted to problems of understanding the gifted child, prepared in collaboration with the American Association for Gifted Children; contains articles on research, special problems, clinical studies, and other topics; gives extensive bibliography.

National Education Association. "High School Methods with Superior Students," *NEA Research Bulletin,* 19: No. 4, Washington, D.C., September, 1941. Describes the general picture in high schools and some specific programs developed to meet the needs of this group.

Strang, Ruth. "Inner World of Gifted Adolescents," *Journal of Exceptional Children,* 16:97-101, 125 (January, 1950). Analyzes, on the basis of compositions written by 300 high-school pupils in English classes who had IQ's over 120, some of the problems they experience in their personal lives. Suggests such compositions as a means of helping teacher or counselor to learn "how it feels to be a gifted adolescent."

Terman, Lewis M., Melita H. Oden, *et al. The Gifted Child Grows Up; Twenty-five Years Follow-up of a Superior Group.* Genetic Studies of Genius No. 4. Stanford: Stanford University Press, 1947. 448 pp. Sets forth the results of a study in which a group of gifted children in elementary schools 25 years ago were followed through to adulthood.

Witty, Paul (ed.). *The Gifted Child.* Boston: D. C. Heath and Company, 1951. Specialists in this field suggest best practice in identifying the gifted child and meeting his needs.

12. The Communication Skills

THE problems of communication are central to instruction in the high school. The student who is deficient in the basic skills of communication may be unable to learn or, what is just as grave a problem, to demonstrate his learning. In the following chapter we will discuss some of the major diagnostic and remedial techniques which can be employed by classroom teachers in these basic skill areas: reading, writing, speaking, listening.

It has been estimated that in the typical high school, "80 to 90% of all study activities require silent reading as a means of gaining knowledge." [1] What then, we must ask, of the student who has not learned to read very well? What can he expect to achieve in high school? And if a student has not learned how to express himself fluently in writing, can he succeed in high school? What about the student who has never learned to listen? What happens to him in high school? And what of the student who cannot speak effectively?

[1] Blair, G. M., *Diagnostic and Remedial Teaching in Secondary Schools* (New York: The Macmillan Company, 1946), p. 3.

Reading in the High School

Several important generalizations can be made at the outset: First, most high-school classes will include students whose reading range will vary as much as, if not more than, their intelligence quotients. Second, the problem of reading is not restricted to the English teacher alone, or to a specialist in remedial reading. Reading is a tool that must be adapted to different kinds of subject matter; the reading of geometry problems is different from reading *A Tale of Two Cities*. Third, skill in reading must continue to be developed throughout the student's schooling. While the basic groundwork is laid in the elementary grades, increasing comprehension and understanding of the material that is read is a responsibility of the high school. In short, every high-school teacher should consider himself a teacher of reading.

There are available some rather startling data about the reading range of an average classroom in the high school to support the first generalization we made. Of 91 entering high-school freshmen in one school, 2 were able to read at a fourth-grade level, and one could read at the level of a college junior. There were 10 who could read at the fifth-grade level, and 7 who could read as well as college sophomores. The rest of the 91 students were distributed in the remaining grade levels. In another instance, 105 out of 950 ninth-grade students were reading at the third- to fifth-grade level.[2] One study of high school graduating seniors shows that on the one hand 9 per cent were reading at or below the average level for ninth-graders, while 7 per cent of the entering freshmen were reading at or above the average for the seniors.[3] The problem, then, is not only that of the great range to be found on any one grade level, but of extensive overlapping between grades.

Now for the second generalization: a student who reads well in one subject does not necessarily read well in another. A student who understands the intricate detail of a history text may do very poorly when asked to read a play. The kind of imagination required to read a play, reading conversation rather than description, may completely baffle the student. It is important, therefore, for the teacher of each subject matter to consider rather carefully the reading problems peculiar to his own field, problems that will face

[2] Blair, *ibid.*, pp. 6, 7.

[3] National Society for the Study of Education. *Reading in the High School and College,* 1948 Yearbook, Part II (Chicago: University of Chicago Press, 1948), p. 18.

the average student, not just the student with special reading problems.

Reading Problems in Subject Fields

What are some of the special reading problems to be found in the different subject fields?

Fiction:

Where fiction is to be read for enjoyment, plus appreciation of specific literary qualities and personal reference, there is a need for the student to be able to read rapidly, to enjoy the story, to read carefully, to note the literary quality, to read thoughtfully, to see the relationship to himself. Foremost, in the reading of fiction, is probably the ability to read fast enough to follow the story. Some students who are used to reading for detail (boys who have followed instructions in making models or performing experiments), often have great difficulty in adjusting their reading to the fast tempo needed to enjoy fiction. So they complain bitterly about having to read novels. Reading for enjoyment has become almost a lost art, except for the vast audience that devours the comic books, the murder mysteries, and the westerns.

Drama:

Here the imagination of the reader is a most necessary adjunct. At the same time this form of writing is least familiar to the average student. It is unfortunate that reading plays is such a difficult task for youngsters. Restricting the reading of plays to those beyond their maturity may account for some of the difficulty. Some teachers have found recordings and motion pictures of good plays a help in developing the ability to reconstruct imaginatively from dialogue.

Poetry:

Much of the antipathy of young people to poetry is due to cultural stereotypes marking them as odd if they admit they enjoy poetry. In addition, the difference between poetry and their usual reading fare is, as in drama, a very great barrier. Nor do they see much poetry being read in their homes. It is important, then, to give them a chance to enjoy poetry. This probably means that we must begin with poetry which brings the most immediate pleasure, with lyrics and ballads, for example. We do not want our students to remain at a primitive level of appreciation, but they must at least gain this level before other levels are possible. Many students probably will not rise to the level where they can enjoy the finest poetry. But it is better to foster honest appreciation, however limited, than to permit outright rejection. Even limited appreciation requires special skill. Reading for detail, imagery, rhythm, rhyme, form, is alien to our usual reading. Skill will come slowly through choral reading, singing lyrics and ballads, listening to the skilled oral reading of the teacher.

Newspapers and Magazines:

Since the newspaper is the principal reading fare of adults, newspapers should play an important role in the educational experience of high-school students. Most high-school students read the comic page, sport page, and front-page headlines. Reading for the details of the news, for information regarding current events, is much less common. Yet careful appraisal of the news is vital to competent adult living. This ability to detect slanted or distorted reporting requires careful training. Learning to read a newspaper should have a place in many classes. In English classes feature articles and reviews of books, plays, and motion pictures can be used. In the social sciences, newspaper reading can be used in forums on world affairs. Newspapers can provide an important source of mathematical problems: the reporting of sports, for example, includes many percentage situations; the stock market and monetary fluctuation reports contain significant data; advertisements of sales and installment proposals furnish good problems for study.

What has just been said about newspaper reading applies equally well to magazine reading. Our students read indiscriminately and uncritically. They read the "easy" magazines. The better magazines are not read because most students are not encouraged and assisted to enjoy them either at home or at school. The reading task has not been studied to help the student in understanding what he reads. The involved abstractions, the special vocabularies, the adult humor, the sophisticated stories—these are not easily accessible to the average high-school student without aid. Yet if such current fare could be made more palatable and enjoyable to more individuals, the *continuing* education of the student as an adult could be assured.[4]

Art:

To see how symbols and color express ideas constitutes an important *reading* skill. The comparison of the graphic and written expression should be exploited in more classrooms. The art teacher can develop the special vocabulary relating to art media and tools, and reading art criticism can develop ability to evaluate and appraise.

Industrial Arts:

Here the teacher needs to instruct his students in habits of accurate reading. The students must be able to follow cryptic instructions; to carry visual images in mind following a brief reading of instructions. The reading of charts, blueprints, maps, and diagrams involves special attention to detail, learning an entirely new set of symbols, and developing a new concept of spatial and symbolic relations. The ability to translate written instructions into a visual image requires practice and help. The industrial-arts teacher who spends some time on these *reading processes* themselves, aiding students with the unfamiliar material, will find that the resultant hand skill is increased because the student has been able to use the mental shortcuts that reading provides.

Homemaking:

To read a recipe and the directions for putting the ingredients together is not an easy task, as any new bride will report! The instructions in knitting books, the instructions that accompany dress patterns, the symbols on the patterns themselves, all these need special skill in interpretation. Students who cannot easily follow such instructions cannot develop skill in the

[4] For details, see Kinney, Lucien B., and Katharine Dresden, *Better Learning through Current Materials* (Stanford: Stanford University Press, 1949).

processes themselves. The homemaking teacher in addition has the wide range of women's magazines to use to develop discrimination in reading about the home arts. After girls leave school it is important they continue to have the desire to read about how their homes and families may be better managed. The homemaking teacher through reading instruction can set the foundations for the continuing education of these future homemakers.[5]

Commercial Subjects:

The material used in business courses is essentially adult. The business forms that are used—contracts, insurance policies, invoices, government forms—all are couched in adult language and are written in a special vocabulary as well as in special grammatical form. The teacher who spends some time in a careful analysis of the reading problems involved in this kind of material will have aided his students immeasurably. It is such a frequent complaint, "But I can't understand the instructions on my income tax blank," that we might well consider this kind of reading instruction a necessity for all students, not only for business students. Being able to follow printed instructions and to fill in forms accurately are necessary skills; they depend on the ability to read carefully, quickly, and meaningfully.

Mathematics:

Some students are easily able to convert word descriptions of problems into meaning and then into number symbols; but many students must go through a lengthy and laborious mental process every time they run into mathematical problems. The word arrangement is different from that of problem statements in everyday life. So the mathematics teacher finds himself teaching reading much of the time. His main problem is to relate a new number vocabulary to old concepts, and to build new concepts about quantitative relationships. Algebraic and geometric problems, for example, are phrased in strange language patterns; the vocabulary has key words never used outside mathematics. Consequently, much careful preparatory work is necessary before the students are able to analyze for essential meanings. The mathematics teacher needs constantly to relate mathematical problem statements to the *daily life* statement of problems; otherwise, when the student meets mathematical problems out of school, he cannot utilize the in-school problem-solving skill. The differences in language patterns are barriers for the student that the teacher must aid in bridging. In mathematics special attention must be given to students with visual difficulty, since this subject area demands meticulous attention to details. Where students are able to read rapidly, to skim material easily, the mathematics teacher will need to slow them down, to help them read for specifics and for key words occuring in close sequence.

Science:

The vocabulary of science is intricate and specialized. The teacher is faced with the problem of helping students recognize, pronounce, and use correctly words that sound as though they came from a foreign language.

[5] *Reading in Home Economics? Certainly!* (Denver: Denver Public Schools, 1950).

Most important is that the student recognize and understand the essential differences in *meaning* of common scientific terms. Reading a science book is not easy; the texts pack a great deal of material into a small space; the presentation of material is not always designed to have intrinsic interest for the student. Furthermore, the inclusion of many mathematical terms, the use of special symbols and problem terminology, the use of diagrams, graphs, and charts to show processes and relationships—these are all *reading* problems for the average student. If approached as such by the teacher, the content will be more understandable to the student.

Foreign Languages:

The teaching of language is facilitated if as much of the work as possible is closely related to the language already known to the student—English. The language teacher needs to know the reading level of the student in his own language prior to attempting to set reading standards for him in a foreign language. Students already highly skilled verbally in English and having extensive vocabularies will obviously do better than those with limited language experiences. Often the foreign word has no meaning to the student because he is not even familiar with it as an English word. Thus, the vocabulary and understanding necessary for reading in the foreign language must be related to where the student is in his own language. Reading fluently in a foreign language depends partly on familiarity with the new words and word arrangements, but it also depends on having adequate training in the skills of good reading—picking out key words and word phrases, using lead and summary sentence to reveal paragraph meaning, finding clues to whole words and sentences through knowledge of word families and word roots. Thus, the foreign-language teacher should first of all be skilled in teaching reading in English, then adapt such instruction to the new area.

It can be seen from this quick overview of the content fields that each teacher must consider himself in some measure a teacher of reading. Some fields obviously have a greater responsibility here than others, but all fields have their unique reading problems.

Enjoying Reading

A recent survey of reading habits among adults showed that only 21 per cent of all the sample questioned in the United States were reading a book, while in England 45 per cent were reading a book. And this in spite of the fact that 53 per cent of the adult population has gone beyond grade school in the United States while only 13 per cent has done so in England.[6] It may be that one of the contributing factors to this rather unflattering picture of reading habits in the United States is a high-school education conditioning adults negatively to reading books. It has been stated that:[7]

[6] Jackson, J. H., *San Francisco Chronicle,* February 26, 1950.

[7] *What the High Schools Ought to Teach* (Washington, D.C.: American Council on Education, 1940), pp. 12-13.

. . . . much of the material which is presented in textbooks is altogether inappropriate for the cultivation of reading habits. When the history of the United States, for example, is condensed into a book of 500 or 600 pages, it has to be compressed to such an extent that the anecdotes which would make it a lively, interesting subject are almost, if not entirely, left out. Every sentence has to carry an idea requiring minute attention. The book is a compact body of factual statements which does not invite or permit fluent reading. Every sentence must be studied analytically. In mastering the contents of the ordinary textbook in history, the pupil cultivates habits of intellectual procedure which may prevent him throughout life from undertaking the type of reading which is appropriate for most of the materials which he will encounter in books and magazines.

Not only is this so, but in most of the recitations which the pupil attends the teachers show ingenuity in torturing the subject studied by asking all kinds of questions which train the pupil in the most deliberate and minute dissection of what he has read. The result is that whenever a pupil takes up a book he begins to ramble in his thinking, indulging in all kinds of speculation as to the possible questions that one might raise. Pupils begin to think that it requires from three to six months to read through a book.

This quotation does not mean that students should not read textbooks. By no means. The textbook is one of the teacher's major helps in guiding learning. But the teacher must recognize that the text could create negative attitudes toward reading if that is all the reading the student is encouraged to do. "Reading for Enjoyment" is a unit sometimes taught in a single English class—as though no other subject field could provide enjoyable reading! Consider the fascinating reading in biography and special historical fiction. It is certainly no more difficult than much of the text material. Many of the books in popular history provide a fascinating picture of the pageant of history. Authors like de Kruif and Peattie have made scientific writing as fascinating as a mystery story. There is abundant current material in the popular magazines on most of the topics taught in high-school science classes. The articles are written so that science becomes an exciting and satisfying experience. For the study of languages the personal anecdotes of travels abroad, of the lives of immigrants of various national groups in America, the translated fiction of the foreign culture are all excellent materials.

One important aspect of reading instruction is the development of skill in the use of the library. There are not many trained librarians in our schools—not nearly so many as we need. There were 24,314 high schools in the United States in 1945–1946; yet there were only 6,599 librarians. In other words, only about one fourth of all high schools will have a trained person in charge of assisting students to understand and use a library.[8] In many instances, therefore, the task devolves upon the individual teacher, assuming of course that the school has a library. Many high schools have no libraries, and many more have poor or wholly inadequate libraries. In such schools the teacher will have to rely on the local public library. In any case, using the library as a place to find enjoyable and informative material is an important part of any reading program no matter what the subject.

Guides to Better Reading

Now that we have seen the reading problems in the different fields of study and the general need to extend reading interests and library skills, we need some guides to action. Here are some suggestions:

1. Diagnose the reading level of reading material provided for the student. The teacher should carefully examine all texts and collateral reading to see what special reading difficulties might be encountered. Clues will of course be found in the introduction to the book itself: Does it say for what grade level this particular book was written? On what basis was this reading level set? In addition, the teacher should read the material to look for some of the special problems encountered in understanding the concepts introduced.

2. Arrange an environment conducive to the enjoyment of reading. See to it that the room is a pleasant place in which to read silently. Color, light, pictures, comfortable tables and chairs, growing plants and other decorative features all will aid in creating a pleasant place in which reading may thrive.

3. Provide a variety of reading materials. After diagnosing the major reading level of the text, the teacher should have at hand books and other reading material that is both much more difficult and much easier than the text. Then the teacher can guide an individual student in terms of his level of skill.

Each room should have its own library of supplementary reading material. Here the teacher can have at hand just the right item for the students without having to go through much of the routines needed in using a larger school or public library. A browsing shelf with new items displayed prominently and invitingly and a lending system so that students may take books home will be of inestimable help in encouraging reading in any subject field. Using student help in organizing and arranging such a library is a very fine way to teach them simple library procedures. Getting students to lend their own books to others will also encourage reading.

4. Assist the students in special problems of reading peculiar to the subject field. Make lists of the specialized vocabulary that will be encoun-

[8] U.S. Office of Education, *Statistics in the Public High Schools, 1945–1946,* Biennial Survey of Education in the United States, Chap. V, pp. 3, 68.

tered in the week ahead and go over it with the class. It is useful to have large lettered charts on which difficult or special words are presented and defined, with both a dictionary definition and a sentence usage definition, plus an illustration if available. Use the blackboard liberally in writing out new words and word phrases and giving pupils opportunity to raise questions of comprehension.

5. Gear class discussion to the kind of reading skill you desire to develop. If reading is to be done for enjoyment, do not kill this attitude by seeking detail and fact and intricate analysis as an outcome of the reading. Raise problems of attitude, feeling, emotion, bias, new ideas, as revealed through the reading.

6. Divide the class into reading levels for some aspects of instruction. Often a teacher can obtain copies of different texts at different reading levels. Since most texts in a given field cover much the same material, though with varying emphases, this comparison could make for very rich learning as each reading group contributes to the total class discussion those aspects of the problem particularly emphasized in their book.[9]

7. Consult the school files regarding reading scores of students in your class. Many schools conduct routine reading tests of all entering students, but teachers do not make adequate use of such information. A teacher can save himself much worry and disturbance by knowing beforehand the reading level of the students in his class. Then the job of planning reading material to meet individual abilities is made easier.

8. Conduct a study of the class about their reading interests and habits. A simple inventory will often provide a teacher with important information about the general interest range and reading level of the class.

Such an inventory might include the following:

1. Do you enjoy reading?
2. What kinds of things do you like to read most?
3. What kinds of things do you least like to read?
4. Do your parents like to read a lot? What do they read?
5. How many books do your parents have at home?
6. Do you take any newspapers at home? What sections do you like to read best?
7. What magazines do your parents take? Do you read them? Which ones?
8. Do you wear glasses now? Have you ever worn glasses?
9. Do you feel you have any special difficulty in reading? If so, what is it?
10. What are your particular special interests or hobbies?

A similar inventory may be sent home for the parents to fill out regarding the student's reading habits and the parents' own attitudes toward reading. On the basis of such information, the teacher can discover where students are having difficulty, and where he may guide them toward adequate adult reading habits. After such a study has been made, the teacher should place the results in the student's counseling folder so that other

[9] For a detailed analysis of using reading groups in class work see: Bond, Guy L., and Bertha Handlan, *Adapting Instruction in Reading to Individual Differences.* Series on Individualization of Instruction, No. 5 (Minneapolis: University of Minnesota Press, 1948), pp. 65-70.

teachers may make use of the same data without having to constantly quiz the students on their interests and habits.

9. Read aloud to your classes. Teachers often forget that reading aloud can be a very exciting teaching technique. If there is some highly dramatic, interesting, or complicated portion of the subject matter, the teacher should take time out to read a few paragraphs. If this is followed by discussion, reading will be a less mysterious process for many students.

Teachers should use reading aloud *by* students with caution. Few are skilled in the technique. For many students oral reading itself is a barrier to developing good silent reading habits. To read aloud with interest is, however, a valuable skill for any future parent and might well be developed as part of a family living course. Where families read aloud together many important personal as well as intellectual values are achieved.

10. Do a case study of a reading problem. Each beginning teacher should focus his attention during one period of his early teaching on this problem. A valuable device is to do a concentrated case study of a student with a reading handicap. Then, through analysis of an individual problem and the remedial and instructional techniques developed to meet that problem, the teacher will gain important insights to carry over to others with reading difficulties.

Retardation in Reading

Retardation in reading is usually due to a complex of causes. Mental, physical, and emotional factors may all be involved. None of these can be treated in isolation but only in association with the others.

The retarded reader may often be identified by clues like the following:

1. The student seems unable to do the necessary reading.
2. He himself is dissatisfied with his reading, revealed either through specific complaint or through objections to any reading assignments.
3. His reading test scores are in the lowest fourth for his grade.
4. He can use words in speaking that he seems unable to comprehend when they are written.
5. Where he is required to do schoolwork that does not call for any reading, he does average or above in achievement.
6. He shows special personal problems, such as poor family attitude toward school; unusual nervousness; extreme hostility toward teachers; extreme apathy toward classroom occurrences; sluggish physical performance.

This list covers general clues. However, the teacher will also want to note students who show special visual difficulty through any of the following ways:

1. Holding the book very close to the eyes.
2. Holding the book very far away.
3. A severe squint.

4. Odd and consistent reversals of words during an oral exercise.

5. Persistent complaint about headaches as an excuse not to study.

6. Falling asleep in class as soon as a study period occurs.

7. Becoming hyperactive as soon as study period arrives.

8. Inconsistent use of glasses; often students with a reading problem will forget or break glasses.

9. Particularly heavy glasses.

10. Cross-eyes or a damaged eye.

11. Lip movements while reading; actual oral reading accompanying silent reading or residual muscle movements from poor habit training in reading.

12. Moving the head to follow the line of the page. A good reader will move the eyes, a poor reader who reads word by word will move the head also. Often by watching the back neck muscles this head movement can be seen even though not perceptible from the front.

13. Monotonous oral reading, which usually indicates word-by-word reading instead of reading for the sense of the phrase.

Using Tests in the Diagnosis of Reading Difficulty

There are many excellent reading tests that will aid the teacher in discovering group and individual reading problems. Some of the most widely used are:

1. Diagnostic Examination of Silent Reading Abilities (Van Wagenen-Dvorak), Educational Test Bureau.

2. Diagnostic Reading Tests (Triggs), Educational Records Bureau.

3. Iowa Silent Reading Tests (Greene-Jorgenson-Kelley), World Book Company.[10]

In addition, the teacher may want to devise a simple reading test of his own. This may easily be done. The teacher chooses a selection of reading matter which seems to be typical of the kind of reading he will expect of his students. He counts the words in the selection carefully. Then he makes duplicate copies of this passage and gives them to the class under optimum conditions of relaxation and motivation. He sets a time limit, asking each student to mark where he finished when time was called. Then he gives the group a set of questions about the selection to test comprehension. The questions should be similar to those that will be asked on reading material in his class. One teacher may seek over-all understanding of mood or point of view, while another may want students to grasp the sequence of thought or retain particular details. A careful checking of several such simple tests will quickly reveal to the teacher individual reading patterns. One student may read slowly, but

[10] For detailed descriptions and reviews of these and other reading tests see: Buros, O. K., *Mental Measurements Yearbook* (New Brunswick: Rutgers University Press, 1948).

grasp all he reads; another may read rapidly but be very confused and vague as to the content of the selection. Others may be able to obtain some kinds of knowledge from reading, and not other kinds. Thus, the teacher will be able to guide individuals in more adequate reading habits for each subject.

General Remedial Procedures

Many schools have special reading classes for seriously retarded readers. Such classes, however, are more the exception than the rule. Teachers specially trained to do remedial teaching are also rare. Thus, the regular classroom teacher may want to provide some kind of special remedial aid to those students who are in most need, over and beyond the general reading instruction that has already been recommended above.

Teachers who wish to help retarded pupils might do additional reading and study in this area. There are numerous excellent guides for those interested, since this field is one where educators have been working intensively for many years. There are also some university centers where summer training may be obtained in special reading skills. One summer spent in such a center is a wise investment of time and will be repaid a hundredfold in greater classroom success. For the beginning teacher and for the student who is looking forward to teaching in the near future, the following remedial techniques may be tried:

1. Develop personal rapport with those students who need remedial assistance. Such students are often very happy to have someone take an interest in their problem, though they are sometimes extremely discouraged about the possibilities of doing anything about it. The teacher will need to set aside some time several days a week for some individual work if a remedial approach is taken.
2. Help the student gain insight into the basis of his own difficulty. After giving him some reading tests, review the results with him. Discuss his study habits with him. Perhaps he has hindered himself from overcoming his handicap because of poor study conditions.
3. Provide for recreational reading. Often the teacher will have to start at a very low level of reading, even allowing the retarded student to work on comic books if that is all he can bring himself to read. The next step is to read some of the more flamboyant paper-bound books or popular magazines, even though the choice of subject matter may leave much to be desired. Most retarded readers are negatively conditioned to any kind of reading, so the classroom teacher will want to permit the student to read widely material of his own choosing, even if choices deviate considerably from the content of the course.
4. Find a problem important to the student requiring him to use some reading skill in order to obtain a solution.

5. Discuss with him the material provided for him to read both before and after he has read it. Through a friendly and informal chat, the teacher may aid the student in looking for meaning in what he reads, reducing initial anxiety when confronted by a printed page, and encouraging him to read for ideas.

6. Use some of the diagnostic devices available. Each student may have a key problem of his own. Diagnostic tests should be used to indicate that problem. Some students have inadequate reading skills that need special corrective exercises. Some students have such limited vocabularies that new words cannot be understood in context. Some students are handicapped because of language confusions developed through learning two languages —one at home and another at school.

7. Concentrate assistance, after rapport has been achieved, upon the on-going work of the class. Do not make the remedial procedures so different that the child feels left out and isolated and cannot understand the essence of daily work. The daily assignments in reading should be part of his reading work and should be the basis for special attention so that he can continue to be a regular member of the class.

8. Discuss the student with his other teachers. It often helps if the cooperation of all his teachers can be enlisted so that he gets support in all of his classes. The confidence gained in one area will not then be undermined through repeated failure in another. It is also important to see that duplication of effort is avoided. If one teacher has better rapport with the student, then that teacher should be the one to undertake the greatest portion of the remedial aid.

Summary

The great emphasis that high school teaching places on ability to read means that more and more classroom instruction must be devoted to the acquiring of adequate reading skills. If we want the student to understand the material provided—if this content is worth learning—then we have an obligation to help him obtain the skills whereby that content may be learned. Heretofore reading instruction ceased at the end of the elementary school, yet the high school demands increased cultivation of old skills and development of new skills. Many students are badly handicapped through poor habits or through poor attitudes. The teacher needs to be fully informed on the reading attitudes and levels of his class before he can offer appropriate instruction.

Writing, Speaking, Listening in the High School

The vast amount of attention given to remedial reading and the whole problem of reading instruction point out one of the basic facts of life in school—the student is expected to learn more by means of reading than by almost any other means. However, this is a condition that we would do well to modify. In both child and adult life learning also goes on through the other senses. In fact, genuine social learning is not only a matter of taking in through sight or hearing (or touch or smell!) but also a matter of giving out, of expressing by way of writing and speaking and gesturing. The student hears, talks, and writes as well as reads. In this section we will consider some of these other special skill areas: writing, speaking, and listening.

A word must be interjected here about the reasons why such problems are included in a discussion of general methods. It might occur to some that these skills are rightfully in the domain of the special-subject teachers, such as teachers of English, speech, music. However, as was indicated in discussing reading, every teacher is involved in communicating and exploring ideas. In any classroom, the students listen, write, or speak, and often they do all three within a very few minutes, repeating the processes day in and day out. Wherever, in any area of the curriculum, the teacher helps the students to learn good habits, progress toward more adult patterns can be expected. Wherever the teacher ignores this aspect of teaching, students with handicaps in listening, writing or speaking will not be able to learn as effectively as others.

Listening Skills

The special problems of the handicapped. Students with marked physical, emotional, or intellectual handicaps present special problems in the communication skills. A student with limited intelligence will not be able to pay attention as well as, or for as long as, a normal student; thus he cannot absorb as much through listening alone. The slow student often misses the essential cues, as in a radio mystery play, and does not understand the reason for the action. The more subtle the cue, whether it be oral or written, the more difficult for the slow learner. The play-on-words type of humor is lost on the dull student. We often notice the look of perplexity that crosses the face of some student who has not seen the joke that is sending the rest of the class into hysterics. Where this occurs time after time, some problem of mental acuity may well be present.

At the same time the teacher must be alert to discover those who are hard of hearing or whose hearing is temporarily impaired. Some school systems provide a hearing test for all entering students, and the information thus obtained is entered on the student's permanent record. Teachers will be informed of the results at the time the test is taken, but, like all such information, it will not be useful in succeeding semesters unless each teacher consults the records for all his students.

The student who constantly says, "But I didn't hear you make that announcement" or "I didn't catch the page number when it was given," may be a genuine case of hearing difficulty. Before the teacher judges such a student as lazy or provocative, he might well check to see if the student has a hearing problem. For example:

> Nancy consistently failed to get her homework in on time. The excuse was, "But I didn't hear you." After audiometer tests were given, Mr. Harvey discovered that Nancy had no hearing at all in one ear. By changing her to another side of the room so that her good ear was in the best position to catch what was said from the front of the room, Nancy's work improved considerably. Nancy herself had not realized that she had a hearing disability until the test was administered.

There is some lack of agreement as to what is meant by deafness and by hearing loss. However, most studies of school children indicate that between 5 and 10 per cent have some definite hearing defect.[11] The available studies on hearing loss make it clear that any such physical limitation will definitely make personal and social adjustment difficult. When so much of the school activity depends upon what can be "heard" the teacher will want to be especially sensitive to this problem.

What can the teacher do about students who are slow learners or whose hearing is impaired? The teacher should employ several methods of making directions clear and of providing materials for learning. A teacher should not only give oral instructions regarding assignments, but should write these upon the blackboard. Thus both sight and hearing may be used to get the important cues.

Room noises. A program for good listening will involve a consideration of the physical environment as well, as witness the following:

> Harry Walters, the new principal, decided to visit classrooms early in the semester. In Miss Avery's class there was a continual hum in the air. It took Mr. Walters some time to find that the heating system was not working so well as it should. Whenever the mechanism was on, the hum began. Mr. Walters made a note to have the system repaired. In Mr. Ringle's room an echo seemed to roll around whenever any-

[11] Barker, R. G., B. A. Wright, and M. R. Gonick, *Adjustment to Physical Handicap and Illness,* Bull. 55 (New York: Social Science Research Council, 1946), p. 163. See also O'Connor, C. D., and Alice Streng, "Teaching the Acoustically Handicapped," Chap. IX in *The Education of Exceptional Children,* Forty-ninth Yearbook, Part II, National Society for the Study of Education (Chicago: University of Chicago Press, 1950), p. 156.

one talked. The slightest sound seemed to be magnified by the room itself. It was very difficult to hear anyone with a high voice. Students were uncomfortable and Mr. Ringle could not quite understand why. Examination disclosed the echo to be a problem of acoustics. Mr. Walters was able to get the advice of a sound engineer. He suggested the room be fitted with sound-absorbent material. The whole atmosphere of the classes changed because something was done about the noise problem.

A word should also be said about out-of-class noises. Often schools are placed beside train tracks, on streets with heavy traffic and street cars, near airports, or next to the school playing field. When such conditions prevail, it is certainly difficult to obtain optimum learning.

Besides the out-of-class noises, there are always some noises originating in the classroom. Furniture is bound to squeak, scrape, and bump; doors slam in the corridor; chords and dischords filter through from the music room. This is not to say that a good classroom is one in which a pin could be heard to drop, although moderately quiet periods are desirable from time to time. Six hours a day the teacher will have to adjust to various kinds and degrees of noise and sound. It will be wise for every teacher to learn early to be tolerant. The class can be relaxed and responsive only if the teacher himself accepts with good humor the inevitable noises of the school and the out of doors.

Classroom Procedures. Let us turn now to the problem of training in listening. Many hours of life are spent in listening to conversation, to speakers, to supervisors, to the radio. In the classroom, being able to follow what is spoken is a great asset! For students continuing to college, the ability to listen and then make intelligible notes, is a skill that can be developed in the high-school classroom. As many students come to the high school deficient in reading skills, so also an equal number come with bad habits of listening. These may be just as great a handicap as inability to read at proper grade level.

Once it is established that the hearing organs of the students are normal, that the acoustics of the room are at least adequate, the teacher will want to check on attention level. After a discussion is started, the teacher should stop and inquire, "Now what was the main point?" or, "Bill, can you trace the steps we have come in our discussion?" Through such devices, the teacher may gauge the attention level of various students. Can they actually follow an oral presentation? The teacher may learn, for instance, that many students are not used to hearing intellectual conversation.

Thus, learning to exchange ideas is akin to learning a foreign language. Cue words, listening for the main idea, getting the sense of an involved statement, these are problems for training.

Next the teacher will want to introduce recordings. Here the speaker is not present, only his words. Watching the faces of youngsters while a recording is being played may tell the teacher a great deal about their listening habits. An oral or written quiz after the recording also may reveal students with a problem in listening.

The teacher will want to tie in out-of-school listening as much as possible. The teacher should be acquainted with the radio and television programs that are current favorites and should make every effort to sample the fare that is enjoyed by their students in order to know what kinds of "educational" influences are at work outside the classroom. If any attempt at all is to be made to develop more discriminating listening in radio and television, it will probably have to be in the classroom.

Many students fail to listen to the more mature programs because of (1) lack of awareness of their existence; (2) lack of encouragement at home; (3) negative conditioning because of inability to understand what is going on; and (4) lack of interest in the subject matter of the programs. The teacher can well afford to work on the latter two problems. Where topics of programs are announced in advance, the teacher may cultivate interest in class through discussion or presentation of the same topic, showing the relevance or significance of the topic to present-day problems.

It is often possible to assign students to listen to programs in much the same manner that they are assigned to read a chapter from a library book. It must be remembered, however, that such an assignment may present difficulty to some students because of lack of a receiving set or interference with the preferences of other members of the family. Such problems should be explored in class by the teacher before making such assignments. It may often be wise to make radio and television listening an alternative to another kind of assignment; for example, reading about the problem. At the same time, the teacher will want to encourage students to do the suggested listening in order to widen their contact with acceptable adult materials.

One major handicap to adequate listening habits is the notion that whenever the student sits still to listen he is to be entertained. Students unfortunately develop a pattern regarding listening that says, in effect, "We are either entertained when we listen, or we are bored; there is no middle ground." It is this attitude that interferes with adequate listening in class and certainly militates against listening to radio and television programs that require some critical reaction.

In brief, each teacher must be aware of the problem of developing adequate listening habits on the part of his students, not only in order to make for more effective learning in the schoolroom, but also to provide a basis for more discriminating and intelligent listening and learning outside of the school.

Writing Skills

> Mrs. Blake had noticed Steve the very first day of class. He was a short, husky fellow with a serious expression. Whenever he spoke, the other students seemed to listen with respect. What he said always made excellent sense, whether it was a problem of classroom management or a discussion about the chapter of the text. Steve was, as Mrs. Blake put it in her own mind, a "natural born leader." He had maturity, intelligence, and evidently could speak the language of the other students. He was the captain of the baseball team, and junior-class president as well. Then came the great blow! The first assignment consisted of answers to questions about the problem area the class had been studying. Steve's paper was shocking. Although his answers were up to his usual level of mature insight and judicious comment, he misspelled, it seemed, every other word. He even confused the letters in "the" so that it came out "eht" or "teh" almost as often as the right way around. Steve readily admitted that spelling just completely baffled him. He spent most of his time in English working on his spelling, but as far as he was concerned, it was hopeless. He was planning to enter the near-by technical school for a year of auto-mechanics training, but he was nearly resigned to the fact that he might not be admitted because of this handicap. He was frightened at the thought of completing an entrance blank because of the spelling involved.

It is a perennial complaint that high-school students today do not know how to write; like all sweeping complaints, it needs some careful scrutiny. Since the high school is now open to all the children of all the people, we find many students whose home backgrounds have not helped to develop writing skills. It is also true that the curriculum of the high school actually has decreased the amount of time spent on learning the skills of communication. Still it is apparent that on the whole American life would be enhanced if written communication were more effective between individuals.

As we consider the demands of adult life upon the majority of our young people, it becomes more and more apparent that training in writing should focus on the kind of communication skill they will use. What, then, should be the goal of the teacher?

Undoubtedly the main objective should be to make writing a pleasant process, to assist those who write to gain in fluency of expression in the conveying of important ideas or emotions.

Classroom procedures. There are several important ways in which the classroom teacher of any subject can assist this process. In the first place, students should be encouraged to write *when they have something important to say.* Too often, students are trying to express ideas that do not interest them, the sole motivation being punishment or fear. The pressure on students to write "because it is required" is as much an inhibiting factor as any other. The teacher would do well to develop some genuine need for students to write. For example, the class itself might try to get a letter on a local issue published in the local paper, or it might want to communicate with the principal or superintendent about a matter of importance to the students. Some incentive that places the stress upon the outcome, rather than on the process of writing, may serve to release many students from the dread of seeing their own handwriting.

The teacher of any subject requiring any kind of written work should use the occasion to develop with students some idea of standards of accomplishment. It is senseless to blame all the students' failings on the English teachers, or, as many high-school teachers are prone to do, on the elementary-school education. Learning continues in the high school. Even though students arrive with handicaps or poor habits, the high-school teacher has not the right to shun responsibility. Like the teaching of reading, the teaching of writing is a problem for all teachers who utilize any kind of written material as a student learning activity.

If students fail to write complete sentences in answering a question in an examination in history, in physics, in Spanish, in commercial law, then that teacher needs to encourage the students to discuss some of the elements in good writing. Through reward and praise, by posting on bulletin boards examples of good written work, by reading aloud to the class some of the better materials turned in by students, by constantly pointing out through marginal comments the good ideas or good phrases that the student used, the teacher can go a long way toward developing a positive attitude towards writing.

Many students, it must be remembered, find writing a painful chore. At best their experience with writing may have been that of only mediocre achievement. This means that in order to get honest student effort and eventual improvement of level of achievement, the teacher must stress both the over-all strengths and the specific sections where the student has been successful in writing. The best practice is to make many comments on the student's written work, pointed most of the time toward recognition of good material. Even where the quality of the work may not be of the best, it is recommended that comments be made at the end of the exercise such as "good try," or "fine start" or "shows considerable improvement," or "good choice of words."

At the same time the teacher should avoid overemphasis on errors. Often when reading examinations or reports the teacher is tempted to circle all spelling errors, to make large red checks to show where incorrect punctuation has been used, to point out the incomplete sentences. The student who spells poorly doubtless has had many years of failure in the subject. To continue to point out all failures to him is probably the least profitable thing the teacher can do in helping him improve. It is worth the effort to assist students to deal with the common words effectively in writing; but class time spent in learning to spell infrequently used words could better be employed in developing ideas, concepts, and attitudes. Large charts with the correct spelling, definitions, and appropriate illustrations help make the important words useful tools for the student, for too often the fear of misspelling a word may keep a student from demonstrating his knowledge. We do not expect anyone to pound a nail without a hammer; let us not expect students to express ideas if we fail to make available some of the essential tools.

At this point we need to repeat a basic concept for good teaching: it is a mistake to make all grades dependent on written examinations, excluding all other modes of evaluation. We know that some people are more expressive orally, some in writing, some in graphic arts. The good teacher will provide many ways for students to demonstrate learning. Overemphasis on writing, to the exclusion of other ways of showing competence, has eliminated many students from school and retarded the growth of others who stayed on.

Speaking Skills

In the average classroom much emphasis is placed on speaking as a way to participate in learning.[13] For this reason the teacher who does have many opportunities for oral expression will need

[13] National Society for the Study of Education, "Teaching Children with Speech Handicaps," in *The Education of Exceptional Children*. 49th Yearbook, Part II (Chicago: University of Chicago Press, 1950), pp. 176-193.

to be aware of some of the problems of those with speech handicaps. In serious cases of speech pathology, the teacher needs expert aid. At the same time there are in every classroom students with normal deviations from the average speech competence. About 1 to 3 per cent of school children are affected by some speech problem. Since almost every classroom makes some public-speaking demands on young people, the teacher who notices a speech problem in a student should follow precautions similar to those noted for other such handicaps.

Classroom procedures. In general, students will do better speaking where the situation is relaxed, where they have something important to impart, and where the "public" nature of the occasion is less significant than the sharing of a vital experience. The use of group work (see Chapter 8) will help to provide opportunities for this kind of speaking. The low level of oral communication skills in most high-school students demonstrates that all teachers need to focus their efforts on aiding students to speak better, to speak more freely, to speak with greater enjoyment.

All speech work in a classroom should be preceded by a class discussion about what makes a good oral presentation. No matter what the subject matter, when a student is asked to impart knowledge to the rest of the class, make an explanation, give directions, report progress, it is important that these situations aid in skill development. This can be assured if teachers and students discuss what goes into a good oral report, then list together criteria which may be used in evaluating these efforts. Then, when agreement has been reached by the class, the list should be posted in a conspicuous place. When a report has been given, the teacher and the class may refer to the list with the question, "How can we improve?" The teacher should at all times find points that were good in the oral presentation and emphasize them.

In the area of oral speaking many students have problems that are individual to them. One particularly important problem exists for the student from a home where a foreign language is spoken most of the time. For this student, learning good habits of expression in English especially is difficult. He will need more sensitive help than the average child particularly in the area of oral communication because of the public nature of such situations.

In setting up a list of good speaking factors, the teacher should use the same criteria that he would apply to himself. The major factors are clarity, interest, ease of audience understanding, directness of contact with audience, poise and relaxation, and absence of distracting mannerisms. A class can quickly and easily build with a teacher a list of such factors. Using an evaluation committee when oral work is in progress, helps also to focus on skill development. But this should not be overdone. The point of oral work is communication to others. It is important not to make adolescents, already highly self-conscious, so much more self-conscious that they are completely tongue-tied and emotionally upset by stage fright.

Summary

Communicating to others is an essential element in adult life. The high school plays a significant role in developing these skills to a level adequate for dealing with later demands in work and college and social intercourse. By recognizing the specific problems that may be met by students in the areas of reading, writing, listening, hearing, and speaking, the high-school teacher can perform a very vital service to the adolescent.

The highly verbal nature of our high-school curriculum makes it imperative that each high-school teacher consider himself not only a teacher of history or biology or music or mechanical drawing, but also a teacher of reading and writing and listening and speaking.

Selected References

Reading

Bond, Guy L. and Eva Bond. *Developmental Reading in High School.* New York: The Macmillan Company, 1941. Written explicitly for the high-school classroom teacher; teaching practices and procedures amply and clearly presented; remedial practices fully covered.

Bond, Guy L., and Bertha Handlan. *Adapting Instruction in Reading to Individual Differences.* Series on Individualization of Instruction, No. 5. Minneapolis: University of Minnesota Press, 1948. Pp. 65-70. A practical guide for teachers in helping individual children in reading.

Gray, William S. (ed.). *Classroom Techniques in Improving Reading.* Supplementary Education Monographs, No. 69. Chicago: University of Chicago Press, 1949. Practical methods by the classroom teacher on the junior and senior high-school level are described.

"Improving Reading Instruction in the Secondary School," *Bulletin of National Association of Secondary School Principals,* Vol. 34, No. 168, February, 1950. Recent recommended practices reviewed.

Kershner, Geneva. "The Slow Learner Reads and Writes," *English Journal,* 35:264-267 (May, 1946). Special procedures with this group are described.

National Society for the Study of Education. *Reading in the High School and College.* Forty-seventh Yearbook, Part II. Chicago: University of Chicago Press, 1948. Basic reference in this field.

Nolan, Esther G. "Reading Difficulty vs. Low Mentality," *California Journal of Secondary Education,* 17:34-39 (January, 1942). This important distinction must be made, and then teaching will be profitable.

National Education Association. "Reading Instruction in Secondary Schools." *NEA Research Bulletin,* Vol. 20, No. 1, January, 1942. A survey of practices, present status, and procedures in the separate subjects.

Reading in Home Economics? Certainly! Denver: Denver Public Schools, 1950. A vivid presentation of reading problems in this field, with many implications for other subjects.

Reading Ladders for Human Relations. Washington, D.C.: American Council on Education, 1947. Excellent annotated bibliography of literature to meet different reading levels.

Rudolf, Katherine B. *The Effect of Reading Instruction on Achievement in Eighth Grade Social Studies.* Teachers College Contributions to Education, No. 945. New York: Bureau of Publications, Teachers College, Columbia University, 1949. Specific aid in reading will improve performance in subject area.

Russell, David H. "Reading Disabilities and Mental Health: A Review of Research," *Understanding the Child,* 26:24-32 (January, 1947). An excellent summary of research indicating where and how emotional factors enter the reading picture.

Reading Guides for High School Students

Kelley, Victor H., and Harry A. Greene. *Better Reading and Study Habits.* Yonkers: World Book Company, 1947.

Knight, Pearle E., and A. E. Traxler. *Read and Comprehend.* Boston: D. C. Heath and Company, 1949.

Witty, Paul. *Streamline Your Reading.* Life Adjustment Booklet. Chicago: Science Research Associates, 1949. A handbook for students.

Other Communications Skills

Brown, James I. "The Measurement of Listening Ability," *School and Society,* 71:69-70 (Feb. 4, 1950). Suggests an approach to diagnosing how well students can listen.

———. "Why Not Teach Listening?" *School and Society,* 69:113-116 (Feb. 12, 1949). A challenging statement.

Dale, Edgar. "Learning by Listening," *The Newsletter* of the Bureau of Educational Research, Ohio State University, Columbus, Ohio, November, 1950. If a student cannot listen in class, he cannot learn; the teacher can help by being aware of aids to listening.

Fernald, Grace. *Remedial Techniques in Basic School Subjects.* New York: McGraw-Hill Book Company, Inc., 1943. See especially for the relationship between visual, auditory, and aesthetic approaches to learning.

Gray, Giles W. "Speech in Every Class," *NEA Journal,* 38:670-671 (December, 1949). Points out how and where every classroom teacher should help develop speech competence.

"Health Bulletin for Teachers, 1947-1948." Metropolitan Life Insurance Co., New York, November, 1948. Includes brief sections on vision, hearing, nutrition, dental care, safety, and behavior problems.

Nichols, Ralph G. "Listening: Questions and Problems," *Quarterly Journal of Speech,* 1:83-86 (February, 1947).

Painter, Margaret. "Guideposts to More Effective Oral Communications," *California Journal of Secondary Education,* 26:135-139 (March, 1951). Basic principles for guiding the classroom teacher in developing speech skills of students.

Silverman, S. Richard. "The Hard-of-Hearing Child," *NEA Journal,* 39:136-137 (February, 1950). Special problems of classroom adjustment are discussed.

"Speech for All American Youth," *Bulletins of the National Association of Secondary School Principals,* Vol. 32, No. 151, January, 1948. Extensive coverage from the point of view of the speech teacher with many practices for general use suggested.

13. Adjustment to School Life: Discipline I

STUDENTS who are misbehaving are not learning the lessons of the classroom. This does not imply that they are not learning; obviously they are learning a great deal. They may be learning how to annoy the girl in the next seat, how to shoot a rubber band so that the ammunition hits accurately, how to tip a chair back just so far before it falls over, how to pile books so that they will topple at just the right moment, and so on. But they are not learning of more important matters: the reasons for the outbreak of the Second World War, or how to figure the board feet required in constructing a garage, or how to evaluate news reporting on television. Just as the slow learner or the student with a sight or hearing handicap requires special assistance, so the chronic troublemaker needs special attention. Not all misbehavior in the classroom is serious, but some students do display far from satisfactory personal adjustment to life in the classroom. In this section we will discuss the role of the teacher faced with minor classroom misbehavior as well as with the more serious problems produced by personality maladjustment.

What Is Discipline?

Few problems loom larger with the beginning teacher than those of establishing and maintaining order in a classroom. It is nonsense to say that a good teacher does not have discipline problems. The better the teaching techniques used, the fewer the problems, true, but student misbehavior is a common hazard for all teachers.

Just why is discipline such a difficult problem? When neighborhood friends are planning a dance, there is remarkably little horseplay or interference with those doing the planning. If there is someone who interferes with what the group wants to do, either the other members of the group quell him or they oust him in no uncertain manner. In such a group it is important to note that, first, the group is actively engaged in an enterprise that is really important to them; second, they chose this activity freely themselves; and third, membership in the group was voluntary.

Now take the typical classroom. The topics of study and the activities for learning are not often selected by the students. Rather, certain subjects and routines must be endured because the teacher, the course of study, the superintendent, or some other remote and nebulous source says so. Nor, for the most part, is the student in school of his own free choice. He knows that there are very drastic social measures that can be taken against him—what, exactly, he is not sure—were he to remain away from school without a genuine excuse. His parents usually insist on his attendance at school. He has no way out except to comply with the requirements of this adult world until he graduates into adulthood himself. Even though students may genuinely desire knowledge, may actually enjoy school more than the aimless hours of vacation—and this attitude is more prevalent than we might suppose—still, the involuntary nature of the situation has its psychological effects.

Major Categories of Discipline Problems

It is not at all surprising that from time to time any student will rebel against alien subject matter, enforced inactivity, involuntary attendance, tasks that are beyond his capacity. This is what might be called "normal" misbehavior. However, sometimes reactions to the ordinary demands of the school are surprisingly violent; individuals seem unable to adjust even for short periods to the expectations of the school. This might be called "abnormal" misbehavior.

The teacher thus has two major tasks in dealing with classroom behavior. First, he needs skill in handling the normal misbehavior situations with tact, understanding, and diplomacy. Second, he needs insight into abnormal misbehavior, with an understanding of what the school can do and what other aid may be requested. The teacher's action in handling both normal and abnormal misbehavior is usually termed "discipline." That "the teacher disciplines the class" is a commonly accepted phrase. By it we mean that the teacher is exercising his authority to produce a classroom atmosphere in which learning may continue, either on the part of an individual or on the part of the group.

Desirable Classroom Disciplines

Most of us carry a mental picture of how teachers in our own experience managed to discipline their classes. Some teachers were stern, cold, forbidding, fearful, others shrilled at the class constantly, and still others lost their tempers on the average of once a week and frightened everyone in the class. But some seemed calm, approachable, unruffled by misbehavior. It may be revealing here to recall incidents in our own school history when we received some form of teacher discipline:

> One future teacher recalled an experience in the third grade. She was sitting in the end of the row in the back of the room, her legs dangling from a too-high seat. She was trying to hear a lengthy reading by the teacher of some remote historical material—she didn't quite remember what. Bored because it just didn't seem to make sense, she started drawing on a piece of tissue paper that just happened to be handy. Abruptly her peace of mind was shattered: "Nancy, you are writing. You are absolutely forbidden to write when I am reading. And you of all people. Come and stand in front of the room until I am all through." Nancy protested. She wasn't writing. She was not even using paper. It was tissue paper. But the teacher was indignant. Shrinking and half sick, Nancy stood with her back to the class beside the teacher's desk for an intolerable ten minutes. On entering teaching herself, Nancy resolved that no matter what happened in her class, she would never, never force a student to stand in front of a class as a method of punishment.

Other beginning teachers may recall similar incidents. It may be worth while to inquire: "How did I feel about this kind of treatment? Why was it that I remember it all so painfully and vividly even to this day? Was the teacher justified? Was the suffering I endured worth it in my more compliant behavior?"

Another important self-inquiry is to examine critically the kind of teacher management we admire. As was suggested in the introduction, there are many kinds of good teachers, and each has his own methods of control. Some teachers establish formal and rather impersonal classroom behavior. Others are free and easy and there is much laughter in their classroom. The kinds of discipline techniques that we can successfully use depend in large measure upon our own personality resources, our normal attitude toward others and our ideal of a classroom. Within such limits as our own personality imposes, there are some general principles for good discipline that can be applied.

While keeping order is the traditional version of discipline, the better professional approach is to develop good motivation, good mental hygiene in the classroom. In other words, a teacher who does a good job of motivating students to do the tasks that have been outlined has good discipline; similarly, a teacher in whose classroom there is a friendly, relaxed atmosphere has good discipline.

Before proceeding with this discussion, let us return for a moment to the criteria for democratic education already presented (see Chapter 3). Essentially these criteria establish the methods of democratic control or, in the terminology of the educator, democratic discipline. Establishing a balance between freedom and security means that rules operate and are respected, but that the individual feels comfortable within the framework of the rules. The rules then are the disciplinary agent; the teacher merely helps students in their observation. But the student does all he can in self-discipline. This concept makes discipline something that is not for the benefit of the teacher, or even for the benefit of the student, but for the benefit of the group. The activity itself imposes its own discipline in the same way that the rules of a game of basketball impose a discipline upon the team.

Sources of Discipline Problems

But this conception is not all there is to the subject of discipline by any means. Several variables must be taken into account. First, we have the problem of teacher personality, teacher reaction to the activities and behavior of immature students. Second, there is the problem of the teacher who lacks teaching and social skills; he is simply untactful, or awkward, or disorganized. These first two may be called *teacher-caused* discipline problems. Third, there is the problem of explosive or provocative personality relations among members of the class. Some students are dynamite only when in combination with certain other students. Others unaided can agitate whole classes. Fourth, there are the problems that reside in the individual personality of the students themselves. With these students disturbances in adjustment at home or school have left their marks, making it more than normally difficult for them to adjust to classroom demands. The latter two may be called *student-caused* discipline problems.

Teacher-Caused Discipline Problems

Discipline problems that arise from inadequacies in the teacher, from his own intolerance or lack of insight into youth, will respond only to critical self-analysis. The inevitable clashes of personality that are to be expected when a random sample of individuals are forced to work together can usually be adjusted by a reasonable facing of the problem.

The problem, in this case, may be subdivided into lack of social skill and lack of teaching skill. Let us list some causes of discipline occurrences under each:

Teachers display lack of social skill in

1. Using sarcasm.
2. Failure to answer reasonable questions.
3. Being insensitive to special problems of students, such as stuttering.
4. Being inconsistent: for example, telling a student who has come in late to ask his neighbor for help, then scolding him for talking.
5. Being impolite, rough.
6. Making personal references about students.
7. Being unfair; having favorites.
8. Making disparaging remarks about social groups in the community.
9. Gossiping about students in public places.

Teachers display lack of teaching skill in

1. Conducting classes in a dull, monotonous way.
2. Speaking in a rasping, irritating voice.
3. Giving vague assignments.
4. Giving assignments too difficult for students.
5. Giving assignments too easy for students.
6. Proceeding with oral work when there is noise in or outside the class.
7. Failure to give attention to light and heat conditions.
8. Being confused about classroom routines, such as distribution of supplies
9. Being subject to student pressure at unpredictable times.
10. Failing to make all learning steps clear.
11. Giving tests on material not covered in class.
12. Rewarding only one kind of aptitude.

Teacher Lacking in Both Social and Teaching Skill

We could probably go on listing many other specifics under each heading wherein the teacher has been at fault, has produced his own trouble. The narrative below gives an example of a teacher grossly lacking in both social and teaching skill. As we read it, we are tempted to say that this is too extreme to be real. Unfortunately the actions are not uncommon; they do not always occur in one class hour but the malpractices are there if we observe long enough. This illustration actually did happen!

It was a lazy warm noon. The first bell had rung. Students began to collect around the locked door of Room 12. Mr. Brown arrived breathlessly about a moment before the last bell sounded. The students pushed into the room.

A locked door! Not a very hospitable beginning; besides, it breeds confusion and rowdiness as a group collects around a door interfering with the orderly passage of other students.

Mr. Brown stood by his desk riffling through a disorderly mass of student papers in search of his grade book. He announced to the class, "While I am taking roll, I want you to fill out these registration cards." He passed out the cards.

Good order, even in the teacher's desk, is basic to good management. The time wasted looking for something is time when the class lacks direction and confusion begins.

No explanation of the cards? What are they for? Even routine forms should be explained so confusion will be minimized.

While he was doing so, two girls came hurrying in.

"You're late, girls," he remarked.

"But, Mr. Brown, we've already been here once. We just went down the hall for a drink of water."

"You're still late. Go to the office and get a pass."

Better to complete distributing the cards and then speak to the girls privately.

The two girls had no sooner gone than another girl opened the door, dropped her books with a clatter on the first desk, and then went out.

This kind of lack of respect for the classroom activity seems to be a prevailing note in Mr. Brown's room. He treats the students with lack of consideration, and they react in kind.

"Mr. Brown," came a voice from the back of the room, "do we fill

An expected reaction due to lack of directions when the cards were these cards out in ink?" No answer. Mr. Brown was checking the roll book, but obviously had heard the remark. "Mr. Brown, pen or pencil?"

passed out. There will always be students who will not know what to do, no matter how often a routine has been gone through.

"You know better than to ask such a question," Mr. Brown finally retorted angrily. "You always fill out things in ink."

Why should the teacher disregard a request for information? If it is a legitimate request, it deserves an answer. If it is an attempt to annoy, the best way to thwart such efforts is to treat them seriously. Certainly telling the student he ought to know better in an angry tone of voice only makes the situation worse.

"But what if you don't have a pen?"
"Then use mine, or borrow one."
"Oh, I have one. I was just wondering what someone who didn't have one would do."
A snicker passed through the room. . . .

This is what disregard for students as human beings will always lead to. The teacher fell into a very neat trap; now his control over the class is in serious jeopardy.

"I'm going to hand back your papers for yesterday," announced Mr. Brown. Immediately everyone began to talk. "You people be quiet."

What is wrong with the students talking at this moment? Of course they are interested in exchanging reactions to this announcement; just like adults!

"Some of you are going to be sent to the office if you're not careful."

The use of threats needs to be carefully weighed. Is "the office" the place to settle minor difficulties? What kind of behavior merits such treatment?

Two girls kept right on talking.

Evidently this threat didn't work, as the students continued to misbehave.

"Have you girls finished your conversation?"

This kind of a question is bound to cause trouble.

"Yes," they answered, with a smirk to their neighbors.

What if the girls had answered, "No"? Then what?

At this point, the three tardy students returned to class. Mr. Brown began to read the answers

Obviously the latecomers could not know what the lesson was, so why ask. The teacher might bet-

to the punctuation exercise. He interrupted himself to ask, "Those of you who came in late, do you know what we are doing?"
"No."

ter have briefly told them what to do, or have asked them to wait and he would tell them later, or have assigned a student to help them quietly.

"Well, find out." The students referred to immediately turned to their neighbors, and for a moment disrupted Mr. Brown's procedure.

He is asking for trouble. Of course, such a remark will only lead to a new source of distraction and confusion. And no one could possibly say that this time the students were at fault.

A discussion arose about one of the exercises. It had to do with the use of a semicolon for a comma. "I don't see what harm there is in using it," one student declared.
"Well, it's wrong, that's all," Mr. Brown said impatiently. "We can't spend much more time on this assignment," he continued, "so I'll hurry through the rest of the answers."

Is this an answer? This is not teaching in any sense of the word. If the subject is worthy of class time, it is worthy of some respect. The teacher by his own attitude is setting a bad example. The students cannot learn to appreciate appropriate speech habits if the teacher himself does not respect them.

While Mr. Brown was reading the rest of the answers, the students wandered up to the waste-paper basket and the pencil sharpener.

A class will show its disinterest by making use of such disturbing actions as throwing away waste paper and sharpening pencils. Either interest the class in the activity or have rules about using these facilities so that class work is orderly.

"I'm going to read some of your themes," he announced next. Voices from the class called out, "Are you going to read the names?" "Please don't read the names."
"If they are good I don't see why I shouldn't," was his reply.
The class began to whisper complainingly. Mr. Brown started to read one of the themes. The whispering continued.

If themes are read aloud, the teacher should abide by the wishes of the class about use of names.

"You students will have to be quiet. You are old enough to know when you are being rude."

Mr. Brown is old enough to know that he has been even ruder himself. Students have personal feelings also.

He finished reading the first theme. The class broke out talking again. Several of the students asked questions. "If you want me to hear you, you'll have to talk one at a time; I can't hear you at all," he said sharply. He started to read another theme; the class continued to fuss and whisper. He looked up.	The class is completely disorganized. The teacher has lost their attention. He tells them he cannot hear them, but fails to recreate some order in the room.
"What did you say, Joan?" "Nothing." "Talking to yourself?" "Uh-huh." Mr. Brown returned to his reading; Joan turned and smiled at the girl behind her. The class snickered. . . . Mercifully, the bell rang.	The teacher baited his own trap. He deserved to be caught.

It is most significant that this teacher seemed unable to predict the consequences of his own actions. When asked why his class was so chaotic and disturbed, he seemed unable to do anything but blame them. Yet a careful report of what went on shows clearly that he contributed most, if not all, of the incentive for the misbehavior.

Below is another example of a teacher whose discipline leaves much to be desired:

> Mr. Green was organizing supplies in the adjoining room when the art class arrived. The class clustered in little groups and chattered about the election which was being held in the school. Mr. Green entered the room and in a loud voice said, "Everyone sit down and be quiet!" He read an announcement of a senior-class meeting. The seniors bounced up and started to leave the room. In a stern voice Mr. Green told them to return to their seats and asked for an assignment due that day. He checked the seniors out one at a time, picking up their assignments as they went out. He continued taking the class roll and checking the assignments. This task took until 9:45; the class was restless with nothing to do. There were several private conversations going on and six or seven students scrambled to their lockers to find the assignment due.
>
> Mr. Green went into the other room to check out paper for the coming assignment. He prefaced this with the remark, "Just ask for the color and size of paper you need, no other questions." This distribution took from 9:45 to 10:05. He returned to the main room, called for order, and announced that the assignments which were overdue would have one letter grade knocked off for each day they

were late. There was time left to help three people individually out of the class of twenty. For most of the students the hour had been spent in waiting and in various diversionary maneuvers.

The Mr. Brown of the first example was alternately rude and inept; Mr. Green tries to be stern and forbidding. But Mr. Green, like Mr. Brown, is having little success in motivating his students to learn. If asked why, Mr. Green would say he had discipline problems: the students did not seem to be able to do their work as requested. This teacher also obviously needs to examine some basic errors in his teaching methods when only three out of a class of twenty get any aid during a 50-minute period.

Teacher Lacking in Teaching Skill

The daily routine—or daily monotony—consists of Mrs. Drew's reading the answers to the previous night's homework, recording the grades orally, and showing the correct answers to those problems in which the students had difficulty. After correcting the problems, either the new day's assignment or review is taken up. After about twenty minutes' discussion, time is given for working the next day's assignment. As far as discipline is concerned, Mrs. Drew runs the class with an "iron hand." The only time that the class was the least unruly was during the study periods. And the one time the teacher went out of class, the following incidents occurred; (1) a boy stood up and shouted to a friend across the room; (2) two other boys threw paper wads at each other; (3) another boy made faces at a girl in the room; (4) three girls started combing their hair and putting on lipstick; (5) one girl hit another on the head with her book. As soon as the teacher returned all was quiet.

This is discipline, with the teacher sitting on a volcano. When she leaves the room, the class explodes. The repressive attitude, the monotony, all lead to discipline problems. These problems are produced by the teacher through poor insight into what makes young people learn. In this example it is obvious that the teacher should overhaul her methods of instruction. Variety of experiences should be offered, use of student problem-solving groups introduced, direction of learning by students encouraged. Repression is accepted only for those moments when the repressive agent is present; the instant the authority is withdrawn, the class erupts.

Here is another description of teacher-made discipline situations:

In the chemistry class everyone was talking so loudly that it was hard to hear what Mr. Kern had to say. He tried to get order by saying: "There will be order in this room." He repeated this twice but it seemed to have no effect. Conversations continued on such topics as the week-end date, the new hair-do, the football team. One of the boys in the class was overheard saying, "Gee, but this class is dull."

Two boys seemed to be the main discipline problems in the room. Mr. Kern tried to kid them and tease them along. He also pointed out that they had done some things wrong and that they should do better or they shouldn't be taking the class. Almost everyone laughed or snickered. The boys enjoyed being the center of attention.

After the bell rang, paper was passed out for a test. Questions were placed on the blackboard. The students were asked to write the chemical formulas for twenty compounds the names of which were written out in long hand on the board. Mr. Kern said that fifteen to twenty minutes would be allotted for this. None of the members of the class looked too happy about the prospect of having a test. There was much cheating during the test which Mr. Kern either did not notice or ignored. At the end of twenty minutes, Mr. Kern asked how many were finished with the test. Most of the class hadn't finished, so Mr. Kern allowed them about ten minutes more. Papers were then exchanged and corrected. Two members of the class scored above 35 points out of 40 on the test. Five others made above 30 points, but the rest of the marks were low. Mr. Kern was very free in expressing his disappointment in the results to the class.

Here, it is evident, Mr. Kern's own lack of teaching skill produces his discipline problems. The class is dull. The teacher does nothing that commands attention. He plays up to students who obtain attention by misbehavior and so increases the incentive to further misbehavior. Finally, by springing a test on the students he arouses student antagonism, and, since the class was evidently unprepared, he promotes and rewards cheating. What does the score on the test mean in this class?

While a parade of horrible examples is not the whole story of discipline, a thoughtful analysis of these descriptions of teacher mismanagement will at least underline some mistakes *not* to make. In the following example, notice how Mr. Joy creates his own troubles:

Before the class had begun Mr. Joy in a very domineering voice ordered John to fix a broken window shade. After a few minutes John took his seat. Roll was then taken. This was a long unorganized process, as the class was noisy and few were paying attention. Upon completing the roll call Mr. Joy noticed the shade was still not fixed to his satisfaction and again commanded John to fix it. All eyes were on John, and there was much amusement on the part of the other students. Finally the shade was fixed to Mr. Joy's satisfaction. He expressed a brief "thanks."

Mr. Joy then began to lecture, but few students were paying attention. Most were either working on tardy reports or doing other assignments. Mr. Joy rebuked Alice on two occasions. When Betty asked a question which was not directly related to the lecture, Mr. Joy spoke to her sharply. A few minutes later he told Ann that if she did

> not close her book and pay attention she could go to the library. Ann insisted she was attentive and need not go to the library. By this time Mr. Joy's harsh voice and sharp tongue had broken down the morale of the whole class.

The teacher deserved all the antagonism he felt in this class. His lack of routine in taking the roll is illustrative of the way in which he allows disorderliness to obscure real learning. He feels ill at ease; his harsh voice and sharp tongue show that he also is unhappy about his teaching.

The next example illustrates the effect of poor teaching skill on the interrelations of students. Here we see a teacher who is insensitive to the kinds of relationships he is forcing on his students, with most serious consequences for all the boys involved:

> After five minutes of calisthenics the boys separated into prechosen touch football teams. The coach handed out the balls to the teams from a bag carried to the field. There were three or four domineering boys on each team. They monopolized all the playing while the other two or three boys on the team centered the ball or blocked—or did nothing. One big boy, who was wearing football shoes, called the plays and carried the ball in almost every play. The coach explained that the boy was a center on the varsity and he allowed him to wear cleats when he didn't have his tennis shoes. On the same team, a small boy, wearing glasses, didn't even bother to get into the huddles. He centered the ball every time and just blocked.
>
> The coach made the statement, "The postwar boys don't seem to have any spirit. They all seem to have too many interests other than learning to play any games or learning fundamentals."

Of course the boys in this class do not play well; the teacher has failed to put them in situations where they will want to play.

Two other pitfalls for unwary teachers should be mentioned here. One is falling prey to his own personal problems and anxieties. The teacher who is moody—sunny one day and a thundercloud the next—induces insecurity and anxiety in his students. While we cannot always do so, it is wise to develop a habit of working in which personal problems are shut out as much as possible. Otherwise, student misbehavior may seem unbearable on one day, and highly humorous the next. This kind of inconsistency is bound to make trouble for the teacher. Students will distrust him and ignore his rules because he himself is unreliable about enforcing them.

The second pitfall is rudeness. Teachers often talk to students and treat them in a way that they would permit no adult to treat them. Calling them "dumb," complaining they are acting like babies, making public personal remarks about their appearance

("Well, Johnny looks as though he finally changed shirts today," or "Mary is trying to be a stand-in for Hedy Lamarr with that hair-do"), hurrying them with impatience and interrupting their conversations or reports in a brusque and unnecessary fashion. As one observer stated, "Watching children play school might well give us pause. Discourtesy, peremptory commands, scoldings, derogatory remarks, are embarrassingly common when they play the role of teachers." We can be quite sure that a rude teacher will be treated rudely by his students.

Guides to Correcting Teacher-Caused Discipline Problems

What measures can be suggested in cases where discipline seems to be a result of the teacher's own mistakes in management? *First,* of course, it would be wise to do a critical analysis of those teacher actions which cause trouble. Assuming that, as in the cases cited here, the teacher himself is at fault, often the analysis must be made by an outside observer. Teachers who bring about their own misfortunes may be unable to see just what it is they do that seems to be so provocative. The student-teaching period for a beginning teacher should be the time during which he is helped to see what actions of *his* promote a smoothly operating class and what are disruptive. *Second,* the quality of instruction should be reviewed. Discipline problems sometimes arise not from anything the teacher does wrong but merely from the sheer dullness of the classwork. *Third,* visits to other classrooms where teachers are successful in discipline may suggest better methods of management. For example, if starting the day is an acute problem for the teacher, he should try to find out how others handle this routine successfully.

The teacher who is the major cause of his own troubles has usually made early mistakes in teaching and has not gone back to analyze his errors. He merely continues to make the same mistakes with the same unfortunate consequences. The skillful teacher says to himself, "Well, that lesson went well; now why did it work so much better in the third period than in the fourth period?" Or, "Why did Johnny look so angry at what I said? What problem in him did I touch?" A persistent self-consciousness about the process of teaching, an objective appraisal of instructional tactics, is necessary to increased competence.

In discussing the contribution that the teacher makes to his own problems of discipline, one additional general principle must be clearly stated and emphasized. Teachers, like all other human beings, will react negatively to anyone who makes life more difficult for them. It would require the teacher to be a kind of super human being to act with loving kindness toward a sixteen-year-old who continually makes irritating remarks in class. The teacher may easily develop a healthy dislike for such a youngster. Under ordinary circumstances, if he were not a teacher, he would be perfectly justified for so doing. But the teaching situation is not an ordinary circumstance, and the teacher is not justified in reacting as he would in a normal social situation. These young people are growing up, and it is a difficult, if not downright hazardous, process in this complicated world of ours. The teacher is one among several special adults who has the peculiar responsibility of helping him grow up in a pattern best suited to his own growth needs. Dislike is a strong impediment to providing such help. Yet the students who need help most are almost always those who are most trying.

The teacher, then, must be emotionally prepared to expect this first reaction of dislike toward those students who are making trouble, and, by seeing it as a normal occurrence, to view it objectively. To the best of his ability, the teacher should consider the student not as one making trouble for the teacher, but as one who, by his misbehavior, makes trouble for himself and thus needs more help, more kindness, more consideration because his pathway to maturity is so much more difficult.

The teacher's role in discipline, then, is to recognize and practice the ordinary amenities of social living, to teach with an optimum level of skill, and to develop insight into his own emotional rejection of students who create trouble. With such preparation, the teacher is then ready to examine carefully the contributions that young people make to classroom disturbances, the subject of the next part of this chapter.

Student-Caused Discipline Problems

In the preceding section of this chapter we have discussed those discipline situations that arise primarily because the teacher has neglected some vital phase of classroom management. In this section, and in the succeeding chapter, we will be concerned with those discipline situations that arise from the students' efforts to adjust to the world around them. Many of the acts of behavior that disturb orderly classroom learning are merely the result of adolescents acting like adolescents; others arise out of the deep unmet needs of personality.

An analysis of the kinds of misbehavior that particularly plague teachers and disrupt classrooms reveals four major categories whose primary cause can be said to lie in the nature of the students themselves. These are:

1. Discipline situations arising from student-student interaction.
2. Discipline situations arising from student reaction to school routines and institutional procedures.
3. Discipline situations that arise from immediate personality needs—"adolescents acting like adolescents."
4. Discipline situations that arise from long-term personality needs.

The first two categories will be discussed in the remainder of this chapter, and the second two will be considered in the following chapter.

Discipline Situations That Arise from Student-Student Interaction

In an earlier section it was noted that a student could no more be expected to behave if seated day after day beside someone he detested than an adult could be expected to control his feelings in a similar situation. A discipline situation may also arise from the reaction of students to others they like very much. The kinds of problems for the teacher that arise in the area of student-student interaction are primarily the following:

1. Continued and disturbing conversations.
2. Passing of notes.
3. Symbiotic relations: where one student depends on another for all his work.
4. Hostility among students.
5. Flirtations.
6. Cheating.

Below are some typical examples:

1. Mr. Gantner was talking, and the conversation of two boys increased to a rather annoying degree. Mr. Gantner stopped and asked, "What is it that you don't understand?" Since the attention of the class was directed toward them, one of the boys managed to ask a question pertinent to the subject. The conversation ceased.

2. Sherman and Gerald were seated one behind the other and were obviously close pals. The two had been assigned, as a joint task, the job of presenting an oral report to the class. Mr. Span asked Gerald to read to the class a portion of a set of printed regulations governing sanitation in restaurants. Gerald didn't reply at once but his friend Sherman volunteered to do it instead. Mr. Span said that he wanted Gerald to read it. Gerald announced that he "guessed" that he had "left it home." Mr. Span told him to speak extemporaneously and tell the class whatever he could remember. Gerald did so. Actually the

printed matter was in his binder on his desk the whole time. Later Mr. Span discovered that Gerald, a ninth-grade student, was to all practical purposes a "nonreader" and very self-conscious about it. His friend Sherman "carried him along," trying to do all his work for him.

3. John was talking to Bill while Miss Swan was discussing the day's work. Suddenly she stopped and asked John if what he had to say was so important that he could afford to be rude to her. If so, Miss Swan said, she would stop and allow him to do the talking. John, with a sheepish smile, opened his book to the day's lesson.

4. A group of ninth-grade girls, including the daughters of two of the most influential families in the district, accused a group of four Spanish-American boys of saying very nasty things to them. The boys denied it. The leader of the group of girls insisted, and, since she had never been known to lie, the boys were talked to, deprived of participation in the baseball game, and their activities restricted to a very small portion of the schoolyard. The next day one of the boys refused to come to school. The others were sulky and rebellious, especially toward the teacher. Mr. Bell, the principal, asked the truant officer to come to talk to them. That afternoon one girl came to Mr. Bell. She told him that the boys had really been speaking Spanish and had said nothing bad. The other girls had not understood and had given the words their own interpretation. Mr. Bell called the boys in and apologized.

5. On Tuesday during a discussing period, Mr. Barr finally asked two students to stop talking. He did this without raising his voice; in fact, he never varied his voice from a rather monotonus low tone. During the two discussion periods during the week, the three overflow students who sat at one of the lab tables were always talking. Once Mr. Barr asked one of these students a question, in a low voice, knowing that the student wouldn't hear him. In a moment the student said, "What was the question?" Mr. Barr said, "I thought you probably wouldn't hear." As an attempt to embarrass the student, it was unsuccessful. After he tried to answer the question, the student soon began talking with his neighbor again.

Several interesting points emerge from these examples. How do good teachers handle students' conversations that are irrelevant to the work of the class? In the first example the teacher assumed that obviously the students would not be talking together unless he, the teacher, had failed to make the instruction clear. But look at example five. Here the teacher has no such confident expectation. On the contrary, he indicates by his weak voice and hopeless attitude that he really does not expect anyone to listen. This action should be contrasted with the assumption underlying the teacher's action in the third example. Here the teacher is using a kind of social blackmail to bring the student into line. After all, no gentleman would be rude, now, would he? This method works, but only up to a point. The teacher is depending on the appeal to loyalty to herself, rather than on an objective need for quiet. Being quiet because the learning job demands quiet lest others miss essential instructions places the emphasis where it belongs.

The fourth example, the problem of the Spanish-speaking students, is a common one wherever a large segment of the school population can speak easily in another language. Teachers as well as students find this a great problem, since it is impossible to know whether or not one is being insulted when one does not know the words! The discipline situations that arise out of this kind of student conflict often involve a total school program. Where the bilingual students are helped to feel at home, respected, accepted, the problems arise more rarely. But where they are subject to social ostracism and repressive rules about speaking their own language, there are bound to be occurrences such as the one given here.

Classroom Procedures

The examples show both poor and good practice in relation to some of the typical disturbances created by interaction of student and student. Let us briefly summarize the teacher's most effective tactics in dealing with them:

1. *Continued and disturbing conversations*

(a) Ignore the conversation if the rest of the class is absorbed in the activity. The students who are talking will be drawn into the group activity eventually without disrupting the rest of the class through a special reprimand.

(b) Walk around the room, and make a point to stand near students who are more likely to talk than others. If a student report is going on, the teacher should quietly place himself wherever he foresees that some trouble may emerge. Thus he can inconspicuously exercise control.

(c) Call the students up for a special conference; discuss the problems they create with the class; ask them for a solution.

(d) Discuss the problem with the whole class, if the disturbance is sufficiently widespread. Ask the class to agree on how to behave, and to set up rules that should be observed. Have the rules posted if need be. Thus attention of offenders can be called to the rule they themselves made.

(f) Study students who talk continually. Have they a special problem? They may genuinely be completely lost in the work. They may have missed class sessions or be beyond their intellectual depth. Or they may have finished all their work and need extra work. Some talkers are exhibitionists and need to learn how to control this bid for attention. These are best handled by giving them ample opportunity to talk before the class rather than by stifling them.

(g) Separating friends who seem to encourage each other to misbehave is futile. Instead of giggling together in the middle of the room, they will communicate across the whole breadth or length of the room and inconvenience that many more students. It is wiser to discuss the matter with the offenders, letting them see the benefits of being allowed to stay together and the possible penalty of separation if they refuse to do some self-disciplining.

2. *Passing of notes*

(a) Ignore the practice but get more variety of activity into the classroom. A teacher can probably get himself into trouble faster with his students by picking up such notes and making an issue out of the matter than by any other means. Only teachers who suspect that notes have unpleasant comments about themselves really get disturbed about such a practice. Like any other student-student disturbance, it is often a symptom of classwork that is boring and lacks challenge. The main problem then is not the note.

(b) Never read a note aloud to a class; it may be highly embarrassing to you. Throwing notes away unread will also earn you the hatred of the student who wrote the note. The rest of the class will not be on your side, either.

3. *Symbiotic relations; overdependence of one student on another* (see example 2 on page 320):

(a) Leave a dependent friendship of this sort alone until a more desirable substitute is ready. The students usually need each other and should not be deprived of help until better relationships with others can be built. Give them joint projects; use group methods to wean them slowly away from each other if it seems desirable. Find some skill on the part of the dependent student and encourage him to develop it.

4. *Hostility between two or more students or between groups of students*

(a) Talk with the hostile students individually. Such a situation needs careful diagnosis rather than immediate action. It is far better to get at the roots of the hostility than to suppress it for a short time. Hostility will only then emerge later in more exaggerated form.

5. *Flirtations*

(a) Do not try to meet the problem head on. A girl intent on attracting the attention of the boys will do so whether permitted to or not. The problem is best met by permitting more, rather than less, socialization, so that students can become acquainted without having to disrupt the class to do so. Then, if the problem continues, the teacher has a firm basis upon which to discuss her actions with the offending girl.

(b) Avoid any public issue. Students will be quick to laugh at the teacher who tries to shame students into ceasing flirtations. The teacher will only gain the reputation of being opposed to human nature and will have made his problem worse.

6. *Cheating*

(a) Reorganize test or assignment structure. Cheating occurs when the teacher has made it impossible for the students either to learn the right answers or to achieve good grades by acceptable means (see example on page 315; also the discussion of cheating in Chap. 16).

(b) Discuss the problem of cheating with the class. Examine the consequences of cheating and suggest that the class think through the problem.

(c) Lift pressure on individuals who consistently cheat. Provide such students with other ways of gaining recognition for achievement.

(d) Provide opportunity to re-do poor work; thus students will not be forced to cheat in order to make good on the one chance provided.

(e) Discuss cooperative learning and how students can help each other to learn without being guilty of cheating.

(f) Remove the temptation to cheat. Use alternate forms of tests.

In order to end the discussion on a positive note, here are some descriptions of teachers dealing adequately with some of the kinds of problem behavior discussed in this section:

> At the start of class Mr. Rung began discussion of new work while drawing a figure on the board. His manner was one of continuing a conversation which had been interrupted sometime previously. One boy in the back of the room was moving about trying to borrow a pencil from someone. A couple were exchanging notes. Mr. Rung, however, gave the activity no apparent notice, and in a few minutes the class's attention was on the new work being discussed. A little later, interest waned on the part of a couple of boys in the front of the room, and they began some extended whispering. This was quashed when Mr. Rung quietly spoke their names, in a simple declarative manner, with no admonishment.
>
> During the study period following the lesson there was low talking among groups, some sitting two in a seat while discussing the work. The instructor circulated about the room helping various individuals. If a problem-working conversation became too noisy or wandered to irrelevant topics, Mr. Rung would just walk by. The noisy one would ask a question (though undoubtedly already knowing the answer), but would then subside to more serious work.

> Just as soon as Mr. MacDonald sensed restlessness, even before it was really noticeable, he would say with good humor, "What's the matter, John?" "Did you have a question, Cornell?" "I wonder if I've made that clear, George." His tone of voice was never accusing or threatening; it was simply a matter of fact. On one occasion he asked Bill to step outside so he could talk to him. When the boy returned he was not belligerent or beaten down; rather, he showed that he accepted the whole incident. Mr. MacDonald felt that Bill would be causing trouble all during class if he were not quieted down immediately. All such situations were treated as incidents rather than issues.

> One morning while a pupil was reading the daily bulletin to the class, there was quite a bit of talking and unnecessary noisemaking. Mrs. Jerome didn't say anything until the pupil had finished reading. Then she explained to the class that they hadn't been fair to those who were interested in what had been said or to the person who was reading. In this way she tried to promote self-discipline among the group members instead of instilling fear of punishment.

Discipline Situations Arising from School Routines

Some discipline problems arise from students all-to-human reaction to the institutional arrangements of our schools. The crucial school situations that seem to make it more than usually difficult for students to control themselves are:

1. The last period of the day on Friday.
2. The last period of the day, usually.
3. The last five minutes of the class just before lunch.
4. The whole day just before a big game, rally, all-school festival.
5. The first part of the period following an exciting rally, school assembly, fire drill.
6. The day just before report cards come out; the day report cards are issued; the day following.
7. At a time of all-school crises, such as death of a popular student, winning the league championship, conflict between students and administration, arrest of students and consequent school scandal.
8. Before a holiday and before extended vacations.
9. The first few days of school.
10. Fridays in general; sometimes the first half of Monday.
11. Appearance of a substitute.
12. The first few minutes of the period.

Probably this list could be extended from the experience of every teacher.

How are students likely to respond to such occurrences? The major symptom is a general restlessness that communicates itself to all of the class: wriggling, giggling, squirming, inattention, inability to stop whispered conversations, short attention span, unexpected bursts of laughter at minor episodes, unusually loud voices, a kind of mass hysteria on a modified level. After all, the students are part of a group, and, as such, group feelings are apt to pervade the classroom. A class can be happy, sullen, gay, silly, excited, voluble, antagonistic, just as a person can. This means that most of the students will react similarly; facial expressions will hold the same kind of look.

Below are some descriptions of such incidents:

> The biggest problem that Mr. Snow had was getting the class quiet after the last bell had rung. It seemed difficult to quiet them without having to remind them continually that the last bell had already rung. First, Mr. Snow just tried to tell them class had begun. When telling them became just a "rumor," he began talking about the homework assignment. The students nearest Mr. Snow heard him and came to attention. But that wasn't the solution. Then he tried calling the roll, only he called them Mr. or Miss and the last name. This worked for

nearly a week, when once again the class had to be told and retold that classwork had begun. At last Mr. Snow just stood before them, ready to begin the lesson. He just stood without uttering a word and looked straight at the few who continually were holding up the class. He did not glare at them, but rather gave them a look of—"Well, I'm ready just as soon as you are."

Students were in the Little Theater viewing films. Some of the films were not very interesting and a chatter set in about a third of the way through. Miss Parry felt that it was unfair to the rest to comment aloud on the actions of a few. However, at length, she felt compelled to speak. It didn't get the desired results. Finally Miss Parry gave up and fortunately was saved by the bell.

One day a comic-musical program was being broadcast over the loudspeaker at the beginning of the hour. Mr. White had a difficult time getting the class's attention at this time. Soon the broadcast terminated and the class settled down to a period of normalcy.

The students were given a short assignment to do in class in which it was necessary to talk to their neighbors. There was some movement about the classroom. When the assignment was finished, there was a hangover of restlessness. Instead of attempting immediately to quiet the class down, Miss Rosenberg went on as best she could with the regular classwork. In a few minutes everything was back to normal and the class was attentive again. Miss Rosenberg had recognized the class reaction and in fact had anticipated it.

Classroom Procedures

In meeting discipline situations arising from student reaction to school routines, the teacher's approach should be one of dealing with the group as a whole instead of individuals. Suggested courses of action are:

1. *Accept the feelings of the class:* The wise teacher recognizes the contagion of restlessness or tension. He does not consider this a personal affront. He does not become aggressive, knowing aggression from him will only bring relative aggression from his class. If he gets angry, the class will get angry in return. Nor does he become worried and let the class observe his insecurity. He may notice with the kind of good humor most natural to him the temper of the class. He may say, "You know, this spring weather makes me restless too, so I've planned an hour especially to take care of all this spare energy I see you have." Or, "Anybody here ever study atomic energy? Have trouble understanding it? Well, here's your chance to study it first hand. There's enough nuclear energy around here today to put Oak Ridge in the shade."

2. *Provide an activity in keeping with the class atmosphere:* Where the reactions of the class are so different from the usual ones, the teacher should not expect to carry on the regular activities. Even if another kind of activity has been scheduled, it is sometimes wiser, when a class is really

very effervescent, to propose instead some active, interesting, and attention-getting device: a drill game (see Chap. 9), group quiz, or some other type of short-group activity (see Chap. 8), general class discussion on a controversial topic of interest. All of these approaches help to utilize the steam that is generated in the students.

3. *Avoid using repressive or anxiety-producing devices:* Some teachers have been known to spring a test on a class when it gets unruly. As a result, the teacher will find the class antagonistic and hostile. His future attempts to win them will be handicapped.

4. *Do not give an assignment the night before a big game, or for the evening of the day when some major school activity is scheduled:* The battles over assignments are cruel enough without provoking worse trouble. One teacher who failed to observe this principle was in continual conflict with his class over its delinquent homework. He seemed to go out of his way to give them lengthy themes the night of the league basketball games. Needless to say, he received few themes the next day.

5. *Discuss the problem with the class:* The teacher who recognizes the feelings of the class and then says, "Well, we feel restless today; but work must go on. There are a number of important things to get done in class today; how should we go about doing it so that our high spirits don't get in the way?" Talking it over with the class will give the teacher an understanding of how they feel, and also permit students to gain an objective view of their own behavior, thus modifying it toward more compliant patterns.

Summary

In this chapter we have discussed several kinds of discipline problems. In one kind, the teacher may contribute to his own problems of classroom control through lack of social skill in human relations, or through lack of teaching skill. A careful diagnosis by the teacher of "What was my contribution to this discipline situation?" will often improve classroom atmosphere. Of course, we must avoid the blunder of assigning exclusive blame to either the teacher or the students for discipline problems; it is not a clear case at any time. It is more important to make a sensitive diagnosis of any continued discipline problem to know what the source might probably be, and then take appropriate action. Too often in such diagnosis the teacher will blame the students; it has been our purpose here to point out the large role played by the teacher himself.

Students, however, do not all adjust equally well to the situations created by the school. Some of them overreact to others and find it difficult to exercise as much self-discipline as the learning situation demands. These discipline situations are of several kinds; in this chapter we discussed those problems that arose from the interaction of student with student and included such things as note passing, continual conversations, cheating. Another kind of discipline situation occurs as students adjust to various aspects of school routines, to the demands of the school as an institution. In this category were included the students' usual responses to the last period of the day on Friday, the day before a big game, the day just before or after a holiday or extended vacation, and other times of the school year.

In dealing with these discipline situations, we recognize that there is no easy solution. However, the teacher who gains insight and understanding into the adolescent personality, who himself is sensitive to the school as an institution, will be able to accept and guide young people in more adequate ways of adjusting to the many conflicting pressures of their school world and the world of their peers.

Selected References

Bibliography on discipline will be found at the end of the next chapter.

14. Adjustment to School Life: Discipline II

THE high-school teacher must live with an average of over 100 students a day. In terms of sheer self-preservation, an atmosphere of relaxation, interest, and quiet order must prevail. But adolescents have many life experiences to explore, understand, and absorb. Many of them come from disorganized and unhappy homes. These pressures, social and personal, make it difficult for many students to accept gracefully the numerous demands of the school and to perform the tasks of learning in compliant and interested fashion. In this chapter, we will discuss the kinds of adjustment to school that arise out of students' adjustment as adolescents in our culture as well as those problems that arise from deeper personality needs of individuals.

Finally, it is important to consider the over-all problem of discipline in terms of a philosophy of discipline. It is vital that teachers assess any line of action purported to create an orderly learning situation in terms of the long range as well as the short-range effects on the human beings involved. Teachers must look at various discipline "policies" in terms of such human effects. It is important to establish a frame of reference that can enable teachers to distinguish effective, mature, constructive, democratic discipline, from repressive, primitive, and destructive procedures.

Discipline Situations That Arise from Immediate Personality Needs

In this section we will consider the discipline situations that arise primarily because adolescents are adolescents. It is important to distinguish these normal personality manifestations of misbehavior from the deeper personality problems and disorders that will be dealt with in the next section. How do you know whether a student misbehavior is merely surface reaction or is deep? Roger Barker[1] has suggested a way of distinguishing these two. The surface misbehavior *can* be disciplined. That is, the surface act of aggression that is merely an expression of ordinary adolescent reaction to adult authority can be dealt with by a firm tone, brief nod, or by being ignored. The student relinquishes the misbehavior easily when the adult toward whom it is directed acts reasonably and confidently. But discipline problems that arise because children are genuinely troubled, either by basic maladjustment in their whole personality structure, or because they must endure impossible home situations are those misbehaviors—

1. that persist; do not respond to normal teacher control;
2. that are manifest in many kinds of unruly actions;
3. that seem to have no logical connection between one misbehavior and another.

A schematic representation may make the distinction clear: the superficial misbehavior comes from the periphery of the personality, if we conceive of the personality as made up of layers of reaction systems. Deep behavior problems come from the central core of the personality. Both may appear similar in their manifestation, but, as stated above, the surface one can be handled by normal teacher control; the deep one cannot.

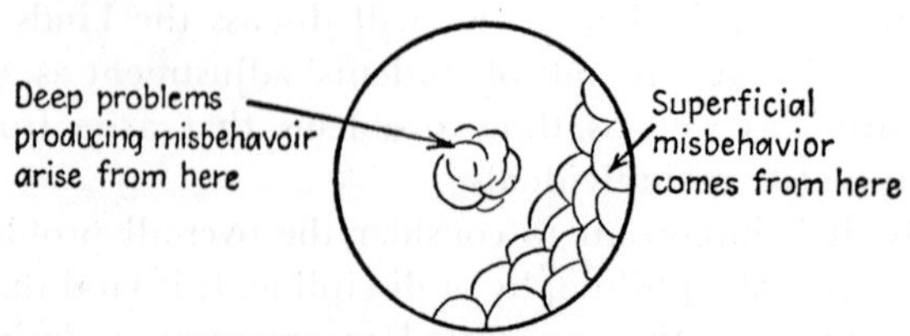

THE PERSONALITY OF THE CHILD

The kinds of superficial misbehaviors that concern us here are the following:

1. Student failure to do homework or assignment.

[1] Barker, Roger, Lecture on Discipline, Department of Psychology, University of Kansas, August, 1950.

2. Student refusal to obey a teacher request.
3. Student impudence.
4. Student-provoked accidents and other minor misbehaviors.

Skillful handling of disciplinary problems like these is a major factor in teacher success.

Student Failure to Do Assignments

The basic problem, of course, is the attitude of the teacher toward what appears to be a breach of discipline. If we view the failure to do an assignment as a personal affront, then punishment is the only recourse. On the other hand, if failure to do an assignment is a problem that concerns both teacher and the student, then the problem is open to mutual discussion. Why do students fail to do assignments?

1. *Unclear assignments.* This is the teacher's fault, and the student is not to be blamed.

2. *Assignments too difficult for this student.* Having one-level assignments for all students will almost always result in failure on the part of the slower students to do the work. After all, none of us likes to spend hour after hour struggling with material that we do not understand or on which we will certainly be given a failing grade even if we do try to do it.

3. *Assignments demanding facilities unavailable to the student.* Sometimes teachers require listening to a radio program as home work. Yet, is it always possible for every student to do this? What if an overbearing parent refuses to give up his program on the one radio in the house so Susan can do her homework? Or what if the student works every hour after school and has no free time for homework?

4. *Assignments basically uninteresting, boring, lacking in genuine intellectual challenge to the lively adolescent mind.* The world of the young person is a very exciting one. If the teacher consistently ignores this fact and asks the students to prepare assignments that are petty, trivial, detailed, and remote from any relation to real life problems there will be a continual problem of forcing the students to do the assignments.

5. *Apathy, laziness, disinterest in the task at hand.* It would be foolish to deny that our classrooms enroll many students who are personally lacking in discipline to do a hard task. School is a way of marking time for them. Grades are not very meaningful. The appeal by the teacher never raises a response, except of indifference or irritation. Often such students cannot be prodded to perform, no matter what the teacher does. Sometimes this is a period of growth, however. A student may demonstrate such behavior one semester and show quite a different attitude the following semester.

6. *A demonstration of rebellion against the authority of the teacher or of the school or of both.* The failure to do an assignment might very well be a refusal to do it. It might be considered a manifestation of the pattern of adolescent revolt that seems typical of our culture. The specific teacher might appear to bear the brunt of this revolt, but probably he stands merely

as a symbol of all authority against which the student is in rebellion as he seeks to attain independence and maturity.

Classroom procedures. In dealing with failure to do assignments, the teacher will want to check those items that stem from his own teaching practices (see section on assignments, Chapter 4), then advance into those which arise from other causes. When the failure is due to these other causes, the best policy is to deal with the problem on an individual basis. Talking with the student about the situation may help. It is important to approach the student from the following point of view: "When you failed to hand in your assignment, John, I wondered if there wasn't something we could do about it. What do you think?" Not: "John, you didn't hand in your assignment; I won't take any excuses. Now, what reasons do you have for this kind of behavior?" The latter approach puts the student on the defensive and is the typical disciplinarian approach. The first approach is the guidance technique, implying that there is a problem of mutual concern to teacher and student.

Since the area of the assignment is one of the major battlegrounds between teacher and student, it may be well to cite a few important strategic errors to avoid:

1. Do not go around the class demanding a public explanation from each student who failed to do his assignment. You will get one. The class clown or his cousin will very quickly rise to the occasion and make a wisecrack that will set the class laughing—at the teacher.
2. Do not argue with one student in front of the entire class regarding what he did or did not do on an assignment. If it appears that a student is going to start an argument, the teacher should immediately divert the discussion by commenting, "Well, Joe, perhaps we had better discuss this later when it won't take time away from the rest of the class. Now . . ." and continue with a comment directing the attention of the class to the work ahead.
3. Do not let failure to do assignments continue without any word of notice on your part. The student may need help. Do not assume that the whole process of self-discipline has been fully learned by every class member. Many need support, specific study aid, and basic understanding to get them farther along the road to maturity. The busy teacher who says, "Well, if they don't get their assignments in, let them suffer the consequences at the end of the semester," is doing a grave disservice to the students and building trouble for himself besides.
4. Do not forget the obligation implicit in giving an assignment. Giving an assignment and then forgetting to collect it, failing to return it, and returning it late are all evidences of poor teaching. Students will not do assignments in such an atmosphere.

Wherever the teacher deals with these more superficial aspects of the teacher-learner situation, it is important to keep a cardinal principle in mind: the teacher must never construe student misbehavior as a personal attack. As soon as the teacher does feel that student misbehavior of whatever sort is an affront to his own personality and authority, he cannot react effectively. We will continue to emphasize this basic principle in connection with the other discipline situations that arise from the periphery of the student's personality.

Student Refusal to Obey a Teacher Request

Here is a typical dilemma:

> Mrs. Jerome was conducting an oral reading period. In a nice manner she asked Phillip to read, just as she had asked others to read. He refused. The first time this happened she passed over it and went on to another student. "But," she asked her neighbor down the hall, "what shall I do the next time this happens?"

The teacher has several ways of dealing with a situation like this. For example:

1. Never call on the student again for that activity. The student may never learn how to read orally, but then, he also is prevented from making a real issue out of it with the teacher.
2. Give him an *F,* tell him so, and continue to call on him when it is his turn.
3. Insist that he do his task as the other students have.
4. Wait until it happens again. If it does, accept his refusal. Then check his cumulative record, talk to other teachers, and finally ask him to talk with you about his schoolwork.

It should be obvious that the fourth course of action is most likely to produce some workable solution. The third solution is an invitation to trouble far more dangerous than any of the others. The student can continue to refuse. Then what?

Classroom Procedures

> Gladys in the back of the room was fussing with the window-shade cord. The sound went click-click-click. The teacher was holding a discussion with the class, but the background rattle of the shade began to distract her and the students also. Finally she said, "Gladys, please stop playing with the shade cord; it distracts us," and continued the discussion. Her tone was firm, pleasant, but insistent. Gladys stopped —for five minutes. Then click-click-click. Was this rebellion? Was this open flaunting of the teacher's authority? It could be. But the teacher refused to act as though it were. Instead, she said, "Gladys, we haven't heard from you on this issue. Those shade cords are awfully tempting. How about moving just for today to this seat here and we will want to call on you soon for your reactions." Gladys moved.

This appeal was hard to resist. But it didn't happen by magic. The teacher had established an atmosphere of regard for others, of response to her politely worded requests given in a firm, clear, unequivocal tone of voice. She didn't pursue the point but returned to the task at hand, making clear by her attitude that of course the student would respond to a reasonable request. This *expectation* of reasonable behavior, of good behavior, is a potent tool in the hand of the teacher. It is particularly effective in dealing with incipient refusal to comply with a teacher request. But the expectation only is effective when the teacher has made the basic assumption that the student is not really trying to harass him, but is revolting against a symbol of adult authority.

But let us examine the refusal-to-obey further. Could the student have possibly had a good reason to refuse in the first example given on page 333? Sometimes, in situations such as oral reading, a boy may have deep reactions of stage fright, or he may be struggling to control a stutter or stammer, or his voice may be changing and be unreliable in pitch. A girl may feel ill or be ashamed of a cheap dress. Refusal may be reasonable and understandable. It is only the consistent or aggressive refusal that warrants action by the teacher. If the teacher follows up a refusal to obey and finds that a student has a reason that is, at least from his point of view, valid, the teacher can express interest or concern or admit that he didn't realize a problem existed. A bond is established then with a student when he is made to realize that the teacher considers personal problems more important than unquestioning conformity.

Should the teacher ever force the issue, insisting that the student obey? We should recognize this situation for what it is—a struggle for power, student against teacher. The teacher feels he must win in order to assure any kind of future authority over the class. A public show-down between two personalities can be highly embarrassing to the teacher, often results in the defeat of the teacher, and, rarely, even if the teacher "wins," helps relationships in the classroom. Show-downs, when necessary, should always be conducted in private. To test the limits of authority, to see how far he can push the authority that surrounds him without getting stopped, is a genuine emotional need for some individuals, particularly young children. They try to find out just how far they can go before mama or daddy rises in wrath. Similarly, some immature adolescents (and some adults) who have found the limits of the authorities in their world somewhat unreliable and inconsistently arbitrary will continue to try out the limits of any authority situation. They will see just how long they can continue aggressive or annoying behavior. The refusal to obey is one such manifestation.

The teacher who understands this need to defy authority responds to it by saying, in effect, "Jane, you seem to want to find out how much you can get away with in this class before I will get angry. Well, I don't get angry. But I think perhaps we might talk together later about how I, and the rest of the class, expect you to behave as a member of our group." And the teacher then proceeds to attend to the problem of the rest of the class. Shortly thereafter a follow-up interview will be needed (see Chapter 18). But the follow-up should take place only after sufficient time has elapsed for the emotional reactions to have passed; then both teacher and student can calmly consider the roots of the rebellion.

Student Impudence

A parent who had visited a school recently made the following observation:

> The trouble with our modern schools is that the kids are just too fresh. Why I heard a student whistle when Miss Green walked by. Another one saw me, waved his hand, and called out, "Hi, Mr. Jenkins," right in the middle of class. These kids are learning disrespect of adult authority; we need more discipline in our schools.

Parents of teen-agers are very vulnerable to adolescent attack. The parent particularly resents his own inability to make the child cease this kind of unpleasant behavior. Therefore, it is quite common to hear such parents call upon the school to do the job of discipline or complain that if the schools had only done a decent job the young people would not be as they are. It is true that in homes where a good working relationship exists between all members of the family the impudent remark is rare, while in a home where there is tension and uncertain authority, young people react to loss of security by being impudent.

Some typical classroom situations are given here:

> 1. Attention was excellent on discussion of four questions. A salutary effect was noted after Mr. Rose caused the wisecracker who said December 20, 1860, was "five days before Christmas," to be expelled from the room. Class paid attention in docile manner.
>
> 2. During a question period, one of the students asked a foolish question that was accompanied by the sudden flash of giggling. This attempt was nipped in the bud by Miss Arto simply by saying, "Bob knows that is a silly question so I won't bother to answer it." With this disciplinary phrase, Bob was halted, and the class returned to the discussion.

3. A boy in the class gave an impression of insolence in his replies to Mr. Basle's questions. Mr. Basle pointed him out to me: "Now take that student. He looks like a bad actor but is really a good student who can do good work and usually does. His surface attitude isn't too encouraging, but if handled right he works hard. It's very important to avoid starting off on the wrong foot with him."

4. One young teacher, dressed in her week-end best, was in charge of keeping the seniors in line on graduation evening. One senior remarked appreciatively, "Say Miss Rolfe, you are much too cute to be a teacher." The rest of the line waited in breathless suspense for her answer. She merely grinned back and told them to watch out because the music was going to start in a moment. No other remarks were made.

These examples were arranged in a sequence from an extreme, arbitrary reaction to the understanding, reasonable, and successful, reaction.

When is the teacher justified in expelling a student? It is highly probable that the teacher in example 1 above was overacting. It was a clever remark, not *necessarily* an impudent one. The teacher turned the remark into an attack upon himself. Perhaps the class remained docile, but it was coerced by fear of arbitrary punishment. Are these students learning anything about self-discipline? Are they learning to like the subject of the course? Are they developing attitudes of regard for the wisdom of adults?

Let us look at the second example. Here the teacher meets the attack head on. He feels that the question is foolish; he suspects that the student knew it; he makes it clear that he is not taken in by it. The tone of voice used by a teacher is the vital factor in the success of this procedure. Unfortunately, it is often a tone heavily loaded with sarcasm, dislike, irritation, or anger. In this incident the idea that the teacher "won't be bothered" gives a somewhat faulty emphasis. It is the *class* whose time should not be taken up to discuss a foolish question. The teacher might more wisely say, "Bob, that seems like a foolish question and we are busy now discussing the really important parts of our topic today."

It is important to remember at this juncture that the teacher's initial reaction to a foolish question may also be at fault. The student may genuinely be seeking a point of information. Therefore the teacher should be careful to leave a loophole for the student to reconsider his question or, if the class reaction differs from that of the teacher, to quickly assess that by a glance around the room and retract the hasty judgment. He can say, "Well, I can see by your faces that that question is in your minds also. I didn't think it was a serious question but I guess I was wrong. Now, Joe, what do you think the answer to Bob's question might be?"

The third example speaks for itself. Here is a teacher recognizing the need of some students to test the limits. This teacher sees that if he, the teacher, can react to the real need of the student and not feel that as a teacher he must be dominant in every relationship, he will be helping the student to outgrow his urge to attack authority.

Classroom Procedures. Nevertheless it is clear that no teacher can stand for consistent "fresh" behavior; the insulting stage-whisper wisecrack; the insolent retort; the deliberate use of vulgar or nearly obscene language; the provocative, needling question. Sometimes this behavior may even take the form of deliberately baiting the teacher. Youngsters try out on teachers the same devices that, unfortunately, work on parents. These are, typically, contrasting one teacher's methods to another, with a clear implication that one is less successful than another teacher; drawing a teacher into a futile " 'tis-'taint" debate, or "Yes, I did, no, you didn't" dispute; arguing a point of behavior in front of the class. The student usually gets the better of this kind of argument, since in this classroom climate the longer he can keep the teacher arguing and away from work the more his fellow students approve. Provocative attacks on the teacher symbol injure more than the teacher's feelings; they injure the teacher's view of himself as a competent adult. When the teacher senses this reaction in either an individual or a group of students, he needs to go through some searching self-examination to detect his own behavioral contribution to the situation:

1. Do I expect insulting behavior?
2. Do I overreact to any sign of attack?
3. Do I lose my sense of humor as soon as I suspect a student is being fresh?
4. Am I inconsistent in my relations with the class—happy one day and tired or harsh or chaotic the next?
5. Do I overreact to the slightest move on the part of a very few students? Are these students who are not in my culture group, that is, are on a low socioeconomic level, nonwhite, of a different ethnic group?
6. Am I easy to bait? Do I get taken in by a student inquiry and descend to an argument with one student while the rest of the class listens with delight to teacher being "taken"?

After such self-inquiry, the next step is to find which individuals in the class seem to be responsible for most of this type of trouble. An examination of office records and comparison of other teachers' experiences may give the teacher some explanation for the behavior of these students. Armed with some prior knowledge, the teacher can provide special recognition in the class on a positive level—a special leadership role, significant class responsibility—to the students who are most prone to being fresh. Then individual conferences should follow. The teacher's role in these conferences should be primarily to help the student recognize his feelings about himself and school which give rise to these outbursts.

Student-Provoked "Accidents" and Other Minor Misbehaviors

1. One day there was a slight disturbance when Jack almost fell into the aisle because his chair back had given way. The pupils near him laughed a little. He blushed and giggled. Mr. Abrams looked at him and smiled. The rest of the class didn't notice what had happened at all.

2. This was a commercial subject and intended primarily for girls. Of the boys who did enroll, most were there because they thought it was an easy course. This was especially true in the case of the one senior in the class. "Red" seemed to be the ring leader in generating some practical jokes. One day he kicked the chair out from under Jeff who was sitting with his chair tilted back. Mr. Roamer asked "Red" if he was the one who kicked the chair. But before "Red" could answer, Jeff said that he had merely slipped. Mr. Roamer gave "Red" a look that implied he knew differently. The class continued its work.

3. Silence had descended on the room. Heads were bowed over the test papers, pencils busily scraping over the desks. Each student was a model of concentration. "Ah-ah-ah-ah-choo!" came from the middle of the room. Everyone looked up, startled. A flurry of giggling passed through the class. Miss Henrich stalked up to Dave and snatched his paper from him. "That was completely unnecessary, young man," she snapped. "Next time you have to sneeze be polite enough to use a handkerchief. The rest of you get back to your test. Dave, you see me after school." Angry, annoyed, and puzzled looks could be observed on the faces of the students.

Classroom Procedures. A sense of humor, an ability to keep from overreacting, and an expectation of compliance with a reasonable request are the major tactics to meet these so-called accidents. For accidents will happen; sometimes just to break the monotony, sometimes out of adolescent deviltry, but often because a book really is too near the edge of the desk, or a chair leg does collapse from overwork, or Susy really does have the hiccups. At any rate, the troublemakers should not be singled out for front-row seats. Teachers sometimes believe these prominent positions inhibit misbehavior. This rarely is the case. Instead, such students now have the whole class behind them to observe their pranks. Incidentally, when teachers talk in front of a group, note where their eyes fall—

not on those in the front row, but rather on the individuals in the middle seats in the middle rows.

Sometimes students substitute bizarre and startling behavior for accidents. Here is a typical incident:

> Miss Laro was correcting sentences on the chalkboard, which had been signed by the translators. She had her back turned, and just as she turned to the class she saw John, who was sitting next to the side board, write someone else's name plus a nickname under his own work. When she came to John's work, she said nothing but drew a line through the fake name.

When incidents like these occur, the teacher should ask himself, "Is this important enough to disturb the process of learning?" Sometimes teachers take so much time in conflict with students over minor behavior disturbances that little time is left for creating a good learning atmosphere. It is often wisest not to see the petty disturbances. However, where the disturbance is apt either to disturb the rest of the class continually or is a symptom of a need on the part of the student to attract attention and gain recognition, the teacher must prepare to deal with the student in the same way as was suggested for "fresh" students. But an isolated expression of adolescent exuberance is not a sign of poor discipline and should not be treated as such.

To close this section, we include two incidents where students were given permission to leave the room but returned late.

> 1. Grace asked permission, just before the start of the class, to go to her locker. Mrs Hope allowed her this privilege and she departed. Some 15 minutes later she re-entered the room, somewhat hesitatingly, to be greeted with these words: "Pardon me, Grace, but just where is your locker? Is it in this building?" The young lady flushed and took her seat amid considerable laughter. Much of the volume came from the left rear corner of the room where the boys clustered.
>
> 2. Every day at 2:30 for a week Tom, one of the older boys in the class, asked for a rest-room excuse. On Friday when Tom asked at the usual time, Mr. Ruml kidded with him and told him this appeared to be quite a habit. Tom was slightly embarrassed. He did not ask for permission to leave in the days that followed.

The public humiliation technique used in the first example is very unwise. The best procedure would be to ignore the late return, to treat it as though it never happened, but make a point of talking to her in private later. At that time, without an audience, the teacher may tactfully suggest that such a prolonged absence should be explained. The teacher should suggest she personally is sure she must have had a very good reason. The teacher expresses, here, the assumption that the student's motives are acceptable. This kind of assumption is the quickest route toward obtaining acceptable behavior. Suspicion on the part of the teacher breeds distrust and defiance on the part of the student.

Now let us look at the second example. Here the teacher is again treading on delicate ground. An inquiry can be made of the school health records to see if there is any indication there, but even if none is discovered, the teacher should be wary of direct attack. The teacher, not the student, may be in the wrong. The teacher might say, in a private conversation, "John, I've noticed you ask for a pass every day at about this hour. It is all right since I know you wouldn't just try to get out of class this way. But I wonder if perhaps you mightn't check with the school doctor if this keeps up. It might indicate a minor infection, you know." And then follow up with a note to the school health department regarding your suggestion.

Special Problems for Men and Women Teachers

The types of student misbehavior considered in this section undoubtedly have a familiar ring. So many of us in our school careers have indulged in just such antics to—provoke? irritate? attract?—the teacher. In addition, there are some special hazards in this discipline area varying with the sex of the teacher:

1. *Special problems for men teachers:* At least once a year a man teacher will find that some girl tries to get out of doing the work, to escape from a general application of the rules, by using what are called "feminine wiles." These often involve coyness and pretentions of fragility and feminine incompetence. Another device that girls use on men teachers is "the weeps." As one male teacher remarked, "I'll do almost anything for a student rather than have her weep; when I see the danger signals, shiny eyes, trembling lip, shaking voice, I just want to run—so I say 'yes' before I know it, and am committed to something unfair to the other students." Of course some students are perfectly sincere, and, since they are emotional in adolescence, tears come because of the stress of feeling. It is important to distinguish, however, between the genuine and the pretended.

2. *Special problems for women teachers:* Women teachers sometimes feel handicapped because of their inability to use the implied threat of physical force to get the bigger boys to behave. Since many women teachers are actually shorter and slighter than the students they have in class, this fear is understandable. But the woman teacher should not use unfair, or psychologically false disciplinary methods. It is possible for a teacher who is a mere five feet tall and weighs all of 103 pounds to be just as poised, calm, reasonable, and firm as a male teacher who is a former football star. Since few schools would tolerate a man teacher who used physical force, it is obvious that force is no real threat to the students. Inner poise and an intelligent

use of good educational practices are a woman teacher's best safeguards. The woman teacher should not be susceptible to the flattery of the mature boys in her classes. They will use many of the wiles of their sisters, but usually are more subtle about it.

Summary

In summary, disciplinary problems arising from immediate student personality needs include:

1. Failure to do homework or assignment.
2. Refusal to obey a teacher request.
3. Impudent behavior.
4. Student-provoked "accidents" and other minor misbehaviors.

Under these headings fall the bulk of the so-called discipline problems. The teacher who hopes to deal adequately with such incidents—and they will occur in every class no matter how competent the teacher is—should in general observe the following principles:

1. Remember that this kind of misbehavior is not a personal attack upon the teacher. It is rather an expression of adolescent exuberance, immaturity, or revolt against adult and school authority.

2. Assume that students are capable of a reasonable response to a reasonable request. This will be more apt to produce reasonable behavior than almost any other technique. Success with this technique demands a basic teacher attitude that no student who is normally adjusting to his world really wants to misbehave all the time. It assumes that an appeal to the desire to be good, to be liked, to be accepted, is the most powerful force motivating student behavior.

3. Underreact rather than overreact to provocative situations. This will provide protection for both teacher and student. No teacher can long survive who is constantly involved in emotional flare-ups in his classes. Nor can students stand emotional attacks for very long and continue to learn and work productively. The sense of humor that recognizes that young people are often very, very funny—even when they don't mean to be—rescues many a teacher from the trap of overreacting.

4. Be discriminating in dealing with misbehavior. Not every breach of classroom regulations is worthy of teacher attention. Choose carefully those situations in which effective class control can be established over the individual. This will build a general atmosphere of control better than dealing severely with every little incident and putting a tight lid on everyone.

5. Remember that students are lively young people, not just names in a roll book. If the pressure is too great, they will explode. Pressure may come from insistence on self-control for too long a period or on too high a level, or on academic success motivated by fear of failure. Misbehavior of students flourishes most under repression.

6. Punishment should be meted out with care. (This will be discussed further at the end of this chapter.) A severe punishment for a mild offense is not appreciated by students. Punishments that ignore students' life situations also are unacceptable (for example, asking students to stay after school when they may have jobs, dental appointments, a school bus to catch).

Discipline Situations That Arise from the Central Core of the Student's Personality

In this section we will consider the problems presented by students whose adjustment to themselves and to their world has been so inadequate that they cannot behave as others do no matter how desperately they may wish to. These are students who are socially maladjusted and emotionally disturbed. Often these students are not classroom disciplinary problems at all, but sometimes they are serious threats to good order.

First, of course, there is need for diagnosis. Using the results of tests of personal-social adjustment (see Chapters 1 and 18), the teacher may detect a future behavior problem before it arises. But other clues are available. To recapitulate the criteria which were given on page 330, serious misbehaviors are those—

1. That persist; that do not respond to normal teacher control;
2. That are manifest in many kinds of misbehaviors;
3. That seem to have no logical connection between one misbehavior and another.

The sources of such misbehavior are varied, as can be seen in the following:

> Steve appeared to be a misfit. He is much smaller physically than his classmates; never volunteers speech or action; "just sits" as if he were not in the classroom at all. Steve transferred to the school three weeks ago and has no friends as yet. He never does anything unless told to, is very shy and retiring.

It is important to remember that students, like other people, have problems. These problems are not left at home when the student comes to school. He brings his troubles with him. And because he is not an adult and consequently has less insight into his troubles, he has fewer ways of dealing with the conditions that interfere with a normal happy life and fewer controls over his emotions. He is more apt to express his troubles freely through his behavior—or rather—misbehavior!

To a teacher every student is a little like an iceberg—only about one-eighth of his life is apparent; the other seven-eighths are hidden from view. The unrevealed portion of the student's life—his personal history, his family constellation, the previous experiences of success or failure in school, his emotional growth in relation to heterosexual adjustment, his fears and anxieties about the future—may produce the classroom misbehaviors.

A student whose problems cause classroom misbehavior might be considered a problem student. Problem students should not be treated in the same way as normal students. In a sense they are maladjusted, sick, out of tune with their world. The teacher who remembers this will not get angry at Johnny because this is the tenth time, it seems, that he has not done his homework. He will remember that Johnny's father has just died and that the boy is deeply angry at a Providence that seems so arbitrary. Or that Johnny is a Negro and feels that because of his status he can never be more than a redcap, so why do the history lessons, or math lessons, or play for the team? Or that Mary Ann is in love with a boy whose parents are anathema to her family; she is forbidden to see him or talk with him, so that most of her energies are devoted to schemes to evade the surveillance of her parents. Or that Ruth has a father who is an alcoholic and a mother who left home for parts unknown a year ago with, so say the neighbors, a stranger in a brown suit; indeed the girl is afraid to go home nights for fear her father will beat her. Knowing that such life problems may surround the "average" student, the teacher is able to be sympathetic, patient, and kind. The difficulties that some adolescents face in growing up in our contradictory world are often so overwhelming that it is surprising that such youngsters are as good as they are!

The teacher needs to remember that there are a few definitely deviant personalities. These we term the "neurotic," "psychotic," or "psychopathic" personalities. There are students to whom reality is so terrifying, so brutal, that escape is imperative, but in seeking to escape, the personality structure becomes distorted and abnormal. The ordinary things of life become major hazards, and a normal response to the demands of daily living becomes impossible. The behavior that the teacher observes is symptomatic: the behavior is not the problem; it is a symptom of something that is disturbing the child. For example, a student who lives in a world of dreams, of fantasy, who seems entirely unaware of what is going on and cares less, is demonstrating symptomatic behavior of a very serious sort. Another student, who seems to get violently ill before any examination, who turns pale with fright at having to answer a simple question, is also overreacting to a normal demand of life.

The teacher is not a diagnostician; he is not trained to deal with neurotic symptoms. However, the teacher should be sensitive to behavior that may be symptomatic of emotional illness. When suspect behavior is observed, the student should be referred to those trained to help in such instances.

One especially irritating form of abnormal misbehavior that many teachers feel powerless to control is that exhibited by the type of student, usually a boy, whom we could call a "clown." This sort of student is doubly a menace to the teacher, not only because he so quickly can upset any and all routines, but also because he is often so genuinely amusing that the rest of the class laughs appreciatively at all his antics. This kind of class support interferes with the teacher's remonstrances. Since the student is getting the kind of satisfaction his personality needs from the class, he will go to great lengths to circumvent the teacher's inhibiting presence. The clown is, however, an unhappy and often tragic case of maladjustment. As one observer notes:

> The child who clowns in the classroom very commonly is found to have a history of teasing by his companions because of his timidity. They call him "sissy," ridicule and torment him. The boy tries to meet the painful situation by actively bringing on the laughter of his companions rather than by waiting to endure it passively.[2]

Other kinds of antisocial or asocial behavior arising from personal maladjustment include the following:

1. Extreme aggression; destruction of books, fighting, breaking of property, lying.
2. Stealing.
3. Sexual offenses.
4. Extreme hostility to peers and adults; truancy.
5. Compulsive behavior; exaggerated fear or anxiety; tics, compulsive arm or leg or bodily movement; inability to sit still.

From this list it can be seen that some of the misbehaviors are directed against others and against the rules of society; others are rooted in the child's own person. Many of the delinquents represent these categories of behavior problems. Their delinquencies are only intensified by teachers who deal with their misbehavior as though the students were "bad," not as though they were in need of help. Where students demonstrate such extreme forms of maladjustment, the teacher must have recourse to trained personnel—psychologists, psychiatrists, psychoanalysts, child guidance workers,

[2] Klein, Emanuel, "Reluctance to Go to School," *Psychoanalytic Study of the Child* (New York: International University Press, 1945), Vol. I, p. 274.

social workers. These specialists are available to the teacher through the immediate school system, the county or state school system, or private or public agencies of the community.

Classroom procedures. What does the teacher do about such students in the classroom? The main object of the teacher's control of such individuals is to prevent the student from injuring others through his behavior and, as much as possible, to prevent him from further injuring himself. Rarely is it possible for the teacher to aid the adjustment of such a student in any fundamental way. He is beyond the help of anyone untrained in the field of psychotherapy. The teacher can only hope not to be one more burden to an already overburdened personality who is attempting to find a way to live in this world.

One aid that lies close at hand, perhaps more accessible than any other, is the utilization of some of the concepts derived from group therapy.[3] The major emphasis in using the group to aid the individual is in establishing an atmosphere of acceptance and permissiveness. The teacher-leader is not a judge or parent substitute; rather, he becomes a stable, accepting, secure individual. The group interactions are the mode by which the individual learns to compromise his own needs against those of others. In the high-school classroom extreme kinds of group therapy are not usually available, although it is possible that one day part of the school's guidance program will include group therapy work. But the individual teacher can, through judicious use of group procedures (see Chapter 19), make more progress in dealing with seriously maladjusted students who create discipline problems than through almost any other teaching technique.

What Discipline Works?

Before concluding this section on discipline we need to evaluate the various concepts of discipline and perhaps indicate the lines upon which the beginning teacher may evolve a philosophy of discipline for himself.

"It may not be the kind of theory they teach you in college, but it works," is a standard comment of many teachers when they defend or describe their modes of obtaining classroom control. Such a viewpoint expresses primarily the idea that discipline is for the teacher's peace of mind. It succeeds because the students do what

[3] Slavson, S. R., *An Introduction to Group Therapy* (New York: Commonwealth Fund, 1943). Also: Slavson, S. R., *Analytic Group Psychotherapy* (New York: Columbia University Press, 1950).

they are told within the four walls of the classroom. But is it successful in a larger sense? Discipline must be related to the purposes that we agree direct our total educational program. Considered in this light, discipline really succeeds only when it contributes to the development of democratic individuals, enabling them to perform satisfactorily the various roles of worker, parent, and citizen. The teacher who is primarily concerned about what works for him in achieving classroom control, "even if it doesn't agree with what is taught in the colleges," denies the larger aims to which our schools are committed.

Let us take some of the common measures that work—punishment, neglect, and emotional blackmail—and see why they negate the broader education goals. Then let us take one uncommon measure that works—democratic group control—and see why it affirms those goals.

Punishment. When does punishment work and when does it not? Can a teacher punish freely? The typical punishments are increased assignments, poor grades, detention after school, dismissal from class, sending to higher disciplinary authority—or threats of all these. Is the effect of such punishments to procure better student-teacher relations? From the point of view of the psychologist, it seems that punishment, by and large, is a very ineffectual way of obtaining genuine compliance. According to Symonds,[4] punishment merely serves—

1. To increase anxiety, which spreads to many other situations;
2. To produce hate of the one punishing and all he stands for.
3. To induce counteraggression.
4. To increase need for more and more punishment out of guilt for wrong doing.
5. To lower the student's self-esteem, making it increasingly difficult for him to feel that he is good enough to do anything that is good.

Olson states:

> Most investigations demonstrate that well-considered praise or approval is superior to reproof in guiding learning. . . . Human studies suggest a greater desirability of reward and approval, partly because of the undesirable emotional involvement that accompanies punishment. Approval gives constructive direction to the nature of the behavior desired, rather than simply negative information about what is to be avoided.[5]

[4] Symonds, Percival M., "Classroom Discipline," *Teachers College Record,* 51:147-158 (December, 1949).

[5] Olson, Willard, *Child Development* (Boston, D. C. Heath and Company, 1949), p. 338.

Classroom procedures. The case against punishment is very well established. Yet we find classroom after classroom dominated by the punishment atmosphere. Detention rooms are a common practice, and individual teachers use many varieties of punishment techniques. Why are these used when they are psychologically unsound? First, because they are at hand; that is, it requires little effort by the teacher to pull a punishment out of the air. Second, because students themselves react toward punishment with a superficial acceptance and subsequent compliance. You see—it works. The question to ask here, as of the other disciplinary approaches, is: it works—but for whom? Punishment works for the teacher insofar as it aids him in maintaining classroom order and surface acceptance of his authority. But as noted above, punishment works against the student as a developing personality. And it must also be remembered that punishment inflicts a subtle injury upon the teacher, involving him in a punitive climate during all his working hours. And few individuals can resist the corrosive effects of such a climate day after day and year after year.

There is another important issue to consider. Children are often conditioned through early family experiences to understand and accept punishment, particularly among lower socioeconomic groups and some culturally less integrated ethnic groups. Among these people the father or mother wields a big stick. The child may be a less adequate person because of these conditions; yet he knows no other sanction that will command his obedience. For this reason many lower-class children simply are amazed at a teacher who expects discipline from them on the basis of any other appeals. Olson's comment on this is very revealing:

> It is quite probable that the differences in disciplinary and educational practices found in the most modern and the most traditional schools are to some extent imposed upon the schools by the cultural tradition of the home and community, and for school persons to act differently would be incongruent with social expectancy. There are also, however, indications that children from homes of lower economic status can be dealt with under conditions which will free them more fully and make them more spontaneous and less apathetic and restrained. The goals of most theories of discipline are more than obedience; they also include concepts of self-reliance, self-control, initiative, and independence of action.[6]

Thus we must conclude that what works for some children will not and should not work for others. Punishment should therefore be used sparingly and only because it is a part of a larger accultura-

[6] *Ibid.*, p. 227.

tion process, which must have as an objective the development in students of an understanding of self-discipline and appreciation of the disciplines of reason, fact, and society.

Isolation

Teachers sometimes discipline students by isolating them in a corner of the room, sending them into the hall for a time or to the library. They may be refused aid. "I'm sorry, but I won't help any student who does not remain in his seat like everyone else." Or, "Stanley, you just don't seem able to resist talking to your neighbors and bothering them; you will have to sit by yourself at the back table." Other methods of isolation are to ignore provocative behavior as though it did not exist.

A child had used a naughty word when talking to his grandmother; she didn't answer him. The child insisted, and finally asked point blank if the grandmother hadn't heard the word he used. The grandmother said, "Why Billy, I didn't even hear you talking to me."

Classroom procedures. Such refusals of attention as we have just described get results. But the same question regarding how they work and for whom must be answered. Provocative behavior is motivated by some need; often it is an effort to gain attention that the child craves. Isolation reinforces the very craving that induced the behavior in the first place, and also makes the individual feel guilty about a need as basic as hunger. It is as though we said to a student: "If you once let me know you are hungry, I will refuse to give you food; if you don't show any hunger then I will feed you." Isolation will probably result in a suppression of the undesirable behavior, but just as probably the cost to the individual will be great. This is not to say that teachers must react on the spot and at the moment when the provocative behavior occurs. Sometimes it is better to wait until there is time for private conference. When it is evident that the student cannot be reached in private conference, it may still be necessary to plan carefully exactly what activities in the classroom will help him become a more acceptable class member. This technique then involves temporarily ignoring the provocative behavior until more strategic measures can be applied. This is quite different from neglecting to react at all.

Emotional Blackmail

In the emotional blackmail climate the teacher "loves" all children and says so at the rate of three times a minute—you don't get punished if you do no wrong, but you know you have to feel like a heel for three weeks afterward. The teacher in this climate produces a tremendous emotional dependence on her, exploiting it as the only source of influence.[7]

This kind of discipline is often utilized by women teachers primarily because the possibilities of physical punishment are remote. Both love and fear of the teacher can be part of the emotional blackmail used by the teacher. Sarcasm is another tool that utilizes emotional relations rather than any actual action. Sarcasm usually digs deeply into the victim's personality weaknesses and exploits his fear of exposure as a means of control. The teacher who develops the feeling of "Now do this for me, because if you don't you will make me so unhappy" is being unfair.

> Discipline was excellent. Mr. Halstead was a young man teacher. He allowed the students to "buzz" a little between each other almost whenever they wished. But if the buzzing became too loud, he would suddenly look very grieved and disgusted. After a moment or two of strained silence he would burst into a mild tantrum in which he would shame the students for not acting their age. He would act hurt that he, who always treated them so well, should be subject to this ungrateful treatment. His whole method of teaching seemed to be geared to a sort of a "proud but grieved parent" attitude.

Young people should be asked to do things in the classroom primarily because it is to their benefit as learners, because they are part of a group endeavor. They should not be constantly reminded that any misbehavior hurts one who loves them dearly.

Discipline for Whom? Individual vs. Group

We have presented thus far three prevalent discipline patterns. There are two more major questions to consider before moving on to a statement of the democratic discipline pattern.

1. Is discipline to be directed against the individual or the group?
2. How can we know if discipline works?

Here is an example where a whole class was punished for the actions of a few.

> A small boy came home with blue pencil designs all over his arms. His mother was quite taken with this decoration and asked him when he had had time to do that in school. He explained that the whole class had had to sit still for half an hour and do nothing because some boys had been throwing oranges in the room. The mother said, "Well, that must certainly have made you mad at those boys who got you

[7] Sheviakov, George, and Fritz Redl, *Discipline for Today's Children and Youth* (Washington, D.C.: Dept. of Supervision and Curriculum Development, NEA, 1944), p. 49.

all punished." "Oh no," answered the boy, "it made us mad at the teacher."

Another instance from the elementary school:

> A teacher divided the class into four groups. Each group worked together on many problems all semester. As each group produced the required work they earned "money." But whenever any member of a group was naughty, the group had a stated amount of "money" taken away. Observing the development of the social climate of the class, one could easily note how this method aroused great antagonisms among the children, suspicion, distrust, and hatred. Child was set against child instead of welding group relationships. The burden of punishment that was given the group was too much for them to handle.

Classroom procedures. These examples can be easily translated into high-school practices. Sometimes in intramural team games so much pressure is put on the team to win that relations within the teams become distorted. Using the group to discipline the individual can be practiced successfully only within carefully defined limits. The teacher can and usually should express the idea, "In this class we just don't interrupt people when they are talking." Or, "Even if you don't feel like studying, Janet, since everyone else is, let's not annoy them." This approach reminds the individual of his obligation to the group and is effective with normal misbehavior.

In most instances of misbehavior that arise from deep sources within the individual, the group approach can only be effective in a therapy situation. Most of the teacher's efforts should be directed to understanding the individual and his problem, since the problem arises from difficulties that extend far beyond *this* classroom and *this* course.

Did It Work?

Now to the most difficult of all the questions that must be answered: Did it work? One of the greatest frustrations of high-school teaching is the lack of continued contact with the students. The teacher has a group for five days a week, an hour a day, for four months; then the students are gone. This contact is very slight indeed, compared with the six hours a day, five days a week for a whole school year that is the privilege of the elementary teacher. The teacher who tries to help a troubled student, who seeks to work with him and give him support and guidance and direction in his attempts to adjust to a confusing and threatening world, finds it discouraging to see him move on to another group of teachers, leaving the teacher with no idea as to how the student is faring. The teacher may be left with the feeling that all his efforts have failed. It is not often that a high-school teacher is in touch with a student after he graduates and takes his place in the world, and this too makes it difficult to assess the effects of the teacher's methods of control. Did they actually make Douglas more self-directing? Did Jane really learn how to control her explosive temper? After all, it is the long-range effects that concern the teacher who desires to utilize democratic methods of discipline. But the teacher is almost invariably denied any knowledge of such long-range effects.

Democratic discipline. Let us then seek to develop some criteria of short-range effects that might guide the teacher here and now in determining whether some long-range good may be developing:

1. Are students developing an ability to obey rules because they understand what is reasonable?
2. Do students help each other in those situations that demand self-control? Does this helping occur because of concern for each other more than a threatened reward or punishment from the teacher?
3. Does the need for the teacher to exercise control diminish as the group continues to work and learn together?
4. Can the students accept a substitute teacher or the unexpected absence of the teacher during the period without becoming disorganized or having to be held down by teacher threats?
5. Can the students develop their own rules of behavior as well as follow them fairly well?
6. Can students and teacher talk calmly together about class disturbances not anticipated in the rules and arrive at mutually acceptable compromises?
7. Are students who seem to be the source of the major problems of discipline being helped by group integration or by outside guidance from teacher or specialists?
8. Does the teacher enter the classroom feeling relaxed and in a mood for work? Does this feeling develop through the semester?
9. Do students enter the classroom feeling relaxed and in a mood for work? Does this atmosphere develop through the semester?

The above list suggests questions that each teacher may use to evaluate the success of his own disciplinary techniques. As can be seen, the questions assume the same basic attitude toward teaching that was developed in the chapter on the democratic classroom. The theory of discipline advanced here is one that conforms to democratic ideals—that discipline is merely the kind of classroom control that is most apt to further the development of democratic personalities.

Test Your Theories

In the following pages are a number of illustrations of discipline situations. Some are well handled, some are poorly handled, some are not resolved at all. It is suggested that each reader think through his own line of procedure in terms of each situation. He should ask himself: What would be the possible consequence of the line of action taken or proposed? Does it jibe with my theory of democratic procedures? Would I feel satisfied if I continued to use such methods day in and day out?

1. When books were supposed to be closed during a conversation based on the assignment, Jane insisted on keeping hers open. The teacher went over to the girl's desk and quietly closed the book, letting the conversation continue.

2. I had trouble with one boy in the class. Why, I don't know. But one day I asked him in Spanish to stand up and recite. He indicated that he didn't understand. This response was repeated often. Finally, I asked him in English to stand up and met with open rebellion. I'm afraid I showed that I was angry with him and said I would report him. At the end of the hour I spoke to him and asked him why he had acted in such a manner. His answer was that he didn't understand me. I accepted this and told him that I was very sorry I hadn't expressed myself more clearly and wouldn't report him. Since that day I haven't had any trouble with this student, even though he is the class cut-up.

3. The class was small, approximately fifteen students. I noticed particularly two cases that could come under the heading of disciplinary problems. The first was a boy about seventeen years old, nice-looking, and seemingly no different in physical appearance or mental ability from the rest of the class. But he continually slouched down in his chair, appearing to have no respect for the teacher and no interest in the class. This occurred every day. Each day Mr. Aman remarked to Jim that his green shirt would look better if it weren't so wrinkled, or he wouldn't get a stiff neck if he sat up straight. Jim would sit up a few minutes, then sprawl once more. When Mr. Aman addressed the remarks to Jim, both laughed, as did the class. So there was no bitterness or tension, but neither was there any long-term success.

One day the class was to be tested. Jim forgot his pencil. There was a school rule that teachers or pupils could not lend pencils. Jim knew this, but without permission spoke up asking for a pencil. Mr. Aman told Jim to leave the room, and with no further remarks went on to administer the test.

The second case was that of a boy approximately sixteen years old, smaller in stature than the other boys in the class and comparatively lower in mentality than the rest of the group. He had a bad complexion, stuttered noticeably, and had a definite twitch in his left eye. To compensate for the above deficiencies, Roger continually whispered and giggled to those nearest him, drew on the blackboard, and was generally inattentive. Mr.

Aman asked him direct questions, trying to bring him into group discussions, but with little success. The boy seldom knew the answers. Frequently Mr. Aman, during study periods, told him to work and snapped his fingers to quiet him down. When Roger was talking, Mr. Aman would say, "Pardon me, Roger, I will have finished speaking in a moment." Mr. Aman had a good sense of humor, which, as somebody says, "is so obviously the most essential characteristic of skillful handlers of discipline problems . . . that its possession must be among the prime requisites for the job."

4. George has had a habit of saying in a most flippant manner when questioned, "What?" instead of "Pardon me." The teacher seized this opportunity to introduce the Spanish words meaning "pardon me" or "excuse me," thereby requiring the whole class to use the phrase.

5. The class came in. Indeed, the class rushed in. Senior boys and girls—shouting, pushing, joking, singing, teasing, arguing. The bell had not rung and things were bound to quiet down with the 10:15 bell. The 10:15 bell rang. Senior boys and girls continued shouting, pushing, joking, singing, teasing, arguing. From 10:15 until approximately 10:30 you could hardly have heard a fire siren. Mr. Burgquist was, for all appearances, oblivious to the pandemonium, and thumbed through his notes unconcernedly. Finally, he had obviously had enough.

"QUIET!"

Wallet passing, note passing, and all talk came to an abrupt halt.

"I've told you a hundred times to keep quiet. . . ."

When some semblance of order had been restored, a certain routine of the class began to operate. Throughout the hour the room was filled with the exaggerated volume of the teacher's voice as he gave out instructions. It seemed to be more of a shout than a normal speaking voice. It had ceased being commanding but had retained its volume, and in a monotone this loud voice continued:

"Now get out your notes on yesterday's panel discussion for me to collect."

This was done, and while the instructor collected the papers from desk after desk, the noise began again. Not so loud as before, to be sure, but it had potentialities.

Fully half the hour had gone by before the actual instruction began. The topic for discussion during this week's class meetings were to be concerned with juvenile delinquency. Each day a report was given by a student on some phase of the problem. As the report was given, the rest of the class took notes on what was being said, which were to be handed in the following day after being transcribed into more readable form.

Isabel, tiny, shy, and nervous, walked to the front of the room and began telling the class of her visit to Girl's State in Sacramento and of the speeches and board meetings there that were directly concerned with delinquency in the state. The class was valiantly attempting to copy down every word Isabel said—or rather read from her notes in the front of the class. She was interrupted repeatedly by the other students, who said she was going too fast, that they couldn't hear her, and would she mind starting over again from the beginning, please. The students for the most part were little concerned with what Isabel had to say except that they had to write it down "to hand in tomorrow." Isabel never did complete the report, for the instructor had some announcements to get out of the way before the bell rang. But what the teacher announced had little effect upon the students, since they didn't have to write it down and hand it back tomorrow. They were, instead, busily engaged in exchanging everything from snapshots to gossip to wallets to notes that read:

> Dear baby,
> Whats the matter with you today and last week. You'll have to change your ways or daddy won't marry you like I said before. But anyway I still loves ya'!
>
> The Mosquito

6. The procedure set up *by* the instructor was that all students should be in their seats by 8:25 A.M. with books open and ready to work. No student would be allowed to sharpen his pencil during the early part of the class hour, as this should have been taken care of prior to the beginning of the class. Any student who wished to use the adding machines had to raise his hand and ask the permission of the instructor prior to walking to the machine. In several cases students lost a considerable amount of their working time awaiting permission to go to the adding machines because the instructor was helping someone else and did not notice their raised hands. The instructor felt that classroom discipline, especially around the adding machines where the students would congregate and talk, was getting lax. He thought he had better crack down now and ease up gradually later on.

Summary

In the preceding two chapters we have discussed some major kinds of discipline situations. From the text of these chapters, it is clear that there is no formula that covers all cases, all students, all times and places. The teacher who seeks to develop an optimal learning situation brings primarily a point of view, an attitude of mind, and a sensitive eye for adolescent attempts at adjustment.

The best preparation for becoming a skillful teacher in the area of classroom control is continual observation of other teachers and continual self-appraisal—"What would I have done differently?" It is also helpful to try some of the crucial teacher-student situations through sociodrama techniques and see what it is *you* can say or do that will create the atmosphere you are seeking. Often by trying several different versions, by seeing others try their ways of dealing with problem situations, teachers gain skill in quickly rising to the needs of the situation.

Democratic classroom discipline is essential to the development of the democratic classroom; one cannot exist without the other, and neither occurs without careful preparation, study, and continual appraisal of progress.

Selected References

Baruch, Dorothy. *New Ways in Discipline*. New York: McGraw-Hill Book Company, 1949. Develops in detail the nondirective approach to discipline.

Fenton, Norman. *Mental Hygiene in School Practice*. Stanford: Stanford University Press, 1943. Chaps. XI and XII, pp. 203-249. Discusses the deeper problems of maladjustment that confront the teacher and counselor.

Fostering Mental Health in Our Schools. 1950 Yearbook, Association for Supervision and Curriculum Development. Washington, D.C.: National Education Association, 1950. Chap. 11, "Shall We Use Rewards and Punishments?" pp. 170-178. Discusses the psychological effects of reward and punishment in terms of long- and short-range effects.

Margolies, Abraham. "A Portrait of George Miles—Problem Child," *High Points*, 28:25-30 (September, 1946). A maladjusted, but intellectually superior boy finds in a high-school social-studies class, with the guidance of a sympathetic teacher, how to overcome his problems and become interested in school activities.

Monash, Louis. "Notes on Mental Hygiene and Preventive Discipline," *Understanding the Child*, 18:19-23 (January, 1949). Lists the characteristics of good discipline and the related class practices and procedures that produce it.

Mowrer, O. H. "Discipline and Mental Health," *Harvard Education Review*, 17:285-296 (Fall, 1947). A psychological inquiry into discipline and how it may be achieved.

Redl, Fritz, and William W. Wattenberg. *Mental Hygiene in Teaching*. New York: Harcourt, Brace & Company, 1951. Recommended for *all* future teachers as basic in understanding how and why children behave as they do.

Robinson, Bruce B. "Neurotic and Normal Discourtesy in the Classroom," *Understanding the Child*, 25:8-14 (January, 1946). Teachers often forget to be as courteous to students as to other individuals; this oversight produces undesirable student reactions.

Sheviakov, George, and Fritz Redl. *Discipline for Today's Children and Youth*. Washington, D.C.: Department of Supervision and Curriculum Development, NEA, 1944. Best coverage of the psychology of various discipline approaches, with many illustrative incidents.

Symonds, Percival M. "Class Discipline," *Teachers College Record*, 51:147-158 (December, 1949). Insightful appraisal of several approaches to discipline.

Wickman, E. K. *Children's Behavior and Teachers' Attitudes*. New York: The Commonwealth Fund, 1932. The classic study in the field that pointed out teacher overconcern of "problem children" as against the real need for attention to children with problems.

15. Testing Instruments

MRS. RAMON was talking with Mr. Davenport. "I am really enjoying the projects we are carrying on in my fifth-period class. I let the class decide how it wanted to study our next unit of work, and the group decided after much talk that it wanted to work as committees. It wants to put all of the findings into a living-newspaper presentation for an assembly. But do you know what worries me? I don't know how much they are learning! They seem to be going full speed and doing an amazing amount of extra reading. I overhear fascinating arguments about the material being collected, but how do I know just *what* is being learned?"

Mr. Davenport was a most appreciative audience. "I know just how you feel. But from what I know of students in the class, they *are* learning something. You must have noticed John England is actually interested in a school subject for the first time since he has been here. And Sue Carrington has stopped her incessant giggling at least long enough to make really first-class posters. And it hasn't just happened to them. I know because I get them the period after you have them and I hear their comments."

This conversation emphasizes what can happen when teachers recognize the differences among their students, and try to provide the group with a variety of materials and activities. It is then that the old measurements of learning fail. They simply will not register all the important changes that come. Full appraisal of these learnings necessitates a whole new concept of evaluation.

The Purposes of Evaluation

Of course, it is still true that teachers and students need to know whether the experiences provided are having desired effects. Even in the most informal activities both may wonder, "How well are we doing?" And, in a larger sense, the school has a basic responsibility to gather evidence that it really is helping youth mature into competent citizens. It is still important to know (1) how well all the youth are progressing along this road; (2) whether some are making generally better progress than others; (3) whether some are making better progress in some aspects of the program and doing poorly in others; (4) whether the school as a whole is contributing a maximum amount to the development of useful citizens; and (5) whether some parts of the school program are doing a better job than other parts. Adequate evaluation means that all of these differences in the quality of learning are recorded and interpreted. In addition, we must add two more: (6) the individual himself wishes to view his own progress in terms of his own capabilities and in contrast to the progress of others; and (7) the teacher seeks knowledge of the comparative effectiveness of various materials and experiences both with groups of children and with individual children. When we think of the evaluation process in this broad sense, we wonder how we can ever collect data to answer all of the questions! Yet it is not only possible, it is essential that we know how well we are doing in terms of these seven major evaluative inquiries. Fortunately we now have techniques that will give us some information on each of these.

In thinking about the ways teachers evaluate student achievement and growth, there appear to be three major areas of concern: (1) The construction and use of tests and examinations in the classroom; (2) grading and reporting student achievement; and (3) developing a point of view toward evaluation—seeing the evaluation process as a whole. This chapter and the two following will consider the three broad areas noted above, with consideration of the best practice in terms of the realities of today's secondary schools.

Constructing and Using Tests

Every teacher will be faced with the problem of making tests, even though it will be clear from the discussion of evaluation to follow that tests provide only one kind of information on student progress. However, this kind of information on achievements in understanding and skill is important and necessary. We will briefly discuss here some of the guide lines in developing testing instruments:

A good test:

1. Is valid.
   (a) The test measures what it is supposed to measure.
2. Is reliable.
   (a) The test is consistent in its measurement.
3. Is objective.
   (a) Two scorers would give the same score to the same response.
4. Has a clearly defined purpose.
   (a) Diagnostic.
   (b) Appraising achievement.
   (c) Motivational.
5. Provides test items consonant with these purposes.
   (a) Diagnostic items reveal strengths and weaknesses.
   (b) Achievement items place students in rank order. Each student occupies a position in relation to other students according to his mastery of those achievements which were listed.
   (c) Motivational items stimulate further study.
6. Provides emphasis on test items according to that which is stressed in teaching.
   (a) If ability to think critically is stressed, the items should not emphasize retention of facts.
7. Uses items of more than one type in order to extend the scope of measurement.
   (a) Completion, multiple-choice, true-false, matching, essay.
8. Arranges items in a progression from easy to difficult.
   (a) Difficult items, if used at the beginning of the test, discourage the less able from trying at all.
   (b) The average student should make 50 per cent of the possible score.
9. Provides for ease of administration and interpretation.
   (a) The directions are clear and succinct.
   (b) The scoring key has been made out in advance so that students can be informed exactly how the items will be scored.

A poor test:

1. Has a jumble of purposes.
2. Is used as threat or punishment.
3. Consistently penalizes some students: those who read slowly, those who handle abstractions with difficulty.
4. Emphasizes rote memory exclusively.
5. Stresses unimportant details.
6. Uses ambiguous questions and methods of scoring.

Tests may serve to corrode the relationships between teacher and student. The atmosphere surrounding tests is often charged with fear. For this reason alone, the teacher should use tests with care and precaution. Learning does not occur where fear of failure is constant. The wrong kind of tests may produce this unhealthy climate.

Using Essay Tests Correctly

Tests, then, must be used with discrimination. Follow-up discussions of just why a given answer was right or wrong or better or worse are mandatory. The essay examination answer, for example, requires great skill in organizing ideas quickly, logically and lucidly, with concomitant writing skills in the manipulation of language. Teachers might well spend several days' time in an intensive study of the essay answer and considerable opportunity in practicing this kind of writing.

In this discussion, teachers and students should consider the advantages and limitations of the essay test, how it is constructed and how it is scored. The following outline indicates important considerations for anyone using essay tests.

1. Limitations
   (a) Low validity
      (1) Limited sampling
      (2) Irrelevant factors considered; handwriting, appearance
   (b) Low reliability
      (1) Subjective scoring: physical and mental condition of scorer, the halo effect of other students' papers
2. Advantages
   (a) Useful in measuring
      (1) Ability to organize, interpret, evaluate, apply
      (2) Ability to summarize, outline; to see relationships and trends
      (3) Ability to write fluently and clearly
3. Precautions in construction
   (a) Increase the number of questions and restrict length of response
   (b) Indicate specifically areas to be discussed
4. Scoring
   (a) Prepare a response in advance to each question; each point should be given a weight for scoring
   (b) Read through once for general organization and again for details
   (c) Note each error and point omitted and write down the amount deducted (making allowance for additional pertinent, but not anticipated, points)
   (d) Grade one question at a time for all papers
   (e) If there is time, divide papers into groups by grades and reread some to see if quality of response is consistent

Examples of Essay Test Items

Here are several examples of essay test items which meet fairly well the listed criteria:

English[1]

She glanced through the fly-specked windows of the most pretentious building in sight, the one place which welcomed strangers and determined their opinion of the charm and luxury of Gopher Prairie—the Minniemashie House. It was a tall lean shabby structure, three stories of yellow-streaked wood, the corners covered with sanded pine slabs purporting to symbolize stone. In the hotel office she could see a stretch of bare unclean floor, a line of rickety chairs with brass cuspidors between, a writing-desk with advertisements in mother-of-pearl letters upon a glass-covered back. The dining-room beyond was a jungle of stained table-cloths and catsup bottles.

She looked no more at the Minniemashie House.

1. What would you say is the writer's own opinion of the Minniemashie House?
2. What method does the writer employ predominantly in attempting to achieve the desired effect?
3. Is that effect successful, and upon what do you base your judgment?
4. What does the writer imply in his reference to "the charm and luxury of Gopher Prairie"? What literary technique is exemplified in this particular part of the passage; that is, what name do we give to this method of conveying one's meaning?
5. What is the meaning of the word "rickety" in line 9?
6. What is the meaning of the word "symbolize" in line 7?
7. The last line is an example of what formal means of achieving emphasis?

General Science[2]

A woman planted some flower seeds beside her house. The plants did not grow very well. The woman next door planted seeds of the same kind of flower. These plants grew very well. The first woman wondered why her flower plants did not grow as well as those of the woman next door. What information must you have before you can tell her why?

Social Studies[3]

The financial position of the national government itself was precarious. It had been impossible to finance the war from current taxation. Between 1812 and 1816 bond issues to a total face value of $80,000,000 were floated. Yet the returns measured in terms of specie were disappointing—only about $34,000,000. By these operations the national debt reached the staggering total of about $125,000,000.

[1] Excerpt from Hawkes, Herbert E., E. F. Lindquist, C. R. Mann, *The Construction and Use of Achievement Examinations* (Boston: Houghton Mifflin Company, 1936), pp. 389-390.

[2] *Ibid.*, p. 236.

[3] *Ibid.*, p. 190.

1. Was the federal "budget" balanced? Explain.
2. Were the government bonds marketed at above or below par? Explain.
3. What was the condition of government credit? Explain.

The Objective Type Test

The so-called objective type of test question is objective only in the sense that there are fewer ambiguities about what constitutes the correct answer. In essay questions the correct answer depends on many subjective factors, which frequently leave the person being graded most insecure. The objection to objective exams is usually less violent and probably can be accounted for by this difference in subjectivity of grading. But the objectivity of the objective examination ends there. Even objective test items are subjectively selected and represent the test maker's ideas about what should be learned. And here teachers and other test makers differ radically. What is vital and significant to one may be dull and trivial to the other. Again and again the teacher who utilizes the objective test must ask, "Is this for which I am testing really worth learning? Should the students retain this understanding or this skill for a week, a month, for five years, for the rest of their lives?"

The major kinds of objective tests are—

1. Completion:
Example: Chlorophyll is usually found in ————.
2. True-false:
Example: T F Edgar Allen Poe lived before Walt Whitman.
3. Multiple choice:
Example: Australia derives its largest income from exporting:
(a) iron
(b) gold
(c) wool
4. Matching:
Example: Match the following individuals with the word that best describes his achievement:

Edison	dynamite
Ford	telephone
Bell	electricity
Clinton	locomotive
	steamship
	automobile

The following table gives in a compact form the chief problems of construction of each of these types, the advantages of each one, and the situations where they can be most effectively used.

	Completion	True-False
1. Situations for which effective	Information: who, when, what, where, how many	1. Beliefs, attitudes, superstitions 2. Only two alternatives 3. General survey of field
2. Advantages	1. Easy to build 2. Requires adequate basis for response (difficult to guess)	1. Easy to build 2. Wide sampling
3. Limitations	1. Subjective scoring 2. Inconvenient to score 3. Emphasizes rote response	1. Ambiguities 2. Guessing
4. Precautions in construction	1. Use brief response 2. Use direct question if possible 3. Avoid textbook language 4. Avoid grammatical clue 5. Provide blank near end, if incomplete type 6. Assure scoring convenience 7. Avoid overmutilation (too many blanks) 8. Avoid indefinite statements 9. Omit only key words 10. Make response lines of same and of adequate length 11. Give credit to any correct response (even if not the desired one)	1. Provide convenient arrangement for scoring 2. Use approximately equal T and F items 3. See that crucial element stands out in item 4. Avoid "traps" 5. Avoid textbook language 6. Avoid clues 7. Don't use subordinate clauses 8. Don't use negatives 9. Remember longer statement is the more likely to be true 10. Make test longer 11. Avoid double negatives 12. Avoid ambiguity 13. Avoid partly true

	Multiple-Choice	Matching
1. Situations for which effective	Most generally applicable	Information: who, what, when, where
2. Advantages	1. Convenient scoring 2. Many adaptations available 3. Easy to give	1. Compact 2. Reduces guessing 3. Ease of construction
3. Limitations	Laborious to construct	1. One group of single words or very brief phrases 2. Probability of clues 3. Related errors
4. Precautions in construction	1. Provide choices at end of statement 2. Remember that question form is better than incomplete sentence 3. Avoid textbook or standardized language 4. Avoid making the longer response always being correct or vice versa 5. Avoid grammatical clue 6. Use plausible distractors 7. Avoid ambiguity 8. Avoid pattern, as in having the third response consistently the correct response 9. Provide at least four choices	1. Keep numbers small (10–15 items) 2. Provide extra responses (especially if less than 10) 3. Provide homogeneity in material (consistency in classification: all men, all battles) 4. Attend to mechanical arrangement keeping responses in alphabetical or some other order 5. Use only one correct matching for each item 6. Place all items on one page

Examples of Objective Tests

Below are given some examples of acceptable test items of each type in a number of different fields. Sample directions are stated for each type. Notice that the answer spaces are provided uniformly at one side of the test paper, which makes it possible to prepare simple scoring keys on strips of cardboard to be placed alongside the answer spaces.

Completion

Each statement below has a blank where a word or number is missing. Write this missing word or number in the space at the left of the statement.

____________ The author who originated the detective story in American literature was ____________.

____________ The title of the short story which tells of the effect of the coming of a child to a Western community of rough and desperate men is ____________.

____________ The section of the United States in which *Death Comes to the Archbishop* is set is ____________.

____________ One way to represent the world is by a map, but a more accurate way is by a ____________.

____________ The legislative program and policies of Franklin D. Roosevelt were known as the ____________.

____________ Car engines should not be run in a small garage with the doors closed because the engine's exhaust contains ____________.

____________ A vitamin whose absence in diet is related to the development of rickets is ____________.

____________ In determining the specific gravity of a liquid we usually use an instrument called a ____________.

True-False

Below is a series of statements. Some are true and some are false. If you believe a statement to be always true exactly as it is stated, circle T; if not, circle F. Do not guess.

T F *The Citadel* and *Arrowsmith* are both novels about college professors.

T F Lincoln Steffens was an American journalist.

T F The Justices of the Supreme Court serve for a term of six years.

T F The "Cross of Gold" in Bryan's famous speech represented income taxes.

T F Eye color is due entirely to heredity.

T F A widely used metal for filaments in electric light bulbs is magnesium.

Multiple-Choice

Below is a series of questions or incomplete statements. They are followed by several words, phrases, or series of numbers. Select the one which answers the question or completes the statement. Place the letter of that word, phrase, or series of numbers in the blank space at the left.

__________ This passage suggests the writings of (a) Browning, (b) Milton, (c) Pope, (d) Addison.[4]

__________ The attitude toward the common people expressed in this is that of (a) Johnson, (b) Pope, (c) Wordsworth, (d) Keats.

__________ The most significant characteristic of Lady Macbeth is (a) fear of moral torment, (b) patriotism, (c) ambition for her husband, (d) gentleness of nature, (e) generosity toward her enemies.

__________ His interest in Italian freedom appears in his writings: (a) Browning, (b) Chaucer, (c) Milton, (d) Shakespeare, (e) Thackeray.

__________ Freedom of the press, as provided in the national Bill of Rights, means that the newspapers have the right to[5]
(a) Comment maliciously on events in the private lives of citizens without fear of being sued.
(b) Print anything whatsoever without restriction.
(c) Send their editors to Washington to lobby for legislation.
(d) Send reporters to all sessions of the legislative, executive and judicial branches of the government.
(e) Criticize the policies of the government without fear of suspension of publication.

__________ Common glass is essentially a mixture of[6]
(a) aluminates (d) borates
(b) sulfates (e) nitrates
(c) silicates

__________ Which of the following is an anesthetic?[7]
(a) calcium oxide (d) nitrous oxide
(b) carbon monoxide (e) sulfur dioxide
(c) mercuric oxide

Matching

In the column at the left below is a series of words and in the column at the right is another series of words. For each word in the column at the left, select from the column at the right the word which most nearly is the same in meaning. In the spaces at the left of the numbers insert the letters of the words selected.

____ 1. arena	(a) amphitheater
____ 2. assassination	(b) chopper
____ 3. cleaver	(c) contest
____ 4. consternation	(d) dismay
____ 5. potency	(e) forerunner
____ 6. preamble	(f) fulcrum
	(g) murder

[4] Objective measurement of comprehension and appreciation may be accomplished by using multiple choice items following a quoted passage.

[5] *Ibid.*, p. 186.

[6] Cooperative Chemistry Test—Revised Series—Form O (New York: Cooperative Test Service).

[7] *Ibid.*, p. 174.

(h) preface
(i) strength
(j) warfare

In the column at the left below is a series of statements and in the column at the right is a series of names. Select the names which correctly identify the statements and place the number of the correct name in the space at the left of the statement.

________	His revolt against the Church probably would have been unsuccessful had the Emperor not been engaged in foreign warfare	1. Henry VIII 2. John Huss 3. Ignatius Loyola 4. Martin Luther 5. St. Dominic
________	His conflict with the Church netted him great economic advantages	
________	He was instrumental in reclaiming a large part of Germany for Catholicism	

For each group of items below, place in the blank before each word or phrase in the left-hand list the letter of the word or phrase in the right-hand list with which it is most directly associated.

______ 1. Anopheles mosquito	(a) bubonic plague
______ 2. Rat	(b) influenza
______ 3. Tsetse fly	(c) malaria
	(d) smallpox
	(e) sleeping sickness

The teacher will spend many hours making tests and marking them. And students will spend many hours preparing to take tests. Certainly, then, tests should be so constructed as to provide both student and teacher with specific information about how much has been achieved in the important learnings which were sought.

Since this part of teaching is so important, we are fortunate that major attention has been given to the measurement of achievement in a large number of *standardized tests.* In the next section of this chapter will be discussed the value and uses of these tests as a supplement to those tests the teacher fashions himself.

Standardized Tests

First, we need to refresh our understanding of what the term *standardized* means.

1. The process begins when the test maker tries to find out what attitudes, understandings, and skills should be represented in ninth-grade arithmetic, or tenth-grade English literature, or twelfth-grade United States history. This information may be obtained from textbook analysis, examination of courses of study, or judgment of experts. In power tests, the information may represent only the author's opinion.

2. Various test items are tried on large numbers of students who represent many geographical areas and many kinds of schools. Those combinations of questions which are able to measure a range of achievement are

retained. Usually several combinations of items are culled out so that more than one form of the test can be constructed.

3. Specific methods for administering the test (directions, time limits) are established.

4. Scoring rules and keys are developed.

5. Norms are prepared indicating where any local scores fall in relation to the national average scores.

This standardization is intended to secure validity, reliability, objectivity, and ease of administration. As we said earlier in the chapter, validity is the crucial element in any test. This process of standardization does not guarantee validity. It is very instructive to check any recognized test in Buros' *Mental Measurements Yearbooks*.[8] Here each test is given reviews by a number of experts in the field. It is the rare test where the experts concur on validity.

The element of tentativity with which the results of these tests must be viewed is increased when we consider local conditions in detail. The class may very well have agreed on additional objectives not contemplated in the test. Especially may this be true in the development of attitudes. Further, the national norms lump together all manner of students in all kinds of schools under all kinds of teachers. A class of superior capacity and environment deserves no special recognition for exceeding the performance of the national average. Nor should a class of inferior capacity and environment deserve strong censure for falling below that average. True, the test maker does not intend to license either reaction. No harm is done so long as administrators, school boards, teachers, parents, and students remember the established standards can only be applied to particular classes with large tolerance. It is important to keep reminding ourselves that in any kind of national average—whether it be average height, weight, physical dexterity, or average achievement in academic matters—individuality is deliberately hammered out.

This is not to say that standardized achievement tests do not have their place in a modern evaluation program. Within the limitations we have noted, the tests indicate where the class stands in relation to other classes. The tests help to diagnose weaknesses in class and individual achievement and so guide future instruction. In short, used with many other means of evaluation, the standardized test serves a useful purpose. Only when these tests are considered almost the sole gauge of learning is there serious damage to good education.

[8] Buros, O. K., *Mental Measurements Yearbook* (New Brunswick: Rutgers University Press, 1949).

A rigid examination scheme, designed to test achievement in certain factual material of traditional rather than genuine value, is likely to keep schools doing the old-time routine program when they ought to be changing with the changing needs of the times.[9]

In the test publishers' catalogues are listed many tests of achievement. Sample tests are available from the publishers at nominal cost. Many teachers find it useful to check test catalogues annually and send for the new instruments in their teaching fields. In this way they keep informed of the new techniques in testing.

What criteria can guide the teacher in selecting appropriate standardized tests? The following list gives some standards to assist teachers in checking tests and the accompanying test manuals:

1. *Validity.*
What is the test supposed to measure? On what basis were these test goals chosen? Was it on the basis of meeting individual and societal needs? What research was used to determine how these needs might be met through this test content?

2. *Reliability.*
Most standardized tests are available in at least two versions. What evidence is presented to show that this test consistently yields a similar score whichever version is used? Test experts usually say that for individual students a test should show a reliability coefficient of about .80. This coefficient indicates the degree of correlation between scores on the various versions of the test. The higher the decimal fraction, the closer the test comes to yielding the same score on its various versions.

3. *Objectivity.*
Good tests ensure that identical scores will be secured with equally competent scorers. Is the test key so precise throughout that no doubt about the correct response exists?

4. *Ease of administration and scoring.*
The directions in the manual should be so clear that tests can be given each time with ease and under comparable circumstances. Does the manual tell exactly how to give and score the test? Or does it leave ambiguities and questions unanswered?

5. *Norms.*
The manual or a supplement should list average or median scores which students have earned where the test has been used. These norms should be regularly revised. The character of the school populations where the norms were derived should be indicated. Preferably the norms should be given for each tenth of the school year, since obviously achievement varies from September to June.

Standardized tests, besides showing achievement in terms of other large groups of students, can provide the teacher with sugges-

[9] Ryan, W. Carson, *op. cit.*, p. 57.

tions for new ways of testing achievement in his own homemade tests. The teacher can find, for instance, how best to word certain kinds of test items. The standardized test has been tried out on many students, and the teacher can therefore be assured that the average student will understand the test items as constructed. Thus a teacher might well select from a standardized test some items to use as models.

In this chapter we have presented so far some of the main considerations that should guide the teacher in making his own tests and in the use and selection of standardized tests. In addition, there are some newer types of examination and test patterns and purposes that should be considered. Such tests can be made by the individual teacher and are also available from commercial publishing firms. These variations in test patterns will be discussed below.

Some Variations in Test Construction

In recent years educators have been increasingly concerned with some of the more intangible outcomes of education such as: "Are students' attitudes changed by course content and experiences?" "Are students developing ability to think logically?" "What is the pattern of social understanding of young people?" Out of such inquiries have come some very stimulating evaluation tools. The tests constructed to evaluate the progress made by students in the Eight Year Study show particular originality and depth of inquiry into the abiding purposes of instruction.[10] An example of a test developed by this study to measure ability to think logically is given below:

PROBLEM III.

A science class was studying methods of caring for the skin. The teacher described the following experiment and stated the conclusion which had been drawn from it. "A large bottle of each of the five leading brands of hand lotion was purchased from a drug store. The lotion in each bottle was thoroughly mixed by shaking the bottle for three minutes. Five exactly similar water glasses, one for each lotion, were set in a row on a table, and a piece of filter paper was placed over the open top of each glass. Each brand of lotion was tested by pouring a half teaspoonful of it on the piece of filter paper. For the first brand of hand lotion, drops appeared in the water glass within thirty seconds. The four other brands all took longer than one minute, and two brands failed to filter through at all." *This experiment shows that the first brand of lotion is absorbed by the skin more readily than any of the others.*

[10] Smith, Eugene, Ralph W. Tyler, and Staff, *Appraising and Recording Student Progress* (New York: Harper & Brothers, 1942).

I. Directions: In this part, you are to do two things:

Select all statements which could logically be used to support the underlined conclusion. Blacken the space under A opposite the number of each such statement.

At the same time, select all statements which might make the underlined conclusion less acceptable. Blacken the space under B opposite the number of each such statement.

In this part of the test, your decision about a statement should not be influenced by whether you believe the idea expressed to be true or false.

(NOTE: Answers to this and question 2 are given in the left-hand column.)

Statements for I and II:

A C	1. The contents of one large bottle of a certain brand of hand lotion are exactly like the contents of any other large bottle of the same brand of hand lotion.
Irrelevant	2. The liquid which is absorbed most readily by the skin is the most effective in softening the hands.
B	3. To be absorbed by the skin a hand lotion need not pass through the skin.
Irrelevant	4. Hand lotions are of doubtful value.
A C	5. The faster a liquid drips through filter paper the faster it will be absorbed by the human skin.
A C	6. The pores of the skin are quite similar to the little holes between the fibers of filter paper.
A	7. Since each bottle was given a thorough shaking, the results for each lotion were typical of the performance of the lotion in that bottle.
B	8. The "pores" in filter paper are constructed quite differently from the "pores" in the human skin.
Irrelevant	9. The experiment was probably intended to make sales for some cosmetics manufacturer.
B	10. Although drops of a liquid first appeared in the water glass, certain ingredients of the first lotion may have been retained by the filter paper.
Irrelevant	11. The speed with which a lotion drips through filter paper is no indication of its effectiveness in softening the skin.
B	12. Water will penetrate filter paper but is not absorbed by the skin.
Irrelevant	13. The obvious way to test the five lotions is to try them on the hands of a large group of people.
A	14. The amounts of lotion placed on each piece of filter paper were very nearly the same.

II. Directions: Select from the statements already marked under A (the supporting statements) those which you would challenge because you are not convinced they are true enough to be used in supporting the underlined conclusion. Blacken the space under C opposite the number of each such statement.

III. Directions: Conclusions A, B, and C are stated below. Choose the one which seems to you to be most consistent with your analysis of the situation described in the problem. In the block at the top of the answer sheet, blacken the space A, B, or C to indicate the conclusion which you choose.

Conclusions:

A. This experiment does not help in deciding which one of the hand lotions would be most readily absorbed by the skin.
B. The experiment suggests that the first brand of hand lotion is absorbed by the skin more readily than any of the others, but the experiment would have to be repeated several times.
C. The experiment shows that the first brand of hand lotion is absorbed by the skin more readily than any of the others.

IV. Directions: Hand lotions are commonly used to replace the oils in the outer layers of the skin which are lost through excessive exposure, washing, and other causes. Hence it may be less important to study the extent to which a lotion penetrates the layers of the skin than to study its effect upon the surface of the skin. The statements presented below describe some activities which have been suggested to study the effectiveness of a hand lotion in keeping the skin soft in the absence of an adequate supply of natural skin oils.

Select all statements that describe activities which you think would help in studying this effect of a hand lotion upon the skin. Blacken the space under A opposite the number of each such statement.

In this part of the test, your decision about a statement should not be influenced by whether you believe the activity described could actually be carried out.

(NOTE: Answers to questions 4 and 5 are given in the left-hand column.)

Statements for IV and V:

A B	15. Secure a description of the structure of the human skin.
Irrelevant	16. Find out the names of the companies which manufacture each of the brands of hand lotion used in the experiment.
A	17. Make a precise laboratory analysis of each of several brands of hand lotion to find out the amounts and properties of its principal ingredients, such as vegetable oils, water, etc.
Irrelevant	18. Repeat the experiment several times with the same five lotions and under exactly the same conditions.
A B	19. Set up an experiment in which ten boys and ten girls apply a hand lotion to one hand and no hand lotion to the other hand once each day for a month and compare the results.
Irrelevant	20. Send out a questionnaire to a large number of users of hand lotion to find out which brand is most popular.
A B	21. Use hand lotions regularly on several parts of the body and compare the results.
A	22. Set up an experiment to compare the natural skin oils to the oils contained in hand lotions.

Irrelevant A B

23. Compare the absorbing power of filter paper and human skin.
24. Look for published information about some of the good and bad effects of using different brands of hand lotion.

V. Directions: Select from the statements already marked under A only things which you think you or your class in high school could actually carry out. Blacken the space under B opposite the number of each such statement.[11]

Even more difficult to measure than the ability to think logically is the development of attitudes. But some promising beginnings have been made in setting up such tests. Below is an example:[12]

IV. Mr. and Mrs. Smith have three children, 18-year-old Jack, 16-year-old Sally, and 13-year-old Mary. They have a car and own their home. All the children are in school. Indicate those of the following statements concerning such families as the Smith with which you agree and those with which you disagree.

. . . . .

17. Jack should be allowed to use the car any evening his father does not need it for business provided Jack has a driver's license, drives carefully, and takes and calls for his sisters when they go out. 17. A D
18. Mr. Smith should spend some time each week with his children no matter how tired or busy he is. 18. A D
19. Mr. and Mrs. Smith should always consider the wishes and welfare of their children before their own. 19. A D
20. Sally should be encouraged to choose her own clothes. 20. A D
21. All three children should have a regular allowance, whether they work part-time or not. 21. A D
22. Mrs. Smith should make the rules concerning the children's personal affairs. 22. A D
23. Mr. Smith should make the rules concerning family financial matters. 23. A D
24. All three children should help decide what courses to take and when they should quit school, even though their parents have planned professional careers for them. 24. A D
25. Jack should not be expected to spend as much time with his family as Sally does. 25. A D
26. Sally and Mary should be at home by 10 P.M. every night; Jack, being a boy and older, should be allowed to stay out as long as he wishes provided he is strong and healthy. 26. A D

[11] *Ibid.*, pp. 136-139.

[12] Excerpts from *Judgments Characteristic of the Socially Competent Person*, Form A (New York: Bureau of Publications, Teachers College, Columbia University, 1936).

27. Sally should be allowed to entertain her friends in the living room whenever she wishes, unless Jack plans to have a party at home. 27. A D
28. Sally should spend a large share of her leisure time with Mary. 28. A D
29. Sally's friends should include both boys and girls. 29. A D
30. The children should spend most of their leisure time with their friends rather than with one another, since the interests of the various members of the family differ considerably. 30. A D
31. All five members of the family should help in choosing activities which include the entire family. 31. A D
32. In selecting clothes, Sally and Jack should consider the opinions of their friends rather than of their family. 32. A D
33. When the children are at home their interests and wishes rather than those of the parents should determine what radio programs are to be heard. 33. A D

These departures from traditional test construction are pioneer efforts in the sense that they are still rarely utilized by the classroom teacher. The tests described in this section have been used primarily by research workers. The classroom rarely sees them. They are difficult to construct, that is true. Problems of test validity and reliability are much more apt to be posed whenever we depart from the pattern, though the same questions could be asked with at least equal pointedness for the common test patterns. If a teacher seeks to depart from the usual pattern and evolve newer and more significant evaluation tools of his own, some working suggestions, given below, will be helpful:

1. *Build a test file of questions and ideas.* Often by continually working up some good test items, good in the sense of being revealing and insightful, instead of waiting until the last moment, the teacher will be able to use them over and over again in varying combinations.

2. *Use students to help build tests.* Often a teacher can pose the problem for the fastest students to prepare new kinds of test items similar to the ones used by the Eight Year Study. These can be filed and used for current and future classes.

3. *Try out new testing devices.* Often a teacher can try out some new device and invite the class to join the experiment. Thus the class is not fearful of a new situation. Their own reactions to, criticisms of, and comments on the "new" type of examination will help the teacher build adequate measures.

4. *Keep informed in the professional literature in general,* and the special subject field in particular. The increasing professional concern over evaluation is seen in many stimulating descriptions of new approaches to evaluation that are repeatedly to be found in the professional literature.

Some exciting ideas in evaluating individual ability have been the outcome of the need in the armed services to select special kinds of individuals for special jobs.[13] Adaptations of some of these ideas to evaluation in teacher education also suggest possible lines of development for high-school classroom use.[14]

Classroom Management and the Giving of Tests and Examinations

Many teachers find that tests and examinations pose some special problems in classroom routines. Will the examination be put on the blackboard, or chalkboard? Will the examination be duplicated? How will the examinations be returned?

Let us look at some of these problems. Where schools have insufficient duplicating equipment, the teacher may have to rely primarily on the blackboard, or chalkboard, or oral tests. If test questions are read, students who finish the question quickly must wait around until the last slow student has finished writing. However, for some kinds of tests, such as true-false, fill-in, very short answer type, the teacher may read the questions. In a room with poor acoustics the loss in audibility may be a severe trial upon some students in poorly located seats. We recall a teacher trying to give a spelling test in a room with a bad echo. The students were doing poorly consistently in the tests. Finally, the teacher had to use another room because of some alterations in the one she had used and found a startling improvement in the spelling. The students had just been unable to understand the words. Under such circumstances, oral reading of a test, particularly a spelling test, must be ruled out. What can we substitute for an oral spelling test? Students may give each other the test, as is often done in elementary schools. The spelling test may be a definitions test, that is, the student fills in the correct word in a sentence where only the required spelling word will fit. This type of sentence may be written on a blackboard, or chalkboard, avoiding the problems of oral testing.

In using the blackboard, or chalkboard, for a test, the teacher will want to have the test ready so that no time is wasted waiting for the test to be copied. Some teachers put the test on before school, then lower a map or chart to cover it until time for the test. Other teachers will put a long question on first, then, while the students are answering that one, continue to put the test on the board.

[13] Office of Strategic Services, *The Assessment of Men* (New York: Rinehart and Company, 1948) and, Harris, Henry, *The Group Approach to Leadership Testing* (London: Routledge & Kegan Paul, 1949).

[14] Grambs, Jean D., "Some New Examination Patterns in Teacher Education," *Educational Administration and Supervision* 36:403-410 (November, 1950).

This means, however, that the teacher is not able to observe the class while it is taking the first part of the test. In a class where the test is crucial to success, the teacher must be very alert to keep students working on their own papers. The wise teacher will of course avoid creating any such provocation or temptation to cheating in the first place.

Where facilities are available, it is most helpful to duplicate tests, since extraneous problems of listening or copying are minimized. More elaborate kinds of tests are also then possible, tests that evaluate larger and more significant areas of learning. After the teacher has made several such tests, he may keep a test-item file and shuffle the items around as appropriate for future classes.

One teacher finds it useful to cut up each test after it has been given, paste the items on separate cards, and cross file them in a card file carefully indexed by subject and purpose. Another teacher builds her tests by having handy a small memorandum pad. Whenever some interesting item comes up in class, she jots down a question or problem that may be used in a test. By the end of a few weeks of study, this teacher has a quantity of possible test items and then merely needs to go back over them and select the best for a test. Some teachers prepare tests prior to teaching the unit, and thus are able to see the focus of their teaching in terms of the content or intellectual skills that will be evaluated.

How do teachers return tests? No test should be given unless, when it is returned, ample class time is given to a discussion of the items of the test, providing correct answers, reviewing ambiguous areas, making sure that the students know what was to have been reported in the test. Some teachers have students re-do those parts of the test that were missed, although this method may not always be the most profitable use of time by students. Of course, sometimes the material may be fundamental and require mastery by every student; then the teacher would do well to have some additional, *different* exercises for the students to complete. The student is then helped to a fresh view, which may assist him to learn the material.

A test should be returned as soon as possible after the students have taken it, so that the material is still fresh and important. The day the test is to be returned, the teacher should plan to use the first ten minutes or so for supervised individual study. Then, while the class is reading or working out problems at their desks, the teacher can go around and quietly return each paper. This gives the teacher an invaluable contact with each student. To Susy, who unexpectedly achieved a superior grade, the teacher can give a word of warm approval; to Harry who turned in another poor test, the teacher can ask if there is some need for some special help—perhaps an after-school conference could be arranged. For each student the teacher, as he returns the paper, should have some personal comment, no matter how slight, that shows that the teacher is aware of, and interested in, each individual's progress. The rewards will be great from this rather simple device of personalizing the returning of papers for the teacher and student alike.

After all papers are returned, the teacher will want to call the class to order, make some general comments as to the class level of achievement, perhaps place a distribution of grades on the board. Then the teacher will ask the class for questions about any items that puzzled them. A rapid review of the questions will be in order, to be sure everyone understood what the answer might have been. After this session, the class might return to the supervised study so that students with individual problems on the test may talk privately with the teacher. It is best for the teacher to avoid public bickering over an answer. A student who thinks he has been graded incorrectly should be given time to talk individually with the teacher. The teacher should always be ready to admit it when a real mistake has been made and adjust the student's grade accordingly. This kind of fairness is prized highly by students.

This procedure in returning tests may be used in returning all written work. If the students have put their time into it, the teacher owes the students a recognition of that effort and an honest evaluaion of it. Probably the worst thing a teacher can do is to require written work, then throw it away, using it merely as a way to keep the youngsters in their seats. The feeling of betrayal experienced by the students will undermine the best morality we can preach.

Tests should be considered not only a means of evaluating progress, but a particularly valuable learning experience. Post-test discussions are often tremendously fruitful in obtaining new insight on the part of students previously puzzled or confused. The real value of an end-term examination is thus often lost.

Summary

Finding how much students have learned from classroom activities and learning experiences is a major task for every teacher. Most evaluation is conducted through tests made by teachers themselves. It is highly important that teacher-made tests be carefully formulated in terms of the purposes of instruction.

Available to the teacher also are a variety of standardized tests that provide valuable instruments to record the growth and achievement of the teacher's own students in relation to others across the nation who are studying similar problems. From the standardized tests and a number of research projects new developments in the construction of tests are emerging. Classroom teachers need to be aware of these promising evaluative devices to measure student learning.

Of course even with the best of tests, the administration of the test is only the beginning. A test is an important classroom activity. The teacher can make it either a valuable learning situation or a source of anxiety and frustration.

Making and using tests and examinations requires many teacher hours. A good testing program is vital to the success of the total teaching function. In this chapter one element in the evaluation program was considered; in the next chapter we will discuss the very important question of grades and grading, and, finally, in Chapter 17, a point of view on evaluation will be discussed.

Selected References

Broening, A. M. (ed.). *Conducting Experiences in English.* New York: Appleton-Century-Crofts, Inc., 1939. Chap. XVII, "Appraising Pupil Growth" pp. 272-292. Includes a check list for teachers to guide them in selecting various tests to use; also includes a student self-appraisal form and a teacher self-rating scale.

Commission on Secondary School Curriculum: See Chapters on Evaluation in the following published in New York, through Appleton-Century-Crofts, Inc.:

Science in General Education (1938), Chap. 9.

Mathematics in General Education (1940), Chap. 13.

The Visual Arts in General Education (1940), Chap. 4.

The Social Studies in General Education (1940), Chap. 9.

The evaluation problems peculiar to each subject field are ably discussed in the specific chapters in the above volumes.

Grambs, Jean D. "Some New Examination Patterns in Teacher Education." *Education Administration and Supervision,* 36:403-410 (November, 1950). Interesting new ways of evaluating behavioral changes that can be easily adapted to high-school classroom use.

Haynes, B. R., M. E. Broom, and M. Hardaway. *Tests and Measurements in Business Education.* Cincinnati: Southwestern Publishing Co., 1940. A comprehensive review of all aspects of testing with special reference to business education.

Keesey, R. N. "How Useful Are Essay Tests?" *The Social Studies,* 42: 13-16 (January, 1951). The pros and cons of essay examinations.

National Association of Secondary School Principals. "Using Tests in Modern Secondary Schools," *Bulletin,* Vol. 32, No. 158 December, 1948.

Emphasizes the role of tests and test results in aiding student adjustment. Very specific, detailed and useful.

National Commission for the Social Studies. *Selected Test Items in Economics.* Bulletin No. 11, 1939. *Selected Test Items in World History.* Bulletin No. 9, 1947. Rev. ed., Washington, D. C. Excellent guides for the classroom teacher in setting up his own tests.

Quillen, I. J., and L. A. Hanna. *Education for Social Competence.* Chicago: Scott, Foresman & Company, 1948. Chap. 14, "Evaluation Techniques" pp. 362-403. Presents in detail the significant features of new-type evaluation devices to measure social growth.

Rivlin, Harry N. *Teaching Adolescents in Secondary Schools.* New York: Appleton-Century-Crofts, Inc., 1948. Chap. 14, "Evaluating the Results of Education," pp. 410-449. Good outline of basic consideration in teacher evaluation.

———. *The Teacher's Role in Achievement Testing.* Test Service Notebook No. 9. Yonkers: World Book Company, n.d. 4 pp. Excellent brief statement of how different kinds of tests help the teacher when used appropriately.

Ross, C. C. *Measurement in Today's Schools.* 2d ed. New York: Prentice-Hall, Inc., 1947. A standard text covering in detail all aspects of evaluation and measurement.

Rulon, Phillip J. *Validity of Education Tests.* Test Service Notebook No. 3. Yonkers: World Book Company, n.d. 4 pp. A clear discussion of validity as it affects test practice.

Schorling, Raleigh. *Student Teaching.* New York: McGraw Hill Book Company, Inc., 1949. Chap. XIII, "The Broader Concept of Appraisal," pp. 315-350. Covers all aspects of evaluation, including grades and report cards, standardized tests, and criteria for utilizing various evaluative devices.

Smith, Eugene, and Ralph W. Tyler. *Appraising and Recording Student Progress.* New York: Harper & Brothers, 1942. Presents many new approaches to evaluating the less tangible aspects of instruction.

Thut, I. N., and J. R. Gerberich. *Foundations of Method for Secondary Schools.* New York: McGraw Hill Book Company, Inc., 1949. Chap. 8, "The Appraisal of Pupil Progress in the Daily Assignment Method," pp. 160-192; Chap. 11, "The Measurement of Pupil Progress in the Subject-matter Unit," pp. 236-268; Chap. 14, "The Evaluation of Pupil Progress in the Experience Unit Method," pp. 318-350. Describes different ways of evaluating pupil growth according to organization of learning materials and experiences.

Wrinkle, William L., and Robert S. Gilchrist. *Secondary Education for American Democracy.* Part 5, "How Can the School Tell How Well it is Doing—What it is Supposed to Do?" New York: Rinehart & Company, 1942. pp. 391-410. Emphasizes current practices in evaluation and how teachers can improve their methods.

16. Grading and Reporting Student Progress

THE crux of the problem for the teacher in the process of evaluation is the giving of grades and the preparing of report cards. No evaluation procedure can work if grading procedures are at variance with it. Yet the area of grading is very sensitive, charged with emotion for student and teacher and usually avoided in textbooks on education! In this chapter we will try to gain insight into the grading complex in order to make more feasible the eventual adoption of a broader evaluation approach.

The Grading Process in Action

Every teacher is involved in the grading process. The high schools of today insist on a semester, term, and year grade for every student in every class. The beginning teacher needs to develop an understanding of the total evaluation process so that he can intelligently adapt himself to different ways of marking and grading students. For whatever the variations in practice, the problems, issues, and challenges in evaluation persist.

Psychologically, the grade is likely to be at best a precarious method of motivation. The grade is often based on a limited type of learning. It is meaningful to those students who want a "good" grade and are able to do those academic tasks in which schools have long specialized. If all of the work in a given class is evaluated through tests on detailed information, students who can memorize will obviously get a high grade. However, students who can memorize detailed information poorly will get poor grades. When this happens often enough, these so-called poor students either refuse to take the test or make only a passing gesture at taking the test. When asked why, they will reply, "Well, we only get *D*'s or *F*'s anyway."

The grade causes the student to regard the teacher, by and large, as a judge, one who hands down a sentence of "Success" or *A*, or "Failure" or *F*. Most of the time the student develops a feeling of helplessness. When asked how he did on a test, the average student will probably reply, "I don't know—I'll have to wait until I get my paper back." In other words, the whole process of grading is a deep dark mystery and the teacher is the only person who has the clues. Where such a condition exists, obviously the student cannot learn a major lesson for competent adult living, that is, to appraise accurately his own achievement. So we hear students remark, "Why I know I did a very good job on that report; I don't see why I only got a *C*," or "I certainly was surprised when I got an *A* on that paper—I hardly spent any time on it, and personally I didn't think it was very good," or, "No matter how hard you try in Mr. Albert's class, you just can't get more than a *B*." No wonder many students never know what good workmanship means—they have never had to judge their own work. They have merely handed it in to a teacher, who passed on it in some mysterious fashion and handed down his dictum, "Good" or "Bad."

Are There Absolute Standards for Grading?

It can be said, of course, that a problem of developing ability in students to judge their own efforts does not confront the mathematics teacher or the science teacher. Either the problems are right or they are wrong; no questions. The very fact that some areas seem to lend themselves to this kind of no-question attitude is very tempting to any teacher. The objective test, for example, often gives the social-science teacher a feeling of being on safe ground. No argument can be forthcoming, he reassures himself, when obviously the right answer is *right* because it is *the* correct date or the one *right* name.

What is the fallacy here? If schools hope to teach young people how to live productively in the modern world, they need to provide education far beyond knowing a few *right* facts. For, as we have said, what teacher or what school administrator is so omniscient that he can say these and these alone are the essential problems to solve.

To return for a moment to the areas of mathematics, and science which seem so exact and *right*. Where the teacher is so absorbed in obtaining the right *answer,* there is very little opportunity for students to experience the right *process.* If mathematics can develop logical methods of problem solving and science can develop a reliance on scientific method for arriving at solutions, then we must focus on the *way* we get in and out of a problem. Too often the over emphasis on the one correct answer encourages lazy thinking, cheating, and merely mechanical manipulation of arbitrary and meaningless symbols. We need to reward accuracy, but let us not exalt this one skill above the real and important other skills that science and mathematics can develop.

Discrimination in Grading

Another indictment must be brought against the typical grading procedure. Studies show rather conclusively that girls get higher school marks and grades than boys, though boys have similar, if not higher, average IQ scores than girls. One study in Cleveland revealed that boys had a statistically significant greater rate of failure than girls; the chance that boys would fail was 2¼ times that of girls. Both men and women teachers tended to give higher grades to girls. The study also showed that teachers who were considered poor teachers by their administrators tended to fail more students, and particularly failed more boys.[1] Another study revealed a similar trend; girls, because of the bias in grading by teachers, were consistently better able to get into the honor society than boys.[2] Still another investigator discovered that while girls excelled boys according to teachers' marks, boys excelled girls by almost the same percentage when an achievement-test score and an IQ score were used as the base.[3]

These studies reveal a pitfall for every teacher. The need to grade means that teachers will undoubtedly be influenced by per-

[1] Schinnerer, M. C., "Failure Ratio: 2 Boys to 1 Girl," *Clearing House,* 18:264-270 (January, 1944).

[2] Swenson, Clifford, "Packing the Honor Society," *Clearing House,* 16:521-524 (May, 1942).

———, "The Girls Are Teacher's Pets," *Clearing House,* 17:537-540 (May, 1943).

[3] Johnson, George, "Girls Lead in Progress through School," *American School Board Journal,* 95:23-26 (October, 1937).

sonal factors that have nothing to do with the actual achievement of boys and girls. The tendency to over-rate girls in terms of teachers' grades needs some careful analysis. It has been suggested that girls mature earlier in the social graces, are more compliant to authority, are more apt to be neat and clean in personal appearance and personal habits. "But behold the boy! Awkward, uncoordinated, loud, untidy, he suffers seriously in any classroom group by comparison with his sisters." [4]

A similar kind of discrimination operates often against students from minority groups and those associated with low socioeconomic levels. A well-documented study of a typical Midwestern community revealed that children from the lowest social class were given most of the low grades and had most of the failures; whereas students from the upper social class groups had no extremely low grades and hardly any failures.[5] And this in the face of data that showed that IQ scores were not unduly weighted toward the top. "Although intelligence was associated significantly with class position, the degree of association was not high enough to account for the concentration of failures" in the lowest class group.[6]

The influence of stereotyped thinking on the teacher's evaluations is thus highly significant. The beginning teacher would do well to understand such unconscious biases and seek to counteract them through adequate evaluation procedures. It would be worth while for a teacher to do some self-research in this area at the end of each year. "Am I giving most of my good grades or marks to girls, to children from the better homes, to those from predominantly Anglo-Saxon groups?" In addition, the teacher would want to ask, "Is the poor grade associated with actual lack of achievement in the subject, or are the students being penalized for being boys, or being poor, or being from a minority group?"

The implication is clear: evaluations of growth in learning must be measures of what the individual himself has accomplished, must not be distorted by the teacher's feelings about groupings to which the individual may belong. We must, however, guard against a tendency to think that if the brighter students, by and large, get the highest grades, then our grading must be all right. Some teachers carry this approach so far that they are convinced that they can actually assign the end-of-term grade to every student at the begin-

[4] Lobaugh, Dean, "Girls and Grades—A Significant Factor in Evaluation," *School Science and Mathematics,* 47:763-767 (April, 1947).

[5] Hollingshead, August B., *Elmtown's Youth* (New York: John Wiley & Sons, Inc., 1949), pp. 172-173.

[6] *Ibid.,* p. 175.

ning of the term, just on the basis of intelligence- and achievement-test scores. In such cases learning and teaching are a travesty. If high-school education is really to serve the needs of society, it is clear that students must all know that an equal chance for a successful educational experience is available to them. The evaluation system, therefore, must be based upon other criteria than just intellectual achievement. Students who grow in social maturity, who learn new cooperative skills, who are able to make progress toward self-direction in their own affairs, must also be recognized. It will do us no good as teachers to believe in educating all the children of all the people if we still persist in grading students on the assumption that only a chosen few may actually attain genuine school success.

Grading and Student-Teacher Rapport

Probably the one aspect of grading that is most crucial and yet most ignored is the effect that grading has upon the interpersonal relations between student and teacher. Teachers by and large would like to be friendly with their students, since it is more pleasant to teach among those who like you and to feel in turn that you like those you teach. One of the prime requisites for teaching has always been a liking for young people. This presupposes that this liking will be reciprocated, that the students will like the teacher. Does this mutual liking occur? If it does, it may be distorted when the teacher must give the student a grade. A study of the fantasy life of adolescents showed that "teachers were almost always stern, threatening, and avenging figures—seldom was any affection shown by or for them." [7] The teacher becomes a symbol of arbitrary judgment, one who can provide either reward—success and high grades, or punishment—failure and low grades. When the basis upon which these grades are awarded is one that the students neither understand nor accept, it is difficult indeed for them to develop positive attitudes toward the giver of grades.

The whole elaborate cultural pattern woven around the process of "apple polishing" and the "apple polisher" is most revealing. Sometimes students make quite a game of this, comparing notes on the appropriate technique to try on the teacher: "If you tell old so-and-so that you think frogs are just fascinating, he'll give you a good grade." Or, "Never argue with that teacher about Hamlet because she flunks students who think Hamlet is dull." Probably

[7] Symonds, Percival M., *Adolescent Fantasy* (New York: Columbia University Press, 1949), p. 223.

most of us can remember when the pretty blonde who giggled so appreciatively at the professor seemed to get a grade completely out of proportion to what she seemed to know. However, the important point is that most students will violently reject anyone who consistently "apple-polishes." So it becomes very difficult indeed for any student to show genuine interest in the subject matter at hand or any genuine liking for the teacher or desire to enter into friendly contact with the teacher.

The student who does really like English or who feels that Mr. Lawrence is a "great guy" is penalized. Either he has to suppress these reactions and, for the public at large—his peer group—pretend that he also despises English and Mr. Lawrence, or, if he expresses his real positive feelings he may be ostracized by the other students. One junior high school, in hopes of producing better deportment, decided that honor letters should be given not only for academic achievement but also for good classroom behavior. It became so that no one wanted a letter; it meant that the student had lived up to the teacher's standard of behavior, had in all probability been a teacher's pet! The school had to change its policy.

Many times the studious, intelligent, interested student is observed wandering alone throughout his high-school career. The other students feel he is not a part of their circle because he really enjoys learning, likes teachers. How very unfortunate! Even on the college and university level it is often "not the thing" to be vitally interested in the content of the classroom. Thus, we may be developing generation after generation of anti-intellectuals who shrink from learning because the grading process has made suspect anyone interested in the importance of ideas.

Effects of Present Grading Practices on Teachers

Teachers are also affected by this atmosphere. They develop a great fear of the students' motives and distrust students who seem appreciative or interested. It is rare that a teacher will not overhear some such cynical remark as reported above and realize with chagrin and anger that he, the teacher, has been "played for a sucker". What happens then? The teacher in turn builds barriers between himself and the student by freezing with suspicion whenever a student makes friendly overtures. After all, the teacher's main function in the life of the student is to induce him to work hard in learning. When the principal emphasis is on grades and not on learning, the student's main function in life becomes one of seeming to learn this material without having to go through all the agony—

to escape failure at all costs. The battle over the grades, then, becomes a fierce and unyielding struggle, where the students attempt to outwit the teacher, and the teacher seeks constantly to anticipate the students.

Where sudents do have successful and important experiences in a classroom, they will of course develop considerable attachment for the teacher. Yet nothing can destroy a long and rewarding friendship more quickly than a poor report mark from a "friend." In fact, the better we know our students, the harder it is to give them low grades. We as teachers feel so guilty, feel that we have betrayed a trust, that we have done something behind the back of a friend who believed in us. This kind of situation produces great ambivalence in both student and teacher. Some teachers escape the problem entirely. One teacher insisted that any student who attended class regularly and was not too unruly would get an *A*. This teacher could not stand to hurt, through grades, the students whom he so genuinely liked. Another teacher may become so cold and distant and unapproachable that students are barely more than names and faces. Then it does not hurt to flunk anyone.

A rather interesting picture is that presented by Waller of the effect of grading upon the teacher:

> There is something in the attitude of grading . . . which makes against change and renders mental growth difficult. One who presumes to rate the performance of another must have a very definite idea of the perfect performance, and he judges other performances not by their inner, groping onwardness, but simply by their resemblance to the perfect performance. . . . Yet the teacher must have in mind a perfect performance. The grading, marking habit assumes increasing importance as one becomes a teacher. The new teacher rarely has definite standards of grading. Often he does not consider that part of his task important. . . . From habit, from the importance which others (especially the persons graded) attach to grades, and from the involvement of the teacher's status feelings with the development of rigorous standards, there arises a change in the teacher's attitudes. His status feelings become involved when he realizes that students believe that he is "easy" and preen themselves upon their ability to deceive him. . . . The teacher must establish standards of grading; he must identify himself with them and make them a part of himself.[8]

What of the function of education in our democratic social order? Can we have a democratic classroom where student and teacher are constantly eyeing each other with this suspicion and distrust?

[8] Waller, Willard, *The Sociology of Teaching* (New York: John Wiley & Sons, 1932 Inc.), p. 393.

Working for Grades vs. Real Learning

Growth occurs only as we know to what degree and in what manner we have achieved goals important to us, in order that we may grow toward increasingly more significant goals. But where evaluation is only a matter of the teacher's giving *grades* and *marks,* then learning is only for the grade. Students who get the *A*'s obtain a spurious feeling of superiority; students who get *F*'s are given a destructive personal view of their incapability to achieve learning. In reviewing the causes for delinquency, it is found that in at least 90 per cent of the cases, the student who became delinquent had a long record of lack of school achievement. This feeling that school success can be measured only by a grade may be highly destructive to the ego picture of those young people who cannot find success in this manner. When the high-school achievement is geared to college entrance, as in many cases it is, the 80 per cent of the school population which has no hope of going on to higher education must thus obtain a very negative view of its own potential as good people (not *A* quality, that is) and a suspicion and hatred for learning and those who symbolize learning.

Grading and Student-Student Relations

What does the grading system do to the interpersonal relations among the students? As has already been mentioned, students who express interest in the classwork are likely to be derided as "apple polishers." Moreover, the competition for a limited number of rewards further divides the students. Since it is clear that only a few will make the top grades, in the usual class, students cannot afford to like each other; after all, their neighbor might win the coveted award away from them. Some students develop a great selfishness regarding what they know. They would not dream of helping a fellow student, because that would minimize their own chances at the top grade. Among the students at the bottom of the heap the reverse is true. Since they are sure that they will not make anything but a low grade, they have no moral compulsions against cheating; to the student, this is merely sharing and helping a fellow unfortunate escape the ultimate disaster of failure. Where the normal curve is used in distributing grades, dooming a large number of students to failure, near failure, and only mediocre success, the teacher may find cheating and exchange of work very common. And why not?

Or so the student reasons in the face of a system which seems to him so completely arbitrary. He feels compelled by force of circumstance to get the grade.

Overcoming the Grading Complex

What can be done to overcome the grading complex? The classroom teacher is inextricably involved in grading year in and year out. There is hardly a school where in some form or other grading problems do not exist. The beginning teacher has a responsibility to try to extend the conventional grade to a more adequate appraisal. A classroom program in evaluation might proceed like this:

1. *Discuss the grading-marking system with the students.* The teacher will find that several class hours spent in discussing grades every semester with every new class will aid immeasurably in bridging this gap between teacher and student. The teacher will want to explain carefully the limits under which he works: for example, in some schools there is a requirement that the final semester examination shall count half of the semester grades.

2. *Provide for variety of achievement.* Every course of instruction has a multitude of possible and important purposes. After being in a mathematics class for a semester, the student should not only have attained some skill in solving problems, but developed ability to draw graphs and charts, write neatly, discuss intelligently, work cooperatively, be responsible for aspects of class management, and so forth. Thus, a student may have more than one avenue to classroom success.

3. *Develop self-evaluation tools.* Here the teacher can use all the steps described above to give the students a technique for looking at their own achievement. A report form should be developed jointly by the teacher and the class or by a class committee for the various phases or units of work. A sample of one such form is given on pages 388 and 389.

STUDENT SELF-EVALUATION CHART

AM I GROWING? [9]

In order to find out how much I am growing this year, I am keeping this chart. In the first column I have indicated those things with an *N* that I need help in very much and with an *A* those I need help in moderately.

In each of the following I have checked with:

X, if I have improved since the last time
O, if I have remained about the same
—, if I have lost ground

[9] *"Instruction in Citizenship in California High Schools," California State Department of Education Bulletin,* Vol. X, No. 11 (December, 1941), p. 41.

1. Extent to which I am growing in my ability to assume responsibility	Date						
a. By regular class attendance...							
b. By having all necessary materials such as pen, pencils, notebooks, ready to carry on work							
c. By voluntarily meeting my obligations for work which I have missed							
d. By not missing class the day a specific piece of work is due							
e. By doing what I have agreed to do							
f. By volunteering things for the class benefit not required in the plan of work...........							
g. By doing things on my own rather than depending on the help of others							

2. Extent to which I am becoming more tolerant toward the ideas of others	Date						
a. By listening attentively to the one speaking even though I disagree with him							
b. By not ridiculing the statements or ideas of others							
c. By being courteous even when disagreeing with others							
d. By asking questions to better understand other points of view							
e. By accepting kindly those who seem "different"							

3. Extent to which I am becoming able to cooperate effectively	Date						
a. By carrying my share of the load when working on a committee							
b. By giving up some of the things I want to do if it conflicts with the wishes of the majority of the class							
c. By suggesting things helpful to others working on a problem							
d. By not "hogging" books, materials, ideas, etc.							
e. By sharing my talents with the class							
f. By not monopolizing the discussion time							
g. By sharing interesting and worthwhile experiences							

This form, when completed by the student, will be kept by the teacher in a folder for the student. The teacher will use it to check his own judgment of the student, and where teacher and student disagree drastically, will use it as a basis for a personal conference. Where the student indicates significant problems and weaknesses, the teacher can easily discuss these with the student.

4. *Develop new evaluation techniques.* Where a teacher gives the same kind of test all of the time—objective, essay, matching, problem-solving—then only students proficient in that kind of skill or in learning material that can be fitted into such a test will be able to do well in the test. This will defeat those who are unable to do that kind of task well and will not challenge those who always succeed. Furthermore, it will encourage cheating, since the student is given only one way to success.

5. *Allow students to share in evaluating each other.* An evaluation committee with constantly rotating membership may be a great asset to a teacher. The students then act in an advisory capacity in judging the quality of their own work. For example, it has been found very rewarding for small groups of students—three or four—to read and evaluate each other's papers. One teacher in a ninth-grade orientation course had the students read their papers in small groups and then select the best one of the three or four read. After several periods of this kind of evaluation, students who had never written a decent paper or report were more conscientious in getting their papers done. The larger the role of the student in the evaluation program, the more effective will the total learning become. The stu-

dents will develop ability to appraise and discriminate and set their own standards and goals for achievement. Teachers can find innumerable situations in the classroom in which students may be active in the evaluation of learning. Some additional suggestions follow.

A. Textbook reading assignments. Instead of pointing textbook reading toward in-class discussion only, students may be asked to prepare some questions on the pages of text that could be used for a quiz on that section. The questions could be part of a classroom review game (see Chapter 9, section on games). The teacher would help the students in understanding what makes a good question by asking the class to look at the learning needed to answer the question. "Is that important for us to know?" would be the recurrent challenge posed by the teacher. A student committee could be asked to screen the questions either for a review game or a quiz; the students might be asked to indicate what they considered a correct answer to each question, and a team of experts from the class could help appraise the judgment of the students, with final over-all review by the teacher.

B. Student presentations. Whenever a group of students or an individual student presents material to the class as a whole, they should be requested to prepare a few questions that the class could and should be expected to be able to answer after the material has been presented. The students responsible for the presentation might then be asked to grade the answers of the class to the questions as a way of self-evaluation. The students who had thus contributed to the class learning would know to what extent they had succeeded in teaching the material.

The class members should also be drawn into the evaluation of each other's performance. After standards of performance have been agreed upon, for example, "What constitutes a good panel discussion?" the members of the class could be asked to fill out some simple form giving their reaction to the presentation:

1. Was the panel discussion interesting?
2. Were the points clearly made?
3. Were charts, graphs, or other displays understandable?
4. Did the panel demonstrate good oral speaking skills?
5. What was the most outstanding contribution of this panel to the class?
6. What suggestions for future panels do you think should be made?

This or another list of questions will help to focus student attention on developing better skills, as well as learning content.

Where committees or individual students take responsibility for bulletin-board displays, the same procedures may be followed. Those posting the bulletin boards will be asked to hand in some questions that students would be able to answer if the bulletin board attracted their attention. Then these questions, when asked of the class, will indicate how well the bulletin board did its job of teaching. The class might be asked to evaluate several bulletin-board displays as to effectiveness, interest, clarity, originality, timeliness, taste, appeal. An evaluation committee might check off the bulletin boards in terms of a list of criteria agreed upon by the class. A few moments at the end of the week might be provided in which each member of the class checked such a list. The results would then be used by the student or committee who put up the bulletin board to discover how others judged their efforts.

C. Group evaluation procedures. Where a group makes a presentation, prepares a test question, and then grades this question as a group, an increased seriousness of interest in the whole process of learning and teaching will be found. The students appreciate more the task that the teacher faces, and they also learn the relation that exists between giving information and learning something important. If the class has been divided into committees, all of which will impart some knowledge to the class, then the examination on the total unit of work may well be such a group examination. Students may read their individual papers and reports in small groups of three or four and make notes on the quality of the reports, or select the best one for posting on the bulletin board.

Where classmates evaluate each other, particularly in a test situation, it is sometimes useful to have students put numbers instead of names on their papers in order to maintain some objectivity on the part of the graders. It is probably more effective to use groups in grading papers than to have individuals grade individual papers, since the group situation will prevent any collusion between the grader and the one whose paper he is grading! Teachers often have students grade each other's papers when the answers (as in a true-false test) are clear and unambiguous. However, this procedure may waste more time than is warranted. A committee of two or three could do it equally well. The membership on the evaluation committee could be rotated frequently in some arbitrary manner to widen the extent of class participation and class support for this procedure.

6. Plan for a conference period with each student to appraise his progress. Such conferences are highly valuable if held early enough in the semester so that the student may have time to improve. And a conference at the end of the semester regarding the final semester grade will help the student accept realistically the teacher's appraisal of his work as it fits into his own self-appraisal. Keeping folders in which students file their work throughout the semester is very helpful. Both student and teacher together can look over several months' work. This method also helps demonstrate growth, rather than making a grade an average of noncomparable periods of work. The teacher should make certain, however, that this collection of student work is not a depressing sequence of *F* and *D* work.

These steps in developing a more adequate grading and marking procedure involve the teacher in considerable planning with his class. The teacher should be fairly skillful in such planning (see Chapters 4 and 8) in order to have a successful grading program evolve. Since this area is one of such deep concern and anxiety to the students, the teacher who wants to do student-teacher planning will find this one place where the planning will be relatively easy.

The Report Card

Report cards are issued quarterly in some schools, twice a year at the end of each semester in other schools. Some schools still adhere to a percentage system—that is, a student will have a report card on which will be listed the subjects he takes, and each teacher then enters a grade. His card reads: History, 65%, English, 90%, Algebra, 83%, French, 87%. Where percentage systems are used, the school usually will have a general agreement as to what the percentages indicate. Some number will refer to a passing score: students receiving 70% or above will be passing in the course, while those receiving less will be failing in the course. Scores over 90% will indicate superior performance, and so forth.

A system that has come into somewhat more common practice today is the use of five letter grades: *A*, superior; *B* good; *C*, average performance; *D*, poor performance; and *E*, or *F*, failing. This is translated into an eight-point scale by many with the addition of plus or minus to all of the letters except *F*. A few schools have adopted a three-point system: *H* for honors; *S* for satisfactory; and *U* for unsatisfactory or failing. This may be reduced further to just two marks, *S* and *U*. Some schools recognize the other learnings, of which we have spoken earlier, with a separate citizenship grade or with a number of grades for various attitudes and behaviors. There is, then, a wide variation among the schools of the country in the kinds of marks assigned. Students who transfer from one school to another sometimes find it difficult to explain just where they are in their work or what level of achievement was reached.

Any system of grading and marking is in part justified, say its defenders, because the marks on a report card are easily entered by a teacher and are easily understood by the parent. A teacher arrives at a summary mark for a student, and puts it in the appropriate box on a report card. This is recorded by the school office staff and the report card is taken home to the parent. The real purpose of the report card has been to indicate to the parent the progress of the student; the question to raise therefore is, "Does the report card actually do this?" As one observer has said, "The mark is inadequate in covering information to the student, his parents and others regarding the progress, achievement, failure, or success of the student." [10]

[10] Wrinkle, William L., "Six Years of an Experiment in Marking and Reporting in the Secondary School of the Colorado State College of Education." Chap. VII in *Guidance in Public Secondary Schools,* Educational Records Bulletin No. 28, October, 1939 (437 W. 59th St., New York).

A study of the school problems of a group of junior Hi-Y boys in Akron, Ohio, showed that 17 per cent of the students reported that they did not like to take home their report cards.[11] The student is involved in translating to his parents the meaning of the school marks on his report card. The typical conversation at home may sound like this:

FATHER: What is this, a *B*— in History? How come you didn't get an *A*? I thought you liked History.

JUNIOR: Well, History is O.K., but you see I got an *A* and a *C*— in a test, so I think my average wasn't so good.

FATHER: Well, you ought to get a better grade than that. Remember, a *B*— is not going to get you into college.

The report card effectually obscures the real purposes of education. In the Eight Year Study it was found that the school marks had directed the attention of students, parents, and teachers toward the symbol of success, the grade, rather than the actual learning or growth that the mark supposedly represented.[12]

Overcoming the Limitations of Report Cards

What can the individual teacher do to overcome the limitations of report cards? First, the teacher should try to understand the psychology of marking as described above, obtaining insight into the current role of marks in the culture of the school and home. Second, with the aid of his class, the teacher should seek to make explicit the meaning of the grade before transmission to the parent. Third, the teacher should devise additional means of communicating with parents regarding the progress of his students.

Let us expand this last point. The average teacher with four or five classes a day with thirty to thirty-five students in each cannot conceivably make very many individual contacts with each parent, either through visits, phone calls, or letters. However, during the course of a semester or a year, the teacher might well schedule at least one such contact with each parent. When the children need special attention, a home visit is helpful (see Chapter 20, section on parent relations). For students who are progressing at a normal rate, a note or a telephone call will help to bring the parent into some better understanding of his child and his child's progress in school. Such notes and telephone calls should include:

[11] Stuber, William D., "The Personal Problems of Jr. Hi-Y Members," *Jr. Hi-Y Ways,* April, 1950 (291 Broadway, New York), p. 1.

[12] Smith, Eugene R., and Ralph W. Tyler, *Appraising and Recording Student Progress* (New York: Harper & Brothers, 1942), p. 489.

1. Some indication of the teacher's genuine interest in the student and his progress.

2. An expression of understanding of problems which may interfere with optimum achievement.

3. A willingness to seek to work with the parents toward the goals that the parent has for his child. Where parents' goals are unrealistic in terms of the student's actual ability, the teacher may sometimes be able to discuss this problem with the parent and produce evidence for the parent to see that supports the teacher's insight. Obviously, this takes tact.

4. Specific statements about areas in which the student has shown genuine progress; specific suggestions about ways in which the student may need to do further work with the aid of his parents.

Here, for example, is a letter that a teacher wrote to the parents of one of his students. You can see how much more meaningful it is than an *A* or *C* on a report card.

Dear Mr. and Mrs. Smith:

After three months of observing Jane in my Biology class, I would like to take this opportunity of telling you something about her progress. I know that Jane has had some difficulty because of her long illness two years ago. This still makes her feel a bit out of things with her classmates because she feels somewhat older than they. However, she has shown consistent progress in her schoolwork with me. I would particularly like to stress her cheerfulness and friendly spirit. Jane works well with others in laboratory study; she is one of the first students that the others come to for help, even though she may not always be as well informed as others in the class. She needs to develop, however, somewhat greater confidence before the class as a whole. We are working now on the presentation of interesting oral reports and Jane, who could be a superior leader as an adult, will only realize this promise if we can help her develop better ease in speaking. With your assistance, I think Jane will be able to work particularly on this part of her class activities. I might also suggest that she sometimes seems too anxious about the quality of her work. She is doing a fine job, studies efficiently, gets her assignments in on time, and does well on examinations. I am sure she will not go on to further work in Biology as her interests are not in this field, but she is doing a quite adequate job now. When she gets too anxious about her work, then it is harder to do well.

We would welcome a visit from you at any time. Next week we are going to have an interesting discussion of conservation. Perhaps you would have a free hour, and if so, we would be most happy to have you. The class meets daily from 10:10 to 11:00 in Room 45.

Sincerely,
Alfred Akrosky

Promotion

To promote or not to promote? We cannot conclude a discussion of grading without considering the problem of failure and nonpromotion. It is customary in the high schools to fail a student in a single subject at a time. Of course, because of failing a single subject, the student may be unable to graduate with his regular classmates and have to continue another semester or year to earn the required credits for graduation. Some schools will require the student to retake the subject that has been failed; other schools merely require that additional units be taken so that a given total is reached before the student can graduate.

What about the individual teacher and failure? When is the teacher justified in failing a student? This point needs careful appraisal. The following statement is challenging:[13]

> When teachers are encouraged to emphasize success experiences, the argument has to be faced that the child must learn to accept failure because he has to live in a competitive society. One answer to this argument is that society is often kinder than the schools by not insisting on the repetition of activities for which the individual is not qualified. When a man fails in a job, he takes the consequences, but usually he goes after a different kind of job. When a pupil fails a school year, he is sometimes sent back to the same class to face failure all over again. Some experience of failure to reach goals is inevitable; in fact, such experiences are so prominent that there is little point in the school's seeking to create any more of them. A better preparation for failure is to have a sufficient backlog of success experiences so that failure is not devastating.

The teacher may, of course, not always have complete freedom in this matter. In one school a principal made continuous studies of the record of achievement of the graduates in their later years in college. It was his contention that if the high school were any good, the high-school group should show the same grade distribution, the same failure proportion as the graduates of his school produced in college. He justified his approach on the basis that high school should be just as selective as college. Such reasoning is questionable. The high school is obligated to take all the children of all the people. The college may set up high barriers to entrance and select only those who can succeed, or have a chance of succeeding, in terms of academic accomplishment. The high school can make no such selection. And when failure means that the student subsequently drops out of school, there is some justification for saying that high school is not fulfilling its function.

A group of school-personnel people (who were concerned with the hiring of teachers) told a group of college-placement officers (who were concerned with helping students find teaching jobs) that

[13] National Society for the Study of Education. Forty-ninth Yearbook, Part I, *Learning and Instruction* (Chicago: University of Chicago Press, 1950), p. 52.

the kind of teachers they wanted were those who could help students feel as though high school had a place for them. The personnel people assumed that teacher candidates know their subject field; what was wanted were teachers who put young people and social needs ahead of mere academic achievement. Any teacher, then, who feels that good teaching means the weeding out of those not academically able should re-examine the broader effects of such a policy.

Furthermore, making a student repeat material that was not grasped at first, may not result in marked improvement. Students may honestly try harder to learn the material, but, on the whole, the failure experience makes it even more difficult to learn on the second try. It has also been noted that students who are regularly promoted despite lack of achievement have, in the main, caught up with their peers if allowed to continue along with them. The material is learned by contagion, so to speak. The gap between the failing and the succeeding student becomes narrower if both students are allowed to progress together and share the same classroom experiences, particularly if the shadow of failure is not imminent for the less able.[14]

Is this soft education? Good education is not soft by any means. Successful achievement still means applying to a task all the student's talents. But the typical grading system forces acceptance of only certain kinds of talent. This makes the judgment of the teacher the end-all of every effort. Very often students who obtain good marks exclaim over the fact that actually such marks were not earned, that they had not done a very good job in their own opinion. But since the teacher was satisfied, why worry!

> In one school the students are not "graded" in the usual sense of the word. While the instructors evaluate each student's performance, such a record is kept highly confidential; the student may not see his record until after graduation or transfer to another institution. At first the students are uneasy and unsure of themselves. They have to learn how to judge their own efforts, and they have to learn how to study and produce at their top level of achievement. After the initial shock has worn off, the students find this new system very refreshing and relaxing. One does not feel in competition with one's fellows; one can afford to like everyone because there is not the pervasive sense of trying to win the few coveted honor grades. By the end of the student's four years of work, he has learned to work and study for the sake of learning, rather than for a grade; students push themselves to better performance, since they themselves are the real judge of how well they have done.

[14] Segel, David, *Intellectual Abilities in the Adolescent Period,* Bulletin No. 6, 1948 (Washington, D.C., U.S. Office of Education), p. 8.

The experiences reported by Wrinkle[15] in an experimental high school produced a similar reaction on the part of the students, according to graduates of the school. The feeling of being free of the grade came as a welcome relief, and the net effect was to step up performance and effort. The teacher in any school system will want, then, to work with the students so that these negative effects of grading are minimized. This will happen to the extent that students judge their own work and are given an opportunity to put to use many kinds of talent in the classroom.

Summary

The task of finding out how well they are doing in their various educational enterprises confronts teachers and students at every turn. The teacher wants to know how well he is doing as a teacher in terms of increasing student insight and ability. He also wants to know how well individual students and groups of students are progressing. It is not an easy task to evaluate something as complex as educational growth. Typically, because it has been so difficult, we have concentrated our evaluation efforts on small, manageable units of information. Yet the significant purposes of education are far more comprehensive. Thus the modern teacher must seek new and more appropriate ways of evaluating learning. The approach to evaluation described in this chapter points a way of helping students grow toward important educational goals.

In this broader evaluation the psychological impact of the grading-report-card complex cannot be ignored. The greater the insight into this crucial area of teacher-student and student-student relationships, the better will the teacher be able to realize a democratic classroom atmosphere. The larger the role given to students in the evaluation of their own progress, the greater is the possibility that the teacher can develop in young people a sense of critical self-appraisal independent of such extrinsic factors as marks and prizes. The best of teaching can be sabotaged by inadequate or inappropriate evaluation procedures. It is highly important that the beginning teacher see the intimate relationship between good teaching and adequate evaluation. In the next chapter we will look closely at evaluation as a total process.

Selected References

Berger, Donald. "When a Class Evaluates," *Educational Leadership,* 6:395-399 (March, 1949). This eleventh-grade class tried to meet coopera-

[15] *Op. cit.*

tively the problem of real learning vs. grades; student-teacher conferences developed as the most useful device.

Burton, William H. *The Guidance of Learning Activities.* New York: Appleton-Century-Crofts, Inc., 1944. Chap. 19, "Marking and Reporting Progress," pp. 479-513. Comprehensive discussion; particular emphasis on use of a descriptive marking system.

Fedder, Ruth. *Guiding Homeroom and Club Activities.* New York: McGraw-Hill Book Company, 1949. Chap. 6, "What the Group Experience Meant to the Boys and Girls: An Evaluation," pp. 328-368. Provides a good answer to the problem of how to evaluate informal socializing activities; a very interesting report.

Otto, Henry J. "Grading and Promotion Policies," *NEA Journal* 40:128-129 (February, 1951). Summarizes research findings to date about what "works" in grading practices.

School Marks and Promotions. Discussion Pamphlet No. 9, Department of Classroom Teachers and Research Division, National Education Association, Washington, D.C., May, 1950. Basic issues regarding grading are presented in a clear and stimulating fashion.

Strang, Ruth. *Reporting to Parents.* Practical Suggestions for Teaching, No. 10. New York: Bureau of Publications, Teachers College, Columbia University, 1947. Current practices described with suggestions for improvement.

Toward Better Teaching. Association for Supervision and Curriculum Development, 1949 Yearbook. Washington, D.C.; The Association, 1949. Chap. 8, "Helping Pupils Evaluate Learning," pp. 226-255. Ways in which students can be brought into active participation in evaluation.

Wrinkle, William L. *Improving Marking and Reporting Practices.* New York: Rinehart & Company, 1947. An excellent and comprehensive discussion of this very complicated and confused area of teaching.

17. A Modern Approach to Evaluation

WHAT do we mean by evaluation in education? The term refers to a broader way of appraising learning than by merely testing. A good evaluation program tries to comprehend the full range of achievement that a student may demonstrate. Evaluation may be thought of as a four-step process: First, what purposes are we trying to achieve by a given activity or unit of work or course sequence? Second, what do we mean by adequate performance in achieving these purposes? Third, under what circumstances can we judge if an individual or group has approached the goals we have set? Fourth, what instruments or tools can we use in judging this performance under these revealing circumstances? An illustration will make this clear:

A teacher in United States history planned to develop a unit on the Civil War. The purposes of such a unit as she saw them were:

1. To learn some basic content regarding important issues and events surrounding the Civil War.
2. To develop critical thinking about important issues in war and civil wars.
3. To develop some skills in writing, speaking, discussing, problem solving, group activities.
4. To increase interest in present-day problems that are related to this historical period.

> Since these were her purposes, it was necessary to think of what she meant by adequate performance. How much of the content should be learned. By all students? By some? How could she judge whether the students were more able to think critically? What did she mean by critical thinking anyway? The idea of development of some skills meant that some students would grow more than others because of greater need or greater ability—adequacy of performance then involved some idea of adequacy of growth. For increased interest it would be hard to set a standard.
>
> The next problem was the need for revealing situations. This meant that in order to learn some content, experience had to be provided with the content; likewise, in terms of critical thinking, skill development, and increased interest, the activities of the classroom had to be planned to allow these things to be learned, as well as reveal to what extent they were being learned. After all, she couldn't expect the students to show increased ability in discussion unless there were opportunities to discuss!
>
> Finally, how was she going to measure what had occurred? The learning of content could be tested by simple recall or other of the usual paper-and-pencil tests. But what about critical thinking? A test of new material where critical evaluation was required could be useful to see if this skill itself had been developed as a carryover into other areas. Writing? Speaking? Group activities? Again, a special tool would have to be set up or a special observation period for evaluating the skill would need to be arranged. How would she measure the increase in interest in the historical backgrounds of modern problems? Could the students themselves evaluate their own growth and learning?

So the evaluation process raises perplexing questions for the teacher. The wide range of purposes that are to be evaluated makes immediately evident the need for many kinds of instruments beyond the paper and pencil test to measure growth. Traditionally, the paper-and-pencil test determined what was taught. For example, if it was known ahead of time that the students were going to take a test demanding recall of minute detail, then obviously during class time the teacher would drill the students on detail. If the test involved an ability to organize and apply ideas, then the students would be drilled in organizing and applying ideas. Thus, the method of testing had very important consequences for the whole teaching-learning process.

Registering growth has equally important consequences for teaching and learning in the evaluation process. But, as we no longer think of registering growth solely in terms of paper-and-pencil tests, we have given new range to kinds of teaching-learning in which we are interested. We have seen from the four-step sequence that we cannot evaluate learning until we know what we hoped would occur as a result of our teaching; then we must calculate how much of these purposes can or should be achieved; next we must provide opportunity for the students to learn and demonstrate this learning in revealing situations; and finally, we need tools of appraisal that are adequately related to our original purposes.

Evaluation as a Starting Point in Instructional Planning

Although we think of evaluation as coming at the end of a course, the approach to evaluation suggested here means that it begins with the very first planning for the course. Consistency in emphasis between learning activities and evaluation technique is very important. If a class has spent all its time in a language class learning verb forms and irregular endings, but is tested on ability to translate, the class will not be evaluated fairly. Here a paper-and-pencil test is appropriate, but the emphasis in the test is inappropriate. On the other hand, if a class has had extensive practice in active oral discussion and then is given a *written* test on principles of discussion, the class will not be evaluated fairly either. The paper-and-pencil test is no longer appropriate. Only an observation record of the students as they discuss is adequate. We cannot measure ability in *oral* discussion by an exercise in *written* discussion.

Before we leave this aspect of evaluation, one more item must be added. What happens after the evaluation has occurred? What does it all mean? It means that the teacher and the institution, as well as the individual pupil, are the subjects of evaluation. After all, if a teacher sought to develop better discussion skills in his students and then discovered that only a few really had developed this skill, he would want to ask, "Is it my fault or theirs?" "Did the training procedures fail to train?" "What new things should I do next time to attain better success with this kind of a class?" Implications for teaching practices are important results of any kind of evaluation, whether it be a simple true-false test or an elaborate series of observations of behavior. The student will want to know what his score means, and the teacher needs to see what techniques in teaching were most efficient and successful both for the class as a whole and for individual students.

In the following section we will present briefly some of the steps the teacher takes in setting up an over-all evaluation program. Essentially this procedure is merely the implementing of a point of view—a basic assumption about education that says: "The significant progress of students must be judged by both informal and formal techniques. Behavior is the primary clue to real learning."

Step 1. Setting Up Appropriate Objectives [1]

Fundamentally, the aims for any school activity are to be found by matching the needs of the pupil and the demands made upon him by society, with the opportunities provided by the activity. This implies—

a. Adequate information about each pupil, his abilities realized and potential, his interests, purposes, background.

b. Adequate information about the demands of society, immediate and future, that will determine the responsibilities of the pupil.

c. The appropriate role of the activity in the total educational program of the pupil, which outcomes it can be concerned with economically and effectively, and which it cannot.

Psychological justification. Such aims, however, must be justified by their *psychological appropriateness.* In a psychological justification the key question is: "Can pupils be stirred to desire these aims as their own?" If they cannot, these aims are only the teacher's aims. At best, they will be but by-products of the goals which pupils can accept as their own. But if these are the aims that pupils can recognize as interesting, appealing, worth while, they are psychologically justified.

In illustration let us examine the following list of aims:

1. *Teaching pupils to multiply by two digits.*

This aim cannot be criticized as a desirable outcome, but it states the intention of the teacher rather than a goal of the pupil. It may well be one of the by-products that the teacher desires to see accomplished while the pupil is pursuing some consummatory objective of his own, but in its present form does not represent a common purpose which the teacher and class can share.

2. *Learning how the state budget is organized.*

This aim has psychological appeal to only a limited group—politicians, college professors, professional civic leaders, and the like. It, too, may well be accomplished as a by-product of some other aim, such as applying for a civil service job or seeking legislative action to reduce high taxes. But to normal children the aim as now stated has very little psychological justification.

3. *Learning how to sail paper airplanes out the window.*

This aim is psychologically sound for almost every school child. Poses an interesting problem and an understandable promise of satisfaction at the end. If child interest were the only criterion, this would rank high.

4. *Learning how to make the city more beautiful.*

This aim may not have instantaneous appeal to all children, but most can be skillfully led to the point of accepting this aim wholeheartedly as their own. It is in accord with the psychology of learning, calling for

[1] This program is adapted from materials developed by Dr. Lucien B. Kinney, School of Education, Stanford University, Stanford, California.

diversified, active behavior, and fulfilling the need for social status through community contribution.

The psychological justification must verify, also, the feasibility of the aim. Is the proposed outcome possible to achieve? Can it be achieved with reasonable expenditure of time and effort? When the development of the trait of honesty is proposed as an outcome in mathematics, we may raise the first of these questions. Some doubt is thrown on the existence of such a general trait by some studies. Hence, the effectiveness of teaching mathematics should not be evaluated on the basis of this outcome until the possibility is verified.

Perfection of handwriting might be questioned as an aim on the basis of the second question. While it might possibly be achieved, it would be at the expense of other outcomes that are more important.

Sociological justification. An aim having psychological appeal may still not be worth seeking. Why is it important to achieve this aim? What is the social significance of this aim? Does it make more of a contribution to the life of the group than some of the other aims which these children could be achieving? About the lowest point in sociological justification is to argue the official course of study requires this aim. More significant points would be to define the likely effects of the achievements of this aim on the general welfare of the group, the social competence of the individual, and the interests of other members of the group.

In illustration here is another list of possible aims:

1. *Learning how to sail paper airplanes out the classroom window.*
Seldom, if ever, does this aim result in a social contribution; at best it may be neutral and harmless in its social significance, in which case it needs to be justified on grounds other than sociological. At its worst it has decidedly negative social significance.

2. *Learning the names of the kings of England in chronological order.*
Seldom, if ever, does this aim result in a social contribution. In some cases it may be neutral and harmless in its social significance, but it requires justification on other grounds (radio quiz programs). In competition with vast range of aims with distinct social importance, it can scarcely be justified.

3. *Learning how to manage a large corporation.*
This aim has a great deal of sociological significance to certain small groups, but lacks general importance. It is sociologically as well as psychologically inappropriate to the lives of most school children.

4. *Learning how to make the city more beautiful.*
This aim has social significance, not only to group welfare, but also to social competence of the individual as well. It represents a responsibility that needs to be accepted by most citizens, including school children. It involves activities which are socially acceptable and desirable.

Step 2. Defining Objectives in Terms of Student Behavior

Once we are satisfied that our aims of instruction are psychologically sound and socially significant, then we need to be able to observe these aims or objectives in terms of actual student behavior. This way of setting down objectives is called an "operational" or "behavioral" statement.

Two questions may be raised in formulating an operational definition:

1. "What are some of the things that pupils do who have achieved growth in this objective?"
2. "How does their behavior differ from that of others who have not achieved such growth?"

Intangible objectives, such as "social effectiveness," "ability to think critically," can be reduced to behavioral terms by such analysis.

The following descriptions of behavior were set up by one science teacher as typical of a pupil on one of his classes who was interested in science:

1. He develops a hobby using science experiences.
2. He reads of his own choice on various phases of science.
3. He displays pleasure in the activities of others in science, as well as his own.
4. He voluntarily seeks information regarding natural life, especially from the point of view of conservation.
5. He brings material to class for analysis or classification on his own initiative.
6. During discussions in class or otherwise he volunteers reasonable generalizations.
7. He uses additional time for research in the field with reasonable effectiveness.
8. He demonstrates ability to define scientific problems.

Such descriptive statements then have real meaning to the teacher who can say, "Why yes, I *know* John learned something because he *did* thus and so." But the usefulness of such statements depends also on their comprehensiveness and ease of utilization.

It is not usually possible to include all objectives. Some forms of behavior are apparent and no formal observation is necessary. Others present a problem of collecting evidence so difficult as to warrant deferral. Many abilities appear to be included as prerequisites in larger outcomes—as ability to read, write, or follow directions—and are assumed to be present when larger outcomes are identified.

They must be investigated, however, if the larger outcomes fail to appear.

It is important that this choice of outcomes be conscious and selective and that those deferred for practical reasons be marked for further study.

Inclusive objectives. In order to check the coverage of objectives, it is helpful to set up large general categories of the behaviors that are sought. This system is necessary because some objectives will be "pervasive," extending through many activities and over long periods; some will be school-wide, others will concern a specific class or unit of work; some will be in the form of attitudes and understandings, others will be skills or techniques. We must develop a form of organization that will group these various types of objectives together so that they can be easily handled in terms of the group concerned, the situations in which growth will be evidenced, or the span of time during which evaluation will take place.

An example of a form of classification is that used by the Evaluation Staff of the Eight-Year Study: [2]

1. Functional information including vocabulary.
2. Reflective thinking.
3. Attitudes.
4. Interests.
5. Appreciations.
6. Work habits and study skills.
7. Social and personal adjustment.
8. Social sensitivity.

Wrightstone[3] uses four general headings:

1. Intellectual factors.
2. Dynamic factors (beliefs and attitudes).
3. Social performance factors.
4. Physiological factors.

Step 3. Deciding What Situations Reveal the Presence or Absence of the Desired Behavior

There are two kinds of situations for revealing desired behaviors: *normal* and *planned* situations.

The normal situation: Often the ordinary acticities of the classroom and the more informal phases of school life afford

[2] Smith, Eugene, Ralph W. Tyler, and Staff, *Appraising and Recording Student Progress* (New York: Harper & Brothers, 1942).

[3] J. W. Wrightstone, *Appraisal of Experimental High School Practices* (New York: Bureau of Publications, Teachers College, Columbia University, 1936), pp. 120-127.

the situations needed for observation. For example, the interest of a pupil in science might be determined by the following:

Behavior	*Technique*
"How much additional time does he use for research?"	Anecdotal record [4]
"How much voluntary reading does he do?"	Interviewing the librarian
"How often does he reveal an ability to define problems?"	Observation, directed by check-sheet

The problem is simply one of recording that information most useful for the evaluation study we are undertaking.

The planned situation: Some behavior is rarely called for in normal routine, and a planned or artificial situation must be devised to discover achievement. (For example, little evidence could be secured by observing the student's normal behavior regarding the use of the arithmetical process of dividing one fraction by another or of the discovery of America by Columbus.) Such special techniques may also be used to get at attitudes or understandings that affect behavior but are difficult to isolate or recognize in a normal situation. In such cases special arrangements for observation must be devised. For example, the teacher of the pupil in science could secure evidence regarding the following behaviors in planned situations:

Behavior	*Technique*
"To what extent does he reveal ability to define problems?"	Interview
"Is he able to draw reasonable generalizations from a given set of facts?"	Test (such as the Eight Year Study test on generalizations)

These techniques will operate within many possible situations—the classroom, the laboratory, the library, the more general and informal school environment, on excursions, going to and from school, in the home, in the individual's own social experiences.

The planned situation, as can be seen, is one set up by the teacher and students to find out: How well are we doing? This leads to step 4.

[4] Anecdotal record: Direct recording of a specific example of a pupil's behavior at the time which it occurs.

Step 4. Finding Appropriate Techniques for Obtaining and Recording Information

The first essential is to use *appropriate* techniques. Using the achievement-test technique just because it gives results in a tangible form is, of course, defenseless.

The problem to be faced in planning what techniques to use is analogous to that of a machinist in attacking a new job. If the standard tool is suitable, it should be used; if not, one must be devised. An expert knows what tools are available, the characteristics of each, and the situations for which they are suitable. Similarly, teachers should be familiar with the available instruments and the situations in which they have been used, as well as the basis for appraising proposed procedures in terms of economy of time and resources and of utility and significance of results.

Some of the techniques that are commonly used are:

For gathering direct evidence of pupil behavior in a normal situation

1. Stenographic reports
2. Sound recordings
3. Pupil products or reports
4. Anecdotal records
5. Time samplings[5]
6. Check list
7. Pupil time charts and diaries
8. Self-rating scales
9. Questionnaires
10. Judgment scales of products

For gathering evidence of specific behavior by short-cut methods in a planned situation designed to gather evidence of special significance to the evaluator

1. Interviews
2. Controlled observation[6]
3. Tests
   Achievement
   Aptitude
   Attitude
   Personality
   Interest

The accompanying chart illustrates a handy technique to use in matching behavioral objectives, situations, and appropriate techniques, in the development of a program of evaluation:

[5] Time samplings: For example, recording behavior of a student over a period of five minutes at the beginning of every hour.

[6] Controlled observations: For example, a planned work situation where certain materials are provided the student while observers record behavior. Or after a study of nutrition, students are observed making choices in the cafeteria.

Objective: Develop student interest in science	Situation							
Behavior	Laboratory	Classroom	Home	To and from School	School Environment	Individual Exploring	Field Trips	Laboratory, Library
1. What, and how many science hobbies has he?	a, b	g	a, b	c	a, b	a, b, c	a, b	
2. How much voluntary reading does he do?	f, h	a, b, g	b					b
3. How often, and in what way, does he demonstrate pleasure in science activities of self and others?	a, b, c	e, g, h	b	b, c	a, b		a, b	
4. How often does he voluntarily seek information about natural life?	d, g	a, f ,g	a, b	c, f	a, b	c	a, b	a
5. How often does he bring material to class on own initiative?	a, b	f						
6. How often does he volunteer reasonable generalizations?	f, g	h						
7. How much additional time does he use for research?	a, b		b, c			c		a, c
8. How often, and to what extent, does he reveal ability to define problems?	a, b	f, g, h	b		a	c		

Techniques for collection of information[7]

(a) Directed observation using a check list
(b) Anecdotal records
(c) Pupil time charts and diaries
(d) Questionnaires
(e) Self-rating scales
(f) Interviews
(g) Written and oral reports
(h) Tests

[7] Adapted from Kinney, Lucien B., and Katharine Dresden, *Better Learning through Current Materials* (Stanford: Stanford University Press, 1949), p. 145.

Many beginning teachers will review the past several pages with a sense of shock: Is there really enough measurement of achievement here? If we remember how much is not measured at all by the typical paper-and-pencil testing, we will see that this program does represent far more comprehensive appraisal. Granted it will not be easy to collect this range of information on student progress, it is still more defensible to do as much as is feasible than to give the false impression of exactness lent by the usual testing program. This is not to say paper-and-pencil tests do not have their place, but that they alone do not provide adequate evaluation.

Summary

As the high school has extended the range of learnings that it tries to develop, a broader program of evaluation has been mandatory. New understandings, new abilities, new attitudes now receive important emphasis in the curriculum. It has become increasingly clear that these broader goals escape the coarse screen of the old testing programs. So the first step taken has been to analyze the new goals into components that can be seen in the actions of students. Curriculum makers have asked of each objective what could a student do if he had achieved it. To answer required defining in terms of observable student behavior such complex abilities as critical thinking or such abstract attitudes as acceptance of minority groups. Obviously the high schools have only begun this task.

The next step has been almost as difficult. It might be stated something like this: If this is the kind of student action desired, under what circumstances can we see the action? Here high-school teachers have been reimpressed with the fact that the learning goes on during all the student's waking hours. It has not been enough to see him in the classroom. What he does in the cafeteria, in the corridor, on the playground, on the way home, at home, in the Community Center must also be known. The result is that high-school administrations are beginning to collect data on the daily lives of high-school students far beyond what has ever been available.

But the task has not ended here. It has still been necessary to devise a range of instruments to record all these student actions in all these revealing situations. Obviously, the paper-and-pencil test, no matter how carefully constructed, does not gather data on this range of action. But many new instruments have come into use: observation check lists, anecdotal records, student diaries and time charts, questionnaires, self-rating scales, interviews. Again, no one has been so brash as to say that these instruments gather, in representative amounts, all the data needed to make a complete evaluation of student growth and development. But it is clear that even with this inadequate battery of instruments, much more can be known about student achievement than has ever been known before.

Beginning teachers often have trouble just devising good paper-and-pencil tests and difficulty in finding time to check and record the tests after they are given. Little wonder then if they are appalled at any addition to the burden. They are not without company among their experienced brethren. It is merely being realistic then to say that beginning teachers can only be expected to extend their programs of evaluation as they gather strength and skill. We need to be concerned about the future of students only if the teachers remain always satisfied with minimal evaluation.

Selected References

Burton, William H. *The Guidance of Learning Activities.* New York: Appleton-Century-Crofts, Inc., 1944. Chap. 17, "The Measurement and Evaluation of Learning Outcomes," pp. 408-448. Theory and practice of the modern concept of the evaluation process.

Educational Policies Commission. *Learning the Ways of Democracy.* Washington, D.C.: National Education Association, The Commission, 1940. Chap. VII, "Evaluation of Outcomes," pp. 379-433. Describes specific techniques that are being used to evaluate education that is directed toward democratic learnings.

Findlay, Warren G. "Educational Evaluation: Recent Developments," *Social Education,* 14:206-210 (May, 1950). How modern teaching has produced a need for new evaluation procedures.

"How Evaluate?" *Educational Leadership,* 8:70-105 (November, 1950) (entire issue). Nine articles on various aspects of theory and practice of evaluation.

Kinney, Lucien B., and Katharine Dresden. *Better Learning through Current Materials.* Stanford: Stanford University Press, 1949. Chap. IX, "Evaluating the Effectiveness of Teaching Procedures," pp. 140-162. A concise statement of evaluation with specific examples on the use of current materials.

National Society for the Study of Education. *The Measurement of Understanding.* Forty-fifth Yearbook, Part I. Chicago: University of Chicago Press, 1946. Good source for an historical overview and a discussion of current issues and problems in evaluation.

Noll, Victor H., and Walter N. Durost. "Measurement Practices and Preferences of High School Teachers." Test Service Notebook No. 8. Yonkers: World Book Company, n.d. 4 pp. An interesting and revealing study of what kinds of tests teachers actually do use.

Quillen, I. J., and L. A. Hanna. *Education for Social Competence.* Chicago: Scott, Foresman & Company, 1948. Chap. 13, "The Meaning and

Significance of Evaluation," pp. 343-361. A well-organized discussion of the principles behind the "evaluation" approach.

Stiles, Lindley M., and Mattie J. Dorsey. *Democratic Teaching in Secondary Schools.* Philadelphia: J. B. Lippincott Company, 1950. Chap. 10, "Appraising Learning and Growth," pp. 205-232. Practical suggestions for developing democratic procedures of evaluation.

18. Techniques of Individual Counseling

NO ONE is more fascinating to an adolescent than himself. During these years he is concerned more exclusively about himself than he has ever been before or probably ever will be again. Commonly the teacher of adolescents is confronted by a divided person. His attention is split between the objective world around him and the subjective world of his own worries, problems, hopes, and conflicts.

In the preceding sections our emphasis was upon the modern approach to teaching in view of the differences among individuals. In this chapter, our emphasis is upon the student as a person, not merely as a student! We see again that the role of the teacher has many facets. To be a competent teacher means more than developing good students. It means understanding the emotional life of young people and helping them to deal more successfully with their personal lives. This is the counselor function.

In all ages, those who were called great teachers were those who were wise and judicious advisers as well as skillful instructors. All of us are grateful for the existence of some person or persons who lend a sympathetic ear to our troubles, large and small. Too often the high-school teacher seems aloof and unsympathetic, a mere giver of assignments and grader of examinations. Few students seek out such a teacher for help and advice. Most schools are fortunate enough to have at least one teacher who is the confidant of many students. Not all of us can be great counselors, for this requires both special training and special personality qualities, but we can at least understand the obligation of the teacher to strive for insight. It has been said that we would have few, if any, delinquents if each student had one teacher in school who gave him warm friendship and understanding.

In this chapter will be discussed some of the tools and techniques that the teacher can use in performing his function as a counselor for the individual student. Succeeding chapters will discuss the special problems of group guidance, vocational and academic counseling, and working with parents on guidance problems of students.

The Counseling Approach

It may be useful to point out the essential difference between the teacher-academician and the teacher-counselor:

Teacher-Academician	*Teacher-Counselor*
Subject matter has priority	Personality is of first concern
Test results determine levels of potential achievement in subject matter.	Test results point out areas of personal need and barriers to successful adjustment
Grades are a function of subject matter learning only	Grades reveal many kinds of achievement other than subject matter alone—social, psychological, aesthetic
Only students who can learn the subject are able to succeed to a high degree	Avenues of success for a variety of talents are vitally important
Few personal interviews are held with students except about academic problems	Many individual interviews are held about personal as well as academic problems
The student's counselor or other teachers are seldom consulted about the progress of an individual	Student problems are often discussed with counselors and other teachers
Few home visits are made and parent conferences at school are avoided	A number of home visits are made and special invitations to individual parents to come to school for conferences are issued
The role of emotion in learning is discounted	Sensitivity to emotional tone in the classroom and with individual students is maintained

It can be seen that taking the teacher-counselor view of instruction will have a significant bearing on human relationships in the classroom. In discussing the democratic classroom (see Chapter 3), it was pointed out that the major concern in such a classroom is what happens to the individuals in it. Similarly, the counseling approach to teaching focuses on individuals in the group. For each student the important question is: Is he being helped to become as adequate an adult as he could?

Diagnosing the Need for Guidance

In order to help young people with their problems the teacher-counselor needs some tools and techniques that help to reveal what these problems are. Research in this field indicates that adolescence is a time when the individual is becoming more and more conscious of the differences between himself and others. The growth that occurs thus produces its own problems. What are the things that adolescents worry about?

54 per cent say they wish they knew how to study more effectively.
40 per cent would like to know more definitely how they are doing in their work.
43 per cent say they worry about tests.
35 per cent say they worry about little things.
27 per cent report they are nervous.
26 per cent have guilt feelings about things they have done.
24 per cent say, "I want to discuss my personal problems with someone."
54 per cent say they want people to like them more.
50 per cent want to make new friends.
42 per cent wish they were more popular.
31 per cent say, "I'm worried about the next war." [1]

There are several check lists of student problems that are useful devices for the teacher to use in familiarizing himself with adolescent concerns. The Mooney Problems Check List, the Science Research Associates Youth Inventory, the check list entitled "High School Youth Look at Their Problems" by L. J. Elias (published by the author, the State College of Washington, Pullman, Wash.) are among those currently in wide use. These lists cover much the same material. Typical statements to be checked are:

I feel sleepy in class even when I've had enough sleep at night.
I need some individual help with my courses.
I often feel lonesome.

[1] *Good Schools Don't Just Happen!* (Pamphlet) (Chicago: Science Research Associates, n.d.).

I feel that I'm not as smart as other people.
People stare at me.
I want people to like me better.[2]

Each teacher may want to adapt these standard scales for his own use. Or he may assign as theme topics certain central problems. Many teachers find topics like these very useful in eliciting guidance data:

1. What I do when I get mad.
2. What I do to get something from my parents that they can't afford.
3. What I do when someone makes fun of me.
4. What my family expects of me.[3]
5. What I remember of the time when I was a child.
6. The person I would most like to be.
7. My happiest (unhappiest) experience.
8. I wish. . . .
9. The worst thing in the world.
10. The kind of boy (girl) I like best is. . . .

Understanding Adolescents

In order better to understand adolescents, the beginning teacher may do well to review in his own mind the adolescent problems he faced himself. Adults tend to forget that the two worlds do not coincide; things of concern to the adult may be very remote to youth while the events that appear crucial to youth often appear inconsequential or even childish to adults. "It is probably fair to say that more teachers are balked in their work with boys and girls because they unwittingly violate adolescents' unformulated codes of behavior than [are balked] because they violate the laws of learning." [4] To work daily with adolescents means to keep freshly in mind the reality of the world in which the adolescent is living. One of our great failures in the schools is that young people come to teachers so seldom with their real problems, because teachers seem too removed from the world of the adolescent, too unsympathetic with those matters of vital importance to youth.

One method of coming closer to the young person, we said earlier, is to recall one's own adolescent problems and difficulties.

[2] From the *SRA Youth Inventory, Form A* (Chicago: Science Research Associates, n.d.).

[3] For specific student reactions to items 1 to 4, see Elizabeth H. Brady, "Children Bring Their Families to School," Chapter 2, *Fostering Mental Health in Our Schools,* 1950 Yearbook (Washington, D. C.: Association for Supervision and Curriculum Development, 1950).

[4] Fedder, Ruth, *Guiding Homeroom and Club Activities* (New York: McGraw-Hill Book Company, Inc., 1949), p. 54.

Talking over these years with other young adults may help to widen the base of our experience and understanding. When we recall the problems we faced as high-school students, it soon becomes apparent that many of them were very personal. We recall conflict at home, worries over physical maturation, insecurity in heterosexual relations, doubt about physical or intellectual competence. At the time, we thought that we alone had these insecure years. Now we know every generation of adolescents undergoes the same period of worry and concern. Of course, we must not project onto others the same problems we had ourselves. After all, if the problem we faced in high school was the self-conscious awkwardness of a stranger in town, that does not necessarily mean that all other adolescents entering a new town feel the same way. No, we do not all have the same problems in adolescence. But what we can gain from remembered feelings is renewed sensitivity to a troubled time of life.

Once we have this feeling for adolescence, we can begin to broaden our perspective. We can accept the experiences of young people without being startled or shocked. Many teachers have lived relatively sheltered lives, yet they must meet and deal effectively with students from a very wide range of backgrounds. For example, if a teacher has never been near the chronic alcoholic, and the kind of family disruption and terror that go along with it, then he may well shy away from the student who has such a problem to face at home. Or he may be unwilling to face the fact that a student comes from a family living in a one-room shanty with no running water. He may want to get away from such problems simply by decrying the way these people live. Obviously that won't help much. Often creative writers have projected the feelings of youth better than educators and psychologists; such books will help teachers to visualize backgrounds which would otherwise be unfamiliar to them.[5] Then, too, anthropologists have made a number of interesting studies of

[5] The following books are recommended: Cather, Willa, *My Antonia* (Boston: Houghton Mifflin Company, 1924). Cronin, A. J., *The Green Years* (Boston: Little, Brown & Company, 1944). Dreiser, Theodore, *An American Tragedy* (New York: Boni & Liveright, 1925). Farrell, James T., *Studs Lonigan* (New York: Vanguard Press, 1935). Griffith, Beatrice, *American Me* (Boston: Houghton Mifflin Company, 1948). McCullers, Carson, *The Member of the Wedding* (Boston: Houghton Mifflin Company, 1946). Mann, Thomas, *Buddenbrooks* (New York: Alfred A. Knopf, 1924). Moravia, Alberto, *Two Adolescents* (New York: Farrar, Straus & Young, 1950). Motley, Willard, *Knock on Any Door* (New York: Appleton-Century-Crofts, Inc., 1947). O'Neil, Eugene, *Ah, Wilderness!* (New York: Random House, 1933). For additional references see *Reading Ladders in Human Relations,* Rev. ed. (Washington, D.C.: American Council on Education, 1949).

young people in other cultures that throw new light on our own ways of doing things.[6] Other social scientists have written biting commentaries upon the American scene, and although we may not agree with all they have to say, nevertheless their insights put new life into old familiar surroundings and jolt us to a sharper vision of the world around us.[7] While it is especially useful to read such commentaries now, early in a teaching career, it is equally important later to keep in touch with what is being written about the American scene. Teachers more than most others must keep abreast of what changing circumstances mean to those who are growing up. After all, the fact that "no one did that when I was a girl" does not mean that it is not accepted fashion now. The mores and attitudes of individuals in the modern world undergo very rapid change, and the teacher, dealing with the young year after year, must be particularly sensitive to changing patterns.

Collecting Personnel Information Preparatory to Counseling

Good counseling assumes knowledge of individuals. But if the high-school teacher has five classes a day, with a minimum of thirty students per class, there are 150 students to get to know each semester, perhaps as many as 300 a year. Now this seems like a staggering number, and indeed it is. Many teachers feel satisfied if they know the names of all their students and know something about a fraction of them. But to know them all intimately is just too much. Yet it has been suggested that one of the reasons why so many students do not like high school, and even drop out of school before they should, is that they feel completely overlooked as individuals.[8]

What is the solution? Some schools give a teacher a class for a two-hour period of time to assist in this process of getting to know the students. Other schools arrange for the teacher to review the cumulative records of all those assigned to his classes before the school year starts (though making even the briefest notes on 150 folders is no easy task). Moreover, teachers may consult school

[6] Mead, Margaret, *From the South Seas,* Studies of Adolescence and Sex in Primitive Societies (New York: William Morrow & Co., 1939).

———, *Male and Female* (New York: William Morrow & Co., 1949).

[7] Gorer, Geoffry, *The American People* (New York: W. W. Norton and Company, 1948).

Horney, Karen, *The Neurotic Personality of Our Times* (New York: W. W. Norton and Company, 1937).

West, James, *Plainville, USA* (New York: Columbia University Press, 1945).

[8] Jersild, Arthur T., *Children's Interests and What They Suggest for Education* (New York: Bureau of Publications, Teachers College, Columbia University, 1949), pp. 76 ff.

counselors to share the data they have collected on the students. Of course the counselors may not have full information about all students, but at least they can offer expert assistance to the teacher on the problems of particularly difficult students. The teacher probably must depend largely on his own resources for observation and analysis, especially in the case of the normal students, those who are not too brilliant, not too slow, not particularly outstanding, those who may get lost in the shuffle because they are so average.

In the first chapter we suggested that the teacher early develop the habit of keeping a personnel file of his own. A small loose leaf binder or a file drawer that holds medium-sized cards would be sufficient for the quick orientation to a new group of students. We recommend a form such as the following, which is easily duplicated:

Name Age

Special physical characteristics (i.e., too tall, short, fat, etc.)

Father's, mother's, occupations:

Test data: (IQ, Achievement, etc.)

School record:

Comments:

Such a brief form can be filled in by the teacher easily and quickly from office records and will give him a start in learning about his class. If the cumulative records indicate special abilities or disabilities, interests, and so on, then these have a place on the teacher's own file. As he gets acquainted with the class, he will want to jot down additional notes on student problems, things for him to watch in dealing with the student and his friends and school activities. As the teacher gets to know his class, he may not need to keep his file up to date, but such a file, started at the beginning of each semester, will go a long way in helping the teacher take the guidance approach to his students. He will know them as individuals, with special family backgrounds, special individual interests, talents, difficulties. Remember, too, that a careful inquiry among other teachers may help to fill in the blank spots.

In the first few days of establishing rapport with the class, a rich prior acquaintance with the students as individuals will help immeasurably. "Knowing the student's likes and dislikes beforehand permits one to establish rapport with him with surprising ease and at the same time enables one to see a deeper meaning in even the casual remarks of the chatting youngster." [9]

The Case Study

There is one especially good way in which teachers can learn about students in order to teach them. This is the *case-study approach* where not only the present status of a student is considered but his personal history and the probable developments in the future. On these three levels, information may be collected about the composition of the family, the family's socioeconomic status, and its social relationships; the qualities of the individual personality, the individual's status within the family, and among his peers; the facts of individual growth and development, the individual's maturity compared to neighborhood playmates and school classmates; the record of health and hygiene; the profile of in- and out-of-school aptitudes, interests, and achievements.

Why make a case study of a student? It takes considerable time and labor, and many teachers wonder if it is worth it. But for a new teacher the case study is an excellent device for becoming informed about the whys and wherefores of problem students. By this means he can often find a reason for behavior that otherwise is quite baffling, and, thus, having a reason, he is better able to work with the problem student in class. One or two case studies a year are a good guarantee of continuing awareness of the real-life situations of young people.

A simple duplicated form may be set up with key data-seeking questions. Suppose we illustrate in just two areas of investigation:

Family:

Where does the student live? Is the house on a par with those of his classmates? Does he have a room of his own? Does he live with his own father and mother?

Do both mother and father work? What do they do? How long has the father held his present job?

[9] Sheviakov, George, "The Necessity of Understanding the Adolescent as a Basis for Curriculum and Guidance," *Journal of the National Association of Deans of Women,* 5:7-12 (October, 1941).

Are there brothers and sisters? Do they live at home? What is his age in relation to them? If employed, what do they do?

What aspirations do father and mother have for their children? With whom does the family associate? What does the family do in its social associations? Are cultural interests encouraged: literature, drama, music, art?

Individual personality:

Do home, school, or youth groups to which he may belong report how he meets or evades his problems? Do they report frequent outbursts of rage or grief? Do they report aggressiveness, submissiveness, shyness, fearfulness? What do they report about strong likes, dislikes, persistent fantasies?

Does he have responsibilities in the family? Do the parents have decided ideas about his vocation? Does he agree? How do they feel about his abilities in comparison to his brothers and sisters? How does he feel about this comparison?

How many friends does he have in and out of school? How do they feel about him? What kind of gang does he belong to? What are his leisure time activities? What are his after-school or vacation jobs? How many hours a day does he work? Pay? What does he do with his money? What do his employers report about him? Does he like the job? Will the job help him make vocational decisions?

Obviously, gathering information in such intimate detail calls for great tact. Neither parents nor students welcome any suggestion of "noseyness." Much of the data cannot be gathered by direct questioning, but only through patient permissive interviews where the information eventually tumbles out. It is often difficult to avoid predisposition so that only wanted data are heard, or, at least, unwanted data are modified as they are recorded. Attitudes of censure and evidence of disapproval of accepted ways of living at a given social level, of course, quickly lead either to rejection of the interviewer or to cessation of the flow of information.

Interpreting Case-Study Findings

Once the data are gathered, the task of interpretation begins. What does all this mean anyway? What possible lines of action can be suggested? What sense can be made of these observations, interview materials, anecdotal records? The teacher needs a framework around which to group the data he has collected so that areas of disturbance, of need, or of conflict may be clearly discerned. A useful outline has been suggested by Prescott:

1. Organic factors that influence growth, development, and behavior:
    a. Health: disease history, corrected and uncorrected defects, nutrition, health habits.

   b. Characteristic rate of energy output; quality of physical endurance and recovery from fatigue.
   c. Growth history, present maturity level, and rate of growth.
   d. Skill in managing body; physical attractiveness.
2. Relationships to others, social roles, and family status:
   a. Social roles of family members in the community.
   b. Interpersonal relations within the family, past and present.
   c. Child's interaction and relations with peers.
   d. Child's interaction and relations with adults outside the family.
3. The child as a developing individual:
   a. Conceptions about physical and social processes; his attitudes toward them.
   b. Conceptions of aesthetic and ethnical principles; his attitudes toward them.
   c. Skill in using symbols in thinking and communication.
   d. Patterns of emotional behavior; situations that evoke them.
   e. Common defense mechanisms.
   f. Present adjustment problems.
   g. Developmental history and present developmental tasks.
   h. Basic evaluation of himself as a physical being, as an object of love, as a social being, and as an individual.
   i. Values and aspirations.
4. Summary: the child's major assets and needs:
   a. As a physical being.
   b. As to personal relations with others.
   c. As to social roles.
   d. As to experience, knowledge, and skills.
   e. As to attitudes, values, and aspirations.
   f. As to his evaluation of himself.
   g. In relation to his adjustment problems and developmental tasks.[10]

Sometimes after trying to organize the data around such an outline, the teacher may find he has ignored or omitted certain important areas, which need to be filled in. Once these areas are covered, there emerges a well-rounded picture of the individual. Then the teacher can see more clearly where the possible centers of trouble may lie: Is it in his relationship to his peers? In his evaluation of himself? In his lack of adequate adjustment techniques? Although the answers to these questions will still be tentative and in the nature of hypotheses, future counseling assistance will at least proceed on a somewhat more substantial basis. The teacher should then know the individual well enough to be able to help the individual know himself. In first attempts at interpreting case studies, beginning teachers can often obtain the assistance of trained counselors and experienced teachers.

[10] Commission on Teacher Education, *Helping Teachers Understand Children* (Washington: American Council on Education, 1945), pp. 431-432.

The real advantage of the case study is that it makes the individual teacher sensitive to the many factors that enter into the life pattern of any given youth. There is then less risk of making glib generalities: "Students from that part of town are just lazy and good-for-nothing"; or, "Boys who are smaller than the average are always trying to compensate for their height." A periodic recheck of the kind of informal appraisal of personality in which teachers indulge every day is probably very healthy; the case study is an essential tool in making such a recheck.

As a teacher-counselor, then, the individual teacher will have a somewhat different attitude toward the problems that students bring to him. As was indicated in the section on discipline in Chapter 13, discipline per se is only a convenient term for a way of handling certain kinds of problems—the surface ones, primarily. But when students have deeper, more personal kinds of problems, then the teacher must take a different point of view. As a matter of fact, some educators insist that if everyone had the guidance approach there would be very little need for discipline. This is an extreme position, but there is a grain of truth in it. When teachers are able to feel that problem behavior is not intended as an attack on them, but rather is evidence of insecurity, they are better able to handle it.

Who Should Counsel Whom?

Logically the question of who should counsel whom might have been one of the first raised in this whole area of counseling. Actually, only as teachers begin to face the real problems of their students does this nettlesome query arise: Am I the one who should consider *these* problems with *this* student? There is no clear-cut answer. In fact, there are many issues and problems still unresolved in this area. First, should teachers do any counseling? Second, if teachers (or counselors) accept the counseling responsibilities thrust upon them, should men and women take on, indiscriminately, all the behavior problems of boys and girls alike? Third, if the teacher does counseling, can he hope for success with those students who are causing him, and him alone, the greatest difficulty in classroom adjustment? Let us look at these three issues:

Should teachers do any counseling at all? It is almost impossible for good teachers to avoid requests for help, advice, and support in many personal problems. This does not mean that guidance experts, where such are available, might not be able to deal more adequately with many of these problems. Indeed, the whole growth of the professional counseling services in the public schools is a phenomenon that is most encouraging. Such experts have specialized training beyond that of the classroom teacher. Furthermore, since they have time to sit down with the individual student for relaxed, unhurried discussions of his problems, constructive solutions are more likely to emerge. The classroom teacher has such opportunities only as he takes them from his out-of-school time. It is sensible then for the beginning teacher to keep always in mind the very real limitations upon his ability to do the total counseling job. Where experts are available, they should certainly be used to the fullest. Unfortunately, in most high schools, the expert, when he is available at all, has a case load far above his capacity to handle. The great bulk of counseling, if it is to be done, must therefore still be carried by the classroom teacher.[11] (See pages 438–440 of this chapter for further discussion of the use of the expert.)

Are men teachers generally able to do a better counseling job with boys and women teachers with girls? There are certain sex-linked problems that a boy or girl would be most reluctant to discuss with an adult of the opposite sex who is a teacher-counselor. A teacher with insight and understanding, however, not only can, but will have to deal with the personal problems of both boys and girls. Being married often helps a teacher understand the personal problems faced by the opposite sex which previous experiences have usually blocked out. By and large boys share few things in the lives of girls and vice versa. Their experiences have been limited to those that concern their own sex most deeply, with only a limited and censored view of the other sex. When a woman teacher feels strongly that a boy in trouble would do better to talk with a man teacher or counselor, she should certainly feel free to suggest to a male colleague that the boy needs help.

Should a teacher try to act as a counselor with students whose problem appears to be most acute only in his classes? If a teacher observes that Susy is really unpleasant and rude in his class only, then it may be that the root of the trouble is a personality clash between them.

> After much trouble with Fred, Mrs. Drake was shocked one day when he suddenly got up, slammed down his books, and stalked out of the room, saying so all could hear, "I just can't stand this any

[11] A good review of the main arguments on both sides of this controversy may be found in the following two references: Chase, Elizabeth, "Oil and Water: Teaching and Guidance Can't Be Mixed," *Clearing House,* 25:210-211 (December, 1950). "Teaching and Guidance Can Be Mixed, A Symposium," *Clearing House,* 25:408-416 (March, 1951).

longer." Later when Mrs. Drake talked with the principal, she learned that Fred had flung himself into the principal's office saying he just had to be taken out of her class. The principal, a patient and understanding person, let Fred talk. After much preliminary letting off of steam, during which time the principal did not try to argue with the student or make any judgmental remarks, Fred finally said, "You know, I think it is because Mrs. Drake is so much like my mother, and I am always in hot water at home. I just hate women teachers." After another half-hour or so of talk, Fred had uncovered much of his own problem and had stated a solution of his own: he would like a few days out of class—he would study the assignments and do the work—and then he would return and behave better, since he saw the problem better himself. The principal relayed the substance of the discussion to Mrs. Drake who was interested and relieved. A later interview and visit with Fred's parents also helped to give insight into Fred's situation; a competing sister also made him resent women. The principal told the P.E. teacher, who was able to give Fred a job as assistant to the student athletic manager in charge of equipment and shower room. This contact with older men and his own male peers did much to help Fred accept the women in his world.

Another case, very similar to this, was reported by a teacher. Here the man teacher had evidently antagonized a girl in his class to such a point that the girl's whole life was being dominated by this one conflict. So critical had this become that the parents finally transferred the girl to another school. Some behavior problems do arise out of this kind of personality clash, and in such cases the aid of another member of the staff may have to be enlisted to gain insight and help.

Finding the Time for Counseling Interviews

Assuming that the teacher has a genuine interest in becoming a counselor-teacher, the problem of finding time for counseling must still be faced. Some teachers are able to use the minutes before and after school for this purpose. Too often, however, before school the teacher is engaged in last-minute preparations. If there is to be a motion picture that day, he must check the projector schedule; see that the motion picture has arrived and tend to countless other small details—perhaps a committee meeting to attend, or book or magazine orders to arrange, or reading material to distribute. These many details may interfere with the preschool half-hour, and thus for many teachers it is wisest to leave it free for last minute replanning.

Many high schools gather the students from a wide radius. Students may arrive by bus just a few moments before the bell and leave just after the last bell rings. In many schools, from one half to two thirds of the student body are immediately excluded from such after- or before-school conference time.

Lunch time? Ah, here is another free period. But teachers, like all other workers, appreciate a few moments of peace and quiet in the middle of the day. Often the lunch hour is only a half or three quarters of an hour, so that even a hurried lunch leaves little time. The teacher's free period? Well, teachers treasure their free period for grading papers, preparing tests, planning for the next day, arranging for films, seeing the principal about some problem. If the teacher can make use of none of these few brief out-of-class hours, arranging for a conference may be difficult indeed.

Even if the proper time is found, there is another problem. Students may be suspicious and on the defensive when called for a special interview by a teacher. "I must have done something wrong" is the first reaction. This natural suspicion can be allayed by rather simple devices. First, the teacher can announce early in his acquaintance with the class that he hopes before the first month is out to have an individual conference with each student, and for that reason he wants to have them fill out a form, such as the accompanying one.

Name:

Class schedule:	*Period*	*Teacher*	*Room*
	1st		
	2nd		
	etc.		

Which of the following times would be best for you if we could schedule a conference at that time?

1. Before school
2. Lunch hour
3. After school
4. Study hall (Hour Room)

On the basis of this information, the teacher can set up a schedule for his students. This record, kept for each student and, if necessary, pasted on the back of his personnel card as described on page 418, will give the teacher a rapid method for getting in touch with any student for special conferences at the time best suited to the student.

A scheduled conference with each and every class member would, of course, require many more hours than any teacher would have. Two alternatives are suggested:

1. Make an assignment early in the semester that requires library research. Arrange for two-thirds of the class to go at one time, and use the class period to interview the other one third.

2. Have the class work in groups during the class hour on projects that will not necessitate every member contributing, and then call to the desk for individual conferences as many students as the time permits.

Finding the Place for Counseling Interviews

If in-class conferences are attempted, several important questions immediately arise. If the teacher is talking with one student, won't there be a hazard of class disorder because his attention will be diverted? Indeed, this will be highly probable unless the teacher has set the stage for the procedure ahead of time. It is important to explain to the class that this disorder is exactly what may happen and that their cooperation is expected, and then to ask them what they think they might do. One factor that will favor the teacher is that, by and large, students respond well to such personal attention. They feel that it is valuable to them, and to the degree that they respect the activity that is going on, they are likely to give the teacher the desired cooperation. Of course, a teacher would be unwise to have such conferences when the class for some reason or other was very excited. For example, the best intentions in the world will not keep a class quiet and orderly on the day of a big game. Such a day demands whole group activity where the attention of the class can be obtained and directed to some expressive activity.

What about being overheard by other class members? A student may be very happy to have a teacher help him with personal problems, but he will not be likely to appreciate an audience of his contemporaries. Some classrooms are entirely too small for any such private discussion. In that case, the teacher should not attempt in-class conferences. He will find that students freeze up and are offended if he seems to ask for private information. The teacher should be very alert to whether the student thinks others can hear what he says.

> Mr. Phillips has his desk at an angle in the corner; on the left, toward the class, he has a three-drawer file. This file gives the desk corner a sort of cozy air; he even has an ivy plant growing luxuriantly on top.

> There are no student desks directly in line with this file since the desk has been placed so far in the corner. However, any student talking to him has to sit behind the file drawer, almost hidden from view by his classmates and with his back toward them. Mr. Phillips can then look over the student's head toward the rest of the class and yet not detract from the kind of semiprivate atmosphere that this desk and file arrangement has provided.

Often, if the teacher's desk is placed at the back of the room, the teacher can assist the feeling that the student is not being watched or listened to by his classmates. Arranging the seats in the class to leave quite a wide aisle around the desk helps. The teacher, of course, must be careful to talk in low tones directly to the student so that only the student can hear him.

Should all teachers conduct in-class interviews? Some teachers may object that such interviewing actually does not affect the kind of teaching they are doing. For example, can the teaching of mathematics be affected by students' personal problems? Yes, indeed! Knowing how a student feels about mathematics, finding out that he has a hobby that could be greatly improved by mathematical skill, learning that his father is very violent on the subject of his mastering mathematics, or that his mother always tells him that no one in their family can do mathematics—such insights into individuals can go a long way toward making mathematics more effectively taught. The same kind of insight will be of aid to any teacher of any subject.

The Interview: Getting Acquainted

The get-acquainted interview as described and recommended here should be simple and exploratory in nature. It is not aimed at therapy. It is aimed at establishing rapport, indicating the interest of the teacher in the student, and gaining some insight into the student as a person. The kinds of questions that might be asked are—

1. Well, John, is history one of your favorite subjects? What are your favorite subjects? Which ones do you do best in? Do you know why you do better in them than in others?
2. What hobbies do you have?
3. Do you work after school? Have any home chores?
4. What do you like best about school? Are you in any of the clubs, teams, or other groups?
5. What do you want to do after you graduate? What does your family think you should do? [This question leads to questions about family or guardians if the student is not living with his family. The teacher should

be careful not to probe; if the student is resistant then it is wisest to go on to the next question.]

6. Have you had any problems so far in the work that we have done in this class?

A structured interview like the above, where certain questions are asked in a certain order, will help, first, to establish rapport, second, to lead naturally into areas of significance for the teacher. It ends naturally on a nonpersonal basis so that the student feels that he has not told too much about himself. The actual questions should not be in front of the teacher. He would do well to memorize them or to have a card with a little key on it to remind him of the sequence of questions. Should he take notes on what he is told? Some students might object, but if the teacher jots down clearly for the student to see only a few such words as "paper boy after school," "prefers science fiction magazines," "has trouble with spelling scientific names," then the student will feel more secure and more willing to talk to the teacher in later, more crucial situations.

The Interview: Meeting Personal Adjustment Problems of Students

Now let us look at interviews that are required for the trouble spots in education. The teacher who finds students who are unable or unwilling to adjust to the school pattern will feel called upon to talk with the student. Yet—

> . . . there is a limiting factor to a teacher's success in an extraclass interview. The actual situation in which the troublesome or significant behavior occurred usually has a very different connotation to all the persons involved than the interview situation in which that behavior is being examined in retrospect. The dynamics in each situation are quite different. It is one thing to be successful in dealing with a child in a face-to-face interview; it is quite another thing to be successful in dealing with that child's troublesome behavior at the moment it is occurring within the classroom.[11]

What happens in the interview between teacher and student may go a long way toward assisting the student to make a more adequate in-class adjustment, but, as the quotation above suggests, often the classroom conditions are still such as to interfere with maximum adjustment. The use of the counseling interview to help a student behave in a more acceptable manner should therefore not be overstressed, nor should too much be expected. After all, if a student is a troublemaker because the other students tease him

[11] Madigan, Betty, and Mary Louise Steadman, "Accepting and Clarifying the Child's Feelings," Chap. 18, *Fostering Mental Health in Our Schools.* 1950 Yearbook, Association for Supervision and Curriculum Development (Washington, D. C.: The Association, 1950), p. 301.

about his family, helping the student see this will still not stop the teasing. The teacher has an obligation, it is true, to help the student see his situation and gain insight into what is occurring, but many of the provocative factors will be beyond the control of the individual student.

The teacher may find that the problem really is rooted in an impossible family relationship, in a physical-growth problem, in a neighborhood gang—problems that the teacher may not be able to deal with at all. In such a case, what should the teacher do? Obviously call on those agencies and facilities that can attack such problems. What these agencies and facilities are will be discussed later and elaborated upon in other sections. The important point here is that the teacher should not put all his trust in an interview or series of interviews. While a useful tool when skillfully utilized, the interview is as limited as any other technique in total solution of problems of students.

Why Interviews Fail

Before we examine some illustrative interviews, we need to re-emphasize that the interview intended primarily to coerce is bound to fail as an effective counseling instrument. Obviously the student does not want to be coerced. The teacher has his ego involved and usually is going to "tell the student just what he had better do." So the atmosphere is far from conducive to a real understanding of why the student caused the trouble. In order, therefore, for counseling to work, the teacher might very well wait until several days have elapsed after a problem incident has occurred, and then call the student in at a time and place convenient for uninterrupted conversation. By this time both student and teacher have re-evaluated their own roles in the problem. If the teacher has used the time wisely, he has checked office records thoroughly about the individual student in order to see if any light can be thrown on the specific difficulty. Perhaps the most unwise thing a teacher can say, after a student has been particularly difficult and after many warnings, is "Well, John, you had better stay after school this evening; it seems that you and I had better have a little talk." Such little talks are usually doomed to failure. How would a better approach sound?

Situation: Barbara has consistently "forgotten" her assignments. Whenever any homework is due, she does not turn it in on time and often fails to turn it in at all if no class time is provided for her to do it. Because she has not done the work she is not informed about the topics the class discusses; so she is very bored; in her boredom she constantly tries to distract the attention of her nearest classmates by chattering, sending notes, turning around in her seat. Miss Cohen has tried to help her and has often had to reprimand her for interrupting. One such incident occurred on Wednesday. Barbara was acting worse than usual and Miss Cohen in desperation asked her to go to the library and complete the last three assignments. For the next several days Barbara has behaved well in class, but still has failed to turn in her classwork.

Miss Cohen says, on the following Monday: "Barbara, I noticed on your program that you have study period right after lunch when I have my free period. Could you meet me here so that we could go over some of these long lost assignments?"

Barbara acquiesces; the problem that she faces has not been ignored—the teacher could not pretend that she just wanted to have a little talk with Barbara, because they are both too aware of the area of trouble. But Miss Cohen has been very careful not to call Barbara in for a conference until the situation between them is as calm and pleasant as possible.

Counseling in Action: Some Typical Interviews

What does the teacher do in an interview with a student? There are two schools of thought here. One approach may be to quickly tell the student how you understand his problem, outline what you consider it to be, and give him direct instruction about what to do. This kind of directive counseling has the advantage of being less time consuming. Furthermore, the student is not uncertain about what is known about him and what is expected of him. However, the method has definite limitations, some of which we will discuss below. The other approach, the nondirective, is a more subtle kind of counseling. Here the teacher merely expresses to the student a feeling that perhaps the student has a problem. The student is encouraged through *interest* and relative *silence* on the part of the teacher to talk about the problem. The teacher gives no judgment regarding what the student says, merely reflects back to the student whatever feeling-tone is manifest. This is intended to allow the student to recognize his problem himself and propose his own solution. We will develop this type of interviewing in more detail below.

Now we are ready to dissect actual conference situations. In the following pages are illustrative interview excerpts,[12] showing good and poor techniques in counseling with students. These are given

[12] Some of the descriptive categories and portions of the conversations are taken by permission of the publisher from: Arbuckle, Dugald S., *Teacher Counseling* (Cambridge, Mass.: Addison-Wesley Press, Inc., 1950), pp. 52–68.

in detail, with analytic commentaries because, as we have stated, the interview is central to all counseling. Skill in interviewing must be learned as one learns any other of the skills that contribute to effective teaching.

The descriptions that follow contrast various types of interviewing approaches and indicate throughout the nondirective, permissive approach to the same problem. The kinds of interview attitudes illustrated, which *do not* result in better student adjustment, are—

1. The disciplinarian.
2. The judge.
3. The moralist.
4. The wishful thinker.
5. The helper.
6. The prober.

In reading these descriptions, it is important to note those words and phrases that contribute to rapport and those that interfere with it; those phases that indicate genuine interest in helping the student understand and solve his own problem; and those that make the student feel helpless and at fault.

Now let us look at these sample interviews.

1. The Disciplinarian

TEACHER: I don't think you have been working as we expect students to work in this class.

STUDENT: I don't know what you mean.

TEACHER: You know very well what I mean; look, here is my roll book. Let me see: No report for last Friday, last Wednesday, the exam—you were absent that day and didn't make it up. You realize this behavior is not acceptable.

The student is being "put on the spot." The teacher is trying to get the student in a corner, with all the advantage on the side of the teacher. If and when the teacher ever gets around to discovering why this series of events occurred, the student will be upset, angry, resentful. Punishment is usually the only outcome of this approach.

Teacher-Counselor

TEACHER: I asked you to stay after school for a few minutes because of your work recently.

STUDENT: I know, I haven't done any, have I? (defiant)

TEACHER: You know what the problem is. . . .

STUDENT: Yeah, I never get my work in. I don't like to do it, it. . . .

TEACHER: Uh, huh. . . .

Here the teacher makes the preamble as short as possible, speaks mildly and unemotionally, does not try to interrupt the student, but rather encourages the student to talk about the central problem that is of first concern. Later some other aspects of this problem will appear, but the teacher lets the student tell what he will in his own fashion, following his own pattern.

2. *The Judge*

STUDENT: I just can't do geometry.

TEACHER: The real trouble is that you waste all your time.

STUDENT: I really try.

TEACHER: You might try, but you don't concentrate when you do. I bet you have the radio on all the time. This is not a good way to study.

STUDENT: But I. . . .

TEACHER: Now, no buts. . . .

No sympathy expressed. The teacher knows much better than the student what his trouble is. There is condemnation without inquiry, without listening to what the student has to say. The student feels on trial; he is always on the defensive with such a teacher; his answers are typically started with "But, I . . ." and he rarely has a chance to finish them. The teacher creates the impression that he is all-knowing, the expert, the superfather.

Teacher-Counselor

STUDENT: I just can't do geometry.

TEACHER: You feel you just can't do geometry . . . .

STUDENT: I don't know. Sometimes I think I am just dumb. My mother tells me I am dumb all the time. I bet she is right.

TEACHER: Your mother tells you you are dumb, . . .

STUDENT: Yeah . . . .

TEACHER: Uh huh . . . .

STUDENT: Yeah . . . but I don't think I am. Anyway, I'm not dumb like old Fatso Grooby—now he's a real stupe. Why do you know . . . .

The teacher reflected back the student's feeling; often this is done in the identical words that the student uses, but the tonal inflection indicates no judgment, no feeling on the part of the teacher, merely interest, slight solicitude perhaps, and often a slightly higher pitch, a slight questioning tone, is an assistance in such an interview situation. Here the student responds well; he is beginning to reveal his feelings about himself, his capacities, his reactions to others. Soon the teacher will have built up a great deal of insight into the problem.

3. *The Moralist*

STUDENT: What do you think I should do?

TEACHER: Well, you are the one that really has to make the decision. You have to be able to face these things and decide for yourself. Later in life no one is

The moralist cannot resist telling the student how to behave in life. He is ready with aphorisms and value judgments for every occasion. He is so full of moral wisdom that no student would willingly come to him with a con-going to make decisions for you.

STUDENT: Well, I wish you would help me.

TEACHER: As I said, you must make your own decisions. Now I think the best thing to do is drop the geometry and take study hall this semester, and then take typing next year.

fession of antisocial behavior in order to get help. This teacher would merely make the students' guilt worse without helping him out of his dilemma. The moralist must give advice because he *knows* he is right.

Teacher-Counselor

STUDENT: What do you think I should do?

TEACHER: You feel that you need help in deciding . . . .

STUDENT: Yeah, I am sort of uncertain myself, and anyway . . . .

TEACHER: Uh huh . . . .

STUDENT: Now I could change majors, couldn't I? But my folks would have a fit. I don't know—if I fail geometry it might even be worse. Is it possible to drop a course?

TEACHER: Yes.

STUDENT: Now maybe if I do that, by next year I can convince Dad I just can't go to college . . . I just hate going to college; we fight about it at home all the time. Dad is so stubborn sometimes; sometimes I think if someone from school could tell him what I can do . . . .

TEACHER: You feel we could tell your father something you can't get across to him . . . .

Notice how the teacher made no judgment at all about what the student said. He recognized the student's feeling of uncertainty; and yet underneath it the student was able to see possible alternatives; even more, an insight has been gained into the real dynamics of the student's problem; it rests with the father, in part. An opening has been given for the school to work directly with the parent in the solution of the student's problem.

4. The Wishful Thinker

STUDENT: I get so worried about not doing well.

TEACHER: Now let's not worry about such things; I am sure everything will turn out all right.

STUDENT: I just feel so blue sometimes and there are so many problems.

TEACHER: Now, now, everything will be all right; we can't let ourselves worry about everything you know; that just makes it worse.

The constant optimist, the wishful-thinker type does not want to admit that things are bad, or cruel, or hopeless, or difficult. Let's all look at the sunny side. Sometimes this type is the jovial, back-slapper, booster kind of person. From him no real counsel is available because he is so aggressively cheery. He sounds patronizing and he usually is. After several such cheery interviews, the student will quickly close up and evade the teacher—"if I feel blue I don't want someone to tell me I don't or shouldn't."

Teacher-Counselor

STUDENT: I get so worried about not doing well.

TEACHER: You are worried about your own success . . . .

STUDENT: Well, yes and no. I don't think it is all my fault. It's these darned depressions I get into. I just want to cry and cry.

TEACHER: You feel like crying . . . .

STUDENT: (Voice shakes) And I do, and I know I am a big sissy; there isn't anything wrong. (Student cries.)

TEACHER: You feel ashamed because you cry for no good reason.

STUDENT: Yeah . . . . Do you think everyone feels this way?

TEACHER: You feel different from other boys and girls.

Again, we can note the way the teacher resists the impulse to sympathize or reprimand. One of the real dangers of this kind of counseling, however, is that students will cry, will get emotional, because this sort of counseling recognizes the real emotions of individuals. The teacher develops skill in meeting these situations —not by getting alarmed, or being sympathetic and saying, "Now, now, Susy, there isn't anything to cry about," but, as the teacher above, merely recognizes that the student has a real trouble here and brings the conversation back to the problem.

5. The Helper

TEACHER: Now you just tell me what is bothering you and I bet I can help you out.

STUDENT: Oh, I don't think anyone can help me. . . .

TEACHER: Now you know we teachers are very happy to do anything we can.

STUDENT: Well, it's that science class. I don't get along with Mr. Dipple. Would you get me changed?

TEACHER: Well, now. . . .

The helper wants to shoulder everyone's burdens; and, as in this case, if the offer of help is taken seriously, the teacher may be in a very bad spot. Often the teacher can really do nothing. The student learns to distrust the offers of help and to suspect that teachers don't mean what they say. Offering to help out leaves the student just as dependent as ever. We need to help young people solve their own problems, rather than solving them for them.

Teacher-Counselor

TEACHER: You want me to help you, Jane?

STUDENT: Well, not exactly. I wish I could get out of this mess myself . . . .

TEACHER: You feel you are in a mess . . . .

STUDENT: (Bursts out) I just hate Mr. Dipple, and I know he hates me.

TEACHER: Uh huh . . . .

STUDENT: He is pretty nice to me, and all that, but those worms and things just give me the creeps.

TEACHER: You feel Mr. Dipple is really all right.

STUDENT: Oh, he is O.K. I guess; I get upset every time I see a worm. Do you think he'd let me off if I explained how they made me feel?

Here the teacher does not offer help, but indicates a recognition of the students need, and, as actually can be seen, the student doesn't want help, but wants clarification. By the end of the conversation, the student has pinned down the problem to her own feelings; has even outlined a possible action.

6. The Prober

TEACHER: Tell me, Agnes, are you sure you are happy at home?

STUDENT: Well, O.K. I guess.

TEACHER: Now be honest; do you get along well with your parents?

STUDENT: Oh, I don't know.

TEACHER: Now we can't get anywhere unless you tell me about yourself. Have you always been moody?

STUDENT: No, just recently and that is why I guess I seem to moon about in class.

TEACHER: Well, now we are getting someplace. You must have some worries you aren't telling me about.

There is a great temptation on the part of some teachers to pry personal information out of the students. But students, like anyone else, protect their own personal lives. This should be respected. The direct attack, as noted here, brings out resistance; this girl is not going to tell anyone anything. The teacher pounces on each new bit of information; even accuses the student of being bad because information is withheld. In this kind of interview no information that the student is not freely willing to give should be deliberately sought.

Teacher-Counselor

TEACHER: Agnes, I have noticed you have been sort of day dreaming in class . . .

STUDENT: Yes, I guess I have.

TEACHER: Do you want to tell me about it?

STUDENT: Gosh, what is there to tell?

TEACHER: You feel the daydreaming is your own problem.

STUDENT: Heck, it doesn't bother anyone else.

TEACHER: Uh huh . . . .

STUDENT: (Long silence) No one ever noticed before.

TEACHER: Uh huh . . . .

STUDENT: (Long silence) There are so many things on my mind. . . . (Bursts out) You know, my parents are going to get a divorce.

TEACHER: You think about your home problem in class . . . .

Another pattern of counseling can be seen here: The student does not want to talk, but the teacher feels an important problem is present. The teacher *allows* the student to remain silent, but indicates interest and no impatience. The feeling conveyed by the teacher is that the student doesn't have to talk at all if he doesn't want to, but here is someone interested in him. It is interesting to note that the student shows some surprise that anyone did notice the behavior. And underlying the symptom is the real cause, which the probing teacher above will never uncover.

Other Counseling Errors

There are other ways, in addition to those just discussed, in which teachers betray the counseling function. There is the teacher who is always in a great hurry; if he talks to a student he fiddles nervously with a pencil, jumps up, looks at his watch, talks briskly, and tries to rush the student along. The student quickly feels that this teacher is only pretending interest, but really has far more important things to do than talk with him. Then the student retreats into his own shell. It is also a serious error to forget the purpose for calling in a student. For example, George appears after school, and Miss Drew looks up, startled, and says, "Did you want something, George?" He replies, "Gosh, didn't you tell me to come in to see you?" What a dash of cold water this is, when the student felt that at last he could obtain a real hearing for his difficulty. Sometimes the teacher finds students coming to him for help of their own volition. To express surprise, resentment, or displeasure at this show of student initiative will kill it in the bud. If the teacher is genuinely busy and cannot talk with the student, a simple statement should be made: "You feel you would like to talk to me, Sam. I won't have the time this afternoon, but let's set a date when we can get together." And an appointment is made then and there, so that the teacher preserves the student initiative for their later interview.

The Nondirective Approach

Let us review what the teacher-counselor was doing in the situations described earlier. The kind of interviewing that was recorded was nondirective in the sense that the teacher encouraged the student to talk as he wished, without attempting to force the student into any preconceived mold or to impose his own ideas and wishes upon him.

Many counselors do not utilize nondirective techniques because of different purposes for the guidance interview, the different outcomes sought, and a different philosophy of guidance. It is suggested here, however, that the classroom teacher probably is best in the guidance function when using the nondirective approach. Of course no one method will fit all individuals. This approach is emphasized here because it is not discussed in much of the literature about teacher counseling. Furthermore, the nondirective approach is somewhat contrary to our usual experience. We are used to being told. As teachers, unfortunately, we are tempted to repeat the pattern. Yet, much of the research in the field demonstrates that when someone is told to do something, he is as likely as not, not to do it. If he makes up his own mind to an action, he is likely to follow through on it. This is the emphasis of nondirective counseling; to promote as many self-decisions as possible, so that the individual is better able to direct his own destiny than before, rather than still be dependent on outside experts.

Some Hazards to Prepare For

The nondirective approach is recommended as most useful to the teacher in the long run, but there are certain hazards in its use that must be anticipated. First, students are not used to such treatment. The result may be more than the teacher bargained for.

> Mr. Gray was just learning how to conduct a nondirective interviewing session. Maryann, who seemed like a very sweet and normal girl, was his first subject. He started by asking her how she liked school. The rapidity with which disturbing material was poured forth startled him. Maryann liked school but was very upset about the high standards she must attain. Her family was pushing her. In the previous school she had attended, success had been easy. In this school, things were much harder, she felt, and it had gotten so that she was almost sick every time she faced a quiz or test. As she went on, her hands got tense, her face became pale, and in a few moments she started to weep violently. Mr. Gray floundered around with words of sympathy, and finally Maryann calmed.

Not only are students unused to such treatment, but teachers as well are shocked by the quick revelation of personal trouble, often accompanied by high emotionality. The consequences may be damaging. The student may bitterly regret having poured out his soul, feel guilty and resentful toward the teacher who let him do it. While individuals appreciate the release of the counseling situation, it is often their first impulse to avoid forevermore the individual to whom they were so revealing. For this reason, the student's teacher may well avoid allowing the student to go too far in a nondirective interview. Gently guiding the student away from personal revelation that may be too damaging, by terminating the interview kindly because of time factors or by referring the student to someone else as soon as it seems a really deep problem exists in the student, will help protect both the student and the teacher.

The emotional impact on the recipient of such confidence must not be underestimated. People who work constantly in such roles as counselors, psychiatrists, and the like, find it emotionally very exhausting. For the same reason, teachers who are under constant emotional challenge from the classroom situation itself, need to watch carefully that excessive demands are not made as a result of such interviewing. The teacher himself may get involved in the student's problem emotionally by being the listener in the interview. This is unfair to the student and can be very destructive of further growth in self-direction on the part of the student.

Another word of caution: the nondirective interview may produce from the student material that only a clinical counselor is equipped to handle or to understand. By allowing such material to be revealed, the teacher may produce more trouble in the student because he allowed the real problem to emerge and then was unable to give the student support in facing it. For this reason the teacher who develops skill in nondirective interviewing would be well advised to watch for danger signals: excessive emotionality on the part of the student, sudden blocks in talking, uninterrupted monologues where the student can't seem to stop himself. The classroom teacher should not try to perform deep therapy. This takes highly skilled and trained individuals. The teacher, however, by showing the kind of insight that nondirective counseling demands, by having the attitude of permissiveness and faith in the individual's ability to find his own solution to his own problem, can do a great deal to help most normal students meet their problems.

Nondirective interviewing requires considerable practice. In order to gain insight into the dynamics of this kind of interviewing, to realize its values as well as the pitfalls, beginning teachers should try out the technique in noncounseling situations. Nondirective interviewing may be used in the gathering of various sorts of opinion. There will be no danger of intruding into the individual's personal life and creating situations that the neophyte interviewer could not handle. But at the same time such practice helps the beginner to concentrate on the feeling tone of the statements that are made, to develop the ability to listen in a neutral fashion, and to acquire the skill needed to close such an interview at the proper time with good rapport. Tape recording of interviews for post-interview analysis is an excellent technique; mistakes made by the interviewer can then be detected and understood.

The Specialist Is Your Ally

We have stressed thus far in this chapter, the role of the teacher in the counseling process and have shown why it is that the counseling burden must inevitably fall upon the classroom teacher. It is, however, highly important that the teacher realize his own limitations in working with individuals and know who is available in his immediate school or in the larger community to assist students. If he is fortunate enough to be in a high school with an enrollment of 750 or more students,[13] he may find a full-time counselor on the staff. In schools of smaller enrollment—making up the bulk of our high schools, incidentally—he may find part-time counselors or none at all. Where there are full-time counselors, the guidance office can provide the teacher with much helpful information about his students and can be utilized for referral of difficult cases. The teacher will want to investigate the total guidance program in his school in order to know exactly what kinds of help are provided, since these vary considerably from school to school.

Furthermore, the teacher will want to check the resources and personnel of the following kinds of school and community specialists:

1. Welfare and attendance personnel. This office will typically be concerned with truancy, drop-outs, and special problems of youngsters that may prevent their regular attendance at school.

2. School social workers. This specialist, sometimes known as the "visiting teacher," has the responsibility of linking school and community services, obtaining the help of community agencies where needed, gathering home data for school use, and in some cases doing tutorial teaching in the home for convalescent students.

3. Child guidance clinics. Here the teacher will usually find a team composed of a psychiatrist, two or more psychologists, several specially trained social workers, psychometrists, and other special personnel in the field of counseling. Some of these clinics are associated with school systems in larger and wealthier communities. More often they are operated by governmental units or privately supported agencies. There are far too few of these excellent institutions to meet the great need for specialized help for children and youth.

4. Family agencies and other social agencies. In most medium-sized and all large-sized communities there is an intricate network of social agencies dealing with many facets of family and child needs. Foster-home placement bureaus, detention homes, family service agencies, county welfare departments, welfare agencies organized by local church groups, and the Salvation Army Homes for unwed mothers—these and countless other agencies should be canvassed by the teacher so that he can, as occasion arises, refer individuals to them for help that the school cannot—and probably should not—provide.

5. Special classes and schools. Finally, there are both public and private agencies specially organized to care for the needs of individuals handi-

[13] *High School Staff and Size of School,* U.S. Office of Education. Circular No. 317 (Washington, D.C.: Government Printing Office, 1949).

capped by physical or emotional problems. Where these are, who can be admitted, and what services are given should be known by the teacher, who can then pass on this information to those who may need it.

It is unfortunately only too true that all the services mentioned above are only staffed and financed to meet the most acute needs. It is also true that those who need such services most usually do not know that they are available. The individual classroom teacher is in a very strategic position to bridge this gap between the agency and the individual, since the school will have almost all the children of most of the people—with their many problems. In orienting himself to his community, then, the new teacher will want to make a special inquiry into the agencies and services mentioned above; he will find such information invaluable in emergencies.

Summary

To recapitulate, we have seen how extensive the responsibility of the teacher is for the individual guidance of the adolescent. The major stress in this chapter has been upon the most effective method of talking with adolescents. These principles should guide the teacher:

1. Establish rapport: have a genuine feeling of friendliness and interest in your students.
2. Let them know what you as an individual teacher can do for them: don't attempt to do too much or claim that you can be of no help whatsoever.
3. Seek out those who need help but do not know it or are too shy or frightened to come for help.
4. Look for problems in all areas of adolescent growth: merely because a student is doing adequate work academically, do not assume that there are no important problems of personal adjustment.
5. Show no shock, no matter what the problem is they want to talk about. Be as matter of fact and objective as possible.
6. Let them talk.
7. Let the student formulate his own solution with your aid; don't take over and give the answers merely because you can analyze the problem so much more quickly; your solution may be very far from the student's own solution.
8. Be content with slow progress, and in some cases with no progress at all.
9. Be concerned with underlying causes, not merely immediate behavior.
10. Call upon specialists to help you.

Besides guidance on personal problems the teacher can offer other kinds of help to students. Group guidance, facing general problems with the whole class, is one source of assistance. This will be discussed in detail in the next chapter.

Selected References

Allen, Frederick H. *Psychotherapy with Children.* New York: W. W. Norton Company, 1942. Excellent presentation of the theory of nondirective therapy in the child-guidance clinic situation.

Arbuckle, Dugald S. "Good Counseling—What Is It?" *Educational Administration and Supervision,* 34:304 (May, 1948). A brief and pointed article.

Arbuckle, Dugald S. *Teacher Counseling,* Cambridge, Mass.: Addison-Wesley Press, Inc., 1950. Basic reference on technique of nondirective counseling in the teaching situation.

Bingham, W. V., and B. V. Moore. *How to Interview.* New York: Harper & Brothers, 1941. 3d rev. ed. A standard guide to all types of interview situations.

Brayfield, A. H. *Readings in Modern Methods of Counseling.* New York: Appleton-Century-Crofts, Inc., 1950. Essays by a wide range of experts on all facets of the counseling picture.

Cassidy, Rosalind, and Hilda Clute Kozman. *Counseling Girls in a Changing Society.* New York: McGraw-Hill Book Company, Inc., 1947. Developed in three main parts: orientation, adolescent girls, and counseling.

Erickson, Clifford E. *The Counseling Interview,* New York: Prentice-Hall, Inc., 1950. Excellent practical and detailed consideration given to all aspects of the interview process.

Keliher, Alice. "The Freedom to Be Different," *Child Study,* 28:3-5 (Spring, 1951). An important statement on one of the central needs of individuals; a crucial problem for adolescents particularly.

Newell, Nancy L. "Mental Health and Ill Health among Youth," *Understanding the Child,* 26:3-6 (January, 1947). Dramatically points out the need to be aware of the danger signs of personal maladjustment.

Rogers, Carl. *Counseling and Psychotherapy.* Boston: Houghton Mifflin Company, 1942. Basic text covering the theory of nondirective interviewing, with a verbatim case study analyzed in fascinating detail.

Snyder, William U. *Casebook of Non-directive Counseling.* Boston: Houghton Mifflin Company, 1947. A number of verbatim records analyzed in terms of the techniques of the counselor.

Student Counseling Bureau of the University of Minnesota. *The Counseling and Guidance Use of Test Scores.* Minneapolis: University of Minnesota Press, 1950. How test scores contribute to counseling when used correctly.

Taba, Hilda, *et al. Diagnosing Human-Relations Needs.* Washington, D.C.: American Council on Education, 1951. Describes such procedures as diaries, parent interviews, open questions, sociometry, and many others.

Wittenberg, R. M. *So You Want to Help People.* New York: Association Press, 1947. Chap. 7, "We Talk Too Much," pp. 98-110. This chapter presents a clear and practical picture of guidance with teen-age groups and individuals in an informal setting.

Wrenn, C. Gilbert, and Willis E. Dugan. *Guidance Procedures in High School.* Modern School Practices Series, No. 1. Minneapolis: University of Minnesota Press, 1950. Overview of what is being done today; shows what the beginning teacher can expect in the field.

19. Techniques of Group Guidance

SO FAR we have been concerned with the counseling of the individual. Now we must look at teacher counseling as a classroom method. The setting in which teachers can perform this kind of group guidance will vary with the school. But remember, every classroom or club situation is a human-relations laboratory and, as such, requires the sensitivity of one schooled in the guidance and counseling attitude. No teacher can be excused from this responsibility.[1] The important point here is that every teacher must be aware of, and sensitive to, the interpersonal aspects of the classroom, whether the subject being taught is mathematics, art, chemistry, or Spanish.

In this chapter we will be concerned primarily with how the teacher can work with the total class in developing personal understanding of the many aspects of adjustment faced by the adolescent. We will discuss the teacher in the homeroom where group guidance is planned for in the school program, the guidance possibilities of orientation courses, counseling as a general classroom method of

[1] Baxter, Bernice, "Getting Along Together," *NEA Journal,* 38:104-105 (February, 1950).

value in any subject field, and finally, the methods that the teacher may use in studying and understanding the interpersonal relationships of the classroom through the use of sociometry and related techniques.

Guidance in the Homeroom

The more formal setting for group guidance occurs in many high schools under the name "homeroom." This administrative device allows one teacher to take major responsibility for a group of thirty to thirty-five students. The teacher may meet with the group once a day for 20 to 30 minutes or several times during the week for an hour. During this homeroom period, the teacher is expected to carry out various routines in connection with arranging schedules, to check attendance and absence, to discuss student government and elections procedures. In addition, the homeroom is often designated as the guidance period, where the teacher is encouraged to discuss with the students the kinds of personal and group concerns that are not covered by standard curricular offerings. It is a place where the teacher seeks to understand better the personal life and problems of each individual. In one junior high school, for instance, the homeroom period for the ninth-grade group was divided by boys and girls. It was felt that much of the teasing and hostility between boys and girls that had tormented the faculty and administration over several years might be better handled if boys were under the guidance of men teachers and the girls under women teachers to discuss over the course of the year some of the heterosexual problems that become crucial at this age. The procedure worked quite well. There was a decrease in boy-girl unruliness. In other schools, it has proved better to keep the sexes together for discussion. Using the homeroom for this kind of help implies special group-guidance techniques. It is not advisable just to have a discussion about personal problems for the sake of discussion. Such a discussion must be specially planned and led with skill.

Several suggestions for such homeroom discussions may be offered. Fedder[2] suggests questionnaires of the students' problems as the basis for group guidance in either homeroom or club situations. For instance, if the group seems to be very interested in learning the proper etiquette for formal dances, then class time may be devoted to discussion of the many problems that arise when boy takes girl. Typically, students are worried over personal and

[2] Fedder, Ruth, *Guiding Homeroom and Club Activities* (New York: McGraw-Hill Book Company, Inc., 1949), pp. 411-448.

interpersonal problems (described on pages 453 and 454). These problems are central for the homeroom teacher.

The homeroom teacher may wish to call upon experts to deal with some of the problems raised. For instance, if there is a question of grooming, a home-economics teacher or a consultant in a local department store might be able to give the students some pointers on improving their personal appearance.

> Miss Snow and her eleventh-grade homeroom committee decided that one homeroom period might be devoted to hair styling. The boys could be brought in to represent the "male viewpoint." So many of the girls did not know what hair style was most attractive for their particular facial type that such a discussion would be very valuable. Miss Snow knew that one of the department stores in a near-by city had a very well informed hair stylist, who often addressed both school and club groups on this problem. The consultant was happy to come, at no charge, since it was considered good public relations by the store. After a very pleasant talk, the consultant asked if anyone would like to have her do over her hair. The girls were reticent, so Miss Snow suggested the consultant start in on her! With a few quick flashes of the brush, the consultant completely changed her hair. The students were amazed and delighted; this was so much more attractive! Miss Snow was a bit taken aback at first, but she has worn her hair that way ever since! The other girls were encouraged then to try to rearrange each other's hair, and the consultant went around the room helping them out. The boys judged the results, and everyone was quite pleased with the session.

Extensive utilization of student-teacher planning (see pages 93 to 96) in the homeroom program is recommended. No grade need be given, and a wide range of subject matter is available. Since the emphasis is on student interests and needs, students should play a major role in deciding the areas of concentration and the way they want to approach them.

What if students select an area in which the teacher feels very insecure? A typical area of this kind would be the problems of sexual adjustment, heterosexual relations, and the physiology of sex. More and more of the high schools today provide for instruction in the physiology of sex in either biology or hygiene courses. However, the growing adolescent has many other problems in this area that concern morality, emotional reactions, problems of marriage, and even child rearing. Rather than deny students an opportunity to gain adult guidance in this area where it is so sorely needed, the teacher who feels unable to lead such discussions should find someone who would do a good job and invite this person in to lead the class. Such a person may be a doctor, a counselor in a family service agency, or another teacher on the faculty. Possibly several of the above individuals could visit the class and answer the questions raised by the students. It would be wise to find what school policy is in such an area; some school systems forbid such instruction, while others make special provision for it. Certain church groups may wish their parishioners to be excused from discussions, and some parents may object. But since the majority of adolescents find sex-related problems most urgent, the teacher should try to meet this basic need in the best possible manner, whether he can carry the full burden or not.

Guidance in Orientation Courses

Some schools provide special courses known as "orientation courses," in which such problems constitute the course of study. Often these orientation courses are for entering freshmen, or, if there is a junior high school, for the sophomore group. Also, courses titled "Senior Problems," "Problems of Everyday Living," "Social Living," usually include large units of time devoted to student problems, similar to the homeroom. Some schools are suggesting that units concerned with student personal problems are of value in many regular subject-matter courses. For example, in tenth-grade English, in the San Diego, California schools, a unit entitled "Getting Along With Others" is recommended. The major topics included are—

1. How can teen-agers make and keep worth-while friendships?
   Developing an interest in others
   Developing social skills—conversation, letter writing, introductions
2. How can teen-agers learn to make and enjoy boy-girl friendships?
   Applying literature to your problems in getting along in boy-girl relations
   Enjoying boy-girl friendships
3. How can teen-agers maintain happy relationships with their families?
   Improving family relations in everyday situations
   Understanding the problems of growing up and your parents' point of view
   Appreciating your parents
   Getting along with your brothers and sisters
4. How can teen-agers learn to appreciate individual differences? [3]

The unit develops the major ideas that should be considered and then points out the literature that will supplement class discussion and provide a focus for such discussion. It is the guidance point

[3] San Diego City Schools, "An Experimental Resource Unit on Getting Along with Others," Grade X, Mimeo, San Diego City Schools, 1950.

of view that has influenced school systems to include such units of instruction. The movement for education for life adjustment[4] has as a basic premise that the content of classroom instruction must be widely re-evaluated in the light of the personal-social needs of adolescents in today's culture.

Developing the Classroom Guidance Situation

The kind of classroom atmosphere under which group guidance takes place most effectively is developed by following much the same procedure set up for the democratic classroom (see Chapter 3). However, these criteria need further amplification here. To carry on adequate group guidance, the teacher must have greater than average ability to create a permissive atmosphere, that is, one in which the teacher actively accepts the way students feel, think, and behave without censure or judgment or disapproval.

> The class was discussing the assignment for the next day. Sidney burst out with: "Aw, I think the old windbag who wrote this book sure must have been a dope." The teacher, instead of chiding him for such an attitude, said instead: "You feel this book isn't very interesting." Susan chimed in: "It is so dull, Miss Andrews." Other students entered the discussion, many expressing similar opinions, with Miss Andrews merely nodding, listening, helping those talk who felt they wanted to, until the class had exhausted its comments about the book and the assignment. The group then rather cheerfully went back to the original assignment and carried on a lively and friendly discussion about the major ideas to be sought in the next chapter. The teacher had used the occasion of Sidney's remark to let the students get rid of some of their antagonisms without scolding them for holding undesirable attitudes; as a result, the class was much better able to continue with the expected work.

The opportunities for group guidance are abundant if the teacher is aware of the feeling tone of a student's remark. In the incident cited above, Miss Andrews could easily have stopped Sidney, prevented any further class comment, and continued with the assignment procedure. But the class would have had all their original feelings about the assignment bottled up inside them. Had a number of students failed to complete the assignment it would have been easily traced to the refusal of the teacher to let them express and face their own negative feelings. As it was, merely listening to their comments in no way meant that the teacher agreed with them; it merely meant that she respected their having such feelings. Her attitude said, in essence: "I understand that many of you may feel a

[4] See Douglass, Harl, *Education for Life Adjustment* (New York: Ronald Press Company, 1950).

dislike for the task at hand. I think it is all right for people to feel that way. We have a job to do here, however, which we can do better together if we understand and respect each other's feelings about it." Thus the class was able to move back to the original assignment without any resentments.

The principles for leading such a discussion with a whole group are much the same as those for individual nondirective counseling.

1. The leader's comments are basically reflections and clarifications of the expressed feelings of the speaker, or a comment which indicates an understanding and acceptance of the feeling.

2. If a student does not wish to speak, he is not pressed to join the conversation.

3. If the conversation lags, the teacher does not direct the thinking of the students in the "right" channels.

4. The leader at no time criticizes, moralizes, or acts as judge.

5. The atmosphere is permissive, so that each student may say as much or as little as he wants.

6. The leader does not answer questions. Instead, he may reflect the confusion of the student who is asking the question or make other comments which are equally effective.[5]

The permissive attitude is essential in any situation where the teacher wants to create a feeling that the students can really decide things for themselves. The school club, for instance, is an area where the teacher-sponsor is merely an adult to give help and advice when requested. Essentially the club should provide a framework within which the students learn independence and have a chance to develop skill in exercising judgment. The teacher then must be able to be neutral, to let the young people talk as they wish about subjects that seem significant at the moment to them. Unless this can be established, the club situation like any other adult-dominated situation will not permit students to learn responsibility.

> The permissive atmosphere is one in which a minimum of information and advice is handed out to the child. This applies not only to advice on personal matters but to advice which is carelessly distributed in the process known as teaching. Some teachers credit the child with having little in the way of latent capacities, and they feel that it is their duty to advise on every matter that may come up. . . . The permissive and understanding atmosphere is one in which independence, rather than dependence, is developed.[6]

It is essential that the teacher do some soul searching himself: "Do I really want young people to grow away from me?" So often the adult who works with the young is meeting some of his own

[5] Arbuckle, Dugald S., *Teacher Counseling,* (Cambridge, Mass.: Addison-Wesley Press, 1950), p. 159.

[6] *Ibid.,* p. 42.

needs to be protective, to be wanted, and thus does not really help the young people to grow away from a need for his help. As we saw earlier (Chapter 3), one of the criteria of democratic education is the concept that the teacher is increasingly dispensable. This attitude pervades the permissive atmosphere, the attitude that "I believe you can solve your own problems without my telling you what to do, that you know better than I do what would be the adequate solution for yourself."

There is danger of overdoing this. In the hands of an unskilled person, the permissive atmosphere may easily degenerate into chaos. The students need the security of an adult to set the limits. Nor do we wish to have this kind of permissive atmosphere in every aspect of school life. A structure for our educational process is imperative. The selection of what is or is not essential in content is the responsibility of the teacher and the community. What the permissive approach emphasizes is a greater responsibility on the part of the student for his own learning and a greater recognition of the emotional aspects of the learning process.[7]

Role Playing as a Guidance Technique

Are there other special classroom techniques that the teacher might use to promote the guidance of students in groups? Let us look at one or two that are of special value. Role playing is particularly useful for guidance. This technique, under the name of sociodrama, has been discussed in Chapter 7. The use of spontaneous role playing for guidance is a tool that the teacher may well want to use where appropriate. Often, for example, if the situation is one revolving around the personal problems of boys and girls, much value is derived from playing out the situation. Suppose that the school realizes that one of its problems is the early school leaving of some of the older boys. A homeroom might play out some of the typical situations involved in this problem. The teacher might introduce the idea, "What is the Value of a High-School Education?" and develop a class discussion about whether it is or is not worth while to stay in high school as long as one can.

> "Well," says Robert, "I've got a good job in Mac's garage for this summer, and if I can make good, I am going to get a work permit to stay out of school."
>
> "You feel it would be better to work than remain in school," says the teacher.

[7] Madigan, Betty, and Mary Louise Steadman, "Accepting and Clarifying the Child's Feelings," Chap. 18 in *Fostering Mental Health in Our Schools,* 1950 Yearbook, Association for Supervision and Curriculum Development. (Washington, D.C.: The Association, 1950), pp. 300-312.

"Yeah, but my old man doesn't agree," responds Robert.

The teacher here takes a cue about an important personal problem, and refers it back to the class.

"Do many of you have ideas different from your parents about what you are in school for?"

A nodding of heads, a look of query and interest, will tell the teacher that he has hit a vital issue in parent-student relations.

"How about trying to understand our own wishes and those of our parents a bit better. Robert, suppose you play yourself for us, and Danny, you come up and be Robert's father. Robert, will you tell us a bit of what your father says when you discuss this with him so Danny will know how to act."

After some few moments of coaching Danny, it may come out that usually Robert's mother enters into the discussion. Helen is called up to be the mother and given some coaching on her role in the discussion.

After a first run through the situation, the teacher will throw it open to the class; comments, reactions, evaluations of the accuracy of role portrayal will come forth. Perhaps a replaying will be necessary, shifting the father role to gain more competence in the words and feeling tones of the arguments. Or the students may start pointing out to Robert that he isn't telling the whole story to his father, that the reason he wants to leave school is that he doesn't work very hard. Out of this may come a reconsideration of the student's stake in his education. Thus, the class as a group has gained insight into an immediate problem, and perhaps Robert has also gained some specific personal help by obtaining a better basis for such a crucial life decision.[8]

It is recommended that such acting out of important real-life problems be based on a well-founded study of the students. For instance, to put Helen in as the role of the mother might have some very important special meanings for Helen. It might influence her attitude toward Robert, but, even more important, it might hurt or help her feelings about herself and her own family. Knowing that Helen is secure in her family, has a jolly and accepting though poorly educated mother, might be highly important in helping to construct the role-playing situation for Robert.

One of the techniques to be described below, the sociometric test, is very helpful to use prior to role playing in order to utilize the relationships that exist in the class for promoting student

[8] An interesting description of sociodrama used for group guidance with teachers is contained in: "Sociodrama Workshops in Puerto Rico," *Understanding the Child,* 19:85-89 (June, 1950). Also, *Creative Dramatics,* The Girls Friendly Society, New York, 1948. Describes teen-age girls' problems that can be worked out and understood through the process of sociodrama. Useful for adaptation to the homeroom guidance period.

growth. It would be relatively sterile to have two students act out a typical snob situation in which some in-group feeling is to be expressed if these two students have no feeling for each other at all. But if two or three clique members are chosen to reveal in-group feeling the clique may see what it does to others. In such an instance, to go out of the way to focus attention on the tight clique might do more harm than good. That is, instead of choosing those clique members who are seriously at fault in this kind of snobbery and thus exposing them to class censure which would do little good and might do damage, the teacher should choose a mildly warm friendship grouping. But the teacher would need to have a good idea of the friendship pattern in the classroom before doing this kind of choosing; the sociometric test will provide this information.[9]

Role playing (or sociodrama) is useful to the extent that the group focuses on those problems that are *representative* of the problems of all the group members and those problems that the group *wants* to explore. Often, problems that seem very common to all the class may not be ones that the class can afford to look at because of reticence, lack of friendly feeling in the group, or adolescent mores that forbid sharing of such problems with adults. The teacher then needs to respect these feelings on the part of the class. Never coax a discussion or a role-playing episode out of a class. If there is a resistance, accept it. Similarly, if a given student is reluctant to take a role, he should never be forced into it. The teacher may return later and make another request, but even then should not force the student into the situation. The techniques of allowing some individuals to play prop roles to get into the picture without too much emotional involvement may ease the reluctance of young people to be expressive. It must be remembered that by the time the student is in high school he has acquired much protective coloration. He has lost much natural expressiveness and ability to be creative and original and has become more self-conscious, conforming, rigid, and incurious. These inhibitions will often interfere with adequate role portrayal for many students and should be respected by the teacher.[10]

[9] Haas, Robert B., "Learning to Read Ourselves and Others: Approach through Sociometry and the Psychodrama," *Claremont Reading Conference,* Thirteenth Yearbook, Curriculum Laboratory, Claremont College, Claremont California, 1948, pp. 14-25.

[10] Jennings, Helen, "Sociodrama as Educative Process," *Fostering Mental Health in our Schools,* 1950 Yearbook, Association for Supervision and Curriculum Development (Washington, D.C.: The Association, 1950), pp. 260-285.

Diagnosing Group Guidance Needs

How can the teacher discover the main problems of the group and of individuals in the group? Jennings[11] suggests a sampling technique to obtain clues about group and individual problems. The following questions could be given to a class or homeroom. Not all questions should be given to any class, but for the particular group the most appropriate should be selected. The wording may be adjusted to fit the maturity level of the group.

1. What situations are there in which you think you don't know how to deal with what happens and in which you wish things would happen differently? When does this situation come up and who is in it with you?
2. In what situations do you find someone doesn't understand you as well as you would like? When does this situation come up and who is in it with you?
3. In what situations do you find someone understands you very well, just as much as you would like? When does this situation come up and who is in it with you?
4. In what situations do you find it hard to decide what to do or to make up your mind what to do or say—seem unable to express yourself? When does this situation come up and who is in it with you?
5. In what situations do you go right ahead and have no difficulty making up your mind what to do or say? When does this situation come up and who is in it with you?
6. What situations come up which make you angry or very much annoyed? When does this situation come up and who is in it with you?
7. What situations happen to you in which someone gets very annoyed or angry at you? When does this situation come up and who is in it with you?
8. What situations happen to you which make you very happy? When does this situation come up and who is in it with you?
9. What situations happen to you which make you very sad? When does this situation come up and who is in it with you?

On the basis of the information obtained through using one or more of the above the teacher can do a *sociodrama role analysis:* He should seek to answer the following:

1. What problems do most pupils face?
2. What roles do most pupils feel they already deal adequately with?
3. What roles are they most in conflict with? (See answers to 2, 4, 6, 7. Do father, mother, sister, teacher appear most often?)
4. In what relationship to them are those individuals who seem to understand the students least? Best? (Do teachers, parents, relatives provide most or least of the understanding as in questions 3, 5, 8?)

[11] *Ibid.*

In this manner, the teacher may learn what problem situations have greatest need for clarification with a given group.

> A group of Spanish-American high-school students who were asked to indicate the problems that concerned them most told of their parents' prohibitions against speaking English at home. The parents did not speak English and felt the young people were trying to hide things from them. By acting out a series of such parent-student conflicts, the students decided that they had been insensitive to their parents and should try to meet this demand at home. The non-Spanish-speaking class members were very interested in this problem and felt a closer bond with Spanish-American students through having seen their own real-life problems with them. They also realized that both groups had a similar parent conflict situation, though it took different forms.

When Is Group Guidance Needed?

Should every teacher of every class be delving into the personal problems of students? Clearly this would be undesirable. It is obvious that any given classroom will afford the opportunities for the teacher to do guidance only insofar as this guidance (1) genuinely aids the students and meets current student needs and (2) fits into the kind of learning expected. As has been suggested, a course in English may well include numerous considerations of human relations through the study of literature. Wherever such a focus occurs, the immediate human relations of students are a useful point of departure, but not the sole consideration. Similarly, in biology the course content may stretch all the way from one-celled animals to problems of nutrition. But only when it is decided that understanding ourselves better is one of the functions of a study of biology should personal problems be studied. In art the teacher and students may want to consider problems of personal taste in home decoration, personal appearance, selection of pictures. These situations involve human relationships and understanding others, and in handling them the guidance approach would be appropriate.

But overconcern for the problems of the adolescents is as dangerous and educationally undesirable as complete unconcern with such problems. It is useful for the beginning teacher to attempt to gauge the extent to which guidance attitudes permeate the classrooms of fellow teachers. If the school has few such teachers, then a new teacher may explore with more assurance than would otherwise be possible some of these areas in order to fill a real need. However, if emphasis is already put on such an approach, the beginning teacher may well leave this kind of guidance in more skilled hands for the time being, without feeling that he is neglecting a major phase of the student's education.[12]

Understanding the Interpersonal Relations in the Classroom

So far our discussion has concerned itself with understanding the emotional problems of the individual and with the techniques for handling these problems individually and in a group. To increase the effectiveness of both individual and group guidance and counseling, it is essential that we know more about the relationships among individuals in the classroom. Where people like each other, feel that others accept them for what they are, are willing to share in the give and take of daily activities, what is known as a "good group atmosphere" exists. If the teacher is aware of this and capitalizes upon it, then the total learning situation will probably be more effective. On the other hand, if the group is one where strong antagonisms exist between one group of adolescents and another, where one individual is the butt of teasing and semi-sadistic actions, where many students have no friends in the group, but feel left out and alone, the teacher will find it difficult to obtain optimum learning.

How can the teacher gain insight into the social structure of the classroom? This view of individual adjustment is relatively new. The development of guidance in the schools came when educators grew concerned about the individual, and when tests were developed that were useful in helping counselors gain insight into individual adjustment. Recently, as observers of the schools recognized how significant the interpersonal relationships are in determining the adjustment of the individual, there has emerged a need to find out just what these relationships with others are.

When Tony entered the eleventh-grade P.E. class in the middle of November, the teacher, Mr. Roderigez, observed that the other boys didn't seem at all interested in him. Often when a new boy came, the other students came around, chatting about where he had come from, giving him a few helpful hints about the school. But Tony was ignored. On the surface he seemed like any other kid: dressed in T-shirt and blue jeans, average height, regular features. But he was quiet, almost sullen. Sitting behind him on the bench, Mr. Roderigez saw Bill come up and sit next to Tony. Bill didn't say anything, just sat. Bill was another lonely boy. The other students ignored him too. He noted their treatment of Tony, and Mr. Roderigez was interested to see a rather silent friendship evolve. Thereafter, Bill and Tony sat on the side lines together, two "outsiders." Mr. Roderigez was still puz-

[12] See Alberty, Harold, "Guidance through Classroom Activities," Chap. XVII in *Reorganizing the High School Curriculum* (New York: The Macmillan Company, 1947).

zled, though. He had no idea what it was that made these two boys seem so isolated. What did they do that made the others shy away from them, leave them alone? Mr. Roderigez tried putting each of the boys on a different team, but they still didn't mix with the others. The only playfulness he ever saw them exhibit was when the two of them would be tossing a ball back and forth together. Then there was much typical kidding and running commentary on each other's skill. But with the other boys this commentary was silent. Why?

The teacher often feels just as puzzled as Mr. Roderigez. Here is Jane, pretty, well-dressed, nice manners, and yet no one seems to claim her as a friend; on the other hand, Jill, sloppy, not too bright, giggly, seems to be the center of a whole group of girls and boys. When the teacher wishes to talk with Jane or Tony or Jill, knowing what it is that lies behind their acceptance or rejection by the group will be important. Similarly, the fact that Joe would like very much to be a friend of Bob's but that Bob isn't aware of Joe's existence may be significant when the teacher comes to set up committees or groups for class enterprises. Perhaps if Joe and Bob do get together and work together, Joe will develop more security in himself and perhaps will do better work in class.

This network of likes and dislikes, prejudices and tolerances, crushes and hatreds, is always present. Wherever a group of people is together long enough to recognize each other, feelings will emerge about the other individuals. The classroom is no exception. The traditional classroom assumes that such interrelations are not important. It is taken for granted that seating students alphabetically to facilitate checking the roll is more important than the fact that, by using an arbitrary arrangement, we have placed Winifred next to Glen of whom she is mortally afraid, and behind Lois who thinks Winifred is "a drip." Life for Winifred may be almost intolerable in this classroom; but the teacher is able to take roll easily. If Winifred's work drops off because of her preoccupation with the feelings she has about those sitting near her, the traditional teacher will not know it or, if he knows it, will discount its importance in the learning process. And if Winifred soon starts missing school, the blame will be on Winifred, not upon the teacher who was so insensitive to her feelings.

As adults will react to those they must work with day in and day out, so students are bound to develop intense feelings about each other. Actually the greater emotionality of the adolescent, the fact that his feelings are much nearer the surface than are those of the mature adult, make it even more important that teachers have real insight into human relationships in their classrooms.

Using the Sociometric and Guess Who? Tests

Several important techniques will be described here that enable the teacher to gain insight into this network of relationships in his classroom. One is the *sociometric test,* and the other is the *"Guess Who?" test.*

As its name implies, the sociometric test measures social relationships.[13] This device is so simple that sometimes its real significance is overlooked. It consists of the following:

> TEACHER: Tomorrow we had planned to set up the groups for our review of the unit we have just finished. It doesn't matter which group you are in because we will all be doing the same thing. However, I know that students work best with those they like. So I am going to ask you to indicate on this slip of paper the three other members of this class that you would like *to work with* in this group:
>
> Put a number one to indicate your first choice, a number two for your second choice, and a number three for your third choice.
>
> Now in case there is anyone you would not like to work with, you might draw a line under your third choice and write the name of this person.
>
> You probably all can't have your first choice, but I will do my best to see that you work with one or more of the persons that you chose.

Notice that the teacher wanted a *work-group* choice. For other situations she might have asked for a *team mate* choice, for a *social-party group* choice, for bus-seat companion, fire-drill line companion, seat partner in the class, laboratory-table partner, problem-solving team choice, assembly-program group choice. The choices the students make will vary, within limits, according to the criteria for the choice. For instance, Elizabeth may be chosen by many students for bus-seat partner, but chosen rarely for work companion because her work in class is not very good, but she is a gay and friendly girl with whom to ride to and from school.

The teacher studies the results of the choices very carefully. A chart such as that on the next page helps to plot the total number of choices a student obtains.

It is important to see the social pattern in another view, however. A sociometric test can be translated into a sociogram which reveals mutual choices, cliques, and isolates and those who are rejected. The illustration on page 457 is a sociogram of a twelfth-grade class.

[13] The earliest discussion of this technique will be found in Moreno, J. L., *Who Shall Survive?* (Washington, D.C.: Nervous and Mental Disease Publishing Co., 1934).

A Sample Sociometric Chart

	Chosen															
Chooser	John	George	Jane	Mary	Henry	Bud	Phillip	Joe	etc.							
John					3	R	2	1								
George																
Jane																
Mary																
etc.																
No. times chosen																
Total score																

John Dodge

The three people I would like to work with in a group are:

Henry—1st
Phillip—2nd
Joe—3rd

I would not like to work with Bud

Directions: To enter the choices made by John Dodge one reverses the weight: a first choice gets a weight of 3, a second choice, 2; a third choice, 1. Then, when all choices have been entered, adding them up gives a quick measure of relative popularity; the higher the score, the more often chosen with first or second choices.

The rejection can be entered in red and added separately.

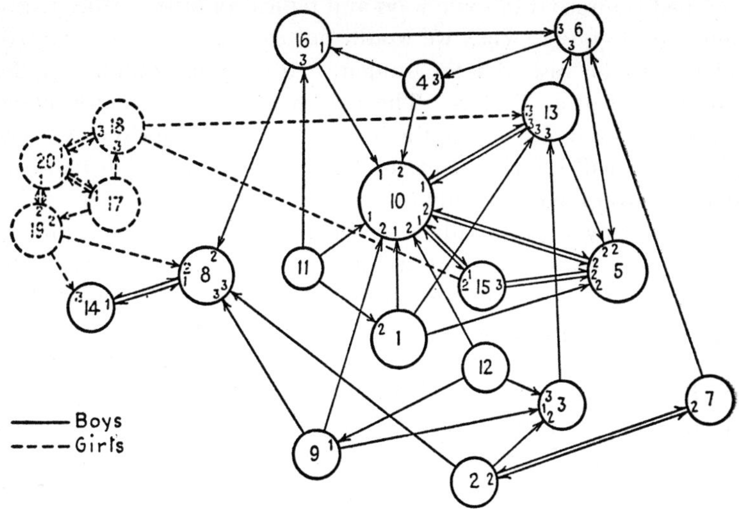

SOCIOGRAM FOR THE CLASS OF TEACHER E

Analyzing a Sample Sociogram

There are several points of immediate interest in this sociogram. First, the large numbers inside each circle refer in code to a student in the class. This helps retain anonymity of the sociogram just in case any outsider happened to see it. Second, the small numbers on the edge of the circle indicate what choice was made: a 3 means that that student was given third choice as a friend. The lines indicate who did the choosing and made the choice. A double line with double arrowhead indicates reciprocal choice. Third, the sociogram is drawn to indicate relative popularity; the larger the circle the more choices, and the more first and second choices. Immediately we notice student 10, a boy who is not only markedly superior in total number of choices but also in first and second choices. Student 5 is also chosen often, but all are second choices. Fourth, the cleavage between boys and girls is worthy of note. Only girls 18 and 19 chose boys. No boys chose girls. Finally, observe the strong clique pattern among both boys and girls. Boys 5, 10, 15 have close reciprocal friendships, with 13 attached on the fringe as a friend of 10. Among the girls, 17 is on the edge of the clique made up of 18, 19, and 20.

In any sociogram we can see all these: *direction* of choice, *intensity* of choice, *reciprocation* of choice, *accumulation* of choice around individuals, and *pattern* of choices. The class we diagrammed is unusual in some ways and typical in others. Since it is a twelfth-grade physics class we would not expect to find many girls, and this is the case. All the students are college bound, and the girls are known as "brains." The two girls chose *boys with whom they had worked.* Usually in the high school even the closest of boy-girl couples will not choose each other *unless* the class has had considerable group work already.

Why is boy 10 so popular? In this instance he was the student-body president and a genuine student leader. He attracts the choices of the other students, although, again, no girl chooses him despite his high prestige. Let us look at some of the other students. Student 8 is a foreign student, shy, with a language handicap. A girl chooses him; so do a number of others. This may be a protective role that the students are taking toward him, since he is so quiet and shy. The teacher did not think he had any friends at all.

There are many students chosen by none or only one other, and they are on the periphery of the class. These isolates will establish few if any friendship ties in a classroom unless aided by the teacher. It would be difficult for any adult to stay long in a job where no one noticed him or was interested or friendly. Yet all too often in high-school classes we ignore similar needs in young people.

Before this test was given, the teacher indicated his idea of the class structure. He picked student 12 as a popular student; but 12 received no votes at all from his fellow students. The teacher felt that no student was disliked; yet student 7 was actively rejected by three students (this is not indicated on the sociogram). Handicapped by these and other errors, this teacher would have difficulty improving the social relationships in his classroom. With the sociometric technique, he, and teachers like him, can do a sounder job of teacher-counseling.[14]

Classroom Procedures: Giving the Sociometric Test

It is clear that this technique is a great aid to the teacher. It is easy to administer, it does not probe into the private worlds of the students beyond what the students are willing to reveal. As a matter of fact, the students welcome the chance to choose:

> In a Senior Problems class, the class had finished one project in which group choices had been based on a sociometric test. The instructor asked the class whether they wanted to choose their group members the way they had before. The class was very enthusiastic in

[14] Sociogram and analysis adapted from materials prepared by Dr. Fred Pinkham, George Washington University, Washington, D.C.

response, since the group experience before had been highly successful. Several students who had made no contribution before had, in a group of close friends, been able to do a very creditable job. The second time the choices were made, the teacher also had a list of topics for group projects and asked them to indicate a choice here, and, finally, to state whether they felt more strongly about working on a given topic, or working with the friends they had chosen. This gave more leeway for individual interests to assert themselves and met the different needs of the group as well.

The importance of the secret vote must be emphasized. Often the voting that is done in a class is by show of hands; students see whom others choose and are swayed or silenced by the will of the dominant members of the class. By being allowed to write down their individual choice and having the teacher the repository of this confidence, genuine relationships are divulged.

It is very important that the teacher respect the privacy of the choices. It would be very damaging to let one student know that a third of the students in the class chose him for best friend and just as damaging to let another student know that no one chose him for work companion. The teacher must use this kind of information with great discretion, since it has the power to hurt infinitely more than a single judgment by a teacher. It is far more crucial for the student to know that none of his peers chose him for teammate, than that the teacher gave him a poor mark in deportment. The teacher is obligated, if a sociometric test is used, to protect the students involved. The papers on which the choices were made should be destroyed as soon as recorded; the sociograms or sociometric charts should be filled in with code numbers or letters rather than actual names of students. Such confidential material should never be left out on a teacher's desk where curious students can have access to it. The information gained should not enter the gossip channels of the school, but should be relayed to the counselor, the principal, and other teachers in a professional manner as a means of furthering the adjustment of students.

A teacher was setting up a group situation for a quiz and asked the class to indicate in what group they would like to be for the test. In the class was a star athlete, a boy whose reputation extended far beyond the town. He seemed like a nice fellow, though irregular in attendance and very quiet and unresponsive in class. He always sat with a group of boys who were also athletes and the teacher had assumed they were buddies. But great was his astonishment to find that the star athlete was not liked by his "friends." Not one of his supposed buddies had chosen him. The teacher sought out the coach and asked him about the student, explaining what had happened. As a result, the coach and the teacher came to understand each other's programs better. Both worked to help this star handle more adequately his fabulous reputation which was hindering, rather than helping, his long-term adjustment.

It is possible that some students will develop great anxiety over the process of choosing, particularly those who fear that they will not be chosen. Choosing sides is often used in elementary schools, and there are always those who are chosen last. For some this may have been traumatic. The use of the sociometric test may suggest to some students these earlier experiences and cause them great perturbation. Consequently, the teacher should reassure the class about the choice situation by making it as casual and unimportant as possible. By proper introduction, the teacher may allay some of these feelings, as in the following:

TEACHER: I am going to ask you to indicate with whom you want to work for next week's project. Remember, you don't have to choose if you don't want to. You can let the choice be up to me, but I think our groups worked so well last time that we might as well continue our procedure. I will try to place you with others whom you choose but with whom you may not have worked before, just so we can all get to know each other better.

There is the possibility that the students will compare notes as to who chose whom, but this can be avoided, at least in part, by having the choices made at the beginning of the period, collecting them rapidly and immediately, and then proceeding to some activity that will effectively absorb the attention of the class. Invariably some students will speculate about the choices, wondering if their current "crush" reciprocated the feeling. Such speculations are no different than they would have been without the use of the sociometric test. The teacher will want to remember that some of the significance of the test derives from the fact that young people are very much interested in friendships just as adults are.

The first sociogram that a teacher makes is bound to be difficult. It is hard to see the relationships indicated by the choices, and manipulating the circles and triangles around the paper, so that the lines of choice are as direct as possible, seems very difficult, particularly with thirty-five to forty students. By making a sociograph first (the chart previously referred to on page 456), the teacher can see some of the reciprocal patterns. It may be that the teacher will want to pick out only two or three students and see what the friendship pattern is that exists around them. A magnetic board[15]

[15] A magnetic board is simply a sheet of metal. Sociogram symbols are attached to small magnets and may be moved about the sheet of metal at will.

may be very helpful in setting up a sociometric pattern easily, since it is an aid to moving the symbols around. Sometimes a felt board[16] may also be used. After doing several, the teacher may not need to make a sociogram for every class, because he will quickly gain skill in analysis of sociometric results. In looking for groupings, he will begin to observe the natural clusters that occur, to spot the "stars" without much trouble, and also to note the isolates and those who are rejected.[17]

Using the Results of the Sociometric Test

After a sociometric test has been administered, the teacher is often amazed at the individuals who emerge as leaders or those who are not chosen. A classic example of such a result is the following:

> A Boy Scout troop faced the problem of dividing up in patrols. When the problem was broached, none of the boys wanted to separate. The leader decided to have them choose on a sociometric test, then he would be able to see what natural groups emerged. Before giving the test, however, he thought it would be fun to rank them in his own mind and see how accurate his ranking was compared with that of the boys. Some of his comments regarding the wide difference in ranking between his judgment and that of the boys are very illuminating:
>
> Take the case of G.B. I had placed him first on the list, while the group placed him third, fifteen points below the first choice. G.B. is a nice, quiet boy and seems to get along with everyone. He is the patrol leader and the kind of a freckle-faced kid I would like to have as a son. In other words *I* liked him so well that I assumed the boys did also. At any rate this seems to be a common occurrence in group selection and has given me a good example for future work on group behavior. . . . The case of D.J. is even more in contrast. I placed him tenth on the list while the sociograph shows him number two. D.J. is a tenderfoot scout who hasn't passed a test in the past year. He is a rather good-looking kid but has the loudest, most irritating voice I have yet to hear from a thirteen-year-old. All in all he usually gets on my nerves before the meeting is ten minutes old. He is a good baseball player and a better umpire baiter, having called me a few classic names as umpire when I called him "out" on first base. At any rate I just didn't like the boy, but never let him know it. He never seemed to have many friends among the boys and since I was prejudiced against him I placed him low on the list. I see now that he is an idol to many of the boys. They admire his looks, his baseball ability, his ability to get along with his peers, and possibly his loud voice. . . . This case also brought home the fact that in order to understand group behavior the observer

[16] A felt board is felt attached to a sheet of cardboard or a strip of wood. The sociogram symbols are glued to strips of felt or coarse sandpaper. The figures then will cling to the felt panel.

[17] See also, *How to Construct a Sociogram* (New York: Bureau of Publications, Teachers College, Columbia University. 1947).

and the leader must integrate himself into the group as a part of that group, and not sit on the side lines and look down.

How reliable are the students' choices? It must be remembered that these choice patterns are always shifting. The grouping one week may differ considerably from that of the following week, and the grouping that occurs for one criterion will be different from that for another. The teacher will want to use sociometric information in order deliberately to influence the groupings in a classroom. Thus one use of the technique can be to check on the effectiveness of developing good human relations by seeing if the isolates have acquired friends. There are some dramatic stories of changing social structures effected by utilizing sociometric insights.[18] Of course, it must be remembered that to understand the many factors that go into the sociometric choice requires years of working with young people. A beginning teacher cannot immediately see the dynamics of choice: why Mary gets ten first choices to Andy's one, or why tenth-graders refuse to cross sex lines in choices. There is also some danger that

> the visual symbolization of the data on a sociogram will convey to the teacher the idea of a fixed and certain scientific reality. We fear that a teacher may think: "This is it. This is the way my pupils feel about each other; this is the way my class is structured." Such a static interpretation of the data is most unsound and unreliable. . . . A sociogram is a most effective starting point and signboard for launching a study of social dynamics in school groups. . . . Child societies change, develop, evolve.[19]

Unlike psychodrama, the sociometric test may be used by all teachers who utilize grouping in the classroom. Usually the adolescents will not consider too much is being asked of them. To use the test for more intensive research into a class entails broadening the criterion questions to include social activities, team activities, and other areas of group living in the total life of the student.

Where a teacher finds a class particularly difficult to handle, where discipline problems are constantly emerging, where teacher-pupil conflict is very much apparent, a sociometric questionnaire is particularly useful. The teacher may thus be aided in identifying leaders, may find the inner groupings of the class, and probably will find that the class itself is composed of one or more

[18] Taba, Hilda, *Elementary Curriculum in Intergroup Relations* (Washington, D.C.: American Council on Education, 1950). Also, Commission on Teacher Education, *Helping Teachers Understand Children* (Washington, D.C.: American Council on Education, 1945).

[19] Commission on Teacher Education, *op. cit.*, p. 362, and all of Chapters IX and X for excellent material on the use of sociometrics.

cliques, with others loosely grouped in the periphery, lonely, unwanted, dissatisfied with their social status. With these indicators, the teacher can proceed to plan various group activities in order to obtain a better social structure, one that decreases the loneliness of those on the fringe and uses the leadership of the cliques for positive goals. Under these circumstances the use of pupil-teacher planning will be held to a minimum; when a class is disorganized, it is futile to try to obtain consensus.

A class will gradually become more organized through using some group activities based on sociometric choice. Group morale will permit more group planning. However, there can be no formula for success in dealing with adolescents. It is up to the teacher to be familiar with the many ways of studying and working with young people and to be flexible in the application of the many kinds of approach suggested in this book.

Identifying Peer Valuations: the Guess Who? Test

Another easily used tool to gain insight into student relationships is the Guess Who? test. This test was used by Tryon in the Adolescent Growth Study to find out what adolescents thought of each other[20] Since then it has been adapted for a variety of purposes in a variety of situations. The typical test will have questions like the following:

Please fill in the blanks in the following questions with the name or names of students who best fit the description. Your answers will be confidential; you are asked not to discuss your answers with anyone. Be as honest as you can. Your opinions here will help us understand you and your classmates better so that our school program may be improved.

[The above introductory paragraph may be changed to suit the situation in which the test is given.]

1. ——————is the best sport in the class.
2. ——————is the student who always knows the answer.
3. The most popular girl in class is——————.
4. ——————is an "apple-polisher."
5. ——————will always help you if you need help.
6. The person no one likes very much is——————.
7. The most popular boy in class is——————.
8. ——————is someone who likes to laugh and be jolly.
9. ——————always brags and boasts.
10. The best-dressed person in the room is——————.
11. ——————has the best ideas for group projects.
12. ——————is the friendliest person in the class.
13. The person who always gets his/her feelings hurt is——————.

[20] Tryon, Caroline M., *Evaluation of Adolescent Personality by Adolescents*, Monograph, Research Society for Child Development, Vol. 4, No. 4, 1939.

14. ————————acts very snobbish.
15. ————————gets mad whenever you say anything.
16. The person who is dirty and sloppy is————————.
17. ————————is a real "glamour girl."

Other questions:
Best athlete
Tells lies
Acts silly
Acts too old for us
Acts too young for us
Is so shy and quiet can't get to know him/her
Always tries to boss everyone
Isn't friendly
Isn't like the rest of us
Is a sissy
Someone who doesn't like me

Additional questions may be added.[21] The teacher may notice some other types of behavior in the classroom and would include descriptions in the Guess Who? test in order to find out how such behavior correlates with the student's rating by his classmates.

Marjorie may be selected in the sociometric test as a star and leader, but what are the characteristics that are associated with this position? From the Guess Who? test the teacher may discover that Marjorie is listed as "friendliest," as "best dressed," as the "most popular," as the one who "likes to laugh." He would know immediately what values were held in high esteem by this group. On the other hand, by seeing Julia's name associated with "dirty and sloppy," "always gets her feelings hurt," "always brags and boasts," and by noticing that Julia was rejected by a number of classmates and chosen by only one as a third choice, the teacher learns some of the personal traits that are interfering with Julia's acceptance by her peers.

It is interesting to note the changes in value placed on traits at different maturity levels; the high popularity accorded one child in the tenth grade for being an athletic star may be reduced as the students move into the eleventh and twelfth grades when social skills and adequacy in heterosexual relationships come to the fore. Moreover, different socioeconomic groups will value different personal traits. Whereas being intelligent and getting high grades may be valued by the college-bound group, the group that comes figuratively from across the tracks may value more aggressive, less school-

[21] College Study in Intergroup Relations, "Who's Who in My Group," College of Education, Ohio State University, Columbus, Ohio. See also Ohio State "Recognition Scale," College of Education, Ohio State University, Columbus, Ohio.

oriented traits. The teacher who sees these group-value differences should be better able to understand the social structure of the class, and the dynamics of interpersonal relations.[22]

The Guess Who? test requires the same safeguards that should surround the sociometric test. The teacher will want to keep in strict confidence the findings from the test. It is advisable to administer the test just before some very exciting event. In this way, the students will quickly forget the test itself and are less likely to compare notes as to who put what for whom. Another precaution might be to have someone who is a stranger to the class come in and administer the test. Then, when this person leaves, he takes with him, literally, whatever the students have written. The psychological situation then is clearer, and the students feel less involved in the responses that were made and less threatened by the evaluations others have made of them or that they have made of each other.

Using Test Results

The classroom uses of the materials gained from these two tests depend largely on the sensitivity of the teacher. That this information is invaluable in the guidance of individuals is clear. But teachers are apt to overlook the interpersonal dynamics of the classroom itself. For this reason, tests such as the two described here are basic in any genuine attempt to use the classroom situation for the improvement of human relations.

The teacher may find, for example, three students without any friendship ties in the class. But all three choose the star of the class for best friend and also choose the other highly popular class members. In grouping the class for some activity, the teacher may, with some probability of success, place these isolated students with those toward whom they have a positive feeling, and then surround the popular ones also with their good friends. Thus an emphasis is provided for positive feelings, for the development of sound human relations.

> In one tenth grade there were only two Negro girls. It happened that in three out of their five class periods they were in the same room. Wherever this occurred, the teachers sat them together "because of course they would feel more comfortable next to someone of their

[22] Tryon, Caroline, "The Adolescent Peer Culture," Chap. XII in *Adolescence,* 43rd Yearbook, Pt. I, National Society for the Study of Education, 1944, pp. 217-239. Also Tryon, Caroline, "Evaluations of Adolescent Personality by Adolescents," Chap. XXXI, pp. 545-566, *Child Behavior and Development,* ed. by Roger Barker, *et al.,* New York: McGraw-Hill, 1943.

own kind." The counselor for the tenth grade was concerned about some discipline cases and so conducted a sociometric test in one of the classes in which the two Negro girls were enrolled. What was his surprise to find that, contrary to the opinion of the teachers, not only were the two Negro girls rejected by many of their classes, but they both rejected the other! The teachers had insisted on putting these two together, yet they had a mutual dislike for each other. On the basis of these findings, the teachers allowed the girls to sit where they wanted and found that, as they became better integrated in the class and also did not have to "live" closely with someone they didn't like, both girls made considerable improvement in class behavior. A later follow-up sociometric test showed that both girls had acquired one or two friends and were no longer rejected by as many students, though they still remained on the fringe of the class society.

An interesting study is reported by Cook[23] in which he shows the sociometric patterning of a class, the utilization of this patterning for individual guidance, and finally the class methods used to develop different group interaction and to achieve a genuine social grouping. The method used in the classroom to produce some classroom changes was to have the class work as a planning group on a scrap drive.

Summary

It is apparent that to do group guidance the content must be more fluid, more available for group thinking and planning; the formal recitation approach cannot result in effective group guidance. The classroom that is seen as a real segment of life, wherein people learn many of the important lessons about themselves and others that have continuing significance into adulthood, is one in which individuals act and interact. But such a situation can occur only when there are real problems to solve and the students are actively engaged in solving them.

In this chapter we have presented some of the ways in which the teacher can gain insight into the interpersonal relationships of the classroom and have indicated also the setting in which such insight might best be utilized—the homeroom and the orientation course. It has also been pointed out that every classroom is rich with human interaction, and that learning proceeds best when such dynamic relationships are accounted for and exploited in the ongoing activity that demands the best energies of the group.

[23] Cook, Lloyd A., "An Experimental Sociographic Study of a Stratified 10th Grade Class," *American Sociological Review,* 10:250-261 (1945).

Selected References

Axline, Virginia. *Play Therapy*. Boston: Houghton Mifflin Company, 1947. Presentation of several significant ways of learning about and dealing with the deep problems of individuals.

Elkins, Deborah. "Students Face Their Problems," *English Journal,* 38:498-503 (November, 1949). Literature used for guidance purposes.

Hallett, Robert W. "The 'Gripe' Session," *The Clearing House,* 16:198-202 (December, 1941). When and how to direct and deal with student complaints.

McKown, Harry C. *Home Room Guidance*. New York: McGraw-Hill Book Company, Inc., 1946. 2d ed. A recent revision of a standard reference on how the classroom teacher performs group guidance functions.

Mersand, Joseph (ed.). *Principles and Practices of Guidance for High School English Classes*. Long Island City, N. Y.: J. Mersand, Publisher, 1951. Many specific instances of guidance practices as part of regular English instruction.

Wright, Barbara. *Practical Handbook for Group Guidance*. Chicago: Science Research Associates, 1948. A very useful practical guide for the teacher who will be doing group guidance.

20. Other Guidance Activities

ADOLESCENCE is a time of great decisions. Shall I go to college? What courses do I need to become an airplane mechanic? How can I best prepare for marriage and parenthood? These are the vital and recurrent questions that adolescents are asking themselves throughout the high-school years. And here is the teacher to whom students come with these immensely important questions; how can he best help his students to answer them? Guidance involves not only gaining insight into one's own personal problems, not only the job of adjusting adequately to a group of one's peers; it also involves making life choices among a plentitude of alternatives leading to responsible adulthood. In this chapter some suggestions will be given for these vocational and academic guidance problems of students.

In working with these problems, we must always bear in mind that adolescents come from a variety of homes, that they have parents who provide security or enforce impossible demands, who surround the individual with affection and regard or continually attack youthful vagaries and flights of fancy. Working with adolcesents implies working also with their parents. Here too the teacher is best equipped who takes the approach of the counselor, seeking to aid others in obtaining insight rather than insisting on any one answer of his. In this chapter, then, we shall conclude our treatment of teacher-counseling with a discussion of the specific skills and understanding needed for work with parents.

Teacher Responsibility in Academic and Vocational Guidance

Is there any real difference between the kind of guidance that has been discussed in the preceding two chapters and vocational and academic guidance? The basic principles are the same in all areas of guidance. The purpose of any guidance procedure is to aid the individual in making his own most mature choices in the light of the best evidence that can be gathered and in terms of his own goals and purposes. For example, to help a student overcome the handicaps of an emotionally disturbed home and to help that student choose between a commercial or a precollege curriculum are often very similar problems. In either kind of guidance, the teacher will find the same skills, understanding, and insights important.

Teachers have no right, then, to be mechanical and arbitrary when it comes to helping students choose courses or to generalize vaguely when it comes to discussing careers. These questions are crucial to the student, and wrong choices or decisions here can be just as tragic and irrevocable as any other personal decision. The availability of a mass of descriptive material—college catalogues that list required high-school courses for entrance, school-program outlines, career bulletins,—does not mean that the student needs no help beyond placing a pamphlet in his hands.

The school counselor, where there is one, may be able to supply a wide selection of the publications that provide information on academic and vocational requirements. With his technical skill, the counselor often is able to prepare digests of these materials and make them available to the classroom teacher. But a job of counseling still remains to be done. It is the rare school where an adequate number of counselors are available to do the whole job. The classroom teacher, for the present at least, will have to help.

Academic Guidance

The importance of academic guidance should not be underestimated. Encouraging a student to sign up for a college-preparatory course or insisting that a boy take beginning machine shop instead of French may set the pattern of his study for years to come.

Studies indicate that students from higher socioeconomic levels and students whose parents have advanced education make up a very high percentage of enrollment in college preparatory courses; while students from lower social groups, students from minority cultural groups, and students whose parents have had a meager education tend, by and large, to take the commercial, general, home-economics, shop, and agriculture courses. Is this a recognition of their ability or is it a response to cultural pressure? Very often it is true that educated parents understand and pass on to their children a desire for more education, while parents with little education themselves do not prize more schooling for their children in the same degree.

Financial ability to send a child to college is a great determiner of who goes to college,[1] irrespective of basic intelligence. The teacher who sits down with his class to work out the future programs that each student should take in high school will need to consider carefully the following points before giving a student an "answer":

1. Will this student get home encouragement for the course of action that seems advised in terms of his ability?
2. Does the student have deep ambition commensurate with his ability and past performance?
3. Does the student have a clear idea of other possible courses besides the one he has in mind?
4. Is the student merely following the crowd, or does he know why he has indicated a particular choice of courses?
5. Does the teacher himself carry a stereotype regarding what students from this part of town or this ethnic group ought to take rather than viewing each individual separately?

Points three and five above require some explanation. Many students take a course of study merely because they have only a vague notion of other alternatives. When the time for making out a program occurs, the teacher should make a special point of discussing at length the various offerings and the advantages and disadvantages of each.

It must be kept in mind that for many students the difference between the elementary-school pattern and the high-school pattern is so great that the students are thoroughly baffled by the new choices. For a teacher with a freshman group, considerable class time should be devoted to a careful consideration of every subject that the student may take over the next four years, showing how each one leads on to another, and what kind of vocational goal is assumed by each course of study sequence.

[1] Warner, W. L., *et al. Who Shall Be Educated?* (New York: Harper & Brothers, 1944), pp. 58-72.

The point regarding the teacher's own bias deserves comment: Is it true that no Spanish-American student can succeed in a college-preparatory course? Should all Negro students be discouraged from the commercial subjects? How about salesmanship courses for a Japanese-American student? There is some evidence that school counselors and administrators as well as individual teachers tend to stereotype students according to membership in some cultural group. They are assigned to curricular patterns on this basis, rather than on the basis of consideration of the individual student's potential.

> Too many counselors automatically pass the children on to shop classes, or cooking, or sewing if there is a Spanish name on the card given them. Sometimes their stereotyped thinking is upset if a child is unusually bright and aggressive and insists on getting into a certain class. But he may have to fight to take some courses even then. Spanish, for instance, is often closed to Mexican-American pupils; commercial classes are also frequently restricted.[2]

Let us view each student as an individual and provide for him the kind of help and guidance that fits his pattern best.

Vocational Guidance

In an earlier era, the high-school program was considered to be all the education needed for many jobs. Specific curricula, such as the industrial arts and agriculture programs, were established to serve the needs of students entering such work areas. Presumably students would obtain in the high school all the requisite education. However, the needs of industry have become so much more elaborate and complex that only a kind of job orientation is now possible in the average industrial-arts program. The boy can obtain a good idea of the complexity of many machines, of the simple safety rules, and of some of the skills of working with electrical, welding, and other shop equipment. But for actual training for a specific job, most industries today plan for from one day to several weeks of on-the-job training of new employees.[3] High schools now serve best by developing an attitude toward work responsibility, an understanding of the role of the worker in society, a familiarity with work routines and work situations, and, finally, an appraisal of the student's own aptitude for a particular kind of work.

[2] Griffith, Beatrice, *American Me* (Boston: Houghton Mifflin Company, 1948), p. 167.

[3] Bell, Howard, *Matching Youth and Jobs* (Washington, D.C.: American Council on Education, 1940), p. 58.

Vocational Guidance in the Subject Fields

In the agriculture programs, extensive use has been made of the 4-H Club work, gearing that into the high-school course. This involves the student in home projects and serves as an excellent bridge between school and home and later vocational pursuit. Similar programs exist in home economics, where girls are encouraged to do home decorating, home canning, and sewing as a part of their education as homemakers. In the commercial courses, elementary typing, bookkeeping, accounting, work with office machines and office forms are better able to equip students with the skills needed for beginning clerical jobs. The other course offerings of the school appear to have little specific job application. In fact, so remote is the subject matter of many academic courses from what the working individual needs that many schools today have had to establish such courses as business English, shop mathematics, business economics, agricultural economics. These are designed to deal specifically with the social, mathematical and communications needs of students headed for a vocation. It is not wholly necessary, of course, that the regular course offerings should be so impractical. It is possible for any teacher to help students see the job applications of any particular unit of work in any course. This does not mean that we teach only concepts that can have specific job application, but wherever what we teach does apply, it is important that we make the bridge explicit.

> As a way of motivating students to work on the apparently unrelated material of algebra, Mr. Jordan asked first for the students to indicate their probable vocational future. He found that members of the class expected to enter the usual professions. A number were going into farming. Many were expecting to enter the skilled trades, such as machine shop and carpentry. Most of the girls were clearly interested in future homemaking. He set up ten groups in the class according to broad occupational categories and then requested each group to interview two or three representatives of that occupational family to see what mathematics that individual needed in his work. The reports from the groups were very interesting. Most of the students had no idea that so much mathematics was needed in everyday life.

Another approach to vocational guidance in the academic classroom is exemplified by the following:

> One bulletin board in the chemistry laboratory was called "Careers for You in Chemistry." Here Mrs. Grant posted articles about chemists that she found from time to time in *Life,* in the *Saturday Evening Post,*

in *Fortune,* in *Science,* in the *Reader's Digest.* She had the current report from the government on opportunities for girls in science. There seemed to be a constant stream of articles that illustrated possible kinds of work for a student interested in chemistry and related fields. At least once a semester she would bring in several individuals who used chemical processes in their occupations to talk to the class about the training needed. One was a laboratory technician from a near-by oil refinery. Another was the chemist from the city water department. A third usually was the soil analyst from the state agricultural college who did extensive traveling around the state. Following this presentation, she would encourage several students to see how many jobs they could discover where a knowledge of chemistry was important. This was then the basis for a discussion about vocations and vocational choices. A number of Mrs. Grant's students found a life-long interest because of this introduction.

The possibilities of using every subject field to introduce to the students some vocational possibilities implicit in that area should be fully exploited. A foreign language teacher should be well informed on the vocational usefulness of foreign language skill. The English teacher should be able to discuss with young people the kinds of jobs where a facility in English is prized. The social-studies teacher should prepare himself to undertake this kind of classroom study with the students. Familiarity with the Strong Vocational Interest Blank, the Kuder Preference Record, and similar vocational interest inventories is important for any teacher who may deal specifically with vocational guidance. Employment-opportunity surveys should be made every few years in the employment area of the school. Follow-ups of graduates on the job will aid the school in keeping instruction realistic and keyed to the changing demands of the job market.

Guidance Through Work Experience

To help young people going out to work, a number of schools have developed work-experience programs. This type of program has been used primarily to help students who needed to work, but it also provided a minimum of schooling. The young student then did not entirely miss high school because of economic necessity. However, some thought should be given to the value of work experience for all youth, whether or not financial assistance is needed. One of the chief complaints about the adolescent who seeks a job today is that he lacks a sense of responsibility and fails to recognize the real demands of the work-a-day world. Work experience could become a vital learning opportunity for many young people at the junior or senior level. It must be geared into the curriculum as part of learning about the world of work, about the reality of one's interests in a job (a girl who likes nursing on a sentimental level may find the reality of the nurse's job not at all appealing), about one's ability to learn what will be needed on the job.

Working with Parents

We cannot complete any discussion of guidance without a consideration of the responsibility of the teacher to work with the parents of the students in his class.

> We plan a conference with the parents of seniors during the first week of school in September followed at one week intervals by meetings with parents of juniors, sophomores, and freshmen. Thus in four weeks, all high school parents have had a chance to visit with the teachers of their children.
>
> Class sponsors prepare parents for social events of the year. The senior trip is outlined as to extent and cost. Also, formal and informal parties—with or without flowers—are agreed upon with the parents.
>
> The dean of students outlines her program of adjustments for students between home and school.
>
> These meetings give the principal a chance to discuss college requirements and the need for high academic achievement.[4]

This school makes a determined effort to work closely with all the parents of all the children. In many schools, only the parents of children who are in trouble are well known by the principal, the counselors, and the teachers. The few parents who are leaders in the PTA are recognized by the teachers; but the great mass of the parents are vague and unknown quantities. Perhaps on Open House Night, or Public Schools Week the teacher will meet several parents of the students in his classes, chat with them for a few brief moments about what a nice boy Johnny is or is not, and that is the end of the teacher-parent contact for another year. Even on these occasions the kind of parents the high-school teacher sees are often just (1) parents of children who are in serious trouble; (2) parents who are active in PTA and community groups; and (3) parents of the superior children in the school.

Normally the teacher will not see (1) parents whose children are of low ability; (2) parents who are on the fringe of community social life; (3) parents with marked foreign accents; (4) parents from the lower socioeconomic levels.

[4] Frank E. Dodge, Superintendent, Public Schools, Bad Axe, Michigan. *NEA Journal,* 39:218 (March, 1950).

Adolescents and Parents

The desire of the high-school student himself very often is to keep his parents as far away from the school as possible. This is understandable. The adolescent is going through the process of becoming independent of his family, and one part of his life which is most truly his own is his school life. Here he is beyond their surveillance. He reports back to them only what he wishes to tell them or what someone else will tell them if he doesn't. So the parents get a highly edited version of the in-school life of the adolescent. Undoubtedly the wishes and needs of the adolescent have acted to reduce the emphasis of the high school on teacher-parent contacts. But is it justified to the extent that it is now practiced? Would students in the long run grow up better and learn more if parents had a closer contact with the school? Much of the adolescent-parent conflict arises out of lack of understanding of each other's worlds. The school has an obligation to aid the parent, who is still a powerful influence in the life of the adolescent, to gain greater insight into the adolescent's problems, as well as to help the adolescent understand the world of the parents.

Values of Talking to Parents

It is also apparent that the best guidance of a student will be nullified if the parents' cooperation and understanding cannot be secured. As has been stated before, the entire burden for such contact can rarely be left to the counselors. Even if the counselors could handle it, it is desirable that classroom teachers do an important share of such parent interviewing. The values of such interviewing may be briefly summarized:

1. The teacher understands better those student problems that may arise due to parental pressure or home conflict.
2. The parents and teacher can plan better together a program to meet the student's needs.
3. A home visit helps to place the student in his most significant environment.
4. Securing the cooperation of the parents is an invaluable aid in any guidance program.
5. The teacher, by talking with the parent, may help bridge the gap between the adolescent and his parents and help them to understand each other better.

Problems in Talking to Parents

As was earlier discussed in connection with student interviews, the average teacher has little time for conferences. To talk with parents is time consuming—a single home visit may take all afternoon. Thus, it is clear that no one teacher can come close to seeing the parents of all of his students or even a major portion of them when his teaching load may be from 100 to 150 students. However, if some teacher cooperation is secured, there could easily be established an interchange of reactions from parent conferences and an assignment of responsibility. Teacher A will take a certain group of parents of students that this teacher feels particular concern about; Teacher B will take another group, until each parent is the particular responsibility of at least one teacher. This teacher may be able to make one or two home calls a year and perhaps have one or more school conferences. The results of such conferences, if summarized and placed in the student's folder, then are available to all the other teachers. Periodic reports on such conferences to the total faculty would also greatly increase the value of the conferences.

The elementary schools have been pushing forward in this area in recent years with conspicuous success. Some schools now dismiss the entire student body for half days for a week in order that the classroom teacher may have a conference with every parent of every child in the class. This sometimes means scheduling conferences in the evening because of working mothers. But the important point is that the elementary school is realizing that a good program cannot exist without the understanding cooperation of the parents, nor can the teacher do an adequate job of instruction without understanding better the student in his family, and the family's wishes, needs, and problems.[5]

The high-school teacher often has the attitude that it is all right for the elementary teachers to work with parents, but that after all, high-school teachers need not be concerned about them. Such an attitude is blind, of course, to the realities of adolescence. However, it must be admitted that by and large the high-school teacher often has difficulty in talking with parents. The training of high-school teachers does not always provide adequate orientation to the personal-social problems of adults in our society. Let us examine briefly some of the problems that parents of adolescents face:

1. The adolescent is challenging severely the authority of the parents.
2. The adolescent is highly critical of his parents.
3. The parents may be entering middle-age, and their own feelings

[5] Eckert, Ralph, and Faith W. Smitter, "Home and School Work Together for Young Children," *Bulletin of the California State Department of Education,* Vol. 18, No. 1, March, 1949.

about themselves may be going through a period of readjustment; they are no longer physically so attractive; there is a loss of vitality; they recognize a limit to their personal ambitions in terms of job, money, or prestige.

4. The mothers in particular may no longer feel so needed; the children are growing up and can take care of themselves; soon they will be out of the home. The housework itself has lost some meaning and actually becomes less time consuming.

5. The parents are fearful of the heterosexual needs of their children; they are particularly anxious that they don't "go bad." The possibility of marriage seems imminent, and many parents feel insecure in the advice and help they have or have not provided their children.

6. Selection of life goals on the part of adolescents is a pressing problem; the common conflict between parent and child desires in terms of vocational choice becomes crucial for many.

7. Parents may feel that they have not done so good a job as they should have in raising their children. It may be a better job than someone else has done with his children, but each parent may feel he has, in some measure, failed some place. As parents, they may be highly self-critical and have few feelings of success. The culture itself provides so many alternatives for the parent that, if one choice is made, there may be the constant feeling that perhaps another might have been better.[6]

Whenever the teacher talks with a parent, then, he should keep in mind the particular sociological and personal situation that surrounds the parent of today's adolescent. He is so much more than "just a parent." He is a person who is going through important periods in his own life that will color his relationship with his child and will also affect the attitudes he takes toward all the other people he meets.

There are a number of basic difficulties in communication between parents and teachers; we list some of them:

1. The teachers may not understand the parent in terms of the kinds of problems and situations as noted above.

2. Parents are more deeply involved emotionally in the child than the teacher, who can afford to be more matter-of-fact and objective. They speak a different language when discussing the child.

3. Parents may approach teachers with ready-made attitudes. Some of these are:

Teachers are superior and I am inferior; the teacher should tell me what to do.

Teachers are peculiar people who have never really lived; I don't think they can tell me much about my child.

[6] Landis, Paul H., *Adolescence and Youth* (New York: McGraw-Hill Book Company, Inc., 1945), Chap. 12, "The Adolescent and Youth in the Parental Home," pp. 233-258.

Zachry, Caroline, *Emotion and Conduct in Adolescence* (New York: Appleton-Century-Crofts, Inc., 1940), Chap. 9, "Changing Relationship with Adults."

Anyone can teach; teaching is merely drilling the child with facts.

Teachers always made me suffer; I am really afraid of teachers.

Teachers are something special; I can't talk to them freely.

4. Both parents and teachers may be unsure of their values; for example do we or do we not want children of different races to treat each other democratically—it may lead to consequences that we are not prepared to face.

5. Teachers may represent new ideas, the broader world; parents may be more provincial, may not be abreast of new ideas.

6. Teachers may be afraid of parents; the parent may be critical, and with reason. The teacher always knows he can and should do a better job of teaching, just as the parent knows he could do a better job of being a parent. Two people who fear each other cannot talk easily.

7. Teachers are not always sure of why they teach what they teach; they do not want someone coming around who may expect a clear statement about "why teach history in units instead of by dates the way we did when I went to school."

Barriers like these interfere with good communication between parent and teacher. It is up to the teacher to gain insight into the problem and attempt to overcome it, since it is clear that parents are in no position to do it for themselves. It is particularly imperative that teachers move ahead in this direction, not only for the welfare of the individual but in order to assure the forward movement of education to meet the needs of society.

The Parent Interview

The individual conference with the parent presents additional difficulties that we have yet to discuss. On the one hand, the teacher is a person of education, usually greater than that of the average parent; and on the other hand, the parent knows a great deal more about the life history of the child than the teacher ever can know. The higher personal stake of the parent in the welfare of the child introduces an element of emotionality that must be recognized. The same principles that operate in the student conference must also prevail in the parent conference. Here are a few warnings:

As a teacher—

1. *Do not put yourself on the defensive.*

   PARENT: Well, Mary certainly got along better last year when she had Mrs. Dale for her English.

   TEACHER: *(Wrong)* Perhaps Mrs. Dale didn't expect her to work very hard.

   (Better) She seemed to get along better with Mrs. Dale. . . .

2. *Do not put parent on the defensive.*

TEACHER: *(Wrong)* Of course, some parents see to it that their children have a place to study at home.

(Better) Mary seems to find it difficult to get some of her work done at home. . . .

3. *Do not, by implication, suggest that parents are doing a poor job.*

PARENT: I just don't know what to do with Mary, she is so rude.

TEACHER: *(Wrong)* You aren't severe enough with her.

(Better) You feel Mary isn't acting well at home. . . .

4. *Do not become omniscient.*

TEACHER: *(Wrong)* Now with students in this ability group we always tell the parents that they should take a vocational course.

(Better) Mary seems to do better work in vocational courses. What do you think about this?

5. *Do not sound like a social snob.*

TEACHER: Now we have another student—his father is a doctor, you know—who is one of our top students.

6. *Do not pry into other people's affairs.*

PARENT: Oh, I am so mad at my husband.

TEACHER: *(Wrong)* Now don't be afraid to tell me your problems; we are here to help you. What did your husband do?

(Better) Sometimes parents disagree. Now I think Mary. . . .

7. *Be prepared to hear unpleasant, disturbing, unexpected things.*

PARENT: *(Weeping)* Oh, you just can't imagine the awful things that boy does. Why the other day. . . .

TEACHER: *(Wrong)* Why Mrs. Jones, you shouldn't say things like that.

(Better) These things can be very upsetting. . . .

8. *Be discriminating in the information given.*

PARENT: Now tell me honestly, is Mary really dumb?

TEACHER: *(Wrong)* Now Mrs. Jones, no one is really dumb.

(Wrong) Mary has an IQ of 80. That means she is probably subnormal. But there is nothing to worry about, really.

(Better) Mary has many assets. She has a good mind for practical and concrete problems, but she does not do so well with vague and abstract things. That is why she is adjusting so well to the new program we planned for her. It is wonderful to see how well she can plan a meal!

9. *Do not become a partisan in family affairs.*

PARENT: To tell the truth, Mary would be all right if her father would only stop nagging at her.

TEACHER: *(Wrong)* Yes, a lot of fathers don't really understand girls very well.

(Better) You feel Mary's father sometimes increases the problem. . . .[7]

These warnings to the teacher preparing to do parent interviewing may be multiplied many times. As in any human relations situation, there are many pitfalls. The teacher with an adequate

[7] Adapted from Smitter, Faith W., Bernard J. Lonsdale, "Interpreting Education," California State Department of Education, Division of Elementary Education, Sacramento, Calif., Mimeographed, April 1, 1947. See particularly pp. 1-4 regarding parent attitudes.

understanding of parents can learn to conduct parent conferences with ease and skill. But it takes experience and a real appreciation of the problems of the parents of adolescents in today's culture. It is suggested that some trial interviews be practiced before doing any actual parent interviewing. Thus, with the help of an audience, one can gain insight into what was strong or weak in one's handling of a parent conference.[8] One suggested structure for a parent interview is as follows:

1. Describe a strength, special ability, or interest of the student and discuss the educational implications of this with the parent.
2. Describe the student's most immediate need. Do not dwell on a weakness about which nothing can be done (low ability, physical handicap). The kind of weakness that can be helped through education is the major objective: improvement of reading, development of hobby interest, finding a vocational objective, and the like. Get the parents' view of this weakness; what the parents think might be done.
3. Discuss what the teacher plans for the student; what the parents plan for the student.[9]

It must be kept in mind that most of the parents whom the teacher will meet will be the mothers. The mother is usually at home during the day, can be reached for appointments at school, and, during most of the child's school life has taken the most active interest in the child's schooling. The father, while interested in the progress of the child, usually cannot be as active in school affairs or find time for daytime conferences. Thus the teacher will want to make a special effort to understand the particular problems of wives and mothers, since he will have to work with them.[10]

Preparing and Planning for the Parent Interview

In preparing for the parent interview, it may help to have examples of the work the student does. If the teacher is wise, his selection of such examples will include both good and poor work, in order that the parent may not get a distorted or hopeless view of his child. If the teacher shows the parent one *D* paper after another and then says, "See what I am up against in trying to work with Susy," irreparable damage may be done to the parent-child relation as well as to the future school progress of the student. As was suggested in the outline for such a parent interview, it is important

[8] For an excellent description of one such program see: Stendler, Celia B., "Let's Look at Parent-Teacher Conferences," *Educational Leadership,* 6:292-299 (February, 1949).

[9] Adapted from Smitter and Lonsdale, *op. cit.*

[10] See, particularly, Cassidy, Rosalind, and Hilda C. Kozman, *Counseling Girls in Today's World* (New York: McGraw-Hill Book Company, Inc., 1947).

to start with positive material, and something concrete to show the parent, such as a report, an examination, a drawing, a comment made by another student. This will provide the parent with a feeling of security. Of course to follow this immediately with negative material may make the parent suspicious—"He just showed me that good paper in order to soften the blow." The teacher must realistically express the feeling: "John does both good and poor work; we are interested, both of us, in helping him do more good than poor work. Here, I have some examples of his work. Let's look at this very good quiz he turned in yesterday. See—it is good because it shows grasp of the facts, it is neat, he had obviously studied and thought about the material. . . ."

Working with parents constitutes a new and needed departure for the secondary schools. The reward in terms of increased school support and improved student attitudes will be considerable. It rests upon the individual teacher to make the initial steps and to make parents an integral part of their child's education.

Visiting the Home

There is no real substitute for the home visit. However, teachers should not drop in on unsuspecting parents. It catches them off guard, places them at a disadvantage, and only increases the tension and distance between school and parents. A note or a telephone call suggesting a time and day for the visit is appropriate. The teacher should previously have approached the student about a home visit. If the student is violently upset at the thought, the teacher should look further into the problem before the visit. The teacher should also reassure the student that the visit is in no way a "checking up" on the student, but a very desirable method of understanding the student better so that he can do his best possible work in school. The same reassurance is needed for the parent. The first reaction of the parent will be, "Oh, oh! John must be in trouble." Thus, the teacher will want to indicate that he is interested in John, that he feels that John is a person worth being interested in, and that the parents can help the teacher to guide John's learning.

Summary

The teacher who sees his role as one of providing guidance to the student will find that there are many ways in which this activity and service is performed. A recurrent need is helping young people choose the proper academic course of study; another is aiding them to select wisely a vocational goal that is fitting. Some thought and sensitivity on the part of the teacher to the special individual problems in these areas can result in significant help to individual students.

But no guidance, whether individual, group, vocational, or academic can ensure individual adjustment if the teacher does not have some communication with the parents of the adolescent. And the parents of adolescents themselves bring special problems to the teacher. In the high school the communication of the teacher and the parent is usually quite limited. Yet the very fact that it is limited is one reason why so many adolescents find home and school offering little of real value in the way of adult help and guidance. A teacher who considers the needs of young people will seek to work closely with their parents and overcome those barriers that traditionally have divided school and home.

Selected References

Vocational and Academic Guidance

American Association of School Administrators. *The Expanding Role of Education,* 1948 Yearbook. "Utilization of the experience of Work in the Learning Process," pp. 149-177. Washington, D.C.: National Education Association, 1948. Emphasizes the need for work experience as basic education.

Bell, Howard. *Matching Youth and Jobs.* Washington, D.C.: American Council on Education, 1940. A basic reference for all teachers who have any responsibility in vocational guidance.

Broadening the Services of Small High Schools. Bulletin No. 9, 1948, U.S. Office of Education, Washington, D.C. One way of extending the educational opportunity of young people in small schools is through work experience programs.

Combs, Arthur W. "Nondirective Techniques and Vocational Counseling," *Occupations,* 25:262 (February, 1947). Provides criteria for the counselor in knowing when to use the nondirective approach in this area.

David, Paul. *Barriers to Youth Employment.* Washington, D.C.: American Council on Education, 1943. Discusses the real factors in the world of work that students and counselors will have to face together in planning a vocational future.

Department of Supervision and Curriculum Development. *Toward a New Curriculum,* 1944 Yearbook. Washington, D.C.: National Education Association, 1944. Chap. 5, "Educating Through Work." The importance of making education a significant contribution to work adjustment.

Douglass, Harl R. *(ed.) The High School Curriculum.* New York: The Ronald Press Company, 1947. Chapter 13, "Occupational Trends, Work Experience, and the Curriculum," pp. 274-294. Points out some of the general problems in the area and how school-work programs are one answer.

Lindquist, E. F., *et al. What Good Is High School?* Life Adjustment Booklet. Chicago: Science Research Associates, 1948. An aid for the teacher doing academic counseling with students.

Myers, George E. *Principles and Techniques of Vocational Guidance.* New York: McGraw-Hill Book Company, Inc., 1941. Discusses such questions as: What is vocational guidance? How is it related to other kinds of guidance, to organized education, and to student personnel work? What services are involved in a comprehensive program of vocational guidance?

Shartle, Carroll L. *Occupational Information.* New York: Prentice-Hall, Inc., 1946. A comprehensive discussion of how to find out about occupations, and the types of information needed.

Occupational Data for Counselors, U. S. Dept. of Labor, Bureau of Labor Statistics, Bulletin No. 817, 1945. Summarizes data on occupations and occupational trends for the vocational advisement of students.

School and Work Programs. Bulletin No. 9, 1947, U. S. Office of Education, Washington, D.C. Brief descriptions of some work experience programs in many places in the United States.

"Your Future Is What You Make It," *You and Industry* Series, No. 4, National Association of Manufacturers, 1947. Useful pamphlet for guidance of high-school students.

Youth and the World of Work. Social Research Service, Michigan State College, East Lansing, Mich., September, 1949. A study of the ideas and attitudes of youth towards their vocational future.

Zapoleon, Marguerite. *Community Occupational Surveys.* Vocational Division, Bulletin No. 223, 1942, U. S. Office of Education, Washington, D.C. A guide for making occupational surveys and a summary of a number of such studies that have been made.

Working with Parents

DelSolar, Charlotte. *Parents and Teachers View the Child.* New York: Bureau of Publications, Teachers College, Columbia University. A significant report on the discrepancies between parent, teacher and child in viewing the concerns, goals, and personalities of the child.

Gabbard, Hazel F. *Working with Parents: A Handbook.* Bulletin No. 7, 1948, U. S. Office of Education, Washington, D.C. Suggests best practice in working to bridge the gap between home and school.

Gardner, George E. "Can Parents Grow Along with Their Teen-agers?" *Child Study,* 28:15-17 (Winter, 1950-1951). Insight into central problem areas of the relation of parents to adolescents.

Guiding the Adolescent. Publication 225, Rev. ed. 1946, Children's Bureau, Federal Security Agency, Washington, D.C. An excellent handbook for parents and teachers to gain understanding of major problems of adolescent growth and development.

Taylor, Katherine W. *Do Adolescents Need Parents* New York: Appleton-Century-Crofts, Inc., 1938. A useful reference to understand the problems that adolescents present to parents; particularly helpful as preparation for parent interviews.

Thompson, Orrin G. "Parents: Unused Allies in Guidance," *Educational Leadership,* 6:536-538 (May, 1949). How parents can be brought into closer relation with the school and their own children.

21. The Teacher in School and Community

SCHOOLS have personalities just as people have. Pinecrest Union is quiet and serious. Teachers have an aloof, preoccupied air. Students rarely smile in their classes. But Glen Park is another matter indeed. The air is easier. Learning is not quite so grim. Even the custodians act different. Then there is Lincoln High where the atmosphere is hard to define. It seems to be several schools mixed in one. Large groups of students seem completely separated from the others. There are the vocational students who spend only a half day in school. The college-bound group keeps to itself in its own classes. A third group, called "general" students, seems not to belong anywhere.

A beginning teacher soon learns the personality of his school. He learns how teachers and students behave. He learns how principals, deans, and department heads act. In brief, he learns his school is a small society, with accepted ways of living for its people.

And the small school society is also part of the larger community society. Community traditions, pressures, desires, all are reflected in the school. The teacher has, as it were, two homes—a home in the school and a home in the community. He needs to know his way around both.

In this chapter we will present some of the key aspects of the individual school structure of significance to the beginner, and then proceed to look at the role of the school in the community.

The New Teacher in the Social System of the School

Even before analyzing the character of the new school, it is important to understand the position of the new teacher. Being a new teacher has special advantages and special hazards. Let us consider the advantages first.

1. Making mistakes is to be expected. Administrators and fellow teachers are tolerantly expecting the new teacher to make a number of mistakes. The new teacher does not, therefore, need to strive to be perfect. He does not have to dwell miserably upon the early ending of a promising career just because third period dissolved into a minor riot. Being new protects the new teacher from major failure *if* he is willing to learn from mistakes, but even the new teacher is not excused from making the same mistake endlessly.
2. Youth means an initial advantage with students. A young teacher may more closely understand and identify, and therefore sympathize, with the problems and potentialities of adolescents. This is an advantage to be exploited.
3. It is easier to try new teaching techniques. The new teacher is unaware of the restrictions of time-worn ways of doing things. It is less difficult to start fresh, because no one knows what the new teacher can do. Therefore, no expectations are set up.
4. Fellow teachers are often eager to help. The more experienced may offer advice, assistance, and many will go out of their way to see that rough spots are smoothed.
5. The new environment is stimulating and interesting. Each day brings surprises and new situations. This sense of new adventure makes teaching engrossing and challenging.

Now, what about the disadvantages:

1. It is possible to be too young for the comfort of the balance of the faculty. Many of the new teacher's associates will have been in teaching for many years. The average age of many high school faculties is well up in the forties. The youth of a new teacher may be a reminder of past promises unfulfilled.
2. Fresh from college, the new teacher may remind some other staff members of their own shortcomings as teachers. Many of the attacks against "new-fangled ideas" or "those fancy notions of college professors that won't work, of course" come out of this resentment against being reminded of old failures. The new teacher is made the scapegoat for feelings of guilt.
3. What is routine to everyone else is a major new learning for the new teacher. Everyone else knows what to do in a fire-drill. The new teacher is as apt as not to march his students down the "up" stairs and bring the amused laughs from students and teachers. It is easy to be unaware of what

is "the thing to do" when the teacher is new. This has to be taken with good humor, and with extra awareness of what the others are doing. The new teacher has to watch his teaching manners in the welter of special conditions that prevail in each school.

4. The new teacher is at the bottom of the pecking order. Where new books are available, they go to the teacher with the longest tenure and greatest prestige. The new teacher takes the cast-offs. Often the poorest rooms—noisy, bad lighting, poor storage facilities—are assigned the new teacher. The study-hall just before lunch may fall to the lot of the hapless beginner. He may have no voice in school councils because he is so "green." He has to watch, be patient, and win his place with his colleagues. He can expect few special favors.

5. Students are aware of his newness. This is one of the horrors that invade the sleepless nights of the prospective teacher. "The students are out to test you," is the traditional comment made to a new teacher. This is only half true; the students do not know what to expect. So they are uneasy likewise. But it is true the students will not "just naturally" follow his directions. He needs to convey his sense of his own security, his interest and competence to them.

While these listings seem to place the new teacher at more of a disadvantage than advantage, it is probably no worse than being new in any job or profession. As a matter of fact, many school systems are going out of their way to make the first years of teaching pleasant and successful in order that the new teacher may learn the best ways of teaching in his first trials and may be wisely guided when he makes his first mistakes:

> Mr. O'Toole reported that his first job was almost too good to be true. He was given two "core" classes—that is, he had two groups a day for two hours each for both English and Social Studies. The rest of his day was free for preparation and counseling with this same group of students. How did this ideal program occur? Because the administration of this system felt that the new teachers needed the additional time for preparation and to get acquainted with the high school age. His second year of teaching Mr. O'Toole was asked to sponsor a club, and also took one additional period of remedial reading with a small group of special students. But that first year of orientation paid off. He refused a higher paying job in a near-by community because he felt that in his original school system he was helped to do the best possible job of teaching. That was more important than a slight salary increase.

The prestige system. The new teacher is almost always at the bottom of the prestige ladder. Of course the hierarchy differs in each school in some of its specifics, but the general relationships are remarkably similar. Science teachers are moving rapidly upward in the hierarchy. The college-preparatory teachers and courses almost invariably have the highest prestige. The coach of the major sport—football or basketball or baseball—may be a powerful personality outside the school if he turns out winning teams, but may have little to say in determining the school policies. Where there is a strong guidance system, the counselors may have high status, but still exercise relatively little influence in curriculum matters. A strong teachers' organization may boost the current president or chairman to a position of high status in school policymaking. Length of tenure has a potent influence on status; an older woman English teacher will outrank a young man teacher of solid geometry any day. But where age is held constant, the man teacher of the academic subject will often carry greater weight. However, many schools are virtual matriarchies because of the dominant position of older women teaching English, mathematics, foreign languages, and history.

The existence of this kind of status ladder is no different in essence from that existing in any business. An institution organizes the relationships of those working on the same program; otherwise, there would be no social order, no channeling of authority, and the result would be social chaos. Every segment of society demonstrates this principle of organization, and the school is no exception. The new teacher will quickly appraise the status situation in the school he enters. He will ask: with whom does power reside? If he tells his troubles to X, does that mean Y will certainly hear about it? Or if he confides in Y, will the news of his problems be discussed with guffaws down in the boiler room when the men have their after lunch smoke? Or, if he waits until he can contact W will he get an immediate helpful reaction, a word spoken on his behalf to the principal, and the way smoothed for him? These are the vital elements of adequate social interaction which most of us accept unconsciously; we have been groomed all our life to make such evaluations of others.[1]

Mistakes of the beginner. The beginning teacher will find working with his colleagues most rewarding when he accepts his own status without annoyance, recognizes the realities of the interpersonal network of his institution, and cheerfully performs his own role. As a new teacher there are a few things *not* to do:

1. Do not complain loudly and at length about the school building, the school program, and school personalities. While old-timers can have all the pleasure they wish out of continual complaints, the newcomer who voices the same sentiments will draw a cold look and an unsympathetic reaction.
2. Do not voice your opinion on matters of teaching, particularly ideas

[1] Redl, Fritz, and William Wattenberg, *Mental Hygiene in Teaching* (New York: Harcourt, Brace & Company, 1951), pp. 251-255.

that are conspicuously "new" or "modern," until after you have earned a reputation of being a competent classroom teacher.

3. Do not keep on talking about "what we did back at old Tuxedo U.," particularly if many of the faculty are from a near-by smaller college.

4. Do not dress at the height of fashion. Dress neatly and in keeping with your usual manner. Do not wear obviously expensive suits or dresses that look as though they were bought on your father's checking account and not on your salary as a teacher.

5. Refrain from gossiping about other teachers. While you can listen to the talk around you, there will not be a very warm reception to your small observations. Keep them to yourself until you are sure that what you say will be understood in the right manner.

6. Do not boast of your great success with the youngsters; but on the other hand, do not always moan about your failures.

7. Do not forget that those who give you advice are often your most devoted champions. Everyone likes to feel that his few words of wisdom are sought and prized. Older members of the faculty have a wealth of experience to share. Ask for their views, but not in a fashion that would call your motives into question. Ask only for the advice you really need and intend to try to follow.

8. Do not always run to the principal with every new idea or new problem. Find one or two other teachers to talk ideas or problems over before seeing the principal. See to it that the principal is informed of your work directly from you, rather than from the grapevine. But this does not mean a daily report on your activities, startling and wonderful as they may appear to you.

9. Do not fret in silence over a classroom boner. If you suspect that something you said or did may cause a serious repercussion, be sure to see the principal first yourself, before an angry student or irate parent distorts the picture.

In summary, the beginning teacher enters an institution that is well structured, having a status system, a system of intercommunication among the members, and a distinctive over-all personality and atmosphere. As a new functioning member of this structure, the beginning teacher has his status quite clearly defined for him. There are certain things he can and cannot do in terms of the particular school and its culture. Let us now turn to two other phases of getting acquainted in the new school; first, the status systems existing among various schools in the system, and second, the role of school traditions in determining the particular culture of the school itself.

Status Systems Among Schools

Personalities of schools come from an inheritance of tradition, location, the building itself, the various dominant personalities in the administration, faculty, and student body whose imprint has been left upon the school. While it may be impossible to assign specific responsibility to any one factor, it is very clear that some schools "rate" and some do not.

> Emerson High School is undoubtedly the dingiest, most time-worn of the five high schools in the city. The building should have been replaced many years ago; the halls are high, dark, echoing; the rooms are inadequate by any modern standard. The desks are scarred deeply by the carvings of generations of students. It is impossible to write on some of them without several thicknesses of paper underneath. The science laboratories are medieval. There is no auditorium and the physical-education classes have to walk two blocks to the playing field. And yet anyone who is anybody wants to go to Emerson High. When Emerson plays its traditional rival, Washington High, the game gets the best spot on the calendar, the Saturday before Thanksgiving. Teachers seek "promotion" to Emerson. There is the essence of a tradition! Emerson has prided itself for years in being the academic college-preparatory high school; it even resisted putting in typing classes until student pressure had its effect. It still has no shop courses, no home-economics courses, only a few business and commercial courses. Students from all over the city are allowed to enroll at Emerson if they signify college ambitions and are recommended by their junior high principal.

The reputation of a school clearly rests on other things besides the building in which it is housed. The socioeconomic level of the school population has a marked effect on setting the status of the school; the wealthier the neighborhood, the higher the school status. The fewer minority-group students there are, the higher is school status. While these rankings are obviously superficial, they do exist and sway the opinions of the public and may even determine the allocation of school funds.[2] New teachers in a large school system may find themselves placed first in the lower ranking schools and then, as they show promise, be promoted to the schools of higher status.

> Jane Anderson, fresh out of college with her secondary certificate, was fortunate in getting the job. It was a large school system, and very few inexperienced teachers were hired. She found herself at Broadway High School with the only other inexperienced teacher in the system. Her classes were small—she thought—until she found out that they were made up of the overflow from other classes; the students nobody else wanted. There were some temporary structures, so called, since they were almost as old as the school, that held classes that could not be accommodated in the big building. All of her classes were in these temporary buildings. Many of her fellow teachers pointed out to her that because she was new and inexperienced, she might not get very easy treatment. The school was on the fringe of the industrial section. The

[2] Warner, L., Robert Havighurst, and Martin Loeb, *Who Shall Be Educated?* (New York: Harper & Brothers, 1944), pp. 75-76.

student body was a mixture of many ethnic groups and from lower socioeconomic levels.

Recognizing the status system within a school organization aids in orienting the teacher to the system in which he is working. Not always will the administration place the "best" teachers in the status schools. In many instances the most creative and imaginative programs occur in the least favored neighborhoods where the public is more receptive to innovations.

The Role of School Traditions

A visitor to Ocean View High School on a Tuesday late in May would have thought everyone had departed his right mind. Down one hall came a girl dressed as the Ace of Hearts. No sooner had she disappeared around the corner than a boy costumed like Li'l Abner appeared. Behind him was a girl dressed like someone out of the Arabian Nights. Indeed, about every tenth student was garbed in a weird and wholly delightful fashion. Of course—it was Senior Jinx Day! At this time all the seniors were to come dressed in some fantastic costume, the funnier and fancier the better. Then a prize for the best costume would be awarded at a school assembly in the afternoon, followed by a variety program put on by the seniors.

In one school the tradition that the Big Game rally is to be broken up by a flying attack from the chief rival has the whole community out to see the fray. In another school the seniors have a Senior Sneak Day, a day when they can cut school without being penalized, usually to go to the beach for a party and have an informal sports dance in the evening. Still another school has a special ritual when a very famous member of the team has graduated and his "number" is retired permanently to take its place in the archives of the school.

The traditions of a school are important. They make the school unique, provide a personality, command loyalty. Not only the traditions, but the rituals of the school are of great significance. To the new teacher, to learn the school song, to remember what the school colors are and what the school symbol is, may not seem at all in keeping with the dignity of being a teacher. Actually knowledge of these traditions helps a new teacher to be accepted.[3]

The Teacher and Other Members of the School Staff

One teacher educator complained sadly, "None of our graduates ever fails in teaching because of lack of knowledge of his subject

[3] Waller, Willard, *The Sociology of Teaching* (New York: John Wiley and Sons, Inc., 1932), Chap. IX, "The Separate Culture of the School," and Chap. X, "The Culture of the School: Ceremonies."

matter, but many do fail because they just can't get along with the rest of the faculty." The human relations of the teacher with his student have concerned us for the major portion of this volume. But it is also important to focus for a time upon the teacher's relations with his fellow teachers, his administrators, and the other adults in the school organization.

It has been pointed out that the new teacher is a special kind of person in the school. But his newness can be forgotten and he can become an accepted part of the group quickly and easily if he is normally observant of the network of human relationships around him.

> The school staff gave a party for the young man who was called into service. The new teacher who had come to replace him had arrived just that evening. At first he felt ill at ease and out of place among this gay room full of utter strangers. Even the principal who had hired him was merely a face and a name met briefly at the placement office. But everyone was having a good time. There was singing and good-natured banter. He didn't know who taught, who was a wife, who a school board member. He began to see that they were pleasant, friendly, and interesting people. He walked over and joined the singing.
>
> A week later when he had gotten to know a few of the people of the faculty one frank woman teacher on the staff said: "I breathed a sigh of relief when I saw you bear down on that barbershop harmony. You looked a bit stiff when you first came in—scared, I guess!—but when you turned on that baritone I had a feeling you would fit in."

The new teacher must remember at all times that he is part of a team engaged in a common enterprise. He is not alone. He must work with others for the good of the young people and the total school program. A good school is a cooperative venture where sharing, mutual help, and the firm support of friendship aid each teacher to perform his task well.

The Individual Teacher and the Subject-Matter Department

The organization of the high school into departments facilitates common programs and projects. It also provides a channel whereby the principal can quickly get information to one group without having to discuss it individually with each teacher. The head of the department usually is the teacher who has greatest seniority, or is the most articulate, or the most politically adroit, or the most competent, or all of these combined. One of the beginner's first tasks is to learn to know this department head and the working relations of the department.

Variations in school policies are infinite. Some departments have great power, some very little; some plan whole curricula; some are merely a convenient administrative device. Some department heads act with the principal in hiring new teachers; some heads are merely titular with no real power at all. In any event, the beginner will find himself working most closely with this group of teachers in his own field. He will often find several points of view expressed, sometimes with resulting bitter feelings as a department divides into opposing camps. There may be a strict expectation of conformity to a set curriculum, in which case the whole department will have a common mold. There may be no curricular expectations at all, in which case each in the department will go his own way. But there is no pattern that can be described as universal. We can only point out here that an understanding of the departmental organization of a school is essential in any attempt to become a working member.

> The work for tenth-grade English included a rather large amount of formal grammar. This program was outlined by the superintendent's office and the English department was expected to follow the outline. Each semester the students moved on to a new teacher. Miss Drew found herself caught in a lock-step progression. No matter what she thought the students might need, the teacher in the department who received them from her next semester would expect that they had learned the required grammar. But Miss Drew found that this class of hers had many very slow readers, students with a great writing handicap, and other problems needing special attention. When she brought it to the attention of the head of the department she was given encouragement to go ahead and work with the students on their special problems. "But remember," said the head, "Miss Scott and Mr. De Paw are going to be upset if most of those students are not ready for their work next semester."

The amount, kind, and direction of flexibility in a school program will derive in large measure from just such human interaction. It is here that change and new programs must have their beginnings. Teachers who can and do work as teams can meet the changing problems of instruction.

Relations with the Administrative Staff

There is one special series of relationships, however, that is of particular concern to the beginner. This concerns his relations with his administrators. During the period of student teaching, the aspiring teacher usually finds himself under the watchful eye, not only of the classroom teacher, but of one of the faculty from his teacher-education institution. Sometimes a student finds himself chafing at the bit, irritated by these other individuals who seek to hold him down. He is unpleasantly surprised that being in his own classroom does not free him from the surveillance of others. And the student who was overdependent on those in charge of his supervision during student teaching is likewise unpleasantly surprised for exactly the opposite reason: There are so many decisions he has to make by himself.

The process of student teaching is useful not only for learning something about the feel of the classroom, but also for learning something about working under and with others. The ability to follow the principle of "alternate assertion and withdrawal" in dealing with professional superiors takes time to acquire. The new teacher learns slowly that there is a time to advance the new idea, make the interesting suggestion, demonstrate initiative. But there is also a time to watch, observe, ask for help, follow instructions carefully, be submissive and accepting. A judicious mixture of these two forms of interaction with others will help the beginner in establishing professional rapport and yet remain aware of his own status.

Many students who have had the opportunity to work as assistant leaders in youth groups, as Sunday-school teachers, as junior members of an office staff, come better prepared to take supervision and direction than those lacking such experiences. The student teacher is part student, part teacher. This in-between, neither-fish-nor-fowl existence is a source of trouble to some beginners. Where new teachers have never held subordinate yet responsible positions, it would be wise to obtain some such experience prior to student teaching or before embarking on the first fulltime teaching job.

The New Teacher and His Principal

The authority hierarchy of the school places the beginning teacher in a subordinate position in regard to school policies, programs, and other school decisions. The principal to a great extent establishes the atmosphere of the school. And the principal can be a person of great educational leadership, working cooperatively with his staff in a continual program of school improvement, or he can be a petty tyrant, wielding an arbitrary authority. The very lack of centralized control in our schools from the county, state, or national level, reinforces the power of the building principal to establish his own school climate.

The principal performs two significant tasks in relation to the teacher, in addition to establishing the administrative atmosphere. The principal provides supervision and acts as a kind of father confessor. While many principals are too involved in administrative matters to give much actual classroom supervision, there is a marked trend toward more and more principal supervision.[4]

Some teachers respond to supervision as though it were an "inspection," as sometimes it is. But most of the time the success of a supervisory visit depends on mutual acceptance of the motives of the visit. The teacher who resents such a visit, who gets agitated and disturbed, can hardly profit from the advice that the principal could give. The beginning teacher in particular should welcome such visits since only by discussing his work with someone who sees the total school program can he learn where his work fits.

Another function of supervision is in the rating of teachers. Some school systems apply rating scales upon which depend the next year's contract and salary. This kind of rating has obvious psychological hazards for the teacher. Probably ratings are more useful for guidance in in-service growth.[5]

In terms of obtaining supervisory assistance, the teacher in the small school is apt to have a great advantage. Here the administrative load, although heavy, is still not as elaborate or time consuming as in a large city school. The new teacher who does need guidance and support in the first years of teaching will find it more often in the small school.

In addition to teaching supervision, the principal often extends guidance on personal problems. The principal, who is sympathetic, understanding, and experienced, is often, to the beginning teacher, the best source of assistance and advice for both teaching and personal problems. This is not a recommendation that the new teacher should run to the principal with every small trouble, but it does mean that where the teacher informs the principal about both his personal and teaching problems he is more apt to find support and receive aid than if he goes his way alone. Because most principals find that a contented faculty is easier to work with, they are willing and eager to be of help wherever they can.

[4] Barr, A. S., W. H. Burton and L. J. Brueckner, *Supervision* (New York: Appleton-Century-Crofts, Inc., 1938).

[5] Reavis, W. C., and D. H. Cooper, *Evaluation of Teacher Merit in City School Systems,* Supplementary Education Monograph, No. 59 (Chicago: University of Chicago Press, 1945). Also see, Association for Supervision and Curriculum Development, *Better Than Rating* (Washington, D.C.: National Education Association, 1950).

The very fact that they are usually older and more experienced and in a position of central authority provides reassurance for the teacher.

The principal may help the beginner combat his feeling of isolation. The teacher closes the door of his classroom at the beginning of the day, and only at lunch and after school does he have an opportunity to talk with another adult. He is quite alone with his classes. This isolation from others is part of the present institutional arrangement in the high school. In some few places where the core program is being used, it has been found worth while to use teams of teachers. Both the social-studies and the English teachers, for example, may be in the same room or rooms with the same classes several times during the week. The more typical isolation often results in lack of security. The new teacher usually is bothered by such things as:

Are they learning enough?

Are students behaving as well with me as with other teachers?

Do all the other teachers have trouble at the same points that I do, or am I just an exception?

It is only when the new teacher checks these uncertainties with the principal that he can gain some insight into his developing competence as a teacher. To keep them bottled up inside for brooding does not contribute to professional growth.

Working with Other Members of the School Staff

There are other professional relationships that are of concern to the teacher. These involve working with:

1. The substitute teacher
2. Non-certificated personnel: custodians, secretaries, clerks, bus drivers
3. Specialists in the school:
   - Librarian
   - Counselor
   - Health service personnel
   - Attendance and child welfare specialists

The Substitute Teacher

In the life of every teacher comes that moment, about 6 A.M.—or it may be 6 P.M.—when he realizes he will be unable to go to school. What happens then! Such emergency absences come only too often without warning:

> Miss Sinclair was finding it harder and harder to finish her lunch. For some strange reason she felt close to tears, and her colleagues around the table swam in front of her vision through a misty haze. She thought this all very odd, and at first decided she was merely too hungry. So she made a valiant effort to eat. But it didn't work. Finally she got up, and hurried out of the room feeling as though pursued by some malignant doom. She luckily found the principal in his office and started to tell him that the world had become very strange, but instead, and to her horror, she burst into tears. The principal quickly deposited her at his desk, and called in one of the women teachers. She felt her forehead, popped a thermometer into her mouth and found a fever of 103°. Five minutes later she was escorted out of the building and home. She remained in bed with a fine case of the flu for three days.

Sometimes it is a sickness at home, or a frantic call from a parent. But it is the rare teacher that can predict when he will be absent. This means that some kinds of teacher preparation are always needed. It is easy for some teachers to plan from day to day, keeping the progress of work in their own minds, but never bothering to write it down or even to inform the students. Such a teacher is the substitute's headache. The preparation that a teacher makes for classwork in order adequately to meet the possible emergencies should include the following:

1. An over-all plan that includes weekly and daily activities in as much detail as fits the teacher's own need, but sufficient to guide a newcomer in the general pattern of the classwork.
2. This plan should be in a workbook that remains in the teacher's desk so that it can be found by someone temporarily taking the teacher's place, and it should be clearly labeled as the workbook for the courses taught.
3. When students have helped to work out these plans the substitute is given guidance because the class knows what is desired.

Sometime during each semester each teacher should consider with the class what is appropriate behavior if a substitute appears. Catastrophes have occurred in classes where such preparation was not undertaken. Students have been unpleasant, unruly, impertinent. This is totally unnecessary, if the regular teacher has the foresight to prepare for inevitable absences. Some teachers may find it worth while to appoint a standing emergency committee to assist substitutes. Such a group of students would be versed in class routines, would be informed as to the week's plans, would know where the plan book was, and would be adept in acting as guide and host to a substitute. It is important that this committee be accepted by the class. This requires developing the idea of such a committee with the class, allowing them to set up the organization and the responsibilities of the committee and of the other class members. The committee may never have to function. But if it is called upon, it can eliminate many unpleasant and trying situations. The committee may also serve as class host to any visitors and be in temporary charge when the teacher is called from the room for a few moments during a regular day.

Relations with Other School Employees

Many students before entering the teaching profession are completely unaware of the significant role played by those who work in and around the school but are not on the professional staff. "If you get the janitor on your side, half your troubles are over," is a common remark of experienced teachers, "but if the janitor is against you, you won't be able to get anything done for your room." Not only the janitor, but the bus driver, the cafeteria employees, the secretaries, and clerical assistants are important to the teacher. While the training of this kind of personnel is usually considerably less than that of the professional staff, they can and do contribute a great deal to the smooth running of the school.

A cooperative, responsible, reliable custodian makes a tremendous difference in the way the school plant can operate. One teacher planned to have a meeting in her room during the period when she was free and there were no classes scheduled for it. However, the janitor was scheduled to clean it at that time. Unless he changed his schedule the meeting would not be possible. Through considerate consultation with the janitor on his schedule, the adjustment was made and the meeting was held. But there are often times when such adjustments cannot be made. The time-consuming cleaning of a school building is accomplished according to a routine that makes for most efficient use of the labor employed. Teachers often complain that this does not take into consideration the most efficient use of the teacher's time in utilizing their classrooms as they wish. Obviously these differences in purposes will have to be compromised. Only when the teacher recognizes the human demands of the non-certificated employee will he be able to achieve satisfactory adjustments. The individual new to authority is apt to abuse it. New teachers are sometimes officious when they should be polite and considerate.

The same principle of considerate treatment applies to the secretaries and clerks. The reputations of many teachers are not helped by what the principal's secretary reports about how they treat her. It is a rare school where such assistants are not always working hard and long hours, usually far beyond that for which they are paid. No teacher is in a position to exact special consideration from them.

Custodians, secretaries, and bus drivers are often experienced observers of the school and student body. A friendly chat with a bus driver can elicit very valuable information about his students to the interested teacher. Similarly, some custodians are themselves almost institutions in the schools they serve. They know more about the inner workings of the organization than many professional staff members. These people are valuable informants for the new teacher in becoming acquainted with who is who and what is what around the school.

Some men teachers when they first begin teaching will find it financially useful and also educationally valuable to act as school bus drivers. This experience is tremendously valuable. The young people are voluble, friendly, uninhibited on the school bus. The quiet observer can glean much of importance about the workings of the adolescent personality. Driving a bus is probably one of the most direct methods for gaining quick access into the student culture of the school.

The Individual Teacher and the Specialists in the School

Early in his career the beginning teacher needs to meet those who provide special services for the school. These include:

1. The librarian and audio-visual coordinator.
2. The counselor.
3. The school nurse and school doctor.
4. The attendance and child welfare worker.
5. The visiting teacher.

The larger the school, of course, the more likely are these specialists to be found. But, unfortunately, in the larger schools the more remote are the specialists from contact with the individual classroom teacher.

Many new teachers lack understanding of the function of these specialists, and how they can aid him in his own daily classroom. Good teachers make maximum use of the resources provided by the personnel of the school itself. The teacher who wishes to meet the variety of interests and needs and abilities of his students will need many books, periodicals, films, slides, and recordings. The librarian and audio-visual coordinator are there to help him get what he needs. The teacher who is sensitive to his guidance function will be more useful and effective with his students if he avails himself of the services of the counseling, health, and attendance personnel. Each specialist has a significant service to contribute. Previous chapters have pointed more explicitly at the need for these services and how they may be used. Here it is our purpose merely to emphasize good personal relationships with these staff members. In working with these specialists, as in the other areas of school relationships, the new teacher should be the one who seeks help, advice, and assistance, rather than the one who tells, criticizes, or objects.

The new teacher should seek an early opportunity to sit down with each specialist and ask him to describe his office, its service to the school, what the individual teacher can utilize and how. Establishing a cordial and friendly relationship will mean easier access to the specialist's help. Too often the new teacher finds when he must make a special demand on the library the librarian does not even know of his existence. Similarly, if a severe behavior problem suddenly explodes in the classroom, the teacher may need the immediate aid of the counseling staff. The assistance will be obtained more quickly if a professional relationship has already been established between the teacher and the counselor.

Extracurricular Duties of the Teacher

A group of students preparing to become teachers were asked early in their professional program to state what was the most outstanding thing they remembered from their high school days. The answers were revealing:

"being captain of the football team"
"being vice-president of the student body"
"winning the interschool debate contest"
"having the lead in the play"
"being editor of the school paper"
"being president of the Hi-Y"
"getting nominated to the exclusive girls' society"

The activities that engage the interest of the high-school boys and girls outside of their regular class routines are of major significance in their lives. In the view of the teacher these are "extras" but in the view of the students, they may be "first." The clubs, the plays, the teams, the contests, the other extracurricular activities command the vital energy of many of the students over and beyond what any classroom can bring forth.

The alert teacher is particularly interested in the kind, the quality and the amount of extracurricular activities that his school sponsors. For some schools such additional activities are considered prime assets of the school. Other institutions have very meager and poorly supported out-of-school activities. In some schools each teacher is asked to sponsor a club or activity of this sort. In others only the energy of the individual teacher introduces any out-of-class activity. For the beginner, these expectations are significant. "Will I have to lead a club or sponsor an activity?" is an important question. Some schools give the new teacher the same, if not a heavier, load in directing activities than the old-timers have. Other schools will not ask a new teacher to undertake additional tasks until he is well integrated into the school program and feels at ease and competent in the classroom. The latter approach is undoubtedly the most successful, although many administrators are forced, because the students want and need adult direction, to ask new teachers to undertake extracurricular leadership.

The kind and variety of extra-class duties are extensive. They include:

1. Clubs and special interest groups.
2. Advising a major school activity: yearbook, newspaper, dramatics.
3. Student government activities.
4. Hall, yard, and cafeteria duty.

Clubs. Let us look first at the club-leadership function. Here the teacher should seek primarily to use the club to develop group self-discipline. A stamp club, for instance, with its own officers and rules of procedure, will plan programs, invite speakers, take trips, exchange stamps. The adult advisor is there primarily to advise, to aid new officers in learning their duties, to be the continuing member from semester to semester, to bring to the officers new ideas and suggestions for programs that may enrich the club activities, and, finally, to be a guide for new students. The teacher serves the same function as the Scoutmaster in a Scout troop, or the adult leader in a YMCA boys' club, or the woman who advises a Campfire Girls group. The club is organized and exists in order that the members may do what they want to do to further their own interests. Whenever teachers dominate a club, the real purpose and significance of this kind of activity are lost. The greater the degree of self-government, the better for the young people.

The art of being adult advisor to a group is learned only by patient observation and a real desire to let the students direct their own affairs. Many of the principles of leadership discussed in Chapter 3 hold true for this kind of leadership also.[7]

Major activities. The more formal school activities, such as the

[7] For an excellent discussion of such leadership, see Wittenberg, Rudolph, *So You Want to Help People* (New York: Association Press, 1947).

production of a school play, the newspaper and yearbook, often put great pressure on the teacher to see to it that the students *produce* something that the public will like. These activities are important to school public relations and as such are particularly under the scrutiny of the administration. When the students bring home prizes or awards, when parents come to view the play or see the school paper in their home, then the community has something whereby it can—and will—judge the school.

The teacher will find at times that this emphasis on producing something for public display may result in undue pressure on students which they do not always appreciate. An uneasy dilemma may confront such an advisor: either become a dictator and run the student group, or attempt to encourage the students to develop their own best talent with the possibility that this may not measure up to public expectations. The wisest use of such extracurricular activities is of course the latter. But it is not always possible. The teacher must bear in mind the position of the school in the community before being disillusioned about what schools must do.

The school requires public support, and this support comes from the recognition by the public that the school is doing an adequate job. It will take time in any community to help the public differentiate between products finished to adult standards and processes contributing to the growth of adolescents. In other words, parents and others must be educated to see that a dramatic production unfinished and uneven in comparison to an adult performance may have in the process of rehearsal developed security, responsibility, and self-direction in the adolescent cast.

Student government. Working with student government activities involves many of the teachers in a school. Often each teacher must provide opportunity in one or more classes for student elections, campaigning, and reporting of student activities. The purposes of such student government in developing and understanding of democratic self-government have been accepted by most of the high schools of the nation. But it is a difficult task to help young people accept the limits of their own power in an adult world, and at the same time learn the significant lessons of responsibility for their own actions. The student government can be a vital and important part of the school, or it can be a farce.

Much of the success of such government depends on the willingness of the faculty to work closely with the young people as guides and advisors. It also means a recognition of the need to educate each new student generation. Every new group relearns the lessons of its predecessors. An honor system, for example, might have been carefully worked out by one student group, but in the space of a few years the whole self-education must be done over again. Genuine student government must be allowed to make mistakes in order to learn the important lessons.

The teacher who does not have central responsibility for student-government activities nevertheless owes a basic obligation to the education of the students to be interested in, to be informed about, and to give support to student-body activities.

Policing duties. The more disciplinary functions of the teacher —being on duty in the hall, cafeteria, or yard during specified times during the day—can be both illuminating and difficult. They are illuminating and helpful to the teacher who uses the opportunity to observe friendship groups, to note who is walking, talking, and playing with whom, and how the group structure shifts and changes. The duties can be useful when the teacher talks informally to students, helps them, answers questions, and in general acts more as a friendly helper than an overseer out to enforce the law. The more nearly school rules are in conformity with reasonable expectations of students, and the more they are written and revised from time to time by the student government, the easier the task of the teacher on these duties will be.

In some schools policing duty can be very difficult. The new teacher will find that many problems can only be solved as total school problems. The wise teacher will not make an issue of every small breach of school discipline but will seek primarily to work with students to win their respect, friendship, and confidence. This is the best way he can influence them to observe those rules that are necessary to the orderly functioning of the school.

In any extraclass duty the teacher must remember that he cannot be a chameleon and get away with it. If he is a stern figure in the classroom he does not change his role in the minds of the students when out of class he attempts to be friendly and relaxed. The students will not respond. Good classroom leadership will lead into good leadership out of class. A relaxed, friendly, interested, and adult relation with students is basic to good in-class and extraclass performance on the part of the teacher.

The Teacher and the Community

Becoming used to the ways of the school confronts the beginner with many new adjustments. Becoming acquainted in a community does not usually present as many perils or unknowns—at least on the surface. Most of us, during the course of growing up and attending school and college, have lived in several communities of varying sizes. The increase in mass communication media has made Main Street look familiar as one travels from corner to corner of our country. But surface appearances can be misleading. Communities vary as people vary. While in many ways American communities have basic values and ways of doing things in common, there are innumerable variations on this theme. Regional differences as well as local differences are apparent as soon as one looks below the surface. And every such difference affects the school and the teachers and teaching program within the school.

It is expected that a good community will produce a good school; but it is also true that a good school can help produce a good community. The process of education in our democratic order should be a two-way road. On one lane the community channels to the school its needs, problems, value systems, traditions, and on the other lane, the school sends out into the community new ideas, tested skills, trained leadership to aid in the solution of local problems. For this essential relationship to be productive of the best for both school and community we need teachers sensitive to community needs, aware of the community as a rich resource for learning, and conscious of the unique ways in which the school must serve the community. In this section some of the techniques for furthering these aims will be discussed.

The Teacher Studies the Community

Alice Bejorsky is going to teach English in Middle Fork Union High School. This is her first job and the prospect is both frightening and exciting. Alice has a friend who taught the year before at Middle Fork and she writes her for some leads on the community. Her friend responds:

You will probably enjoy teaching at Middle Fork; I did. The town is not as large as the one you have been living in the past several years while at State Teachers College, but at least it has two movie houses. The best people in town only go to the Bijou; but the kids seem to like the Star better as it has all the Westerns. There is only one paper, a weekly, but I would advise you to subscribe to it because it has all the local gossip; who has a baby, who is going to be married, who died, who went to the Lodge meeting Tuesday night, etc. I'd keep an eye out for old Mrs. Stripe because between you and me she really runs this town. I think she is related to every official that was ever elected—maybe that's why they were elected! Anyway, she is a real nice old soul but I'd try not to get in her way. There are a couple of apartments that you might get if you share one with another teacher, but Mary Small lived alone last year and the tongues really wagged. Be sure to bring lots of warm clothing as it is terribly cold in the winter and I think they skimp on heat in the school. You will like most of the faculty as long as you don't try to tell them how much you know. The principal is really a great guy and will give you a lot of help. Keep an eye out for Bob Brown; they say he is a wolf but I wouldn't know!

Best Wishes,
Sue

After her first few months at Middle Fork, Alice writes Sue:

Your preliminary bird's-eye view was not very far wrong. You were right about Mrs. Stripe. But Sue—the things there are that you have to find out about a new community! I read the weekly sheet avidly because it tells me a lot about the juniors I have in my three English classes and two math classes. But you know, you didn't tell me the town was so bitter about not winning the football pennant last year. I'm afraid that poor Joe will lose his job as coach. Also, there is a strike at the cannery, and it is impossible—I think—to read and discuss that short story in our literature anthology about the labor leader that is so dramatic. I really don't dare at this point. It amazes me how weather can affect you—here the weather conversation is all about the effect of the rain on the sub-soil water level as it seems to be sinking, or something. At home we didn't worry about rain except if it was going to spoil a picnic! I guess that is the difference between a farm town and a suburban town. I didn't get an apartment, but was able to get room and board with one of the older married teachers, Mr. and Mrs. Denny. They are very nice to me and I certainly get all the school scoop. But I don't think the principal is quite the wonderful fellow you thought him; at least he hasn't bothered much about me. The students certainly are interested in my private life. I think I will scream if another one coyly asks if I am engaged or not!

More later,
Alice

There is a moral to be drawn from these two letters. Each community looks different to different people. While someone who knows a town can give you some idea of what it is like, it is true that each person sees some things and neglects others. However, a cursory observation of the town will not provide the future teacher with what he needs to know about the community.

Each of us carries a memory of his own home town and assesses others against it. Yet what we know of our own home town is its real inner life; we know who is who, who counts and who doesn't. When we go into a new and strange community, all we see is the outer appearance. Unfortunately, if New Town looks like our own home town, we may delude ourselves into thinking it probably is very much the same, the kind of town we would, or would not, like to work and live in. Appearances are so deceiving! A nice maple-lined Main Street may look comfortable and inviting; yet the town may be smug, indifferent to the school, dominated by ingrown provincial leadership. On the other hand, a barren, dusty, wind-swept community that looks as though no one stayed long enough to grow a sun flower may be a vital, interesting, sophisticated place in which to teach.

The teacher, for his own personal seeking after the "good life" or, perhaps, to be more specific, the good teaching life, needs to be able to get below surfaces, to be sensitive to the real community. This is the only way he can know if this is where he ought to teach and the only way he can judge whether the community will accept him and his ideas about teaching. To see for oneself, then, is to see with a trained eye. Some suggestions as to what to look for will be given later on. But first, an aside to those who are married. One principal remarked,

> In our community we have begun a practice of interviewing the wives of prospective teachers, not just the men themselves! Our community is a good one, for some kinds of people. It is isolated. The social life is not very extensive. You have to be the kind of person who is happy tending your own garden or joining in the simple pleasures of an evening of bridge, or you won't like it here. So many of our teachers have left because their wives were not happy, through no fault of the community, but just because they were big city gals and this is a small oil town.

The community is important to the teacher's family, and the happiness of the teacher's family is vital to his success in teaching. It is often wise for a beginning teacher to arrange for his wife (or husband, as the case may be) to get a chance to see what lies ahead and agree with him (or her) about the community.

And a warning to the unmarried! The girls going out into teaching will be looking forward to marriage with or without a continuance of their careers. And if marriage is equal in importance to a career, or of greater importance, then the girl should consider the communities in which she chooses to teach accordingly. Going to an isolated rural community means that contact with eligible educated bachelors will be limited, very limited. The stereotype of the "old maid school teacher" has a firmer grip on the more remote hamlets and crossroads. The unmarried woman teacher might well choose a lesser-paying position or one less advantageous in other ways but offering wider opportunity for meeting marriageable young men. In lesser degree the unmarried man must also exercise care in his choice of community.

Responsibilities of the School to the Community

The modern teacher recognizes the limits that the community places upon the school, although it is more appropriate to term these limits the *responsibilities* that the school has to the community. In one town the schools are the leaders in community progress; in an adjoining community the schools may be so far behind the times that the citizens are beginning to complain. But whether the schools lead, follow, or preserve the status quo, the individual teacher must clearly know what the role of this school is in this community. The beginning teacher leaves the college with many ideas and ideals regarding teaching, but he will be doomed to bitter disappointment if he does not realistically appraise the communities in which he teaches. He must sense how much of his idealism can be operative or how far short of community needs his own view of education may be. In one community a unit on personal grooming may be very welcome to the parents and students; in another such a unit would be considered an affront to the students or an invasion of the prerogatives of the parents. Thus, selection of content and also methods is often a function of community expectations and acceptances.

For personal orientation, the beginning teacher seeks answers to questions like these:

1. How does the community feel about the high school? What does it like in the school? Of what is it critical? Which teachers seem to have the highest prestige in town?
2. What are the sensitive spots in this community? Unions, minority groups, working mothers, slums, old-timers vs. new residents, migrants, foreign-language groups, town improvements, public vs. private utilities, industry vs. agriculture?
3. What are the "prevailing sentiments?" [8] What are the attitudes toward national policy issues, toward foreign relations, toward local institutions?
4. What are the major community loyalties? What forces tie the community together, if any? Who are the local leaders? What do they represent? How stable is this leadership? What major community groups are not represented?

Deliberate education can occur when the teacher is well informed about the community in terms of questions like these. The community might have a conflict between industrial and agricultural interests, which is interfering with community growth. Yet children of both groups are in the school. The teacher with a long-

[8] Leighton, Alexander, *The Governing of Men* (Princeton: Princeton University Press, 1945).

range view would be sure to study the role of both industry and agriculture in building the nation. He would develop the idea that both groups can work together and would help students read critically in local sources about local problems that impinge on this conflict. Then coming generations would not be ignorant heirs to the mistakes of their forebears.

Guides to Understanding the Community

The major sources for gaining such intimate community knowledge are easily accessible. The following guides are suggested for a beginning teacher:

1. What does the school community look like? Walk down Main Street first thing in the morning—are the commuters rushing to the trains, or are the farmers coming in for early morning shopping? Walk down the street again at dusk, again at midnight. Who is in town during the week late at night; what is the night life over the week-end?

Drive slowly around all the neighborhoods. Where do the Best People live? Where are the slums? Where do the newcomers buy homes? Are there large apartment house districts? Where are the restricted areas for Negroes and other out-groups?

Drive the school bus routes. How different are the environments of the town and country students? Is this a rich area, or are there rural slums?

2. Read the local newspaper. Long before a teacher moves to town, if he subscribes to the local newspaper, he can quickly get a vivid picture of the "real" news of the community. What kinds of events make the front page? What columnists are syndicated for this community? What are the editorial attitudes? What school news seems important? To find the leaders of the local social whirl the teacher can quickly find out "who counts" by keeping a little notebook in which he jots down the names of those who make the society news frequently. He will soon find out that Mrs. X is very active, and Mr. Y is prominent in local organizations. He should also look for groups whose news does *not* appear: union news, minority group affairs, and the like.

3. Interview local leaders. The new teacher should make a point of talking casually or formally with the major individuals in the school community. The larger the city, the harder this will be to do, of course, but in a moderate-sized city it is very useful for the teacher to know what are the sentiments of those who count in local life. In such an interview the leading question should be, "I am a newcomer here; what is it important for me to know about this town?"

4. Locate sources of descriptive and statistical materials. Visit the Chamber of Commerce, city hall, library, planning commission. This will yield important data regarding the history and present status of the community. The Chamber of Commerce will be able to point out what the community is most proud of. The library will have documents and materials on local celebrities and local history. Locating the community in the U.S. Census reports is helpful.

There are a number of school systems that recognize the value of such community orientation so well that a special program is outlined for new teachers. Special booklets are prepared and sent to the new teacher prior to coming to the town. Such programs are very useful, but they are still rare enough that the teacher cannot depend on this to do the job for him. Furthermore, such an introduction, valuable as it may be, can show only a select side of the community. Each new teacher will therefore want to see the community for himself, form his own judgments, and then check these against the experiences and judgments of those who have lived and taught in the community for a number of years.

Using Community Information in the Classroom

The application of the information and understandings gained from a community orientation to the actual classroom teaching is the important next step. "So what?" asks the beginning teacher. "If I know that the community is very recreation-minded and spends more per capita on playgrounds than any other city its size, what effect does that have on my teaching?" Such questions are very pertinent. The community-oriented teacher does make use of his knowledge. He would know that a study of recreation in a senior problems class would be welcomed by the community. If he led a hobby club after school, he would know the community would support it eagerly. He would know that having students conduct opinion polls about the recreation program would be given wide cooperation. He would know that a unit on family recreation, personal recreation, developing wide recreational interests, in English, art, history classes would probably not be criticized. He would know that he could use statistics about recreation programs, local and national, in his mathematics class, and critics of "modern" education would accept the practice as "sound." Knowing something about what the community prizes guides the teacher into new resources for learning. The many ways in which the community can be used to enrich classroom learning have been described in detail in Chapter 6. The wise teacher will orient himself to the community as part of his job, and then select those community resources which can best be utilized in the light of his growing knowledge of the total community.

Community Education as a Continuing Process

Before concluding this section, it might be well to develop briefly two closely related concepts. First, in each community where the teacher goes to teach, learning about the community must be begun all over again. And second, in order to understand adolescents and their culture, the teacher must periodically immerse himself in *their* culture, as it is manifest in the larger community.

Teachers sometimes yield to the fallacy that, having known one community well, others are merely variations on the same theme. This is of course only a partial truth. Teachers may, by learning about one community, learn best *how* to learn about communities, but the answers they obtain will never be the same twice running. Thus, the process of community understanding will always remain necessary whenever one enters a new teaching community.

But it is not only necessary that teachers learn about the adult community. Margaret Mead has wisely suggested that one of the basic needs for continuing professional competence is to go out, as a teacher, every few years, and relearn the peer culture that so potently presses upon the young. Where cultural change on some levels is as rapid as it is in our society, the teacher, above all others, must be aware of the direction and pattern of change.[9]

Summary

In this chapter we have discussed some of the special relationships of the teacher and other members of the staff and some of the special out-of-class demands. The new teacher enters an institution in which relationships are fairly well ordered and follow a hierarchical pattern. As a newcomer he finds himself at the bottom of the order. He is an outsider in terms of the school and its culture; its traditions are new and strange and sometimes difficult to fathom. He moves into a series of new personal commitments to others of his professional peers and administrative superiors. Still it is significant that the high school is, by and large, encouraging to the newcomer. He finds many others dedicated to their tasks, working far beyond anything remuneration could cover, and eager to enroll the beginner as an important addition to the over-all process of educating the young citizen for a democratic social order.

The school community, however, is an integral part of the larger community. It is only as the teacher learns about the ways of life outside the school that he can most effectively understand and educate the youth who are a product of that community.

[9] Mead, Margaret, *The School in American Culture* (Cambridge: Harvard University Press, 1951).

Selected References

The New Teacher

Barrell, E. A. "The New Teacher Shouldn't Forget," *NEA Journal,* 39:438 (September, 1950). A list of things to remember to avoid trouble the first year.

Holman, Mary V. *How It Feels to Be a Teacher.* New York: Teachers College, Columbia University, 1950. Excellent introduction to the more subjective aspects of teaching for the beginner.

Lamb, Marion. *Your First Year of Teaching.* Monograph 45. Cincinnati: Southwestern Publishing Company, 1939. 35 pp. Down-to-earth advice written in a sprightly fashion.

Metropolitan School Study Council. *The Newly Appointed Teacher.* New York: Bureau of Publications, Teachers College, Columbia University, 1950. 49 pp. How schools can help the new teacher adjust.

Spears, Harold. *The High School for Today.* New York: American Book Company, 1950. Chap. 13, "The Teacher with the Full Vision," pp. 227-242. A rapid survey of many important factors in good teaching in terms of the teacher as a person.

Other School Personnel

Chamberlain, Leo M., and Leslie W. Kindred. *The Teacher and School Administration.* New York: Prentice-Hall, Inc., 1949. Chap. 18, "Participating in School Administration," pp. 513-543. Points out what *can* be done, rather than what is now common practice.

Changing Conceptions of Educational Administration. Forty-fifth Yearbook, Part II, National Society for the Study of Education. Chicago: University of Chicago Press, 1946. See especially Chap. IV, "Organizing the Personnel of a Democratic School" for a good discussion of the relations of the teacher to the administrative process.

Cooper, Shirley. "Not a 'Flunky'," *NEA Journal,* 40:203-204 (March, 1951). Describes the importance and duties of the school custodian.

Educational Policies Commission. *Social Services and the Schools.* Washington, D.C.: National Education Association, 1939. Describes the services of the school to the community and visa versa.

Grambs, Jean D. "Do Classroom Teachers Really Want Democratic Administrators?" *Nation's Schools,* 46:40-41 (November, 1950). Democratic administrators can only function where teachers likewise desire a democratic relationship.

Krail, Jack B. "Common Errors of Student Teachers," *Clearing House,* 25:232-235 (December, 1950). A good discussion of common hazards in student teaching that should be avoided.

Leadership at Work. Fifteenth Yearbook. Department of Supervisors and Directors of Instruction, Washington, D.C.: National Education Association, 1943. How teachers, supervisors and other school personnel can work together in many situations. See Chap. 1 for a particularly effective story of democratic leadership.

Moehlman, Arthur B. *School Administration.* Boston: Houghton Mifflin Company, 1940. Chap. 24, "Secondary Administration," pp. 543-577. Comprehensive coverage of school administrative practices and problems on the secondary level.

"School Social Workers," *Understanding the Child,* 19:1-32 (Entire issue), (January, 1950). An important specialist and how she contributes to individual student adjustment.

Smith, B. O., O. W. Stanley, and J. H. Shores. *Fundamentals of Curriculum Development.* Yonkers: World Book Company, 1950. Pp. 688-695. Points out the significance of the school hierarchy and status system.

Extracurricular Activities

Alexander, William M., and Galen J. Saylor. *Secondary Education.* New York: Rinehart & Company, 1950. Chap. XVIII, "Out-of-Class Activities," pp. 451-477. A well-organized presentation of the teacher's many avenues for education out of the classroom.

Douglass, Harl (ed.) *The High School Curriculum.* New York: The Ronald Press Company, 1947. Chap. 17, "Extra-curricular Activities and the Curriculum," pp. 358-376. Good overview of the extent and variety of out-of-class activities to be found in many high schools.

Fedder, Ruth. *Guiding Homeroom and Club Activities.* New York: McGraw-Hill Book Company Inc., 1949. Discusses the importance of the guidance and leadership function of the teacher in student clubs.

Heiss, Elwood D., Ellsworth S. Oburn, and Charles W. Hoffman. *Modern Science Teaching.* New York: The Macmillan Company, 1950. Chap. 10, "Extra-curricular Activities in Science," pp. 233-244. Shows how many clubs and other extraclass activities can be developed by the science teacher.

Jones, Anna May. *Leisure Time Education.* New York: Harper & Brothers, 1946. Describes ways in which the teacher can use school and community resources for enriching avocational pursuits of young people.

National Society for the Study of Education. *Science Education in American Schools.* Forty-sixth Yearbook, Part I. Chicago: University of Chicago Press, 1947. "Science Clubs" pp. 229-233. A variety of activities to develop special science interests and abilities can be achieved through science clubs.

Shufelt, Laura M. (ed.). *Developing Citizenship through School Activities.* Bulletin No. 22, 1949, National Council for the Social Studies, Washington, D.C. Describes a number of school club and council activities that are of value in service to the community and in developing improved citizenship understandings of students.

Strang, Ruth. *Group Activities in Colleges and Secondary Schools.* Rev. ed. New York: Harper & Brothers, 1946. A standard work on school groups and how the value of these activities may be extended.

Tompkins, Ellsworth. *Extraclass Activities for ALL Pupils.* Bulletin No. 4, 1950, U.S. Office of Education, Washington, D.C. Indicates how a high school can plan extraclass activities that meet the needs of all students and gives statistics on current practices.

22. Becoming a Teacher

TEACHING is more than techniques. The best knowledge of all of the ways of conducting a class will not alone produce a teacher. There is even a school of thought that proclaims, "Teachers are born, not made." If this were true, there would be no need for courses in education, there would be no science of education, no educational research. We would merely have to develop a routine that could separate those who were born teachers from those who were not. But we know that this is far from being the case. Those who seem to be born teachers actually have often had better opportunities to be "teachers" during their years of growing up: leading groups, helping their own brothers and sisters, tutoring other students because the teacher needed help. They learned through experience the feel of teaching. Most of us, however, have had few teaching opportunities. As adults we face in teaching something very different from any other experience we have had. What are some of the unique characteristics of this teaching experience?

Fears of the Beginning Teacher

Mr. Gordon faced his class alone for the first time. He looked at thirty-five adolescents, of all shapes, sizes, and appearances. Visions of the horror stories that he had heard from other teachers about the wild mischief these students could perpetrate rose before his eyes. "What if they won't keep still when I ask them to? What if a boy starts getting fresh? What will I do if a girl bursts out crying?" These

> thoughts flashed through his mind in the instant that the final bell rang. "I'll get them busy at something, then they can't get into trouble—anything to keep them in their seats, quiet . . . ."

Another teacher reported:

> The first time I met the other faculty members they said to me, "Be stern the first month. Don't smile or be easygoing. Then you can relax and take it easy. But you have to be tough with them immediately or they will try to get away with all kinds of things."

Still another:

> As the teacher of the "special class" in which were placed the worst behavior problems, Miss Smith had a rigid daily routine. The boys—and they were always boys—were given more problems to work than anyone could finish. These were turned in every day. She always threw most of them out; but about once a week she would correct a set of them and scold the class roundly for doing such poor work. "I know it is mostly busy work," she said, "but if I don't keep them as busy as possible they will get into all kinds of mischief."

These incidents point to one of the central problems of beginning teachers: fear of the teaching situation. For many years we have been students—receiving the assignments, more or less conscious of the rest of the class, seeing the teacher as a rather remote, sometimes pleasant, sometimes unpleasant person. Suddenly the positions are reversed. As the teacher, we are acutely aware of the thirty or so different personalities that must be kept together as a group. We remember all too vividly the kinds of trouble that we gave teachers in times past; and subconsciously we are troubled often enough by memories of the hatred, antagonism, resentments that we felt toward teachers. We wonder what the students are thinking about us. We wonder what unexplored avenue of experience they may open where our incompetence may be revealed. We recognize belatedly that we may have been rather introverted, bookish people throughout our lives. We think ruefully that we have held only modest leadership roles. We are dismayed at our temerity in choosing teaching at all.

It is encouraging to learn that these feelings are common. Most beginning teachers are frightened of the class; and most beginning teachers soon get over it. But gaining an understanding of the common fears, facing and acknowledging them, will aid the beginner when they are faced in actuality.

The beginning teacher may gain further reassurance by remembering the years of conditioning that have already occurred. The students are not likely to rebel very much. As was discussed in the section on discipline (Chapter 13), trouble comes when trouble is expected; where a teacher has a thorough expectation of harmony and workmanlike atmosphere, good order is more likely to develop. Teachers who expect trouble may be tempted to resort to punitive methods. "They work," they say. "I try to be nice to them and I just get chaos, but when I crack down, then everything is orderly." Dictatorships *are* orderly. But as a people we are committed to a different way of living. In the classroom we cannot teach the words of democracy and live the life of autocracy. It *is* more difficult to secure good order through good management in which students share responsibility, but it is the only defensible course to take. This is not to say that the teacher should abdicate his leadership (see Chapter 3), but it must not be rigid and unyielding. The best psychological preparation for good leadership is to admit frankly, "I may have some fears, but they are not going to betray me into becoming a petty tyrant."

Motives for Entering Teaching as a Life Work

Once this hurdle has been faced, the beginning teacher will want to re-examine his motives for choosing teaching. Most choose teaching because of an interest in service, and because of the contribution they can make to society.[1] Other important factors that encourage individuals to enter teaching are the influence of others who are teachers in their immediate family, an admiration for a teacher they have known, opportunity to work closely with young people.[2] Interestingly enough, most of the studies of motivation for entering the profession give a rather low ranking to purely selfish interests: security, long vacations, improving social position.

For the family man or woman the profession of teaching offers far greater opportunities to be an active parent than most other jobs in today's world. To anyone with a deep interest in his own children, the opportunity to work closely with young people is an important consideration. Teaching is also one of the few professions that permit a married woman to share school vacations with her children. Many women students who remain out of teaching during the early years of their children's growing up return to teaching with

[1] Threlkeld, C. H., "Problems in the Recruitment and Adjustment of Teachers," *Bulletin of National Association of Secondary School Principals,* 32:169-175 (March, 1948).

[2] Stroh, Margaret, *et al., Better Selection of Better Teachers* (Washington, D.C.: Delta Kappa Gamma, 1943).

the happy feeling that in this way they deepen their understanding of young people.

Many teachers are motivated to enter the profession because of teachers they knew. One teacher became an English teacher because she was convinced that English could be vital and interesting; she wanted to prove this because of the dull and deadly English teachers she herself had had. More often the decision to enter teaching has been influenced by the memory of a well-loved teacher. One precaution is important when beginning teachers try to model themselves after the memory of some special teacher. If the student has a similar personality all may be well; but often as youngsters we admire deeply those who are least like us. Thus, we may want to be the gay, sparkling, understanding teacher that helped so much when we were in school, when we are really rather slow, quiet people. The effort to be like the model might lead to discouragement because anything less than this ideal might appear as failure. It is wisest to capitalize on personality strengths already developed.

Others enter teaching because there have been teachers in the family. For some, living up to a family tradition can be very challenging; for others, it may be very discouraging. The choice of entry into teaching may not have been freely made. "All girls in our family are teachers", may actually be emotional blackmail exercised upon one who is not interested in, or stimulated by, teaching. In that case, recognizing frankly both one's own unwillingness to become a teacher and the compulsion of powerful family or group pressures may mitigate the conflict. Accepting this life decision, even though in some respects it is not a first choice, may help remove one barrier to effective teaching.

In discussing this whole problem of motivation on the part of the teacher, it is clear that good teaching occurs when the teacher's needs and feelings do not conflict with those of the students. If the students desire to learn, but the teacher resents his role as instructor, it will be difficult to create a good learning situation. There need not be conflict, of course. The good teacher derives genuine satisfaction from teaching and the students gain real satisfactions from learning and living in his classroom.

Some future high-school teachers may be attracted into teaching because of the power and authority that can be exercised. This is different from becoming a tyrant because of fear of disorder. This is becoming a tyrant because one enjoys ordering others around. It is necessary, of course, that the teacher accept his own authority. Good order rarely prevails in the classrooms of teachers who really do not want to have responsibility and authority. But we must repeat: domination for its own sake will not aid young people to acquire skill in making their own decisions. And in our culture, we prize that ability highly.

Then there are the high-school teachers who may be called the "frustrated Ph.D.'s." These students have been successful as undergraduates in their own specialized academic fields. But because of financial or other problems they have turned to high-school teaching. Deep in the minds of these teachers, however, is the feeling that those who really succeeded are those who were able to enter college teaching. To these teachers most high-school students are disappointments. They are distressingly uninterested in the more specialized concepts of a field of knowledge. This type of teacher can pattern his teaching in one of three ways: (1), he can teach his subject only for those chosen few who are bright and interested enough to respond; or (2), he can teach in a comfortable rut; or (3), he can find new stimulation in making his chosen subject important to the average and slow student as well as the brilliant.

Psychological Barriers Between Teacher and Students

As the teacher stands before his class he appears the symbol of all teachers. What does this mean, exactly? As we go out to teach we want to be the friend of our students. Is this possible? If by "friend" we mean one who confides completely in us and accepts in turn our complete confidence, we may well doubt if such a relation is possible with students. Certainly a firm and happy relation is possible. But our position does not permit the uninhibited interchange that may be characteristic of close friendships. We are friends as fathers and mothers can be the friends of their children.

The teacher, because he is a teacher, has some barriers between himself and the students. For one thing, the teacher does have important authority over the student (see Chapter 3 on democracy), and this places him in a special world apart. Some beginning teachers expect to be "buddies" of their students. They should be warned ahead of time that more often than not they may be met with suspicion and distrust. Students want teachers to act like teachers. They are uneasy around the teachers who act, dress, talk too much like people their own age.

Teachers are also the source of rewards and punishments (see Chapter 16 on grades). Most students have an ambivalent attitude toward the teacher, knowing that one day he can reward them most highly, but the next day may punish them drastically. We do not develop close friendship with a person who has such power. We may have friendship in the sense of mutual respect. But few students put their full personalities in the hands of a teacher as they do with a trusted friend. Students are reminded constantly that the teacher is studying his growth, his learning, his motives, his interests, in terms of some "standard." This the student expects from a parent or a teacher, but not from a close friend. If the beginning teacher encounters seeming coldness on the part of students, lack of response to friendly overtures, he would do well to remember that it is probably because he as the teacher stepped out of role.

Teachers serve as the "cultural conscience" for the student. No matter how sympathetic a teacher may be with adolescent pranks and misdeeds, he is obligated both by the culture and the students' needs to judge such behavior by accepted standards. The culture expects the teacher to convey accepted moral values and behavior patterns to the young; a teacher who did not do this probably would not last very long in his job. This support for an adult value system carries even into the kinds of language and word usage that is considered proper in the school. Some of the ways in which we expect children to talk, if used at home, would call down the ridicule of parent and playmate. Yet, in the classroom other students would be shocked if the teacher did not correct consistent grammatical mistakes! In the classroom it is almost criminal to use a plural verb with a singular noun. Since he is a cultural conscience, the teacher finds that the students cannot share with him the experiences that the culture outlaws.

Although the teacher must exercise authority, must grade his students, must pass on the cultural expectations of good and bad, he can still be the kind of friend who helps, who understands, who offers sound advice. In return, the teacher can expect loyalty, support, and the kind of affection that is built from respect and admiration. The major satisfactions of teaching are long term. They come from watching students grow toward responsible maturity; from seeing one change his view of himself from that of a failure to that of one who can succeed; from seeing another in a happy marriage; and from hearing now and then, perhaps indirectly, how he once helped.

Mistaken Efforts to Remove Psychological Barriers

While they are still in school, students are wary of their praise for teachers. It is too much like apple-polishing to tell a teacher how much a class may be enjoyed. The teacher will have to resign himself to seeing only the little cues of student appreciation and rarely having the students actually express how they feel. "How can I tell if the students like me?" is a recurrent complaint of the beginning teacher. We need the reassurance that students do like us, but they will not often tell us so. In the search for reassurance, some teachers are apt to go to extremes in winning student approval. In almost any school there will be one teacher whose popularity with the students is only a degree removed from undesirable familiarity. In trying to make sure that students will like them, some teachers are guilty of one or more of the following:

1. Overgrading students when work is clearly not adequate.
2. Using colloquialisms in speech that are appropriate for teen-agers but not for teachers.
3. Dressing sloppily in a mistaken notion that this is being informal.
4. Allowing students to call them by their first names or nicknames.
5. Confiding in students: talking about the teacher's personal problems before the class or with groups of students.
6. Helping or permitting students to break rules under the impression that this will help the teacher win the students' favor.
7. Agreeing with students in criticizing other teachers or the school administration.
8. Gossiping with students about their personal lives and that of school personnel; hinting in class about personal incidents relating to individuals in the class that are known to the teacher.
9. Making personal comments on their appearance to students.
10. Joking with the students on their own level.

These actions reveal a lack of security. Few teachers actually win lasting satisfaction from the relations they develop by these means. While students appreciate a teacher who is genuinely interested in them, who is not a "stuffed shirt" or a "bluestocking", they still insist that adults act like adults. A teacher who has a circle of his own friends, or who has a family, rarely needs this extreme kind of reassurance. The hazard for the beginning teacher arises from starting to teach in an unfamiliar situation where one has neither friends nor family. But it is wiser to seek friends among the faculty and townspeople than to look to the high-school students to fill this emotional need.

Student Crushes on Teachers

Sometimes high-school students develop a "crush" on a teacher. It is a kind of puppy-dog admiration in which the adolescent perpetually tags around after the teacher. One explanation for this attachment: "The young person who is very insecure may turn to crush and hero-worship relationships with exaggerated devotion in effort to gain, outside the home, satisfaction which he has been unable to find there." [3] Sometimes the adulation is for a teacher of the same sex, sometimes for one of the opposite sex. The student may go to embarrassing extremes in trying to make himself known to the teacher and in doing things for the teacher:

> The young adolescent girl tends to identify herself wholeheartedly with the admired older girl or woman. She usually shows less reluctance than the boy to recognize that she is infatuated with her teacher, for example. She is likely to be more interested in her experience than in the object of her affection. Among her girl friends she sings the praises of her "crush," blushes if her name is mentioned, and enjoys being teased about her devotion. To the object of her fondness she is likely to show her feelings openly—writing notes, giving presents.[4]

What should the teacher do about it? If the teacher he selects is understanding and emotionally mature himself, then the adolescent will move on to the next stage in his emotional development: finding a partner of the opposite sex and making warm friends among both sexes. However, for the teacher who himself needs such devotion and so forgets why the adolescent acts the way he does, there may be unhappy consequences. The adolescent obviously needs to outgrow the crush. The teacher who perpetuates the crush may doom the student to immature emotional responses for many years to come. This is not to say the teacher should retain a kind of dignified aloofness. The middle-of-the-road course is the wisest. The teacher should show genuine kindness, accept the attention, but not encourage the crush or expect it to last. The teacher might well go out of his way to help the student mix more with his classmates, arranging class leadership roles for the student to ensure him more recognition.

The student needs to be accepted by the individual whom he has identified as his model, because it becomes more possible for him to emulate adult traits. If the teacher rejects him, then the student may be confused about the proper kind of adult he wishes to become. Some teachers may be offended and possibly disturbed by the homosexual overtones that may be present in some of the crushes, where an obviously "sissy" boy trots after the debate coach like a devoted puppy, or where the masculine girl can hardly be pried out of the door long after all other students have gone home.

It is possible that for a minority of such students a grave problem of finding their appropriate sex roles is present. Again, reject-

[3] Zachry, Caroline, *Emotion and Conduct in Adolescence* (New York: Appleton-Century-Crofts, Inc., 1940), p. 336.
[4] *Ibid.*, p. 114.

ing the student because of drives that are personally repugnant to us will only make it less possible for the individual to work out his problem. The understanding teacher will seek outside help from trained psychologists and psychiatrists wherever available, but meanwhile will try gently and kindly to wean the student away from this overdevotion.

Identifying Personal Teaching Strengths and Weaknesses

While it is true that teachers must accept some definite limits in their relationships with students, the picture need not be too bleak. After all, good teachers work in a satisfying atmosphere of mutual respect. This means that the beginning teacher assesses his qualifications for teaching to discover where his strengths lie. As a rough guide to this appraisal we will sketch three major teacher "types." Probably no beginning teacher is a pure type, but he may be closer to one than to either of the others.

Type A. This type might be called the *academic teacher*. He is primarily interested in subject matter. He would have liked to continue study in his own field. Meanwhile, he tries to keep up with new developments in it. When he goes back to summer school, he much prefers to take courses in his own subject field than in further professional courses. He is often a brilliant teacher of his subject. He is very sensitive about maintaining high standards of workmanship and scholarship; his criteria are usually of college-preparatory level. He does his best job with college-bound students, since they are more likely to do well in his subject and to find it interesting. He does not do much counseling with his students; often knows very little about their home background; is impatient with psychological explanations for poor student work which he is prone to term "excuses." He flunks students with a clear conscience.

Type B. This type might be called the *counselor-teacher*. He is first of all interested in students. He uses subject matter mainly as a way of working with young people; in fact, he often throws traditional subject matter out the window if he finds a substitute that comes nearer to the interests or needs of students. Sometimes his teaching is a little dull in the classroom because he didn't spend enough time preparing for it. Most of his attention is devoted to students and their problems and only incidentally to the chores of teaching. He would rather pass all students than fail anyone. He gives grades almost intuitively, because of the effect on the student rather than for any measurable attainment. He is apt to drive Type A teachers mad on this account, since they can never understand each other's different view of the function of grades and standards. Type B teachers are sometimes extroverts who seem happiest when with a group of people. Sometimes they are highly sensitive and easily hurt because of their awareness of people, their emotions and motives.

Type C. This kind of teacher might be called the *inspirational type*. Like Type A, he loves his subject field, but on an emotional basis primarily. He is convinced that if people only loved to play music, to paint, to play on the team, then all the ills that troubled them would probably fade away. This is the kind of teacher who will put on marvelous plays and have constant wrangles with the rest of the faculty for insisting that the students be released from any and all classes for rehearsals. Obviously taking part in a dramatic production (or playing on the team, or being in the band, or participating in a debate, or putting out the school newspaper, or decorating the gym for a fiesta) is more rewarding to the student's total personality than any class! These teachers are likely to get support from Type B teachers, but Type A teachers resist them to the last breath. A running battle usually goes on all year between this kind of teacher and those who have the students in other academic classes. The inspirational-type teacher usually asks only that students feel the spark, share his enthusiasm for the activity. Then even lack of skill may be forgiven. This teacher, however, may sometimes be impatient with the unskillful and devote most of his time and energy to those who are enthusiastic and talented.*

Some teachers have strengths of all three kinds, while others are definitely one type or another. It is not necessarily wrong to be any one kind of teacher. We cannot be all things to all students, and we should not feel a sense of personal failure on this account. It *is* wrong, however, to refuse to recognize the other kinds of strengths. We do have two major responsibilities: First, to do well that kind of teaching in which we have the greatest talent, whether it be of the academic, counseling, or inspirational type; and, second, to strive to do justice to those students who are not going to respond to our major strength.

As a counseling teacher, for instance, we may find students who plainly do not care to have the teacher inquire into their personal lives, students who are academically oriented and happy in this role. For them, the counseling teacher would do well to keep hands off, to be kind and patient, but not offended if such students do not respond well to counseling overtures. Similarly, as an academic-type teacher, we must make allowances for those students who do not excel in our subject field and make an effort to help them succeed at their level in some facet of the subject that interests them. The gravest mistake we can make in teaching is to assume that students who are not like ourselves are of a lower order of human beings.

The examples of teachers at work presented in the *Introduction* of this book illustrate how different teachers approach the teaching job; each is good in his own right, each has a value to offer the educational system. If schools were staffed with one kind of teacher only, school would be a deadly place indeed for those students who did not respond to that kind of teacher. A wise administrator tries

* This discussion is adapted from materials prepared by Dr. Robert N. Bush, School of Education, Stanford University, California.

to achieve balance in his faculty, with all types of teachers well represented, thus making it possible for almost every student to find some teacher who can give him personal support and assist him in effective learning. It must also be remembered that as a member of a school faculty the teacher must work with teachers of all three types and combinations of them.

The kind of school program that is best for the students must be a compromise among the various points of view. Although it is often difficult for Type A teachers to understand Type B and C, and vice versa, a recognition of their genuine contribution to the education of adolescents will help to reduce conflict and provide some workable compromises. The method of working that is right for us is not, *ipso facto,* right for everyone else, though a kind of personal devotion often deludes us into thinking so. We tend also to project onto others those things we know best in ourselves and assume that their motives and ways of working are similar to ours. This is far from true. Awareness of the real differences among teachers will aid the beginning teacher in finding his own forte.

Another way of looking at teacher-student relationships has been aptly presented by Abel.[5] She sets up some suggestive categories that define different ways of dealing with ideas:

Ways of Thinking and Teaching

Logical Thinking	Autistic Thinking
Ideas that come from factual understanding. Tends to ask questions of fact or causation.	Ideas that "come from nowhere." Not too concerned about the factual or logical basis for an idea.
Objective Ideas	**Subjective Ideas**
Ideas do not produce excitement; remains calm throughout discussions; tends to shy away from ideas that come too close to his ego.	Interested primarily in topics of close concern to him, disinterested in others. Gets excited and enthusiastic about such ego-involving ideas.
Socialized Modes of Expression	**Egocentric Modes of Expression**
Is concerned about getting his ideas across; will modify his ways of talking if not understood.	Assumes he is understood by others; is apt to be careless about pronouns; unaware of gaps in communication between himself and others; surprised when these occur.

[5] Abel, Theodora M., "Modes of Thinking and Classroom Adjustment," *Journal of Social Psychology,* 9:287-298 (August, 1938).

Rigidity of Thinking	Fluidity of Thinking
Slow to modify or adopt ideas; may develop logic tight compartments and often fails to see consistency or inconsistency of ideas.	Easily modifies ideas in the light of new facts or experiences; is sensitive to inconsistencies; may seem flighty in skipping from idea to idea.

Compulsive Thinking	Noncompulsive Thinking
It is important to finish a task, get the solution to the problem, finish reading the book. Unfinished tasks bother him.	Drops a task if it appears unimportant or a new and more challenging one turns up. Unfinished task does not worry him. Sometimes never finishes anything.

Knowledge Attitude toward Learning

Seeks ideas based on fact or knowledge; oftentimes seems to seek knowledge for its own sake.

Appreciation Attitude toward Learning

Ideas are predominantly evaluative or emotional; tends to react to facts or knowledge in terms of effect.

Use Attitude toward Learning

Examines all ideas in terms of practical value; tends to be impatient with theories and philosophy or beauty.

These categories suggest an important idea to the beginning teacher, namely, that his modes of thinking may be far different from that of students. Judgments which fail to recognize these differences may be fallacious. For example, a teacher who himself is eager to try new ways of doing things may be surprised by students who object, who prefer the usual, albeit dull, routines. The teacher probably is more fluid in his thinking, whereas the students may be more rigid. A teacher who complains of a student, "He always wants to know why; he won't take anything on faith!" probably is prone to autistic thinking, whereas the student works by means of a more logical mode of thinking. Where a student may say of a poem, "How exciting!" the teacher may say, "Look at the perfection of meter and the elaborate rhyme structure." The teacher and student here would obviously be talking around each other. Each might wonder what was wrong with the other. Teachers who suffer from egocentric modes of expression may produce great anxiety in their students because they cannot communicate. These teachers may well find their greatest value in extensive use of student leadership which can help them with the job of communication.

Since so much of our teaching is concerned with ideas and ways of arriving at new ideas, it is important for the teacher to be sensitive to his own modes of thinking and try to avoid pushing all students into his own pattern. By aiding students to recognize their modes of thinking and appreciating the contributions each type can make to the solution of problems, the teacher can do much toward building in each student genuine self-respect. Too often the imaginative, creative, intuitive student is lost in the academic shuffle—at great personal cost.

Some of the barriers that exist between student and teacher, then, derive from the variations in human personality and as such can be used to enrich rather than to impede the educational process. At the same time it is essential to good mental hygiene in teaching to recognize the factors that mark teachers off from the students, to remember the special quality of teacher-student relationship. This relationship can be meaningful and significant when it is understood objectively.

How Do Teachers Feel About Teaching?

One of the important factors in job satisfaction is that the individual likes his job and likes himself for having such a job. To what extent do teachers like being teachers? There is considerable evidence of both a positive and negative nature. On the one hand, during the Second World War thousands of teachers left teaching voluntarily to enter industrial or other jobs that were newly created. Many expressed relief at a chance to escape from teaching. On the other hand, teachers give constant testimonial to the stimulation and reward of teaching and command genuine community respect for their talent, skill, and education. A recent survey inquiring among employed men about their satisfaction with their job found that while only 1 per cent of the men teachers who were polled stated, "I seldom enjoy teaching," 7.2 per cent of employed men in general said their work was dull or boring.[6]

In the average university or liberal arts college the education departments and courses are very likely to be viewed as academically inferior. Much as this may be resented, and untrue as many of the accusations may be, the fact remains that in the atmosphere that influences student thinking the education majors are often looked down upon. In the colleges that are primarily teacher-

[6] Monroe, W. S., Jr. (ed.), *Encyclopedia of Educational Research* (New York: The Macmillan Company, 1950) (Rev. Ed.).

education institutions or in which industrial and agriculture programs are also included, this attitude may be less in evidence. But even here undergraduates may be heard saying, "I don't tell my friends that I am going to get a credential; they will think I am crazy," or, "I find myself agreeing with people about the low quality of my education courses even when I know that this isn't really the case." Some students cannot withstand this pressure, and, if they remain in education at all, are apt to be cynical about work in professional education.

> To be sure, there is an age-old prejudice against teaching. Teachers must share with doctors the world's most celebrated sneers, and with them also the world's unbounded hero-worship. Always and everywhere, "He is a school teacher" has meant "He is an underpaid pitiable drudge." Even a politician stands higher, because power in the street seems less of a mockery than power in the classroom. But when we speak of Socrates, Jesus, Buddha, and "other great teachers of humanity," the atmosphere somehow changes and the politician's power begins to look shrunken and mean. August examples show that no limit can be set to the power of a teacher, but this is equally true in the other direction: no career can so nearly approach zero in its effects.[7]

Of course, no one enjoys being in a low status position. In the ranking studies of professions, teaching comes below doctor, lawyer, and engineer, but ahead of nursing and library work. The reason for this is obscure. It may be because the early school teachers in America were often ignorant and ill-educated, or it may be that in the past, the women who went into teaching were often socially isolated. They were considered old maids who, in the stereotype of many decades ago, were prudish and eccentric. Undoubtedly the low status has been modified by the recent interest in improved professional standards, by the entry of men in greater numbers into high-school teaching, by employment of married women teachers, and by greater freedom for the unmarried woman teacher. But the old stereotype is not completely gone: an examination of cartoons and fiction about teachers shows the teacher to be very often a scowling, old-fashioned, prim old maid. Some men entering high-school teaching, resenting this stereotype, relieve their feelings in a kind of general deprecation of the whole teaching profession. Such an attitude can hardly produce a satisfied and satisfying teacher. We need to be aware of these common attitudes about teaching, but we do not have to bow down to them.

[7] Barzun, Jacques, *Teacher in America* (Boston: Little, Brown and Company, 1945), pp. 4-5.

Community Expectations of Teachers

Beginning teachers are often concerned about what a teacher can or cannot do in a given community. There are numerous instances in the literature of several decades ago of teaching contracts specifying how many times a month a teacher could leave the community or prohibiting card playing and dancing. There are still places where married women teachers are not employed or a teacher is dismissed if she marries. The prevailing trend, however, is toward fewer and fewer community restrictions.

Probably dislocations of the war years have had a marked effect on what communities expect from teachers. One study by Lichliter[8] shows some of the expectations in smaller communities regarding women teachers. Although on the whole few contracts were specific regarding such things as church attendance, teachers often felt bound to participate because of advice from school board members or from community pressure. However, it was noted that of all the women teachers replying from a sampling of communities of 12,000 or less from all over the nation, 61 per cent of the communities expected *nothing* of the teachers in church or community activities. Only three kinds of social restrictions were sufficiently common to cause a heavy proportion of the teachers to mention them at all—drinking, dating students, and smoking.

No one questions the community objection to dating students. The prohibition against drinking and smoking applies principally to indulgence in public places. It is only fair to observe that smaller communities apply the same restriction on smoking and drinking to all women of the community, not only women teachers. Restrictions, then, are fewer than usually supposed. The facts do not warrant feeling that entering teaching is becoming subhuman.

It is heartening, also, to note that the younger generation of teachers, having successfully revolted against many older concepts of adolescent behavior, is less apt to be overly sensitive to community pressures. The beginning teacher might well find for himself the middle pathway between completely ignoring community expectations, and complete subjection to the slightest raising of an eyebrow. More self-respect on the part of beginning teachers, more feeling of adult responsibility for their own behavior, will do much to help re-educate communities into the acceptance of teachers as mature adults.

[8] Lichliter, Mary, "Social Obligations and Restrictions Placed on Women Teachers," *School Review,* 54:14-23 (January, 1946).

Some school systems make a practice of favoring local residents for new positions. For an individual to return to a high school where he was known as a student only a matter of four or five years previously may interfere with his complete acceptance as a full-fledged teacher. He may find that other members of the staff still consider him a "kid" and winning his place as a respected member of the school faculty may be that much more difficult. On the other hand, returning to familiar ground also means that he does not have the same feelings regarding social restrictions. He knows the community's foibles; he is well aware of the sharp eye and sharper tongue of the town gossip. He knows how to avoid her, and how to handle the inquiries she makes about his personal affairs. To a stranger this would seem intolerable prying, but home-town products expect it. What is felt to be a restriction by a newcomer may be so much a part of the town pattern that one raised in the community is unaware of it.

Community pressure, then, is how you see it. The present-day trend is to extend the anonymity of the urban community to more and more portions of our society. What a person does is his own business. Many teachers remark on the seeming lessening of attention to the minutiae of their daily lives. As a profession, teaching is probably not any more confining than most of the professions; it is just that more people are aware of what teachers do. The recent trend of more and more men entering the ranks of teaching on all levels also may have a marked effect on the social expectations of teachers.

The attention that the community pays to the teacher bears, of course, an inverse ratio to the size of the community; the smaller the town the more the people will notice what the teacher does. However, communities also have been criticized by beginning teachers because they ignore the teacher.

> This upper-class suburban community seemed, to the new teacher, to be an attractive place in which to teach. But it turned out to be very lonely, too. While she could hear the gay laughter from the parties across the street, no one invited her. Social affairs of all sorts seemed to occupy the energies of the bright young couples she met daily in the streets. But the only invitations she received were from the other teachers. Soon she discovered that her friends would come only from this closed circle. However, as she came to know her colleagues, they developed into fine and interesting people. After the first feeling of being left out, she soon came to enjoy her fellow educators. After several years, when she had entered a few community activities—community theater, a fly-casting club, and so forth—she widened her circle

of friendships and met a number of the local community residents. But it took time.

In all types of communities the beginning teacher will find his first friends on the faculty. It is important, therefore, to learn quickly who they are, to talk with them, to be agreeable and friendly. Some of the problems of the new teacher on the faculty have been discussed in Chapter 21.

In summary, the process of becoming a teacher starts within the individual. Techniques of teaching, knowledge about students and schools, are the outward polish that professional education provides. But to be a teacher means more than that; it means the acceptance of the role of the teacher, the recognition of the feeling of being a teacher, the ability to accept the social expectations of teachers.

The Teacher Cannot Afford To Be Prejudiced

Becoming a teacher means rubbing shoulders with all kinds of people. For many students this will come as a shock, but to others it will be one of the chief rewards of the profession. Probably most of us have found our friends among others in the same social sphere as ourselves; if we were reared in a city, our circle of friendship grew out of the occupational level of our parents and we met few from other occupation levels or social strata. Similarly, our associations have been limited by the church we attended, by the neighborhood we lived in, by the elementary and high schools we attended, by the college we chose. Those from smaller cities and towns may have a wider social acquaintance, but for close association again, they rarely step outside a rather narrow boundary. Going to college cuts us off even more from many kinds of people in a community. Even more significant, few of us have known at all well individuals of other racial or ethnic groups. They are rarely close friends; in school we seldom had prolonged contact with them, and certainly we did not visit in their homes or attend church with them. Thus such minority individuals (who, if they are all counted, constitute a majority of our nation) are unknown quantities. We do not know how they feel or act or live. Similarly, those from minority groups have had limited personal experiences with the major white Protestant "old resident" group in the community, and may feel ill at ease and outside it all.

As teachers, however, we do not pick and choose our students. If there is a large Negro community, a significant number of recent immigrants from Europe, a neighborhood only recently built up of new residents from out of state—all of these people will send their youngsters to school. As a high-school teacher, our feelings about these groups deserve close examination.

The accompanying questionnaire might be useful in assessing our own feelings of separation from such minority groups. It might be useful to fill out both parts independently of each other, then compare what is said.

Part I. Place before each of the groups named below the number of the statement that most nearly expresses the way you would feel about having children from any of these groups in your classes. You should regard these children as representing an average socio-economic status (not the best you have known, nor the poorest) (Do not leave any blanks):

1. I would go out of my way to ask for classes consisting of a large number of these children.
2. I would welcome children from this group in my classes.
3. I wouldn't care one way or another if children from this group were in my classes.
4. I'd rather not have any children from this group in my classes, at least not more than one or two.
5. If I had a class made up mostly of children from this Group, I would request a transfer or resign.

NUMBER	*GROUP*	*NUMBER*	*GROUP*
______	1. Italian	______	10. Armenian
______	2. English	______	11. Protestant
______	3. Jewish	______	12. "Okie" or "Arkie"
______	4. Negro	______	13. Canadian
______	5. Scandinavian	______	14. Japanese
______	6. Polish	______	15. Mexican
______	7. German	______	16. Chinese
______	8. Catholic	______	17. Portuguese
______	9. Filipino	______	18. Latin-American

Part II. You are going to be a teacher in a community new to you. You have to find a place to live; you are also going to be called upon to have some contact with the parents of children in your classes. Place before each of the groups listed below the statement that would most nearly express your feeling. (Again, consider the groups as representing an average socio-economic status) (Do not leave any blanks):

1. I would go out of my way to board in the home of people in this group.
2. I would welcome having these people as neighbors.
3. I do not have strong feelings one way or another about social contacts with people in this group.
4. I would accept a dinner invitation from parents of children in class who were in this group, but I would prefer not to live in the same neighborhood with them.
5. I would be willing to talk to parents of children in this group if they came to the school or even make an afternoon visit to their home, but I would not accept any other contact.

NUMBER	GROUP	NUMBER	GROUP
______	1. Jewish	______	10. Italian
______	2. German	______	11. "Okie" or "Arkie"
______	3. Polish	______	12. Japanese
______	4. Latin-American	______	13. Canadian
______	5. Negro	______	14. Portuguese
______	6. Scandinavian	______	15. Protestant
______	7. Mexican	______	16. Armenian
______	8. English	______	17. Filipino
______	9. Chinese	______	18. Catholic

If there is a marked discrepancy between the scores, then we might examine the implications of this picture. It has been found fairly typical for students entering teaching to feel quite unemotional about members of minority groups as children in their classes, but to have very definite feelings about such groups when it came to living arrangements. The question to ask here would be, "If I couldn't visit with a feeling of ease in the homes of these people, really, how can I genuinely feel that my classroom attitudes toward their children will be similar to those I have for all other children?"

It is difficult indeed to divorce these out-of-class feelings from in-class behavior. The teacher who recognizes these reactions—and our culture makes it difficult for us to escape these feelings—will be a long way on the road toward reducing their impact upon students. If the prospective teacher feels so strongly about one or another group in the national community that it would drastically interfere with his ability to handle the group fairly, then it may be wisest to avoid teaching altogether.

Prejudice has no place in the classroom. Our obligation to society is to provide equal opportunity for all. Our own feelings can interfere with this equality if we are blind to them ourselves.[9] It is not easy, understandably, for us to deal with a mixed class if all of our background has been without such experiences. How does a Negro feel? Can one discuss religion objectively when there are Catholics and Jews in the same class? How about the problems of the immigrant in America when Joe and Susy and Fred have foreign-born parents who do not even now speak English? These problems are acute for the sensitive teacher. One way out is to avoid all such controversial areas. We do not discuss tolerance because it immediately means discussing prejudice, and we might inadvertently step on someone's toes. This is the ostrich approach.

[9] Grambs, Jean D., "Are We Training Prejudiced Teachers," *School and Society*, 71:196-198 (April 1, 1950).

The teacher who faces for the first time interracial or intercultural groups, or both, would do well to follow the suggestions made by the YWCA on the basis of extensive experience with interracial and intercultural groups:

1. The teacher should be keenly aware of group interrelationships over and above specific interracial problems.
2. The teacher should be familiar with the local school program and what progress has been accomplished in this area.
3. The teacher should know how all peoples live in his community: housing, employment, community attitudes.
4. The teacher should seek to develop warmth in his relationships with all in his group; if they disagree with his policies, they can let him know without fear of censure or retaliation.
5. The teacher will seek to get acquainted with the leadership of all segments of the community: know the Negro church leaders as well as the white church leaders.
6. The teacher should be an educator in this area—not a propagandist: being all hot for "equality" may be the best method of offending those with whom one must work.
7. The teacher should understand how the members of minority groups think and feel as well as seeing into the roots of majority prejudice; by genuine seeking for information from minority leaders the teacher can often gain valuable insights, but always remembering the problem is a two-way road.
8. Talk over mistakes with someone who can help you analyze what you have said or done: if minority-group students do not seem to respond to the program as set up, an outsider may see what has been wrong.
9. Do not deal with members of other groups in a special manner.
10. Avoid saying "Oh *you* are all right" to an individual of another group, as though implying that they are different or better than others of their group toward whom you have a stereotyped approach.[10]

Meeting these human relations problems takes more than just following democratic classroom procedures mechanically. Human relations need the free sanction of the teacher's feelings. This emotional acceptance is much more difficult to obtain than mere intellectual assent. One of the problems, then, of becoming a teacher is recognizing this new demand for dealing freely and equally with all kinds of children from diverse origins and backgrounds and overcoming in ourselves our own cultural provincialism or prejudice.

Getting the Job

Obtaining a job depends on several interrelated factors: Is there a current oversupply of secondary teachers? If so, what is the de-

[10] Height, Dorothy I., "Step by Step with Interracial Groups" (New York: YWCA, The Women's Press, 1948), 56 pp.

mand for any particular specialty? If, as has been the case over several recent years, there is an oversupply of secondary teachers, the individual enters a competitive market. He is at an advantage if his area of specialization is in short supply. However, regional factors play a part too. If he is highly trained in an area where most teachers are highly trained, he has a better opportunity if he migrates to a portion of the country where most teachers are not so well trained. Finally, he will be at an advantage if he has a number of hobbies and skills which will enable him to fit into several parts of the school program. For instance, a teacher with a social-studies major and an English teaching minor may find the competition intense; but he will certainly enhance his employability if he also can coach swimming, or has made an extensive hobby of photography, or has taken enough physics to feel at home in the field, or is willing to drive the school bus, or can operate and repair motion-picture projectors. The same holds true of a woman prepared to teach languages who is an expert seamstress as well, who may have had experience as a librarian, who can teach home nursing or upholstering, who has a hobby of nature study. The real use for talents is one of the advantages of teaching. Likewise, teachers with wide travel and work experiences are likely to be favored over those who have stayed in the cloister and know their way only around the home town and the library stacks. The added maturity and independence that comes from work experience and travel are almost always significant to an administrator.

Placement agencies. In seeking a job, the beginner should make use of local placement facilities. Such facilities are maintained by most colleges and universities for the benefit of their own graduates. The placement function of the teachers college is so important that many such institutions require students to register at the placement office before they may be certified for a credential. Others set up a special office for the placement of teachers only and offer another facility for other graduates. Only nominal registration fees are charged.[11] Such offices will gather confidential letters of recommendation, make contacts with administrators in the field, and help students with placement advice. It is suggested that where such facilities are available, the student inquire regarding placement trends early in his career in education. Often a student may choose a more ad-

[11] National Institutional Teacher Placement Association, *Current Practices in Institutional Teacher Placement,* Published by the Association (no place of publication given), 1941. Gives additional details on practices across the country in teacher placement.

vantageous course preparation if told early enough that in a given locality a journalism minor might be better than straight English, or corrective speech preparation better than general speech training. Such offices usually have on file the latest statistics regarding occupational trends. Advice and guidance are also available regarding best localities for job opportunities, proper procedure in job applications, and best interview practice.

What about private placement agencies? During times of oversupply of teacher personnel, it is often necessary for the individual to utilize the services of private teacher placement agencies. Some college placement offices will furnish such agencies with the information gathered by the college, others will not. The private agency charges anywhere from 5 per cent to 10 per cent of the first year's salary, and thus may be a heavy financial drain on the individual. Although most such agencies are highly reputable and ethical in their practices, some are not. The student would be well advised to consult his own placement office or a member of his faculty regarding the merit of such private agencies before using their services. Some states have placement offices operated by the teachers' association. These generally charge a small percentage of salary and are highly reputable.

Some students may wish to canvass the field independently. This may be profitable; on the other hand, it is costly in time and energy. A consultation with the college's placement office and with the faculty known to the student is a useful preliminary procedure. Letters sent ahead to the individuals to be contacted are always helpful.

Job interviews and applications. In obtaining a teaching job, the job interview is so important that beginning teachers should make every effort to gain skill and poise in the interview situation. Appropriate dress, general appearance, ability to talk with an administrator on a professional level, evidence of maturity and poise —all of these are important. Administrators are concerned with the success the student has had in student teaching and related teaching experiences, such as recreation playground work, work with boys and girls clubs and groups, Sunday-school teaching. They are also interested in the personableness of the future teacher. It is assumed that the candidate is prepared to teach his field; there is rarely a question about adequacy of preparation.

Students may have occasion to write letters of application for a job. While these should be simple, formal, and direct, it is only too easy to make gross mistakes. It is wise never to send such a letter until it has been read by another person with experience in writing this kind of letter. Included with a letter of this sort should be a brief sketch of experience, education, and individuals for reference. Any letter of recommendation sent by the applicant will be suspect; obviously no one is going to be frank if he knows the subject of the letter will see it. Thus, the confidential letter of recommendation is much more valuable.

In choosing individuals to act as references, the student should carefully select those who know him in a professional relationship. The home town banker may attest to the student's personal character and this, of course, has its place, but the administrator is much more interested in professional character. Students sometimes make the mistake of asking faculty members to act as references when they have had only slight acquaintance or when faculty members may not have been too favorably impressed. A few favorable references are far better than many lukewarm ones. Students should particularly seek out those who have observed them in action with young people or in leadership roles in adult groups. The qualities demonstrated in these situations impress administrators as having a direct carry-over to high-school teaching.

The student who has always made excellent academic grades will find that this is not enough. Some administrators are wary of the so-called "brain" who is so wrapped up in the higher mysteries of his field that he can never come to earth and deal with average high-school students. A student who is Phi Beta Kappa quality would do well to make a special effort to have in his recommendations evidence of leadership activities, of wide work experience, of intimate and successful work with young people. Critics of the high school often decry this prejudice against the very bright as teachers, but there is unfortunately some evidence that one whose interests are purely scholarly may not be cut out for the hurly-burly and the rough give and take of the high school. The public high school of today demands trained intelligence, but trained in the realities of everyday living, not merely the intricacies of a reference library.

Accepting the job. The ethics of job commitment are important. Teachers should not accept a job as insurance until a better offer comes along. They will quickly lose the backing of any placement office if it is found that they have been "playing the field". A statement of acceptance is binding, and only the gravest of personal situations permits the teacher to ask to be released from a contract. Even if a better job is offered with higher pay and other inducements, in the long run it is wiser to abide by the original contract. Such breaches of faith are quickly known among administrators and will do the individual no good. The new teacher is often so flattered by the first offer of a job that he jumps at it. But it is probable that if there is one offer early in the placement season, April, May, and June, then others will come. The beginning teacher should think several times before accepting the first offer, unless it is very close to what has been desired.

Partly for these reasons the student would do well to plan his student teaching in advance of entering the job market. Many of the best positions will be filled early; the administrator is more likely to take one who has already proved his ability in student teaching than one who is a "dark horse" and merely has good academic or personal recommendations.

Sometimes the high school will select one or more of its replacements from among the student teachers who have been placed there. The alert student will see his student teaching as a possible avenue to placement. He will attempt to act more like a professional teacher than a college student and will try to understand the workings of the high school in a serious and interested fashion. He will see to it that the administrator knows that he is around. The principal will not welcome a daily diary from a student teacher, but he will be favorably impressed by one or more professional interviews that seek to gain advice and information about teaching in general and the problems of this school in particular.

The Teacher on the Job

While this book is designed primarily as a working guide for students prior to entering teaching, it may be well to discuss some of the ways to make on-the-job teaching more satisfying.

In the school systems of America there is growing emphasis on in-service education. Alert leaders in education recognize the importance of helping the teacher to help himself. However, this is not enough. The individual teacher who seeks to grow in service, to continue to derive personal satisfaction out of his job, has several possibilities for his own continuing professional education. First, he can join the professional organizations in his field of special interest; second, he can join professional organizations of a general nature; and third, he can utilize vacation periods to gain further education in professional or academic subject areas.

Today the teacher in the high school has available several national organizations in each subject field, many of which have local units that meet monthly or quarterly to exchange professional ideas. Such association is invaluable to the teacher. Probably the best investment that the beginning teacher can make is subscribing to the journal that is devoted to the teaching problems of his special field. He will also want to read one or more general education journals. This monthly reminder of the new thinking and research in his special area and in the broader fields of education keeps the teacher alive in his work. He will find many suggestions which have immediate carry-over to his daily tasks in the classroom. The stimulation of reading about what others are doing will go a long way toward making teaching creative and satisfying.

The teacher is not a finished product when he completes his formal college requirements. Only a part of the educational job has been done. The rest has to be done on the job. It is foolish to assume that we can or should learn no more. Teaching has too many responsibilities to brush off lightly the continuing demands to maintain a high level of competence.

The summer vacation has always been important to continued professional growth. Some systems insist that each teacher during a certain number of years accumulate a minimum of college credit. This forces the teacher to go back to school whether he wishes to or not. Often teachers object to this procedure; its values are, however, unquestioned if the teacher makes a wise choice of college work. The beginning teacher in particular will find great need for special course work during the first few years of teaching to meet some of the obvious gaps in his preparation. Many teachers, for instance, recognize the problem of remedial reading in their classes only after having taught. A summer session in a reading workshop may be invaluable.

Postscript

When we finished writing this chapter, we realized that we had not touched it up with the usual bright promises to beginning teachers. We had said little about job security, salary schedules with regular increments, long vacations. We hadn't said much about these because these are not the significant considerations. The significant considerations reside in the nature of the work itself and not in the appurtenances thereto, pleasurable or no. This is work of basic importance to human welfare. No modern society can long survive without trained people devoted to the work of education.

Because we feel so strongly about the importance of good

education to people, we have been unwilling to gloss over the hard facts. Sometimes it may seem that pessimism has permeated these pages. It is not pessimism—but realism. Today teachers need more than cheery expectations of a bright future. They need to have practical training in the everyday tactics of the classroom. But more than that, they need to know that, however skilled they are as tacticians, there will be obstacles, problems, and anxieties. It would be convenient for teachers if we could somehow line the walls of the classroom with lead and shield the students from the radiations of the larger world. It would be convenient for teachers and disastrous for students. But we cannot shut out any of society's inconsistency, indecision, and conflict. They are all there with us everyday as we teach. We are better off knowing that they will be our constant companions than to delude ourselves with rosy illusions. We will know then from the beginning that society's unwillingness to carry out consistently the principles it says it believes in will plague us when we try to practice those principles in the classroom. Students will rebel. Parents will complain. The words are all right, they will say in effect, but we don't live that way. And we will be discouraged and disheartened. We should expect to be —many times. But this gives us no license to turn away from the long task of good education—to say we know that's all right in theory but it won't work. It will work if enough of us keep working at it, keep clearly in view what the obstacles are, keep alive and growing our training for the job ahead. And this is the only bright promise we make you—that the job is tough and long. But no job is more important.

Selected References

Securing a Position

Chamberlain, Leo M., and Leslie W. Kindred. *The Teacher and School Oranization.* New York: Prentice-Hall, Inc., 1949. Chap. 6, "Securing a Position," pp. 143-186. A detailed and practical presentation.

National Education Association. "Teacher Personnel Procedures: Selection and Appointment," *NEA Research Bulletin,* Vol. 20, No. 2 (March, 1942). Reviews general practices in selecting teachers: eligibility, interviewing procedures, contracts, and orientation practices.

Suggestions for Securing Teaching Positions. Circular No. 224, 1950, U.S. Office of Education, Washington, D.C. A very good guide to all aspects of placement problems.

Wrinkle, William L., and Robert S. Gilchrist. *Secondary Education for American Democracy.* New York: Rinehart & Company, 1942. Part 6,

Section 46, "How to Get a Position," pp. 493-514. Practical advice for the beginner.

The Teacher as a Person

Barzun, Jacques. *Teacher in America.* Boston: Little, Brown & Company, 1945. Provocative and often controversial, but always witty, comments on education and teaching.

Beale, H. K. *Are American Teachers Free?* New York: Charles Scribner's Sons, Inc., 1936. Important survey of the pressures on teachers from many sides that limit teacher freedom.

Caswell, Hollis L. (ed.) *The American High School.* 8th Yearbook, John Dewey Society. New York: Harper & Brothers, 1946. Chap. X, "Teachers for Tomorrow's High School," pp. 183-214. Outlines needed attitudes and training for future teachers.

Donovan, Frances R. *The Schoolma'am.* New York: Frederick A. Stokes, 1938. An unvarnished commentary on the situations teachers meet in daily life, with good suggestions for meeting many kinds of problems.

Douglass, Harl R., and Hubert H. Mills. *Teaching in High School.* New York: The Ronald Press Company, 1948. Chap. 27, "The Teacher as a Person," pp. 568-589. Describes specific personal needs and understandings of teachers.

Elsbree, Willard. *The American Teacher,* New York: American Book Company, 1939. An historical presentation of the teaching function in America.

Highet, Gilbert. *The Art of Teaching.* New York: Alfred A. Knopf, Inc., 1950. Stimulating essays on the "feeling" of good teaching with good advice thrown in.

Holman, Mary. *How It Feels to Be a Teacher.* New York: Bureau of Publications, Teachers College, Columbia University, 1950. Unusually insightful.

Mort, Paul R., and William S. Vincent. *Modern Educational Practice.* New York: McGraw-Hill Book Company, Inc., 1950. Pp. 413-417. Comprehensive list of films on teaching and teaching techniques, and problems of student adjustment.

Quillen, I. James and Lavone A. Hanna. *Education for Social Competence.* Chicago: Scott, Foresman & Company, 1948. Chap. 16, "The Teacher of the Social Studies," pp. 426-442. Competences needed specifically for the teacher of the social studies.

Redl, Fritz and William Wattenberg. *Mental Hygiene in Teaching.* New York: Harcourt, Brace & Company, 1951. Chap. X, "The Psychological Roles of the Teacher." A new and stimulating concept of the teacher in action.

Riley, John W., Jr., *et al. The Student Looks at His Teacher.* New Brunswick: Rutgers University Press, 1950. Presents the viewpoints of some 5,000 students on what makes a good teacher.

"Teachers as Individuals," *Educational Leadership,* 3:250-283 (entire issue) (March, 1946). Teachers have problems and also are a basic resource for the building of good schools.

Teachers in Fiction

Burlingame, Roger. *Cartwheels.* New York: Doubleday & Company, 1935. A headmaster in a private school struggles to modernize the school program—a vivid report.

Ellis, H. F. *The Vexations of A. J. Wentworth, B.A.* Boston: Little, Brown & Company, 1950. An amusing tale of a schoolmaster in an English school.

Fisher, Dorothy Canfield. *Seasoned Timber.* New York: Harcourt, Brace & Company, 1939. The conflict between the ideals of an educator and community pressure in a small Vermont town.

Hilton, James. *Good-Bye, Mr. Chips.* Boston: Little, Brown & Company, 1934. A quiet, classic study of the realization by a teacher of the true rewards of teaching.

MacRae, Donald. *Dwight Craig.* Boston: Houghton Mifflin & Company, 1947. A sharp and rather bitter report of the life history of an educator; some good insights into the hazards of self-delusion and power seeking.

Rives, Fern. *Friday, Thank God.* New York: G. P. Putnam's Sons, 1943. The dramatic things that can occur in a typical American high school.

Rosten, Leo C. *The Education of Hyman Kaplan.* New York: Harcourt, Brace & Company, 1941. Highly amusing and insightful anecdotes of a night-school class for immigrants; a *must* book for all teachers.

Scott, V. J. *The Hickory Stick.* New York: William Morrow & Company, 1948. A bitter story of the conflict between a teacher's ideals and the faculty and community where he teaches. Picture is overdrawn, but many aspects are well portrayed.

Stuart, Jesse. *Thread That Runs So True.* New York: Charles Scribner's Sons, Inc., 1949. Autobiography of a teacher in the isolated mountain communities of the Eastern United States. Vivid and amusing.

Winsloe, Christa. *The Child Manuela.* New York: Rinehart & Company, 1933. The tragic emotional relationship of a teacher and a student.

Wood, Playsted. *The Presence of Everett Marsh.* New York: Bobbs Merrill Company, 1937. The life in a Wisconsin high school seen through the main character role of the principal.

Appendix

Suggested Activities

CHAPTER 1

1. Administer a questionnaire to determine the differences in a class of high-school students. Here are some illustrative items. You will want to add others.

   1. Background: Father's occupation; education; place of birth
   Mother's occupation; education; place of birth
   Your place of birth
   Other places you have lived
   Your hobbies
   Part time jobs
   Things you like best about school
   Things you like least about school
   What would you like to be doing ten years from now?
   What groups in and out of school do you belong to?

   Analyze the differences you find. What implications could these differences have for you if you were teaching this class?

2. Examine the cumulative records in a local high school. Look for the following items for a single high-school class:
   Health records: type, items entered
   Family background data: socio-economic level, number of brothers and sisters
   Scholastic records: strengths and weaknesses
   Anecdotal material from teachers: characteristic behavioral patterns
   Counselors' reports: indications of personal problems
   Standardized test reports: recency, consistency of scores

What help do the records provide to the classroom teacher? Give specific examples. What further information would be useful?

3. Administer a standardized achievement, aptitude, or intelligence test to a high-school class. Score and interpret findings.
4. Review and compare ten intelligence or aptitude tests reported in the most recent *Mental Measurements Yearbook.* (O. K. Buros, editor. Published by Rutgers University Press.)

   1. How was the test validated?
   2. How easy or difficult is it to administer and score?
   3. Is it useful for group or individual predictions? How can you tell?
   4. What possible interpretive hazards might be present?

5. Write a short autobiographical essay covering the following:

   1. Your first impressions of high school
   2. Did your high-school experience live up to your expectations?
   3. What were the outstanding experiences in your high-school years?
   4. If you went to more than one high school, which one did you like best?

   Does this help you understand present-day high-school youth? In what way?

6. Write a description of your most successful high-school friend. Also of the one you thought was least successful. How do you account for the differences? What could the high school have done for the one who was the least successful?
7. Order several copies of the *Wetzel Grid.* In cooperation with the school health or physical education department, arrange to collect the needed data with a group of high-school students. What findings are revealed by the results? How could these influence your teaching?

CHAPTER 2

1. Obtain the class schedule of a high school. Analyze it and compare with the recommendations of the Harvard Report and the Educational Policies Commission Report, *Education for All American Youth.* What changes would you like to see in the course offerings?

2. Collect the arguments pro and con on one of the proposals for curriculum revision discussed in this chapter. Analyze them for validity and feasibility. What obstacles would need to be overcome in your local high school in order to implement this kind of curriculum revision?
3. Interview three to five teachers regarding their attitudes towards a core curriculum. Prepare for this interview by finding a model core program from the available literature that seems to you to be most feasible for a local high school or community school.
4. Interview ten or more recent graduates of the local high school. Ask the following questions or comparable ones:

    1. What jobs have you had since leaving high school?
    2. What are you doing now?
    3. Are you satisfied with the way you are doing your present job?
    4. What in your high-school career prepared you best for what you are now doing or expect to be doing?
    5. What aspect of the high-school program could have been strengthened to help you to do a better job today?
    6. In what ways would you like to see the high school change for the coming generation?

5. Analyze the content of your own major teaching field and list all those attitudes, concepts and skills that meet the criteria suggested by *Life Adjustment Education.*
6. Examine model courses of study or examples of such courses of study in your teaching field as found in the professional literature. List the educational objectives for your subject area. Take this list and visit at least three classrooms in which this subject is being taught. Identify the specific content and methods which are designed to achieve the stated objectives. Evaluate the success to which the classroom experiences seem to be meeting these objectives.

CHAPTER 3

1. Take the suggested check list for the democratic classroom and use it in making observations of an elementary and a secondary class. Compare the findings. Which classroom seems to be most democratic? How do you account for the differences?

2. Attend a faculty meeting. What kind of leadership do you observe? To what extent are the relationships democratic? What are the limitations on school democracy?
3. Observe a leader of some youth group activity (Scouts, YM or YWCA, Sunday School, Campfire, etc.) and compare with classroom teachers of the same age groups. Which situation seems most democratic? Why? What variations in student behavior do you observe in the different situations?
4. Review the classroom situations you have actually been in. Which of the democratic behaviors listed in this chapter were most frequently ignored? Which were observed most often? Arrange the skills demanded of a teacher in fostering democratic behavior in an order from least difficult to most difficult. What does this imply for you in your teaching?
5. In recalling the history of your own learning, which teacher did you like best? What did this teacher do for you? For others in the classroom? How did this teacher's classroom compare with the democratic classroom described in this chapter?
6. List the democratic classroom behaviors as given in this chapter in terms of your own feeling as to which ones you could do first, which second, and so forth in your own classroom, in striving to make it more democratic.

CHAPTER 4

1. Prepare a resource unit, including the following:

    1. Purposes
    2. Problems
    3. Activities
    4. Materials
    5. Evaluation.

2. Select a chapter from a textbook commonly used in your subject field. Expand the material covered into a resource unit as given above. Collect as many as possible of the actual materials you would use.
3. Observe a classroom. Record all motivational techniques used by the teacher and the reaction of students to them.
   Analyze the motivational pattern observed. Will this produce positive outcomes or will the outcomes be negative?

4. Prepare a lesson plan. Indicate every point where student-teacher planning might occur. Show what possible alternatives would need to be foreseen by the teacher.
5. Select several lesson plans. Give the specific assignments that would be necessary, following the assignment pattern given on pp. 98–101. Indicate what material would be needed to make the assignment pattern function.
6. Observe a classroom. As your observation proceeds, sketch out what you believe to be the plan for the lesson. When the lesson is over, interview the teacher regarding his plan for the period. Compare the discrepancies and account for them.
7. Prepare several assignments in your own subject area as usually taught. Present them, orally or in writing, to fellow classmates. Ask them to react to them in terms of:

    1. Highly interesting; I would like to go to work on this
    2. Not very interesting; sounds dull
    3. Not at all interesting; sounds like much work for what will be learned.

CHAPTER 5

1. Prepare some one of the following instructional materials designed to motivate students in attacking a problem: a poster, bulletin board display, slide sequence, strip film, exhibit, etc.
2. Evaluate some commercially produced instructional materials: films, film strips, recording, free materials, slides, exhibits.
3. Examine and evaluate the teaching aids provided by *Scholastic* (Teacher's edition), *Time, Reader's Digest, Newsweek.*
4. Prepare an extensive and organized picture-and-article file taken from current magazines, for use in your major teaching field.
5. Select radio and television broadcasts that should be called to the attention of students for subject matter enrichment.
6. Survey a number of classrooms with regard to the kinds and usefulness of various free and inexpensive materials. Ask teachers concerned which materials are most helpful to them. What are their objections to materials recommended but not utilized?
7. Examine the professional magazines in your teaching field. Collect a bibliography of teaching materials reviewed and listed over a period of not less than three months, preferably for the preceding year.

8. Visit the nearest county, university or city Instructional Materials Center. Report on materials and services available to you if you were teaching in this area. Evaluate the extent of utilization of the Center by interviewing the director or the assistant.

CHAPTER 6

1. Select an area of content in your subject field. Canvass the local community for all resources that might be used. Use a resource file card as given in this chapter or devise one for yourself.
2. Find a community resource suitable for a field trip. Outline in complete detail everything that you would do to prepare for, conduct, and follow-up the trip. Include classroom discussion topics and evaluation tools.
3. Interview several possible resource visitors. Evaluate each such interview in terms of the classroom preparation necessary to make optimum use of this person. What possible difficulties do you foresee? Outline in detail one classroom presentation of a resource visitor, including preparation, presentation and follow-up.
4. On the basis of the community survey guides listed in the bibliography or others available in your library, compile a minimum master list of questions suitable for a survey conducted by high-school students. Relate this proposed survey to a specific content area in your subject field. Show briefly how such a survey might be carried out in your class in relation to the content covered.
5. Prepare a sample questionnaire in some area of special interest to you (student opinion, general public opinion, etc.) and go through the complete cycle of pretesting, final administration, tabulating, and analysis of results. Review this experience critically in light of what you might do differently next time.
7. Interview the principal or vice-principal of a local high school regarding service projects currently under way or contemplated. Also inquire about the school's record in regard to community service. Recommend further projects to tie in with the content area of your special interest.

CHAPTER 7

1. Using the discussion pattern charts given in this chapter, analyze several class discussions in either a college or high-school classroom. Compare the different kinds of charting patterns in the different classrooms. How do you account for differences in the observed patterns?
2. Apply the criteria for good discussion questions to a discussion you have listened to in a classroom. How would you modify the discussion to comply better with the criteria given?
3. Make a list of possible discussion questions in your subject field. Give the questions to friends not majoring in your field. Which questions do they rate first? Why? Present the same list to a group of adolescents. Which questions would they like to discuss? Why?
4. Make an exhaustive list of all controversial areas and issues in your subject field. Which are essential in the education of adolescents? Which can more profitably be left for adult consideration? Why? Plan in detail the strategy you would employ for presenting to a high-school class one controversial issue noted above.
5. Select five possible issues that might lend themselves to sociodrama treatment in your subject area. Describe briefly the characters and the starting situation, plus any other details such as the desired outcome. If possible, try one such situation in your college class or in a high-school class. Evaluate the results. Were the directions clear? Did the individuals chosen to play the parts do a good or poor job? Did the situation develop as you had expected? What was the reaction of the audience? What would you do differently next time in setting up the same sociodrama?
6. Set up some role-playing situations relating to problems you expect to face in student teaching or are facing now in a teaching situation: The student who refuses to do an assignment; the other teacher who criticizes your idea; the parent who comes to complain about how much work you are giving the class, etc. Try these in class with several different students giving their solutions to the problem. What different versions were given? How did the role-playing give you new insight into the problem you faced?
7. Sooner or later every teacher must sponsor class plays, preside at school assemblies, or assist in putting on radio or television shows. To gain skill in rapid skit writing, use the sociodramatic

technique described in this chapter to write a skit for your college classmates, revolving around teacher preparation, going out to get a job, your first day as a student teacher, etc.

CHAPTER 8

1. Select a content area which you will be teaching. Outline a lesson plan covering several days or weeks in which you will use either short- or long-term groups. Give the specific instructions that you will furnish the class in setting up the groups.
2. Using one of the group analysis forms given in this chapter, or to be found in the literature. (See Bales, Robert F., *Interaction Process Analysis,* Addison Wesley Press, Cambridge, Mass., 1950; Meil, Alice, "A Group Studies Itself to Improve Itself," *Teachers College Record,* 49: 31-44, Oct., 1947; Bernstein, Saul, *Charting Group Progress,* Association Press, New York, 1949). Analyze the record you obtain in terms of the suggestions made in this chapter.
3. Observe either a formal or informal group. Write a brief anecdotal record of what the group was doing. Identify the group roles that you observed and give specific behaviors that support your analysis.
4. Write a brief description of your own behavior in a recent group situation. What role did you take? How did you feel about the other members of the group? What might you have done differently in order to help the group move forward? With what kinds of individuals in the group did you find it easiest to work? Which were the most difficult? Why?
5. In your own college class, or in a class of high-school students, plan for and try out several different kinds of group situations. Evaluate the method. Some suggested situations are: Buzz groups to make suggestions for a class project; a group reading exercise; a group test in which all members cooperate in giving one answer; test questions made up by groups; group sociodrama presentations to illustrate a current topic; buzz groups on a highly controversial issue.

CHAPTER 9

1. Select those items in your subject area which probably need drill procedures to be learned. Defend the importance of these items in terms of psychological and sociological rationales.
2. In addition to the games suggested in this chapter, list further methods that can be used to provide necessary drill situations.
3. Make a study-habit inventory covering such items as: Amount of study required in different courses; number of hours the student usually studies; kinds of study problems he finds most difficult; time of day and place where he studies most, etc. Administer this schedule to ten or more adolescents, either as an interview or a paper-and-pencil response situation. What study-habits training seems indicated by the results of this questionnaire?
4. Interview two or three teachers, parents and students, regarding the question: is homework valuable? Compare the answers of the three groups. What seems to be the major value and function of the homework? What kinds of homework seem to be preferred by the three groups? What homework procedure do you believe should be followed?
5. Analyze your own study habits. Compare them to the way in which you studied in high school. What changes have occurred? What do you find to be your most difficult problem when you are studying? Compare your study habits with those of several friends taking the same courses. What common problems do you find? How, as a teacher, would you set about to help students overcome these problems?

CHAPTER 10

1. Observe several teachers. Note all classroom routines that recur in each classroom every day. How does the teacher provide for those routines? Do the routine events interrupt classroom learning? What use is made of student help in taking care of routines? What suggestions would you have for better management of routine situations?
2. Interview several teachers regarding their clerical duties. What methods have they evolved for handling these duties?
3. Plot several model room arrangements. Describe the merits of

your suggested arrangement in terms of better organization of materials, supplies and total environment, all of which would promote learning.

4. Arrange to visit some of the newest elementary or high-school classrooms in your area. Note all improvements that are in line with the best practice and that make possible a flexible laboratory situation for learning. To what extent have these newer classrooms not included desirable items?
5. Review several issues of a number of professional journals, for example, *School Executive, Nation's Schools, American School Board Journal.* Look for articles and advertising on room equipment and school arrangement. Summarize the data that refer to modern high-school classrooms.
6. Often teachers are faced with the difficult problem of making over an old classroom to coincide with modern ideas of learning, without spending any money. A group of students can adopt a classroom, with the consent of the teacher and principal involved, and see how much can be done to improve it. Often high-school students, parents and other interested individuals will be glad to help. A renovated classroom, complete with estimated and actual budget, would be a worthwhile semester project.

CHAPTER 11

1. Select a unit of study in your teaching field. Prepare a list of instructional materials that will provide for a wide range of abilities.
2. Keep a list of the assignments, both in and out of class, given by a teacher for a week. If the class is a heterogeneous group, what provisions have been made for slow and fast learners? If it is a homogeneous group, how well calculated are the assignments for the group?
3. Interview a very bright and a very slow student as identified by either a teacher or a counselor. Compare their attitudes toward: school, the future, their families, teachers, social activities, the world of work, college current events. What common attitudes do you find? What are the major differences? Can these be attributed primarily to differences in intelligence?
4. Read and review four or more articles on each side of the issue of homogeneous grouping. What are the arguments for such

grouping? What are the arguments against? Draw your own conclusion about which is the better practice and defend it.

5. Interview a teacher or teachers who have been primarily responsible for slow groups. What particular problems or difficulties have they met? What methods do they use? In general do they favor grouping or oppose it? Interview teachers who instruct mainly fast groups asking the same questions. What conclusions regarding grouping can you draw?

CHAPTER 12

1. Using a description of reading problems in your content field, outline a course of action you would undertake in your own classroom in order to meet these problems.
2. Analyze three textbooks used in your content field. Apply one of the readability formulas (Lorge, Flesch, Dale-Chall) or make informal appraisals of readability. Which text do you consider most readable?
3. Select at least two units of instruction taught in your subject field. Make a list of reading materials at different levels of reading difficulty for each area. Try to achieve a wide range of difficulty.
4. Make a reading test in your own content area. If possible, administer it to a group of high-school or college students. What do you find of significance regarding reading abilities and reading problems.
5. List and review at least five reading tests covered in the current issue of *Mental Measurements Yearbook.*
6. Give a standard reading test to a high-school group. Score and analyze the results. Compare reading-test scores with other data obtainable on the students such as IQ, school grades, socio-economic status.
7. Make a time study of several high-school classrooms. What proportion of the time is spent in listening? What problems in attention and retention do you observe in the classes with the highest amount of listening, as against those with the lowest?
8. What are the differences in the listening problems in two content areas? List and analyze. What kinds of classroom procedures would you recommend to teachers in these two areas to meet the listening needs of the students?

9. Arrange for a recording of your own speaking voice. What improvements are needed?
10. Have several of your colleagues rate you on a typical teaching presentation. Analyze their findings in terms of your strengths and weaknesses in speech.

CHAPTERS 13 AND 14

1. Collect several anecdotes of discipline situations in the high-school classrooms you are observing. In which category, as given in these two chapters, do these situations belong?
2. Analyze some discipline situations in terms of teacher-student interaction. What did the teacher do? What did the student do? What should the teacher have done differently?
3. Evaluate the way in which a teacher handles a discipline situation in terms of "did it work?" and "for whom did it work?"
4. Recall your own educational history. What kinds of discipline situations were you involved in? What did the teacher do? How did you feel about it? What were the long-term effects of these discipline situations?
5. Interview a high-school student who has been involved in some discipline situations. Attempt to learn what the student believes to be the problem. (Do not try to enforce any discipline yourself; seek to obtain the *student's* view.) What action would you suggest for future classroom handling of this student on the basis of the information obtained?
6. Review the kinds of discipline situations given in these two chapters. Which do you feel you would have greatest trouble handling? Why? What can you do to prepare yourself to handle them?
7. Describe a typical discipline situation. If this behavior occurred any place but in school, what would be the reaction: in the home? In an office? In a youth group? What kinds of behavior cause trouble in all such situations? What kinds are problems only in school? What are the implications of this analysis?
8. Interview several teachers about student behavior. Which student behaviors are most difficult to handle, which occur most frequently, which annoy them most? Ask for advice on how to administer discipline in the classrom. Compare these findings with the point of view discussed in these chapters.

CHAPTER 15

1. Make sample test items in one content area for each of the following types:

   True-false
   Completion
   Multiple-choice
   Matching
   Essay.

   Which kind of questioning do you prefer? What different kinds of knowledge do the different questions seek?
2. Following one of the patterns suggested in the section entitled "Some Variations in Test Construction," write at least one complete test in your content area.
3. List and review at least ten standardized tests in your content area as given in the current *Mental Measurements Yearbook.*
4. Give a standardized test in your own content area to a high-school class. What do the results indicate? What recommendations would you make on the basis of these results? What dangers do you see in the use of such tests to serve as goals for instruction?
5. Compose a complete test covering a unit of instruction. Administer this test to a high-school class. Score and interpret the results. Return the test to the class and discuss the results with them. Describe your whole procedure critically. What would you do differently next time?

CHAPTER 16

1. Collect sample report cards from as many elementary and secondary-school districts as are immediately available. What are the outstanding features of these cards? How do they differ by grade level? What changes would you suggest on the high-school level?
2. Interview several teachers regarding their philosophy of grading. Describe your own point of view.
3. Interview ten high-school students of varying ability and representing different years in school regarding their attitudes to-

wards grading. Which teacher's method do they prefer in this respect? What major complaints do they have? How do those who are succeeding best view grading as compared with students who are failing?

4. Analyze the school records of ten boys and ten girls chosen at random. Are there any trends evident to support the research cited in the chapter regarding the over-grading of girls? Obtain the names of those in the honor society. Which sex is predominant?
5. Obtain the achievement record of several students. Write a model letter for each student in which you inform his parents regarding his progress. Outline a possible interview with one parent covering the things you would say in discussing the progress of his child. (The parent interview could be presented as a sociodrama to your college class. Have the class evaluate it in terms of parent response and of the realism of the problem.)

CHAPTER 17

1. Select a significant learning outcome in your field of teaching. Construct an evaluation chart in behavioral terms following the pattern given in this chapter.
2. List the major purposes to be achieved by instructing students in your area of teaching content. Defend each purpose psychologically and sociologically.
3. Compare the principles and theory underlying the measurement movement and the evaluation movement.
4. With the help of your instructor, select an area of instruction in the course in which you are presently enrolled. Construct an evaluation sequence for this content. If possible, try it on the class and obtain reactions.

CHAPTER 18

1. Make two case studies, one of a normal student and the other of a student who is having difficulties of some sort in school. Obtain all the information you can from school records, teacher interviews, student interviews. If possible, make a home visit. Does

further investigation show the normal student to have significant personal problems? How would you interpret the material on the student having difficulties?

2. Arrange to make a recording of one or more student interviews. Try to be non-directive. Use as a subject "How do you like high school?" Analyze the transcription to find out to what extent you were actually able to achieve a non-directive situation. (See Rogers, Carl, *Counseling and Psychotherapy,* Houghton, Mifflin, 1942, for an example of how to analyze a transcription.)
3. List all the resources available in your community for the guidance of students—other than school guidance services. Interview the director or professional worker in each such agency. Obtain information as to what service is available, who may use it, and what are the referral channels. (If in a large city, obtain the names of at least five such agencies and arrange interviews.)
4. Arrange for at least an hour's interview with one of the school counselors in your area. Make inquiries regarding testing programs, in-service program for teachers, counselor case-load, types of cases typically handled, the guidance philosophy held by the school personnel, problems encountered in the guidance program.
5. Observe several classrooms. What guidance did the teacher exert? What guidance opportunities existed that the teacher did not fully exploit?

CHAPTER 19

1. Arrange to observe and interview a homeroom or an orientation course teacher. What group guidance is done? How is it handled? What topics are covered? How successful does the program seem to be?
2. List some role-playing situations that could be used for group-guidance purposes. If possible try these in either a high-school or college class. Describe what occurred and evaluate the success of the technique for both participants and observers.
3. Administer one of the diagnostic devices described in this chapter: the three wishes, open questions, autobiography outline. What guidance needs become apparent on an analysis of the material obtained? Outline a possible group-guidance project in your subject field to meet the most crucial guidance needs revealed.

4. Administer a sociometric test, with the cooperation of the classroom teacher, to a high-school class. Prior to giving the test, list the students according to what you, or the teacher, think their order of popularity will be and who will choose whom in the test situation. Compare your list with the results of the test. What discrepancies do you note? How do you account for them? What new insights did you gain from the sociometric pattern?
5. Make and administer a "Guess Who" test. Analyze it in the same fashion as suggested for the sociometric test in item 4 above.

CHAPTER 20

1. Arrange to interview three high-school students regarding their vocational plans. Discuss their school program with them in light of their objectives. Analyze this experience in terms of vocational and academic guidance needs of youth.
2. Interview the school counselor about the kinds of vocational guidance he provides in individual conferences. Ask also about the vocational information available in the guidance office. Seek his advice on the kind of assistance classroom teachers can give in vocational guidance.
3. Interview the personnel in the local branch of your State Employment Office about vocational opportunities for youth. Also interview personnel directors of industries in the area and officials of private employment agencies.
4. Interview a random group of five business men in the community who employ high-school graduates. Secure their reactions to the training provided by the high school, further programs that might be useful and the general employability of high-school graduates.
5. If the school conducts any work-experience programs, interview the director of the program, several students who are participating, and several of their employers. How well is this program working? What contributions does it make to the usual high-school curriculum?
6. List as exhaustively as possible the vocational opportunities unique to your field. Show what the trends are regarding these opportunities and where current information may be obtained.
7. In a series of sociodramas practice parent interviews. Then arrange with the local high school to interview some parents.

Report these interviews and analyze their strengths and weaknesses.

CHAPTER 21

1. Interview the new teachers in the local high school. What special problems do they face? What suggestions do they have for beginning teachers?
2. Identify the special traditions and rituals of the local high school. Compare these with the traditions of your own high school.
3. By interviewing the administrators of the local high school, inquire into expectations of new teachers. For what do administrators look in determining the success of a new teacher? In their opinion what are the marks of an unsuccessful teacher?
4. Arrange to ride on several of the bus routes of a local high school. What do you note about community differences as you ride along the route? (If in a large city follow a group of high-school students via a public transportation system.)
5. Obtain permission to attend a faculty meeting and a departmental meeting in a local high school. What group atmosphere do you note? Are relations democratic or authoritarian?
6. Arrange to interview some of the school specialists serving the local high school. Include such personnel as the school nurse, librarian, counselors, welfare and attendance personnel, curriculum coordinator, audio-visual coordinator, etc. Obtain information regarding services rendered to the school as a whole and to the individual classroom teacher.
7. Visit at least once a representative group of extracurricular activities, for example a club meeting, a dance, a sports event, an assembly, a meeting of the student council, a meeting of the school paper staff, etc. Who participates? Who supervises the activities? Which activities could you learn to supervise? What should you do to prepare yourself?

CHAPTER 22

1. Write a detailed autobiography. Analyze your teaching potential, your strengths and your weaknesses.

Index

1. Arranging the facts in accordance with an organizing framework for information.
2. Checking the facts.
3. Looking for clues and uncovering blind spots.
4. Identifying and testing recurring situations and patterns of behavior.
5. Spotting significant, unique events.
6. Forming a series of hypotheses to account for particular patterns of behavior.
7. Relating hypotheses about different patterns of behavior to each other in order to understand the youth as an organized whole and as a developing personality.
8. Checking hypotheses against an organizing framework of explanatory principles in order to discover contradictory, oversimplified, or biased interpretations.
9. Planning practical ways to help the individual.
10. Evaluating hypotheses and plans on the basis of the effects of practical attempts to help the individual.[10]

Differences in Interests

Stemming from these needs are patterns of interest which research has identified. Since motivation is a prime problem in learning, knowledge of these characteristic interests is most useful. Teachers who do not point these latent sources of energy toward important learning needlessly handicap themselves.

For convenience, we may distinguish three main interest structures: interest in intellectual and aesthetic achievement; interest in the current social scene; interest in the cultural heritage. Perhaps we may best gain a sense of continuity if we follow each of these structures as it changes during the high-school years.

Intellectual and aesthetic achievement. On entering adolescence, responsiveness to sensory impressions is intensified. Neither interest nor ability in fashioning understandings is strong unless closely allied to direct experience through the senses. It is a rare young adolescent whose interest is captured for long by purely intellectual or aesthetic appeals. By mid-adolescence an upsurge in interests often occurs in intellectual and aesthetic matters. This interest is commonly expended in many directions with no single direction very well defined.

Depth and continuity of interest in dealing with abstract considerations come usually with the later adolescent years. Mature reasoning ability can consequently be expected more confidently. This new proficiency is often directed toward crystallizing and specializing vocational aims.

[10] *Ibid.*, p. 426.

Current social scene. As adolescence approaches, interest in group cooperation is more readily engaged. Then experience in group action toward goals quite removed from the immediate peer culture but of importance to the larger community may profitably be begun. Given this earlier guidance, by mid-adolescence group activity should be increasingly self-directed, and by late adolescence groups should be able to focus on social issues with a minimum of teacher direction.

Concurrently with this enlarging interest in group solution of social problems runs the much publicized interest in boy-girl relationships. Neither teachers nor parents need research to remind them how engrossing this interest can be. And yet it is strange how little constructive guidance either teachers or parents give to this interest. Both groups recite countless moral strictures about what cannot be done, but neither is willing to take time to show what can be done to develop understandings in these crucial human relationships.

The cultural heritage. Even in early childhood there is often considerable interest about the facts regarding past societies, but it is usually about the time of adolescence before a consistent understanding that this age stands on the shoulders of other ages is developed. There is commonly a wide interest in the fact that men make the culture in which they live. This budding interest can be nurtured if the drama and adventure of the long struggle is brought to them. It often withers in the arid climate of purely political chronicles.

This description of interest structures is couched in broad generalizations. It can only be a very general guide to the kind of interest patterns which are often found around the adolescent years. Now there is nothing inviolate or sacred about interests. The good teacher does not haphazardly follow the interests of students. Instead, he plans with them to use what he can of those interests which seem to be most common and most abiding and most important. There are thousands of fleeting interests passing through the adolescents he teaches which will not be helpful for learning. Nor does the teacher discharge his responsibilities unless he helps arouse some common abiding and important interests. Someone has said: "What interests the students bring are our opportunity; what interests the students carry away are our responsibility." Ingenious teachers almost literally strew the course of instruction with interesting items to stumble over. Gathering information about interests will be undertaken willingly by students if they are convinced this is a necessary prelude to planning with the teacher how best their class can be conducted. It is vital that from the beginning students accept the idea that they have heavy responsibility for the quality of their education.

The use of student interest may seem a remote possibility in some classes—mathematics for example—but even in this field the teacher can relate mathematics to future vocational goals (see Chapter 20), can determine if any students are puzzle fiends, and even perhaps develop a mathematics hobby club.

Assembling the data. Ways of ascertaining just what interests are already present in a specific class are numerous. One of the best is to encourage the students themselves to take a census of interests. Hobby exhibits are also useful in discovering interests. Participation in extracurricular activities (perhaps better called co-curricular), sports, and out-of-school clubs should also be noted. Sometimes a time log that lists for each student his activities for the week and how he budgets his time is revealing.

Differences in Abilities

Needs develop interests. Interests channel abilities, and these abilities, in turn, develop further interests. Some abilities have been recognized early in the student's school career, especially those which were engaged to advantage in school activities. But other abilities may be dormant, at least as far as the school is concerned.

Here it may be useful to classify abilities on two levels: (1) aptitudes—potentialities that *will* profit by training; and (2) achievements—measurements attesting that students *have* profited by training. Common instruments for indicating aptitudes include intelligence tests, musical aptitude tests, and mechanical aptitude tests. There are achievement tests available in all the usual subject-matter areas; for example, English, social studies, mathematics, science.

Research has indicated that intelligence tests are very good indices to potentialities that will profit from academic training, especially where that training requires linguistic ability and the ability to manage abstract ideas. This theory is applicable from the elementary school through college. Thus, at any level of education, students of high intelligence quotients generally do superior work in written composition, reading, spelling, English, social studies, science, and mathematics. But where mechanical aptitude is a more important component of the training, the prediction of talent by means of these instruments is not nearly so marked. For example, aptitude in handwriting, arts and crafts, or drawing is not clearly singled out.

Intelligence quotients are also closely related to ability to master vocational tasks of increasing complexity. Not only does this relationship exist between different vocational groups, but within vocational groups as well. That is, the intelligence quotient will usually indicate whether the student can learn the job of a shipping clerk or the job of an accountant—jobs in different vocational groups. Furthermore, the tests will usually distinguish between ability to do bookkeeping and accounting—jobs within the same vocational group.

On the other hand, the correspondence is only fair between intelligence and social skills: understanding, getting along with, directing other people. Indeed, those who score the very highest on intelligence tests often are not "big wheels" socially. Characteristically, these students are somewhat at a loss to understand why they are different from the ordinary students, and, in turn, the ordinary students find them a little odd.

Similarly, social adjustment, in the sense of lack of involvement in delinquency and crime, is not too well indicated by intelligence tests. Although delinquents as a group are somewhat below average, delinquency occurs along the whole range of intelligence.

Probably out of all this research about the predictive qualities of intelligence tests, one conclusion needs special emphasis. The intelligence quotient does not comprehend the whole complex of abilities that men and women need to live satisfying, effective lives. There is no body of significant data which licenses teachers to relegate those who score below average on this single instrument to a kind of second-rate status in the classroom. Teachers need to remember that we do not have a differential tally at the ballot box. The so-called "dull normal" also elects congressmen. He has a right to a fair share of time, skill, and consideration from his teachers and a right to the opportunity to develop *his* capacities, some of which may register very imperfectly on intelligence tests. All too often an intelligence quotient that is below average brands the student in the eyes of the teachers. Over a period of years he may be invested with a reputation that makes it psychologically impossible for him to gain equitable opportunity to learn. And his teachers, if asked to explain his fringe existence in the classroom, simply point to the IQ penciled in red in the classbook. "What do you expect?" they say. "Look at his IQ."